26th International Conference on Computational Linguistics (COLING 2016)

System Demonstrations

Osaka, Japan
11 – 16 December 2016

ISBN: 978-1-5108-3336-4

Printed from e-media with permission by:

Curran Associates, Inc.
57 Morehouse Lane
Red Hook, NY 12571

Some format issues inherent in the e-media version may also appear in this print version.

Printed by Curran Associates, Inc. (2017)

Association for Computational Linguistics
209 N. Eighth Street
Stroudsburg, Pennsylvania 18360

Phone: 1-570-476-8006
Fax: 1-570-476-0860

acl@aclweb.org

Additional copies of this publication are available from:

Curran Associates, Inc.
57 Morehouse Lane
Red Hook, NY 12571 USA
Phone: 845-758-0400
Fax: 845-758-2633
Email: curran@proceedings.com
Web: www.proceedings.com

COLING 2016

The 26th International Conference on Computational Linguistics

Proceedings of COLING 2016: System Demonstrations

December 11-16, 2016
Osaka, Japan

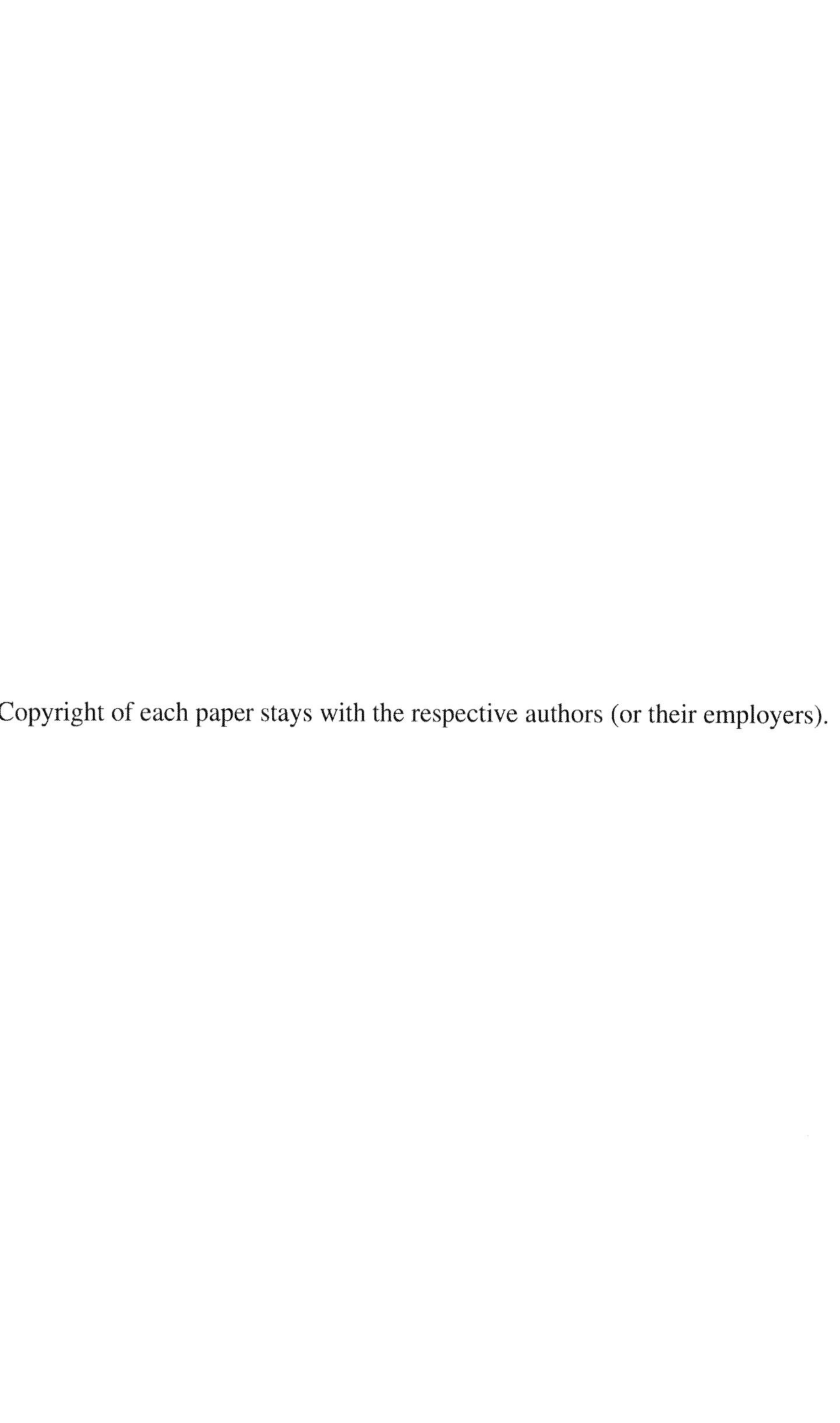

Preface

This volume contains papers from the system demonstration sessions of the 26th International Conference on Computational Linguistics (COLING 2016) held in Osaka, Japan. The conference is organized by the Association of Natural Language Processing (ANLP) and held at the Osaka International Convention Center from 11th to 16th December 2016, under the auspices of the International Committee on Computational Linguistics (ICCL).

The demonstration sessions complement the conference's presentation and poster sessions and aim at showcasing working software systems in a wide range of the conference topics. The demonstration sessions also provide opportunities to exchange ideas gained from implementing NLP systems, and to obtain feedback from NLP experts.

As a result of a review process, we accepted 64 papers out of 86 submissions. The program committee consisted of 32 members and one chair. The number of submissions largely exceeded than the previous COLING 2014 and each member performed hard work, that is, evaluated five or six papers, which amounted to two reviews per paper. During the selection process, we accepted the top-quality papers that showed the best utility and demonstrability potential.

First and foremost I would like to thank the program committee for their dedicated efforts to the tough review work. My special thanks also go to the people who organized COLING 2016 and made this volume possible. I thank General Chair, Prof. Nicoletta Calzolari, and Program Chairs, Prof. Yuji Matsumoto and Prof. Rashmi Prasad, and Local Chairs, Dr. Eiichiro Sumita, Prof. Takenobu Tokunaga, and Prof. Sadao Kurohashi, and Publication Chairs, Prof. Hitoshi Isahara, and Dr. Masao Utiyama for their great support.

Hideo Watanabe
COLING 2016 Demonstration Program Chair
6th November 2016

Organisers

Chair

Hideo Watanabe, IBM Research – Tokyo

Programme Committee

Ai Ti Aw, Institute for Infocomm Research
Eiji Aramaki, Nara Institute of Science and Technology
Riza Batista-Navarro, NaCTeM, University of Manchester
Kay Berkling, Cooperative State University, Karlsruhe
Hervé Blanchon, Université Grenoble Alpes – Laboratoire LIG
Christian Boitet, CLIPS-IMAG équipe GETA
Hailong Cao, Harbin Institute of Technology
Michael Carl, Cophenhagen Business School
Vittorio Castelli, IBM Research
Luong Chi Mai, Institute of Information Technology (IOIT)
Tsuneaki Kato, The University of Tokyo
Hideto Kazawa, Google Inc.
Mitesh M. Khapra, IBM Research - India
Genichiro Kikui, Okayama Prefectural University
Mamoru Komachi, Tokyo Metropolitan University
Mathieu Lafourcade, The Montpellier Laboratory of Informatics, Robotics and Microelectronics
Séamus Lawless, ADAPT Centre, Trinity College Dublin
Young-suk Lee, IBM Research
Qun Liu, Dublin City University
Teruko Mitamura, Carnegie Mellon University
Shinsuke Mori, Kyoto University
Kiyonori Ohtake, National Institute of Information and Communications Technology
Stefan Riezler, Heidelberg University
Hammam Riza, Agency for the Assessment and Application of Technology (BPPT)
Manabu Sassano, Yahoo Japan Corporation
Koichi Takeda, IBM Research - Tokyo
Takaaki Tanaka, Nippon Telegraph and Telephone Corporation
Lamia Tounsi, ADAPT Centre, Dublin City University
E Umamaheswari Vasanthakumar, Nanyang Technological University
Jason D. Williams, Microsoft Research
Youzheng Wu, iQIYI
Hai Zhao, Shanghai Jiao Tong University

Table of Contents

Conference Program

December 13th, 2016

11:00–12:30 Demo Session 1

An Interactive System for Exploring Community Question Answering Forums
Enamul Hoque, Shafiq Joty, Lluís Màrquez, Alberto Barrón-Cedeño, Giovanni Da San Martino, Alessandro Moschitti, Preslav Nakov, Salvatore Romeo and Giuseppe Carenini

NLmaps: A Natural Language Interface to Query OpenStreetMap
Carolin Lawrence and Stefan Riezler

A Reading Environment for Learners of Chinese as a Foreign Language
John Lee, Chun Yin Lam and Shu Jiang

A Post-editing Interface for Immediate Adaptation in Statistical Machine Translation
Patrick Simianer, Sariya Karimova and Stefan Riezler

Word Midas Powered by StringNet: Discovering Lexicogrammatical Constructions in Situ
David Wible and Nai-Lung Tsao

'BonTen' – Corpus Concordance System for 'NINJAL Web Japanese Corpus'
Masayuki Asahara, Kazuya KAWAHARA, Yuya TAKEI, Hideto MASUOKA, Yasuko OHBA, Yuki TORII, Toru MORII, Yuki TANAKA, Kikuo Maekawa, Sachi KATO and Hikari KONISHI

A Prototype Automatic Simultaneous Interpretation System
Xiaolin Wang, Andrew Finch, Masao Utiyama and Eiichiro Sumita

MuTUAL: A Controlled Authoring Support System Enabling Contextual Machine Translation
Rei Miyata, Anthony Hartley, Kyo Kageura, Cecile Paris, Masao Utiyama and Eiichiro Sumita

Joint search in a bilingual valency lexicon and an annotated corpus
Eva Fučíková, Jan Hajic and Zdenka Uresova

Experiments in Candidate Phrase Selection for Financial Named Entity Extraction - A Demo
Aman Kumar, Hassan Alam, Tina Werner and Manan Vyas

December 13th, 2016 (continued)

14:00–16:00 Demo Session 2

December 15th, 2016

10:30–12:30 Demo Session 3

CATaLog Online: A Web-based CAT Tool for Distributed Translation with Data Capture for APE and Translation Process Research
Santanu Pal, Sudip Kumar Naskar, Marcos Zampieri, Tapas Nayak and Josef van Genabith

Interactive Relation Extraction in Main Memory Database Systems
Rudolf Schneider, Cordula Guder, Torsten Kilias, Alexander Löser, Jens Graupmann and Oleksandr Kozachuk

An Open Source Library for Semantic-Based Datetime Resolution
Aurélie Merlo and Denis Pasin

TASTY: Interactive Entity Linking As-You-Type
Sebastian Arnold, Robert Dziuba and Alexander Löser

What topic do you want to hear about? A bilingual talking robot using English and Japanese Wikipedias
Graham Wilcock, Kristiina Jokinen and Seiichi Yamamoto

Annotating Discourse Relations with the PDTB Annotator
Alan Lee, Rashmi Prasad, Bonnie Webber and Aravind K. Joshi

Opinion Retrieval Systems using Tweet-external Factors
Yoon-Sung Kim, Young-In Song and Hae-Chang Rim

TextPro-AL: An Active Learning Platform for Flexible and Efficient Production of Training Data for NLP Tasks
Bernardo Magnini, Anne-Lyse Minard, Mohammed R. H. Qwaider and Manuela Speranza

SideNoter: Scholarly Paper Browsing System based on PDF Restructuring and Text Annotation
Takeshi Abekawa and Akiko Aizawa

Sensing Emotions in Text Messages: An Application and Deployment Study of EmotionPush
Shih-Ming Wang, Chun-Hui Scott Lee, Yu-Chun Lo, Ting-Hao Huang and Lun-Wei Ku

Illinois Cross-Lingual Wikifier: Grounding Entities in Many Languages to the English Wikipedia
Chen-Tse Tsai and Dan Roth

December 15th, 2016 (continued)

14:00–16:00 Demo Session 4

A Meaning-based English Math Word Problem Solver with Understanding, Reasoning and Explanation
Chao-Chun Liang, Shih-Hong Tsai, Ting-Yun Chang, Yi-Chung Lin and Keh-Yih Su

Valencer: an API to Query Valence Patterns in FrameNet
Alexandre Kabbach and Corentin Ribeyre

The Open Framework for Developing Knowledge Base And Question Answering System
Jiseong Kim, GyuHyeon Choi, Jung-Uk Kim, Eun-kyung Kim and KEY-SUN CHOI

Linggle Knows: A Search Engine Tells How People Write
Jhih-Jie Chen, Hao-Chun Peng, Mei-Cih Yeh, Peng-Yu Chen and Jason Chang

A Sentence Simplification System for Improving Relation Extraction
Christina Niklaus, Bernhard Bermeitinger, Siegfried Handschuh and André Freitas

Korean FrameNet Expansion Based on Projection of Japanese FrameNet
jeonguk kim, younggyun hahm and key-sun choi

A Framework for Mining Enterprise Risk and Risk Factors from News Documents
Tirthankar Dasgupta, Lipika Dey, Prasenjit Dey and Rupsa Saha

papago: A Machine Translation Service with Word Sense Disambiguation and Currency Conversion
Hyoung-Gyu Lee, Jun-Seok Kim, Joong-Hwi Shin, Jaesong Lee, Ying-Xiu Quan and Young-Seob Jeong

TopoText: Interactive Digital Mapping of Literary Text
Randa El Khatib, Julia El Zini, David Wrisley, Mohamad Jaber and Shady Elbassuoni

ACE: Automatic Colloquialism, Typographical and Orthographic Errors Detection for Chinese Language
Shichao Dong, Gabriel Pui Cheong Fung, Binyang Li, Baolin Peng, Ming Liao, Jia Zhu and Kam-Fai Wong

A Tool for Efficient Content Compilation
Boris Galitsky

December 16th, 2016

10:30–12:30 Demo Session 5

December 16th, 2016 (continued)

14:00–15:30 Demo Session 6

CaseSummarizer: A System for Automated Summarization of Legal Texts
Seth Polsley, Pooja Jhunjhunwala and Ruihong Huang

WISDOM X, DISAANA and D-SUMM: Large-scale NLP Systems for Analyzing Textual Big Data
Junta Mizuno, Masahiro Tanaka, Kiyonori Ohtake, Jong-Hoon Oh, Julien Kloetzer, Chikara Hashimoto and Kentaro Torisawa

Multilingual Information Extraction with PolyglotIE
Alan Akbik, laura chiticariu, Marina Danilevsky, Yonas Kbrom, Yunyao Li and Huaiyu Zhu

WordForce: Visualizing Controversial Words in Debates
Wei-Fan Chen, Fang-Yu Lin and Lun-Wei Ku

Zara: A Virtual Interactive Dialogue System Incorporating Emotion, Sentiment and Personality Recognition
Pascale Fung, Anik Dey, Farhad Bin Siddique, Ruixi Lin, Yang Yang, Dario Bertero, Yan Wan, Ricky Ho Yin Chan and Chien-Sheng Wu

NL2KB: Resolving Vocabulary Gap between Natural Language and Knowledge Base in Knowledge Base Construction and Retrieval
Sheng-Lun Wei, Yen-Pin Chiu, Hen-Hsen Huang and Hsin-Hsi Chen

PKUSUMSUM : A Java Platform for Multilingual Document Summarization
Jianmin Zhang, Tianming Wang and Xiaojun Wan

Kotonush: Understanding Concepts Based on Values behind Social Media
Tatsuya Iwanari, Kohei Ohara, Naoki Yoshinaga, Nobuhiro Kaji, Masashi Toyoda and Masaru Kitsuregawa

Exploring a Continuous and Flexible Representation of the Lexicon
Pierre Marchal and Thierry Poibeau

Automatically Suggesting Example Sentences of Near-Synonyms for Language Learners
Chieh-Yang Huang, Nicole Peinelt and Lun-Wei Ku

Kyoto-NMT: a Neural Machine Translation implementation in Chainer
Fabien Cromieres

An Interactive System for Exploring Community Question Answering Forums

Enamul Hoque[†‡], Shafiq Joty[†], Lluís Màrquez[†], Alberto Barrón-Cedeño[†], Giovanni Da San Martino[†]
Alessandro Moschitti[†], Preslav Nakov[†], Salvatore Romeo[†], and Giuseppe Carenini[‡]
[†]ALT group, Qatar Computing Research Institute, HBKU, Qatar Foundation
[‡]Department of Computer Science, University of British Columbia
[†]{sjoty,lmarquez,albarron,amoschitti,gmartino,pnakov,sromeo}@qf.org.qa
[‡]{enamul,carenini}@cs.ubc.ca

Abstract

We present an interactive system to provide effective and efficient search capabilities in Community Question Answering (cQA) forums. The system integrates state-of-the-art technology for answer search with a Web-based user interface specifically tailored to support the cQA forum readers. The answer search module automatically finds relevant answers for a new question by exploring related questions and the comments within their threads. The graphical user interface presents the search results and supports the exploration of related information. The system is running live as a part of the Qatar Living forums.

1 Introduction

Community Question Answering (cQA) forums, such as StackOverflow and Quora, are becoming more and more popular these days.[1] They represent effective means for communities of users around particular topics to share information and to collectively solve their information needs. cQA forums typically organize their content in the form of multiple topic-oriented *question–comment threads*, where a question posed by a user may be answered by a possibly very long list of other users' comments.

Many such on-line forums are not moderated, which often results in noisy and redundant content. Users tend to initiate new questions or engage in discussions that easily deviate from the original topic. Additionally, the same questions may be posted repeatedly with minor variations. This near-duplicity is very difficult to track for users, who are usually offered simple search capabilities by the forum interface. Finding existing good answers to newly-posed questions (i.e., never asked in exactly this way before) is a real challenge for cQA, since they may be scattered around multiple related conversations and buried among a large number of comments. Recently, automatic systems have been proposed to address this problem in the framework of the SemEval-2015 and SemEval-2016 tasks on cQA (Nakov et al., 2015; Nakov et al., 2016).[2]

In this paper, we present an interactive system tailored to help users to find good answers to a new question and we apply it to the Qatar Living forum. The system integrates search and NLP modules to (*i*) find related questions in the forum, and (*ii*) rank by relevance the comments within the thread for each such related question. The top suggested answer to the original question is found by a combination of these two processes. The core NLP part of our system is the answer ranking module. This is an improved version of the state-of-the-art classifier with which we participated in SemEval-2016 Task 3 (Barrón-Cedeño et al., 2016).

Our system integrates a Web-based interface to address the further challenges that arise in presenting the results to the user. The interface allows the user to start with a new question, then to explore the related threads to find the ones that are most relevant to his/her information needs, and eventually to navigate through the comments of a thread looking for relevant answers to the question.

[1] http://stackoverflow.com, https://www.quora.com
[2] http://alt.qcri.org/semeval\{2015,2016\}/task3/

Proceedings of COLING 2016, the 26th International Conference on Computational Linguistics: System Demonstrations, pages 1–5, Osaka, Japan, December 11-17 2016.

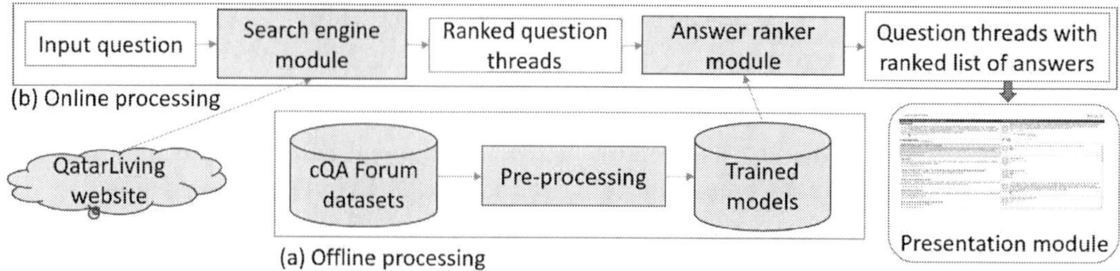

Figure 1: Overview of our interactive system for supporting community question answering.

2 System Overview

An overview of our system is shown in Figure 1. We first perform some offline steps to process the data and to train the rerankers (Subfigure a). The proper on-line system is illustrated in Subfigure b. In the remainder of this section, we briefly discuss these steps.

Offline Processing In order to build the system, we obtained a recent dump of the Qatar Living forum (from March 2016), and we performed several formatting pre-processing steps. We also used the cQA dataset from SemEval-2016 Task 3 (subtask A), where the comments in the threads are annotated with `good` vs. `bad` labels indicating how well the comments answer the question in the thread. Using this dataset, we extracted features and we trained a kernel-based comment classifier (cf. Section 3). The trained models are used to provide goodness scores for each comment in each thread.

Online Processing When a user types a new question q, the system performs the following three steps on the fly: (*i*) *Retrieving related questions with a search engine module*, where Google local search is invoked to retrieve the top-n question threads in the Qatar Living forum that are most similar to q; (*ii*) *Ranking the answers*, where all the comments from these top-n question threads are ranked based on their relevance with respect to q (see Section 3 for detail); (*iii*) *Visualizing the results*, where the presentation module takes the related questions' threads together with the ranked lists of comments and the overall best selected answer, and presents them to the user within an interactive Web interface (see Section 4 below).

3 Ranking Answers with Respect to the Input Question

We compute the relevance score of a comment c in a question thread q' with respect to the original question q by multiplying: (*i*) the relevance of q' to q (we use the inverse rank in the list returned by the Google search engine) by (*ii*) the goodness score for c with respect to q' (produced by the comment classifier, and indicating how well comment c answers q'). The resulting score is used to rank all the comments from the retrieved question threads to obtain the best overall answer to the input question. The core NLP component of this architecture is the comment classifier, which is briefly described below.

The Comment Classifier Given a question and a set of comments associated with it, the task is to assign a relevance score to each of the comments according to their *goodness* at answering the question. This very problem was set at SemEval-2016 Task 3 (Nakov et al., 2016). We trained a Support Vector Machine (SVM) classifier on the SemEval-2016 subtask A dataset to distinguish between `good` and `bad` comments. The kernel function in our SVM is a linear combination of four functions: two linear kernels over numeric features and embeddings, and two tree kernels over shallow syntactic trees.

Numeric Features They include three types of information: (*i*) a variety of textual similarity measures computed between the question and the comment, (*ii*) several Boolean features capturing the presence of URLs, emails, positive/negative words, acknowledgments, forum categories, long words, etc., and (*iii*) a set of global features modeling dialogue and user interactions in the thread. More detailed descriptions of these features can be found in (Barrón-Cedeño et al., 2015; Nicosia et al., 2015; Joty et al., 2015).

Embedding Features We learn embeddings for questions and answers by training a convolutional neural network (CNN) on the comment classification task following (Severyn and Moschitti, 2015). Specifically, the input to the CNN is formed by two matrices containing word embeddings for the question and for the answer, respectively. The CNN performs a *convolution* and a *max-pooling* operations on the word embeddings and on the convoluted feature maps, respectively, to produce the question embedding q_e and the answer embedding c_e. These embeddings are then combined to produce a similarity value using a similarity matrix. The similarity and the embeddings along with other additional similarity features are then passed through a hidden layer and next to the output layer for classification. The q_e and c_e are learned by backpropagating the (cross entropy) errors from the output layer. q_e and c_e vectors are finally concatenated and used as features in our SVM model.

Tree kernels We use tree kernels to measure the syntactic similarity between the question and the comment. First, we produce shallow syntactic trees for the question and for the comment using the Stanford parser (Klein and Manning, 2003). Following Severyn and Moschitti (2012), we link the two trees by connecting nodes such as NP, PP, VP, when there is at least one lexical overlap between the corresponding phrases of the trees, and we mark those links using a specific tag. The kernel function K is defined as: $K((t_1, t_2), (c_1, c_2)) = TK(t_1, c_1) + TK(t_2, c_2)$, where $TK(t, c)$ is a tree kernel function operating over a pair of question (t) and comment (c) trees.[3]

Classification Performance We evaluated our comment classifier on the SemEval-2016 Task 3 test set with the official scorer, obtaining the following results: MAP=77.66, AvgRec=88.05, MRR=84.93, F_1=66.16, Acc=75.54. Compared to the systems that took part in the competition, our system would have ranked in second position according to the official MAP evaluation metric (-1.5 points below the best). In contrast, we achieve better F_1 (+1.8) and better Accuracy (+0.4) than the top system. For a full comparison to the SemEval-2016 Task 3 results see (Nakov et al., 2016).

4 The System in Action

The design of our visual interface was guided by previous research on designing interfaces for exploring online conversations (Hoque and Carenini, 2016); however, in this new design we took into account specific features of cQA data and tasks. Our interface consists of the following components: a search bar, a *question list view* that shows the top-most relevant questions to the user's question; and a *conversation view* showing the question followed by the answers for a particular question thread (see Figure 2).

Questions list view: After the system finds the related questions to the user's question, it presents the top relevant questions in a scrollable list view (see Figure 2, left). Each item within the question list view represents a question thread, showing the original question, the posting date, and a stacked bar with the distribution of useful comments. In this way, the user can get a sense of which threads seem to be more relevant and which threads may contain the most useful answers. The questions are ordered by their relevance rank by default, but the user can change this order by selecting criteria from the popup menu 'Order by'. For instance, s/he can order the question threads based on the number of useful answers within each of these threads. Finally, at any time, the user can filter out less useful comments by using the slider of the legend at the top. Note that on top of the question list view, the interface also shows the comment that has received the best score with respect to the new question ("Best Answer"). This way, the user may be able to find a very good answer to his/her question immediately, without having to open any question thread and then navigating to a good answer within that thread.

Conversation view: When the user selects a particular question thread from the list, the system presents the corresponding thread in the conversation view (see Figure 2, right). On top of this conversation view, the original question along with a visual overview of the entire thread is presented, followed by the list of detailed comments.[4] The thread overview visually encodes the comments using a sequence of rectangles from left to right, where each rectangle represents a comment. A set of five sequential colors was used in a perceptually meaningful order, ranging from dark green (highly useful) to white (not useful) to encode the classification score for each comment.

[3]We use Partial Tree Kernel and Syntactic Tree Kernel (Moschitti, 2006; Collins and Duffy, 2001) to instantiate TK.

[4]Note that the red rectangle in Figure 2 is only used to highlight the thread overview; it is not displayed in the real interface.

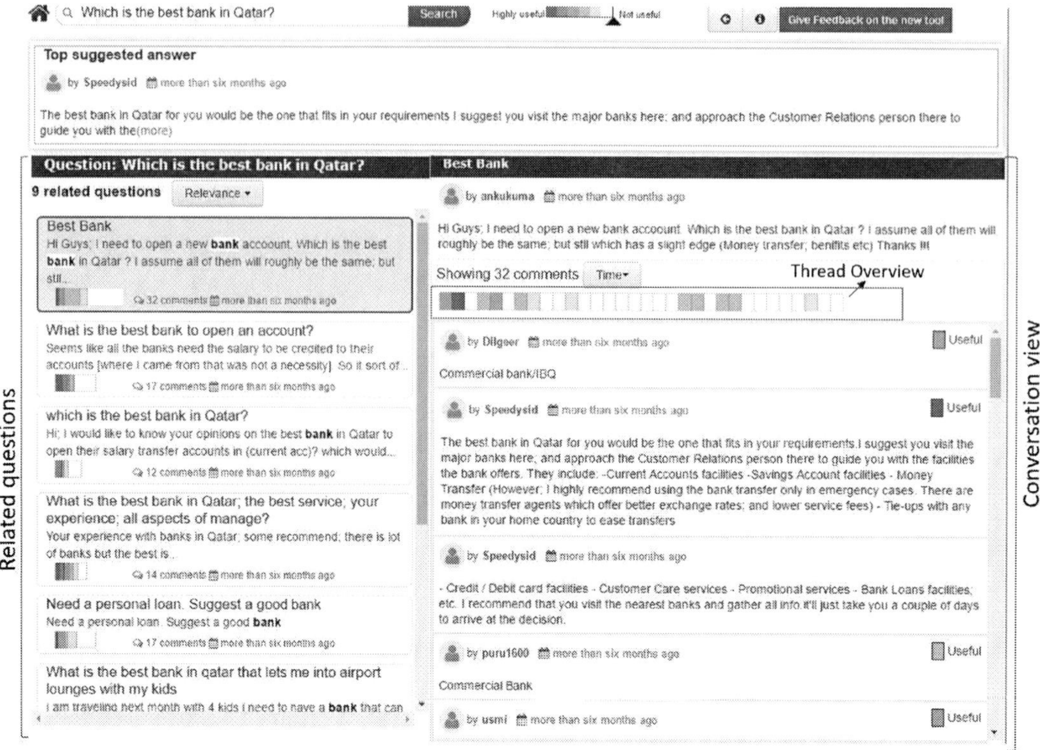

Figure 2: A screenshot of the interface showing the top answer and related questions for a user's question. As the user selects a related question (marked by the blue rectangular boundary), the interface shows the corresponding thread in the conversation view (right).

From the thread overview, the user can quickly notice which comments seem to be more useful and then can immediately navigate to a particular comment by clicking on the rectangle representing that comment. Note that hovering on a rectangle in the thread view highlights the corresponding comment in the detailed view (by scrolling if needed) and vice-versa.

Implementation The system is implemented as a Java Web application and runs on an Apache Tomcat Server. The back-end of the system is developed using Java. The presentation module, on the other hand, is implemented in Javascript (using the D3 and JQuery libraries). The system is sufficiently fast to respond in real time to the user's actions. A key factor for the efficiency is the fact that we precomputed and stored the goodness scores for all the comments in all the question-threads from the static snapshot of the Qatar Living database. Thus, at running time there is no need to classify the comments of the already stored question-comment threads.

5 Conclusion

We have presented an interactive system that supports users to find good answers to newly-posed questions using pre-existing questions and their answer threads in community question answering forums. In particular, we implemented a Web-based demo trained on data from SemEval-2016 Task 3 and allows users to ask questions and to get real-time answers using data from the Qatar Living forum. The demo has already been deployed in Qatar Living.[5] It provides a graphical interface, which allows users to navigate in the set of related questions (question-list view) and in the set of comments in a thread (conversation view). Internally, the system uses state-of-the-art NLP tools and search capabilities to effectively retrieve and rerank a set of comments with respect to the new question.

[5] http://www.qatarliving.com/betasearch/

In future work, we will evaluate the demo interface by running user studies with real Qatar Living users. We also plan to further improve all the classifiers of our system.

Acknowledgments

This research was performed by the Arabic Language Technologies (ALT) group at the Qatar Computing Research Institute (QCRI), HBKU, Qatar Foundation. It is part of the Interactive sYstems for Answer Search (Iyas) project, which is developed in collaboration with MIT-CSAIL. We thank Scott Cyphers and Mitra Mohtarami for their help in designing and implementing the initial demo architecture.

References

Alberto Barrón-Cedeño, Simone Filice, Giovanni Da San Martino, Shafiq Joty, Lluís Màrquez, Preslav Nakov, and Alessandro Moschitti. 2015. Thread-level information for comment classification in community question answering. In *Proceedings of the 53rd Annual Meeting of the Association for Computational Linguistics and the 7th International Joint Conference on Natural Language Processing (Volume 2: Short Papers)*, ACL-IJCNLP '15, pages 687–693, Beijing, China.

Alberto Barrón-Cedeño, Giovanni Da San Martino, Shafiq Joty, Alessandro Moschitti, Fahad Al-Obaidli, Salvatore Romeo, Kateryna Tymoshenko, and Antonio Uva. 2016. ConvKN at SemEval-2016 Task 3: Answer and question selection for question answering on Arabic and English fora. In *Proceedings of the 10th International Workshop on Semantic Evaluation*, SemEval '16, pages 896–903, San Diego, California, USA.

Michael Collins and Nigel Duffy. 2001. Convolution kernels for natural language. In Thomas G. Dietterich, Suzanna Becker, and Zoubin Ghahramani, editors, *Advances in Neural Information Processing Systems*, NIPS '01, pages 625–632, Vancouver, British Columbia, Canada. MIT Press.

Enamul Hoque and Giuseppe Carenini. 2016. MultiConVis: A Visual Text Analytics System for Exploring a Collection of Online Conversations. In *Proceedings of the 21st International Conference on Intelligent User Interfaces*, IUI '2016, pages 96–107, Sonoma, California, USA.

Shafiq Joty, Alberto Barrón-Cedeño, Giovanni Da San Martino, Simone Filice, Lluís Màrquez, Alessandro Moschitti, and Preslav Nakov. 2015. Global thread-level inference for comment classification in community question answering. In *Proc. EMNLP*, pages 573–578.

Dan Klein and Christopher D. Manning. 2003. Accurate unlexicalized parsing. In *Proceedings of the 41st Annual Meeting on Association for Computational Linguistics - Volume 1*, ACL '03, pages 423–430, Sapporo, Japan.

Alessandro Moschitti. 2006. Efficient convolution kernels for dependency and constituent syntactic trees. In *Proceedings of the 17th European Conference on Machine Learning*, ECML'06, pages 318–329, Berlin, Germany.

Preslav Nakov, Lluís Màrquez, Walid Magdy, Alessandro Moschitti, Jim Glass, and Bilal Randeree. 2015. Semeval-2015 task 3: Answer selection in community question answering. In *Proceedings of the 9th International Workshop on Semantic Evaluation*, SemEval '15, pages 269–281, Denver, Colorado, USA.

Preslav Nakov, Lluís Màrquez, Alessandro Moschitti, Walid Magdy, Hamdy Mubarak, abed Alhakim Freihat, Jim Glass, and Bilal Randeree. 2016. SemEval-2016 Task 3: Community question answering. In *Proceedings of the 10th International Workshop on Semantic Evaluation*, SemEval '16, pages 525–545, San Diego, California, USA.

Massimo Nicosia, Simone Filice, Alberto Barrón-Cedeño, Iman Saleh, Hamdy Mubarak, Wei Gao, Preslav Nakov, Giovanni Da San Martino, Alessandro Moschitti, Kareem Darwish, Lluís Màrquez, Shafiq Joty, and Walid Magdy. 2015. QCRI: Answer selection for community question answering - experiments for Arabic and English. In *Proceedings of the 9th International Workshop on Semantic Evaluation*, SemEval '15, pages 203–209, Denver, Colorado, USA.

Aliaksei Severyn and Alessandro Moschitti. 2012. Structural relationships for large-scale learning of answer re-ranking. In *Proceedings of the 35th International Conference on Research and Development in Information Retrieval*, SIGIR '12, pages 741–750, Portland, Oregon, USA.

Aliaksei Severyn and Alessandro Moschitti. 2015. Learning to rank short text pairs with convolutional deep neural networks. In *Proceedings of the 38th International Conference on Research and Development in Information Retrieval*, SIGIR '15, pages 373–382, Santiago, Chile.

NLmaps: A Natural Language Interface to Query OpenStreetMap

Carolin Lawrence
Computational Linguistics
Heidelberg University
69120 Heidelberg, Germany
lawrence@cl.uni-heidelberg.de

Stefan Riezler
Computational Linguistics & IWR
Heidelberg University
69120 Heidelberg, Germany
riezler@cl.uni-heidelberg.de

Abstract

We present a Natural Language Interface (nlmaps.cl.uni-heidelberg.de) to query OpenStreetMap. Natural language questions about geographical facts are parsed into database queries that can be executed against the OpenStreetMap (OSM) database. After parsing the question, the system provides a text-based answer as well as an interactive map with all points of interest and their relevant information marked. Additionally, we provide several options for users to give feedback after a question has been parsed.

1 Introduction

OpenStreetMap (OSM) provides a map of the world, annotated by volunteers with GPS points (*nodes*) that they consider relevant, and with as much corresponding information as is deemed of interest. For example, such nodes mark restaurants, hotels, schools or hospitals. Each node can be assigned various tags, usually from a pool of agreed upon tags by the OSM community, such as "*tourism=hotel*", "*amenity=school*" or "*name=Heidelberg University*". Alternatively, a node may be used to form a *way*, such as a road, in conjunction with other nodes. Nodes and ways in turn can be grouped together to form a *relation*, for example to mark several buildings as belonging to the same institution.

The resulting database is vast, with over 3.4 billion objects, but only offers limited searchability. For example, the search tool on the main website [http://www.openstreetmap.org] finds for the search term "*Gare du Nord*" the train station Gare du Nord in Paris, and returns it as the first search result. For "*Where are 3 star hotels in Paris*", no search result is found, even though the database contains objects marked with the tags "*tourism=hotel*" and "*stars=3*". To be able to find these objects, one would have to use the Overpass API [http://wiki.openstreetmap.org/wiki/Overpass_API] which requires extensive knowledge of not just the OSM tags used, but also of the Overpass query language. A query in this case would read "*area[name='Paris']→.a;node(area.a)[tourism= 'hotel'][stars='3'];out;*" which is not feasible for everyday use for the average user.

To be able to ask exactly such questions, we developed a semantic parser for the OSM domain that maps natural language questions to a Machine Readable Language formula (MRL) which can be executed against the OSM database. Also, we created an interface (see Figure 1 for a screenshot) that makes the parser available for online use. Furthermore, we extended our framework with various conveniences such as location detection and an interactive map that connects the text-based answer from the parser with clickable markers on an interactive map via hyperlinks. With the help of a feedback formula, the users can help us to improve the parser and to extend it to other languages in the future.

A few examples of questions that our interface can answer are:

```
What is the closest bank with ATMs from the Palace of Holyroodhouse in
Edinburgh?

Which driving school is closest to Mannheimer Straße in Heidelberg and where
is it?
```


Proceedings of COLING 2016, the 26th International Conference on Computational Linguistics: System Demonstrations, pages 6–10, Osaka, Japan, December 11-17 2016.

Figure 1: A screenshot of the user interface after a question has been processed, and the underlined link in the answer box was clicked to open up the corresponding marker's popup.

```
Where are the closest bank and the closest pharmacy from the Rue Lauriston
in Paris?
```

In the following, we present a semantic parsing approach that uses hard constraints to search a geographic information system that can cope with complex spatial expressions, such as "*nearby*" or "*in walking distance*". The type of questions that can be answered, may be found in Table 2.

The system can be freely accessed by anyone and all components of the semantic parser are publicly available. For detailed license notes of the individual components see `nlmaps.cl.uni-heidelberg.de`.

To the best of our knowledge, this is the first approach of a natural language interface to OSM using semantic parsing. Overpass-turbo[1] supplies a wizard that uses a simple set of rules to match a few basic natural language words to Overpass, e.g. "*tourism=museum in Vienna*". Other purely string matching approaches are Nominatim[2] and GeoNames[3].

2 System Architecture

Area Recognition. The interface offers the users a text field to type in their question and to submit it to the system. Once the system receives such a submitted question, the processing pipeline is started. First, possible area references (locations that are areas) mentioned in the question need to be identified. For example, the system will recognize "*Heidelberg*" as a city name in "*Which cuisines are there in Heidelberg?*". Words following "*in*" and "*around*" are marked as area references. Additionally, we mark a word as an area reference if it is preceded by "*of*" and if the previous word was "*vicinity*" or a cardinal direction ("*Where are restaurants in the east of Heidelberg?*").

In a next step, the identified area references are mapped to an OSM object. This is accomplished using the OSM tool Nominatim [`http://wiki.openstreetmap.org/wiki/Nominatim`] which,

[1] `http://overpass-turbo.eu/`
[2] `http://wiki.openstreetmap.org/wiki/Nominatim`
[3] `http://www.geonames.org/`

given a search term, searches the name and address fields of all OSM objects and returns a ranked list. The object has to be either a way or a relation, as a single node (i.e. a GPS point) does not span an area. The ranked list is searched until either a way or a relation is found. The resulting object will then be used to constrain the search for objects of interest to lie within the area spanned by said object. One main drawback of this strategy is that a name which applies to several cities will only ever match the first city found. Thus a person living in Heidelberg, Pennsylvania, will always be disappointed with answers that concern Heidelberg, Germany. Because of this, we offer two alternative input methods to the user. The first is a text field where the user can specifically enter the area that shlould be searched. If "*Heidelberg, Pennsylvania*" is entered, then Nominatim will return the correct area. To alleviate the effort required on the user's part, we offer another option which can be selected by clicking the button "*Use my location*". This will ask the Geolocation API [`http://www.w3schools.com/html/html5_geolocation.asp`] to locate the user's device. Of course, the user is first asked for permission. Once the user's GPS location has been determined, Nominatim's reverse geocoding feature can provide the name of the city in which the GPS coordinates lie.

Semantic Parsing. After these preprocessing steps have been accomplished, the question is sent to a semantic parser. The parser employed here is a SMT system that translates from natural language to a machine readable language (MRL), following an approach introduced by Andreas et al. (2013). A MRL for the OSM domain as well as a corpus, NLMAPS, containing 2,380 question-MRL pairs was introduced by Haas and Riezler (2016) [`http://www.cl.uni-heidelberg.de/statnlpgroup/nlmaps/`]. Using this corpus, split into 1,500 training examples and 880 test examples, a SMT system can be trained, using GIZA++ (Och and Ney, 2003) and the SMT framework CDEC (Dyer et al., 2010), including a MERT run. Finally, the MRL returned by the SMT system is executed against the OSM database using an extension of the Overpass API, OVERPASS NLMAPS [`https://github.com/carhaas/overpass-nlmaps`]. All relevant information is collected from the returned database objects and is then compiled into 2 different output formats.

Answer Presentation. Answers are returned in the interface's answer box in text format. Additionally, the output, formatted in GeoJSON, is used to place markers in the appropriate GPS locations on an interactive map. If a marker is clicked, this output supplies further information that may be of interest to the user in a popup. It first provides the object's name. Second it lists information directly related to the text-based answer. In the example of Figure 1, this would be the cuisine served at the restaurant the marker points to. Further it provides the exact latitude and longitude of the objects but also, again using Nominatim's reverse geocoding feature, a human readable address (due to resource reasons this is currently only supported for selected countries). Lastly, it lists all values of an OSM tag's key-value pair ("*amenity=restaurant*") which were used in the query that returned the object.

To browse the results, the users can now move around the map and click on markers for more information. Alternatively, they can, if applicable, click on an element in the text-based answer which will then open all relevant markers' popups. In the example in Figure 1, the user clicked "*malaysian*" and all restaurant markers that serve malaysian food where opened.

Backoff. Should the semantic parser not find an answer, then the system backs off and queries Nominatim. If Nominatim now finds an answer, that information is then presented to the user.

3 Semantic Parser Training

For the semantic parser to work in this setting we extended the parser described in Haas and Riezler (2016) in several ways[4].

Area IDs. One of the issues of the original model is its difficulty to generalize to area references not seen during training. It purely relies on the word to be passed through. Our first parsing model alleviates

[4]Their model labelled "*+intersect +stem +cdec +pass +cfg*" is called "*original*" in Table 1 and the extensions are added consecutively onto that model.

NLMAPS		Precision	Recall	F1
1	original	89.90	64.02	74.78
2	+IDs	88.67	66.17	75.78
3	+SE	89.56	65.67	75.71
SE		Precision	Recall	F1
1	original	71.56	39.27	50.71
2	+IDs	63.32	40.4	49.29
3	+SE	90.86	71.64	80.11

Table 1: Semantic Parsing results on the NLMAPS and SE test sets for the models introduced. Results are an average over 3 runs because the tuning algorithm MERT introduces randomization.

Type	Example
aggregation	How many...?
GPS location	Where...?
existence	Is there...?
specific key search	What is the name/website/...?
distance	How far apart...?
cardinal direction	...in the north of...?
closest	closest hotel
radius search	hotels in walking distance
exclusive or	a bar or restaurant
union	a butcher and a bakery

Table 2: An overview of the questions types the system has seen during training.

this issue by the area reference recognizer and lookup components described above. For example, the question "*Where are restaurants in Heidelberg?*" is changed to "*Where are restaurants in 3600285864*" by the area recognizer and lookup components. We thus modified the MRLs in the training corpus to reflect this change accordingly.

Search Engine Queries. A first test of the system showed that people tend to enter, search engine style, short queries, rather than fully grammatically correct sentences. The discrepancy between the training data and these queries causes a significant drop in performance. We thus changed the complex sentences of NLMAPS into these shortened forms, resulting in a second data set, SEARCHENGINE (SE). The current parser model performs very badly on this new test set (see Table 1), confirming the reports of the first testers. Training a new model on both the original and the new training data shows a big increase in performance (model "+*SE*"). The model is now better on the SE test set than on the NLMAPS test set. We attribute this to the fact that all words that are not strictly necessary are removed in a search engine style query, allowing the model to exclusively focus on the important words.

4 User Feedback Mechanisms

To be able to improve our system in the future, we implemented mechanisms that allow us to gather user feedback after a question has been answered. The most direct feedback option is directly integrated into the answer box. It asks for single point feedback to the question "*Was that helpful?*" where the user can select the "*Yes*" or the "*No*" button.

Alternatively, the user can click the "*More*" button which then opens another window that overlays the previous. Here the user can provide more detailed feedback. The questions become progressively more complex, in the sense that the further the user progresses, the more detailed knowledge is required about OSM, the Overpass query language, and the MRL. Each question asks the user if an intermediate result from various steps in the pipeline is correct or not. The intermediate result is printed in a text box which the user can edit if it is wrong. Alternatively, the user can also merely indicate if it is correct or not, using buttons next to the text box. The user can stop at any time, thus submitting an incomplete form, or close the feedback window without answering any questions at all.

If a user can correct the MRL, then this highest level feedback equals a training example with a gold answer. Any supervised learning can be used to further improve the parser. However, this type of feedback is by far the hardest to give. A more likely scenario is one, where a user who regularly used the Overpass query language, visits the site and corrects the Overpass query in the feedback form. This would still provide a high quality supervision signal, though only partial. The same holds true for the other feedback questions where the correct output or the 0/1 feedback can be seen as a partial supervision signal of varying degrees of detail.

We will use this feedback to test various algorithms for response-based learning (Kwiatowski et al. (2013), Berant et al. (2013), Goldwasser and Roth (2013), Szepesvári (2009), Bubeck and Cesa-Bianchi

(2012), *inter alia*) to improve the parser. A new challenge will be to incorporate the different levels of feedback into one algorithm.

5 Conclusion

We presented an online interface with which the OSM database can be queried using natural language. While the parser is not yet close to answering every question posed, it already shows promising results. Considering that previously a simple question like "*Where are 3 star hotels in Paris*" needed detailed knowledge of OSM and the Overpass query language, we think that the interface takes a large step towards making the vast and interesting knowledge of the OSM database available to the everyday user.

In the future, we will use feedback gained from the users to improve the system further, using algorithms for learning from partial feedback. Additionally, we want to extend our system to work for multiple languages. To this end, we will train SMT systems that translate the question into English, which can then be parsed with the current system. To improve the translations into English by the SMT system, we can again make use of the feedback users provide by employing response based learning algorithms, particularly the algorithms introduced by Riezler et al. (2014). The user feedback as well as the question logs will also be used to further improve the system in future work.

Acknowledgments

We would like to thank the OSM developers Roland Olbricht and Martin Raifer for their support. The research reported in this paper was supported in part by DFG grant RI-2221/2-1 "Grounding Statistical Machine Translation in Perception and Action".

References

Jacob Andreas, Andreas Vlachos, and Stephen Clark. 2013. Semantic parsing as machine translation. In *Proceedings of the 51st Annual Meeting of the Association for Computational Linguistics (ACL)*, Sofia, Bulgaria.

Jonathan Berant, Andrew Chou, Roy Frostig, and Percy Liang. 2013. Semantic parsing on Freebase from question-answer pairs. In *Proceedings of the 2013 Conference on Empirical Methods in Natural Language Processing (EMNLP)*, Seattle, WA.

Sébastian Bubeck and Nicolò Cesa-Bianchi. 2012. Regret analysis of stochastic and nonstochastic multi-armed bandit problems. *Foundations and Trends in Machine Learning*, 5(1):1–122.

Chris Dyer, Adam Lopez, Juri Ganitkevitch, Johnathan Weese, Ferhan Ture, Phil Blunsom, Hendra Setiawan, Vladimir Eidelman, and Philip Resnik. 2010. cdec: A decoder, alignment, and learning framework for finite-state and context-free translation models. In *Proceedings of the 48th Annual Meeting of the Association for Computational Linguistics (ACL)*, Uppsala, Sweden.

Dan Goldwasser and Dan Roth. 2013. Learning from natural instructions. *Machine Learning*, 94(2):205–232.

Carolin Haas and Stefan Riezler. 2016. A corpus and semantic parser for multilingual natural language querying of OpenStreetMap. In *In Proceedings of the North American Chapter of the Association for Computational Linguistics (NAACL)*, San Diego, California, June.

Tom Kwiatowski, Eunsol Choi, Yoav Artzi, and Luke Zettlemoyer. 2013. Scaling semantic parsers with on-the-fly ontology matching. In *Proceedings of the Conference on Empirical Methods in Natural Language Processing (EMNLP)*, Seattle, WA.

Franz Josef Och and Hermann Ney. 2003. A systematic comparison of various statistical alignment models. *Computational Linguistics*, 29(1):19–51.

Stefan Riezler, Patrick Simianer, and Carolin Haas. 2014. Response-based learning for grounded machine translation. In *Proceedings of the 52nd Annual Meeting of the Association for Computational Linguistics (ACL)*, Baltimore, MD.

Csaba Szepesvári. 2009. *Algorithms for Reinforcement Learning*. Synthesis Lectures on Artificial Intelligence and Machine Learning. Morgan & Claypool.

A Reading Environment for Learners of Chinese as a Foreign Language

John Lee, Chun Yin Lam, Shu Jiang
Department of Linguistics and Translation
City University of Hong Kong
jsylee@cityu.edu.hk, mickey1224@gmail.com, jshmjs45@gmail.com

Abstract

We present a mobile app that provides a reading environment for learners of Chinese as a foreign language. The app includes a text database that offers over 500K articles from Chinese Wikipedia. These articles have been word-segmented; each word is linked to its entry in a Chinese-English dictionary, and to automatically-generated review exercises. The app estimates the reading proficiency of the user based on a "to-learn" list of vocabulary items. It automatically constructs and maintains this list by tracking the user's dictionary lookup behavior and performance in review exercises. When a user searches for articles to read, search results are filtered such that the proportion of unknown words does not exceed a user-specified threshold.

1 Introduction

"Free voluntary reading" — i.e., recreational reading, or reading for pleasure — promotes reading competence and vocabulary development (Krashen, 2005). Since it plays such an important role in second language acquisition, students benefit from reading a wide range of texts, inside and outside the classroom.

We present a mobile app that facilitates reading among learners of Chinese as a foreign language. The app includes a text database that offers over 500K articles from Chinese Wikipedia, covering a wide range of topics. These articles have been word-segmented. The app provides a supportive reading environment by linking each word to its entry in a Chinese-English dictionary. It also automatically generates review exercises for each word. Further, the app estimates the reading proficiency of the user based on his "to-learn" list of vocabulary items, and maintains this list by tracking user behavior in dictionary lookup and performance in review exercises. When a user searches for articles to read, search results are filtered such that the proportion of unknown words does not exceed a user-specified threshold.

The rest of the paper is organized as follows. Section 2 summarizes the features of the app; these features rely on a user proficiency model, which is presented in Section 3. Section 4 then describes implementation details and evaluates the quality of the review exercises. Section 5 compares this app with other computer-assisted language learning systems. Finally, Section 6 concludes.

2 System Features

The app toggles among three modes — Search, Read, and Review. In addition, there is a "Settings" page for user customization.

2.1 Search Mode

The start page of the app presents a search interface for reading materials (Figure 1a). The user can enter keywords to search for articles on the desired topic. Below the search field, the page displays words that are currently in the user's personal "to-learn" list. By highlighting these keywords, the app steers the user to articles that can reinforce or expand his vocabulary knowledge.

Proceedings of COLING 2016, the 26th International Conference on Computational Linguistics: System Demonstrations, pages 11–15, Osaka, Japan, December 11-17 2016.

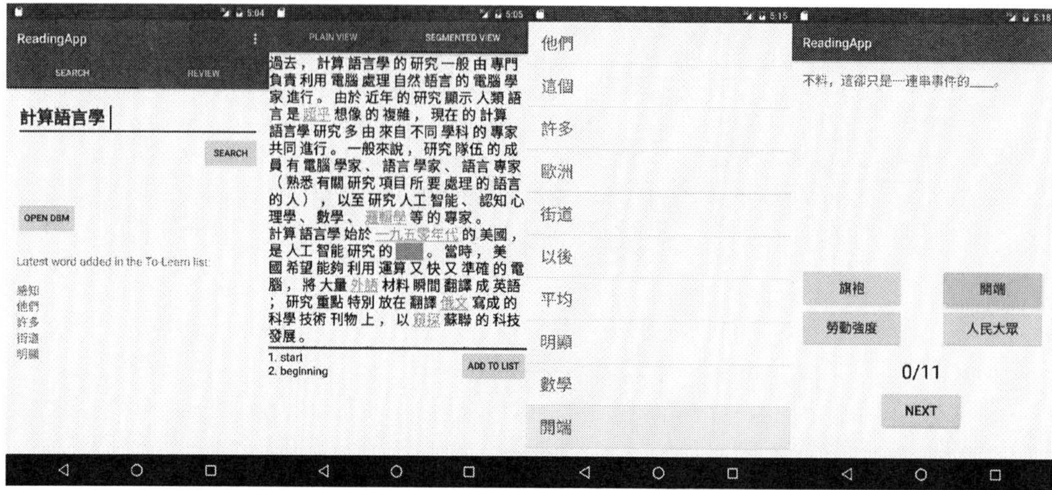

Figure 1: From left to right: (a) **Search Mode** (Section 2.1): The user enters the keyword *ji suan yu yan xue* 'computational linguistics' to search for articles on that topic; below the search field, the user's personal "to-learn" list is shown to provide suggested keywords. (b) **Read Mode** (Section 2.2): One of the retrieved articles is displayed with word segmentation. Words predicted to be unknown to the user are highlighted in orange. The user taps on the word *kai duan* 'beginning' to consult its dictionary entry in English. (c) **Settings page** (Section 2.4): The user views his "to-learn" list, to which the word *kai duan* has been added. (d) **Review Mode** (Section 2.3): A fill-in-the-blank item is offered for the word *kai duan*, with three other distractors.

Previous research suggests that learners need to know 95% to 98% of the words in a text in order to understand it well (Laufer, 1989; Hu and Nation, 2000; Schmitt et al., 2011). While the user should not be overwhelmed with difficulty words, he might nonetheless desire articles that stretch his vocabulary. By default, the search results are filtered such that the proportion of unknown words does not exceed 20%. This percentage can be adjusted by the user to suit his preference (Section 2.4). The app dynamically estimates the user's vocabulary level (Section 3), so that search results keep pace with his increasing proficiency.

2.2 Read Mode

When the user taps on a search result, the app enters the Read Mode and initially displays plain text with no reading aid. The user may choose to request word segmentation and English translations for Chinese words. As shown in Figure 1b, word boundaries are indicated with space, and words predicted to be unknown to the user are highlighted in yellow. When the user taps on a Chinese word, the app shows its English translation at the bottom, and also prompts the user to add the Chinese word to his "to-learn" list.

2.3 Review Mode

At any time, the user can request review exercises for words in his "to-learn" list. We will refer to the word being reviewed as the "target word". The app offers two kinds of exercises:

- ***Translation exercises***: The user is shown the target word and three possible choices of its English translation. One of these choices is the definition extracted from the English dictionary (Section 4.1). The other three are distractors, drawn randomly among other entries in the dictionary. These exercises start with easy words in the "to-learn" list and proceed to the more difficult ones, as estimated by word frequencies in Chinese Wikipedia.

- ***Fill-in-the-blank exercises***: The system randomly draws a sentence from the text database (Section 4.1) that contains the target word. It blanks out the target word and offers four choices. One choice is the target word itself; the other three are distractors, chosen such that they have the same part-of-speech and similar word frequencies as the target word (Coniam, 1997). Figure 1d shows a fill-in-the-blank item for the word *kai duan* 'beginning'.

If the user picks the right answer for either exercise, the target word is removed from the "to-learn" list, and the user proficiency model is updated (Section 3).

2.4 Settings

On the Settings page, the user can view and adjust three parameters:

- ***"To-learn" list***. The user can view and optionally remove words from the "to-learn" list (Figure 1c).
- ***Vocabulary coverage percentage***: This parameter specifies the minimum percentage of words that must be known to the user in an article, to filter out reading material that would require excessive dictionary lookup. It is set at 80% by default and can be adjusted by the user.
- ***User proficiency level***: The app estimates the user's vocabulary proficiency level (Section 3). The level is shown to the user on a 20-level scale. Level 1 assumes knowledge of the 1000 most frequent words in Chinese Wikipedia. Each subsequent level adds the 1000 next most frequent words, up to Level 20. At this highest level, with the default vocabulary coverage percentage of 80%, the user would be able to read 82.2% of the articles in Chinese Wikipedia. The user can manually adjust his proficiency level in order to obtain easier or more difficult reading material.

3 User Proficiency Model

In order to retrieve texts that challenge the user, yet not overwhelmingly difficult, the app attempts to estimate the user's proficiency level. Automatic proficiency assessment is a difficult task and needs to consider a wide range of factors. Since previous research has shown significant correlation between proficiency and vocabulary level (Laufer and Nation, 1995; Coniam, 1999), we focus on the user's vocabulary size. Specifically, the app estimates the number of Chinese words that the user knows. We rank the words in the user's "to-learn" list according to their frequency in Chinese Wikipedia. The user is then estimated to know all words that have higher frequency than the median word in the list.

A new user is estimated to know 5000 words, the breadth required for the highest level of the *Hanyu Shuiping Kaoshi* (HSK), a widely adopted proficiency test for Chinese. The estimate then dynamically changes according to the set of words in the "to-learn" list. In Read Mode, when the user looks up the English translation of a Chinese word, that word is added to the list. In Review Mode, when the user successfully completes an exercise on a target word, that word is removed from the list. The user can also directly edit the "to-learn" list and/or the proficiency level in the Settings page (Section 2.4).

4 Implementation

4.1 Text Database

We used Solr, a high performance search server that supports full-text search, to construct our database. We extracted a total of 524,543 articles from Chinese Wikipedia to be included in the database. On average, each article has 370 characters and 12 sentences. We segmented all texts with the Stanford Chinese segmenter (Manning et al., 2014). CC-CEDICT, a Chinese to English dictionary with 114,291 entries, supplies English translations for Chinese words in the texts.

4.2 Fill-in-the-blank Exercises

For each target word, the app generates fill-in-the-blank items (Section 2.3). Each item consists of a carrier sentence with a blank, and four choices for the blank. The generation process is as follows:

- ***Carrier sentence selection***: The sentence must contain the target word, and must be between 10 and 20 words long. Further, other words in the sentence must not be more difficult (i.e., have lower frequency) than the target word. Within these constraints, for each target word, ten sentences are selected as carrier sentences.

- ***Distractor generation***: While the key for the item is the target word, the three distractors must be generated. We follow largely the same criteria as Coniam (1997), requiring the distractors to have similar word frequency and the same part-of-speech as the key. It is crucial that a distractor be an unacceptable answer. We evaluated 100 fill-in-the-blank items, randomly chosen from all 20 levels. Overall, 92% of these items had a unique answer (i.e., the target word), while the remaining 8% contained two correct answers.

5 Previous Work

Current systems that support reading in a foreign language mostly focus on English. The user can search for web pages with the *Read-X* tool, which classifies them in real time according to theme and to difficulty level (Miltsakaki and Troutt, 2008); the text is then displayed in the *Toreador* tool, which underlines unknown vocabulary according to the user-specified grade level. Another system, *REAP*, allows the user to search a database of downloaded web pages (Heilman et al., 2008). Similar to our system, *REAP* offers fill-in-the-blank exercises, but they are human-crafted rather than automatically generated.

Fewer systems are available to learners of Chinese as a foreign language. Many focus mainly on teaching characters and words (Shei and Hsieh, 2012). Others, such as *Clavis Sinica* (clavisinica.com) and *Du Chinese* (duchinese.net), use pre-selected texts, vocabulary exercises and translations. The *Smart Chinese Reader* (nlptool.com) allows the user to input any text, and then automatically performs word segmentation and links the words to CC-CEDICT. In addition, it supports automatic sentence translation, and helps the user maintain a "to-learn" word list. Distinct to the systems cited above, our system automatically generates vocabulary review exercises (Section 2.3), and dynamically estimates the user's proficiency level to personalize search results (Section 3).

6 Conclusions and Future work

We have presented an app that offers a reading environment for learners of Chinese as a foreign language. It helps the user search for reading material at an appropriate vocabulary level, and automatically generates review exercises. In future work, we would like to further develop this app in a number of areas. First, we intend to implement more sophisticated criteria for choosing sentences for the review exercises (Kilgarriff et al., 2008). Second, we aim to refine the estimation procedure for the user's vocabulary level (Miltsakaki and Troutt, 2008; Ehara et al., 2012; Ehara et al., 2013). Lastly, we plan to take into account the syntactic complexity of a text when assessing its difficulty level (Heilman et al., 2007).

Acknowledgements

This work is funded by the Language Fund under Research and Development Projects 2015-2016 of the Standing Committee on Language Education and Research (SCOLAR), Hong Kong SAR.

References

David Coniam. 1997. A Preliminary Inquiry into Using Corpus Word Frequency Data in the Automatic Generation of English Language Cloze Tests. *CALICO Journal*, 14(2-4):15–33.

David Coniam. 1999. Second Language Proficiency and Word Frequency in English. *Asian Journal of English Language Teaching*, 9:59–74.

Yo Ehara, Issei Sato, Hidekazu Oiwa, and Hiroshi Nakagawa. 2012. Mining Words in the Minds of Second Language Learners: Learner-specific Word Difficulty. In *Proc. COLING*.

Yo Ehara, Nobuyuki Shimizu, Takashi Ninomiya, and Hiroshi Nakagawa. 2013. Personalized Reading Support for Second-Language Web Documents. *ACM Transactions on Intelligent Systems and Technology*, 4(2):31.

Michael Heilman, Kevyn Collins-Thompson, Jamie Callan, and Maxine Eskenazi. 2007. Combining Lexical and Grammatical Features to Improve Readability Measures for First and Second Language Texts. In *Proc. NAACL-HLT*.

Michael Heilman, Le Zhao, Juan Pino, and Maxine Eskenazi. 2008. Retrieval of reading materials for vocabulary and reading practice. In *Proc. Third Workshop on Innovative Use of NLP for Building Educational Applications*.

Marcella Hu and I. S. P. Nation. 2000. Unknown Vocabulary Density and Reading Comprehension. *Reading in a Foreign Language*, 13(1):403–430.

Adam Kilgarriff, Mils Husák, Katy McAdam, Michael Rundell, and Pavel Rychlý. 2008. GDEX: Automatically Finding Good Dictionary Examples in a Corpus. In *Proc. EURALEX*.

Stephen Krashen. 2005. Free Voluntary reading: New Research, Applications, and Controversies. In Gloria Poedjosoedarmo, editor, *Innovative Approaches to Reading and Writing Instruction, Anthology Series 46*, pages 1–9, Singapore. Southeast Asian Ministers of Education Organization (SEAMEO) Regional Language Centre (RELC).

Batia Laufer and P. Nation. 1995. Vocabulary Size and Use: Lexical Richness in L2 Written Production. *Applied Linguistics*, 16(3):307–322.

Batia Laufer. 1989. What Percentage of Text-Lexis is Essential for Comprehension? In Christer Laurén and Marianne Nordman, editors, *Special Language; from Humans Thinking to Thinking Machines*, pages 316–323, Clevedon. Multilingual Matters.

Christopher D. Manning, Mihai Surdeanu, John Bauer, Jenny Finkel, Steven J. Bethard, and David McClosky. 2014. The Stanford CoreNLP Natural Language Processing Toolkit. In *Proc. ACL System Demonstrations*, pages 55–60.

Eleni Miltsakaki and Audrey Troutt. 2008. Real time web text classification and analysis of reading difficulty. In *Proc. Third Workshop on Innovative Use of NLP for Building Educational Applications*.

Norbert Schmitt, Xiangying Jiang, and William Grabe. 2011. The Percentage of Words Known in a Text and Reading Comprehension. *The Modern Language Journal*, 95(i):26–43.

Chris Shei and Hsun-Ping Hsieh. 2012. Linkit: a CALL system for learning Chinese characters, words and phrases. *Computer Assisted Language Learning*, 25(4):319–338.

A Post-editing Interface for Immediate Adaptation in Statistical Machine Translation

Patrick Simianer[†], **Sariya Karimova**[†*], **Stefan Riezler**[†‡]
Department of Computational Linguistics[†] & IWR[‡], Heidelberg University, Germany
[*] Kazan Federal University, Russia
{simianer,karimova,riezler}@cl.uni-heidelberg.de

Abstract

Adaptive machine translation (MT) systems are a promising approach for improving the effectiveness of computer-aided translation (CAT) environments. There is, however, virtually only theoretical work that examines how such a system could be implemented. We present an open source post-editing interface for adaptive statistical MT, which has in-depth monitoring capabilities and excellent expandability, and can facilitate practical studies. To this end, we designed text-based and graphical post-editing interfaces. The graphical interface offers means for displaying and editing a rich view of the MT output. Our translation systems may learn from post-edits using several weight, language model and novel translation model adaptation techniques, in part by exploiting the output of the graphical interface. In a user study we show that using the proposed interface and adaptation methods, reductions in technical effort and time can be achieved.

1 Introduction

Since the earliest beginnings of MT research, it has been obvious to many researchers and practitioners that automatic translation is an outstandingly hard problem and may need human participation for sufficient quality. Accordingly, about 70 years later, systems are not (yet) able to produce perfect, or, depending on the domain, comprehensible translations without human intervention. But, as for example shown by Guerberof (2009), the current quality is sufficient to be used in CAT scenarios, i.e. interactive MT or post-editing. CAT has gained more and more interest from the research community in recent years (Tatsumi, 2010; Koponen, 2016), and now (2016), commercial translation system providers implement and successfully use adaptive MT systems in production[1][2].

Most previous studies in CAT were either evaluated by simulating user behavior or did not consider adaptive translation systems. We seek to conduct studies that examine real user behavior in an adaptive environment. Adapting MT systems to specific users can be advantageous in numerous ways: In simulated experiments of adaptive systems large improvements were shown by taking reference translations as a stand-in for post-edits – significantly reducing the cost of high quality translation; Frustrations, rooted in repeated errors of MT systems, are mitigated and acceptance of MT can be improved; Domain adaptation in MT is capable of greatly improving translation quality; And lastly, translators expect and demand adaptiveness of their tools, as translation memories implement it naturally. To enable studies of user behavior in adaptive environments, we present a post-editing toolkit which can support different types of (adaptive) MT engines, and provide a graphical user interface which includes alignments between sources and their translations. The alignments are extracted from the output of the MT engine and permit novel and precise adaptation methods. Additionally, we provide tools to examine the translation system and the adaptation process, as well as detailed statistics of users' performance in terms of various measures relevant to post-editing.

[1] https://e2f.com/case-study-lilt-travel-portal/

[2] http://blog.translationzone.com/sdl-trados-studio-2017-transformation-translation/

Proceedings of COLING 2016, the 26th International Conference on Computational Linguistics: System Demonstrations, pages 16–20, Osaka, Japan, December 11-17 2016.

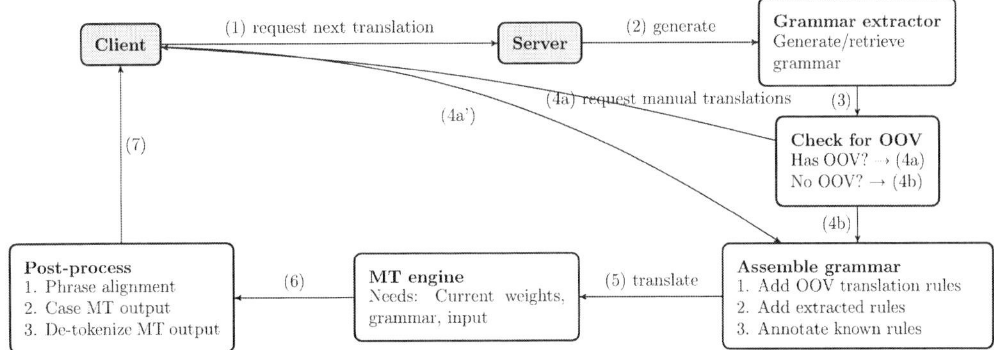

Figure 1: Overview of the steps required to produce a translation that is acceptable for post-editing: After the client (top left) requested a translation of the next segment (1), first the grammar extractor is invoked (2) to produce the grammar (grammars can also be pre-generated), then the input is checked for words that the system is not able to translate (3). If there are untranslatable words, the process returns to the client with a request for translation of the out-of-vocabulary items (OOV) (4a). Then, the grammar can be assembled with all rules that were previously extracted (4a' or 4b). With this grammar, the current weights and the input the MT engine can produce a translation (5), which needs to be processed before it is shown to the user (6, 7).

2 Related work and motivation

Post-editing of MT output is an old idea, going back until the first steps in MT, see e.g. the overview in Koponen (2016). But actual user studies were relatively seldom, as they are expensive to conduct, even more so in the 1960s: The earliest user study to our knowledge describes an offline experiment, which compared comprehensibility of machine translations, post-edits and human made translations (Orr, 1967). With the rise of statistical MT user studies of CAT have gained considerable traction (Casacuberta et al., 2009; Alabau et al., 2013; Federico et al., 2014). Many different toolkits and user interfaces have been used in these studies, for example graphical interfaces for interactive MT specialized for patent translation (Pouliquen et al., 2011), interfaces for predictive translation memories (Green et al., 2014; Koehn, 2009), tools for monitoring post-editing efforts (Aziz et al., 2012), full workbenches supporting post-editing or interactive MT for translators (Alabau et al., 2013; Federico et al., 2014; Casacuberta et al., 2009), or also test-beds for post-editing (Denkowski, 2015). The latter being most similar to our work, even providing a small user study on potential effects of adaptive MT in post-editing.

In most aforementioned interfaces users operate on the string-level and the MT engine is treated as a static black box. Denkowski (2015) is a notable exception, incorporating effective adaptation methods. These, however, also operate only on surface strings, and use a static word alignment model. In contrast, we propose a novel graphical interface that enables efficient and precise resolution of errors in the adaptive MT engine by leveraging user corrected alignments of translation units (e.g. phrases), in conjunction with standard adaptation methods.

3 System overview

Our system can be disassembled into two distinct steps: generation of the output of the MT engine[3], and secondly the adaptation step. The first step is described in Figure 1. The second step, which is comprised of updating the models, is described in Section 5.

[3]Throughout this paper the engine is assumed to be a hierarchical phrase-based SMT engine following Chiang (2007), with a SCFG as the core of its translation model.

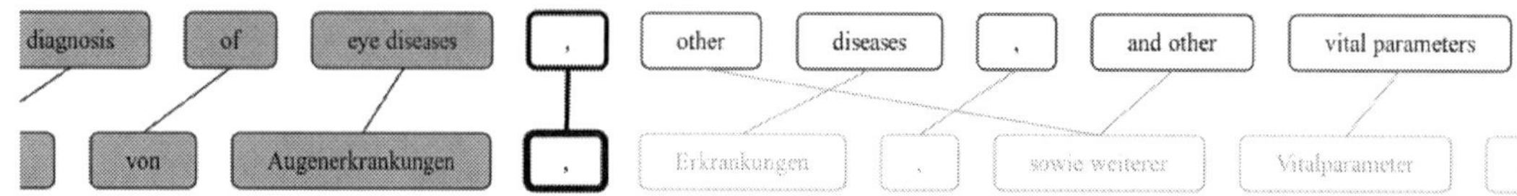

Figure 2: Detail of the graphical user interface, translating from English (top row) to German. Phrases are shown as boxes, alignments are displayed with connecting lines. All target phrases may be interactively moved, deleted, or edited, as well as the alignment links. New phrases can also be added to the target side, only the source side and its segmentation are fixed. The active phrase has a bold border, finished phrases have a dark background.

4 Interfaces

There are two user interfaces implemented: a standard text interface and a graphical interface for enriched presentation of the translation. The text interface consists of two simple input boxes: one contains the source sentence to be translated, the other one is for producing the translation. The target input box can either be pre-filled with a machine translation or left empty for translation from scratch.

In the graphical interface (an example is shown in Figure 2) we show the user not only the target string, but also the latent segmentation and alignment which leads to the translation. The user is invited to not only produce a correct translation, but also to make a sensible alignment of source and target. What is shown can differ between MT approaches: In word-based or current neural MT systems we could simply show the (soft) alignments of words. In phrase-based systems, the source and target are segmented into phrases, and for the hierarchical phrase-based paradigm phrases may be discontinuous, resulting in many-to-many alignments. Our approach not only enables usage of richer structures for adaptation, it has already been shown that visualized word-alignment alone can positively affect users (Schwartz et al., 2015).

From the user-corrected alignment, the MT engine can explicitly learn native corrections to its translation units, which are very valuable compared to updates that only use the surface data (strings). To evaluate and compare different adaptation approaches, the system collects timing information, as well as the number of clicks and keystrokes, all stages of input and output, and weight and model differentials.

5 Adaptation

Our proposed MT engine adaptation partially follows (Denkowski, 2015), using the same adaptive language model and a similar weight adaptation technique, but differs in the adaptation of the translation model. With the graphical interface one is not limited to a simple string pair of source and target translation to adapt the system, but one can also exploit the alignments between the translation units. The chronological sequence of adaptation steps in our implementation is as follows: (1) As shown in Figure 1, OOV is avoided by asking the user for translations of unknown words prior to decoding. (2) After post-editing a sentence, the phrase-segmented and aligned post-edit is compared to the initial machine translation, and lexical corrections and new rules are immediately added to the current grammar. (3) The source is then re-decoded with the augmented grammar, generating a k-best list which is re-ranked by BLEU+1 using the post-edit as reference translation. Weights are updated based on this list with pairwise ranking as described in Simianer et al. (2012). (4) Additionally, we implemented a rule extraction that closely follows the grammar extraction described in Chiang (2007), but instead of words it is using full phrases from the phrase alignment. This results in a large number of additional rules, as all rules (also with gaps) that are compatible with the phrase alignment are extracted for each post-edit provided by the user. To prevent overfitting[4], extracted rules are added to the system in a leave-one-out fashion (i.e. only to subsequent grammars). (5) Before the translation of the next sentence the adaptive language model described by Denkowski (2015) is updated with the string of the current post-edit.

[4]Each translation rule has an associated weight, the same feature set as in Simianer et al. (2012) is used.

response var.	est. Δ	
HBLEU+1	$+6.8 \pm 2.0$ [%]	$p < 0.001, \chi^2(1) = 11.748$
HTER	-5.3 ± 1.9 [%]	$p < 0.01, \chi^2(1) = 7.8741$
norm. time	-118 ms	—

Table 1: Results of the LMEM analysis. Estimated differences in the response variables contrasting non-adaptive to adaptive systems are given in the Δ column along with their associated p-values, if $p \leq 0.05$. Significance is tested with likelihood ratio tests of the full model against the model without independent variable of interest.

6 User Study

We conducted a user study to test whether our proposed adaptation methods could lead to reduced technical effort or translation speed. For the study we recruited 19 students to use our system in five 90 minute sessions. The group of students was diverse: six study computer science, 13 are prospective translators; the mother tongue of nine students is German, the others were native Italian (7), Spanish, Arabic and Russian (each 1) speakers. The study took place in a controlled environment, all subjects used the same hardware in a computer pool. As translation material we selected patents (Wäschle and Riezler, 2012), where baseline translation performance is good even using smaller, faster models. Since patent claims and descriptions tend to be complex and long, they are not suitable for translation by non-experts. We therefore used titles and abstracts for both training and test. Development and test data are limited to documents with an overall maximum length of 45 tokens per sentence. The data split was done by year and by family id to avoid possible overlaps. Translation direction was English-to-German. The test data were automatically grouped into clusters by cosine similarity of their bag-of-words tf-idf source representations and length, to obtain clusters of related documents with an approximate source token count of 500, which is appropriate in a post-editing setup given the available time limit of 90 minutes. This way, each cluster contained the titles and complete abstracts of 3-5 documents. Two sessions were used to familiarize the subjects with the interface and the translation material using the same task setup as used in the controlled experiments. Each task consists of a document cluster, as described above, which has to be translated within the given time limit. Per session, each cluster is shared by another subject to account for translator variability. Each user uses a dedicated translation system. A session without the proposed adaptation is contrasted to two sessions in which adaptation was enabled. This way, 978 per-sentence measurements were achieved.

Analysis is carried out with linear mixed effects models[5] (LMEM), which are well suited for experimental setups that involve several non-independent measurements, e.g. from multiple responses by the same subjects. Technical translation effort is approximated by HBLEU+1 and HTER, comparing MT outputs to post-edits, and time is normalized by the number of characters in the final post-edits. Raw time cannot be used as response variable since the translation condition (non-adaptive vs. adaptive), the independent variable of interest, is tested with different sets of sources. Random effects (with random intercepts) are subject and source sentence ids, fixed effects are a binary variable separating mother-tongue speakers of German from non-native speakers, and an indicator for source sentence length, which is binned into three distinct levels. Results contrasting the translation condition are given in Table 1. We see significant improvements in HBLEU+1 and HTER, as well as a non-significant time reduction. Quality of post-edits in terms of average BLEU+1 scores with respect to reference translations is stable at 39.6 ± 0.4 [%] across sessions.

7 Conclusions

We presented a toolkit comprised of a text interface, a novel graphical interface and an adaptive MT engine which opens up a wide range of possibilities to carry out interesting post-editing experiments. Our system implements a feedback mechanism to bypass the OOV problem, and with the graphical

[5]Using the implementation of Bates et al. (2012) for R.

user interface, it supports editing of structured MT output which can be leveraged for novel adaptation methods. It also uses and supports existing adaptation techniques, for updating weights, translation and language models. We additionally provide tools to examine the MT engine, as well as the adaptation process, and enable users to evaluate their output in contrast to existing reference translations, and in terms of various measures relevant for post-editing performance. In a user study we could show that adaptive MT engines can significantly reduce technical translation effort in terms of metrics such as HTER or HBLEU+1. The source code is licensed under the LGPL and freely available[6].

References

V. Alabau, R. Bonk, C. Buck, M. Carl, F. Casacuberta, M. G. Martínez, J. González, P. Koehn, L. Leiva, B. Mesa-Lao, D. Ortiz, H. Saint-Amand, G. Sanchis, and C. Tsoukala. 2013. CASMACAT: An open source workbench for advanced computer-aided translation. *The Prague Bulletin of Mathematical Linguistics*, 100.

W. Aziz, S. Castilho, and L. Specia. 2012. Pet: a tool for post-editing and assessing machine translation. In *Proceedings of the 8th International Conference on Language Resources and Evaluation.*

D. Bates, M. Maechler, and B. Bolker, 2012. *lme4: Linear mixed-effects models using S4 classes.*

F. Casacuberta, J. Civera, E. Cubel, A. L. Lagarda, G. Lapalme, E. Macklovitch, and E. Vidal. 2009. Human interaction for high-quality machine translation. *Communications of the ACM*, 52.

D. Chiang. 2007. Hierarchical phrase-based translation. *Computational Linguistics*, 33.

M. Denkowski. 2015. *Machine Translation for Human Translators.* Ph.D. thesis, Carnegie Mellon University.

M. Federico, N. Bertoldi, M. Cettolo, M. Negri, M. Turchi, M. Trombetti, A. Cattelan, A. Farina, D. Lupinetti, A. Martines, A. Massidda, H. Schwenk, L. Barrault, F. Blain, P. Koehn, C. Buck, and U. Germann. 2014. The matecat tool. In *Proceedings of the 25th International Conference on Computational Linguistics.*

S. Green, J. Chuang, J. Heer, and C. D. Manning. 2014. Predictive translation memory: A mixed-initiative system for human language translation. In *ACM User Interface Software & Technology.*

A. Guerberof. 2009. Productivity and quality in mt post-editing. In *Proceedings of the MT Summit XII Workshop: Beyond translation memories: New tools for translators.*

P. Koehn. 2009. A process study of computer-aided translation. *Machine Translation*, 23.

M. Koponen. 2016. Is machine translation post-editing worth the effort? a survey of research into post-editing and effort. *The Journal of Specialised Translation.*

D. B. Orr. 1967. Comprehensibility of machine-aided translations of russian scientific documents.

B. Pouliquen, C. Mazenc, and A. Iorio. 2011. Tapta: A user-driven translation system for patent documents based on domain-aware statistical machine translation. In *Proceedings of the 15th International Conference of the European Association for Machine Translation.*

L. Schwartz, I. Lacruz, and T. Bystrova. 2015. Effects of word alignment visualization on post-editing quality & speed. In *Proceedings of MT Summit XV.*

P. Simianer, S. Riezler, and C. Dyer. 2012. Joint feature selection in distributed stochastic learning for large-scale discriminative training in SMT. In *Proceedings of the 50th Annual Meeting of the Association for Computational Linguistics.*

M. Tatsumi. 2010. *Post-Editing Machine Translated Text in A Commercial Setting: Observation and Statistical Analysis.* Ph.D. thesis, Dublin City University.

K. Wäschle and S. Riezler. 2012. Structural and Topical Dimensions in Multi-Task Patent Translation. In *Proceedings of the 13th Conference of the European Chapter of the Association for Computational Linguistics.*

[6]`https://github.com/pks/lfpe`

Word Midas Powered by StringNet: Discovering Lexicogrammatical Constructions *in Situ*[1]

David Wible
National Central University
No.300, Jhongda Rd. Jhongli City,
Taoyuan County 32001, Taiwan
wible@stringnet.org

Nai-Lung Tsao
Tamkang University
No.151, Yingzhuan Rd., Tamsui Dist.,
New Taipei City 25137, Taiwan
beaktsao@stringnet.org[2]

Abstract

Adult second language learners face the daunting but underappreciated task of mastering patterns of language use that are neither products of fully productive grammar rules nor frozen items to be memorized. Word Midas[3], a web browser extension, targets this uncharted territory of lexicogrammar by detecting multiword tokens of lexicogrammatical patterning in real time *in situ* within the noisy digital texts from the user's unscripted web browsing or other digital venues. The language model powering Word Midas is StringNet, a densely cross-indexed navigable network of one billion lexicogrammatical patterns of English. These resources are described and their functionality is illustrated with a detailed scenario.

1 Background

Some of the most persistent yet underappreciated challenges in learning a second language are to be found not within the purview of highly productive grammar rules nor in particular lexical items whose behavior is well described by those rules and by traditional dictionary entries. They lie rather in a vast and poorly charted middle ground between items and rules, a territory of semi-productive and lexically picky patterns, what Halliday referred to as "lexis as most delicate grammar" (1961) and others call lexico-grammatical constructions (Kay, 1997). In addition to escaping coverage in traditional knowledge resources, this cline of lexicogrammar often skirts the awareness of language teachers. In the absence of reference books and teachers, children learn these elusive and variegated patterns in their first language by some combination of immersive encounters with tokens of language in use and their uncanny acumen in distilling abstract patterns from these tokens. Rare is the adult second language learner, however, who shares the child's urgency and immersion in target language input or the child's capacity for detecting patterns from it. The tools we present in this paper address basic challenges posed to adult learners and their teachers by this intermediate territory of lexicogrammar.

As an example of the challenge, the string *a wide range of issues* conforms to maximally general rules of English grammar, and so that would seem adequate to a command of this expression. This is misleading, however. Simpson-Vlack and Ellis (2010) identified the 4-gram *a wide range of* as the top-ranked item on their corpus-derived academic formula list. This shows that the co-occurrence of the words in that 4-gram is the result of more than simply general combinatorial rules of syntax and that it deserves more attention from learners than grammar alone would indicate. Our point is that here, as in so many patterns that pervade language, the expression is neither a frozen, one-off item nor simply a product of maximally general rules combining words. Rather, *a wide range of* is part of a tight nexus of limited but inter-related variations: *a [wide/broad/whole/vast] range of*; *a wide [range/variety/array/spectrum] of*.

[1] This research was supported by Taiwan's Ministry of Science and Technology, grant #105-2511-S-008-008.

[2] The work reported here was first done when Nai-Lung Tsao worked at National Central University.

[3] Word Midas can be downloaded for free from Google Chrome Store.

Proceedings of COLING 2016, the 26th International Conference on Computational Linguistics: System Demonstrations, pages 21–24, Osaka, Japan, December 11-17 2016.

The problem we address is this: With current resources, it is virtually impossible for situated learners to get any sense of which strings in their input are instantiations of lexicogrammatical patterning and, for those that are, what variations on those strings are possible. The system we present, called Word Midas, detects tokens of such patterns in noisy digital text of the readers' choice and shows the paradigmatic variation that is not present in the text but which constitutes the possibilities available there that are part of a mature language users grasp of the language. In what follows we describe the components of the system and illustrate its workings with a detailed scenario.

2 The System

The system has two basic components: (1) an existing, corpus-derived English language model called StringNet (nav4.stringnet.org), consisting of over one billion unique lexicogrammatical patterns; (2) a web browser plugin tool called Word Midas, which detects multiword strings in digital text that are instantiations of any of the lexicogrammatical patterns from the language model (StringNet).

2.1 The Language Model: StringNet

StringNet (Wible and Tsao, 2010; 2011) contains not only n-grams extracted from the British National Corpus (BNC) such as the trigram *as good as,* but also what Wible and Tsao (2010) call "hybrid n-grams," that is, more abstract n-grams where grams can include part-of-speech categories, for example, *as [adj] as*. The gram types that can compose hybrid n-grams fall into one of four levels of abstraction: word form (*made, makes*), lemma (**make**, subsuming *make, makes, made, making*), detailed part of speech (V-past), and rough part of speech (V). StringNet is a relational network in which the one billion unique hybrid n-grams are those from 2 to 6 grams in length instantiated in BNC with 5 or more tokens. These are cross-indexed for subsumption and inclusion relations. Thus, the n-gram *as good as* is indexed to its more abstract counterpart *as [adj] as* and to its longer counterparts, for example *as good as his word*; *as good as [poss pro] word*; and ***be*** *as good as his word*. Slots in hybrid n-grams differ in how open or selective they are in the words that can appear in them. The selective slots can be detected computationally within the more than one billion hybrid n-grams in StringNet and have served as contextual clues flagging slots of semantically similar words, what Tsao and Wible (2013) call "constructional selection."

2.2 The *In Situ* Tool: Word Midas

The basic conception of a browser-based tool that identifies multiword patterns in real time within texts that the user freely browses was first implemented in a tool called Collocator that detected two-word collocations (Wible et al., 2011). In the present paper, Word Midas extends the conception to the immensely more complex challenge of detecting lexicogrammatical patterns. Recall a fundamental challenge which language input poses to learners and which Word Midas aims to address: the tokens of word strings that a user encounters in input do not directly signal the lexico-grammatical pattern(s) that they betoken. This severely limits the value of such tokens and such encounters for learning unfamiliar patterns of the language behind them. Word Midas provides a reader in real time with links from the tokens in a text to the patterns they instantiate.

We illustrate the workings of Word Midas through a scenario for its use. This involves a person browsing web content with Word Midas installed on their browser as a Chrome extension or a plug-in. The user can select any word or string of words found in that web page in order to discover whether it is used there as part of a pattern and if so what variations are possible that are not there in that text. Figure 1 shows a webpage where the user has paused at the string "In a region where many people eat chocolate on a daily basis..." and wonders about the string *on a daily basis* here or simply about one of the words in that string as used here. Word Midas is activated from a context menu that appears by right-clicking on any word in that string. Activating Word Midas from that context menu launches a search for patterns that include the selected word and fall within a nine-word window of context surrounding it. The results are listed in a popup as shown in Figure 1.

Word Midas results are derived in three steps. First, string matching identifies all n-grams that include the user-selected word and match the context of that word in the text where the user found it. Then, an adapted edit-distance algorithm identifies abstract hybrid n-grams that also describe n-grams identified in the first step (see Wible and Tsao 2009 on this adaptation of edit distance). Third, pruning and ranking algorithms evaluate these patterns using weighted features (including edit distance scores) that assess two competing requirements: their closeness of match to the target text and their productivity in wider use (see Wible and Tsao 2010 for details on this pruning and ranking of StringNet patterns). To see the significance of this, we return to the example.

The popup in Figure 1 lists the hybrid n-gram patterns that describe strings found surrounding the selected word and, for each pattern, gives its frequency in BNC and links to a concordance of sentences containing that pattern. In this case, the top three patterns listed (with their frequencies) are: *[noun] on a daily basis* (60); *[noun sg] on a daily basis (35)*; *on a daily basis* (150). The prominent frequency of the third pattern (*on a daily basis*) invites further exploration.

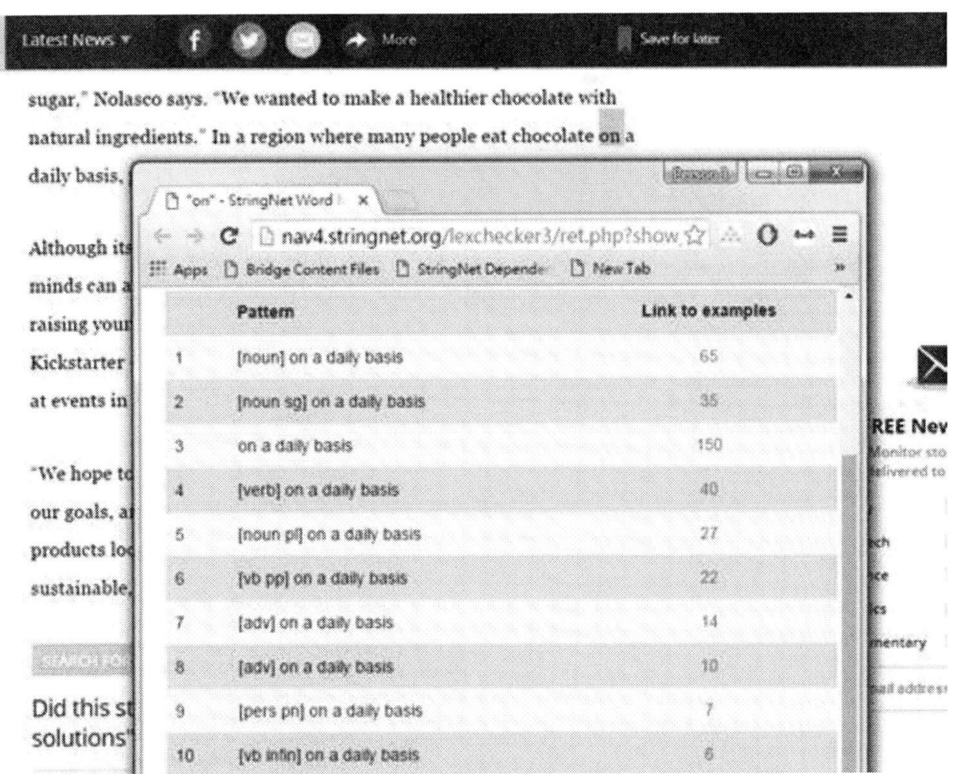

Figure 1. Patterns found by Word Midas from webpage text.

From here, Word Midas helps answer key question about lexicogrammatical patterning that an unaided reader cannot: What variations of this string are possible? Clicking on any word in the pattern *on a daily basis* where it appears in the popup list shows the user the paradigm of all words attested in that slot, indicating whether the word there is the only option or replaceable, and if replaceable, whether variation is relatively open or restricted. This can be done for each word in the sequence. In this case, the first word in *on a daily basis*, the preposition *on*, is shown to be the only attested word in its slot as is the indefinite article *a* which follows it. In turn, the noun *basis* in this frame, while replaceable, is hands down the most likely word in its position; its frequency there is 150 while the second most frequent noun, *rate*, has a frequency of only three. The limited substitutability in this four-word sequence for these three slots --*on*, *a*, and *basis*--demonstrate Sinclair's "idiom principle," that is, they are cases of tight limitations on lexical choice far more restrictive than grammar can account for. Turning to the adjective *daily* in this sequence, however, we discover a different phenomenon. Word Midas shows that the word *daily* in the sequence *on a daily basis* is occupying a slot that exhibits a dramatically wider variation than any of the other slots in this string, with 469 different adjectives attested in that position: *on a [adj] basis*. This can be seen in the paradigm for that slot shown partially in Figure 2. Thus, we can discover that *on a daily basis* is just one member in a family of variations, and that the locus of variation is concentrated in the [adj] slot.

on a [daily/regular/voluntary/day-to-day/part-time/temporary...] basis

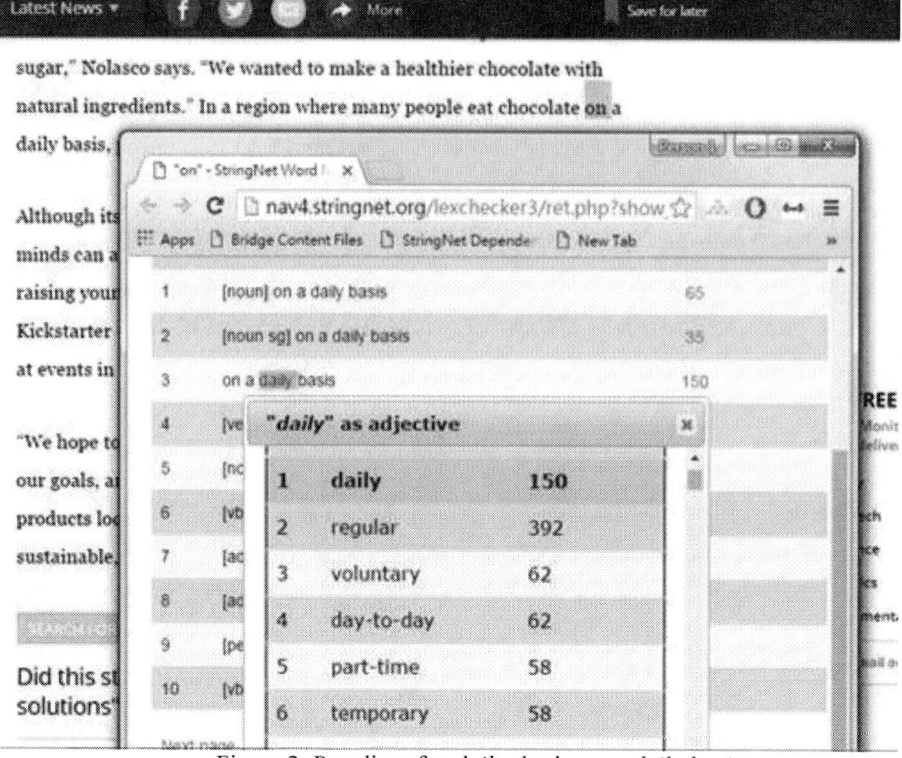

Figure 2. Paradigm for *daily* slot in *on a daily basis*.

3 Conclusion

There are some major points to note from this extended example. The relative freedom exhibited in the slot occupied by *daily* in the string *on a daily basis* and the corresponding lack of freedom in its co-occurring slots are symptomatic of the regularity and idiomaticity that comingle in lexicogrammatical constructions. This mix of features is undetectable from simple encounters with multiword tokens in text and unrepresented in dictionaries and grammar references. Access to these features requires access to the paradigmatic dimension of input. That access is what StringNet and Word Midas aim to provide to situated, unscripted users in real time for any part of noisy text they wish to explore.

References

M.A.K. Halliday. 1961. Categories of the theory of grammar. *Word*, 17(3): 241-292.

Paul Kay. 1997. *Words and the Grammar of Context*. Stanford: Center for the Study of Language and Information Publications, Stanford, California.

Anne L.-E Liu, David Wible and Nai-Lung Tsao. 2011. A Browser-based Approach to Incidental Individualization of Vocabulary Learning. *Journal of Computer Assisted Learning*, 27: 540-543.

Rita Simpson-Vlach and Nick C. Ellis. 2010. An Academic Formulas List: New Methods in Phraseology Research. *Applied Linguistics*, 31(4): 487-512.

Nai-Lung Tsao and David Wible. 2009. A Method for Unsupervised Lexical Error Detection and Correction. *Proceedings of the NAACL Workshop on Innovative Uses of NLP for Building Educational Applications,* 51-54.

Nai-Lung Tsao and David Wible. 2013. Word Similarity Using Constructions as Contextual Features. Joint Symposium on Semantic Processing, Trento, Italy.

David Wible and Nai-Lung Tsao. 2010. StringNet as a Computational Resource for Discovering and Investigating Linguistic Constructions. *Proceedings of the NAACL HLT Workshop on Extracting and Using Constructions in Computational Linguistics*, 25-31.

David Wible and Nai-Lung Tsao. 2011. Towards a New Generation of Corpus-derived Lexical Resources for Language Learning. In F. Meunier (ed.) *A Taste of Corpora*. John Benjamins, Amsterdam.

'BonTen' – Corpus Concordance System for 'NINJAL Web Japanese Corpus'

Masayuki ASAHARA♢ Kazuya KAWAHARA♠ Yuya TAKEI♠
Hideto MASUOKA♠ Yasuko OHBA♡ Yuki TORII♡
Toru MORII♡ Yuki TANAKA♡ Kikuo MAEKAWA ♢
Sachi KATO ♢ Hikari KONISHI♢
♢ National Institute for Japanese Language and Linguistics,
National Institutes for the Humanities, Japan
♠ Retrieva Inc., ♡ Everyleaf Corporation

Abstract

The National Institute for Japanese Language and Linguistics, Japan (NINJAL) has undertaken a corpus compilation project to construct a web corpus for linguistic research comprising 25 billion words. The project is divided into four parts: page collection, linguistic analysis, development of the corpus concordance system, and preservation. This article presents a corpus concordance system named 'BonTen', which enables a ten-billion-scaled corpus to be queried by string, a sequence of morphological information or a subtree of the syntactic dependency structure.

1 Introduction

The National Institute for Japanese Language and Linguistics, Japan (NINJAL) has compiled a ten-billion-word scale Japanese web corpus named 'NINJAL Web Japanese Corpus' (hereafter 'NWJC')(Asahara et al., 2014). This paper presents the web-based corpus concordance system 'BonTen' – *Brahman*[1] for NWJC. The system designs are based on the string search mechanisms of the web-based search system 'Shonagon' [2], which is used to search 'the Balanced Corpus of Contemporary Written Japanese' (hereafter 'BCCWJ')(Maekawa et al., 2014). Shonagon enables a short unit sequence search to be carried out on the web-based corpus concordance system 'Chunagon' for BCCWJ, and a dependency search to be performed on the corpus management system 'ChaKi.NET' (Matsumoto et al., 2005; Asahara et al., 2016). Because the system functions as a web application, the user only requires a web browser to access the corpus. The user interface design [3] is based on that of 'ChaKi.NET'. The back-end search system is based on 'Sedue for Bigdata' and was developed by Retrieva Inc. [4]. The search system can effectively search the ten-billion-word scale corpora at practical speeds.

2 'NINJAL Web Japanese Corpus' (NWJC)

NWJC is a web corpus for Japanese linguistic research comprising ten billion words.

Page collection is performed by employing remote harvesting using the Heritrix crawler. [5] Our web crawler processes one hundred million URLs every three months to provide fixed-point observations for one year. The list of URLs is changed annually.

In linguistic analysis, we perform *normalisation*, *Japanese morphological analysis*, and *Japanese dependency analysis*. The crawled pages are normalised by nwc-toolkit-0.0.2 [6] to remove HTML tags and convert character encoding, after which they are split into sentences. The periods (Kuten), exclamation marks, and question marks are removed during the sentence splitting process. Sentences are collected according to types rather than by tokens to alleviate duplication issues on the web. Sentences are paraphrased for type unification purposes by using the uniq command (with sort). We use the MeCab-0.996

[1] The name originated from a form of 'Bengalese finch'.
[2] http://www.kotonoha.gr.jp/shonagon/
[3] the user interface is developped by Everyleaf Corpolation http://everyleaf.com/
[4] http://retrieva.jp/
[5] http://webarchive.jira.com/wiki/display/Heritrix/Heritrix/
[6] http://code.google.com/p/nwc-toolkit/

Proceedings of COLING 2016, the 26th International Conference on Computational Linguistics: System Demonstrations, pages 25–29, Osaka, Japan, December 11-17 2016.

morphological analyser [7] and the UniDic-2.1.2 dictionary [8] to conduct Japanese morphological analysis (word segmentation and POS tagging). We also use the dependency analyser CaboCha-0.69 [9] with UniDic head rule options [10] for Japanese dependency parsing.

We preserve the data collected for linguistic studies to monitor any future changes. The corpus is archived in WARC format (ISO 28500:2009) by the Heritrix crawler. The data will be harvested in online backup as open source wayback software and in offline backup as LTO tapes.

Japanese copyright law prevents us from making the corpus publicly available. However, the data will be accessible by search engine to enable the user to search for query strings, morphological information, and syntactic dependency subtrees. The result shows the links to the original pages. The search engine includes data crawled from October 2014 to December 2014 (2014-4Q) by the types of sentences. The statistics for the data are provided in Table 1.

Table 1: Statistics :2014-4Q

No. of URLs	83,992,556
Tokens of Sentences	3,885,889,575
Types of Sentences	1,463,142,939
No. of Bunsetsus	8,736,741,719
No. of Short Unit Words	25,836,947,421

3 Functions of the corpus concordance system 'BonTen'

This section describes the functions of the BonTen corpus concordance system 'BonTen'. We aimed to utilize existing user interface designs for query building. However, some functions such as regular expression matching are omitted in order to work on a ten-billion-word scale corpus.

Below, we introduce three query systems: string search, short unit search, and dependency search. We also present the display of retrieval results.

3.1 String Search

A string search is the most fundamental query function for accessing the corpus and returns sentences that include the exact same query string. The result can be refined by the last two parts of the URL domain.[11]

BonTen cannot use regular expressions such as concatenation, alternation, and Kleene star, because the length of Japanese words tends to be shorter than other languages.

Because the data is stored in the form of sentences, we cannot throw a query across sentence boundaries. Although some preceding systems use a history function to liset previous user queries, this function was not implemented in BonTen. The history function will not be implemented until the end of 2016.

We demonstrate the two formats in which retrieval results are displayed. Authenticated users will be able to use the rich display. We present the display itself in Section 3.4.

3.2 Short Unit Search

The short unit search is a function that is very similar to the short unit search function in Chunagon and tag search function in ChaKi.NET. The function can throw queries based on sequences of morphological information. Figure 1 shows the on-screen display of an example query. The boxes correspond to the morphemes (short units) in the sentences. We can determine the relative positions of the boxes. Relative position '0' denotes a centred word in the KWIC. A relative position with a negative value indicates the left side of the centred word. A relative position with a positive value indicates the right side of the

[7] `http://mecab.googlecode.com/svn/trunk/mecab/doc/`

[8] `https://osdn.jp/projects/unidic/`

[9] `https://taku910.github.io/cabocha/`

[10] `./configure --with-posset=UNIDIC`

[11] Internet top-level domain such as .com and .jp, and second-level domain such as .co.jp and ac.jp.

centred word. The two numbers on the box denote the relative positions between the boxes, in which the number on the left is the minimum (left-most) relative positions and the number on the right is the maximum (right-most) relative positions.

The box can specify the following morphological information: Surface form: (〈表層形〉) the form appearing in the sentence; POS1, POS2, POS3, POS4: 〈品詞 1〉, 〈品詞 2〉, 〈品詞 3〉, 〈品詞 4〉 parts of speech in the hierarchical tag; Conjugation type: 〈活用型〉; Conjugation form: 〈活用形〉; Lemma – reading: 〈語彙素読み〉 the reading form of entry data in the UniDic, which should be transcribed using Katakana; and Lemma: 〈語彙素読み〉 the writing form of entry data in the UniDic.

The POSs, Conjugation type, and Conjugation form are listed by clicking the ▽ icon.

Because the data is stored in sentence form, we cannot throw a query across sentence boundaries. Althogh some preceding systems use a history function to list previous user queries, BonTen has not implemented a history function. The history function will be not implemented until the end of 2016.

The boxes can be expanded by clicking '+', reduced by clicking '×', or cleared by clicking the eraser icon.

In the example, we specify a centred word of the POS type 'Noun, Proper Noun, Place Name' followed by the lemma '語 (*language*)'.

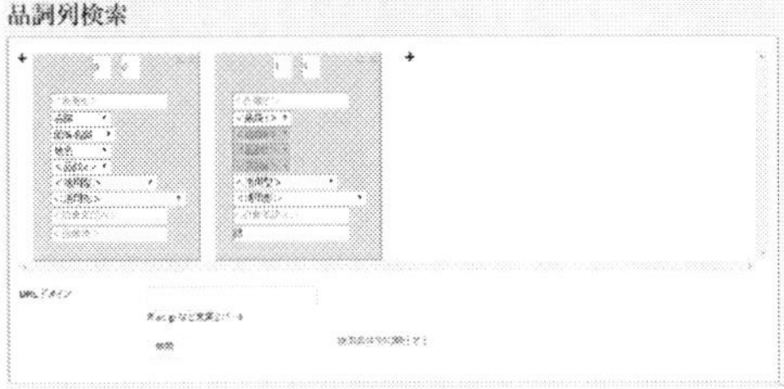

Figure 1: Short unit search query

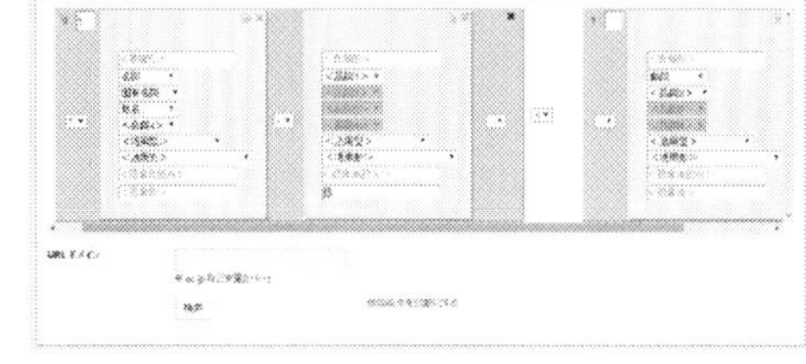

Figure 2: Dependency search query

3.3 Dependency Search

The dependency search function is nearly the same as that in ChaKi.NET. The function can be used to search for 'Bunsetsu (*Japanese base phrase*)'-based dependency structures. The query can be specified by providing a subtree of the Bunsetsu-based dependency structure, such as morphological information, the relative position in a Bunsetsu, the relative positions between Bunsetsus, and the dependency relation.

Figure 2 shows a screen displaying an example query. The green and orange boxes specify the Bunsetsus. The numbers on the upper left side of the colored boxes specify the ID of the Bunsetsu (to the left of the colon) and the ID of the head Bunsetsu (to the right of the colon). The ^ sign in the figure indicates the left (Bunsetsu) boundary. The – sign in the figure indicates that the two (morpheme) units are adjacent. The < sign in the figure indicates that the two (Bunsetsu) units occur in this linear order. We can also use the $ sign as the right (Bunsetsu or Sentence) boundary. The + sign is for increasing the size of a morpheme or Bunsetsu box.

In this example, we define two Bunsetsus: the first Bunsetsu includes a word of the POS type 'Noun, Proper Noun, Place Name' as the left-most word followed by the lemma '語 (*language*)', whereas the other Bunsetsu includes a word of the POS type 'Verb'. The two Bunsetsus appear in this order and have a dependency relation.

3.4 Displaying the retrieval results

The retrieval results show the number of query hits, and the example sentences. Fifty example sentences are displayed using pagination. We prepared the following two displays of retrieval results. The first is a simple example in which only the sentences are rapidly displayed. The second is a rich example (Figure 3) in which sentences are shown together with the morphemes and Bunsetsus segmented according to the top level of the POS tag. In the figure, the mouse cursor is on the morpheme/Bunsetsu 'する' (in the yellow background) of the fourth example. The morphological information appears in a pop-up box

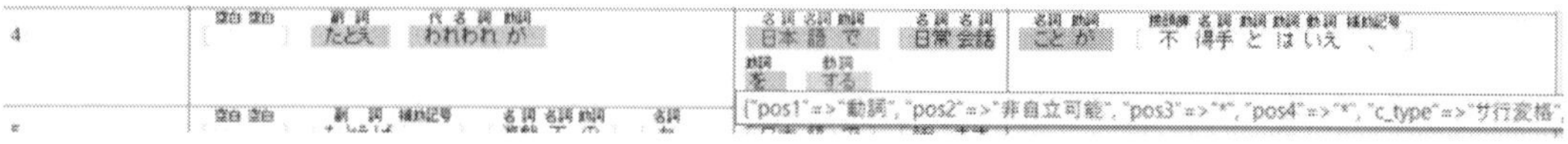

Figure 3: Rich display of retrieval results

Table 2: String Search Evaluation

query	English translation	Hit number	Response Time (simple display)	Response Time (rich display)
さくら	cherry blossoms	137,680	0.717 sec.	11.387 sec.
フランス語	French	15,214	0.692 sec.	9.376 sec.
国立国語研究所	NINJAL	106	1.239 sec.	5.420 sec.
じゅげむじゅげむ ごこうのすりきれ	a phrase (in Buddhist scripture)	13	0.460 sec.	0.998 sec.

and is displayed against a white background. The Bunsetsus that appear against a blue background are dependants of those highlighted in yellow, whereas a Bunsetsu highlighted in pink is the head of the Bunsetsu highlighted in yellow.

We also provide two services to download the results. The first enables 50 example sentences to be displayed with the morphological information and syntactic dependency structure in the format of the syntactic dependency parser CaboCha. The second service allows the user to download the retrieved sentences (max. 100,000 sentences) in tsv format (without any linguistic annotation). Both of these types of data are displayed with a URL list. The line ending code can be specified as CRLF (Windows), LF(Linux), or CR(Mac OS). The character encoding is fixed as UTF-8.

4 Evaluations

We evaluated the response time of the corpus concordance system using the Firefox 40.0.1 browser with HttpWatch Basic Version 10.0.44 [12]. The computer was connected to the Internet via optic fibre for home use and the evaluation was performed in March 2016.

Table 2 shows the results of the string search in two display modes. The simple display mode produces results reasonably quickly, with the network latency being the main cause of time loss. The rich display mode needs time to construct visualization of linguistic annotations, including morphological information and dependency structures. Tables 3 and 4 show the results of a Short Unit Search and Dependency Search, respectively. The dependency subtree search on the ten-billion-word scale web corpus takes less than one minute, and includes rich annotation information.

Table 3: Short Unit Search Evaluation

Query	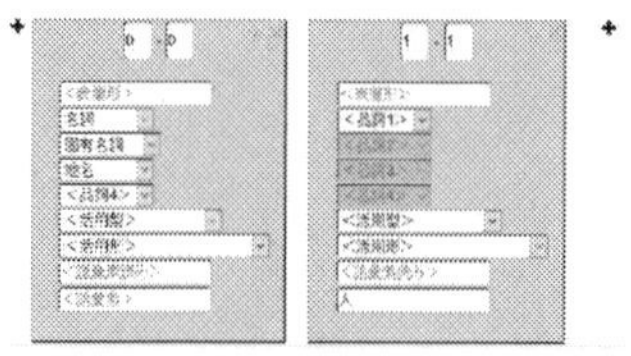	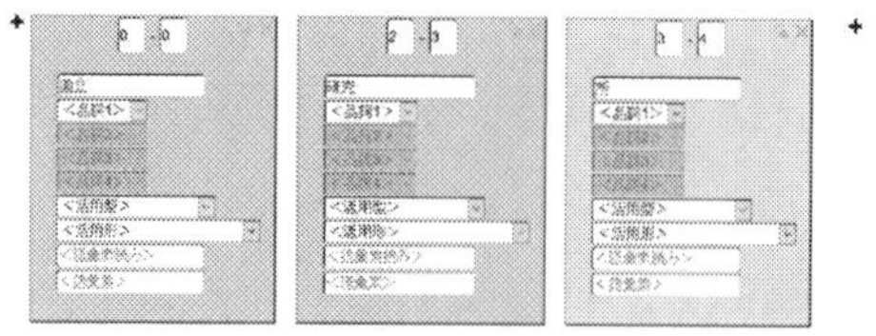
Hit number	412,763	2,067
Response Time (rich display)	16.567 sec.	10.702 sec.

[12]https://www.httpwatch.com/

Table 4: Dependency Search Evaluation

Query	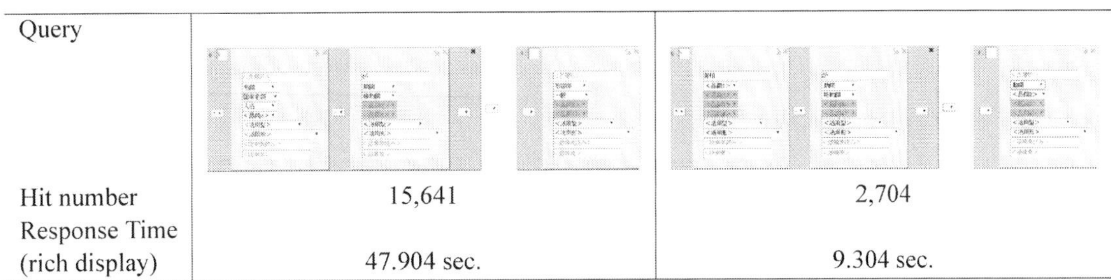	
Hit number	15,641	2,704
Response Time (rich display)	47.904 sec.	9.304 sec.

The Demo Video: `https://youtu.be/jYxeLYbnd3k`

Both searches can only be carried out in the rich display mode. The first query in Table 3 is a pattern of words of the POS type 'Noun, Proper Noun, Place Name' as the left-most word followed by the lemma '人 *(people)*'. The second query in Table 3 involves a pattern containing one or two words (wildcards) between the word 'National' and the compound word 'Research Institute'. Both queries need less than 20 seconds to fetch the results. The first query in Table 4 relates to a pattern consisting of two Bunsetsus with a dependency relation in the following linear order. The first Bunsetsu includes a word of the POS type 'Noun, Proper Noun, Person Name' as the left most word followed by the surface form 'が' and the POS is a Case Particle (Subject marker). The second Bunsetsu includes a word of the POS type 'Adjective General'. Because there are no lexicalized content words among the content words, the query takes nearly one minute to display a result. The second query in Table 4 again involves a pattern consisting of two Bunsetsus with a dependency relation in the following linear order. The first Bunsetsu includes the surface form 'Prime Minister' as the left-most word followed by the surface form 'が' and the POS is a Case Particle (Subject marker). The second Bunsetsu includes a word of the POS type 'Verb'. Thus, one lexicalized entry reduces the query time.

5 Conclusions

The paper presents the functions of the BonTen corpus concordance system. The system has the ability to process queries using strings, morphological information sequence, and by using a subtree of the dependency structure for the ten-billion scale web corpus.

Acknowledgments

The work reported here is a result of the "Choo-daikibo koopasu" (ultra-large scale corpus) project of the Center for Corpus Development, NINJAL (2011-2015).

References

Masayuki Asahara, Kikuo Maekawa, Mizuho Imada, Sachi Kato, and Hikari Konishi. 2014. Archiving and Analysing Techniques of the Ultra-large-scale Web-based Corpus Project of NINJAL, Japan. *Alexandria*, 25(1-2):129–148.

Masayuki Asahara, Yuji Matsumoto, and Toshio Morita. 2016. Demonstration of ChaKi.NET – beyond the corpus search system. In *Proc. of COLING-2016 (Demo Session)*.

Kikuo Maekawa, Makoto Yamazaki, Toshinobu Ogiso, Takehiko Maruyama, Hideki Ogura, Wakako Kashino, Hanae Koiso, Masaya Yamaguchi, Makiro Tanaka, and Yasuharu Den. 2014. Balanced Corpus of Contemporary Written Japanese. *Language Resources and Evaluation*, 48:345–371.

Yuji Matsumoto, Masayuki Asahara, Kou Kawabe, Yurika Takahashi, Yukio Tono, Akira Otani, and Toshio Morita. 2005. ChaKi: An Annotated Corpora Management and Search System. In *Proceedings from the Corpus Linguistics Conference Series*.

A Prototype Automatic Simultaneous Interpretation System

Xiaolin Wang **Andrew Finch** **Masao Utiyama** **Eiichiro Sumita**
Advanced Translation Research and Development Promotion Center
National Institute of Information and Communications Technology, Japan
{xiaolin.wang, andrew.finch, mutiyama, eiichiro.sumita}@nict.go.jp

Abstract

Simultaneous interpretation allows people to communicate spontaneously across language boundaries, but such services are prohibitively expensive for the general public. This paper presents a fully automatic simultaneous interpretation system to address this problem. Though the development is still at an early stage, the system is capable of keeping up with the fastest of the TED speakers while at the same time delivering high-quality translations. We believe that the system will become an effective tool for facilitating cross-lingual communication in the future.

1 Introduction

Interpretation is the oral translation of speech from one language to another. Simultaneous interpretation is one type of real-time interpretation where the interpreter performs the translation within the time permitted by the pace of source speech. Compared to another type of interpretation – consecutive interpretation – where the speaker pauses after completing one or two sentences, simultaneous interpretation has the advantages of saving time, and also not interupting the natural flow of the speaker [1].

Simultaneous interpretation is an effective way to bridge language gaps. A good example of events where simultaneous interpretation is used are the United Nations and European Union conferences. The interpreter sits in a soundproofed booth and speaks into a microphone, while clearly seeing and hearing the speaker. The delegates in the meeting room select the relevant channel to hear to interpretation in the his or her native language [2]

Simultaneous interpretation is an expensive service due to the cost of interpreters. First, the number of simultaneous interpreters is small, because the job requires many years of experience and subject matter expertise. Second, for a real-world event, employing one interpreter is normally insufficient, because the task demands so much concentration that any individual can only hope to be effective for periods of 20 minutes or less. Several interpreters are required for continuous service of more than two hours [3].

Inspired by both the merits and the demands of simultaneous interpretation, we have developed a fully automatic simultaneous interpretation system, as presented in this paper. Recently some other simultaneous interpretation systems such as (Müller et al., 2016) have also been presented. Unfortunately, cross-comparison is currently not possible without access to these systems, and will hopefully become interesting future work. This paper first explains how the system works (Section 2), then describes how to use the system (Section 3), then shows how well the system works (Section 4), then presents an example of the system's performance on a TED talk (Section 5), and finally concludes with a description of future work (Section 6).

2 The System in a Nutshell

The simultaneous interpretation system is a fully automatic speech-to-speech system that is currently capable of English-Japanese bidirectional interpretation. The method is general, and can be applied to other language pairs directly.

[1] https://en.wikipedia.org/wiki/Language_interpretation

[2] http://ec.europa.eu/dgs/scic/what-is-conference-interpreting/simultaneous/index_en.htm

[3] http://www.londontranslations.co.uk/our-services/simultaneous-interpreters/

Proceedings of COLING 2016, the 26th International Conference on Computational Linguistics: System Demonstrations, pages 30–34, Osaka, Japan, December 11-17 2016.

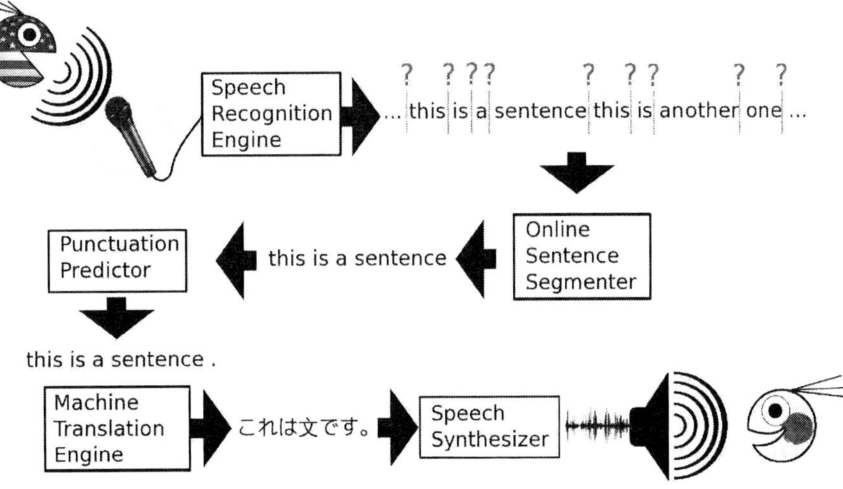

Figure 1: Architecture of the Simultaneous Interpretation System

Figure 1 illustrates the architecture of the system. The key element in the design is an online sentence segmenter that bridges the speech recognition engine and the machine translation engine. The whole system is a pipeline of six components: a speech recognition engine, a sentence segmenter, a punctuation predictor, a machine translation engine, and a speech synthesizer.

The **Speech Recognition Engine** converts audio signals into a stream of words. The current implementation is an online decoder based on the Kaldi open source toolkit (Povey et al., 2011)[4]. We plan to integrate our own in-house speech recognition engine – SprinTra (Shen et al., 2014) in the future.

Our system is able to perform speech detection. That is to say the system is always listening, and will respond to any speech it hears (see Section 3 for details). Speech detection is done by applying a threshold to the energy of the input audio signals. We determined empirically that this heuristic works well in actual use. In the case when loud noises exceed the threshold and trigger the system, the speech recognition engine normally outputs no words, thus little damage is caused.

The **Online Sentence Segmenter** converts the stream of words into sentences. The implementation is based on the method proposed in (Wang et al., 2016a). The implementation uses a linear combination of a language model, a length model and a prosodic model to calculate the confidence of segmentation boundaries, and uses a threshold-latency-based heuristic to make decisions.

The **Punctuation Predictor** converts an un-punctuated sentence into a punctuated sentence. The implementation is based on the findings in (Wang et al., 2016b). It uses a hidden N-gram model (Stolcke et al., 1998; Matusov et al., 2006), which is available in the toolkit of SRILM (Stolcke, 2002), to insert punctuation.

The **Machine Translation Engine** translates a source-language sentence into a target-language sentence. The implementation is our in-house pre-ordering translation system, called the General Purpose Machine Translation (GPMT) engine. The system is publicly accessible through a Web API [5]

The **Speech Synthesizer** converts sentences into speech. The implementation is based on the HTS open-source toolkit (Tokuda et al., 2013)[6]

[4] `https://github.com/kaldi-asr/kaldi`
[5] `https://mt-auto-minhon-mlt.ucri.jgn-x.jp/`
[6] `http://hts.sp.nitech.ac.jp/`

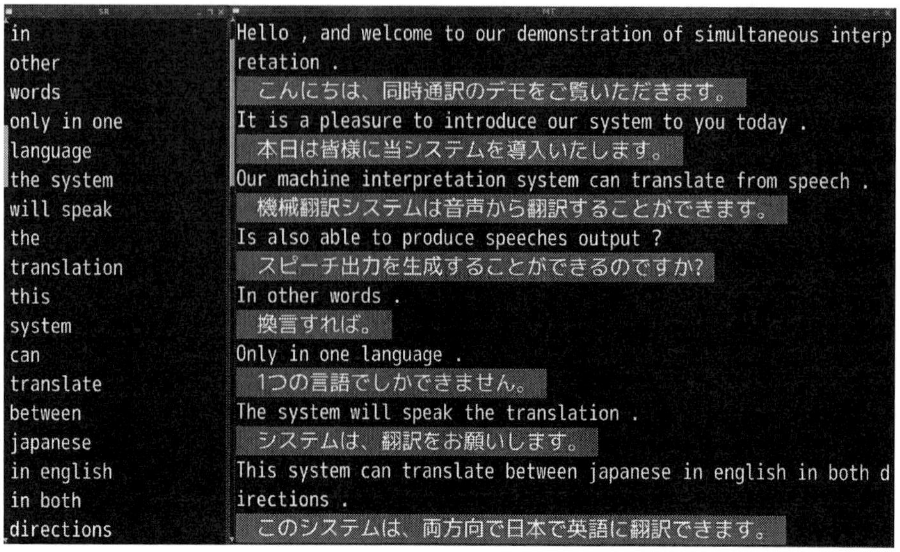

Figure 2: Logs of Simultaneous Interpretation System: Speech Recognition (left) and Machine Translation (right).

3 Usage

The system is designed to work in exactly the same manner as a human interpreter working in multilingual conferences. Once launched, the system can work continuously for hours or days without intervention. In operation, it receives audio signals constantly from its microphone. If no one is speaking, the system will produce no output. If someone is speaking, the system will speak out the translation, normally, in only a few seconds.

In addition to the speech output, two logs can be used to monitor the running of the system: the speech recognition log and the machine translation log (Figure 2). The speech recognition log shows the recognized words from the speakers. The machine translation log shows the recognized sentences and their translations. The content of both logs is updated in realtime.

4 Performance

The performance of our method was measured in (Wang et al., 2016a). Experiments were performed on translation between Japanese and English in both directions. The time efficiency was measured by average latency per source word using the definition given in (Finch et al., 2014). The translation quality was measured by the BLEU of end-to-end translation. Because the segmented source sentences did not necessarily agree with the oracle, translations were aligned to reference sentences through edit distance in order to calculate BLEU (Matusov et al., 2005).

The results of the measurement are presented in table 1. Different sentence segmentation methods were compared. Our system adopted the threshold-latency method which generally outperformed the other methods on both time efficiency and translation quality.

5 Example Analysis

Here is an example of interpreting a TED talk from English to Japanese by the system. The talk is "Your elusive creative genius " given by Elizabeth Gilbert in 2009[7]. The oracle transcript is,

> I am a writer. Writing books is my profession but it's more than that, of course. It is also my great lifelong love and fascination. And I don't expect that that's ever going to change. But, that said, something kind of peculiar has happened recently in my life and in my career ...

[7] `https://www.ted.com/talks/elizabeth_gilbert_on_genius?language=en`

Sentence Segmenter	Dev. Set		Test Set	
	BLEU	Latency	BLEU	Latency
Japanese-to-English				
Oracle	13.82	NA	13.67	NA
Hidden N-gram †	13.30	NA‡	12.97	NA‡
Fixed-length	11.71	16.66	11.55	16.63
Threshold-based	**13.38**	14.20	13.16	13.68
Latency-based	13.21	18.04	13.20	18.03
Threshold-latency (our System)	**13.38**	**12.98**	**13.28**	**12.89**
English-to-Japanese				
Oracle	13.84	NA	14.15	NA
Hidden N-gram†	12.85	NA‡	13.10	NA‡
Fixed-length	11.86	8.19	12.15	8.20
Threshold-based	12.93	**7.13**	13.19	**7.18**
Latency-based	**13.18**	12.25	13.38	12.26
Threshold-latency (our System)	**13.18**	10.01	**13.42**	10.11

Table 1: Performance of interpretation systems that use different sentence segmenters. The confidence scores in threshold-based, latency-based and threshold-latency-based segmenters were calculated using Equation 4 in (Wang et al., 2016a). † Employed the segment tool from the SRILM toolkit (Stolcke, 2002). ‡ The method is not online since it operates on a whole sequence of words, thus the measurement of latency is not applicable.

Recognized Sentence	Translation	Post Edited	Lat.(s)
I am a writer .	私は作家です。	私は作家です。	1.5
writing books is my profession .	書く仕事です。	本を書くのが私の仕事です。	3.3
but , it's more than that of course it is also my great lifelong love and fascination .	しかし、それはまた、私がたいへん好きや魅力のものより多い。	ですが、それは仕事以上のもので、私がずっと大好きで魅了されていることなのです。	2.5
and I don't expect that that's ever going to change .	そして私はそれが変わるのです、とは思っていません。	そして、今後もそれは変わらないと思っています。	2.1
but that said , something kind of peculiar has happened recently in my life , and in my career .	しかしそうは言っても、最近変わった体験をし私の人生において、ました。	ですが、最近、公私に渡り変わった体験をしました。	1.8

Table 2: Example of Simultaneous Interpretation System Working on an TED Talk

The result of the system is shown in Table 2. The system works rapidly, and can easily keep with up the speaker, with a latency ranging from 1.5 to 3.3 seconds for these sentences.

For analysis, the output was corrected by a professional translator ('Post Edited' in Table 2). The first sentence was translated perfectly; the second was good but omitted the translation for the word *books*. The third sentence's translation resolved the pronouns incorrectly, and this was subjectively the worst translation. The fourth sentence was semantically correct, but it is more natural to say: 'I expect not *X*' rather then 'I didn't expect *X*' in Japanese. The fifth sentence was also quite good but the word *career* was not translated. Overall, the translation quality is impressive, given the difficulty of translation between English and Japanese.

Note that although speech recognition errors rarely happen on this speech. Recognition error rate is speaker dependent and proved to be one of the main sources of errors in our tests. Therefore we believe that further improvements in speech recognition are vital for the future development of simultaneous interpretation systems.

6 Conclusion

This paper presents a prototype automatic simultaneous interpretation system. The system adopts a robust and effective pipeline framework. It is designed to behave like a human interpreter, and is very easy to use. In real-world use it is capable of producing useful translations while keeping up with the fastest of speakers.

Our system is still in early-stage, and we hope that by demonstrating this system we can encourage both academic research and industrial development in this field. In the future, we will constantly improve the system with an emphasis on the quality of final output. Future efforts may include handling disfluencies, applying neural networks to the task of sentence segmentation, integration with our in-house speech recognition engine of SprinTra, and improving our GPMT in-house machine translation engine.

References

Andrew Finch, Xiaolin Wang, and Eiichiro Sumita. 2014. An Exploration of Segmentation Strategies in Stream Decoding. In *IWSLT*.

Evgeny Matusov, Gregor Leusch, Oliver Bender, Hermann Ney, et al. 2005. Evaluating machine translation output with automatic sentence segmentation. In *IWSLT*, pages 138–144. Citeseer.

Evgeny Matusov, Arne Mauser, and Hermann Ney. 2006. Automatic sentence segmentation and punctuation prediction for spoken language translation. In *Proceedings of 3rd International Workshop on Spoken Language Translation*, pages 158–165.

Markus Müller, Thai Son Nguyen, Jan Niehues, Eunah Cho, Bastian Krüger, Thanh-Le Ha, Kevin Kilgour, Matthias Sperber, Mohammed Mediani, Sebastian Stüker, and Alex Waibel. 2016. Lecture translator - speech translation framework for simultaneous lecture translation. In *Proceedings of the 2016 Conference of the North American Chapter of the Association for Computational Linguistics: Demonstrations*, pages 82–86, San Diego, California, June. Association for Computational Linguistics.

Daniel Povey, Arnab Ghoshal, Gilles Boulianne, Lukas Burget, Ondrej Glembek, Nagendra Goel, Mirko Hannemann, Petr Motlicek, Yanmin Qian, Petr Schwarz, Jan Silovsky, Georg Stemmer, and Karel Vesely. 2011. The Kaldi speech recognition toolkit. In *IEEE Workshop on Automatic Speech Recognition and Understanding*, December.

Peng Shen, Xugang Lu, X Hu, N Kanda, M Saiko, and C Hori. 2014. The NICT ASR system for IWSLT 2014. In *Proceedings of the 11th International Workshop on Spoken Language Translation.*

Andreas Stolcke, Elizabeth Shriberg, Rebecca A Bates, Mari Ostendorf, Dilek Hakkani, Madelaine Plauche, Gökhan Tür, and Yu Lu. 1998. Automatic detection of sentence boundaries and disfluencies based on recognized words. In *Proceedings of 5th International Conference on Spoken Language Processing*, pages 2247–2250.

Andreas Stolcke. 2002. SRILM - an extensible language modeling toolkit. In *Proceedings of the 7th International Conference on Spoken Language Processing*.

Keiichi Tokuda, Yoshihiko Nankaku, Tomoki Toda, Heiga Zen, Junichi Yamagishi, and Keiichiro Oura. 2013. Speech synthesis based on hidden markov models. *Proceedings of the IEEE*, 101(5):1234–1252.

Xiaolin Wang, Andrew Finch, Masao Utiyama, and Eiichiro Sumita. 2016a. An efficient and effective online sentence segmenter for simultaneous interpretation. In *(to appear)*.

Xiaolin Wang, Masao Utiyama, Andrew Finch, and Eiichiro Sumita. 2016b. A study of punctuation handling for speech-to-speech translation. In *Proceedings of 22nd Annual Meeting on Natural Language Processing*, pages 525–528.

MuTUAL: A Controlled Authoring Support System Enabling Contextual Machine Translation

Rei Miyata
The University of Tokyo
rei@p.u-tokyo.ac.jp

Anthony Hartley
Rikkyo University

Kyo Kageura
The University of Tokyo

Cécile Paris
Data61, CSIRO

Masao Utiyama
NICT

Eiichiro Sumita
NICT

Abstract

The paper introduces a web-based authoring support system, **MuTUAL**, which aims to help writers create multilingual texts. The highlighted feature of the system is that it enables machine translation (MT) to generate outputs appropriate to their functional context within the target document. Our system is operational online, implementing core mechanisms for document structuring and controlled writing. These include a topic template and a controlled language authoring assistant, linked to our statistical MT system.

1 Introduction

For improved machine translatability, a wide variety of controlled language (CL) rule sets have been proposed (Kittredge, 2003; Kuhn, 2014). Evidence of reduced post-editing costs when a CL is employed is provided (Bernth and Gdaniec, 2001; O'Brien and Roturier, 2007), and several controlled authoring support tools, such as Acrolinx[1] and MAXIT[2], have been developed. The fundamental limitation of the CLs proposed hitherto is, however, that they are defined at the level of the sentence rather than at the level of the document (Hartley and Paris, 2001). In fact, the notion of functional document element (see Section 2.1) does figure in some CL rule sets. ASD Simplified Technical English (ASD, 2013), for example, specifies writing patterns linked to functional roles of the document elements; the recommended maximum length of sentence is 20 words for 'procedural' writing and 25 words for 'descriptive' writing. Yet, the granularity of the elements is not high enough to enable detailed definitions of linguistic patterns within the elements. Thus it is necessary to formalise a document-level framework which enables context-dependent CL specification.

In this paper, we introduce an integrated web-based system, **MuTUAL**, which implements a suite of controlled authoring support modules, combined with our statistical machine translation (SMT) system. At the document level, document structuring modules help authors create well-organised documents. At the sentence level, controlled writing modules help them write source texts (ST) consistent with source-language CL rules. The principal innovation in the system is to contextualise the CL rules in the document structure to enable MT to generate outputs consistent with the target-side CL for a given functional element. While the current system supports the creation of municipal procedural documents in Japanese and their translation into English, it is extensible to other language pairs and text domains.

2 Contextual Translation

MuTUAL starts from the observation that the same source sentence should be translated as different target sentences depending on its location within the functional elements of the document. Let us consider this example Japanese sentence from a procedural technical manual: '文書を印刷する/*bunsho o insatsu suru*'. This sentence can appear as a task title in a section heading or as a step description in an itemisation, and should be translated, respectively, as 'To print a document' or 'Print the document'. That is, the translation depends on the item's functional role within the document.

[1]http://www.acrolinx.com/

[2]http://www.smartny.com/maxit.html/

Proceedings of COLING 2016, the 26th International Conference on Computational Linguistics: System Demonstrations, pages 35–39, Osaka, Japan, December 11-17 2016.

	DITA element in **Body** (default)	Specified functional element
Prereq	information the user needs to know before starting	**Personal condition** **Event condition** **Item condition**
Context	background information	**Explanation (Summary, Purpose, Expiration of validity, Penalty, Related concept)**
Steps	main content: a series of steps	**Necessary items to bring** **Place to go** **Form(s) to complete**
Result	expected outcome	**Result (Period for procedure, Items to be issued, Contact from local government)**
Postreq	steps to do after completion of current task	**Guidance to other procedures**

Table 1: Instantiation of the DITA Task topic

To realise contextual translation using MT, we (1) formulated a document structure for municipal procedures based on the Darwin Information Typing Architecture (DITA) framework (OASIS, 2010), and (2) defined context-dependent CL rules in both source and target languages according to the functional document elements, in combination with ST transformation rules.

2.1 Functional Task Elements

DITA is an XML architecture for authoring and publishing technical information which supports structured authoring to help writers compose a modularised chunk of information, called *topic* (Bellamy et al., 2012). A topic has a hierarchical structure of functional elements, i.e., elements which play certain communicative roles within the documents, and, at the highest level, is composed of the common elements: **Title**, **Short description**, **Prologue**, **Body** and **Related-links**.

According to topic types, DITA further defines more specific elements under the **Body** element. DITA provides by default several topic types such as *Concept topic*, *Reference topic* and *Task topic*. We focus here on the Task topic, which is designed for describing technical procedures, because what we are concerned is mainly municipal procedures. The left column in Table 1 shows the functional elements under the **Body** of Task topic (OASIS, 2010).

Note that the functional elements of the Task topic as defined in DITA are still too coarse-grained to properly organise municipal procedures and specify detailed linguistic patterns for each element. However, DITA allows for 'specialisation', so we undertook a genre analysis of actual municipal documents and assigned fine-grained sub-elements (the right column of Table 1).

2.2 Context-dependent CL with Pre-translation Processing

At this stage, the DITA structure provides a language-independent functional framework, which helps authors identify what information should be included. It is, however, still unclear how to write and translate each element. In order to instantiate the elements as texts, we defined context-dependent CL rules, i.e., desired linguistic patterns, for each element on both source and target sides.

For example, **Event condition** requires a conditional clause such as '日本に来たとき/*nihon ni kita toki*' (when you arrive in Japan). We also assigned a rather strict pattern for **Steps** element, polite speech style with declarative form 'します/*shimasu*' in Japanese and imperative form 'do' in English, such as '以下の書類を持参します/*ika no shorui o jizan shimasu*' (Bring the following documents), while the constraint is relaxed in **Context**, **Result** and **Postreq**.

The problem here is that a CL-compliant ST segment does not always generate a desired linguistic form in the target language. To resolve such incompatibilities, we introduce background pre-translation processing to transform the ST into an internal form amenable to the chosen MT system. Figure 1 depicts an example flow of this process for the **Steps** element: **ST1** is the CL-compliant original sentence, in polite speech style with the declarative '*shimasu*'. Since the MT output **MT1** is not a desirable result, **ST1** is transformed internally into **ST2**, with the imperative '*shiro*'. This then enables MT to produce

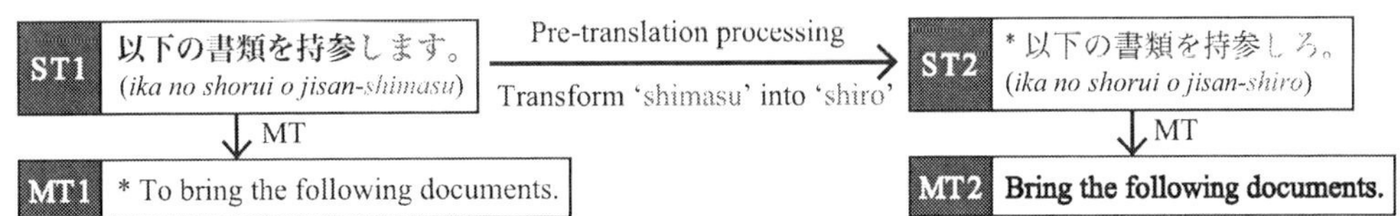

Figure 1: Pre-translation processing for **Steps** (* undesirable sentence)

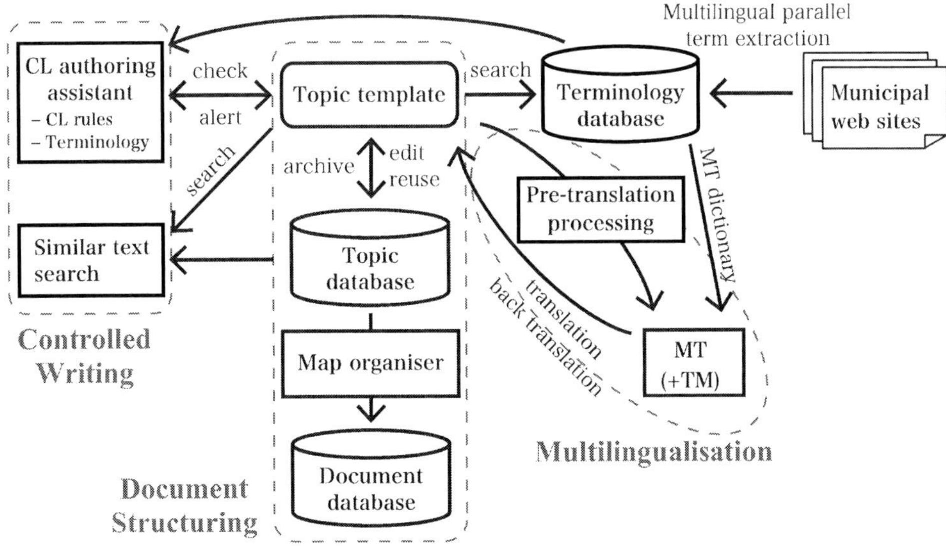

Figure 2: Modules of MuTUAL

MT2, which complies with the target side CL rule, with the use of the imperative form 'do'. **ST1** is served to Japanese readers and **MT2** to English readers. This process can be fully automated by defining simple transformation rules based on the morphological analysis of ST,[3] on condition that the linguistic patterns of the ST are sufficiently controlled in conjunction with functional elements.

3 The MuTUAL System

The MuTUAL system comprises modules for document structuring, controlled writing, and multilingualisation (see Figure 2). The following modules realise the contextual translation we have outlined:

- **Topic template** is the core interface for authoring self-contained topics in a structured manner. The left pane in Figure 3 provides the basic DITA Task topic structure for composing municipal procedural documents.
- **CL authoring assistant** analyses each sentence in the text box and highlights any segment that violates a local CL rule or controlled terminology, together with diagnostic comments and suggestions for rewriting (shown at bottom centre in Figure 3) (Miyata et al., 2016). In addition, we have implemented a preliminary rewriting support function with several of the features advocated by Mitamura et al. (2003). For a particular CL-noncompliant segment, the function offers alternative expressions; clicking one of the suggestions automatically replaces the offending segment in the text box above.
- **Pre-translation processing** automatically modifies source segments in the background following transformation rules defined for each functional element, and then **MT** produces the translation and back-translation at the same time.

[3]We used a Japanese morphological analyser MeCab. http://taku910.github.io/mecab/

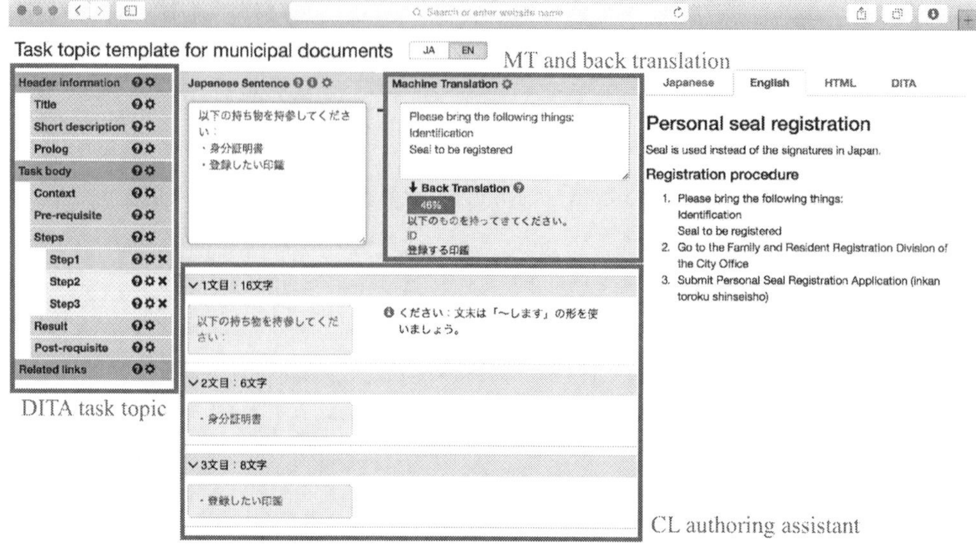

Figure 3: Task topic template for authoring municipal procedures

The key mechanism for enhancing authoring and translation is to invoke the CL authoring assistant tuned to the current functional element. For example, only for the **Steps** elements of the template, it implements the rule 'use declarative form *shimasu* at the end of the sentence'. Then the pre-translation processing for **Steps** transforms the declarative '*shimasu*' into an imperative '*shiro*' for our MT system to produce the desired imperative form 'do' on the target side.

The modules above are implemented in PHP and JavaScript, and can be accessed through the usual web browsers. The topic template seamlessly connects with our SMT system, TexTra,[4] the dictionary of which is customised by municipal terminology we maintain. We plan to publish an open-source version of the system through our project website.[5]

4 Conclusions and Future Work

We have presented a web-based support system for authoring municipal procedural documents. The principal novel feature of the system is that it makes use of document structuring based on the DITA framework, which affords a basis for fine-grained context-dependent CL rules coupled with pre-translation processing. It consequently enables MT to generate outputs appropriate to their functional context without degrading the quality of the source.

MuTUAL is currently operational online, focusing on the Task topic for creating municipal procedural documents in Japanese and English. The implemented CL rules were shown to be effective in triggering more appropriate outputs from our SMT system (Miyata et al., 2015). Also, a preliminary user evaluation revealed that the controlled authoring assistant module helped reduce time correcting CL-violations by more than 30%. As a future evaluation plan, while previous work has tended to focus on sentence-level text quality, we intend to evaluate the document-level quality of the system products by adopting task-based methods (Colineau et al., 2002). We will eventually make the system available to municipal departments and assess its usability in actual work scenarios.

[4]TexTra is a state-of-the-art SMT system particularly intended for Japanese as source language, and provides free API. https://mt-auto-minhon-mlt.ucri.jgn-x.jp

[5]The MuTUAL Project, http://www.mutual-project.com

Acknowledgements

This work was supported by JSPS KAKENHI Grant Number 16J11185 and by the Research Grant Program of KDDI Foundation, Japan.

References

ASD. 2013. ASD Simplified Technical English. Specification ASD-STE100, Issue 6. http://www.asd-ste100.org.

Laura Bellamy, Michelle Carey, and Jenifer Schlotfeldt. 2012. *DITA Best Practices: A Roadmap for Writing, Editing, and Architecting in DITA*. IBM Press.

Arendse Bernth and Claudia Gdaniec. 2001. MTranslatability. *Machine Translation*, 16(3):175–218.

Nathalie Colineau, Cécile Paris, and Keith Vander Linden. 2002. An evaluation of procedural instructional text. In *Proceedings of the International Natural Language Generation Conference*, pages 128–135, New York.

Anthony Hartley and Cécile Paris. 2001. Translation, controlled languages, generation. In Erich Steiner and Colin Yallop, editors, *Exploring Translation and Multilingual Text production*, pages 307–325. Mouton, Berlin.

Richard Kittredge. 2003. Sublanguages and controlled languages. In Ruslan Mitkov, editor, *Oxford Handbook of Computational Linguistics*, pages 430–437. Oxford University Press, Oxford.

Tobias Kuhn. 2014. A survey and classification of controlled natural languages. *Computational Linguistics*, 40(1):121–170.

Teruko Mitamura, Kathryn Baker, Eric Nyberg, and David Svoboda. 2003. Diagnostics for interactive controlled language checking. In *Proceedings of the 4th Workshop on Controlled Language Applications (CLAW 2003)*, pages 237–244, Dublin, Ireland.

Rei Miyata, Anthony Hartley, Cécile Paris, Midori Tatsumi, and Kyo Kageura. 2015. Japanese controlled language rules to improve machine translatability of municipal documents. In *Proceedings of the Machine Translation Summit XV*, pages 90–103, Miami, USA.

Rei Miyata, Anthony Hartley, Cécile Paris, and Kyo Kageura. 2016. Evaluating and implementing a controlled language checker. In *Proceedings of the 6th International Workshop on Controlled Language Applications (CLAW 2016)*, pages 30–35, Portorož, Slovenia.

OASIS. 2010. Darwin Information Typing Architecture (DITA) Version 1.2. http://docs.oasis-open.org/dita/v1.2/os/spec/DITA1.2-spec.html.

Sharon O'Brien and Johann Roturier. 2007. How portable are controlled language rules? In *Proceedings of the Machine Translation Summit XI*, pages 345–352, Copenhagen, DK.

Joint search in a bilingual valency lexicon and an annotated corpus

Eva Fučíková **Jan Hajič** **Zdeňka Urešová**

Faculty of Mathematics and Physics
Charles University in Prague, Czech Republic
Institute of Formal and Applied Linguistics
{fucikova,hajic,uresova}@ufal.mff.cuni.cz

Abstract

... so I say to you ... search, and you will find ...

In this paper and the associated system demo, we present an advanced search system that allows to perform a joint search over a (bilingual) valency lexicon and a correspondingly annotated linked parallel corpus. This search tool has been developed on the basis of the Prague Czech-English Dependency Treebank, but its ideas are applicable in principle to any bilingual parallel corpus that is annotated for dependencies and valency (i.e., predicate-argument structure), and where verbs are linked to appropriate entries in an associated valency lexicon. Our online search tool consolidates more search interfaces into one, providing expanded structured search capability and a more efficient advanced way to search, allowing users to search for verb pairs, verbal argument pairs, their surface realization as recorded in the lexicon, or for their surface form actually appearing in the linked parallel corpus. The search system is currently under development, and is replacing our current search tool available at http://lindat.mff.cuni.cz/services/CzEngVallex, which could search the lexicon but the queries cannot take advantage of the underlying corpus nor use the additional surface form information from the lexicon(s). The system is available as open source.

1 Introduction

For linguistic research and for manual inspection of corpora, treebanks and lexicons, many different search tools exist (PML Tree Query[1] (Štěpánek and Pajas, 2010; Bejček et al., 2010), KonText (Klyueva and Straňák, 2016),[2] NoSketch Engine[3] (Rychlý, 2007), Tgrep,[4] BNC-search,[5] LAPPS Grid,[6], and many others. Every electronic lexicon (monolingual or bilingual) also comes with a basic search, typically allowing to search for headwords, or within any text using some form of fulltext search. Specifically both valency lexicons developed at the Institute of Formal and Applied Linguistics, PDT-Vallex[7] (Urešová, 2011b; Urešová, 2011a) and VALLEX[8] (Lopatková et al., in print; Žabokrtský and Lopatková, 2007), come with a search-allowing interface.[9]

However, we are not aware of any system that would allow structured search (a) in both a lexicon with rich information and an annotated corpus at the same time, *and* (b) bilingually. This could be caused also by the lack of parallel (bilingual or multilingual) corpora that are annotated by such rich lexicon entries

[1] https://ufal.mff.cuni.cz/pmltq
[2] https://ucnk.ff.cuni.cz/intercorp/?req=page:manual_kontext_en, http://ufal.mff.cuni.cz/lindat-kontext
[3] https://nlp.fi.muni.cz/trac/noske
[4] https://tedlab.mit.edu/~dr/Tgrep2
[5] http://www.natcorp.ox.ac.uk
[6] http://galaxy.lappsgrid.org
[7] https://ufal.mff.cuni.cz/pdt-vallex-valency-lexicon-linked-czech-corpora
[8] http://ufal.mff.cuni.cz/vallex/3.0
[9] http://lindat.cz

Proceedings of COLING 2016, the 26th International Conference on Computational Linguistics: System Demonstrations, pages 40–44, Osaka, Japan, December 11-17 2016.

(usually, the corpora contain - in some cases - lemmas, which can be then searched for in *independent* lexicons). Our task was to make the Prague Czech-English Dependency Treebank (PCEDT 2.0) (Hajič et al., 2012) efficiently searchable, aiming to be a help for various applications of computational and traditional linguistics as well as for NLP studies. The PCEDT is a bilingual corpus that contains both rich dependency and predicate-argument annotation itself, as well as links to valency lexicons used (not only) for predicate-argument annotation consistency. In this respect, it is similar to the PropBank (Palmer et al., 2005), which annotates predicate-argument structure on top of the Penn Treebank (Marcus et al., 1993), indexing also by pointing to the frame files, from which additional information about the predicates (verbs) can be extracted. However, PropBank is a monolingual resource. Also, because English is not a very morphologically rich language, PropBank's frame files do not contain much more than a list of arguments and sense distinctions; in contrast, Czech language is quite rich in this respect, and consequently, the Czech valency lexicon entries (Urešová, 2011b) contain additional information on the required form of verb arguments in terms of case, prepositions to be used, etc. Fig. 1 shows a simple example of a valency entry for the Czech verb *kalkulovat*, which has two senses: a *compute sth* sense, and a more abstract sense on *counting on something, on somebody* (*to happen*). In the first sense, it adds an optional third argument *to compute ... from something*, and both senses also differ in the possible surface form - the second, more abstract sense requires a particular preposition and case (specified by `s+7`, lit. `with`, and `7` for instrumental case), while the deep object of the former sense is a simple direct (prepositionless) accusative (specified by `4`, as cases are typically numbered in Czech).

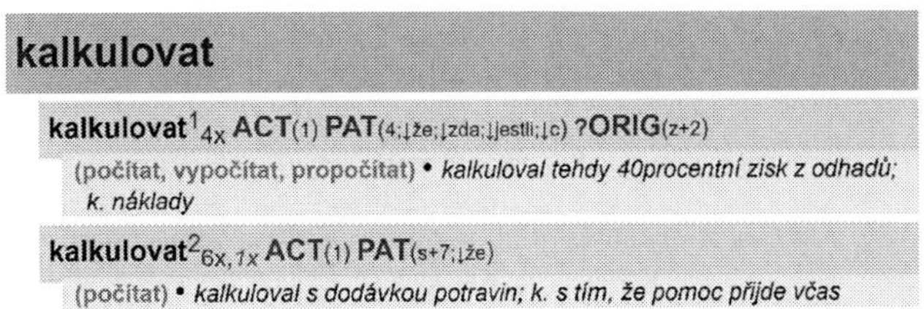

Figure 1: Czech Valency lexicon (PDT-Vallex) entry (two senses of "kalkukovat": lit. "compute" and "count on *sth/sb*")

In addition, not only the Czech and English treebanks are aligned in the PCEDT, but so are the associated valency lexicons for Czech - PDT-Vallex[10] (Urešová, 2011b) and English - EngVallex[11] (Cinková, 2006), forming a bilingual parallel CzEngVallex lexicon (Urešová et al., 2016) which explicitly aligns verb senses as well as verb arguments between the two languages.

What was missing after having explicit alignments annotated was a tool that would allow inspection of the resulting corpus and lexicons, allowing cross-lingual queries with reasonable flexibility to support linguistic studies, NLP tasks, manual check of results of automatic tools, etc.

In our previous work (Fučíková et al., 2015), we have developed a tool that can search the lexicon(s) in a cross-lingual manner, allowing to formulate queries such as *show me all pairs of verbs and their translations where the English verb is a phrasal verb, while the Czech one is not.* Fig. 2 shows the old interface (taken from (Fučíková et al., 2015)), and the result of such a query.

The tool did not allow the user to formulate the query over the associated parallel corpus, but it was at least showing the associated examples with the bilingual lexicon entries found. While useful as such, there was a demand both from linguists and from computer researchers to allow for more detailed queries: specifically, to be able to use the surface form constraints in the lexicon, and also constraints on the actual use in the associated parallel corpus.[12] For example, there was no way to specify exactly which particular phrasal verb the user wants to find (cf. Fig. 2). The new tool presented here answers to such demands

[10]http://lindat.mff.cuni.cz/services/PDT-Vallex

[11]http://lindat.mff.cuni.cz/services/EngVallex

[12]This has been in part due to the fact that the English valency lexicon unlike the Czech lexicon does not often contain any information about the required form, such as required or typical prepositions, and thus the corpus is the only place where such information is available.

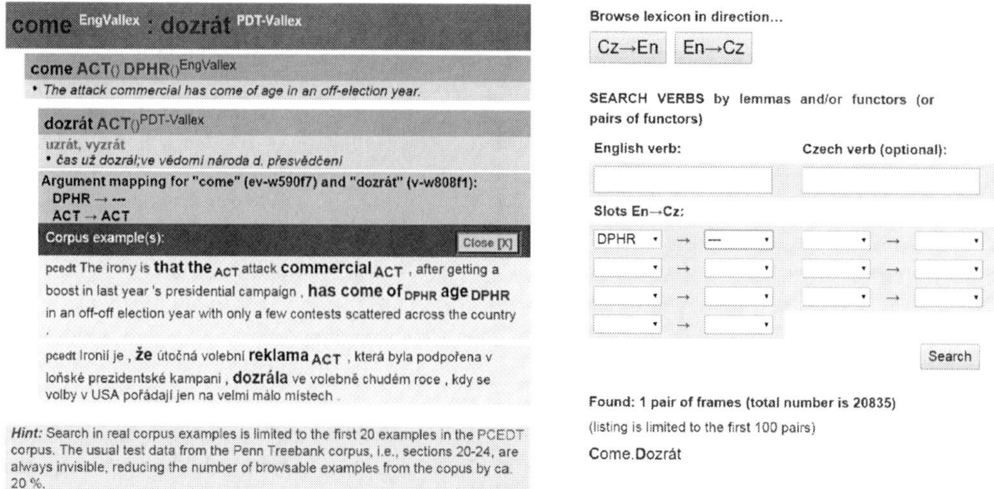

Figure 2: The old search interface

by implementing the possibility to search for the surface form constraints in the lexicon as well as in the corpus, in a bilingual setting.

2 System overview

Fig. 3 depicts the new search interface. We demonstrate the new system capabilities on the displayed example.

The query interface is on the right-hand side, the results appear left to it. In this case, the user searched for all Czech verbs—paired with the English verb *to cater (to)*—which express the corresponding argument (a deep object) by a prepositional phrase using the Czech preposition `o` (lit. `about`) with accusative, or by a subordinate clause introduced by the conjunction `aby` (lit. `so that`). There was only one result (*starat se*, lit. *to take care*) in Czech. One example from the PCEDT is also shown (which fully corresponds to the requirement that the English verb occurrence in the corpus has to be complemented by a prepositional phrase with `to`).

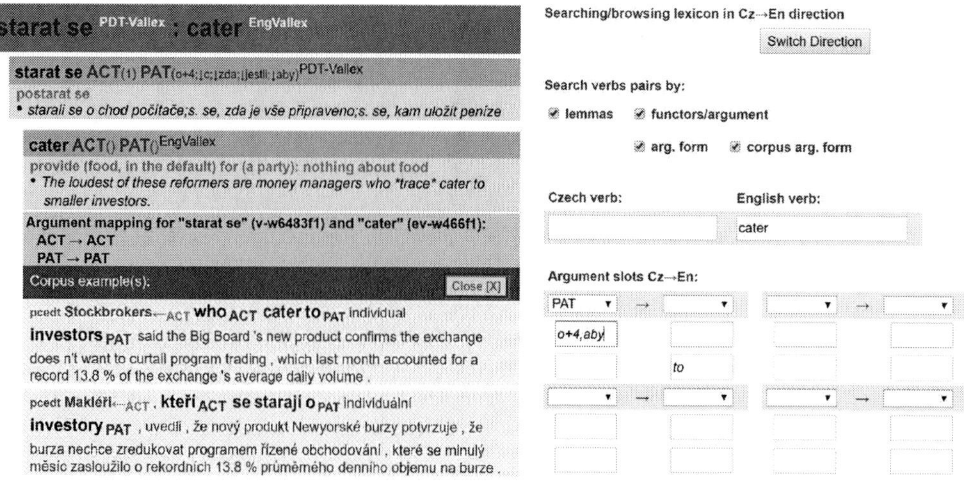

Figure 3: The new search interface and a result of search query

Let's have a closer look at the query: the checkboxes (lemmas, functors, arg. form, corpus arg. form) are all checked, bringing up the corresponding search fields to be filled. There is always a pair of these fields - Czech on the left, English on the right.[13] Apart from lemma, there are three search fields for each language: selector for the argument label ("functor"), lexicon argument form specification, and field for specifying the required corpus argument form. In Fig. 3, the user selected `PAT` as the argument label on the Czech side, limiting the search results to "deep objects" (label: `PAT`) of the Czech verb while leaving the field on the English side empty (any label - actor, deep object, addressee, ... could be paired with the Czech `PAT` on the English side). In addition, the (surface) argument form of the Czech `PAT` has been restricted to an accusative prepositional phrase headed by `o` (lit. `about`) which is expressed by `o+4`. As an alternative for this arg. form, the user allowed for this argument to be a subordinate clause headed by the conjunction `aby`, (lit. `to`), expressed as `aby`.[14] On the English side, the user has put the preposition `to` on the second line of the two form fields, since it is to be found in the *corpus*, not in the English valency lexicon.[15] These expressions are a shorthand for fully expressing the exact dependencies of the verb and its arguments; the relatively complex expansion of these fields and execution of a proper match of the treebank data is performed by the search engine.

In general, it is possible to use also much more complicated queries, using the usual logical operators ("and", "or") grouping and precedence, all combined with the possibility of using regular expressions on the literals (strings, whether lemmas, forms, or tags).

At query time, the search engine does not use the treebank (PCEDT) and the bilingual lexicon (CzEng-Vallex) directly, but they are pre-processed and indexed to make the search efficient. It also re-formats the treebank annotation to a linear annotation within the text (as can be seen in the examples), to make it more readable and avoid the need for additional visualization for the trees.[16]

Information about every pair of verbs is collected into a separate `.php` file (which also includes CSS-based formatting). In addition, information about the form for each argument of each valency frame for both PDT-Valex and EngVallex is extracted to another file for efficient search; similar index is created for the parallel corpora. There is also one more set of `.php` files for the display of dictionary examples, one file for each valency frame pair.

3 Conclusions and Future Development

We have described a search system over a bilingual lexicon and a parallel corpus. The tool builds on our previous simple search system, but substantially extends it for the use of surface form both as recorded in the lexicon as well as allowing to restrict the search to particular forms of argument expression in the associated corpus.

In the future, we intend to add more search possibilities, such as the option to search for particular form combinations in verb argument description, statistics (occurrence counts etc.) and their visualization.

The system is open, but at the moment its adaptation to other similar treebanks will require certain amount of work, namely to converts and index such treebanks and lexicons to the form which the search system uses at search time. This factorization allows, on the other hand to accommodate diverse corpora to be used, without regard to original formats or exact annotation schemas.

The system is available from the LINDAT/CLARIN language resource repository[17] as open source, as is the current system and the associated lexicons and corpora. The search interface can be used openly through any browser.

Acknowledgments

This work has been directly supported by the grant No. DG16P02019 of the Ministry of Culture of the Czech Republic.

[13] The direction can be switched for convenience.

[14] Czech prepositions do not overlap with conjunctions, so their lexical forms can be used without ambiguity in the queries.

[15] Which typically do not have the required preposition marked.

[16] For those interested in the annotation itself, there are other tools, such as the PML-TQ search system, see above.

[17] `http://lindat.cz`

In addition, it has also been using language resources distributed by the LINDAT/CLARIN project of the Ministry of Education of the Czech Republic (projects LM2010013 and LM2015071), which also hosts the resulting software.

References

Eduard Bejček, Václava Kettnerová, and Markéta Lopatková. 2010. Advanced searching in the valency lexicons using PML-TQ search engine. In *Text, Speech and Dialogue. 13th International Conference, TSD 2010, Brno, Czech Republic, September 6-10, 2010. Proceedings*, pages 51–58.

Silvie Cinková. 2006. From PropBank to EngValLex: Adapting the PropBank-Lexicon to the Valency Theory of the Functional Generative Description. In *Proceedings of the 5th International Conference on Language Resources and Evaluation (LREC 2006)*, pages 2170–2175, Genova, Italy. ELRA.

Eva Fučíková, Jan Hajič, Jana Šindlerová, and Zdeňka Urešová. 2015. Czech-English Bilingual Valency Lexicon Online. In *14th International Workshop on Treebanks and Linguistic Theories (TLT 2015)*, pages 61–71, Warszawa, Poland. IPIPAN.

Jan Hajič, Eva Hajičová, Jarmila Panevová, Petr Sgall, Ondřej Bojar, Silvie Cinková, Eva Fučíková, Marie Mikulová, Petr Pajas, Jan Popelka, Jiří Semecký, Jana Šindlerová, Jan Štěpánek, Josef Toman, Zdeňka Urešová, and Zdeněk Žabokrtský. 2012. Announcing Prague Czech-English Dependency Treebank 2.0. In *Proceedings of the 8th LREC 2012)*, pages 3153–3160, Istanbul, Turkey. ELRA.

Natalia Klyueva and Pavel Straňák. 2016. Improving corpus search via parsing. In Nicoletta Calzolari, Khalid Choukri, Thierry Declerck, Marko Grobelnik, Bente Maegaard, Joseph Mariani, Asunción Moreno, Jan Odijk, and Stelios Piperidis, editors, *Proceedings of 10th LREC 2016*, pages 2862–2866, Paris, France. ELRA.

Markéta Lopatková, Václava Kettnerová, Eduard Bejček, Anna Vernerová, and Zdeněk Žabokrtský. in print. *Valenční slovník českých sloves VALLEX*. Nakladatelství Karolinum, Praha.

Mitchell P. Marcus, Beatrice Santorini, and Mary Ann Marcinkiewicz. 1993. Building a Large Annotated Corpus of English: The Penn Treebank. *COMPUTATIONAL LINGUISTICS*, 19(2):313–330.

Martha Palmer, Daniel Gildea, and Paul Kingsbury. 2005. The Proposition Bank: An Annotated Corpus of Semantic Roles. *Computational Linguistics*, 31(1):71–106.

Pavel Rychlý. 2007. Manatee/bonito - a modular corpus manager. In *1st Workshop on Recent Advances in Slavonic Natural Language Processing*, pages 65–70, Brno. Masarykova univerzita.

Jan Štěpánek and Petr Pajas. 2010. Querying diverse treebanks in a uniform way. In *Proceedings of the 7th International Conference on Language Resources and Evaluation (LREC 2010)*, pages 1828–1835, Valletta, Malta. European Language Resources Association.

Zdeňka Urešová, Eva Fučíková, and Jana Šindlerová. 2016. CzEngVallex: a bilingual Czech-English valency lexicon. *The Prague Bulletin of Mathematical Linguistics*, 105:17–50.

Zdeňka Urešová. 2011a. *Valence sloves v Pražském závislostním korpusu*. Studies in Computational and Theoretical Linguistics. Ústav formální a aplikované lingvistiky, Praha, Czechia.

Zdeňka Urešová. 2011b. *Valenční slovník Pražského závislostního korpusu (PDT-Vallex)*. Studies in Computational and Theoretical Linguistics. Ústav formální a aplikované lingvistiky, Praha, Czechia.

Zdeněk Žabokrtský and Markéta Lopatková. 2007. Valency information in VALLEX 2.0: Logical structure of the lexicon. *The Prague Bulletin of Mathematical Linguistics*, (87):41–60.

Experiments in Candidate Phrase Selection for Financial Named Entity Extraction - A Demo

Hassan Alam
BCL Technologies
San Jose, CA 95128
Hassana@bcltechnologies.com

Aman Kumar
BCL Technologies
San Jose, CA 95128
amank@bcltechnologies.com

Tina Werner
BCL Technologies
San Jose, CA 95128
twerner@bcltechnologies.com

Manan Vyas
BCL Technologies
San Jose, CA 95128
mvyas@bcltechnologies.com

Abstract

In this study we develop a system that tags and extracts financial concepts called financial named entities (FNE) along with corresponding numeric values – monetary and temporal. We employ machine learning and natural language processing methods to identify financial concepts and dates, and link them to numerical entities.

1 Introduction

We developed a baseline system called Automatic Extraction of Financial Data from Text (AEFDT) that tags and extracts financial concepts based on the natural language text from a financial document such as 10Q, 10K and analyst's reports.

Such financial entities (FNEs – Financial Named Entities, numerical entities, and semantic tags) are useful to multiple audiences. On one hand these extracted financial concepts are useful to analysts and internal users who can benefit from a simplified overview of the financial health of a company and in writing financial reports and making budgetary decisions; on the other, it will help consumers who are interested in reviews about a company for a product, job-related news and other financial aspects. In addition, such a system will help public companies meet the SEC.gov filing requirements in an automated fashion that is less prone to errors.

A snap-shot of the working architecture of the AEFDT system is given Figure 1.

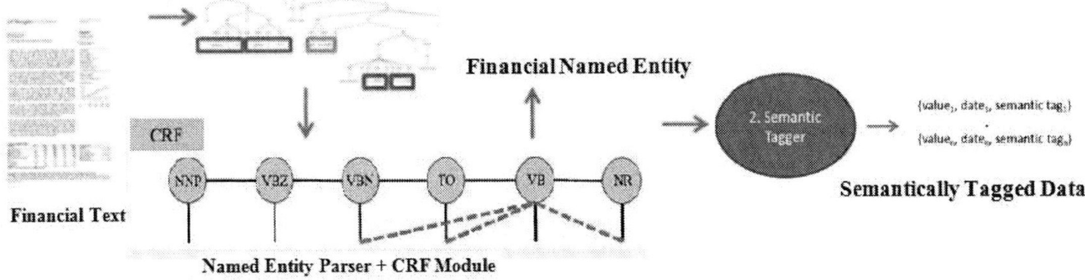

Figure 1. Flow chart of the AEFDT system

Proceedings of COLING 2016, the 26th International Conference on Computational Linguistics: System Demonstrations, pages 45–48, Osaka, Japan, December 11-17 2016.

2 Methodology

We have modelled our system as a Named Entity Recognition (NER) [Nadeau et al., 2007] problem. NER is an important subtask within information retrieval that locates and tags entities in text into categories such as the name, organization, location, time, quantities, etc.

Our current FNE identification system is a customized version of Stanford NER [Finkel, 2005]. Stanford NER is a Java implementation of a Named Entity Recognizer that provides a framework for training and inference of *Conditional Random Field* (CRF) model. In addition, it has the capability to incorporate other existing NLP tools like syntactic parser, Semantic Role Labelling (SRL), part-of-speech tagger, etc. We utilized our domain knowledge based on financial reports (10-Q, 10-K, etc.) to extend Stanford NER for a high precision system.

2.1 Data Collection and Annotation

We have collected around 6 MB of data in the form of 10Q/10K and non-SEC documents. We wrote programs in C++ and Python to crawl the sec.gov page. Once the sentences (from the Notes section of a 10Q document), labels, semantic tags, and numeric values are mined the training corpus is created by annotating the corpus with *labels* for training toward FNEs and creating attributes for semantic tags and numbers. Here's a snapshot of the label annotations of a part of a 10Q document (Notes section).

> **<FNE>** *Amortization expense* **</FNE>** *for the three* months ended **<Date1>** *January 31, 2013* **</Date1>** *and***<Date2>** *2012* **</Date2>** *was* **<NV1>** *$5.0 million* **<NV1>** *and* *<NV2>* *$5.2 million***</NV2>**, *respectively.*

Our training dataset has 8000 and 2000 annotated sentences for training and testing, respectively. These datasets were obtained by randomly shuffling entire corpus and partitioning them in 80:20 ratios.

The three methods that we implemented are: (1) *CRF+No Dictionary*; (2) *CRF+Dictionary*; (3) *CRF+Dictionary+Features*. *CRF+No Dictionary* refers to the method where we just have the conditional random field model that tags the tokens (words) in a sentence with FNE or not (o). *CRF+Dictionary* is applied when we have dictionary built and we do basic statistical analysis of the dictionary items, and *CRF+Dictionary+Features* method uses post-processing linguistic rules for tagging.

3 Evaluation and Results

Three trained subject matter experts manually evaluated the results for accuracy. We tested the models on unseen 2000 sentences from a 10Q file crawled from the sec.gov webpage. The results of the preliminary system are given in Table 1.

	CRF+No Dictionary	**CRF+Dictionary**	**CRF+Dictionary+Features**
FNE % accuracy	61.33	77.82	88

Table 1. Preliminary results of the FNE identification system with three models using CRF parser

3.1 Discussion

The CRF+Dictionary+Features model gives the best results. That tells is that if we refine our heuristics and feature selection, we are likely to getter better results in future revisions. For the current set of heuristics, we have used the following feature rules for clustering and classification.

Surface Feature Selection for FNE identification system:

- Current word
- Next word
- Previous word
- Current POS (part-of-speech) Tag
- Previous POS Tag
- Next POS Tag
- Base POS tags
- Custer of "related" words
- Relative positions with numerical entity etc.
- Trigger word

In addition, we extracted features from parse tree like extracted NP sub-tree etc. As semantic features, we used semantic tree annotations extracted from Stanford parsed tree (De Marneffe et al. (2006)). We extracted a dictionary of FNEs from filed 10Qs at sec.gov and employed that as trigger words.

4 Conclusions

In this study we performed a feasibility study to tag and extract financial concepts called *financial named entities* (FNE). We employed machine learning and natural language processing methods to identify financial concepts and link them to numerical entities. The best model records an accuracy of 88% in 10Q/K files from the sec.gov webpages.

References

1. Ananiadou, S. and McNaught, J.(eds) Text Mining for Biology and Biomedicine, 2006, Artech House.
2. Bishop, Christopher M. Pattern recognition and machine learning. springer New York, 2006.

3. Cohn, Trevor. "Efficient inference in large conditional random fields." Springer, 2006.

4. De Marneffe, Marie-Catherine, MacCartney, Bill, Manning, Christopher D and others. "Generating typed dependency parses from phrase structure parses." Proceedings of LREC. 2006. 449-454.

5. Finkel, Jenny, Dingare, Shipra, Nguyen, Huy, Nissim, Malvina, Manning, Christopher and Sinclair, Gail. "Exploiting context for biomedical entity recognition: From syntax to the web." Proceedings of the International Joint Workshop on Natural Language Processing in Biomedicine and its Applications. Association for Computational Linguistics, 2004. 88-91.

6. Finkel, Jenny Rose, Grenager, Trond and Manning, Christopher. "Incorporating non-local information into information extraction systems by gibbs sampling." Proceedings of the 43rd Annual Meeting on Association for Computational Linguistics. Association for Computational Linguistics, 2005. 363-370.

7. Lafferty, John, McCallum, Andrew and Pereira and Fernando CN. "Conditional random fields: Probabilistic models for segmenting and labeling sequence data." International Conference of Machine Learning. 2001.

8. McCallum, Andrew and Li, Wei. "Early results for named entity recognition with conditional random fields, feature induction and web-enhanced lexicons." Proceedings of the seventh conference on Natural language learning at HLT-NAACL 2003-Volume 4. 2003.

9. Minkov, Einat, Wang, Richard C, Tomasic, Anthony and Cohen, William W. "NER systems that suit user's preferences: adjusting the recall-precision trade-off for entity Extraction." Proceedings of the Human Language Technology Conference of the NAACL, Companion Volume: Short Papers. Association for Computational Linguistics, 2006. 93-96.

10. Nadeau, David and Sekine, Satoshi. "A survey of named entity recognition and classification." Lingvisticae Investigationes, 2007: 3-26.

11. Ratinov, Lev and Roth, Dan. "Design challenges and misconceptions in named entity recognition." Proceedings of the Thirteenth Conference on Computational Natural Language Learning. Association for Computational Linguistics, 2009. 147-155.

12. Silla Jr, Carlos N and Freitas, Alex A. "A survey of hierarchical classification across different application domains." Data Mining and Knowledge Discovery, 2011: 31-72.

13. Vapnik, Vladimir and Cortes, Corinna. "Support vector machine." Machine learning, 1995: 273-297.

Demonstration of ChaKi.NET – beyond the corpus search system

Masayuki ASAHARA◇ Yuji MATSUMOTO♣ Toshio MORITA ♠
◇ National Institute for Japanese Language and Linguistics,
National Institutes for the Humanities, Japan
♣ Nara Institute of Science and Technology, Japan.
♠ Sowa Research Co., Ltd.

Abstract

ChaKi.NET is a corpus management system for dependency structure annotated corpora. After more than 10 years of continuous development, the system is now usable not only for corpus search, but also for visualization, annotation, labelling, and formatting for statistical analysis. This paper describes the various functions included in the current ChaKi.NET system.

1 Introduction

The corpus management tool ChaKi[1] (Matsumoto et al., 2005) was originally released in 2004. In version 3.0, the user interface was rewritten using the .NET framework, and was renamed ChaKi.NET.

The system was originally created as a corpus search system for dependency-analysed Japanese corpora. The String Search, Tag Search, and Dependency Search functions can be used to search dependency-parsed corpora at the string, POS-tag and dependency structure levels. A dependency-parsed corpus is converted into an SQLite DB file or stored on a MySQL server. In the case of SQLite DB files, corpus database files are shared by simply copying them to a new system. The system has been enhanced continuously and used for other purposes such as corpus visualization, annotation, labelling, and formatting for statistical analysis. In this paper, we present these functions of ChaKi.NET.

2 Visualization

2.1 Visualization of Dependency Tree

ChaKi.NET was originally developed as the viewer for the output of a dependency analyser named CaboCha [2]. Figures 1 and 2 show the diagonal and horizontal visualization modes, respectively. The extended CaboCha format and CoNLL-X format[3] can be imported into ChaKi.NET. The Japanese examples are from the BCCWJ-DepPara syntactic dependency and coordinate structure annotation of the Balanced Corpus of Contemporary Written Japanese (BCCWJ) (Maekawa et al., 2014). Because Japanese is a strictly head final language, the diagonal mode is often used for annotation. The lower panel of Figure 2 shows a Universal Dependency tree (German). In the ACL community, the direction of dependency relation arrows is from head to dependent. However, in the Japanese NLP community, we prefer the one from dependent to head, regarding the dependency relation as the modification relation. In ChaKi.NET, the direction of arrows can be specified by the user.

2.2 Visualization of SEGMENT, LINK, and GROUP

We believe that most annotations on text corpora can be abstracted into the following three types: SEGMENT, LINK, and GROUP. SEGMENTs are regions in a sentence such as phrases and named entities. LINKs are directed relations between two SEGMENTs; these can indicate syntactic dependency, semantic dependency (predicate argument relation), and temporal relationships between two events. GROUPs are equivalence classes determined by an equivalent relation between SEGMENTs; these include coordinate structures and coreferences.

[1] https://en.osdn.jp/projects/chaki/releases/
[2] https://taku910.github.io/cabocha/
[3] http://ilk.uvt.nl/conll/#dataformat

Proceedings of COLING 2016, the 26th International Conference on Computational Linguistics: System Demonstrations, pages 49–53, Osaka, Japan, December 11-17 2016.

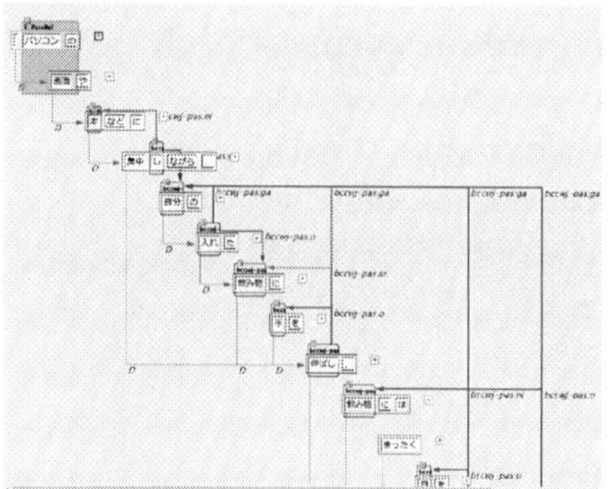

Figure 1: Diagonal mode for dependency tree visualization

Japanese Example: arrow direction is from dependent to head

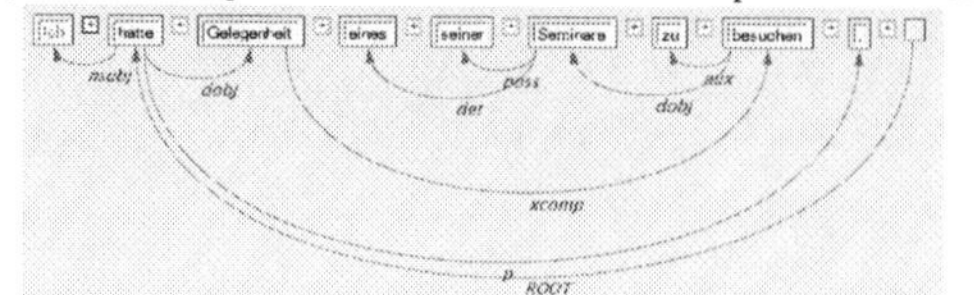

German Example: arrow direction is from head to dependent

Figure 2: Horizontal mode for dependency tree visualization

Figure 3 shows a visualization example from BCCWJ-DepParaPAS, i.e., the dependency structure with predicate-argument relations and coreference relations for BCCWJ. A thick blue arrow denotes a 'ga' relation, which is a subject-predicate relation. A thick purple arrow denotes an 'o' relation, which is an object-predicate relation.

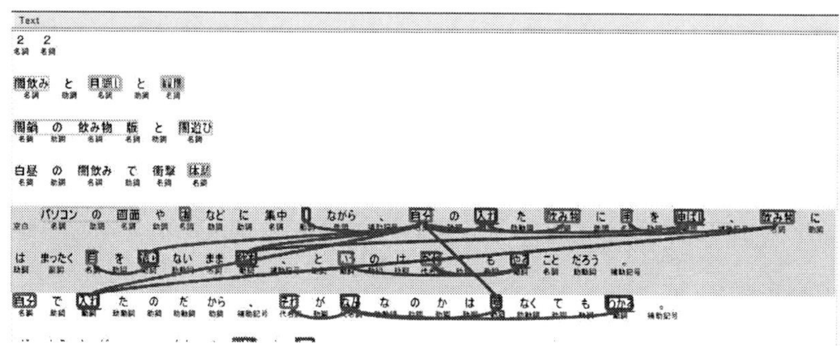

Figure 3: Text mode for visualization of predicate argument structure

2.3 Visualization of Projection

ChaKi.NET can import more than one corpus with alignment information into one database. We refer to this as 'projection' from one image to another in relational algebra. Parallel corpora can be visualized using the projection function. The aligned words are highlighted by colours.

The projection functions can be used for various types of parallel analysis:

- Word segmentation variation (BCCWJ): `https://youtu.be/L-Arl9oDUm8`
  BCCWJ includes two units – 'Short Unit Word' and 'Long Unit Word' (Figure 4).
- The Japanese-English parallel corpus (BCCWJ-Trans): `https://youtu.be/SZL8P5_Z-Xg`
  The corpus is word aligned (Figure 5).
- Dialect (Kitakyushu, Fukuoka, Japan) and standard Japanese: `https://youtu.be/_b1zLHMK_i8`
  The dialect corpus is Bunsetsu-segmented with Katanaka transcription. The dialect is translated into standard Japanese, which is POS tagged and dependency parsed (Figure 6).

We also plan to use this function with a historical Japanese corpus containing translations into contemporary Japanese.

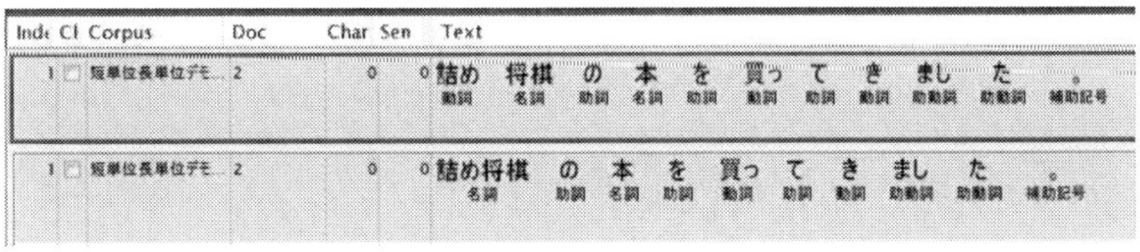

Figure 4: Visualization of two word segmentation standards

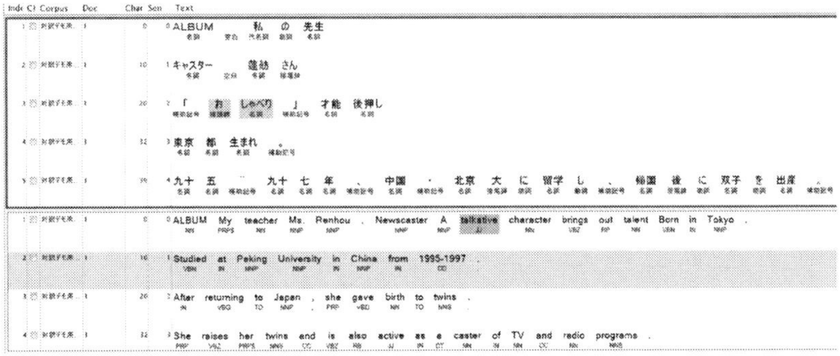

Figure 5: Visualization of Japanese-English parallel corpus

2.4 Visualization of Time

ChaKi.NET can store the start time, end time, and duration of words or morphemes for speech transcription corpora. The demo for 'Corpus of Spontaneous Japanese' (CSJ) (Maekawa et al., 2000) can be accessed at `https://youtu.be/Qod6J14X9mU`.

2.5 Combination of Projection and Time

The BCCWJ EyeTracking Corpus (Asahara et al., 2016) contains the reading time data of 24 experiment subjects, obtained from BCCWJ samples. We can define two word orders – the reading order of the subject and the word order in the original text. For the former order, we can define the start time, end time, and duration. For the latter order, reading time is aggregated into the following three duration types: first pass duration, regression path duration, and total duration. First pass duration is the time spent in a word region before moving on or looking back. Regression path duration is the time from

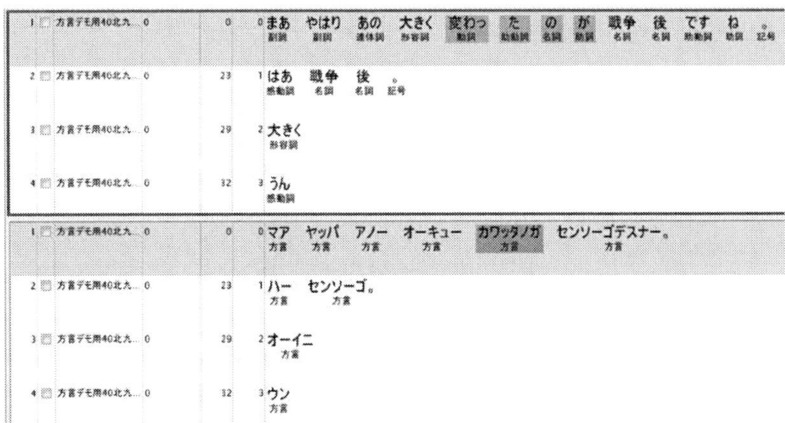

Figure 6: Visualization of dialect and standard Japanese parallel corpus

the time that the eye first enters a word region until the time it moves beyond that region, and includes regression time. Total duration is the sum of all fixations in a word region. Figure 7 shows a visualization of the BCCWJ EyeTracking Corpus. The demo for the BCCWJ EyeTracking Corpus can be viewed at `https://youtu.be/H2ySz09n_sA`.

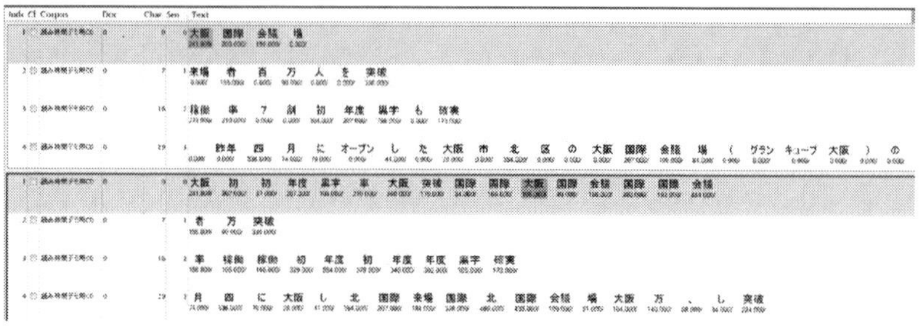

Figure 7: Visualization of BCCWJ EyeTracking Corpus

3 Annotation and Labelling

3.1 Annotation

ChaKi.NET can call a morphological analyser (MeCab) [4] and a Japanese dependency analyser (CaboCha); this functionality is invoked when a user drags and drops a text file onto ChaKi.NET's menu bar. The word segmentation and POS tags of the analyser output can be corrected by a morpheme panel.

Using a mouse operation, the dependency structure can be modified via the dependency tree panels shown in Figures 1 and 2. SEGMENT, LINK, and GROUP are also modified using the panels.

3.2 Labelling

The corpus search functions (query) can define the patterns of strings, sequences of morphological information, and subtrees of dependencies. The search results can be exported into a Microsoft Excel spreadsheet or CSV file. However, we occasionally need to annotate a label to the searched results.

On the Scripting Panel, we can use Ruby or Python code to execute a labelling action based on the pattern of the query. We can use set of predefined scripts, or write any specific purpose code. The following sample Ruby code assigns the label 'NE' to a region:

Ruby code to assign label 'NE' `CreateSegmentAll.rb`

```
...
records.each do |r|
   svc.Open(corpus, s, nil)
   ...
   c = r.GetCenterCharOffset()
   w = r.GetCenterCharLength()
   svc.SetupProject(0)
   svc.CreateSegment(c, c+w, "NE")
   svc.Commit()
   ...
end
```

The `CreateSegment(startPos, endPos, tagName)` method assigns the label `tagName` to the region between the `startPos` and `endPos-1`. The leftmost offset of the matched pattern can be obtained by the `GetCenterCharOffset` method. The rightmost offset is calculated from the length of the matched pattern given by the `GetCenterCharLength` method.

We perform the following cycle (Figure 8) to assign labels to the corpus. ChaKi.NET enables us to perform this cycle via mouse clicks on the user interface.

[4] `http://taku910.github.io/mecab/`

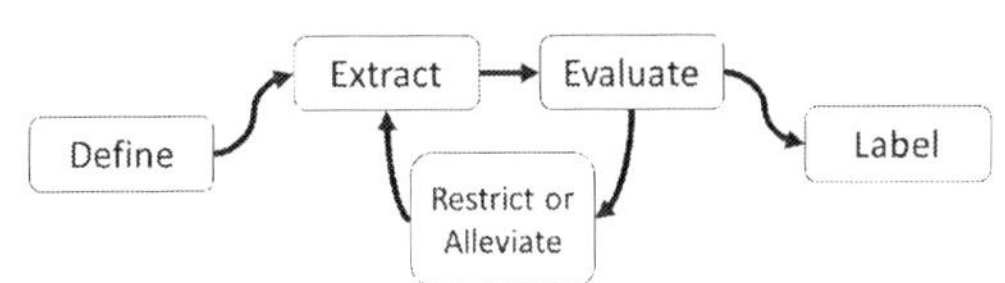

Figure 8: Labeling cycle

1. Define: define the query pattern

2-a. Extract: extract the matched examples

2-b. Evaluate: evaluate the matched examples

2-c. Restrict or Relax: restrict or relax the pattern

3. Label: assign labels to the matched examples

4 Statistical Analysis Aids

The original Collocation functions of ChaKi.NET can extract collocations using various frequencies or statistics, including co-occurrence frequency, MI score, various cooccurrence measures, [5] and N-gram frequency[6].

We can compose a term document matrix without writing a program code by using Word List functions. The demo `https://youtu.be/yWE0z-bd5ME` shows the output of the term document matrix. The original data is from BCCWJ-SUMM, which is a BCCWJ-based summarization corpus containing data from more than one hundred experimental participants.

The matrix can be exported as a Microsoft Excel spreadsheet or R data frame file.

When we define a query of word sequences using a tag search, we can also extract an n-gram/p-mer document matrix (Demo: `https://youtu.be/Ossr5if8cKI`). When we define a subtree query using a dependency search, we can also extract a dependency subtree document matrix (Demo: `https://youtu.be/XwJNEBEzcBw`).

5 Summary and Future Directions

We presented newly installed ChaKi.NET functions. The software is free for any purpose, including commercial use. We hold tutorials of the system periodically in Japan. The copyright-free data for ChaKi.NET can be downloaded from `http://chaki-data.ninjal.ac.jp/`. The BCCWJ-related data can be downloaded from `https://bccwj-data.ninjal.ac.jp/mdl/`. In our future work, we plan to develop new corpus query functions for any annotation, including SEGMENT, LINK, and GROUP.

Acknowledgments

The work reported in this article was supported by the NINJAL research project of the Center for Corpus Development.

References

Masayuki Asahara, Hajime Ono, and Edson T. Miyamoto. 2016. Reading-time annotations for the "Balanced Corpus of Contemporary Written Japanese". In *Proc. of COLING-2016*.

Kikuo Maekawa, Hanae Koiso, Sadaoki Furui, and Hitoshi Isahara. 2000. Spontaneous speech corpus of Japanese. *Proc. LREC2000 (Second International Conference on Language Resources and Evaluation)*, 2:947–952.

Kikuo Maekawa, Makoto Yamazaki, Toshinobu Ogiso, Takehiko Maruyama, Hideki Ogura, Wakako Kashino, Hanae Koiso, Masaya Yamaguchi, Makiro Tanaka, and Yasuharu Den. 2014. Balanced Corpus of Contemporary Written Japanese. *Language Resources and Evaluation*, 48:345–371.

Yuji Matsumoto, Masayuki Asahara, Kou Kawabe, Yurika Takahashi, Yukio Tono, Akira Otani, and Toshio Morita. 2005. ChaKi: An Annotated Corpora Management and Search System. In *Proceedings from the Corpus Linguistics Conference Series*.

[5] MI score, MI3 score, Dice score, log-log score, and Z score.

[6] Also requires a sequence pattern mining algorithm.

VoxSim: A Visual Platform for Modeling Motion Language

Nikhil Krishnaswamy
Brandeis University
415 South Street
Waltham, MA 02453 USA
nkrishna@brandeis.edu

James Pustejovsky
Brandeis University
415 South Street
Waltham, MA 02453 USA
jamesp@brandeis.edu

Abstract

Much existing work in text-to-scene generation focuses on generating static scenes. By introducing a focus on motion verbs, we integrate dynamic semantics into a rich formal model of events to generate animations in real time that correlate with human conceptions of the event described. This paper presents a working system that generates these animated scenes over a test set, discussing challenges encountered and describing the solutions implemented.

1 Introduction

The expressiveness of natural language is difficult to translate into visuals, and much work in text-to-scene generation has focused on creating static images, e.g., Coyne and Sproat (2001) and Chang et. al (2015). Our approach centers on motion verbs, using a rich formal model of events and mapping from an NL expression, through Dynamic Interval Temporal Logic (Pustejovsky and Moszkowicz, 2011), into a 3D animated simulation. Previously, we introduced a method for modeling motion language predicates in three dimensions (Pustejovsky and Krishnaswamy, 2014). This led to VoxML, a modeling language to encode composable semantic knowledge about NL entities (Pustejovsky and Krishnaswamy, 2016), and a reasoner to generate simulations involving novel objects and events (Krishnaswamy and Pustejovsky, 2016). Our system, **VoxSim**, uses object and event semantic knowledge to generate animated scenes in real time without a complex animation interface. The latest stable build of VoxSim is available at `http://www.voxicon.net`. The Unity project and source is at `https://github.com/nkrishnaswamy/voxicon`.

2 Theoretical Motivations

Dynamic interpretations of event structures divide motion verbs into "path" and "manner of motion" verbs. Path verbs reassign the moving argument's position relative to a specified location; for manner verbs, position is specified through prepositional adjunct. Thus, *The spoon falls* and *The spoon falls into the cup* result in different "mental instantiations," or "simulations" (Bergen, 2012). In order to visualize events, a computational system must infer path or manner information from the objects involved or from their composition with the predicate.

Visual instantiations of lexemes, or "voxemes" (Pustejovsky and Krishnaswamy, 2016), require an encoding of their situational context, or a *habitat* (Pustejovsky, 2013; McDonald and Pustejovsky, 2014), as well as afforded behaviors that the object can participate in, that are either *Gibsonian* or *telic* in nature (Gibson, 1977; Gibson, 1979; Pustejovsky, 1995). For instance, a cup may afford containing another object, or being drunk from. Many event descriptions presuppose such conditions that rarely appear in linguistic data, but a visualization lacking them will make little sense to the observer. This linguistic "dark matter," conspicuous by its absence, is thus easily exposable through simulation.

Proceedings of COLING 2016, the 26th International Conference on Computational Linguistics: System Demonstrations, pages 54–58, Osaka, Japan, December 11-17 2016.

3 Architecture

VoxSim uses the Unity game engine (Goldstone, 2009) for graphics and I/O processing. Input is a simple natural language sentence, which is part-of-speech tagged, dependency-parsed, and transformed into a simple predicate-logic format. These NLP tasks may be handled with a variety of third-party tools, such as the ClearNLP parser (Choi and McCallum, 2013), SyntaxNet (Andor et al., 2016), or TRIPS (Ferguson et al., 1998), which interface with the simulation software using a C++ communications bridge and wrapper. 3D assets and VoxML-modeled entities are loaded externally, either locally or from a web server. Commands to the simulator may be input directly to the software UI, or may be sent over a generic network connection or using **VoxSim Commander**, a companion iOS app.

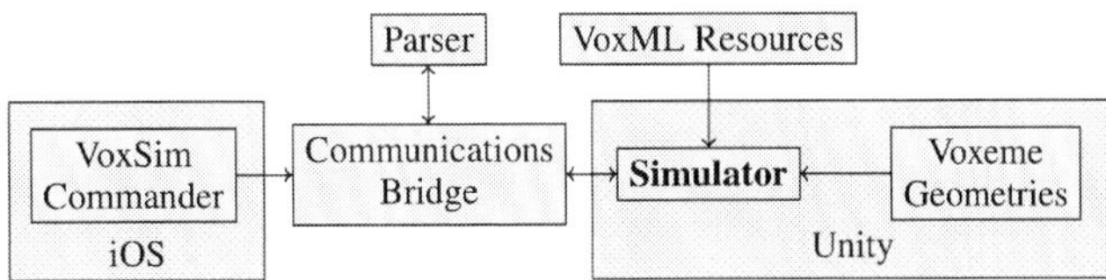

Figure 1: VoxSim architecture schematic

3.1 Processing Pipeline

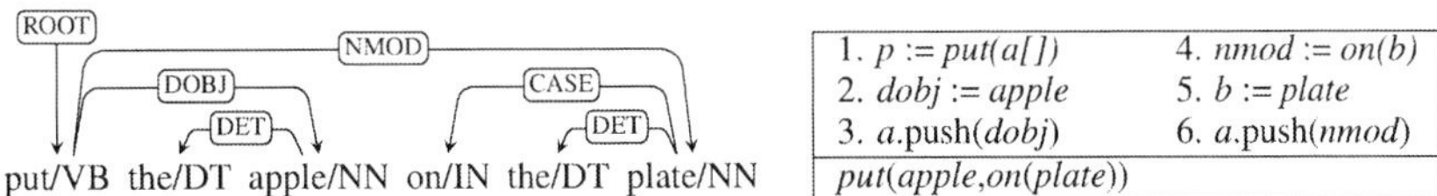

Figure 2: Dependency parse for *Put the apple on the plate* and transformation to predicate-logic form.

Given a tagged and dependency parsed sentence, we can transform it into predicate-logic format using the root of the parse as the VoxML PROGRAM, which accepts as many arguments as are specified in its type structure, and subsequently enqueuing arguments that are either constants (i.e. VoxML OBJECTs) or evaluate to constants at runtime (all other VoxML entity types). Other non-constant VoxML entity types are treated similarly, though usually accept only one argument.

4 Semantic Processing and Compositionality

Rather than relying on manually-specified objects with identifying language, we instead procedurally compose voxemes' VoxML properties in parallel with their linked lexemes.

A VoxML entity's interpretation at runtime depends on the other entities it is composed with. A cup on a surface, with its opening upward, may afford containing another object, so to place an object $in(cup)$, the system must first determine if the intended containing object (i.e., the cup) affords containment by default by examining its affordance structure (figure 3).

If so, the object must be currently situated in a habitat which allows objects to be placed partially or completely inside it (represented by RCC relations PO, TPP, or NTPP, as shown in the VoxML for in). cup's VoxML TYPE shows a concave object with rotational symmetry around the Y-axis and reflectional symmetry across the XY and YZ planes, meaning that it opens along the Y-axis. Its HABITAT further situates the opening along its positive Y-axis, meaning that if the cup's opening along its +Y is currently unobstructed, it affords containment. Previously established habitats, i.e., "The cup is flipped over," may activate or deactivate these and other affordances.

Finally, the system must check to see if the object to be contained can fit in the containing object in its current configuration. If so, it is moved into position. If not, the system attempts to rotate the contained object into an orientation where it will fit inside the container. If it can, the object is rotated into that orientation and then moved. If no such orientation exists, the system returns a message stating that the requested action is impossible to perform.

$$
\left[\begin{array}{l}
\textbf{put} \\
\text{TYPE} = \left[\begin{array}{ll}
\text{HEAD} = \textbf{process} & \\
\text{ARGS} = & \left[\begin{array}{l} \text{A}_1 = \textbf{agent} \\ \text{A}_2 = \textbf{physobj} \\ \text{A}_3 = \textbf{location} \end{array}\right] \\
\text{BODY} = & \left[\begin{array}{l} \text{E}_1 = grasp(A_1, A_2) \\ \text{E}_2 = [while(hold(A_1, A_2), \\ \quad move(A_2))] \\ \text{E}_3 = [at(A_1, A_3) \rightarrow \\ \quad ungrasp(A_1, A_2) \end{array}\right]
\end{array}\right]
\end{array}\right]
$$

$$
\left[\begin{array}{l}
\textbf{in} \\
\text{TYPE} = \left[\begin{array}{ll}
\text{CLASS} = \textbf{config} & \\
\text{VALUE} = \textbf{ProperPart} \parallel \textbf{PO} & \\
\text{ARGS} = & \left[\begin{array}{l} \text{A}_1 = \textbf{x:3D} \\ \text{A}_2 = \textbf{y:3D} \end{array}\right]
\end{array}\right]
\end{array}\right]
$$

$$
\left[\begin{array}{l}
\textbf{cup} \\
\text{TYPE} = \left[\begin{array}{l}
\text{HEAD} = \textbf{cylindroid[1]} \\
\text{COMPONENTS} = \textbf{surface,interior} \\
\text{CONCAVITY} = \textbf{concave} \\
\text{ROTATSYM} = \{Y\} \\
\text{REFLECTSYM} = \{XY, YZ\}
\end{array}\right] \\
\text{HABITAT} = \left[\begin{array}{l} \text{INTR} = [2]\left[\begin{array}{l} \text{UP} = align(Y, \mathcal{E}_Y) \\ \text{TOP} = top(+Y) \end{array}\right] \end{array}\right] \\
\text{AFFORD\_STR} = \left[\begin{array}{l}
\text{A}_1 = H[2] \rightarrow \\ \quad [put(x, on([1]))] \\ \quad support([1], x) \\
\text{A}_2 = H[2] \rightarrow \\ \quad [put(x, in([1]))] \\ \quad contain([1], x) \\
\text{A}_3 = H[2] \rightarrow \\ \quad [grasp(x, [1])]
\end{array}\right]
\end{array}\right]
$$

Figure 3: VoxML typing, habitats, and affordances for "put", "in", and "cup"

Figure 4: Execution of "put the spoon in the mug"

Currently VoxSim implements RCC relations (Randell et al., 1992; Galton, 2000; Albath et al., 2010), but can be extended to other QSR approaches, including the situation calculus (Bhatt and Loke, 2008), and Intersection Calculus (Kurata and Egenhofer, 2007).

We augment this approach with an embodied agent that simultaneously enacts the same program as the manipulated object, composing the object motion ("object model") and the agent motion ("action model") into a single "event model," allowing for both agent-free and agent-driven actions.

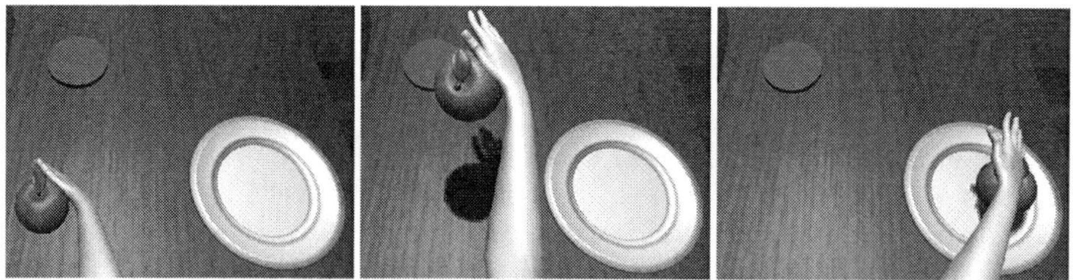

Figure 5: Execution of "put the apple on the plate" using embodied agent

Once all parameters requiring specification have values assigned to them, VoxSim executes the program over its arguments, rendering the visual result each frame, which provides a trace of the event from beginning to end. Note that the precise running time of the generated animation is variable and dependent on the values calculated for the aforementioned parameters, including the total distance an object must move from its starting position to its target, any preconditions that must be fulfilled before the commanded event can be executed, and others.

5 Conclusions

VoxSim provides a method not only for generating 3D visualizations using an intuitive natural language interface instead of specialized skillsets (a primary goal of programs such as WordsEye), but also a platform on which researchers may conduct experiments on the discrete observables of motion events while evaluating semantic theories, thus providing data to back up theoretical intuitions. Visual simulation provides an intuitive way to trace spatial cues' entailments through a narrative, enabling broader study of event and motion semantics.

VoxSim currently handles an expanding lexicon of voxemes (a "voxicon"), with many primitive objects and behaviors encoded in VoxML and available for composition into macro-entities. The current voxicon status is given in table 1. No distinction is made here between primitive and macro-entities.

Objects (18)	**Programs** (17)	**Relations** (6)	**Functions** (12)
block	grasp	on	edge
ball	hold	in	center
plate	touch	against	top
cup	move	at	bottom
disc	turn	support	back
spoon	roll	containment	front
book	slide		left
blackboard	spin		right
bottle	lift		corner
grape	stack		diagonal
apple	put		above
banana	lean		below
table	flip		
bowl	close		
knife	open		
pencil	reach		
paper sheet	push		
box			

Table 1: Current voxicon contents

Scene visualization work is not well-reflected in current evaluation, due to sparsity of datasets and lack of a general-domain gold standard(Johansson et al., 2005), so we are developing two human-driven evaluation methods, augmented by an automatic method. Human evaluation asks subjects to make a pairwise similarity judgement over a generated simulation and a set of possible labels, going both ways (i.e. a judgement on one simulation to many labels and on one label to many simulations). Automatic evaluation measures the vector distance from a generated simulation to a preconceived "prototype" of the input event descriptor. The results of these experiments are currently being evaluated.

We are also planning on building links to lexical semantic resources such as VerbNet (Kipper et al., 2006) to allow us to leverage existing datasets for macro-program composition, and to expand the semantic processing to event sequences, to simulate narratives beyond the sentence level.

Acknowledgements

We would like to thank the reviewers for their insightful comments. This work was supported by Contract W911NF-15-C-0238 with the US Defense Advanced Research Projects Agency (DARPA) and the Army Research Office (ARO). Approved for Public Release, Distribution Unlimited. The views expressed herein are ours and do not reflect the official policy or position of the Department of Defense or the U.S. Government. All errors and mistakes are, of course, the responsibilities of the authors.

References

Julia Albath, Jennifer L. Leopold, Chaman L. Sabharwal, and Anne M. Maglia. 2010. RCC-3D: Qualitative spatial reasoning in 3D. In *CAINE*, pages 74–79.

Daniel Andor, Chris Alberti, David Weiss, Aliaksei Severyn, Alessandro Presta, Kuzman Ganchev, Slav Petrov, and Michael Collins. 2016. Globally normalized transition-based neural networks. *arXiv preprint arXiv:1603.06042*.

Benjamin K. Bergen. 2012. *Louder than words: The new science of how the mind makes meaning*. Basic Books.

Mehul Bhatt and Seng Loke. 2008. Modelling dynamic spatial systems in the situation calculus. *Spatial Cognition and Computation*.

Angel Chang, Will Monroe, Manolis Savva, Christopher Potts, and Christopher D. Manning. 2015. Text to 3d scene generation with rich lexical grounding. *arXiv preprint arXiv:1505.06289*.

Jinho D. Choi and Andrew McCallum. 2013. Transition-based dependency parsing with selectional branching. In *ACL (1)*, pages 1052–1062.

Bob Coyne and Richard Sproat. 2001. Wordseye: an automatic text-to-scene conversion system. In *Proceedings of the 28th annual conference on Computer graphics and interactive techniques*, pages 487–496. ACM.

George Ferguson, James F Allen, et al. 1998. Trips: An integrated intelligent problem-solving assistant. In *AAAI/IAAI*, pages 567–572.

Antony Galton. 2000. *Qualitative Spatial Change*. Oxford University Press, Oxford.

J. J. Gibson. 1977. The theory of affordances. *Perceiving, Acting, and Knowing: Toward an ecological psychology*, pages 67–82.

J. J. Gibson. 1979. *The Ecology Approach to Visual Perception: Classic Edition*. Psychology Press.

Will Goldstone. 2009. *Unity Game Development Essentials*. Packt Publishing Ltd.

Richard Johansson, Anders Berglund, Magnus Danielsson, and Pierre Nugues. 2005. Automatic text-to-scene conversion in the traffic accident domain. In *IJCAI*, volume 5, pages 1073–1078.

Kara Kipper, Anna Korhonen, Neville Ryant, and Martha Palmer. 2006. Extensive classifications of english verbs. In *Proceedings of the 12th EURALEX International Congress*, Turin, Italy.

Nikhil Krishnaswamy and James Pustejovsky. 2016. Multimodal semantic simulations of linguistically underspecified motion events. *Proceedings of Spatial Cognition*.

Yohei Kurata and Max Egenhofer. 2007. The 9+ intersection for topological relations between a directed line segment and a region. In B. Gottfried, editor, *Workshop on Behaviour and Monitoring Interpretation*, pages 62–76, Germany, September.

David McDonald and James Pustejovsky. 2014. On the representation of inferences and their lexicalization. In *Advances in Cognitive Systems*, volume 3.

James Pustejovsky and Nikhil Krishnaswamy. 2014. Generating simulations of motion events from verbal descriptions. *Lexical and Computational Semantics (* SEM 2014)*, page 99.

James Pustejovsky and Nikhil Krishnaswamy. 2016. VoxML: A visualization modeling language. In Nicoletta Calzolari (Conference Chair), Khalid Choukri, Thierry Declerck, Sara Goggi, Marko Grobelnik, Bente Maegaard, Joseph Mariani, Helene Mazo, Asuncion Moreno, Jan Odijk, and Stelios Piperidis, editors, *Proceedings of the Tenth International Conference on Language Resources and Evaluation (LREC 2016)*, Paris, France, May. European Language Resources Association (ELRA).

James Pustejovsky and Jessica Moszkowicz. 2011. The qualitative spatial dynamics of motion. *The Journal of Spatial Cognition and Computation*.

James Pustejovsky. 1995. *The Generative Lexicon*. MIT Press, Cambridge, MA.

James Pustejovsky. 2013. Dynamic event structure and habitat theory. In *Proceedings of the 6th International Conference on Generative Approaches to the Lexicon (GL2013)*, pages 1–10. ACL.

David Randell, Zhan Cui, and Anthony Cohn. 1992. A spatial logic based on regions and connections. In Morgan Kaufmann, editor, *Proceedings of the 3rd Internation Conference on Knowledge Representation and Reasoning*, pages 165–176, San Mateo.

TextImager: a Distributed UIMA-based System for NLP

Wahed Hemati
Text Technology Lab
Goehte-Universität Frankfurt

Tolga Uslu
Text Technology Lab
Goehte-Universität Frankfurt

Alexander Mehler
Text Technology Lab
Goehte-Universität Frankfurt

{hemati,uslu,mehler}@em.uni-frankfurt.de
http://www.hucompute.org

Abstract

More and more disciplines require NLP tools for performing automatic text analyses on various levels of linguistic resolution. However, the usage of established NLP frameworks is often hampered for several reasons: in most cases, they require basic to sophisticated programming skills, interfere with interoperability due to using non-standard I/O-formats and often lack tools for visualizing computational results. This makes it difficult especially for humanities scholars to use such frameworks. In order to cope with these challenges, we present TextImager, a UIMA-based framework that offers a range of NLP and visualization tools by means of a user-friendly GUI. Using TextImager requires no programming skills.

1 Introduction

Computational humanities and related disciplines require a wide range of NLP tools to perform automatic text analyses on various levels of textual resolution. This includes, for example, humanities scholars dealing with repositories of historical documents, forensic linguists analyzing unstructured texts of online social media to create digital fingerprints of suspects or even doctors using clinical NLP to support differential diagnosis based on physician-patient talks. However, established NLP frameworks still require basic to sophisticated programming skills for performing such analyses. This hampers their usage for users who are not sufficiently trained neither in computational linguistics nor in computer science. Further, these frameworks often lack interoperability due to using non-standard I/O-formats. We present TextImager to cope with these challenges. The longer-term goal of TextImager is to provide a platform into which any open source/access NLP tool can be integrated. To this end, TextImager provides a web-based GUI whose usage does not require any programming skills while making accessible a range of tools for visualizing results of text analyses. In order to ensure standardization and interoperability, TextImager is based on the *Unstructured Information Management Applications* (UIMA) framework. Currently, the scope of TextImager ranges from tokenizing, lemmatizing, POS-tagging, text similarity measurements to sentiment analysis, text classification, topic modeling and many more.

2 Related Work

Frameworks of computational texts analysis have already been introduced and are now common in industrial use. This includes, for example, UIMA (Ferrucci and Lally, 2004), DKPro (Eckart de Castilho and Gurevych, 2014), OpenNLP (OpenNLP, 2010) and Gate (Cunningham et al., 2011). Note that these frameworks do not provide visualization interfaces and require versatile programming skills for set up. Thus, they cannot be recommended for being used by computationally less trained users. We provide the TextImager to cope with this problem while integrating most of the components of these frameworks. On the other hand, Voyant Tools (Bird et al., 2009; Ruecker et al., 2011), WebNLP (Burghardt et al., 2014) and conTEXT (Burghardt et al., 2014) are web-based NLP tools including visualization components. In order to combine the best of both worlds, TextImager additionally subsumes the functionalities

Proceedings of COLING 2016, the 26th International Conference on Computational Linguistics: System Demonstrations, pages 59–63, Osaka, Japan, December 11-17 2016.

of these tools. It also shares functionalities with WebLicht (Hinrichs et al., 2010). However, unlike WebLicht, TextImager is based on open UIMA and, thus, complies to an industrial standard of modeling text processing chains.

3 System Architecture of TextImager

TextImager consists of two parts, front-end and back-end. The front-end is a web application that makes all functionalities and NLP processes available in a user-friendly way. It allows users for analyzing and visualizing unstructured texts and text corpora. The back-end is a highly modular, expandable, scalable and flexible architecture with parallel processing capabilities.

3.1 Back-end

Figure 1 shows the architecture of TextImager. Every NLP component of TextImager implements a UIMA interface. Every UIMA compatible NLP-component can easily be integrated into TextImager. Even modules not compatible with UIMA can be integrated with just a slight effort. Amongst others, we have integrated DKPro (see Section 2), which offers a variety of UIMA-components. We also integrated the *UIMA Asynchronous Scaleout* (UIMA-AS)[1] add-on.

TextImager allows users for dynamically choosing NLP components in a pipeline. To this end, we extended UIMA-AS by initiating components without XML descriptors by means of uimaFIT[2]. We extended this framework by allowing for dynamic instantiations of pipelines. These extensions make our framework highly flexible, adaptive and extensible during runtime.

All TextImager components are configured as UIMA-AS services, which may run standalone or in a pipeline. All services are located on servers to allow for communication among them. Note that we are not limited to run these components on a single server; rather, they can be distributed among different servers (see Figure 1). We developed a mechanism that automatically selects and acquires components and their resources: it arranges components into pipelines and grants the ability to parallelize them. Thus, components that do not depend on each other can run in parallel. For this we developed an advanced UIMA flow controller. Take the examples displayed in Fig.2: suppose that vertices in these examples denote NLP components; suppose further that the corresponding arcs denote interdependencies between these components. In Fig. 2a, the components C_1, C_2 and C_3 do not depend on each other. Thus, they can run in parallel. In Fig. 2b, components C_1 and D_1 do not depend on each other, but on C and D, respectively. Thus, C and D can run in parallel as can do the components C_1 and D_1. In Fig. 2c, C depends on C_1, C_2 and C_3. Thus, running C has to wait on the termination of C_1, C_2 and C_3. Within TextImager, dependency hierarchies of components as exemplified by these three examples are generated from information provided by each of the components supposed that their input and output types have been defined appropriately (cf. the class specifications of type `org.apache.uima.fit.descriptor.TypeCapability`). In this way, TextImager allows for realizing a wide range of processing chains.

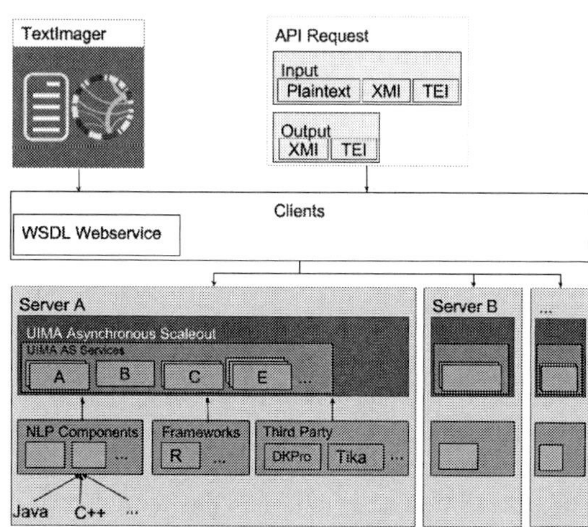

Figure 1: TextImager's back-end.

One advantage of our framework is that it does not rely on a central repository. Rather, TextImager can be distributed across multiple servers. This allows developers for setting up their own TextImager

[1] `https://uima.apache.org/doc-uimaas-what.html`

[2] `https://uima.apache.org/uimafit.html`

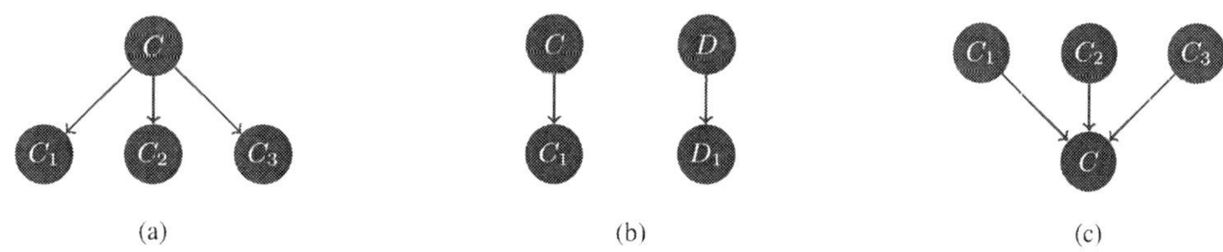

(a) (b) (c)

Figure 2: Component dependency types.

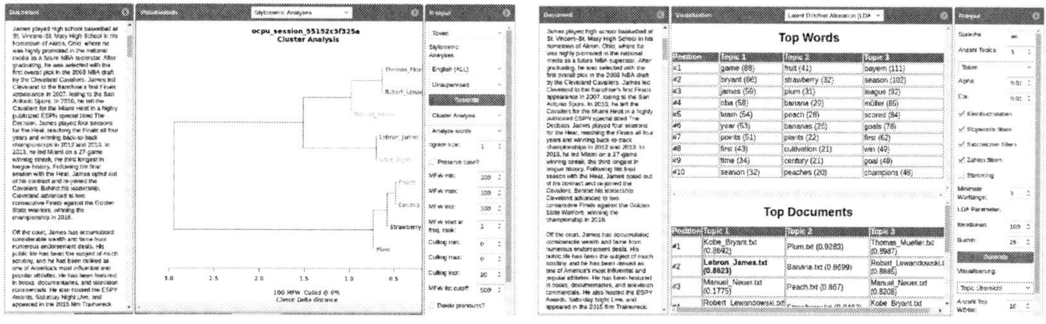

(a) Stylometric R-Module (b) LDA R-Module

server and to distribute their own NLP tools within the TextImager ecosystem.

TextImager can be used within a web application that offers a graphical user interface. Alternatively, TextImager can be used via a WSDL webservice client.

3.2 Front-end

The front-end gives access to all NLP tools integrated into TextImager without requiring any programming skills. This is done by means of a GUI that even provides three-dimensional text visualizations (see Figure 4b). All visualizations are interactive in the sense of allowing for focusing and contextualizing results of text analysis (e.g., the macro *reference distribution of sentence similarity across multiple documents* exemplified in Figure 4d). The GUI contains a text and a visualization panel. One of TextImager's guiding principles is to enable *bidirectional interactivity*. That is, any interaction with the visualization panel is synchronized by automatically adjusting the content of the text panel and vice versa. The front-end is based on *Ext JS*, a JavaScript framework for building interactive cross platform web applications. The visualizations are done by means of *D3.js*[3] and *vis.js*[4] to enable browser-based visualizations while handling large amounts of data.

Figure 4 exemplifies TextImager. With a focus on close reading, TextImager supports the interpretation of single texts by determining, for example, their central topics or by depicting their unfolding from constituent to constituent (see Figure 4g, 4a, 4h). Regarding distant reading (Jänicke et al., 2015), TextImager provides more abstract overviews of the content of text corpora. Here, visualizations provide summary information as exemplified in Figure 4b, 4c, 4d, 4f.

Last but not least, TextImager provides a generic interface to *R*[5]. The aim is to give access to any NLP-related package in R *once more without requiring programming skills*. This is especially needed for scholars in digital humanities who are not trained in using script languages for modeling statistical procedures, but expect a versatile tool encapsulating this computational complexity. Thus, TextImager users can process input texts using R packages like LDA (see Figure 3b), network analysis or stylometrics (see Figure 3a) without the need to manipulate or to invoke any *R* script directly. All these R packages

[3] https://www.d3js.org
[4] http://visjs.org
[5] https://www.r-project.org

are given a single entrance point in the form of TextImager. See (Mehler et al., 2016) for a recent research study based on TextImager.

4 Future Work

In already ongoing work, we extend the functionality of TextImager. This includes covering all features of tools like conTEXT. In contrast to many current frameworks, we will make TextImager's source code open-source as soon as the framework reaches a stable and documented version. We are going to specify a comprehensive model for component specification. The model will contain specifications of general components and their dependency hierarchy. This model will help defining where new NLP components are settled within the NLP landscape.

5 Scope of the Software Demonstration

A beta version of TextImager's web application can be found at `http://textimager.hucompute.org`. A preprocessed demonstration can be found at `http://textimager.hucompute.org/index.html?viewport=demo`. A tutorial on how to set up TextImager's backend services on codebase and a list of available components and options can be found at `http://service.hucompute.org`.

Acknowledgment

We gratefully acknowledge financial support of this project via the BMBF Project CEDIFOR (`https://www.cedifor.de/en/`).

References

Steven Bird, Ewan Klein, and Edward Loper. 2009. *Natural Language Processing with Python: Analyzing Text with the Natural Language Toolkit*. O'Reilly, Beijing.

Manuel Burghardt, Julian Pörsch, Bianca Tirlea, and Christian Wolff. 2014. WebNLP – an integrated web-interface for Python NLTK and Voyant. In *KONVENS*, pages 235–240.

Hamish Cunningham, Diana Maynard, Kalina Bontcheva, Valentin Tablan, Niraj Aswani, Ian Roberts, Genevieve Gorrell, Adam Funk, Angus Roberts, Danica Damljanovic, Thomas Heitz, Mark A. Greenwood, Horacio Saggion, Johann Petrak, Yaoyong Li, and Wim Peters. 2011. *Text Processing with GATE (Version 6)*.

Richard Eckart de Castilho and Iryna Gurevych. 2014. A broad-coverage collection of portable NLP components for building shareable analysis pipelines. In *Proceedings of the Workshop on Open Infrastructures and Analysis Frameworks for HLT*, pages 1–11, Dublin, Ireland, August. ACL and Dublin City University.

David Ferrucci and Adam Lally. 2004. UIMA: an architectural approach to unstructured information processing in the corporate research environment. *Natural Language Engineering*, 10(3-4):327–348.

Erhard Hinrichs, Marie Hinrichs, and Thomas Zastrow. 2010. Weblicht: Web-based LRT services for German. In *Proceedings of the ACL 2010 System Demonstrations*, ACLDemos '10, pages 25–29, Stroudsburg, PA, USA. Association for Computational Linguistics.

Stefan Jänicke, Greta Franzini, M Cheema, and Gerik Scheuermann. 2015. On close and distant reading in digital humanities: A survey and future challenges. *Proc. of EuroVisSTARs*, pages 83–103.

Alexander Mehler, Tolga Uslu, and Wahed Hemati. 2016. An image-driven approach to differential diagnosis. In *Proceedings of the 5th Workshop on Vision and Language (VL'16) hosted by the 54th Annual Meeting of the Association for Computational Linguistics (ACL), Berlin*, pages 80–85.

OpenNLP. 2010. Apache OpenNLP, `http://opennlp.apache.org`.

Stan Ruecker, Milena Radzikowska, and Stéfan Sinclair. 2011. *Visual interface design for digital cultural heritage: A guide to rich-prospect browsing*. Ashgate Publishing, Ltd.

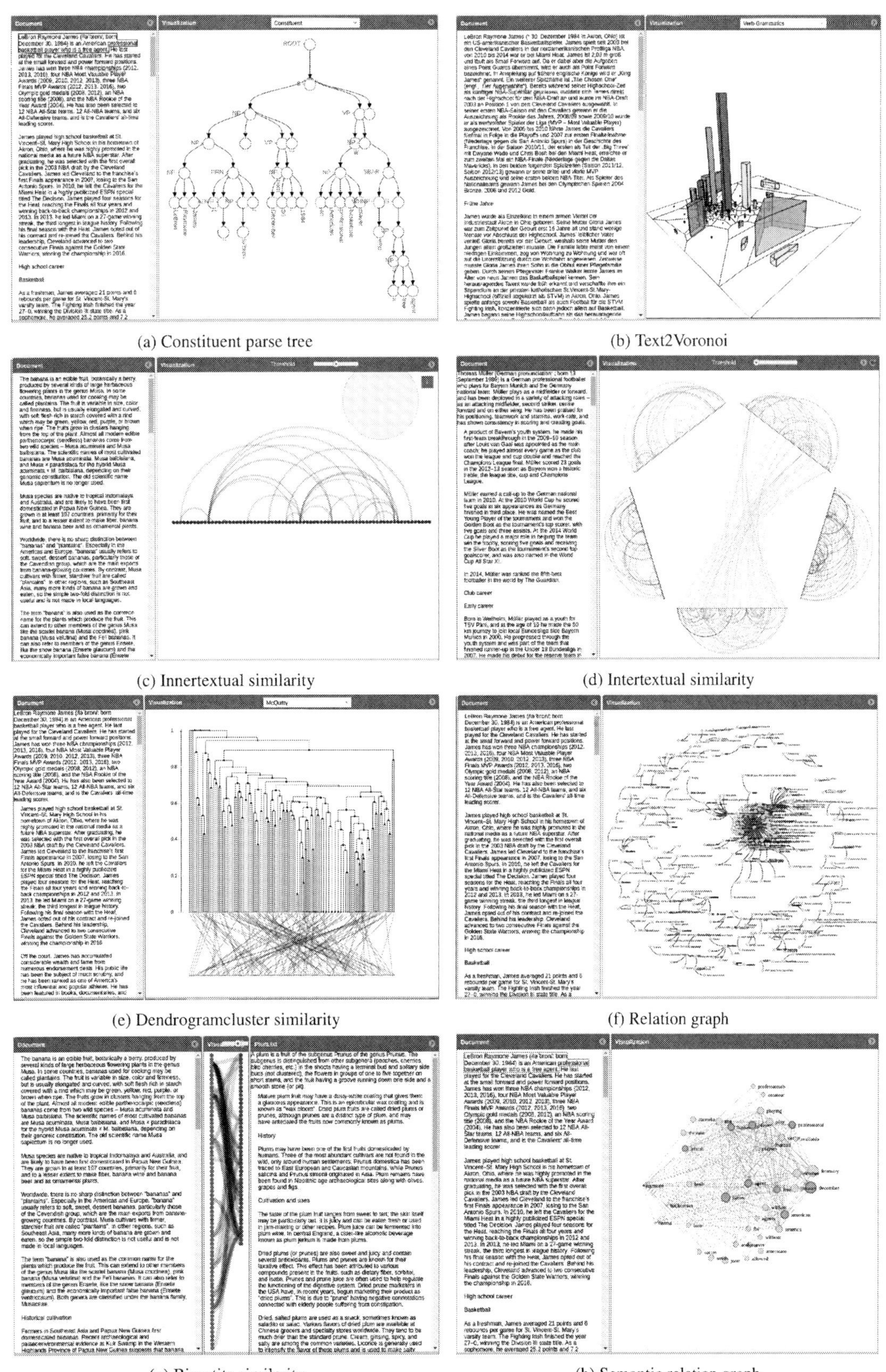

(a) Constituent parse tree

(b) Text2Voronoi

(c) Innertextual similarity

(d) Intertextual similarity

(e) Dendrogramcluster similarity

(f) Relation graph

(g) Bipartite similarity

(h) Semantic relation graph

Figure 4: Visualization Examples

DISCO: A System Leveraging Semantic Search in Document Review

Ngoc Phuoc An Vo, Fabien Guillot, Caroline Privault
Xerox Research Centre Europe
Meylan, France
{an.vo, fabien.guillot, caroline.privault}@xrce.xerox.com

Abstract

This paper presents Disco, a prototype for supporting knowledge workers in exploring, reviewing and sorting collections of textual data. The goal is to facilitate, accelerate and improve the discovery of information. To this end, it combines Semantic Relatedness techniques with a review workflow developed in a tangible environment. Disco uses a semantic model that is leveraged on-line in the course of search sessions, and accessed through natural hand-gesture, in a simple and intuitive way.

1 Introduction

Complex information seeking tasks frequently involve exploratory search activities. Although they can be characterized in many ways (see (Wildemuth and Freund, 2012), or (Marchionini, 2006) where they are grouped into "Learn" and "Investigate" activities), the next aspects are frequently used to describe exploratory scenarios: a) task description is ill-defined: it is broad or under-specified, or on the contrary multi-faceted; b) task is dynamic: relevance, object, targets evolve over search time; c) Information need is ill-defined: initial searchers' knowledge may be insufficient or inadequate and will also evolve over time. A remarkable consequence is that searchers have more latitude in directing their search. They can follow mixed strategies of searching, where they alternate between exploration phases and lookup/iterative phases. In the latter, items are systematically searched or reviewed (e.g. by attribute or simple keyword), whereas during exploration the search is expanded to new data, sources or domain of information, or to the development of new search criteria or strategies.

The development of search tools and interfaces to support exploratory search activities present a range of design challenges (e.g visualization, interaction, or relevance feedback). Recently search interfaces have been designed on multi-touch devices (smart phones, tablets (Klouche et al., 2015) or large surfaces). However, user studies reveal the need for search systems to increase the level of explorative search versus iterative search; otherwise, users tend to actually engage in exploring and learning from the data set, but in a rather limited way despite the availability of advanced UI layout and features. Search tools should then specifically encourage users to engage into exploratory phases, and facilitate the switch between lookup and exploratory phases.

Disco is a prototype developed to support knowledge workers in exploring, reviewing and sorting collections of textual data. We present how semantic relatedness is leveraged to sustain explorative search and increase information discovery. Our system is targeted at every user including non-technical users and is not domain-specific.

2 System Description

2.1 Disco Functionalities and Tangible User Interface

Disco combines a tangible user interface (TUI) with machine learning and advanced search capabilities (Privault et al., 2010; Xerox, 2010). At session startup, the user loads a collection of documents that is displayed on a touchscreen in a "Wall view": each document is represented by a tile on the wall. The user can explore the data set by using unsupervised text clustering, ML text categorization, automatic term

Proceedings of COLING 2016, the 26th International Conference on Computational Linguistics: System Demonstrations, pages 64–68, Osaka, Japan, December 11-17 2016.

extraction and keyword-based filtering. When the user locates a subset of documents that seem worth further reviewing, the subset can be sent to a dedicated area called the "Document Dispenser" (DD) and the user can switch to the "Document View". In the DD, documents are queued and can be opened by the user on a simple tap. Documents open in standard A4 format, just like paper sheets for ease of reading. The user can drill down one by one to decide which documents are relevant to the search, and which ones are non-relevant. Touching the "relevant" tab on the order of a document will tag that document and move it to a container called the "relevant bucket" (at the bottom right of the touchscreen); and touching the "non-relevant" tab will do the same but to the "non-relevant bucket" (at the bottom left corner).

To identity and locate potentially interesting data, the user can manipulate specific search widgets called "Virtual Magnets" (VM): a VM needs first to be populated with a term chosen by the user; then the user can move the magnet widget close to a group of documents (e.g. a cluster), which pulls out all the documents holding the chosen term. The tiles representing these documents are attracted around the magnet which helps users quickly visualize how many documents meet their search criteria, (see Figure 1). A swipe on the group of tiles gathered around the magnet automatically opens a random sample of documents, that the user can read to further decide if the subset is worth inspecting. To further review the subset, the user moves the document subset, from the magnet location to the Document Dispenser, through a 2 hand gesture.

Magnet Widgets can be populated in three different ways: a) *Static keywords:* a tap on a magnet opens a wheel menu displaying user-predefined terms; a tap on a term closes the magnet menu and populates the VM with the chosen term that appears on top of the widget; b) *Extracted keywords:* user chooses among keywords automatically extracted from each cluster by the clustering algorithm (or named entities) and displayed on the touchscreen; by touching with one finger a term listed to the right side of a cluster, and subsequently touching with the other hand a VM widget, the user can see the chosen term navigating to the magnet widget, and finally appearing displayed on top of the widget; c) *Highlighted keywords:* the user can directly highlight some text segments with his/her finger from a document displayed in paper format on the screen; when the user's finger is released from the document, a magnet pops-up with the selected text appearing on top of the widget.

In Disco the user switches easily between iterative/lookup search and exploratory search: an Iterative Search will correspond to a systematic drill down on documents stacked in the DD, by opening, reading and tagging them to the relevant or non-relevant bucket. An Exploratory Search will correspond to an expansion of the search to new areas of the document wall or groups of data, using clustering, categorization, or term-based filtering via VMs. At any time, users can interrupt an iterative search, and switch to an exploration phase. This typically happens as the review session unfolds and documents are read and labelled: knowledge is acquired and new information is discovered; interest drifts occur that can lead to new exploration phases. In this work we focus on using semantic relatedness in order to increase the level of exploration of the data in a simple and intuitive way.

2.2 Generating a Model for Semantic Relatedness

The notion of "Semantic Relatedness" is meant to quantify the semantic relationship between words, sentences or concepts, in a broad sense, covering relations beyond similarity such as: *"is-a-kind-of", "is-a-part-of", "is-a-specific-example-of", "is-the-opposite-of", etc.* Word embeddings are used to build semantic language models that can be afterwards deployed to obtain the semantic information on input terms: either getting the level of relatedness between 2 input words (or phrases), or finding lists of most semantically related terms given an input word.

We applied Semantic Relatedness for semantic search. It is important here to make a distinction with the notion of Semantic Web (SW): the SW, (which has been around at least since 2001) is a web of linked data with a semantic structuring achieved by ontologies and supported by several technologies and standards (i.e. RDF, OWL, SparQL, etc). A number of SW search engines are available, such as Siren built on top of Lucene™/Solr[1].

In contrast, when building a semantic model through word embeddings, the attempt is to learn the

[1] https://github.com/sirensolutions/siren

Datasets	Pearson	Spearman
ALL	0.65045	0.6699
MC30	0.7904	0.7835
RG65	0.7614	0.7626
MTurk	0.7020	0.6738
WordSim353-Sim	0.6696	0.7183
WordSim353-Rel	0.5147	0.5386

Table 1: Model evaluation on different datasets.

context of words in an unsupervised way from unstructured raw corpora. In this work, we used Google's word2vec toolkit[2], see (Mikolov et al., 2013a; Mikolov et al., 2013b; Mikolov et al., 2013c). As a large dataset is required to build a model generic enough to serve in different domains, we collected a large set of data (approximately 40GB) using the following sources:

- The training monolingual news crawl in 2012 & 2013 of the 9th Workshop on SMT.[3]
- The 1-billion-word language model benchmark.[4]
- The UMBC webbase corpus.[5]
- The latest Wikipedia dump file.[6]

To integrate data of heterogeneous format, we applied some pre-processing: firstly, converting all texts to lower case and removing special characters; secondly for the Wikipedia data, keeping only the body text in <text> tags, (removing xhtml tags, image links, etc) to get a dataset of 28GB.

We generated the semantic model via the Google's word2vec toolkit using the combination of Skip-Gram and Negative sampling as recommended as the best strategy (Mikolov et al., 2013b). In addition, we used the "word2phrase" function to get a model supporting also n-grams. Finally, we obtained a model of 4.4GB.

For model evaluation, as we wanted to evaluate the model capability of finding semantically related words to be used in our semantic search, we tested the model on the task of computing the semantic similarity/relatedness between words. We build the evaluation data from several datasets: MC30 (Miller and Charles, 1991), RG65 (Rubenstein and Goodenough, 1965), MTurk (Radinsky et al., 2011), WordSim353 Similarity and Relatedness (Agirre et al., 2009). It contained 837 word pairs in total with human annotation for semantic similarity and relatedness. However, since these datasets were developed and annotated by different people and annotation guidelines, the semantic similarity/relatedness scores were specified in different scales; thus we normalized annotation score via Feature Scaling[7] to [0-1]. We used the Pearson[8] and Spearman[9] correlation methods for evaluation metrics. Table 1 shows the results of our model evaluation on different settings of datasets. It shows that our semantic model obtains good results on several datasets compared to other models reported on this site[10]. The semantic model is further used in Disco to assist users during search sessions on collections of text documents. The next section explains how the model is loaded and queried by the searchers.

2.3 Loading and Querying the Model in Disco

Semantic relatedness capabilities are provided by the "Disco Semantics" Java library, that can: a) load a model in memory; b) query the model from an input term, to get a list of most related words/phrases; c) compute the semantic relatedness score between two words. The model is loaded at application start-up to ensure users can access it in real-time during a search session. Loading can take a few minutes (e.g.

[2]https://code.google.com/archive/p/word2vec

[3]http://www.statmt.org/wmt14/translation-task.html

[4]http://www.statmt.org/lm-benchmark/1-billion-word-language-modeling-benchmark-r13output.tar.gz

[5]http://ebiquity.umbc.edu/redirect/to/resource/id/351/UMBC-webbase-corpus

[6]https://en.wikipedia.org/wiki/Wikipedia:Database_download

[7]https://en.wikipedia.org/wiki/Feature_scaling

[8]https://en.wikipedia.org/wiki/Pearson_product-moment_correlation_coefficient

[9]https://en.wikipedia.org/wiki/Spearman%27s_rank_correlation_coefficient

[10]http://aclweb.org/aclwiki/index.php?title=Similarity_(State_of_the_art)

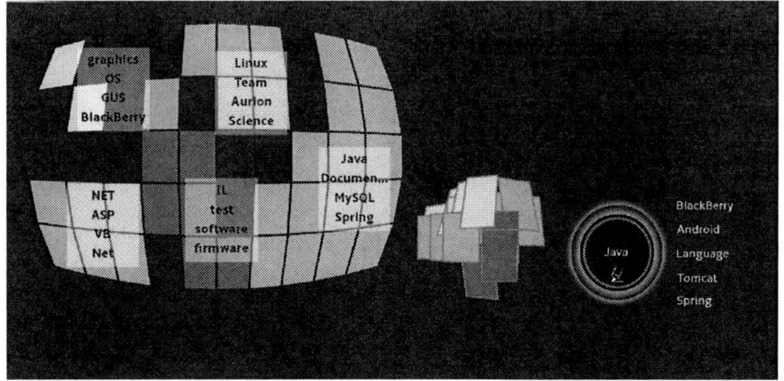

Figure 1: Result of a magnet query in semantic mode from the term "Java".

at the worst case, $\approx 6mn$ for the 4.4GB model on an ordinary computer - 8Gb ram); then computing the relatedness score for a word-pair is fast (less than 1s, again on an ordinary machine).

Online requests to the semantic module are made using the virtual magnet widgets: the user selects a word, phrase or text fragment as input to populate a magnet, that can operate in a "semantic relatedness mode". The searcher can select the input from 3 different sources: *Static keywords* (user predefined terms via magnet menus); *Extracted keywords* (discovered by the system via clustering/entity extraction, and displayed on the screen); *Highlighted keywords* (directly selected from document contents by the user). The reuse of existing text through natural hand gesture for formulating queries on the TUI is particularly convenient, and it facilitates exploratory search behaviour by enabling sequential search (see section 2.4).

Once the magnet is populated in semantic mode, the system computes on-the-fly the list of semantically related terms to form an expanded query. An animated glow effect on the widget indicates that it is ready for searching for new documents. When moved close to a group of documents, the magnet attracts all documents that match one or several of the terms from the expanded query, (see Figure 1). The searcher can choose to further inspect the retrieved documents by sending them to the Document Dispenser for a systematic review. The magnet can also be applied to other groups of documents to locate other sources of information in the data space.

2.4 Visualizing Related Terms and Formulating Subsequent Queries

On the touch screen, the list of "semantically related words" is displayed next to the magnet that operated the query, so that the searcher can instantly visualize and access them: users can scroll and select items, each item showing a related word. The displayed items are ranked by distance, i.e. the top item is the one most similar to the input word populating the magnet, etc. Whenever the user drags the magnet to another location on the screen, the list stays close to the magnet, following its movement. The maximum number of "related words" displayed and used during a query is defaulted to 10 which can be configured (upfront or on the fly). As the items displayed in the list of semantically related terms are also selectable, they can be used in turn for populating a new magnet, then launching a new query through 10 other semantically related terms computed on the fly, and so on, enabling in this way to run sequential semantic searches.

2.5 Implementation

Disco is based on a client-server architecture: the client TUI is developed in Adobe Air; the server orchestrating the text mining components (ML categorization, clustering, rule-based entity extraction, semantic search) is implemented in Java. The Disco Semantics component uses Deeplearning4J (http://deeplearning4j.org/) which is a Java open-source deep-learning library distributed under Apache license. We use it for querying the semantic model, whereas the model itself is off-line generated using word2vec.

3 Conclusion and Future Work

Technology-Assisted Review tools find applications in various domains and can be embedded in a range of industrial services, (e.g. in eDiscovery). With Disco, we combine semantic search and a specific design approach on a TUI, to increase information discovery on collections of textual documents. We aim at making semantic relatedness techniques available to all - and especially nontechnical-users, in a simple, generic and effective way. User studies show that a specific system design associated with touch capabilities can lead to more active search behaviours, (in addition to shortening system learning curve and allowing for faster adoption). We plan now to set-up a user study to collect feedback on the usability of the information provided by the semantic model, and the interaction design built to leverage semantic relatedness in search sessions.

References

Eneko Agirre, Enrique Alfonseca, Keith Hall, Jana Kravalova, Marius Paşca, and Aitor Soroa. 2009. A study on similarity and relatedness using distributional and wordnet-based approaches. In *Proceedings of Human Language Technologies: The 2009 Annual Conference of the North American Chapter of the Association for Computational Linguistics*, pages 19–27. Association for Computational Linguistics.

Khalil Klouche, Tuukka Ruotsalo, Diogo Cabral, Salvatore Andolina, Andrea Bellucci, and Giulio Jacucci. 2015. Designing for exploratory search on touch devices. In *Proceedings of the 33rd Annual ACM Conference on Human Factors in Computing Systems*, pages 4189–4198. ACM.

Gary Marchionini. 2006. Exploratory search: from finding to understanding. *Communications of the ACM*, 49(4):41–46.

Tomas Mikolov, Kai Chen, Greg Corrado, and Jeffrey Dean. 2013a. Efficient estimation of word representations in vector space. *arXiv preprint arXiv:1301.3781*.

Tomas Mikolov, Ilya Sutskever, Kai Chen, Greg S Corrado, and Jeff Dean. 2013b. Distributed representations of words and phrases and their compositionality. In *Advances in neural information processing systems*, pages 3111–3119.

Tomas Mikolov, Wen-tau Yih, and Geoffrey Zweig. 2013c. Linguistic regularities in continuous space word representations. In *HLT-NAACL*, pages 746–751.

George A Miller and Walter G Charles. 1991. Contextual correlates of semantic similarity. *Language and cognitive processes*, 6(1):1–28.

Caroline Privault, Jacki O'Neill, Victor Ciriza, and Jean-Michel Renders. 2010. A new tangible user interface for machine learning document review. *Artificial Intelligence and Law*, 18(4):459–479.

Kira Radinsky, Eugene Agichtein, Evgeniy Gabrilovich, and Shaul Markovitch. 2011. A word at a time: computing word relatedness using temporal semantic analysis. In *Proceedings of the 20th international conference on World wide web*, pages 337–346. ACM.

Herbert Rubenstein and John B Goodenough. 1965. Contextual correlates of synonymy. *Communications of the ACM*, 8(10):627–633.

Barbara M Wildemuth and Luanne Freund. 2012. Assigning search tasks designed to elicit exploratory search behaviors. In *Proceedings of the Symposium on Human-Computer Interaction and Information Retrieval*, page 4. ACM.

Xerox. 2010. Inside innovation at xerox: Smart document review technology. `https://www.youtube.com/watch?v=ZwPU51j5qoU`.

pke: an open source python-based keyphrase extraction toolkit

Florian Boudin
LINA - UMR CNRS 6241, Université de Nantes, France
florian.boudin@univ-nantes.fr

Abstract

We describe pke, an open source python-based keyphrase extraction toolkit. It provides an end-to-end keyphrase extraction pipeline in which each component can be easily modified or extented to develop new approaches. pke also allows for easy benchmarking of state-of-the-art keyphrase extraction approaches, and ships with supervised models trained on the SemEval-2010 dataset (Kim et al., 2010).

1 Introduction

Keyphrase extraction is the task of identifying the words and phrases that represent the main topics of a document. Keyphrases have been shown to be useful for a variety of natural language processing applications such as document indexing (Gutwin et al., 1999), text categorization (Hulth and Megyesi, 2006) or summarization (Qazvinian et al., 2010). Recent years have witnessed increased interest in keyphrase extraction (Gollapalli et al., 2015), and several benchmark datasets have become available in various domains and languages (Hasan and Ng, 2014). Yet, there are few tools available for automatic keyphrase extraction, and none of them offer implementations of current state-of-the-art approaches nor the suitability for rapid prototyping like the python-based Natural Language Toolkit (nltk) (Bird et al., 2009) does. In this demonstration, we describe an open source python-based keyphrase extraction toolkit, called pke, which 1) provides implementations of existing supervised and unsupervised keyphrase extraction approaches; 2) can be easily extended to develop new approaches; 3) ships with a collection of already trained models, which are ready for use. The pke toolkit is open source under the GNU GPL licence and available at https://github.com/boudinfl/pke

2 Architecture

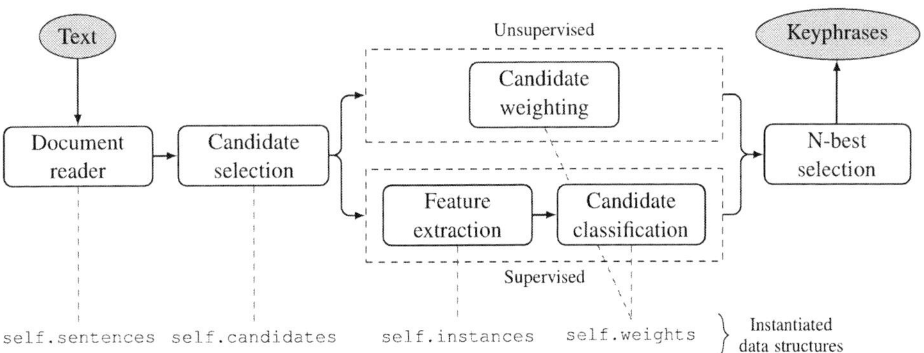

Figure 1: Overall architecture of pke.

Proceedings of COLING 2016, the 26th International Conference on Computational Linguistics: System Demonstrations, pages 69–73, Osaka, Japan, December 11-17 2016.

The overall architecture of pke is depicted in Figure 1. Extracting keyphrases from an input document involves three steps. First, keyphrase candidates (i.e. words and phrases that are eligible to be keyphrases) are selected from the content of the document. Second, candidates are either ranked using a candidate weighting function (unsupervised approaches), or classified as keyphrase or not using a set of extracted features (supervised approaches). Third, the top-N highest weighted candidates, or those classified as keyphrase with the highest confidence scores, are selected as keyphrases.

Document reader: three input formats are supported: raw text, preprocessed text[1] and Stanford CoreNLP XML (Manning et al., 2014). When raw text is provided, preprocessing (i.e. tokenization, sentence splitting and POS-tagging) is carried out using nltk. Preprocessed text files are expected to use POS tags from the Penn Treebank tagset. Document logical structure information[2], used as features in some supervised approaches, can by specified by incorporating attributes into the sentence elements of the CoreNLP XML format.

Implemented approaches: The pke toolkit currently implements the following approaches, each consisting of a unique combination of candidate selection and candidate ranking methods.

Unsupervised	TfIdf: we re-implemented the TF×IDF n-gram based baseline in (Kim et al., 2010). By default, it uses 1, 2, 3-grams as keyphrase candidates and filter out those shorter than 3 characters, containing words made of only punctuation marks or one character long[3]. SingleRank (Wan and Xiao, 2008): keyphrase candidates are the sequences of adjacent nouns and adjectives. Candidates are ranked by the sum of their words scores, computed using TextRank (Mihalcea and Tarau, 2004) on a word-based graph representation of the document. TopicRank (Bougouin et al., 2013): this model improves SingleRank by grouping lexically similar candidates into topics and directly ranking topics. Keyphrases are produced by extracting the first occurring candidate of the highest ranked topics. KP-Miner (El-Beltagy and Rafea, 2010): keyphrase candidates are sequences of words that do not contain punctuation marks or stopwords[4]. Candidates that appear less than three times or that first occur beyond a certain position are removed. Candidates are then weighted using a modified TF×IDF formula that account for document length.
Supervised	Kea (Witten et al., 1999): keyphrase candidates are 1, 2, 3-grams that do not begin or end with a stopword. Keyphrases are selected using a naïve bayes classifier with two features: TF×IDF and the relative position of first occurrence. WINGNUS (Nguyen and Luong, 2010): keyphrase candidates are simplex nouns and noun phrases detected using a set of POS filtering rules. Keyphrases are then selected using a naïve bayes classifier with a large set of features including document logical structure information.

Already trained models: to promote benchmarking of current state-of-the-art keyphrase extraction approaches on new datasets, we make available supervised models for Kea and WINGNUS, as well as document frequency counts, trained on the training part of the SemEval-2010 dataset (Kim et al., 2010).

Non English languages: while the default language in pke is English, extracting keyphrases from documents in other languages is easily achieved by inputting already preprocessed documents, and setting the language parameter to the desired language. The only language dependent resources used in pke are the stoplist and the stemming algorithm from nltk that are available in 11 languages[5]. Examples of use for other languages are provided in the documentation.

[1]whitespace-separated POS-tagged tokens, one sentence per line.
[2]We use the classification categories proposed by Luong et al. (2012).
[3]This filtering process is also applied to the other models.
[4]We use the stoplist in nltk, http://www.nltk.org
[5]http://www.nltk.org/_modules/nltk/corpus.html

3 Elementary Usage

Python Library: pke can be imported as a Python module, which is its primary use. Figure 2 gives a complete example of use, showing the typical three-step process involved in keyphrase extraction. Particular attention was paid to modularity: each method instantiates a different data structure (see Figure 1), thus making it easier to develop new approaches by modifying the behaviour of only some components. Modifying the example to apply another approach is quite straightforward: replace TopicRank at line 4 with another model (e.g. TfIdf).

```
1  import pke
2
3  # initialize TopicRank
4  extr = pke.TopicRank(input_file='/path/to/input')
5
6  # load the content of the document
7  extr.read_document(format='raw')
8
9  # step 1: candidate selection
10 extr.candidate_selection()
11
12 # step 2: candidate weighting
13 extr.candidate_weighting()
14
15 # step 3: N-best selection
16 keyphrases = extr.get_n_best(n=10)
```

Figure 2: Example of keyphrase extraction using TopicRank with pke.

Figure 3 illustrates how to train a new supervised model in pke. The training data consists of a set of documents along with a reference file containing annotated keyphrases in the SemEval-2010 format[6]. Candidate classification is performed using the implementations available in scikit-learn [7].

```
import pke

# load document frequency counts (DF) as a dictionary
df_counts = pke.load_document_frequency_file('/path/to/file')

# train new Kea model
pke.train_supervised_model(input_dir='/path/to/input/directory/',
                           reference_file='/path/to/reference/file',
                           model_file='/path/to/model/file',
                           df=df_counts,
                           model=pke.Kea())
```

Figure 3: Training a new Kea supervised model with pke.

Command Line: the pke toolkit also includes a command line tool that allows users to perform keyphrase extraction without any knowledge of the Python programming language. An example of use is given below.

```
python cmd_pke.py -i /path/to/input -f raw -o /path/to/output -a TopicRank
```

Here, unsupervised keyphrase extraction using TopicRank is performed on a raw text input file, and the top ranked keyphrase candidates are outputted into a file.

4 Benchmarking

We evaluate the performance of our re-implementations using the SemEval-2010 benchmark dataset (Kim et al., 2010). This dataset is composed of 244 scientific articles (144 in training and 100

[6] http://docs.google.com/Doc?id=ddshp584_46gqkkjng4
[7] http://scikit-learn.org

for test) collected from the ACM Digital Library (conference and workshop papers). Document logical structure information, required to compute features in the WINGNUS approach, is annotated with ParsCit (Kan et al., 2010)[8]. The Stanford CoreNLP pipeline[9] (tokenization, sentence splitting and POS-tagging) is then applied to the documents from which irrelevant pieces of text (e.g. tables, equations, footnotes) were filtered out[10].

We follow the evaluation procedure used in the SemEval-2010 competition and evaluate the performance of each implemented approach in terms of precision (P), recall (R) and f-measure (F) at the top N keyphrases. We use the set of combined author- and reader-assigned keyphrases as reference keyphrases. Extracted and reference keyphrases are stemmed to reduce the number of mismatches. Detailed results for each approach are presented in Table 1.

Approach	**P**	**R**	**F**
`TfIdf`	20.0	14.1	16.4
`TopicRank`	15.6	10.8	12.6
`SingleRank`	2.2	1.5	1.8
`KP-Miner`	24.1	17.0	19.8
`Kea`	23.5	16.6	19.3
`WINGNUS`	24.7	17.3	20.2

Table 1: Performance of each approach computed at the top 10 extracted keyphrases. Results are expressed as a percentage of precision (P), recall (R) and f-measure (F).

5 Related Work

Most of the tools available for automatic keyphrase extraction only implement one approach, and are often outdated with respect to the current state-of-the-art. These tools also rely on in-house text preprocessing and candidate selection/filtering pipelines, which makes it difficult to compare results across several approaches. One notable exception to this is the DKPro Keyphrases Java framework (Erbs et al., 2014), which provides a UIMA-based workbench for developing and evaluating new keyphrase extraction approaches. However, this framework requires users to learn UIMA before they can get started, and does not provide supervised approaches that are known to perform better (Hasan and Ng, 2014).

6 Conclusion

We presented `pke`, an open source python-based keyphrase extraction toolkit that provides an end-to-end pipeline in which each component can be easily modified to develop new models. `pke` includes implementations of state-of-the-art supervised and unsupervised approaches, and comes with a collection of already trained models. It is our hope that this toolkit will help researchers to compare, build upon and devise keyphrase extraction approaches.

Acknowledgments

This work was partially supported by the TALIAS project (grant of CNRS PEPS INS2I 2016, `https://boudinfl.github.io/talias/`). We thank the anonymous reviewers for their comments.

References

[Bird et al.2009] Steven Bird, Ewan Klein, and Edward Loper. 2009. *Natural language processing with Python*. O'Reilly.

[8] We use ParsCit v110505.

[9] Use use Stanford CoreNLP v3.6.0.

[10] Further details about preprocessing can be found at `https://github.com/boudinfl/semeval-2010-pre`

[Bougouin et al.2013] Adrien Bougouin, Florian Boudin, and Béatrice Daille. 2013. Topicrank: Graph-based topic ranking for keyphrase extraction. In *Proceedings of IJCNLP*, pages 543–551.

[El-Beltagy and Rafea2010] Samhaa R. El-Beltagy and Ahmed Rafea. 2010. Kp-miner: Participation in semeval-2. In *Proceedings of SemEval*, pages 190–193.

[Erbs et al.2014] Nicolai Erbs, Pedro Bispo Santos, Iryna Gurevych, and Torsten Zesch. 2014. Dkpro keyphrases: Flexible and reusable keyphrase extraction experiments. In *Proceedings of ACL*, pages 31–36.

[Gollapalli et al.2015] Sujatha Das Gollapalli, Cornelia Caragea, Xiaoli Li, and C. Lee Giles, editors. 2015. *Proceedings of the ACL 2015 Workshop on Novel Computational Approaches to Keyphrase Extraction.*

[Gutwin et al.1999] Carl Gutwin, Gordon Paynter, Ian Witten, Craig Nevill Manning, and Eibe Frank. 1999. Improving Browsing in Digital Libraries with Keyphrase Indexes. *Decision Support Systems*, 27(1):81–104.

[Hasan and Ng2014] Kazi Saidul Hasan and Vincent Ng. 2014. Automatic keyphrase extraction: A survey of the state of the art. In *Proceedings of ACL*, pages 1262–1273.

[Hulth and Megyesi2006] Anette Hulth and Beáta B. Megyesi. 2006. A study on automatically extracted keywords in text categorization. In *Proceedings of COLING/ACL*, pages 537–544.

[Kan et al.2010] Min-Yen Kan, Minh-Thang Luong, and Thuy Dung Nguyen. 2010. Logical structure recovery in scholarly articles with rich document features. *Int. J. Digit. Library Syst.*, 1(4):1–23.

[Kim et al.2010] Su Nam Kim, Olena Medelyan, Min-Yen Kan, and Timothy Baldwin. 2010. Semeval-2010 task 5 : Automatic keyphrase extraction from scientific articles. In *Proceedings of SemEval*, pages 21–26.

[Luong et al.2012] Minh-Thang Luong, Thuy Dung Nguyen, and Min-Yen Kan. 2012. Logical structure recovery in scholarly articles with rich document features. *Multimedia Storage and Retrieval Innovations for Digital Library Systems*, 270.

[Manning et al.2014] Christopher Manning, Mihai Surdeanu, John Bauer, Jenny Finkel, Steven Bethard, and David McClosky. 2014. The stanford corenlp natural language processing toolkit. In *Proceedings of ACL*, pages 55–60.

[Mihalcea and Tarau2004] Rada Mihalcea and Paul Tarau. 2004. Textrank: Bringing order into texts. In *Proceedings of EMNLP*, pages 404–411.

[Nguyen and Luong2010] Thuy Dung Nguyen and Minh-Thang Luong. 2010. Wingnus: Keyphrase extraction utilizing document logical structure. In *Proceedings of SemEval*, pages 166–169.

[Qazvinian et al.2010] Vahed Qazvinian, Dragomir R. Radev, and Arzucan Ozgur. 2010. Citation summarization through keyphrase extraction. In *Proceedings of COLING*, pages 895–903.

[Wan and Xiao2008] Xiaojun Wan and Jianguo Xiao. 2008. Collabrank: Towards a collaborative approach to single-document keyphrase extraction. In *Proceedings of COLING*, pages 969–976.

[Witten et al.1999] Ian H. Witten, Gordon W. Paynter, Eibe Frank, Carl Gutwin, and Craig G. Nevill-Manning. 1999. Kea: Practical automatic keyphrase extraction. In *Proceedings of the Fourth ACM Conference on Digital Libraries*, pages 254–255. ACM.

Langforia: Language Pipelines for Annotating Large Collections of Documents

Marcus Klang
Lund University
Department of Computer Science
Lund, Sweden
Marcus.Klang@cs.lth.se

Pierre Nugues
Lund University
Department of Computer Science
Lund, Sweden
Pierre.Nugues@cs.lth.se

Abstract

In this paper, we describe **Langforia**, a multilingual processing pipeline to annotate texts with multiple layers: formatting, parts of speech, named entities, dependencies, semantic roles, and entity links. Langforia works as a web service, where the server hosts the language processing components and the client, the input and result visualization. To annotate a text or a Wikipedia page, the user chooses an NLP pipeline and enters the text or the name of the Wikipedia page in the input field of the interface. Once processed, the results are returned to the client, where the user can select the annotation layers s/he wants to visualize.

We designed Langforia with a specific focus for Wikipedia, although it can process any type of text. Wikipedia has become an essential encyclopedic corpus used in many NLP projects. However, processing articles and visualizing the annotations are nontrivial tasks that require dealing with multiple markup variants, encodings issues, and tool incompatibilities across the language versions. This motivated the development of a new architecture.

A demonstration of Langforia is available for six languages: English, French, German, Spanish, Russian, and Swedish at `http://vilde.cs.lth.se:9000/` as well as a web API: `http://vilde.cs.lth.se:9000/api`. Langforia is also provided as a standalone library and is compatible with cluster computing.

1 The Demonstration

Langforia is a multilingual annotation and visualization platform available as a web service and as a standalone library. Figure 1 shows the interface, where the user chooses the language and tool chain s/he wants to use from the drop-down menu to the left. Depending on the language and the availability of components, the annotations can range from tokenization to dependency parsing, semantic role labeling, and entity linking. The user then either enters a text or writes the name of a Wikipedia page and presses the "Annotate" button. If the document to analyze is a raw text, it is sent directly to the server; if it is a Wikipedia page name, the client first fetches the HTML content of this page from `https://www.wikipedia.org/` and then sends it to the Langforia server. Figure 2, left part, shows the resulting annotations for the *Osaka* article from the Swedish Wikipedia for three layers, tokens, named entities, and dependency relations, while the right part of the figure shows the entity linking results.

2 Motivation and Significance

We designed Langforia with a specific focus for Wikipedia, although the pipeline can process raw text. Wikipedia has become an essential encyclopedic corpus used in many NLP projects. In translation (Smith et al., 2010), semantic networks (Navigli and Ponzetto, 2010), named entity linking (Mihalcea and Csomai, 2007), information extraction, or question answering (Ferrucci, 2012), Wikipedia offers a multilingual coverage and an article diversity that are unequalled. However, processing articles are non-trivial tasks that require dealing with multiple markup variants, encodings issues, tool incompatibilities

Proceedings of COLING 2016, the 26th International Conference on Computational Linguistics: System Demonstrations, pages 74–78, Osaka, Japan, December 11-17 2016.

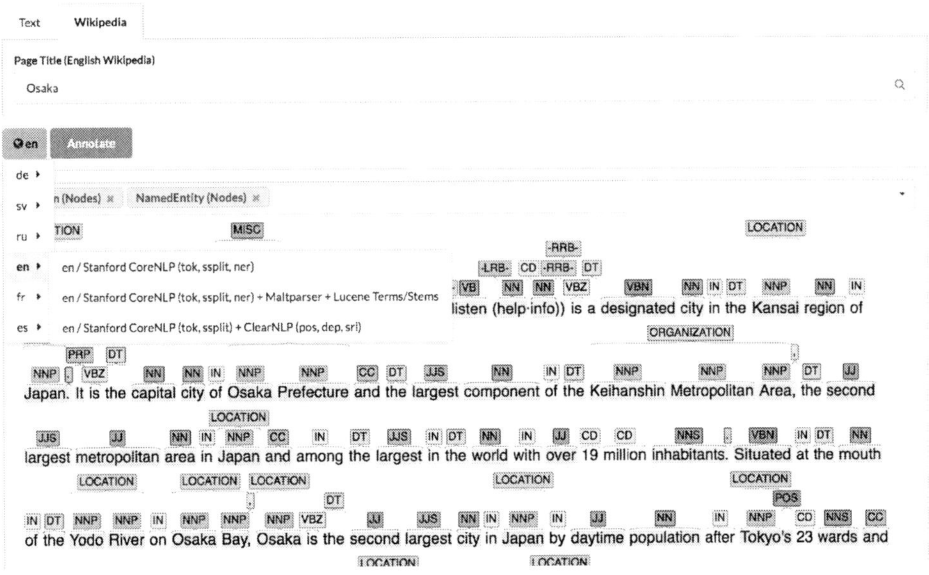

Figure 1: The Langforia interface. The upper part of the figure shows the input box, where the user either selects a Wikipedia page (Wikipedia tab), here the article on Osaka in English, or enters a raw text (Text tab); The center part shows the language selection menu with six languages (de, en, es, fr, ru, sv), here English, and submenus to choose the toolchain (three toolchains for English); and the Annotate button; The lower part shows the annotated text, where the annotation layers are selectable from a drop down menu in the block just above (black triangle to the right), here the tokens and named entities

across the language versions and significant processing capacities. In addition, the scale and heterogeneity of the Wikipedia collection makes it relatively difficult to do experimentations on the whole corpus. These experimentations are rendered even more complex as, to the best of our knowledge, there is no available tool to visualize easily annotation results from different processing pipelines.

Langforia builds on a document model (Klang and Nugues, 2016) that stores the linguistic annotations and enables the pipeline to abstract the components across the languages and tools. This model consists of layers, where each layer is a sequence of ranges describing a specific annotation, for instance the parts of speech or the syntactic dependencies. It provides a format common to all the pipelines that makes them insensitive to the input/output features of a tool.

The list of annotated layers varies depending on the tool availability for a specific language. The layers common to all the versions are compatible with the Wikipedia markup: They include the text, paragraphs, text styles, links, and page sections. Using this document model as input, we created a client visualizer that let users interactively visualize the annotations. Beyond the demonstration, Langforia is available in the form of a library that provides a uniform way to process multilingual Wikipedia dumps and output the results in a universal document model. This could benefit all the projects that use Wikipedia as a corpus.

3 System Architecture

Langforia consists of three parts: A set of language processing components assembled as tool chains; a multilayer document model (MLDM) library; and a visualizer.

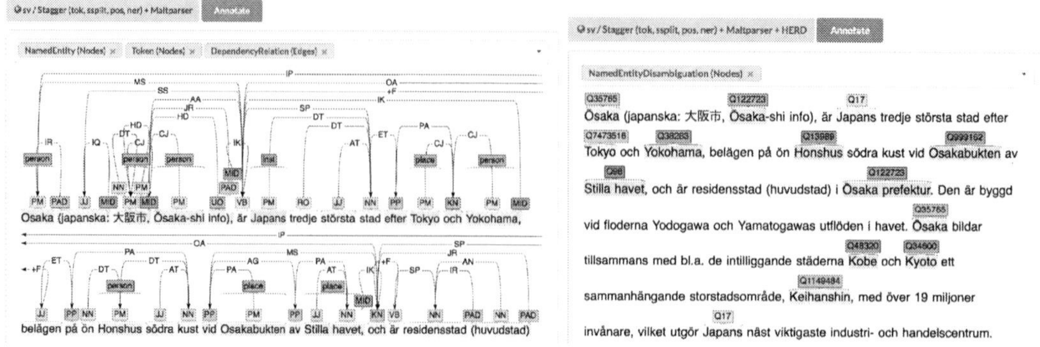

Figure 2: Left part: Visualization of three layers: Tokens, named entities, and dependency relations from the *Osaka* page in Swedish; right part: Visualization of named entity linking with Wikidata identifiers

3.1 Tool Chains

We annotate Wikipedia HTML pages into MLDM records using an annotation pipeline: a sequence of processing components. The first step converts the HTML documents into DOM trees using jsoup[1]. The second step extracts the original page structure, text styles, links, lists, and tables. We then resolve the links to unique Wikidata identifiers. Wikidata is an entity database[2], part of Wikimedia, which assigns unique identifiers across all the language editions of Wikipedia. The city of Osaka, for instance, has the unique id: Q35765 that enables the system to retrieve the article pages in English, French, Swedish, or Russian. We keep the original links occurring in the Wikipedia pages and we resolve them using Wikidata identifiers, when they exist, or to normalized page names as a fall back. These steps are common to all the language editions we process. If the input is plain text, we skip these steps.

The annotation tool chains are specific to the languages. We abstracted these chains so that they are instances of a generic annotator. For English, Spanish, and German, we use CoreNLP (Manning et al., 2014) or ClearNLP (Choi, 2012). For French, we use CoreNLP for tokenizing the text and MATE for parsing (Björkelund et al., 2010). For Swedish, we use Stagger (Östling, 2013) and MaltParser (Nivre et al., 2006). For Russian, only the tokenization is available for now. We also link mentions of named entities and concepts to unique Wikidata identifiers. To carry this out, we reimplemented a variant of TAGME (Ferragina and Scaiella, 2010).

3.2 The Document Model

The MLDM library[3] (Klang and Nugues, 2016) defines a model for storing, querying, and extracting hypertextual information common to many NLP tasks in a standalone package. We designed this model so that it could store the original Wikipedia markup, as well as the subsequent linguistic annotations: Part-of-speech tagging, coreference resolution, named entity recognition and linking, dependency parsing, semantic role labeling, etc.

The model consists of multiple layers, where each layer is dedicated to a specific type of annotation. The annotations are encoded in the form of graph nodes, where a node represents a piece of data: a token, a sentence, a named entity, etc., delimited by ranges. These nodes are possibly connected by edges as in dependency graphs. This data structure used is similar to a property graph.

3.3 Visualization

The interactive visualization tool enables the user to examine the results. We designed it so that it could handle large documents with more than 10,000 tokens with a fast rendering of the annotations and allow cross sentence annotations, such as for paragraphs and sections. The layers are selectable from a dropdown menu and the supported visualizations are the ranges and relationships between them.

[1] `http://jsoup.org/`

[2] `http://www.wikidata.org`

[3] `https://github.com/marcusklang/docforia`

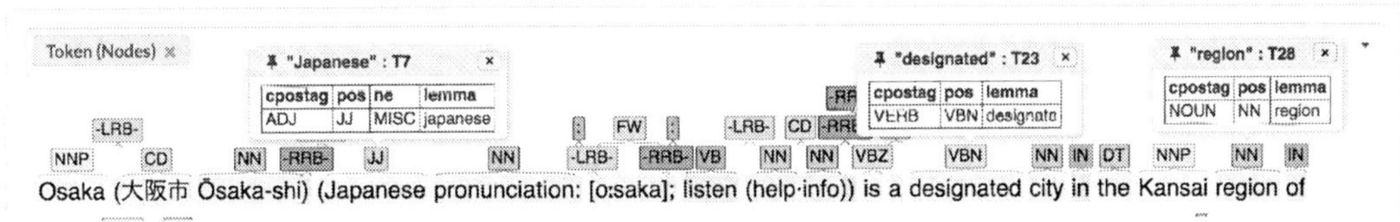

Figure 3: The properties attached to the words *Japanese*, *designated*, and *region*, in the form of tooltips

In Fig. 3, we selected the token layer that by default displays the parts of speech of the words. If we hover over the words, the visualizer shows the properties attached to a word in CoNLL-like format in a tooltip that the user can fix, move, and discard. Figure 3 shows the properties of the words: *Japanese*, *designated*, and *region*. Finally, we estimated the rendering speed (time to interactive use) on 30,000 annotations (tokens) with Intel Core i7, 2.3 GHz, with 16 GB RAM running a Chrome browser and we obtained the figure of 7.7s seconds, i.e. 3,800 annotations per second.

4 Related Work

The UIMA project (Ferrucci and Lally, 2004) provides an infrastructure to store unstructured documents. In contrast, the MLDM library and Langforia emphasize on simplicity, portability, ease of integration, minimal dependencies, and efficiency. Other toolchains include CoreNLP (Manning et al., 2014). However, CoreNLP cannot process the Wikipedia markup or easily integrate external tools. In addition, CoreNLP does not provide a storage model and its data structures are primarily meant to extend its functionalities. In contrast to CoreNLP, Langforia builds on Docforia that provides dynamic and typed annotations as well as multiple sublayers such as gold and predicted. Finally, CoreNLP does not provide a query API for its data structures.

The Langforia visualization tool is similar to the brat[4] components (Stenetorp et al., 2012) for the text visualization. Brat produces good visual results and has support for multiple layers of information. However, to the best of our knowledge, it lacks tooltip support in the embeddable version and it does not handle line-wrapped annotations well. In addition, it revealed too slow to render a large number of annotations in the documents we tested.

5 Conclusion and Future work

We described Langforia, a multilingual tool for processing text and visualizing annotations. Langforia builds on a multilayer document model (MLDM), structured in the form of a graph and unified tool chains. It enables a user to easily access the results of multilingual annotations and through its API to process large collections of text. Using it, we built a tabulated version of Wikipedia (Klang and Nugues, 2016) that can be queried using a SQL-like language. When applied to Wikipedia, MLDM links the different versions through an extensive use of URI indices and Wikidata Q-numbers.

6 Availability

The Langforia demonstration is accessible at: `http://vilde.cs.lth.se:9000/` and the web API at: `http://vilde.cs.lth.se:9000/api`. The source code is available from github at: `https://github.com/marcusklang/`.

Acknowledgments

This research was supported by Vetenskapsrådet, the Swedish research council, under the *Det digitaliserade samhället* program.

[4] `http://brat.nlplab.org/`

References

Anders Björkelund, Bernd Bohnet, Love Hafdell, and Pierre Nugues. 2010. A high-performance syntactic and semantic dependency parser. In *Coling 2010: Demonstration Volume*, pages 33–36, Beijing, August 23-27.

Jinho D. Choi. 2012. *Optimization of Natural Language Processing Components for Robustness and Scalability*. Ph.D. thesis, University of Colorado at Boulder, Boulder, CO, USA. AAI3549172.

Paolo Ferragina and Ugo Scaiella. 2010. Fast and accurate annotation of short texts with wikipedia pages. In *Proceedings of CIKM'10*, Toronto.

David Ferrucci and Adam Lally. 2004. UIMA: an architectural approach to unstructured information processing in the corporate research environment. *Natural Language Engineering*, 10(3-4):327–348, September.

David Angelo Ferrucci. 2012. Introduction to "This is Watson". *IBM Journal of Research and Development*, 56(3.4):1:1 –1:15, May-June.

Marcus Klang and Pierre Nugues. 2016. Wikiparq: A tabulated Wikipedia resource using the Parquet format. In *Proceedings of LREC 2016*, pages 4141–4148, Portorož, Slovenia.

Christopher D. Manning, Mihai Surdeanu, John Bauer, Jenny Finkel, Steven J. Bethard, and David McClosky. 2014. The Stanford CoreNLP natural language processing toolkit. In *Proceedings of 52nd Annual Meeting of the Association for Computational Linguistics: System Demonstrations*, pages 55–60, Baltimore, Maryland.

Rada Mihalcea and Andras Csomai. 2007. Wikify!: Linking documents to encyclopedic knowledge. In *Proceedings of the Sixteenth ACM Conference on CIKM*, CIKM '07, pages 233–242, Lisbon, Portugal.

Roberto Navigli and Simone Paolo Ponzetto. 2010. Babelnet: Building a very large multilingual semantic network. In *Proceedings of the 48th annual meeting of the ACL*, pages 216–225, Uppsala.

Joakim Nivre, Johan Hall, and Jens Nilsson. 2006. MaltParser: A data-driven parser-generator for dependency parsing. In *Proceedings of LREC-2006*, pages 2216–2219.

Robert Östling. 2013. Stagger: an open-source part of speech tagger for Swedish. *Northern European Journal of Language Technology*, 3:1–18.

Jason R. Smith, Chris Quirk, and Kristina Toutanova. 2010. Extracting parallel sentences from comparable corpora using document level alignment. In *Human Language Technologies: The 2010 Annual Conference of the North American Chapter of the Association for Computational Linguistics*, HLT '10, pages 403–411.

Pontus Stenetorp, Sampo Pyysalo, Goran Topić, Tomoko Ohta, Sophia Ananiadou, and Jun'ichi Tsujii. 2012. brat: a web-based tool for nlp-assisted text annotation. In *Proceedings of the Demonstrations at the 13th Conference of the European Chapter of the Association for Computational Linguistics*, pages 102–107, Avignon, France, April. Association for Computational Linguistics.

Anita: An Intelligent Text Adaptation Tool

Gustavo Henrique Paetzold and **Lucia Specia**
Department of Computer Science
University of Sheffield, UK
{g.h.paetzold,l.specia}@sheffield.ac.uk

Abstract

We introduce Anita: a flexible and intelligent Text Adaptation tool for web content that provides Text Simplification and Text Enhancement modules. Anita's simplification module features a state-of-the-art system that adapts texts according to the needs of individual users, and its enhancement module allows the user to search for a word's definitions, synonyms, translations, and visual cues through related images. These utilities are brought together in an easy-to-use interface of a freely available web browser extension.

1 Introduction

Readers who suffer from reading impairments find it difficult to understand certain types of texts which, to an average reader, would not pose any challenge. Low literacy readers and second language learners, for example, often have very limited vocabulary (Watanabe et al., 2009; Aluisio and Gasperin, 2010), while those with Dyslexia may have problems understanding the meaning of rare and/or long words (Ellis, 1993; Rello et al., 2013b). Other notable examples of such conditions are Aphasia and some forms of Autism, which can also hinder the patient's capability of comprehending sentences made up of a large amount of words and/or complex syntactic constructs (Devlin and Tait, 1998; Barbu et al., 2015).

Previous work has proposed a wide array of approaches that aim to adapt texts for these audiences. Text Simplification strategies are good examples of that. While Lexical Simplification approaches handle vocabulary limitations by replacing complex words with simpler alternatives (Devlin and Tait, 1998; Paetzold and Specia, 2016a), Syntactic Simplification approaches address the problem of long, complex syntactic constructs by re-structuring them (Siddharthan, 2006; Paetzold and Specia, 2013). Text Enhancement approaches can also help: Devlin and Unthank (2006), Watanabe et al. (2009) and Azab et al. (2015) adorn the words of a text with definitions, images and synonyms in order to facilitate their comprehension. Rello et al. (2013a) reveal that while simplification tends to increase a document's readability, enhancement tends to improve its comprehensibility.

One important limitation of the state of the art Text Adaptation systems is that they are not available for download and/or use. Online demos are provided for some, but they only allow the processing of small snippets of text through online interfaces. Another limitation is that the adaptations made by these systems are not personalised i.e. they will be the same for each and every user, regardless of their profiles and backgrounds.

There are, however, commercial reading/writing assistance tools, such as Simplish[1], texthelp[2] and Fast ForWord[3], which provide high quality services for those with reading difficulties. These tools are not free and most of them focus on text-to-speech capabilities, which makes them limited in functionality and inaccessible to the wider public.

In this contribution, we introduce Anita: a freely available Text Adaptation tool that, unlike previous work, tailors the provided assistance with respect to the needs of each user. In the sections that follow,

[1]http://www.simplish.org

[2]https://www.texthelp.com

[3]http://www.scilearn.com/products/reading-assistant

Proceedings of COLING 2016, the 26th International Conference on Computational Linguistics: System Demonstrations, pages 79–83, Osaka, Japan, December 11-17 2016.

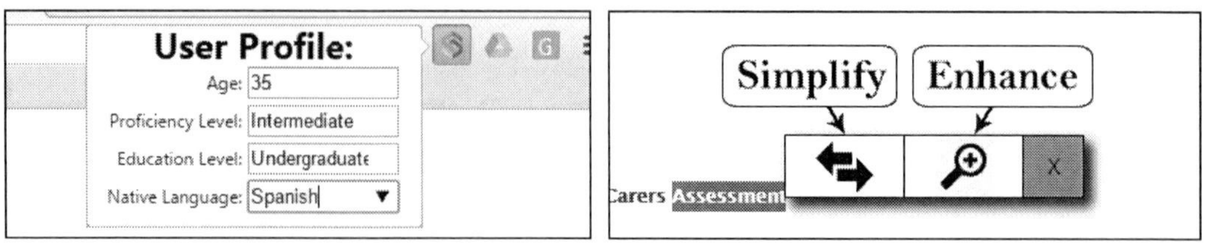

(a) User profile interface

(b) Reading assistance wizard

Figure 1: Interface components of Anita

we describe Anita and its two main modules.

2 System Description

Anita is a Google Chrome extension that aims to assist individuals from various target audiences, such as non-native speakers and the poorly literate, to read and understand the content of web pages. Anita innovates by providing a minimalistic, user-friendly interface, as well as a wide array of state of the art Text Adaptation solutions for English, including an intelligent Lexical Simplification module.

In order to use Anita, the user must download and install the extension. Once installed, the tool can be configured with respect to the user's profile information, which will help in the assistance customisation process. Figure 1a illustrates the tool's profiling interface.

With a profile at hand, the tool is ready to provide personalised reading assistance. To launch it, the user must select a word they do not understand. The reading assistance wizard depicted in Figure 1b will then pop-up. Anita currently offers two types of adaptation: Simplification and Enhancement.

3 Simplification Module

Anita's simplification module attempts to replace the selected word with a simpler alternative. To do so, Anita first finds the sentence containing the selected word and then sends this information to the remote server where Anita's Lexical Simplification engine is running. The engine runs a state-of-the-art Lexical Simplification system powered by the LEXenstein framework (Paetzold and Specia, 2015). The strategy used here has been shown to outperform all other simplifiers from previous work (Paetzold and Specia, 2016a). Upon receiving a simplification request for a word, Anita's simplifier performs the following steps:

1. **Generation:** A context-aware word embeddings model trained over 7 billion words which accounts for grammatical information (Paetzold and Specia, 2016b) is used to produce candidate substitutions for the word.

2. **Selection:** The Unsupervised Boundary Ranking approach (Paetzold and Specia, 2016b) is used to select the candidates that best fit the context of the complex word.

3. **Ranking:** The selected candidates are ranked using a Supervised Boundary Ranking approach (Paetzold and Specia, 2015). The ranker is trained over a dataset composed of simplicity rankings produced by hundreds of non-native English speakers with different backgrounds, and checks the user's profile to determine which candidate best fits the user's simplification needs.

4. **Replacement:** Finally, the simplifier returns a response from the remote server to the chrome extension with the highest ranked candidate. The chrome extension then temporarily modifies the website's content for the user by replacing the selected word with the alternative provided.

Once the word is simplified, Anita highlights it, as illustrated in Figure 2a. If the highlighted word is selected again, the user will be presented with the interface in Figure 2b, which allows to either undo the simplification or enhance it. If the user chooses to undo the simplification, Anita will send a report to the

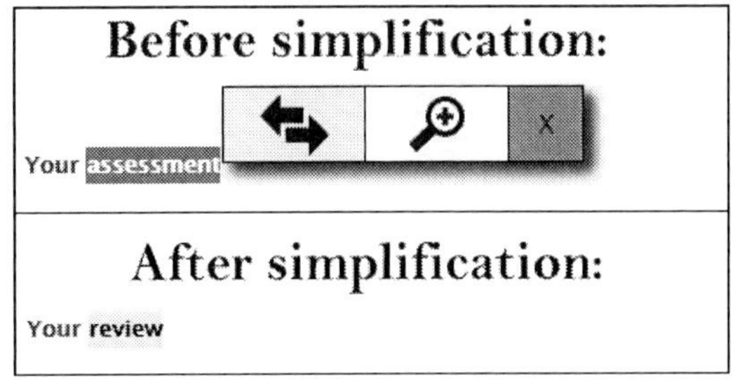

(a) Simplification example

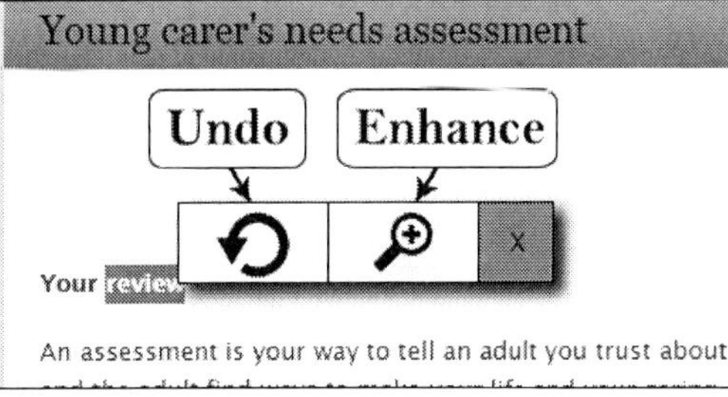

(b) Reading assistance wizard for simplified word

Figure 2: Anita's Simplification module

remote server containing the rejected simplification. The content of the report is then fed as a negative training instance to Anita's Lexical Simplification system, which is periodically re-trained to improve prediction for specific users' needs.

4 Enhancement Module

Anita's enhancement module allows the users to learn more about the words they find complex. Unlike in simplification, enhancement does not require the website's content to be modified in any way. As discussed in (Devlin and Unthank, 2006; Rello et al., 2013a), enhancements can help "jog" the memory of the user, and consequently increase comprehensibility. They are also preferred by many as a better alternative to "dumbing down" the language: by explaining a complex concept instead of replacing it by a simpler one, the reader is given the opportunity to learn about a new concept.

When the user requests an enhancement, they will be presented with the interface illustrated in Figures 3a through 3d. The enhancement interface offers the following services, all of which can be customised:

- **Definitions:** Shows dictionary definitions of the word. In the demo version of the tool, the definitions are queried from the Merriam Dictionary and Thesaurus[4], which provides a free API.
- **Synonyms:** Shows synonyms of the word. In the demo version of the tool, synonyms are also queried from the Merriam Dictionary.
- **Translations:** Shows machine translations of the word and of its synonyms. The language in which the translations are presented is defined in the User Profile interface (Section 2). Translations are currently produced by the Yandex API[5], which is also free.
- **Images:** Shows images related to the word. In the demo version of the tool, the images are freely available thumbnails queried from the Getty Images API [6].

Anita's word enhancements are customised through ranking: definitions, synonyms and translations are ranked so that the most helpful among them are featured at the top of the list. To do so, Anita employs the same Supervised Boundary Ranking strategy used in its Simplification module to rank synonyms and their translations by simplicity, based on the user's profile. In order to rank definitions, it first ranks the simplicity of all words in every one of them, then places definitions with the highest average word simplicity at the top of the list.

5 Final Remarks

We introduced Anita, an intelligent Text Adaptation tool composed of a Simplification module, which continuously learns how to adapt its simplifications to the users' needs, and an Enhancement module,

[4]http://www.merriam-webster.com
[5]https://www.yandex.com
[6]http://www.gettyimages.com

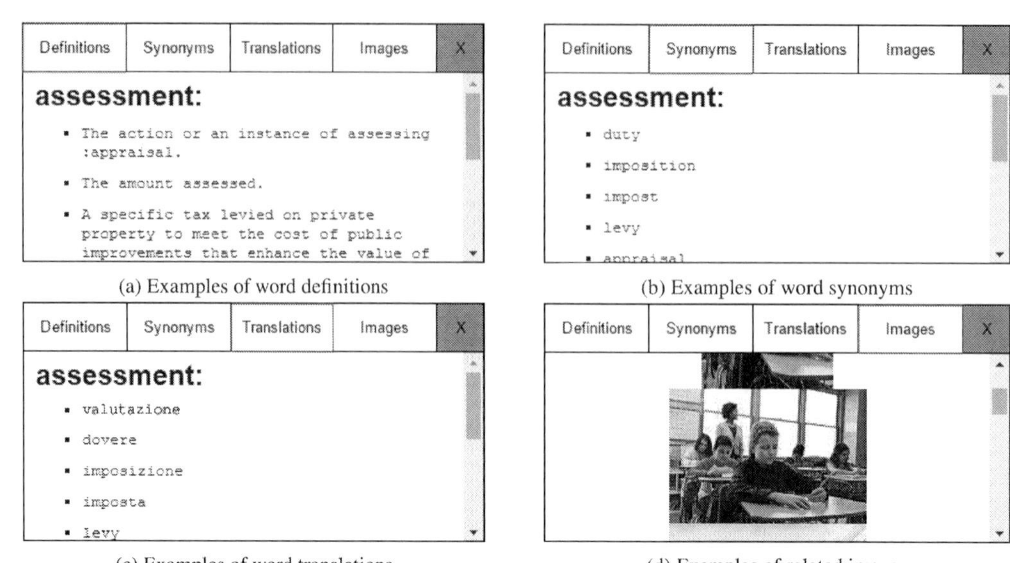

(a) Examples of word definitions

(b) Examples of word synonyms

(c) Examples of word translations

(d) Examples of related images

Figure 3: Anita's Enhancement module

which allows the user to query for different types of information about words. Anita is an open-source tool from the SIMPATICO project[7] that will be released under a permissive BSD license. In the future, we will extend the tool by adding syntactic and semantic simplification functionalities. We also intend to follow the efforts of (Rello et al., 2013a) and conduct studies in order to investigate how the Anita utilities affect readability and comprehensibility for users.

Acknowledgements

This work has been partially supported by the European Commission project SIMPATICO (H2020-EURO-6-2015, grant number 692819).

References

Sandra Aluisio and Caroline Gasperin. 2010. Fostering digital inclusion and accessibility: The porsimples project for simplification of portuguese texts. In *Proceedings of the 2010 NAACL*, pages 46–53.

Mahmoud Azab, Chris Hokamp, and Rada Mihalcea. 2015. Using word semantics to assist english as a second language learners. In *Proceedings of NAACL*, pages 116–120.

Eduard Barbu, M Teresa Martín-Valdivia, Eugenio Martínez-Cámara, and L Alfonso Ureña-López. 2015. Language technologies applied to document simplification for helping autistic people. *Expert Systems with Applications*, 42:5076–5086.

Siobhan Devlin and John Tait. 1998. The use of a psycholinguistic database in the simplification of text for aphasic readers. *Linguistic Databases*, pages 161–173.

Siobhan Devlin and Gary Unthank. 2006. Helping aphasic people process online information. In *Proceedings of the 8th SIGACCESS*, pages 225–226.

A.W. Ellis. 1993. *Reading, Writing and Dyslexia: A Cognitive Analysis*. Open University Press.

Gustavo H. Paetzold and Lucia Specia. 2013. Text simplification as tree transduction. In *Proceedings of the 9th STIL*, pages 116–125.

Gustavo Henrique Paetzold and Lucia Specia. 2015. Lexenstein: A framework for lexical simplification. In *Proceedings of The 53rd ACL*, pages 85–90.

[7]http://www.simpatico-project.eu

Gustavo Henrique Paetzold and Lucia Specia. 2016a. Benchmarking lexical simplification systems. In *Proceedings of the 10th LREC*.

Gustavo Henrique Paetzold and Lucia Specia. 2016b. Unsupervised lexical simplification for non-native speakers. In *Proceedings of The 30th AAAI*, pages 3761–3767.

Luz Rello, Ricardo Baeza-Yates, Stefan Bott, and Horacio Saggion. 2013a. Simplify or help?: text simplification strategies for people with dyslexia. In *Proceedings of the 10th W4A*, pages 1–10.

Luz Rello, Ricardo Baeza-Yates, Laura Dempere-Marco, and Horacio Saggion. 2013b. Frequent words improve readability and short words improve understandability for people with dyslexia. *Human-Computer Interaction*, pages 203–219.

Advaith Siddharthan. 2006. Syntactic simplification and text cohesion. *Research on Language and Computation*, 4(1):77–109, March.

Willian Massami Watanabe, Arnaldo Candido Junior, Vinícius Rodriguez Uzêda, Renata Pontin de Mattos Fortes, Thiago Alexandre Salgueiro Pardo, and Sandra Maria Aluísio. 2009. Facilita: reading assistance for low-literacy readers. In *Proceedings of the 27th ACM*, pages 29–36.

HistoryComparator: Interactive Across-Time Comparison in Document Archives

Adam Jatowt
Kyoto University
adam@dl.kuis.kyoto-u.ac.jp

Marc Bron
University of Amsterdam
marc.bron@gmail.com

Abstract

Recent years have witnessed significant increase in the number of large scale digital collections of archival documents such as news articles, books, etc. Typically, users access these collections through searching or browsing. In this paper we investigate another way of accessing temporal collections - *across-time comparison*, i.e., comparing query-relevant information at different periods in the past. We propose an interactive framework called *HistoryComparator* for contrastively analyzing concepts in archival document collections at different time periods.

1 Introduction

The role of history and cultural memory in shaping today's society cannot be overestimated. We often refer to the past for variety of reasons including supporting decision making processes (Gilovich, 1981). Up to recent years analyzing large samples of historical documents was difficult due to the nature of the materials studied, e.g., paper records stored in physically distributed archives. Now, with the availability of large digitized collections, academia and industry are looking into the utility of using computational methods on large samples of digitized records to study human history and culture (Odijk *et al.*, 2012). Understanding and making use of such collections often necessitates across-time comparison to elucidate commonalities and differences between entities existing at different times. Comparison is in fact a common tool used by historians and social scientists for insightful analysis. *Comparative history* (Halperin, 1982), in particular, often relies on across-time comparative analysis presuming that nothing can be correctly understood without proper comparison and grounding (even a timeline is a comparison tool, albeit, a very simple one).

We propose in this paper an interactive framework called *HistoryComparator* for across-time comparison of query result sets within archival document collections. Rather than comparing individual documents, our framework contrasts temporal slices of corpora containing documents related to a query (e.g., entity or event). The proposed system is build on the top of a retrieval engine and offers two basic comparison modes, *contrastive term cloud view* and *contrastive graph view*. The former generates comparative text summaries in the form of term clouds, while the latter aligns networks composed of the top query-related terms. Provided functionalities include, among others, *keyword in temporal context*, *time-based term adjustment* and *sentiment-level correlation* of collection snapshots. In addition, a range of *synchronization facilities* are provided for facilitating effective comparison.

Relatively little research focused on interactively comparing collections of archival text documents. Odijk *et al.* (2012) demonstrated interactive environment to visualize information on volume and correlation of words and documents over time. *Texcavator* (van Eijnatten *et al.* 2014) is a framework integrating analytical tools such as concept clustering, sentiment mining, and named entity recognition to produce world clouds, timelines and other visualizations. The closest work to ours is perhaps an interactive tool for exploratory search in document collections proposed by Bron *et al.* (2012). Like our system, theirs uses the concept of double columns and term clouds for finding interesting information. However, it does not provide the same comparative facilities like our system, neither it offers graph-based contrastive interface.

Proceedings of COLING 2016, the 26th International Conference on Computational Linguistics: System Demonstrations, pages 84–88, Osaka, Japan, December 11-17 2016.

2 HistoryComparator

We employ dual-column visualization (Bron *et al.*, 2012) (see Fig. 1). The side-by-side composition allows immediate comparison alleviating cognitive burden of spotting commonalities and differences. A user enters two queries (they can have the same syntactic form for representing the same concept or they can rather represent two different things) and sets the corresponding time periods in both the left and the right column. The queries are next issued against an underlying document collection subject to the input time constraints. Based on the returned documents the results are displayed in each column.

2.1 Contrastive Term Cloud View

In the first mode the system displays the key terms related to the input query as term clouds of both the collection subsets (see Fig. 1). Term clouds are convenient technique for summarizing large text collections where sizes of terms denote their importance (Bateman *et al.*, 2008). Summarizing a collection of a few thousands documents by selecting whole sentences is not effective since query terms occur in a multitude of possible contexts, and, hence, presenting all such contexts as sentences would lead to prohibitively large summaries. On the other hand, term clouds have been found useful for quick and effortless overview of large portions of textual data (Bateman *et al.*, 2008). In our system, terms in both the columns are color-coded to emphasize differences and similarities. While the font size of each term is bound to its relative frequency in a given time period, the color is associated with the relative difference of frequencies. That is, terms prevailing more in one time period and less in the other are either more red or more blue depending on the column they are shown in (blue for left and red for right). Black color indicates terms with similar rate of occurrence in both the compared periods. Font size and color selection can be set based on either linear or logarithmic scales. Furthermore, the following options are provided:

- Adjustable number of terms to be shown in each column by manipulating sliders
- Choice of term ordering: alphabetically or by frequency
- Grouping separately colored and black terms.

Fig. 1 shows the results of example query: `world trade center` (WTC) at the time immediately after the buildings' collapse (left column) and at about 10 years later (right column). We next list and discuss the key components of the contrastive term cloud view.

Keyword in temporal context. Upon clicking on any term displayed in either column, HistoryComparator displays term's contextual information in a popup window as portrayed in Fig. 2. If the same term is also listed in the results of the other column, the second popup window will automatically be shown in that column enabling term's contexts' comparison across the two columns. The context of the term is reflected by three representative text snippets. These are selected from all the snippets that contain both the clicked term and the query words. The selection is done by averaging the minimum distances expressed as the number of words between each of the query words and the selected term with additional penalty in case of missing query terms. The selected term and the query words have backgrounds colored for their easy spotting in the displayed sentences. Additional information about the term includes its frequency and sentiment score. The pop-up windows shown in Fig. 2 have been generated from the results of Fig. 1 after a term `construction` has been clicked. Sentences in the left column refer to the information about construction materials used in the former WTC building or to the National Construction Safety Team investigating the location of the buildings, while the same word in the right column refers to constructing a new building in the area of the former WTC.

Similar terms. Besides information about the context of a selected term, the system also displays terms with similar contexts to it in both the columns (Fig. 2). Term similarities are computed as the overlap of the sets of the top co-occurring words found by applying Jaccard Coefficient. The top 5 similar terms to the target term are displayed in each column.

Time-based term adjustment. Sometimes changes are due to outside-driven effects rather than due to the change of the compared query (e.g., entity) across time. A new term may appear simply because of the time passage and, hence, not due to the change specific (related) to the query. For example, a term `computer` is considered as novel in the present time in the results of a query unrelated to computers (e.g., `tokyo`) when compared to some past period for this query, merely, due to the recent significant increase in the use of computers. For capturing the effect of time, we utilize background document collections which are built on the random sample of documents (unrelated to the queries) collected from each time period set by the user. Three options are provided in the system in regards to the time effect:

- *No adjustment*: no adjustment done (default option).
- *Term normalization*: the frequency of each term within the foreground sub-collection is normalized by dividing it by its corresponding frequency in the background sub-collection.
- *Visual indication*: in this option an additional visual signal is added to each term (see Fig. 3) to explicitly inform about term's dependency on the above-discussed time effect. In particular, a rectangle frame surrounding each term is added. The width of the frame is bound to the term's frequency in the corresponding background collection while its color depends on the relative difference of the term's background frequencies across both the compared time periods. These inform users to what extent the term frequency in each column and its column-wise difference are affected by time. Frame sizes and colors can be based on either linear or logarithmic scales.

Note that when selecting the visual indication mode, in total, four signals are visible about each term in either time period (column): term's normalized frequency in the foreground collection (i.e., font size), the difference of term's foreground frequency in the target time period and foreground frequency in the other time period (i.e., font color), term's normalized background frequency (i.e., frame width) and the difference of the term's background frequencies in both the compared time periods (i.e., frame color).

Popularity trend. The popularity of queries in each time period is also shown above the term clouds in the form of two time series corresponding to both the time periods (see Fig. 1). Furthermore, a user can also click on any term in the term clouds to display its popularity across time.

Sentiment analysis. Temporal changes in sentiment associated with query at different times can constitute complementary information for more exhaustive analysis. To study fluctuations in emotional factors across time we utilize SentiWordnet[1]. Sentiment orientations in relation to the query are calculated by summing sentiment scores of terms in the returned results for each time period (each column). The bottom bar displays in each column the rate of positive vs. negative orientations. A user can thus observe the change in sentiment value across time. In the example shown in Fig. 1 we can notice that the recent context in which the world trade center is mentioned is slightly more positive than the context in which it was mentioned during and right after the building's collapse.

Lastly, hovering mouse over the positive (negative) parts of the sentiment bar highlights positive (negative) terms in the corresponding column to explain reasons behind a particular sentiment rate.

2.2 Contrastive Graph View

Term clouds cannot capture changes in relations between terms over time. To compare the inter-word relations, we provide the second view, *contrastive graph view*, as portrayed in Fig. 4. In this view the top frequent words are positioned as nodes in two force-directed graphs in the columns. To inform about the term importance, the node size is dependent on the term frequency. Terms that frequently co-occur with each other are connected by the edge whose width is determined by the value of Jaccard coefficient computed on their co-occurrence and occurrence rates. The graphs are then composed of the top important nodes and the top high-scored edges linking them. Same as in the contrastive term cloud view, the color of a node in a given column depends on the relative frequency difference of a term underlying the node across both the columns. In addition to the node coloring, the color of edges conveys information on whether the connected nodes have similar or different affinity across the compared periods. To enable effective comparison, the positions of nodes in both the graphs are aligned. In other words, the terms which are same in both the graphs are placed in the same relative positions.

---

[1] http://sentiwordnet.isti.cnr.it/

Selecting any node triggers automatic selection of an identical node/edge in the other column. The nodes can also have their positions rearranged. As the graphs are synchronized, any displacement in one column results in an equal displacement in the other column.

Dynamic adjustment of node and link counts. Too many nodes or links may clutter the view. The proposed system provides then an easy way for adjusting the number of nodes or edges by manipulating sliders in each column. Less important nodes or edges can be then increasingly added to either graph by incrementing sliders. When the sliders are synchronized (synchronization option), the change in one column triggers the same change in the other column. This allows for synchronized comparison of node and edge importance. Such progressive edge increment permits also observing gradual additions of edges starting from the most important to less important ones.

Similar nodes detection. Like in the contrastive term cloud view, a user can select a node by double clicking on it in order to see its most similar nodes in the other column.

3 Architecture

The system is implemented using Perl 5.10 and works in the client-server mode. The Web interface depends on Mojolicious Web Application Framework[2]. We use jQuery as foundation for JavaScript design together with D3[3] visualizations. The time plots are generated using jQuery plugin called jqPlot[4]. The user-specified time periods are used for constructing time-constrained queries. These time periods can be set to be divided into L non-overlapping equal-size time units (by default, $L=1$). L queries would be then sent to the underlying search engine together with associated time constrains. The latter are defined by the starting and ending points of each of L units. By issuing L ($L \gg 1$) queries over smaller, consecutive time units, instead of a single query over the entire chosen time period, the system effectively "forces" the search engine to retrieve documents more or less uniformly over time rather than from only one of few time points. As underlying data sources, currently, our system uses the New York Times Article Archive on Solr, Google News Archive and Google Blog search engines. The content of each collected document is subject to stop word removal, tokenization and normalization.

4 Conclusions

To support effective search and discovery in text archives, we have introduced in this paper a novel framework for the comparative analysis of historical document collections both on the term (contrastive term cloud view) and term association (contrastive graph view) levels. In future, we plan to suggest relevant and interesting time periods for contrasting entities by comparing term distributions over time.

Acknowledgments

This work has been partially supported by Grant-in-Aid for Scientific Research (No. 15K12158) from MEXT of Japan and by the JST research promotion program Presto/Sakigake.

References

Bateman, S., Gutwin, C., Nacenta, M.: Seeing Things in the Clouds: The Effect of Visual Features on Tag Cloud Selections. Proceedings of the HT 2008, pp. 193–202, 2008.

Bron, M, van Gorp, J., Nack, F., de Rijke, M., Vishneuski, A., and de Leeuw, S. A Subjunctive Exploratory Search Interface to Support Media Studies Rearchers. Proceedings of the SIGIR 2012, pp. 425-434, 2012.

van Eijnatten, J., Verheul, J., Pieters, T. TS Tools: Using Texcavator to Map Public Discourse. TS: Tijdschrift voor Tijdschriftstudies, issue 35, pp. 59-65, 2014.

Gilovich, T. 1981. Seeing the past in the present: The Effect of Associations to Familiar Events on Judgments and Decisions. Journal of Personality and Social Psychology, 40(5):797.

---

[2] http://mojolicio.us/
[3] https://d3js.org/
[4] http://www.jqplot.com/

Halperin C.J. et al. 1982. Comparative History in Theory and Practice: A discussion. The American Hist. Rev., 87(1):123–143.

Odijk, D., Santucci, G., de Rijke, M., Angelini, M., and Granato, G. Exploring Word Meaning through Time. Proceedings of the TAIA 2012 Workshop in conjunction with SIGIR 2012. Portland, USA.

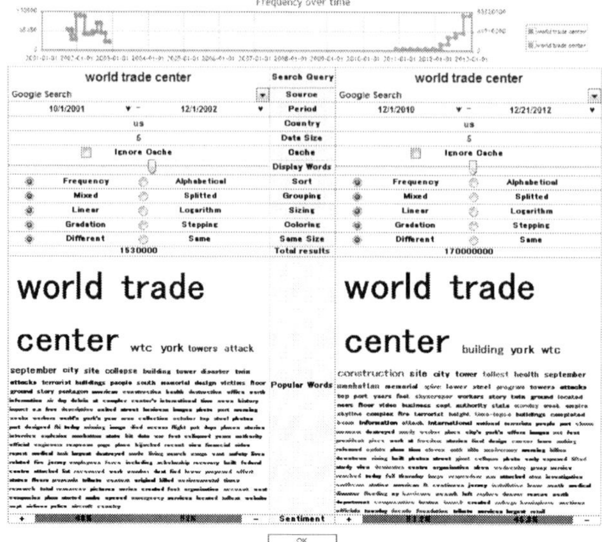

Figure 1: System interface and output for query `world trade center`.

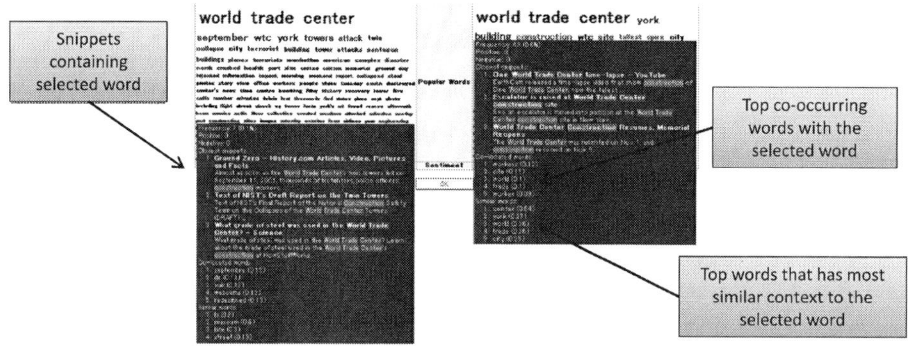

Figure 2: Popup windows due to highlighting term `construction` in the left column of Fig. 1.

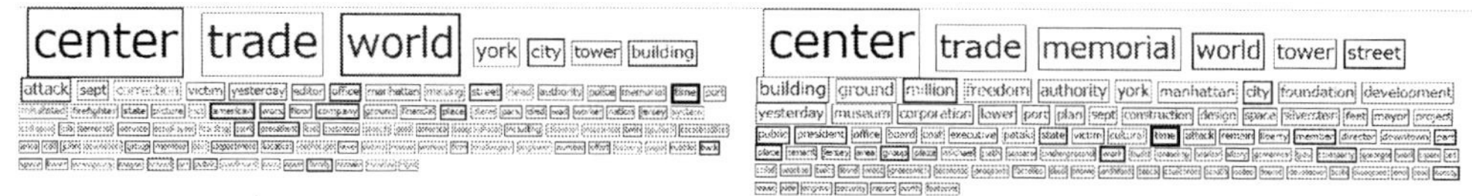

Figure 3: Snapshot of term clouds with visual adjustment of time passage effect.

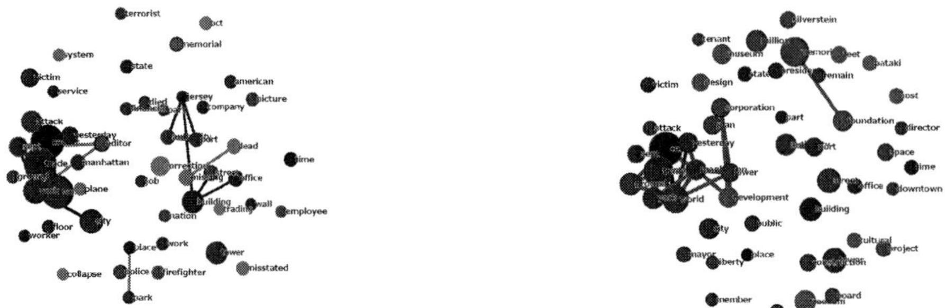

Figure 4: Snapshot of the contrastive graphs in the contrastive graph view.

On-line Multilingual Linguistic Services

Eric Wehrli LATL / University of Geneva
Yves Scherrer LATL / University of Geneva
Luka Nerima LATL / University of Geneva
{Eric.Wehrli, Yves.Scherrer, Luka.Nerima}@unige.ch

Abstract

In this demo, we present our free on-line multilingual linguistic services which allow to analyze sentences or to extract collocations from a corpus directly on-line, or by uploading a corpus. They are available for 8 European languages and can also be accessed as web services by programs.

1 Introduction

Linguistic information is useful for a wide-range of applications dealing with natural language. In a large number of cases, lexical disambiguation and part-of-speech (POS) assignment is all that is needed; in some other cases, additional information, such as phrase-structure representations or dependency structures, grammatical functions or multiword expressions may also prove useful.

To satisfy such needs, we have developed an on-line platform of linguistic services offering a multilingual parser/tagger for 8 European languages[1] (English, French, German, Greek, Italian, Portuguese, Romanian, Spanish), as well as a collocation extraction tool for the same languages. Those services can be freely accessed either directly on a dedicated webpage (`http://latlapps.unige.ch`), or (in the case of the parser/tagger) by programs interacting with the services (an example of a Python script is given below). While several open systems are available for POS-tagging and dependency parsing[2] or terminology extraction[3], their integration into an application requires some – sometimes non-trivial – computational competence. Furthermore, none of the parsers/taggers handles MWEs very satisfactorily, in particular when the two terms are distant from each other or in reverse order. Our tools, on the other hand, are specifically designed for users with no particular computational literacy. They do not require from the user any download, installation or adaptation if used on-line, and their integration in an application, using one the scripts described below is quite easy. Furthermore, by default, the parser handles collocations and other MWEs, as well as anaphora resolution (limited to 3rd person personal pronouns). When used in the tagger mode, it can be set to display grammatical functions and collocations (see below for details).

The following sections give a short description of the Fips parser, which is at the core of all the tools, some specific details and descriptions of the parser/tagger tool, and finally a description of the collocation extraction tool.

2 The Fips parser/tagger

The Fips multilingual parser (Wehrli, 2007; Wehrli & Nerima, 2015) is a grammar-based constituency parser using both attachment rules (to build phrase-structure representations) and specific procedures

[1]The parsing quality is not identical for all languages. The best results are achieved with English and French, then German, Spanish, Italian, then Portuguese and Greek, and finally Romanian.

[2]For instance, the Stanford parser (Klein & Manning, 2003; Chen & Manning, 2014), the MaltParser (Nivre et al. 2007), TreeTagger (Schmidt, 1995), Mate Tools (Bohnet et al., 2013), SyntaxNet (Andor et al, 2016), Marmot (Mueller et al, 2013).

[3]The Sketch engine (Kilgarriff et al., 2014), mwetoolkit (Ramisch, 2015).

Proceedings of COLING 2016, the 26th International Conference on Computational Linguistics: System Demonstrations, pages 89–92, Osaka, Japan, December 11-17 2016.

to compute properties such as long-distance dependencies, argument-structure building, coordination structures, and so on. It uses an information-rich lexical database containing inflected words, lexemes and collocations.

The Fips parser/tagger is a powerful tool to analyse textual corpora. It can display results in several modes, ranging from phrase-structure representation (along the lines of Chomskyan generative grammar), to easier to read or to process part-of-speech representations, which can be optionally augmented with grammatical functions, dependency relations and collocations. By default, we use the universal tagset, but a richer tagset is also available, displaying number, gender, case, tense, modality, etc. Fips computes several analyses in parallel, but only the best analysis is dispalayed in the on-line service.

Figure 1, below shows a screenshot of the results returned by the Fips service for the short German example *Türkische Panzer rücken nach Syrien vor. 'Turkish tanks move forward towards Syria'* . In this example, Fips is selected with the Tagger output and rich POS tagset. The results show the words in column 1, the rich tags in column 2, the position of the first letter of each word with respect to the beginning of the sentence in column 3, the lexeme[4] in column 4. Column 5 displays the grammatical function associated with the syntactic head of each constituent (SU for subject, PO for prepositional object) and the argument structure of the predicate (the particle verb *vorrücken* 'move forward') with the grammatical function labels and the (semantic) head of each argument.

Türkische	ADJ-PLU-MAS-NOM-ACC	1	türkisch		
Panzer	NOM-PLU-MAS-NOM-ACC-GEN	11	Panzer	SU	
rücken	VER-IND-PRE-3-PLU	18	vor|rücken		SU:Panzer PO:Syrien
nach	PRE	25	nach	PO	
Syrien	NOM-SIN-NEU-DAT	30	Syrien		
vor	PART	37	vor		

Figure 1: Fips German analysis in Tagger mode

3 Collocation extraction

The collocation extraction tool is based on the Fips parser. In a nutshell, the input corpus is first parsed, sentence by sentence. For each parsed tree, all the word pairs in a given syntactic configuration (eg. adjective-noun, noun-noun, noun-preposition-noun, verb-object, subject-verb, etc.) are extracted as potential collocations and stored in a database. At the end of the process, the database is filtered by means of an association measure – by default log-likelihood (cf. Dunning, 1993)– and the results can be displayed[5]. As pointed out by Seretan (2011), the main advantage of this syntax-based method is (i) a much better precision than other systems and (ii) better recall with collocations likely to have the two terms separated by several words and/or in reverse order, such as verb-object, subject-verb or particle verb (for instance in German).

Figure 2 shows the web page for collocation extraction. The user selects a language and uploads the desired corpus, either in ANSI or UTF-8 format. Optionally the user can choose another association measure, a minimal score for association measure and the minimal number of occurrences. As the treatment of a large corpus can take several minutes or more, the user can also leave an e-mail address to receive a notification when processing is completed, along with the link to the results.

Figure 3 shows the results obtained by the extraction process on a small sample of the Europarl corpus (0.5 MB) for collocations of type verb-object. By clicking on a collocation type, the user will see all the occurrences of that collocation in the corpus.

[4]The lexeme associated with the word *rücken* is the particle verb *vorrücken* ("to move forward"). We inserted a vertical bar to make it explicit.

[5]See Seretan (2011) for a thorough description of the extraction method and comparison to other extraction tools.

Collocation extraction

Language: English

Association measure (AM): Log Likelihood Ratio

AM score (min.): 0.0

Occurrences (min.): 3

Input file:

Choose File ep-00-02-15.txt

File encoding: ANSI, UTF-8. Size limit: 500 000 words. The extraction method is described here.

[Optional] Enter an e-mail address if you wish to be notified when processing is completed: luka.nerima@unige.ch

Extract

Figure 2: The Collocation extraction web page

7;	60.81;	answer;;question;	Verb-Object;
9;	60.19;	take;;step;	Verb-Object;
9;	58.76;	make;;effort;	Verb-Object;
10;	52.96;	address;;issue;	Verb-Object;
8;	50.44;	meet;;challenge;	Verb-Object;
5;	46.56;	play;;role;	Verb-Object;
8;	44.68;	make;;decision;	Verb-Object;
6;	44.57;	close;;debate;	Verb-Object;
3;	38.38;	pay;;attention;	Verb-Object;

Figure 3: Verb-object collocations

4 Accessing the online services programmatically

We provide both a Python and a PHP scripts to integrate the linguistic services into existing pipelines[6]. The Python script accesses the parser/tagger tool and provides the same parameters as the web version. Its usage is as follows:

```
python latlapps.py application language inputfilepath outputfilepath
```

where the `application` parameter accepts the same values as the web version. The `language` parameters specifies the language of the input data in the form of the two-letter ISO code. The third and fourth parameters specify the path to the file to be analyzed, and to the file to be created with the results of the analysis. Both files are expected to be in UTF-8 encoding. On Unix systems, these two parameters can be replaced by standard input and standard output pipes.

The script sends the input text line by line to the linguistic service. Therefore, it is important that each line corresponds to a linguistically meaningful entity such as a sentence or a paragraph. Figure 4 shows an example of the use of the Python script for our German sentence.

```
$ echo "Türkische Panzer rücken nach Syrien vor" | python latlapps.py Tagger de
```

Figure 4: Usage example of the latlapps.py script

The input sentence is communicated to the script by standard input, and the result –same as the one

[6]Both scripts are available on the site `http://latlapps.unige.ch`.

given in Figure 1 above– is written on standard output (the terminal). The application is 'Tagger' and the language code is 'de', which stands for German.

For PHP, two scripts are provided: one to be used from a command line with the same parameters as the Python script, while the second is designed to be used in an HTML file, as in the example below.

```
<form name="form1" id="form1" method="post" action="latlapps4html.php" >
```

The link to the script is done through the `action` attribute of the `form` tag. In the definition of the form, the application field name must be `ap` and the language field name must be `ln`.

References

Andor, D., Ch. Alberti, D. Weiss, A. Severyn, A. Presta, K. Ganchev, S. Petrov & M. Collins, 2016. "Globally Normalized Transition-Based Neural Networks", *Proceedings of ACL 2016*, 2442-2452.

Bonnet, B., J. Nivre, I. Boguslavsky, R. Farkas, F. Ginter & J. Hajic, 2013. "Joint Morphological and Syntactic Analysis for Richly Inflected Languages", *Proceedings of TACL* 1, 415-428.

Chen, D. and Ch. Manning, 2014. "A Fast and Accurate Dependency Parser using Neural Networks", *Proceedings of EMNLP 2014.*

Kilgarriff, A., V. Baisa, J. Busta, M. Jakubicek, V. Kovar, J. Michelfeit, P. Rychly, V. Suchomel, 2014. "The Sketch Engine: ten years on", *Lexicography*, vol. 1, Issue 1, 7-36.

Klein, D. & Ch. Manning, 2003. "Accurate Unlexicalized Parsing" *Proceeding of ACL 2014*, 423-430.

Mueller, T., H. Schmid & H. Schütze, 2013. "Efficient Higher-Order CRFs for Morphological Tagging", *Proceedings of EMNLP 2013*, 322-332.

Nivre, J., J. Hall, J. Nilsson, A Chanev, G. Eryigit, S. Kubler, S. Marinov & E. Marsi, 2007. "MaltParser: language-independent system for data-driven dependency parsing", *Natural Language Engineering* 13.2, 95-135.

Petrov, S., D. Das & R. McDonald, 2012. "A Universal Part-of-Speech Tagset", in *Proceeding of LREC 2012*, 2089-2096.

Ramisch, C. 2015. *Multiword Expressions Acquisition: A Generic and Open Framework*, Theory and Applications of Natural Language Processing, Springer.

Schmidt, H. 1995. "Improvements in Part-of-Speech Tagging with an Application to German", *Proceedings of the ACL SIGDAT Workshop*, Dublin.

Seretan, V. 2011. *Syntax-based Collocation Extraction*, Springer.

Wehrli, E. 2007. "Fips, a "deep" linguistic multilingual parser" in *Proceedings of the ACL 2007 Workshop on Deep Linguistic processing*, 120-127.

Wehrli, E. & L. Nerima, 2015. "The Fips Multilingual Parser", in N. Gala, R. Rapp, and G. Bel-Enguix (eds.), *Language Production, Cognition and The Lexicon.* Text, Speech and Language Technology 48, Springer, 473-490.

A Customizable Editor for Text Simplification

John Lee, Wenlong Zhao
Dept. of Linguistics and Translation
City University of Hong Kong
Hong Kong SAR, China
jsylee@cityu.edu.hk
wenlzhao@gmail.com

Wenxiu Xie
Cisco School of Informatics
Guangdong University of Foreign Studies
Guangzhou, China
vasiliky@outlook.com

Abstract

We present a browser-based editor for simplifying English text. Given an input sentence, the editor performs both syntactic and lexical simplification. It splits a complex sentence into shorter ones, and suggests word substitutions in drop-down lists. The user can choose the best substitution from the list, undo any inappropriate splitting, and further edit the sentence as necessary. A significant novelty is that the system accepts a customized vocabulary list for a target reader population. It identifies all words in the text that do not belong to the list, and attempts to substitute them with words from the list, thus producing a text tailored for the targeted readers.

1 Introduction

The task of *text simplification* aims to rewrite a sentence so as to reduce its lexical and syntactic complexity, while preserving its meaning and grammaticality. Consider the complex sentence "The professor, carrying numerous books, entered the room." It can be rewritten into two simple sentences, "The teacher entered the room." and "He was carrying many books." The rewriting process involves both syntactic and lexical simplification. The former decomposes the complex sentence, extracting the participial phrase "carrying numerous books" and turning it into a separate sentence. The latter replaces the word "professor" with the simpler word "teacher", and "numerous" with "many".

It is well known that sentences with difficult vocabulary, passive voice or complex structures, such as relative and subordinated clauses, can be challenging to understand. Text simplification has been found to be beneficial for language learners (Shirzadi, 2014), children (Kajiwara et al., 2013), and adults with low literacy skills (Arnaldo Candido Jr. and Erick Maziero and Caroline Gasperin and Thiago A. S. Pardo and Lucia Specia and Sandra M. Aluisio, 2009) or language disabilities (John Carroll and Guido Minnen and Darren Pearce and Yvonne Canning and Siobhan Devlin and John Tait, 1999; Luz Rello and Ricardo Baeza-Yates, 2014). To cater to these target reader populations, language teachers, linguists and other editors are often called upon to manually adapt a text. To automate this time-consuming task, there has been much effort in developing systems for lexical simplification (Zhu et al., 2010; Biran et al., 2011) and syntactic simplification (Siddharthan, 2002; Siddharthan and Angrosh, 2014).

The performance of the state-of-the-art systems has improved significantly (Horn et al., 2014; Siddharthan and Angrosh, 2014). Nonetheless, one cannot expect any single system, trained on a particular dataset, to simplify arbitrary texts in a way that would suit all readers — for example, the kinds of English words and structures suitable for a native speaker in Grade 6 are unlikely to be suitable for a non-native speaker in Grade 4. Hence, human effort is generally needed for modifying the system output.

To support human post-editing, a number of researchers have developed specialized editors for text simplification. While the editor described in Max (2006) shares similar goals as ours, it requires human intervention in much of the simplification process. The Automatic Text Adaptation tool suggests synonyms (Burstein et al., 2007), but does not perform syntactic simplification. Conversely, the *Simpli-*

Proceedings of COLING 2016, the 26th International Conference on Computational Linguistics: System Demonstrations, pages 93–97, Osaka, Japan, December 11-17 2016.

fica tool, developed for Brazilian Portuguese, does not perform lexical simplification. Other packages for lexical simplification, such as LEXenstein (Paetzold and Specia, 2015), are not designed for post-editing.

To fill this gap, we developed a customizable, browser-based editor for simplifying English text. Besides performing automatic lexical and syntactic simplification, it facilitates user post-editing, for example in choosing candidate substitutions or undoing sentence splits. Importantly, the user can supply a vocabulary list tailored for a target reader population. This list serves to specify which words are considered "simple," thus guiding the system in tailoring lexical substitution for the target readers.

2 Lexical Simplification

The lexical simplification task generally consists of three steps (Paetzold and Specia, 2015). The first step, substitution generation, produces a list of candidate words to substitute for the target word w. Typically, the context of w in the input sentence is not considered in this step. In the second step, substitution selection, the system selects the best candidates to replace w in the input sentence. Finally, the substitution ranking step re-ranks the candidates in terms of their simplicity.

Often, the expected vocabulary level of a target reader population is explicitly prescribed. For example, many governments have drawn up graded vocabulary lists to guide students of English as a foreign language; likewise, developers of machine translation systems have specified controlled languages with restricted vocabulary. In this context, lexical simplification can be defined as follows: to rewrite a sentence by replacing all words that are not in the given vocabulary list (and hence presumed to be difficult for the reader) with those from the list (and hence presumed to be simple). For example, Kajiwara et al. (2013) performed lexical simplification based on 5,404 words that elementary school children are expected to know.

2.1 Algorithm

By default, the editor uses a list of approximately 4,000 words that all students in Hong Kong are expected to know upon graduation from primary school (EDB, 2012). However, the user can also upload his or her own vocabulary list. Given an input sentence, we first identify the target words, namely those words that do not appear in the vocabulary list. Following Horn et al. (2014), our system simplifies neither proper nouns, as identified by the Natural Language Toolkit (Bird et al., 2009), nor words in our stoplist, which are already simple. In terms of the three-step framework described above, we use the word2vec model[1] to retrieve candidates for substitution in the first step. We trained the model with all sentences from Wikipedia. For each target word, the model returns a list of the most similar words; we extract the top 20 in this list that are included in the user-supplied vocabulary list. In the next step, substitution selection, we re-rank these 20 words with a language model. We trained a trigram model with the kenlm (Heafield, 2011), again using all sentences from Wikipedia. We then place the 10 words with the highest probabilities in a drop-down list in our editor[2]; for example, Figure 1 shows the ten candidates offered for the word "municipal". If none of the candidates are appropriate, the user can easily revert to the original word, which is also included in the drop-down list; alternatively, the user can click on the text to directly edit it.

2.2 Evaluation

We evaluated the performance of our algorithm on the Mechanical Turk Lexical Simplification Data Set (Horn et al., 2014). This dataset contains 500 manually annotated sentences; the target word in each sentence was annotated by 50 independent annotators. To simulate a teacher adapting an English text for Hong Kong pupils, we used the vocabulary list from the Hong Kong Education Bureau (EDB, 2012). To enable automatic evaluation, we considered only the 249 sentences in the dataset whose target word is not in our vocabulary list, but whose human annotations contain at least one word in the list. Precision is at 31% for the top candidate; it is at 57% for the top ten candidates. In other words, for 57% of the target words, a valid substitution can be found in the drop-down list in the editor.

[1]http://code.google.com/archive/p/word2vec/

[2]We regard all words in the vocabulary list to be sufficiently simple, and do not perform the third step, substitution ranking.

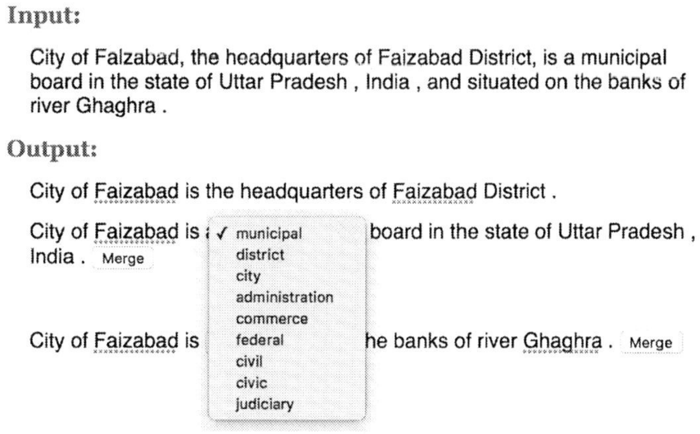

Input:

City of Faizabad, the headquarters of Faizabad District, is a municipal board in the state of Uttar Pradesh , India , and situated on the banks of river Ghaghra .

Output:

City of Faizabad is the headquarters of Faizabad District .

City of Faizabad is ✓ municipal board in the state of Uttar Pradesh , India . Merge

district
city
administration
commerce

City of Faizabad is federal he banks of river Ghaghra . Merge

civil
civic
judiciary

Figure 1: The input sentence is "City of Faizabad, the headquarters of Faizabad District, is a municipal board in the state of Uttar Pradesh, India, and situated on the banks of river Ghaghra." For syntactic simplification (Section 3), the system first splits its coordinated clauses into two sentences, S_1="City of Faizabad ... state of Uttar Pradesh, India."; and S_2="City of Faizabad is situated on the banks of river Ghaghra". It then further extracts the appositive phrase "the headquarters of Faizabad District" from S_1, and turns into a separate sentence. For lexical simplification (Section 2), the system offers eight substitution candidates for the word "municipal" in a drop-down list.

3 Syntactic Simplification

The editor performs automatic syntactic simplification for seven grammatical constructs. In a complex sentence, it identifies relative clauses, adverbial clauses, coordinated clauses, subordinated clauses, participial phrases and appositive phrases; it then splits the sentence into two simpler ones. Further, it transforms passive voice into active voice when the agent is explicitly mentioned. Examples of these constructs and their simplifications are listed in Table 1.

3.1 Algorithm

The system follows the three-step framework of analysis, transformation and regeneration, as laid out in Siddharthan (2002). In the analysis step, it parses the input sentence with the Stanford dependency parser (Manning et al., 2014). In the transformation step, it scans the parse tree of the input sentence to match subtree patterns that have been manually crafted for each of the seven constructs in Table 1. In Figure 1, the input sentence matches the subtree pattern for coordination; it is therefore split into two shorter sentences, S_1="City of Faizabad ... India." and S_2="and situated ... river Ghaghra". Since S_1 then matches the pattern for appositive phrase, the phrase "the headquarters of Faizabad District" is taken out to form its own sentence. If the user finds a sentence split to be inappropriate, he or she can click on the "Merge" button to undo the split. Finally, in the regeneration step, the editor restores the subject (e.g., "City of Faizabad") to newly formed sentences. Often, this step also requires generation of referring expressions, determiners, conjunctions and sentence re-ordering. Since most of these tasks require real-world knowledge, the editor currently leaves it to the user for post-editing.

3.2 Evaluation

We evaluated the quality of syntactic simplification on the first 300 sentences in the Mechanical Turk Lexical Simplification Data Set (Horn et al., 2014). For each sentence, we asked a professor of linguistics to mark the types of syntactic simplification (Table 1) that are applicable, without regard to regeneration requirements. Compared with this human gold standard, the system achieved 79% precision and 64% recall.

Type	Example
Coordination	"I ate an apple and he ate an orange." → "I ate an apple. He ate an orange."
Subordination	"Since he was late, I left." → "He was late. So, I left."
Adverbial clauses	"Impatient, he stood up." → "He was impatient. He stood up."
Participial phrases	"Peter, sweating hard, arrived." → "Peter arrived. He was sweating hard."
Relative clauses	"Peter, who liked fruits, ate an apple" → "Peter liked fruits. He ate an apple."
Appositive phrases	"Peter, my friend, ate an apple" → "Peter was my friend. He ate an apple."
Passive voice	"An apple was eaten by Peter" → "Peter ate an apple."

Table 1: Types of syntactic simplification supported by the editor.

4 Conclusions and Future Work

We have presented a browser-based editor that performs lexical and syntactic simplification and supports human post-editing. The editor takes a customized vocabulary list as input, such that its lexical substitutions are tailored to the needs of the target reader population. Evaluation shows that, for a majority of sentences in a test set, the editor is able to propose appropriate word substitutions and to split up complex syntactic structures. In future work, we aim to further improve the quality of simplification, and to offer annotations for difficult words that cannot be simplified.[3] We also intend to perform empirical studies, to measure the editor's effectiveness in assisting teachers in language lesson planning.

Acknowledgements

This work was supported by the Innovation and Technology Fund (Ref: ITS/132/15) of the Innovation and Technology Commission, the Government of the Hong Kong Special Administrative Region.

References

Arnaldo Candido Jr. and Erick Maziero and Caroline Gasperin and Thiago A. S. Pardo and Lucia Specia and Sandra M. Aluisio. 2009. Supporting the Adaptation of Texts for Poor Literacy Readers: a Text Simplification Editor for Brazilian Portuguese. In *Proc. NAACL-HLT Workshop on Innovative Use of NLP for Building Educational Applications.*

Or Biran, Samuel Brody, and Noémie Elhadad. 2011. Putting it Simply: a Context-aware Approach to Lexical Simplification. In *Proc. NAACL-HLT.*

Steven Bird, Edward Loper, and Ewan Klein. 2009. *Natural Language Processing with Python.* O'Reilly Media Inc.

Jill Burstein, Jane Shore, John Sabatini, Yong-Won Lee, and Matthew Ventura. 2007. The Automated Text Adaptation Tool. In *Proc. NAACL-HLT Demonstration Program.*

EDB. 2012. *Enhancing English Vocabulary Learning and Teaching at Secondary Level.* http://www.edb.gov.hk/vocab_learning_sec.

Kenneth Heafield. 2011. KenLM: Faster and Smaller Language Model Queries. In *Proc. 6th Workshop on Statistical Machine Translation.*

Colby Horn, Katie Manduca, and David Kauchak. 2014. Learning a Lexical Simplifier Using Wikipedia. In *Proc. ACL.*

John Carroll and Guido Minnen and Darren Pearce and Yvonne Canning and Siobhan Devlin and John Tait. 1999. Simplifying Text for Language-Impaired Readers. In *Proc. EACL.*

Tomoyuki Kajiwara, Hiroshi Matsumoto, and Kazuhide Yamamoto. 2013. Selecting Proper Lexical Paraphrase for Children. In *Proc. 25th Conference on Computational Linguistics and Speech Processing (ROCLING).*

Luz Rello and Ricardo Baeza-Yates. 2014. Evaluation of DysWebxia: A Reading App Designed for People with Dyslexia. In *Proc. W4A*, Seoul, South Korea.

[3]For example, Burstein et al. (2007) used marginal notes.

Christopher D. Manning, Mihai Surdeanu, John Bauer, Jenny Finkel, Steven J. Bethard, and David McClosky. 2014. The Stanford CoreNLP Natural Language Processing Toolkit. In *Proc. ACL System Demonstrations*, pages 55–60.

Aurélien Max. 2006. Writing for Language-Impaired Readers. In *Proc. CICLing*.

Gustavo Paetzold and Lucia Specia. 2015. LEXenstein: A Framework for Lexical Simplification. In *Proc. ACL-IJCNLP System Demonstrations*.

Solmaz Shirzadi. 2014. Syntactic and Lexical simplification: the Impact on EFL Listening Comprehension at Low and High Language Proficiency Levels. *Journal of Language Teaching and Research*, 5(3):566–571.

Advaith Siddharthan and M. A. Angrosh. 2014. Hybrid Text Simplification Using Synchronous Dependency Grammars with Hand-Written and Automatically Harvested Rules. In *Proc. EACL*.

Advaith Siddharthan. 2002. An Architecture for a Text Simplification System. In *Proc. Language Engineering Conference (LEC)*.

Zhemin Zhu, Delphine Bernhard, and Iryna Gurevych. 2010. A Monolingual Tree-based Translation Model for Sentence Simplification. In *Proc. COLING*.

CATaLog Online: A Web-based CAT Tool for Distributed Translation with Data Capture for APE and Translation Process Research

Santanu Pal[1], Sudip Kumar Naskar[2], Marcos Zampieri[1], Tapas Nayak[2], Josef van Genabith[1,4]
[1]Saarland University, Germany, [2]Jadavpur University, India,
[4]German Research Center for Artificial Intelligence (DFKI), Germany
{santanu.pal, marcos.zampieri, josef.vangenabith}@uni-saarland.de
tnk02.05@gmail.com, sudip.naskar@jdvu.ac.in

Abstract

We present a free web-based CAT tool called *CATaLog Online* which provides a novel and user-friendly online CAT environment for post-editors/translators. The goal is to support distributed translation where teams of translators work simultaneously on different sections of the same text, reduce post-editing time and effort, improve the post-editing experience and capture data for incremental MT/APE (automatic post-editing) and translation process research. The tool supports individual as well as batch mode file translation and provides translations from three engines – translation memory (TM), MT and APE. TM suggestions are color coded to accelerate the post-editing task. The users can integrate their personal TM/MT outputs. The tool remotely monitors and records post-editing activities generating an extensive range of post-editing logs. Compared with current state-of-the-art CAT tools, *CATaLog Online* provides an enhanced interface, an option to integrate APE and more informative logs to help translation process research.

1 Introduction

Machine translation (MT) technology has improved substantially over the past few decades. MT output is no longer used just for gisting but also for post-editing by professional translators as an important part of the translation workflow. Several studies confirm that post-editing MT output increases translators' productivity and improves translation consistency (Guerberof, 2009; Plitt and Masselot, 2010; Zampieri and Vela, 2014). Alongside classical TM matches, computer-aided translation (CAT) Tools that integrate MT and TM output are a trend in the translation and localization industries providing translators more useful suggestions. Another important trend is the development of web-based CAT tools which require no local software installation and allow teams of translators to work on the same project simultaneously (e.g., WordFast Anywhere[1], MateCat[2] (Federico et al., 2014), and Wordbee[3], Lilt[4] etc.).

This paper presents *CATaLog Online*, a web-based CAT tool that provides translators MT, TM and APE output and ensures data capture for APE development and translation process research. The MT and APE systems integrated in *CATaLog Online* are based on Pal et al. (2015) and Pal et al. (2016b), respectively. In this paper, we present the key features implemented in *CATaLog Online* and their importance to translation project managers, translators, and MT and APE developers. Compared to state-of-the-art CAT tools (e.g., MateCat, Lilt) *CATaLog Online* offers the following advantages: (i) color coded TM translation suggestions (highlighted TM source and corresponding target fragments are shown in the same interface), (ii) a wide range of editing logs, (iii) alignment between source, TM/MT/APE and the results of human PE, (iv) improved TM similarity measure and search technique (Pal et al., 2016a), and (v) additional translation option from APE which learns from human post-edited data.

The paper is organized as follows. Section 2 presents the desktop version of the *CATaLog* tool. Section 3 describes in detail the main functionalities of *CATaLog Online*. Section 4 outlines APE and translation

[1]https://www.freetm.com/
[2]https://www.matecat.com/
[3]http://www.wordbee.com/
[4]https://lilt.com/

Proceedings of COLING 2016, the 26th International Conference on Computational Linguistics: System Demonstrations, pages 98–102, Osaka, Japan, December 11-17 2016.

process research with *CATaLog Online*. Section 5 concludes and provides avenues for improving the CAT tool further.

2 CATaLog

CATaLog (Nayek et al., 2015) is a TM-based CAT tool which provides core functionalities for *CATaLog Online*. What distinguishes *CATaLog* from existing TM-based CAT tools is a set of newly introduced features targeted towards improving post-editing experience in terms of both performance and productivity. These include an improved TM similarity measure, searching and a novel coloring scheme. The color coding introduced into *CATaLog* guides the user during the translation (or post-editing) process. The matching parts in the TM source matches, as well as their translations in the target, are displayed in green, while the non-matching parts in both the TM source and target suggestions are displayed in red. Unaligned words are shown in orange. Similarly, when the user clicks on one of the 5 TM suggestions to start the post-editing task, the corresponding matching and non-matching parts in the input segment are also displayed in green and red, respectively. The color coding scheme not only helps the user to choose the most suitable TM suggestion for post-editing, it also helps the user to identify which parts of a TM match require more post-editing effort and which fragments are reliable translations.

3 CATaLog Online

CATaLog Online provides a novel and user-friendly online CAT environment for post-editors and translators to reduce post-editing time and effort and improve the post-editing experience. The basic TM fuctionalities in *CATaLog Online* follow *CATaLog*'s color coding scheme. *CATaLog Online* is a freeware software that can be used through a web browser (works best in Mozilla Firefox) and requires only a simple registration. The tool remotely monitors and records translator/post-editor activities generating a wide range of post-editing logs (cf. Section 3.5) that are a fundamental source of information for APE and translation process research. *CATaLog Online*, produces multiple translation options for an uploaded input text file. It is a language independent tool that enables users to upload their own translation memories.

On the main user interface[5], users can translate a single segment after choosing the source language and the target language (cf. "Quick Translation" in the main interface). The suggested translations are generated by three different engines: MT, TM and APE. The TM output is color coded. Unlike other existing CAT tools, *CATaLog Online* provides many facilities including file translation, CAT tool environment, user management, project management, translation data capture, TM/MT and APE support, as well as distributed translation, where teams of translators working on the same job, etc.

3.1 File Translation

CATaLog Online provides facilities for batch mode file translation[6], i.e., a user can input a source file. The *CATaLog Online* batch mode file translation option provides a post-editing environment which allows the user to post-edit the selected translation from among the three translation suggestions (MT, TM and APE). The user has to choose the source–target language pair and upload a text file which contains a set of source segments. The tool translates this text file at the back end by creating a project and then assigns a unique job identification number (Job ID) to the user which is displayed on the large red button in the interface (cf. Figure 3). Each project/job is associated with a unique job URL. The user can either keep this Job ID for future reference or directly go to the job page by clicking on the recent Job ID (i.e., the red button marked with the Job ID). To recover a project/job, the translator has to search the project/job using the corresponding Job ID (cf. Figure 3). The File translation interface provides on-the-fly user guidance regarding the "usage" and "tool functionality" in terms of message services.

[5]`http://santanu.appling.uni-saarland.de/CATaLog/`

[6]`http://santanu.appling.uni-saarland.de/CATaLog/GeustTranslation.jsp`

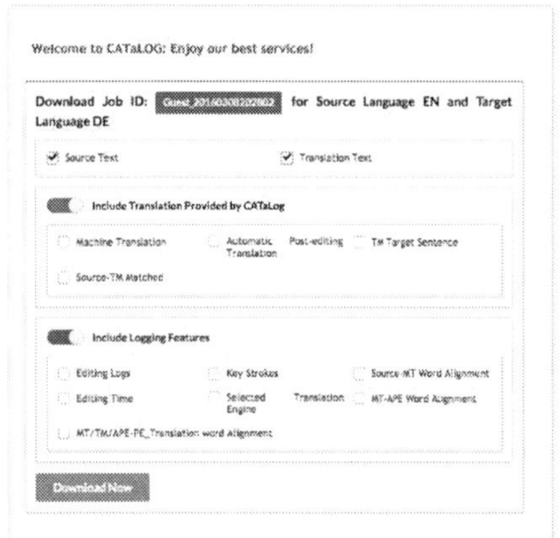

Figure 1: Job download interface

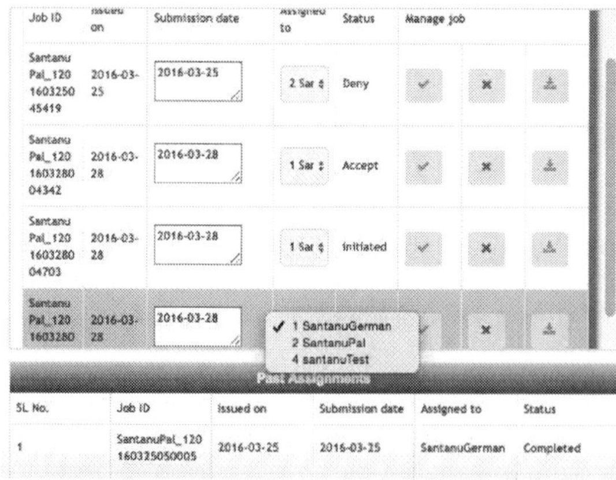

Figure 2: Project Management interface for PM

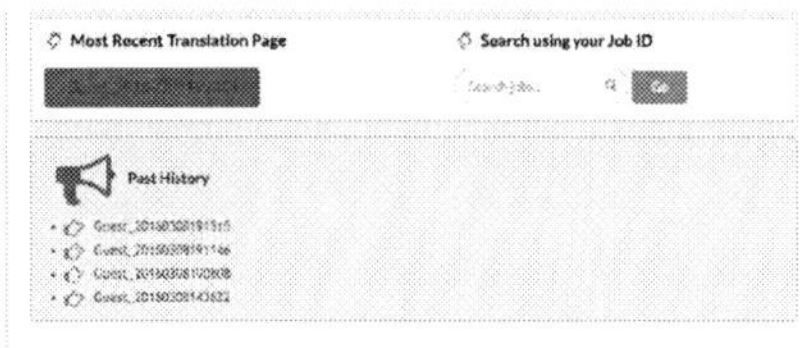

Figure 3: Job search interface

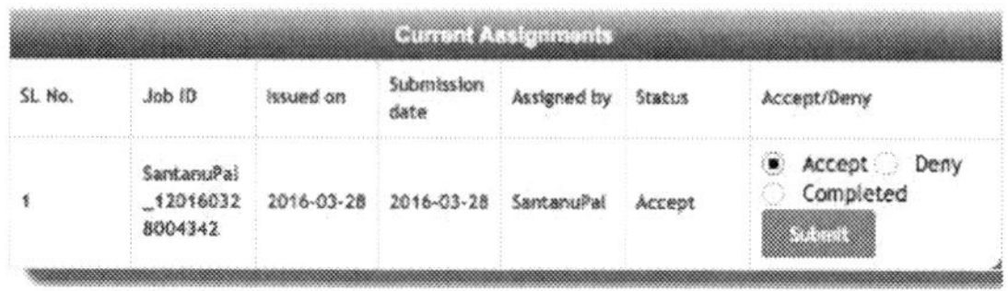

Figure 4: Project Management interface for translators

3.2 CAT Tool

The CAT Tool interface[7] is similar to the File Translation interface described in Section 3.1, however, it differs in terms of features and functionalities. Users can upload their own translation memories as tab separated text files. The tool is language agnostic and allows the user to upload files in any language. Users have full freedom to use MT translations generated by their own MT systems or third party MT engines (up to two alternatives are supported in the current version. Additionally, the tool provides color coded translations from the back end TM. When uploading finishes, the system provides a unique Job ID; the functionality is similar to that described in Section 3.1.

3.3 Project Management and Distributed Translation

The *CATaLog Online* project management system supports basic project management activities. A registered Project manager (PM) creates a translation project for a specific language pair by uploading a source file. Once a project/Job has been created, a Job Id appears in a row of the job assignment table. Additional information is associated with the Job Id, including issue date, submission date, available translators for that particular language pair, etc. The PM can review the job and assign translation sub-jobs to any of the available translators supporting concurrent distributed translation management including submission deadlines (cf. Figure 2).

As soon as the PM assigns a sub-job to a particular registered translator, the translator can see and review that job. The interface provides three options to the translator by which the translator can set the status of his/her activity for that particular job. A translator can either delete the assigned job from his/her profile by setting a "Deny" status or can accept it by setting the "Accept" status (cf. Figure 4). After finishing a translation task, the translator sets the corresponding job status as "Completed" which is directly updated in the PM's job status where the PM can see the completed and pending jobs. Finally, after reviewing, the PM can download the completed job and deliver it to the client.

[7] http://santanu.appling.uni-saarland.de/CATaLog/CATTool.jsp

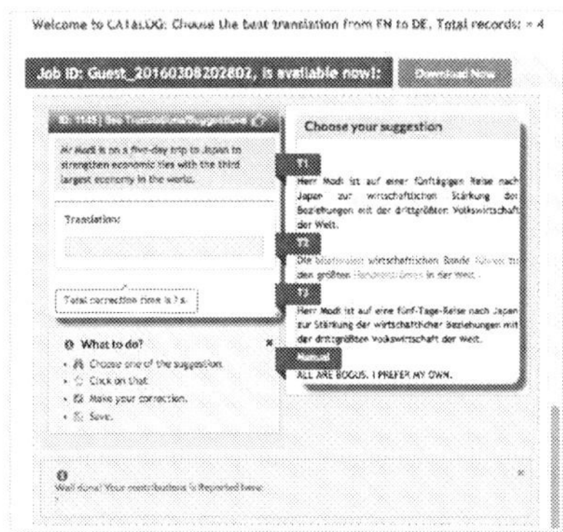

Figure 5: Job interface

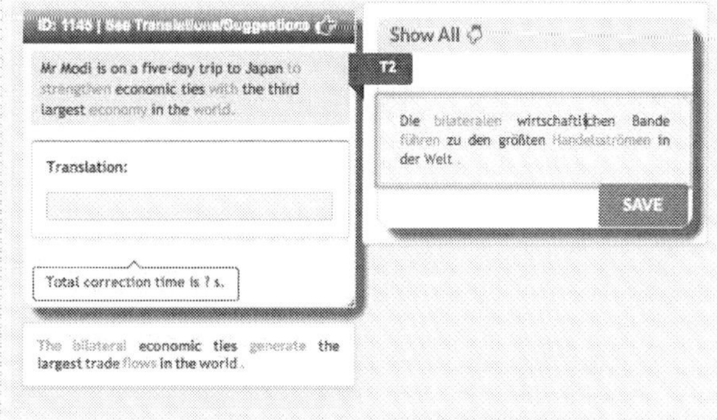

Figure 6: Job interface of TM selection

3.4 Job Management

A job is created when the PM or a guest user uploads a source file. The job interface provides three different translation alternatives for each source segment (cf. Figure 5).The TM translation alternative is color coded. The other two outputs are from MT and APE engines provided by *CATaLog Online* (cf. Section 3.1) or the uploaded third party MT engine outputs (cf. Section 3.2). As shown in Figure 5, source segments are listed in the blue panel on the left and the corresponding translation suggestions appear on the right panel upon clicking a link shown above the source segment. The translator chooses one of these suggestions and post-edits it. Figure 6 shows the interface when the translator selects the TM suggestion. The final translation appears in the green panel on the left when the translator presses the "Save" button. The editing time (in seconds) is also shown below the final translation panel. After finishing each translation, an editing summary shows the number of editing operations performed by the translator. *CATaLog Online* provides an on-the-fly editing guide throughout the translation process. In case of re-editing a translation, the previously stored final translation is shown as the first translation suggestion in the suggestion panel.

3.5 Editing Log

For a given input segment, the post-editor edits the best translation suggestion which may contain errors. The system records the user activities such as key strokes, cursor positions, text selection and mouse clicks. The tool provides analytical summaries of post-editing activities during translation and presents well structured XML formatted logs which can be customized according to the user's choice, e.g., the user can download the entire logs or some specific logs for a particular translation job (cf. Figure 1). The tool also provides word alignment which is also a part of the XML logs. *CATaLog Online* records word alignments between source–MT, MT–APE and source–HPE (human PE). The source–MT and MT–APE word alignments are established based on the decoding traces. The MT–HPE and APE–HPE alignments are recorded from the keystroke logs based on whether the user edits the MT output or APE output. Finally, the source–HPE alignments are generated by combining the transitive links between source–MT, MT–APE and APE–HPE in case of editing on the APE output or as the combination of source–MT and MT–HPE. These alignments and post-editing information are beneficial for translation process research.

4 APE and Translation Process Research using CATaLog Online

The post-editing logs collected during the translation process are a valuable source of information for translation process research as well as APE research and development. These user activity data logs not only help to assess the performance and understand the behavior of the translators, they also provide crucial information about cognitive aspects of post-editing. The logs can be used to model APE to improve quality and productivity.

User Perspective: *CATaLog Online* generates a summary for every completed translation task which includes translator productivity in terms of number of words translated per minute and time taken per word. From the logs it is also possible to generate a report on translator style and behavior which can include, e.g., number of keystrokes per (effective) character editing, repetitive typing, preference for certain function words, etc.

Research Perspective: *CATaLog Online* records word alignments between source–MT, MT–APE, source–APE and source–HPE. These alignments and related post-editing information are beneficial for incremental MT/APE. Moreover, the source–HPE word alignments gathered by the tool can serve as a potential source for terminology extraction.

5 Conclusions and Future Work

CATaLog Online is a novel and user-friendly online CAT tool offering new features developed with the objective of improving translation productivity and experience. The tool provides a wide range of logs and data which serve as important information to translation process researchers, MT developers, and APE developers. The success of the two editions of the APE shared task in WMT (Bojar et al., 2016) indicate that APE is one of the important directions that research in MT is moving to. Post-editing tools, such as CATaLog Online, are able to provide crucial information for APE development. We would like to further expand and improve the tool by including additional features, e.g., interactive translation prediction in the form of on-the-fly translation suggestion, terminology extraction, option for compiling corpora, auto-suggestion for words, on-click pop-up terminology view, etc. Finally, we would like to model user behaviour and implement incremental MT/APE using the edit logs provided by the tool.

Acknowledgments

Santanu Pal is supported by the People Programme (Marie Curie Actions) of the EU Framework Programme (FP7/2007-2013) under REA grant agreement no 317471. Sudip Kumar Naskar is supported by Media Lab Asia, DeitY, Government of India, under the Young Faculty Research Fellowship of the Visvesvaraya PhD Scheme for Electronics & IT. Josef van Genabith is supported by funding from the EU Horizon 2020 research and innovation programme under grant agreement no 645452 (QT21).

References

Ondrej Bojar, Rajen Chatterjee, Christian Federmann, Yvette Graham, Barry Haddow, Matthias Huck, Antonio Jimeno Yepes, Philipp Koehn, Varvara Logacheva, Christof Monz, et al. 2016. Findings of the 2016 Conference on Machine Translation (WMT16). In *Proceedings of WMT*.

Marcello Federico, Nicola Bertoldi, Mauro Cettolo, Matteo Negri, Marco Turchi, Marco Trombetti, Alessandro Cattelan, Antonio Farina, Domenico Lupinetti, Andrea Martines, et al. 2014. The Matecat Tool. In *Proceedings of COLING*.

Ana Guerberof. 2009. Productivity and Quality in the Post-editing of Outputs from Translation Memories and Machine Translation. *Localisation Focus*, 7(1):133–140.

Tapas Nayek, Sudip Kumar Naskar, Santanu Pal, Marcos Zampieri, Mihaela Vela, and Josef van Genabith. 2015. CATaLog: New Approaches to TM and Post Editing Interfaces. In *Proceedings of the NLP4TM Workshop*.

Santanu Pal, Sudip Naskar, and Josef van Genabith. 2015. UdS-Sant: English–German Hybrid Machine Translation System. In *Proceedings of WMT*.

Santanu Pal, Marcos Zampieri, Sudip Kumar Naskar, Tapas Nayak, Mihaela Vela, and Josef van Genabith. 2016a. CATaLog Online: Porting a Post-editing Tool to the Web. In *Proceedings of LREC*.

Santanu Pal, Marcos Zampieri, and Josef van Genabith. 2016b. USAAR: An Operation Sequential Model for Automatic Statistical Post-Editing. In *Proceedings of WMT*.

Mirko Plitt and François Masselot. 2010. A Productivity Test of Statistical Machine Translation Post-Editing in a Typical Localisation Context. *The Prague Bulletin of Mathematical Linguistics*, 93:7–16.

Marcos Zampieri and Mihaela Vela. 2014. Quantifying the Influence of MT Output in the Translators' Performance: A Case Study in Technical Translation. In *Proceedings of the HaCat Workshop*.

Interactive Relation Extraction in Main Memory Database Systems

Rudolf Schneider **Cordula Guder** **Torsten Kilias** **Alexander Löser**
Jens Graupmann **Oleksandr Kozachuk**
Beuth University of Applied Sciences, Luxemburger Straße 10, 13353 Berlin, Germany
Exasol AG, Neumeyerstraße 22, 90411 Nürnberg, Germany
{ruschneider,s57515,tkilias,aloeser}@beuth-hochschule.de
{jens.graupmann, oleksandr.kozachuk}@exasol.com

Abstract

We present INDREX-MM, a main memory database system for interactively executing two interwoven tasks, declarative relation extraction from text and their exploitation with SQL. INDREX-MM simplifies these tasks for the user with powerful SQL extensions for gathering statistical semantics, for executing open information extraction and for integrating relation candidates with domain specific data. We demonstrate these functions on 800k documents from Reuters RCV1 with more than a billion linguistic annotations and report execution times in the order of seconds.

1 Introduction

Relation Extraction (RE) is the task of extracting semantic relations between two or more entities from text. Often these relations are loaded into a relational database system for further exploitation. One line of approaches to RE is rule-based, where users manually define rule-sets consisting of extraction patterns that if observed point to instances of a relation. These approaches are easy to debug, permit the user a high level of direct control over the extraction process and can outperform machine-learning based state-of-the-art models (Chiticariu et al., 2013). However, writing rules is a time consuming and iterative process, in particular for extracting uncommon relationship types with high recall and precision.

Our task: Complement existing in-house relational data with insights from text. While browsing news, a supply chain analyst performs research on suppliers of a car rental company, product recalls. She desires to complement an existing table *productrecall(supplier, product)*, with relations extracted from news text. Currently, the user performs these task with two separate systems, a system for extracting a relation *productrecall(supplier, product)*, such as (Krishnamurthy et al., 2008), and a relational database management system (RDBMS) for joining, grouping, aggregating and ordering. In a typical work flow, the user ships existing tables from the RDBMS to bootstrap text and ships back extracted relations to the RDBMS for analytical queries. This costly work flow is iterated until an analytical query shows desired results. Moreover, the user must learn to manage both systems.

Contribution. Ideally, users could execute both, analytical and relation extraction tasks, in a single database system and could leverage built-in query optimizations. Another crucial requirement is interactive query execution, in particular for extracting rare relation types with high recall and precision. We demonstrate INDREX-MM[1], a Main-Memory Relational Database System (MM-RDBMS) that permits this functionality, either as fast back-end for interactive relation extraction applications, such as (Michael and Akbik, 2015), or on command line. INDREX-MM provides a broad and powerful set of SQL-based query operators for declarative relation extraction. These include query predicates for detecting span proximity, predicates for testing overlapping spans or span containment, scalar functions for returning the context of a span, or user defined table generating functions for consolidating spans. Further, the system supports executing regular expressions and built-in operators from the RDBMS, such as joins,

[1]see our online demonstration at `http://dbl43.beuth-hochschule.de/html/indrex-mm/`

Proceedings of COLING 2016, the 26th International Conference on Computational Linguistics: System Demonstrations, pages 103–106, Osaka, Japan, December 11-17 2016.

unions or aggregation functions. These additional operators permit the user basic operations for *looking up* words in sentences describing entities or other potential relation arguments. The system also supports the user *learning* about potential open relation candidates where these words appear in, or about distributions of potentials synonymous relation names. Finally, we support the user in *investigating* new relations. Our work in (Kilias et al., 2015) shows details and extensive performance evaluations. INDREX-MM bases on EXASOL, a parallel main-memory and column-oriented database. It permits integration via standard interfaces, such as JDBC, or business intelligence tools, like *Tableau*.

2 Demonstration Outline

We demonstrate how INDREX-MM supports the user in three elementary steps during the declarative relation extraction process, for which figure 1 gives a high-level overview. Each of these steps 'filters out' irrelevant sentences and only keeps sentences containing relations of the type *productrecall(supplier, product)*.

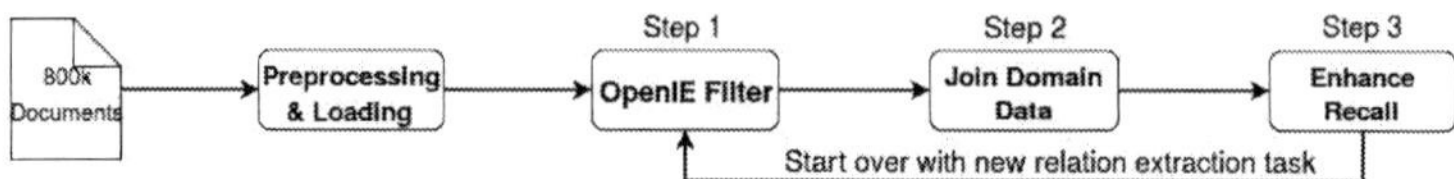

Figure 1: Relation Extraction process using Open Information Extraction in INDREX-MM.

Batch loading base annotations in a flat, sparse and cache affine data structure. Text mining workloads rarely require full scans of all table data, but do often require full scans of a small subset of the columns. Our base table layout from (Kilias et al., 2015) supports such work flows. This schema partitions data per *(document, span)*; we denote a span with its beginning and ending character. Many operations on text are 'local' on a single document. Hence, our partition scheme permits a MM-RDBMS to ship data for a single document 'close' to the CPU and in orders of magnitudes faster cache structures. For each span we provide additional attributes denoting annotation types, such as tokenization, sentence recognition, part-of-speech tagging, named entity recognition, user-defined types, dependency tagging, or noun- and verb-phrase chunking.[2] We add attributes for referencing spans to containment relations in the same document. For example, a span for a sentence may contain additional spans denoting organisations. Such a flat and sparse table layout pre-joins data already at data loading time and avoids most joins at query execution time. Because of the columnar layout in a MM-RDBMS, *NULL values* in attributes do not harm query execution time.

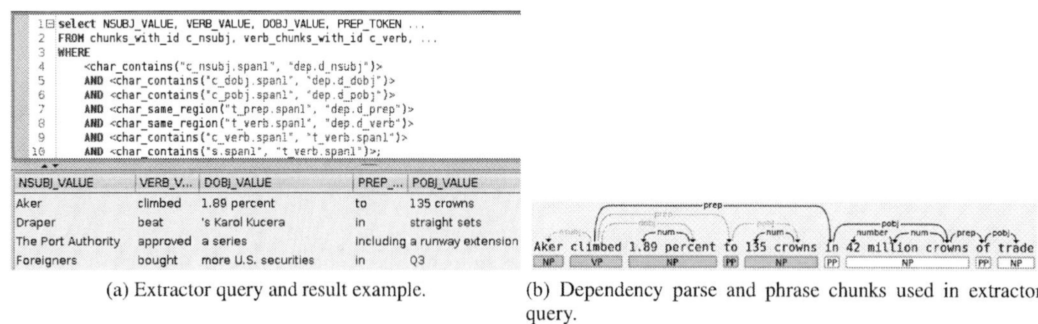

(a) Extractor query and result example.

(b) Dependency parse and phrase chunks used in extractor query.

Figure 2: Query example of an Open Information Extraction pattern.

Step 1: Filtering relation candidates with Open Information Extraction. Open Information Extraction (OIE) is the task of extracting relations from large corpora and without requiring a pre-specified vocabulary. Relations are n-ary and arguments do not follow a pre-defined type set. From the perspective of a database, we understand OIE as selective filters connecting arguments in sentences. Recent work in clause-based OIE (Del Corro and Gemulla, 2013) shows effective filters for n-ary relations. INDREX-MM supports OIE as black box or as customizable and debuggable database views: One approach is

[2]We use Stanford CoreNLP 3.6 for this task.

executing OIE outside a MM-RDBMS as a black box, load results into an OIE table and reference spans to the annotation table. We noticed that such black boxes are difficult to debug, break with the programming paradigm of the database, and if the code does not match the corpus requirements of the user, she must wait for an update of the OIE system. Contrary, we provide the user in INDREX-MM a set of 'ready-to-use' OIE filters in SQL as views as shown in figure 2. The user can add SQL-predicates from additional OIE approaches, such as (Angeli et al., 2015), can debug directly on her corpus, while the MM-RDBMS takes over on optimizing the execution.

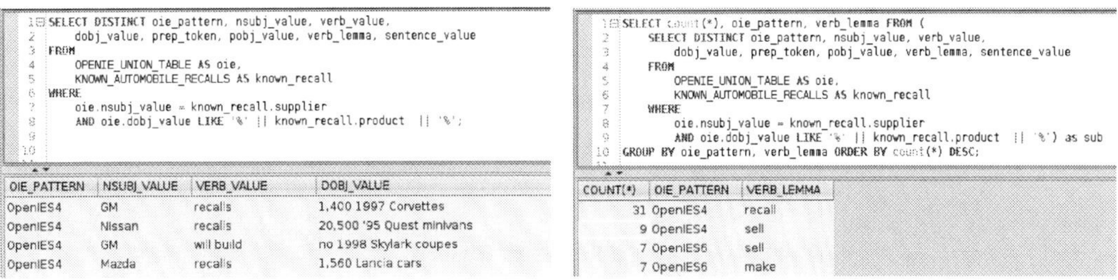

(a) Join of the Union OIE table with in house data regarding known product recalls of the company's suppliers.

(b) Relation candidates grouped, counted and ordered by pattern and verb. The most frequent combination is OIE-Pattern 4 and the verb "recall".

Figure 3: Use of in-house data to spot patterns of product recall mentions in the OIE schema.

Step 2: Joining OIE relations with domain data into a universal schema and spotting patterns. After step 1 relations connect two or more relation arguments. However, we need to filter out irrelevant relations and only keep relations that belong to our desired relation type *productrecall*. For example, we keep relations connecting a company with predicates, such as 'recalls', 'withdraws' and discard relations with 'sold' or 'has refused'. For executing this task and analogue to universal schemas (Riedel et al., 2013), we join arguments of OIE-relations with in-house domain specific relations representing the same semantic type, such as a table describing product recalls of the suppliers of a company. As a result, our universal schema represents relations, mainly candidate patterns of our desired relation type, and few patterns for other semantic types (see figure 3a). The fast execution performance of INDREX-MM permits the user to filter out these irrelevant patterns manually. For example, she aggregates, groups and counts patterns with standard SQL, orders patterns by frequency and marks unsuitable patterns (see figure 3b). For spotting additional semantic patterns, we provide synonyms from Wordnet. INDREX-MM also supports loading existing lexical patterns from the literature in a table, such as Hearst patterns (Hearst, 1992) or patterns from ConceptNet 5[3]. The user can execute a join and utilize these patterns as additional filters for OIE candidates. Focus of our current research is applying in-database-analytics for pattern generation, such as clustering techniques (see our work in (Akbik et al., 2012)).

Step 3: Applying selectional restriction and enhancing recall. For further enhancing recall, the user keeps lexical patterns for predicates from the last step but applies various selectional restrictions to arguments. INDREX-MM supports selectional restrictions to one or many argument types. For example, the user may keep the company name of relations from step 2, but relaxes the second argument. As a result, she may spot new relations of *productrecall(supplier, product)*, in particular relations between previously known companies and previously unknown products.

3 Discussion

Execution on one billion annotations in seconds. We measure the relation extraction process from above in INDREX-MM on Reuters RCV1 with 800k documents and 1.2 billion annotations. For each of the four steps mentioned above we measure the execution time and how selective each filtering step prunes sentences. For evaluating precision, we asked two independent students to draw a sample of 100 sentences randomly after each step and to count the number of correct relations for our desired type.

[3] *http://conceptnet5.media.mit.edu*

Step	Time	Relations	RL100	Examples
BL	180 min	15.785.155	0	-
1 OIE	9,9s	13.695.006	10	All OIE pattern (Mitsubishi, raised its production plan, October)
2 PR	49ms	134	31	**Product recall**(GM, recalls, 1,400 1997 Corvettes)
3 PR	619ms	921	61	**Product recall**(Tensor, recalls, halogen bulbs)
2 AL	16.64s	662	35	**Alliance**(LUKoil, signed, a $2-billion deal, with SOCAR)
3 AL	2.505s	3.265	91	**Alliance**(Xillix, signed, an agreement, with Olympus)
2 AC	5.643s	112	41	**Acquisition**(Quaker, reviews, Snapple)
3 AC	7.031s	1654	73	**Acquisition**(Quaker, acquired, Snapple, for, $1.8 billion)

Table 1: Performance for each step. After phase BL, we loaded 15.7 Mio sentences and estimate one relation per sentence. In step 1, we extract OIE relations from sentences using the 7 basic patterns from ClausIE resulting in slightly fewer OIE relations than sentences. For phase 2 and 3 we show results for *productrecall(supplier, product)*, *alliance(company, company)* and *acquisition(company, company)*. We count correct relations on a randomly taken sample of 100 sentences (RL100).

Table 1 shows our measurements and example sentences. One-time batch loading (denoted with *BL* in Table 1) takes roughly 180 minutes, because the MM-RDBMS executes compressions and builds index structures before we can run queries. In a streaming scenario the MM-RDBMS uses delta indexing techniques and permits hitting queries while new data is inserted.

INDREX-MM exploits data locality and leverages multi-core shared memory architectures. Declarative relation extraction systems, such as SystemT (Krishnamurthy et al., 2008) or GATE[4], need to conduct expensive data shipping between different NLP components and databases. Such data shipping is a major performance bottleneck. Contrary, INDREX-MM avoids data shipping, rather ships functionality to data, and even leverages multiple built-in optimizations of main memory RDBMSs, such as massive parallel execution with multi-cores, compression techniques and columnar based table layouts, cache affine data structures, single instruction multiple data (SIMD) or result materializations.

Acknowledgements Our work is funded by the German Federal Ministry of Economic Affairs and Energy (BMWi) under grant agreement 01MD16011E (Project: Medical Allround-Care Service Solutions).

References

Alan Akbik, Larysa Visengeriyeva, Priska Herger, Holmer Hemsen, and Alexander Löser. 2012. Unsupervised discovery of relations and discriminative extraction patterns. In *COLING*, pages 17–32.

Gabor Angeli, Melvin Jose Johnson Premkumar, and Christopher D. Manning. 2015. Leveraging linguistic structure for open domain information extraction. In *ACL*, pages 344–354.

Laura Chiticariu, Yunyao Li, and Frederick R. Reiss. 2013. Rule-based information extraction is dead! long live rule-based information extraction systems! In *EMNLP 2013*, pages 827–832.

Luciano Del Corro and Rainer Gemulla. 2013. Clausie: clause-based open information extraction. In *World Wide Web*, pages 355–366.

Marti A. Hearst. 1992. Automatic acquisition of hyponyms from large text corpora. In *COLING*, pages 539–545.

Torsten Kilias, Alexander Löser, and Periklis Andritsos. 2015. INDREX: In-Database Relation Extraction. *Information Systems*, 53:124–144.

Rajasekar Krishnamurthy, Yunyao Li, Sriram Raghavan, Frederick Reiss, Shivakumar Vaithyanathan, and Huaiyu Zhu. 2008. Systemt: a system for declarative information extraction. *SIGMOD Record*, 37(4):7–13.

Thilo Michael and Alan Akbik. 2015. SCHNAPPER: A web toolkit for exploratory relation extraction. In *ACL, System Demonstrations*, pages 67–72.

Sebastian Riedel, Limin Yao, Andrew McCallum, and Benjamin M. Marlin. 2013. Relation extraction with matrix factorization and universal schemas. In *HLT-NAACL*, pages 74–84.

[4] *https://gate.ac.uk/ie/*

An Open Source Library for Semantic-Based Datetime Resolution

Aurélie Merlo, Denis Pasin
Jam, 80 rue de Cléry, 75002 Paris, France
{firstname}@hellojam.fr

Abstract

In this paper, we introduce an original Python implementation of datetime resolution in French, which we make available as open-source library. Our approach is based on Frame Semantics and Corpus Pattern Analysis in order to provide a precise semantic interpretation of datetime expressions. This interpretation facilitates the contextual resolution of datetime expressions in timestamp format.

1. Introduction

Jam is an artificial intelligence supervised by humans answering to questions of young French people (18-30 years old) on activities to do during their spare time (sport, movies, restaurant, travel...). Adapted to French, the AI classifies the user messages sent by text message among a list of needs. Each need is associated with a list of metadata. A metadata is a qualitative data in an incoming message. This data provides relevant informations (datetime, location, price...) in order to search for contents (restaurant, movie, air ticker...) through APIs (Booking, Yelp).

Our users communicate in natural language. We need a system able to identify and translate various possible formulations of a metadata into a data understandable by an API. For example, the system has to be able to make all these datetime constructions interoperable in timestamp format: *departure on August 26, a nice evening for Halloween, departure about August 26, I don't know when, only on September 2.*

TIMEX3 (Pustejovsky & al., 2010) and libraries using this standard annotation (GUTime (Verhagen et al., 2005), HeidelTime (Strötgen & Gertz, 2010), SUTime (Chang & Manning, 2012)) fail to provide a satisfactory contextual resolution outside explicit datetimes. For example in (1), TIMEX3 does not account for approximative datetimes:

(1) *départ vers le 8 mai* "departure about May 8"
départ vers <TIMEX3 tid="t1" type="DATE" value="XXXX-05-08">le 8 mai</TIMEX3>

TIMEX3 fails also to define a datetime against an event (*two days before Christmas*) and does not account for compositionnality (Bethard & Parker, 2016). For example in (2), datetime expression should be interpreted as a date associated with a time and not as two TIMEX3 tags:

(2) *vendredi 10 avril à 15h* "Friday April 10 at 3PM"
<TIMEX3 tid="t3" type="DATE" value="XXXX-04-10">vendredi 10 avril</TIMEX3> à <TIMEX3 tid="t6" type="TIME" value="XXXX-XX-XXT15:00">15h</TIMEX3>

The relevance of the content that we send to our users depends heavily on the understanding we have of their needs. Faced with the lack of precision and the incompleteness of TIMEX3, we developed a python library for identification, interpretation and contextual resolution in timestamp format of French datetime constructions. Datetime resolution is not a new task in NLP. Our approach is original because it is based on the works of the Frame Semantics (Fillmore 1976) and the Corpus Pattern Analysis (CPA) (Hank 2004). Our library provides a rich semantic interpretation of datetime constructions which enables to resolve them in timestamp format. The library and its documentation are available under MIT license and on https://github.com/blackbirdco/time_extract.

2. Semantic-Based Approach

2.1. Frame Semantics and Corpus Pattern Analysis (CPA)

In order to take into account datetime compositionnality, we based our approach on Frame Semantics. According this semantic theory, the meaning of a word or an expression is determined above all by its context. A frame consists of Frame Elements (FEs) and a list of lexical units which call a frame. In FrameNet, we identified two frames that describe datetime:
- Calendric_Unit : Unit FE (*Tuesday*), Whole FE (*Tuesday of next week)* and Relative_time FE (*next Tuesday*)
- Time_vector : Direction FE and Distance FE (*in two days, two days ago*).
Frame Semantics does not offer a complete description of all datetime constructions and it only lists the FEs without explain how they are combined. Furthermore, Relative_time FE lacks precision for contextual resolution. *Next Tuesday* cannot be resolved similar to *Last Tuesday* in timestamp format.

CPA, influenced by Frame Semantics, is a method of corpus analysis for lexicographic purpose. Meaning is viewed as a pattern. Each pattern consists of ontological categories called semantic type. A semantic type is a general category representing a shared property by concepts. With CPA it is possible to describe datetime constructions using patterns. For example, we can describe the frame timeModified corresponding to a timeline modification using this pattern:

datetime expressions: *before Monday, after Monday*
frame: timelineModified
pattern: before or after dayOfWeek

dayOfWeek is a semantic type because all of its concepts (Monday, Tuesday, Wednesday…) share the property to be modified by a timeline modifier (before, after, around, not, only).

2.2. Datetime Ontology

We extracted from our database 1200 incoming messages for annotation. The purpose of annotation was to identify frames and patterns for datetime expressions. We show succinctly the highest frames and patterns of our datetime ontology[1]:

- datetimeGeneralUsageTerm
    - datetimeElementTerm
        - dateTerm
            - explicitDateTerm
                - pattern: dayOfWeekItem (*Monday)*
                - pattern: dayOfWeekItem monthValueItem dayValueItem (*Monday August 28*)
                - pattern: dayOrdinalItem dayOfWeekItem monthValueItem YearValueItem (*second Monday of January 2017*)
                - …
            - modifiedDateTerm
                - beforeDateTerm (*before Monday*)
                - afterDateTerm (*after Monday*)
                - approximativeDateTerm (*around Monday*)
                - constraintDateTerm (*only on Monday*)
                - negativeDateTerm (*not on Monday*)
            - vectorDateTerm
                - futureVectorDateTerm (*in two days*)
                - pastVectorDateTerm (*two days ago*)
            - urgencyDateTerm (*it's urgent*)
            - indeterminateDateTerm (*I don't know when*)
            - anyDateTerm (*no matter when*)
        - hourTerm
            - explicitHourTerm (*at 3 PM*)
            - modifiedHourTerm (*before 3 PM*)

[1] The complete ontology is in the library documentation.

- vectorHourTerm (*in two hours*)
- indeterminateHourTerm
- anyHourTerm

- datetimeGroupElementTerm (*August 7 and 10*)
- datetimeAlternativeElementTerm (*August 7 or in two days*)

- datetimeTravelUsageTerm
  - departureDatetimeTerm (*departure on Monday*)
  - returnDatetimeTerm (*return before August 10 2016*)

3. Implementation

3.1. Semantic interpretation module

Intepretation module takes an user message in French (Il y a quoi au ciné lundi vers 15h? "what are the movies on Monday around 3PM?"). The message is cleaned (addition of missing spaces, multi-word expressions tagging) and lemmatized with TreeTagger. Lemmas in datetime semantic lexicon are tagged with a semantic type (Monday [firstDayOfWeekItem]). The semantic tagged message is used as an input for a semantic rule-based chunker. We created a semantic grammar which represents frames and patterns above. The output of interpretation module is a semantic tree with an extracted datetime expression:

```
(metadata
 (datetimeTerm
  (datetimeGeneralUsageTerm
   (datetimeElementTerm
    (dateTerm
     (unmodifiedDateTerm
      (calendarDateTerm
       (dayOfWeekTerm lundi "Monday"/firstDayOfWeekItem))))
    (hourTerm
     (modifiedHourTerm
      (approximativeHourTerm
       vers "around"/approximativeItem
       (unmodifiedHourTerm
        (numericHourTerm 15/numeralItem heure "hour"/hourUnitItem)))))))))
```

Our approach has several advantages. It reports the semantic compositionnality of datetime expressions. It allows to infer implicit informations (August 7 or 8 (August implicitly)). Our approach is quite flexible to give a semantic interpretation even the most complex datetime expressions. The contextual resolution in timestamp format is facilitated by the richness of tree analysis. Finally, the library adaptation to other languages can be done only by translation of semantic lexicons, the grammar being language-independant.

3.2. Contextual resolution module

As shown in the introduction, talking to other machines, services or customers require a standard format that is understandable by them. You can't really use "next Monday" to talk to them but "1468250471" will work. That's why we introduced a parser from information tree to JSON. So Monday is stored as the timestamp of Monday:

{"text": "next Monday", "timestamp": 1468250471}.

We also added multiple fields to enhance this timestamp and make it more "precise". It's quite easy to do when the date is well expressed ("September 12, 2017") but, with oral-like text it's almost never the case.

Relative datetime case: *I'm looking for a bar this evening.* When does the evening start exactly? We solve the problem of relative datetime by adding a "approximate" filed and a "radius" one. We also fixed times for each kind of "special" times like evening which is 9pm. Regarding to the 'time-object' granularity we have different radiuses. For example, this evening is hourly based so the radius is 2 hours around the decided time:

{"text": "this evening", "timestamp": 1468250471 (the time of today at 9pm), "approximate": true, radius: 7200}.

Group and alternative datetime case: *I'm free this Monday or next one.* We should look for something either this Monday or one week later? We solve the problems of group and alternative datetimes by adding an id to each "time" object. Then the script returns a super object containing an array of time object and a logical string:

{"times":
[{"id": 1, "text": "this Monday", "timestamp": 1468250471 (the time of next monday), "approximate": false},
{"id": 2, "text": "next one", "timestamp": 1468855271 (the time of next Monday), "approximate": false}],
"logic": "1 || 2"}.

Urgency datetime case. There's sometimes notion of urgency in datetimes: *I need a cab right now.* We forward through a particular field:

{"times": [{"id": 1, "text": "right now", "timestamp": 1468250471 (the time of next Monday), "approximate": false, urgent: true}], "logic": "1"}.

4. A brief evaluation

We evaluated our approach with a corpus of 639 incoming messages extracted from our database. The messages contain datetime expressions. The aim of the evaluation was to measure semantic interpretation efficacy checking frames and patterns in analysis tree. For the evaluation, the measures of precision, recall and F1 are used. We obtained a high recall (0,994), precision (0,814) and F1 score (0,895) in interpreting datetime expressions.

5. Conclusion

We presented an open-source library for datetime resolution in French. In future work, we plan (i) to add new temporal notions as period, duration and set, (ii) to make a more detailed evaluation and (iii) to translate the semantic lexicons in order to adapt library for other languages.

References

Bethard S. and Parker J. (2016). "A Semantically Compositional Annotation Scheme for Time Normalization". In: *Proceedings of the Tenth International Conference on Language Resources and Evaluation (LREC 2016).*

Chang A. X. and Manning C. D. (2012). "SUTIME: A Library for Recognizing and Normalizing Time Expressions". In: *Proceedings of the 8th International Conference on Language Resources and Evaluation (LREC 2012).*

Fillmore C. (1976). "Frame semantics and the nature of language". In: *Annals of the New York Academy of Sciences: Conference on the Origin and Development of Language and Speech.*

Hank P. (2004). "Corpus Pattern Analysis". In: *Proceedings of the 11th Euralex.*

Pustejovsky J., Lee K., Bunt H., and Romary L. (2010). "ISO-TimeML: An International Standard for Semantic Annotation". In: *Proceedings of the 7th International Conference on Language Resources and Evaluation (LREC 2010).*

Strötgen J. and Gertz M. (2010). "Heideltime: high quality rule-based extraction and normalization of temporal expressions". In: *Proceedings of the 5th International Workshop on Semantic Evaluation (SemEval 2010).*

Verhagen M., Mani I., Sauri R., Knippen R., Jang S. B., Littman J., Rumshisky A., Philipps J. and Pustejovsky J. (2005). "Automating temporal annotation with TARSQI". In: *Proceedings of the 43th Annual Meeting of The Association for Computational Linguistics (ACL 2005).*

TASTY: Interactive Entity Linking As-You-Type

Sebastian Arnold **Robert Dziuba** **Alexander Löser**
Beuth University of Applied Sciences
Luxemburger Straße 10
13353 Berlin, Germany
{sarnold,s58345,aloeser}@beuth-hochschule.de

Abstract

We introduce TASTY (Tag-as-you-type), a novel text editor for interactive entity linking as part of the writing process. Tasty supports the author of a text with complementary information about the mentioned entities shown in a 'live' exploration view. The system is automatically triggered by keystrokes, recognizes mention boundaries and disambiguates the mentioned entities to Wikipedia articles. The author can use seven operators to interact with the editor and refine the results according to his specific intention while writing. Our implementation captures syntactic and semantic context using a robust end-to-end LSTM sequence learner and word embeddings. We demonstrate the applicability of our system in English and German language for encyclopedic or medical text. Tasty is currently being tested in interactive applications for text production, such as scientific research, news editorial, medical anamnesis, help desks and product reviews.

1 Introduction

Entity linking is the task of identifying mentions of named entities in free text and resolving them to their corresponding entries in a structured knowledge base (Hachey et al., 2013). These two steps are often executed as batch process *after* the document has been written by the author. Contrary, doctors during a medical anamnesis, technicians writing supportive manuals or assistants in help desks desire entity linking *during* writing. Ideally, a machine could highlight relevant information about recognized entities while the author is typing the text and gradually adapt the results to complement his task.

Contribution. TASTY is such a novel text editing interface for fine-grained tagging of text articles as part of the writing process. Figure 1 shows an example of the editor in use. While the author is typing characters, a contextual sequence learner immediately recognizes mention boundaries, tags them in-line, resolves associated articles and displays them beside the document. When more context is written, the system reacts and refines boundaries and associations without interrupting the process. The author can *add*, *remove* and *disambiguate* tags according to his task and knowledge. Tasty's extraction model recognizes multi-word mentions and can identify entities that are both in and outside the knowledge base. It does not require linguistic features and is robust to misspelled or out-of-vocabulary words. To our knowledge, Tasty is the first system that implements an interactive entity linking task for manifold scenarios. We apply it to German and English language for encyclopedic and medical text without any change of hyperparameters. In the rest of this paper, we guide through the user interface using a medical examination scenario in Section 2, explain the process of interactive entity linking in Section 3, and conclude in Section 4 with an evaluation and discussion. A live demo and video of Tasty can be found at http://dbl43.beuth-hochschule.de/demo/tasty/

2 Demonstration Scenario

TASTY supplies doctors with supplemental materials. As demonstration example we showcase a medical *History and Physical Examination (H&P)* write-up, where doctors write text about a patient's

Proceedings of COLING 2016, the 26th International Conference on Computational Linguistics: System Demonstrations, pages 111–115, Osaka, Japan, December 11-17 2016.

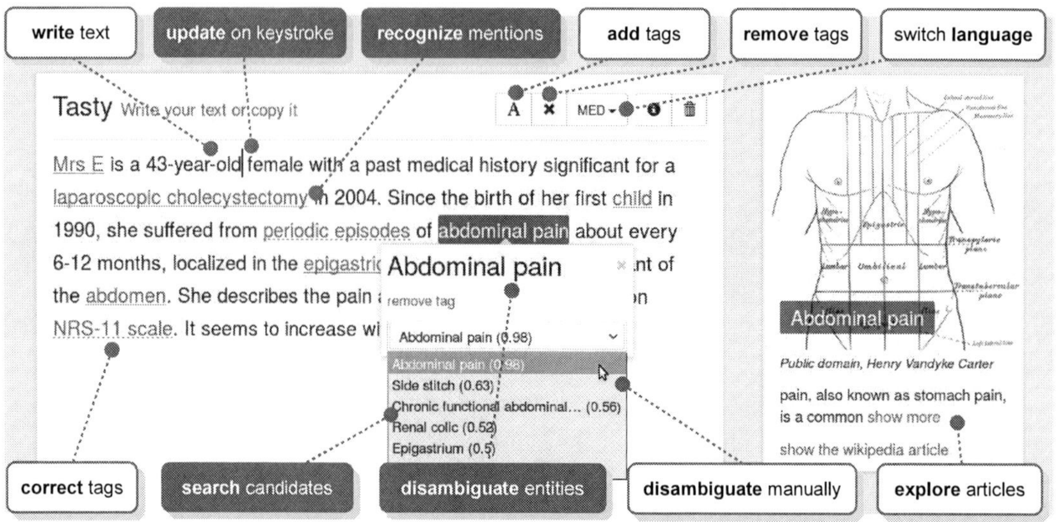

Figure 1: Example of writing a text in Tasty's user interface. Named entities are displayed as tags, articles appear on the right side. White boxes denote interaction operators, filled boxes show system actions.

history and conditions. Tasty can recognize these medical conditions and link them to Wikipedia articles. Other possible targets are e.g. research papers or relevant archived doctor letters. As a result, a doctor may learn from these documents additional insights for sharpening her focus in the write-up.

We showcase the following scenario as an example H&P (see Figure 1): The doctor starts by writing the first sentence about her patient: "Mrs E is a 43-year-old female with a past medical history significant for a laparoscopic cholecystectomy". Tasty responds to key strokes, recognizes mentions, searches for candidates and displays a complementary article for *cholecystectomy* next to the document. The doctor might explore the article and incrementally learn about important aspects of this condition. She might continue writing "she suffered from periodic episodes of abdominal pain localized in the epigastric region" and manually select a more precise disambiguation for the phrase *abdominal pain*. She may correct further tagging errors, e.g. remove the unwanted tag *Mrs E*. In case of a missing tag, the doctor can edit a phrase, e.g. NRS-11 pain scale and tag it manually. The system reacts and returns a disambiguation.

3 Interactive Entity Linking Process

We implement interactive entity linking using *mention recognizer*, *candidate searcher* and *link disambiguator* stages (Hachey et al., 2013). We extend the process by an interactive cycle that includes *partial update* and *user feedback* operators, as shown in Figure 2. We implement Tasty as demonstrator for English (EN) and German language (DE) and a specialized medical scenario (MED).

Step 1: Update while the author is typing. Tasty's user interface is based on a lightweight rich text editor[1] that we extend to display named entity mentions as in-line tags. Tasty captures the author's key strokes and detects word boundaries after space or punctuation characters. We split a document of length n into a sequence of word tokens $d = (w_1, \ldots, w_n)$ using a language-independent whitespace tokenizer[2]. In a partial update step, we analyze only the changed portion $\tilde{d} = (w_b, \ldots, w_e)$, $1 \leq b < e \leq n$ of the document. We expand indexes b and e to sentence boundaries and omit any further linguistic processing.

Step 2: Recognize mention boundaries. We define a mention m as the longest possible span of adjacent tokens that refers to a an entity or relevant concept of a real-world object, such as epigastric region. In Tasty, we further assume that mentions are non-recursive and non-overlapping. The objective of this step is to detect all mention spans $M_{\tilde{d}} = \{m_i\}$ in the document portion. We model this task as

[1]We use Quill v1.0.0-beta.11 `http://quilljs.com`

[2]We use PTBTokenizer from Stanford CoreNLP 3.6.0 `http://stanfordnlp.github.io/CoreNLP/`

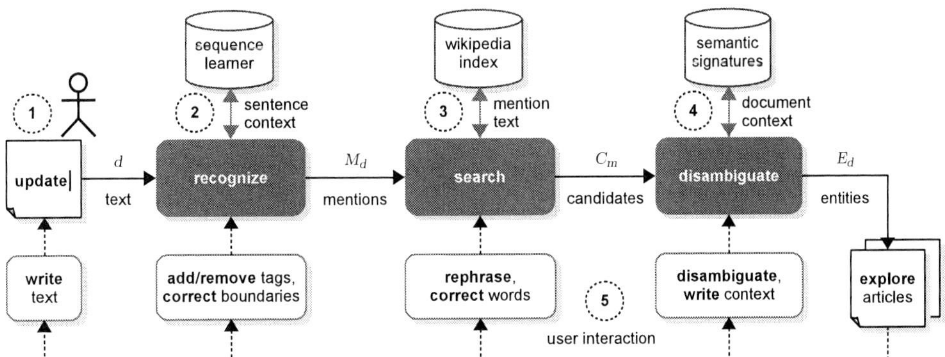

Figure 2: Overview of the interactive entity linking process in Tasty. While the author is writing a text, the system recognizes mentions, searches for entity candidates and disambiguates the mention to its corresponding Wikipedia article. The author is able to interact with every stage of the extraction process.

context-sensitive sequential word labeling problem. We predict for each token $w_t \in \tilde{d}$ a target label $\hat{y}_t$ according to the BIOES tagging scheme (Ratinov and Roth, 2009) with respect to its surrounding words (Eq. 1). From these labels, we populate $M_{\tilde{d}}$ in a single iteration. For the prediction task, we utilize long short-term memory (LSTM) networks (Hochreiter and Schmidhuber, 1997), which are are able to capture long-range sequential context information with short answer times. The input is a sequence of word feature vectors $x(w_t)$ with three components: First, we use lowercase letter-trigram word hashing (Huang et al., 2013) to encode word syntax on character level. This technique splits a word into discriminative three-letter 'syllables' with boundary markers, e.g. cell $\rightarrow$ {#ce, cel, ell, ll#} to make the bag robust against misspellings and out-of-vocabulary words. Second, we utilize word embeddings (Mikolov et al., 2013)[3] to represent word semantics in dense vector space. Third, we encode surface form features by generating a vector of flags that indicate e.g. initial capitalization, uppercase, lower case or mixed case.

$$\hat{y}_t = \underset{l \in \{B,I,O,E,S\}}{\arg\max} \; \mathrm{p}\big(y_t = l \mid x(w_b), \ldots, x(w_{t-1}), x(w_t), x(w_{t+1}), \ldots, x(w_e)\big) \tag{1}$$

We pass through $\tilde{d}$ bidirectionally using a stacked BLSTM+LSTM architecture (Arnold et al., 2016)[4]. Our recognition component can be trained 'end-to-end' with only few thousand labeled sentences. For the demonstration, we provide three different pre-trained models: EN is trained to recognize named entities (persons, organizations, locations and misc) in English encyclopedic text, DE captures proper nouns (untyped) in German encyclopedic text, and MED recognizes biomedical terms in scientific text.

Step 3: Search for candidate links. Our next step is to resolve a subset of Wikipedia article candidates C_m for each of the detected mentions m. We especially aim to capture a large number of candidates for highly ambiguous terms such as scale or child. For this task, we create an index of 4.5M English and 1.6M German Wikipedia abstracts[5]. We use redirects and anchor phrases to capture alternative writings and synonyms (Hachey et al., 2013). We apply a dictionary-based technique described by Ling et al. (2015) and query the index for candidates $C_m = \{c_j \mid \forall m \in \tilde{d} : c.\text{title} \approx m.\text{span}\}$ using phrase queries with BM25 similarity[6] for retrieval. In case of an empty result, we return NIL (non-linkable entity).

Step 4: Disambiguate associated articles. From the set of candidates C_m, we want to pick the most likely entity associations $E_d = \{(m_i, \hat{c}_j)\}$. We do this by picking the candidate $\hat{c}$ with maximum score depending on the mention and current document context (Eq. 2). As scoring function, we utilize short text similarity (Kenter and de Rijke, 2015) between mention context $m.d$ and a candidate article $c.d$. We

[3]We trained a 150-dimensional lowercase word2vec model using English and German CoNLL2003 and Wikipedia articles
[4]We implement the network using Deeplearning4j 0.6.0 with CUDA backend `https://deeplearning4j.org`
[5]We use DBpedia version 2015-10 `http://wiki.dbpedia.org/datasets`
[6]We use the implementation in Lucene 6.1.0 `http://lucene.apache.org`

stage	Recognize (EN)			Recognize (DE)			Recognize (MED)			Disambiguate (EN)		
dataset	CoNLL2003 NER			TIGER Treebank			GENIA Corpus			DBpedia Spotlight		
corpus	Reuters RCV-1			Fr. Rundschau			Medline abstracts			Wikipedia		
language	English			German			English			English		
domain	newswire			newswire			biomedical			encyclopedia		
annotation	named entities			proper nouns			medical terms			Wikipedia IDs		
	Prec	Rec	F1	Prec	Rec	F1	Prec	Rec	F1	Prec	Rec	F1
Stanford NER	**96.4**	73.6	83.5	68.9	31.7	43.4	31.7	7.6	12.3	–	–	–
Lingpipe	69.0	50.3	58.2	–	–	–	**91.8**	**93.8**	**92.8**	–	–	–
DBpedia Spotlight	66.6	58.6	62.4	–	–	–	–	–	–	**82.0**	62.1	**70.7**
Babelfy	44.2	62.7	51.8	–	–	–	–	–	–	57.7	46.7	51.6
TASTY	90.3	**92.0**	**91.1**	**82.7**	**83.9**	**83.3**	77.5	79.5	78.5	66.1	**64.9**	65.4

Table 1: Evaluation of Tasty's recognition and disambiguation stages (micro-averaged exact span match).

utilize word embeddings to calculate vectors $v(w_t)$ for every token in the document and aggregate them into a normalized mean document vector that we use as semantic signature $s(d)$ (Eq. 3). We finally use cosine similarity between the semantic signatures as scoring function (Eq. 4).

$$\hat{c} = \arg\max_{c \in C_m} \text{score}(c|m,d) \quad (2) \qquad s(d) = \frac{1}{n} \sum_{w_t \in d} v(w_t) \quad (3) \qquad \text{score}(c|m,d) = \frac{s(m.d) \cdot s(c.d)}{\|s(m.d)\| \|s(c.d)\|} \quad (4)$$

Step 5: Feed back user interaction. Tasty offers seven feedback operators that enable an author to interact with every component in the extraction process. All operators are based on typing or text selection. Using **write**, the author emits more context and the system reacts to word boundaries by triggering a partial update. The author might also **rephrase** single words, triggering the system to update surrounding annotations. Using the **add** button, the author is able to correct false negative predictions from the recognition component. The system will tag the selected mention, generate candidates and decide for an associated article. The **remove** button deletes selected tags to correct false positive predictions. The author can **correct** boundaries of an existing tag, and the system will update the link if necessary. If the boundaries of a tag are correct, but the link is not, the author can **disambiguate** by assigning a different candidate from the drop-down menu. Finally, the author benefits from several operators to **explore** the articles. Corrections are directly executed in the local session and fed back as training data to our model.

4 Evaluation

We evaluate Tasty's recognition and disambiguation stages compared to four state-of-the-art annotators: Stanford NER[7] and LingPipe[8] implement text chunking classifiers with pre-trained models. DBpedia Spotlight (Mendes et al., 2011) and Babelfy (Moro et al., 2014) are comprehensive systems specialized for entity linking and word sense disambiguation. We run the experiments in an isolated offline setting using the GERBIL evaluation framework (Usbeck et al., 2015) and measure micro-averaged precision, recall and NER-style F1 score for exact span match. For the recognition stage, we use test splits from English CoNLL-2003 shared task (Tjong Kim Sang and De Meulder, 2003), German TIGER Corpus (Brants et al., 2004) and biomedical GENIA Corpus (Ohta et al., 2002) datasets. For the disambiguation stage, we utilize the English DBpedia Spotlight NIF NER Corpus (Mendes et al., 2011).

Result discussion. Table 1 shows the evaluation results. We notice that Tasty's recognition stage is able to adapt to English (91.1% F1) and German newswire (83.3% F1) and English biomedical texts (78.5% F1) using small training sets of only 4000 labeled sentences and without any change of hyperparameters. This result for 'raw' mention recognition is on par with state-of-the-art text chunkers (Arnold et al., 2016) and achieves significantly higher recall on news datasets. The fact that we cannot achieve best results on biomedical text is due to generalization: while the pre-trained LingPipe model is strongly overfitted to GENIA dictionaries, Tasty leverages context and typical syllables and therefore is able to

[7]We use English CoNLL 4-class distsim CRF and German dewac CRF models `http://nlp.stanford.edu/software/CRF-NER.shtml`

[8]We use MUC6 CharLmRescoringChunker and GENIA TokenShapeChunker `http://alias-i.com/lingpipe/`

scenario	**Research**	**Editorial**	**Diagnosis**	**Help Desk**	**Shopping**
example	report writing	news authoring	anamnesis	customer support	product order
subtasks	pin topics	annotate paragraphs	lexicon search	FAQ search	price comparison
	find sources	identify topics and tags	patient history	related tickets	feature infobox
	lookup	thesaurus	side effects	manuals	user reviews
	explain	style suggestion	medical compatibility	expertise search	purchase advice

Table 2: Examples of Tasty's application in five scenarios and potential exploratory subtasks.

detect mention boundaries even if the word is misspelled or not priorly known to the system, e.g. "we treat the XYDKF34 cells with high-dosed srscklartamin." Furthermore, Tasty's disambiguation stage shows comparable performance to the comprehensive systems on the English disambiguation task (65.4% F1).

Applying TASTY. We showcased Tasty's editor with pre-trained models to 21 experienced professionals and learned about exciting application scenarios which are shown in Table 2. A large group of users applied the results of in-line entity linking to subtasks with *exploratory search intention* (Marchionini, 2006): *look up* facts or definitions for entities in the text, *learn* from complementary articles, *compare* written text against text in archives, *verify* information, *integrate* with existing tagging schemes. For future implementations, users suggested the application of *investigatory* subtasks: *evaluate* text to fit a desired tone or vocabulary, *discover* alternatives or get *advice* from user reviews or experts. For realizing these application scenarios, in our future work we will extend Tasty with powerful cross-document coreference capabilities and specialized retrieval models for a broader set of data sources.

Acknowledgements Our work is funded by the Federal Ministry of Economic Affairs and Energy (BMWi) under grant agreement 01MD15010B (Project: Smart Data Web).

References

Sebastian Arnold, Felix A. Gers, Torsten Kilias, and Alexander Löser. 2016. Robust Named Entity Recognition in Idiosyncratic Domains. In *arXiv:1608.06757 [cs.CL]*.

Sabine Brants, Stefanie Dipper, Peter Eisenberg, Silvia Hansen-Schirra, Esther König, et al. 2004. TIGER: Linguistic Interpretation of a German Corpus. *Research on Language and Computation*, 2(4):597–620.

Ben Hachey, Will Radford, Joel Nothman, Matthew Honnibal, and James R. Curran. 2013. Evaluating Entity Linking with Wikipedia. *Artificial intelligence*, 194:130–150.

Sepp Hochreiter and Jürgen Schmidhuber. 1997. Long Short-Term Memory. *Neural Comput.*, 9(8):1735–1780.

Po-Sen Huang, Xiaodong He, Jianfeng Gao, Li Deng, Alex Acero, and Larry Heck. 2013. Learning Deep Structured Semantic Models for Web Search using Clickthrough Data. In *CIKM'13*, pages 2333–2338. ACM.

Tom Kenter and Maarten de Rijke. 2015. Short Text Similarity with Word Embeddings. In *CIKM'15*, volume 15, page 115. ACM.

Xiao Ling, Sameer Singh, and Daniel S Weld. 2015. Design Challenges for Entity Linking. *ACL'15*, 3:315–328.

Gary Marchionini. 2006. Exploratory Search: From Finding to Understanding. *CACM*, 49(4):41–46.

Pablo N Mendes, Max Jakob, Andrés Garcia-Silva, and Christian Bizer. 2011. DBpedia Spotlight: Shedding Light on the Web of Documents. In *I-Semantics 2011*, pages 1–8. ACM.

Tomas Mikolov, Kai Chen, Greg Corrado, and Jeffrey Dean. 2013. Efficient Estimation of Word Representations in Vector Space. *arXiv:1301.3781 [cs.CL]*.

Andrea Moro, Alessandro Raganato, and Roberto Navigli. 2014. Entity Linking meets Word Sense Disambiguation: A Unified Approach. *ACL'14*, 2:231–244.

Tomoko Ohta, Yuka Tateisi, and Jin-Dong Kim. 2002. The GENIA Corpus: An Annotated Research Abstract Corpus in Molecular Biology Domain. In *HLT'02*, pages 82–86. Morgan Kaufmann.

Lev Ratinov and Dan Roth. 2009. Design Challenges and Misconceptions in Named Entity Recognition. In *CoNLL'09*, pages 147–155. ACL.

Erik F. Tjong Kim Sang and Fien De Meulder. 2003. Introduction to the CoNLL-2003 shared task: Language-independent named entity recognition. In *CoNLL'03*, pages 142–147. ACL.

Ricardo Usbeck, Michael Röder, Axel-Cyrille Ngonga Ngomo, Ciro Baron, Andreas Both, et al. 2015. GERBIL: General Entity Annotator Benchmarking Framework. In *WWW'15*, pages 1133–1143. IW3C2.

What topic do you want to hear about?
A bilingual talking robot using English and Japanese Wikipedias

Graham Wilcock
CDM Interact, Finland
University of Helsinki, Finland
gw@cdminteract.com

Kristiina Jokinen
University of Tartu, Estonia
University of Helsinki, Finland
kristiina.jokinen@helsinki.fi

Seiichi Yamamoto
Doshisha University, Japan
seyamamo@mail.doshisha.ac.jp

Abstract

We demonstrate a bilingual robot application, WikiTalk, that can talk fluently in both English and Japanese about almost any topic using information from English and Japanese Wikipedias. The English version of the system has been demonstrated previously, but we now present a live demo with a Nao robot that speaks English and Japanese and switches language on request. The robot supports the verbal interaction with face-tracking, nodding and communicative gesturing. One of the key features of the WikiTalk system is that the robot can switch from the current topic to related topics during the interaction in order to navigate around Wikipedia following the user's individual interests.

1 Introduction

The WikiTalk system for Wikipedia-based spoken information access dialogues is described by Jokinen and Wilcock (2012a) who also presented information access with robots in a tutorial at COLING 2012 on *Open-domain conversations with humanoid robots* (Jokinen and Wilcock, 2012b). Different aspects of the implementation of WikiTalk on Nao robots (Figure 1) are discussed in several papers, including Csapo et al. (2012) on integration of the technologies, Meena et al. (2012) on the use of gestures in interaction, and Han et al. (2012) on the use of visual, sonar and other non-verbal information.

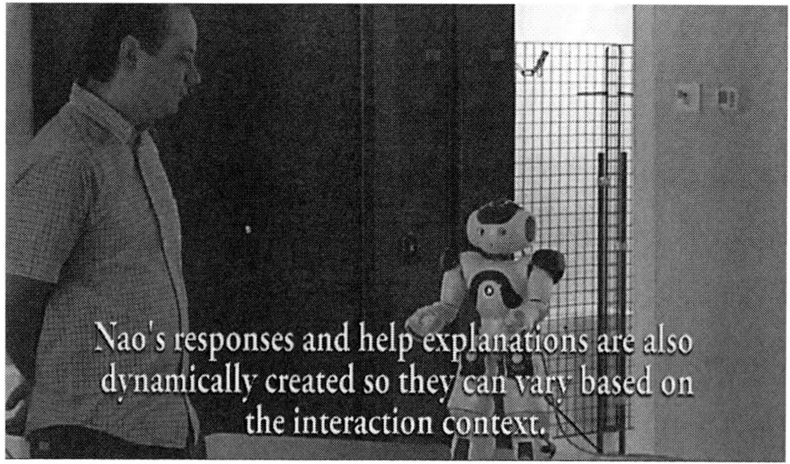

Figure 1: The first demo of English WikiTalk on a Nao robot at Supélec, Metz, in July 2012 (https://drive.google.com/open?id=0B-D1kVqPM1KdOEcyS25nMWpjUG8).

Proceedings of COLING 2016, the 26th International Conference on Computational Linguistics: System Demonstrations, pages 116–120, Osaka, Japan, December 11-17 2016.

WikiTalk was also demonstrated at SIGDIAL 2013, using a Nao robot for spoken information access dialogues with English Wikipedia (Jokinen and Wilcock, 2013). Although the speech recognition in 2012 and 2013 often gave low confidence scores, users were able to obtain spoken information from the robot about their desired topics and were able to navigate by speech from topic to topic. An evaluation of WikiTalk was published in 2013 by Anastasiou et al. (2013), showing that the robot was regarded as a lively and exciting interaction partner with future potential as an interesting agent interface, although the users' expectations about fluent speech interaction were higher than the robot's actual capabilities.

We subsequently developed multilingual capabilities for WikiTalk by adapting techniques for internationalisation and localisation of software systems to our spoken dialogue system, as described by Laxström et al. (2016). The first two localisations were for English and Finnish. A Finnish-speaking robot using WikiTalk was first demonstrated at EU Robotics Week 2014 in Helsinki. A video report by Iltalehti newspaper titled "This robot speaks Finnish and can tell you what is a robot" can be seen at `http://www.iltalehti.fi/iltvdigi/201411290140927_v4.shtml`.

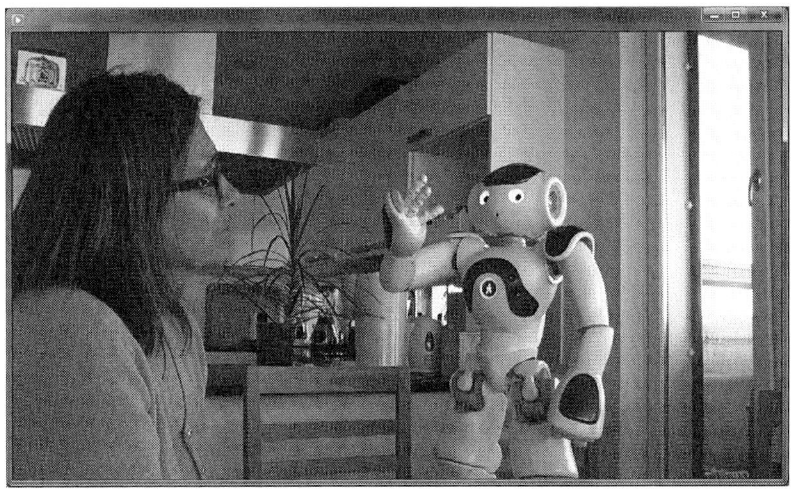

Figure 2: A robot talking in Finnish about a wide range of topics in a domestic setting (`https://drive.google.com/open?id=0B-D1kVqPMlKdY05JakMtMFJwRnc`).

The video in Figure 2 shows a robot in a domestic setting talking in Finnish about a wide range of topics using information from Finnish Wikipedia. Recent improvements in speech recognition can be seen by comparing the video in Figure 1 with the more recent videos (Figures 2 and 3). In the earlier video the robot often has low confidence scores for speech recognition and in that case is programmed to ask the user for confirmation, often asking for example "Did you mean *enough*?". In the later videos this almost never happens. Also in the earlier video the user leans forward to speak as close as possible to the microphone located in the robot's forehead, but this is not necessary in the more recent videos.

A localised Japanese version of WikiTalk developed in 2015 is described by Okonogi et al. (2015). At SIGDIAL 2015 we presented a video (Wilcock and Jokinen, 2015) showing a robot speaking English and Japanese, getting information from English and Japanese Wikipedias, and switching languages on demand. The dialogues with the robot in this video are described in Section 2.

At COLING 2016 we will demonstrate English and Japanese WikiTalk with a bilingual Nao robot, showing the improved speech recognition capabilities and focussing on unscripted user interaction and the system's ability to shift smoothly from the current topic to related topics to follow the individual user's interests. The demonstrated system is described in Section 3.

Future plans, including a system that can be configured for Nao and Pepper robots and also for robots that use ROS, the open source Robot Operating System, are briefly described in Section 4.

2 The robot dialogues in the video shown at SIGDIAL 2015

The video in Figure 3 shows information access dialogues with English and Japanese WikiTalk, using a bilingual Nao robot that switches language on demand. This video was shown at SIGDIAL 2015 and is described by Wilcock and Jokinen (2015).

Figure 3: Annotated video of an English-Japanese language-switching robot
(`https://drive.google.com/open?id=0B-D1kVqPMlKdRD1kVHh4Z2tUTG8`).

The video lasts just over 14 minutes. The robot speaks English with an English-speaking user in the first 7 minutes, then speaks Japanese with a Japanese-speaking user for 5 minutes, and finally switches back to English for the same English-speaking user for the last 2 minutes.

At the beginning the robot identifies a human face and makes eye-contact. When the human moves, the robot uses face-tracking to maintain eye contact. It explains in English that it can talk about any topic in Wikipedia, and suggests some favourites such as Shakespeare and Manchester United. It briefly switches to Japanese to invite the user to select Japanese, but the human ignores the offer and the robot switches immediately back to English.

The user asks for "Shakespeare", one of the suggested topics. The robot connects to Wikipedia via wifi, downloads the latest version of the article about the selected topic, processes the information to produce sentences suitable for speaking, and begins talking about Shakespeare. The robot continues talking about this topic for some time, but after completing a paragraph-sized chunk of information with no interruption by the user, the robot stops and asks explicitly whether to continue or not.

The user asks to "continue" and the robot continues telling more information about Shakespeare. After another paragraph-sized chunk of information about the same topic, the robot does not simply ask whether to continue, but explains some of the dialogue options by telling the user "You can change to other topics related to Shakespeare simply by saying them". The user then asks about Shakespeare's son Hamnet so the robot shifts topic and starts talking about Hamnet Shakespeare.

After the robot mentions Shakespeare's play Julius Caesar, the human asks about "Julius Caesar" and the robot starts talking about the play. Interestingly, the robot mentions the historical person Julius Caesar while talking about the play with the same name. Next the human again asks about "Julius Caesar", and this time the robot starts talking about Julius Caesar the person, not the play, as the person is more recently mentioned.

Soon the English-speaker stops interacting and goes away, and a Japanese-speaker approaches the robot and says "Nihongo" (the name of the Japanese language in Japanese). The robot switches to Japanese, makes eye-contact with the new person, and explains in Japanese that it can talk about any topic in Wikipedia, suggesting some favourite topics. The Japanese user also selects Shakespeare, and this time the robot gets information about Shakespeare from Japanese Wikipedia.

The robot talks about Shakespeare in Japanese, and also explains the Japanese versions of various commands and interactions. The Japanese-speaking user asks in particular about Romeo and Juliet. After 5 minutes he decides to stop and then the English-speaker returns. He simply says "English" and the robot switches back to English speech. The video ends during this part of the interaction.

3 Description of the demonstrated system

The demonstrated system addresses the problem of open-domain interaction, i.e. how to enable robots to talk fluently about an unlimited range of topics. Given that companion-type interactive applications are expected to become more popular in the future there is a need for systems that can chat and entertain the human users on an unlimited range of topics, and the system's ability to change topics fluently and find relevant information is important. The impact of multilingual robot agents which are capable of talking in such situations is huge, not only from the technological point of view but also considering how they affect human life: such interaction skills will make the world more complex but also extend human cognitive, physical and interaction capabilities.

Comparing the demo with existing systems, there are other systems that can read Wikipedia articles aloud, but WikiTalk also smoothly shifts topics in the middle of an article when prompted by the user. For example, as shown in the English-Japanese video (Figure 3), if the robot is talking about Japan and mentions "kanji" when explaining the Japanese name for Japan, the user can say "kanji?" and the system smoothly switches topics and starts talking about kanji after getting information from Wikipedia about this new topic. Details of the implementation of smooth topic shifting in WikiTalk are given by Wilcock (2012). In addition, WikiTalk switches languages smoothly on demand.

One novel aspect of the approach concerns internationalisation. Developers of devices where spoken dialogue systems are used, such as robots, can help internationalisation by providing better interfaces to enable better synchronisation of different modalities, for example audio and gestures or modules for detecting the gender of the user. This enables the robot system to address better the unique functional property, namely to talk about an unlimited range of topics using Wikipedia. Another aspect is that the system uses reliable and up-to-date information written and edited by humans in Wikipedia. Detailed discussions of internationalisation and localisation are given in (Laxström et al., 2016).

The system is also being applied in the revitalisation of endangered languages by the use of language and speech technologies. In Finland, the DigiSami project (Jokinen et al., 2016) is developing a Sami-speaking robot application based on WikiTalk, in order to encourage the North Sami language community in Lapland to view their language as a language with a future as well as a past. This SamiTalk application is described by Wilcock et al. (2016).

4 Future plans

Future versions of WikiTalk are likely to include new language localisations such as French, German and Dutch versions, which will use information from French, German and Dutch Wikipedias. WikiTalk will be developed by CDM Interact (`www.cdminteract.com`), a Finnish social robotics company.

WikiTalk will also be available for Pepper robots, which use the same Naoqi operating system used by Nao robots. Previously, Pepper robots were only available in Japan and at first they only spoke Japanese, but now Pepper robots are available in Europe and speak several European languages like Nao robots. Of course, the bilingual English and Japanese version of WikiTalk which is already available on Nao is very suitable for Pepper robots in Japan.

Future plans also include a version of WikiTalk for ROS, the open source Robot Operating System (Wikipedia, 2016), which is used by a wide range of robots from different manufacturers. A ROS version of WikiTalk will therefore be able to run on many different future robot models.

Although a ROS version of WikiTalk will not be restricted to Nao robots, it will still be usable with Nao by means of the `naoqi_bridge` interface which is part of ROS. This interface allows ROS components to invoke the functions of the Nao robot, to control for example its walking and talking using its Naoqi operating system. The same `naoqi_bridge` interface also means that ROS WikiTalk will be usable with Pepper robots, which also use the Naoqi system. ROS WikiTalk will be able to use the robots' own face-tracking, nodding and gesturing capabilities to support interaction management and the presentation of new information on humanoid robots like Nao and Pepper.

There are many application opportunities for this type of system, where a talking robot is connected to internet-based digital information sources. For example, one area is in applying new technology to education, and another is in providing robot companions for elderly people.

Acknowledgements

We thank Niklas Laxström for his work on the internationalization of WikiTalk and the localized Finnish version, and Kenichi Okonogi for his help with the localized Japanese version.

References

Dimitra Anastasiou, Kristiina Jokinen, and Graham Wilcock. 2013. Evaluation of WikiTalk - user studies of human-robot interaction. In *Proceedings of 15th International Conference on Human-Computer Interaction (HCII 2013)*, Las Vegas.

Adam Csapo, Emer Gilmartin, Jonathan Grizou, JingGuang Han, Raveesh Meena, Dimitra Anastasiou, Kristiina Jokinen, and Graham Wilcock. 2012. Multimodal conversational interaction with a humanoid robot. In *Proceedings of 3rd IEEE International Conference on Cognitive Infocommunications (CogInfoCom 2012)*, pages 667–672, Kosice.

JingGuang Han, Nick Campbell, Kristiina Jokinen, and Graham Wilcock. 2012. Investigating the use of non-verbal cues in human-robot interaction with a Nao robot. In *Proceedings of 3rd IEEE International Conference on Cognitive Infocommunications (CogInfoCom 2012)*, pages 679–683, Kosice.

Kristiina Jokinen and Graham Wilcock. 2012a. Constructive interaction for talking about interesting topics. In *Proceedings of Eighth International Conference on Language Resources and Evaluation (LREC 2012)*, Istanbul.

Kristiina Jokinen and Graham Wilcock. 2012b. Open-domain conversations with humanoid robots. In *COLING 2012 Tutorial*, 24th International Conference on Computational Linguistics (COLING 2012), Mumbai.

Kristiina Jokinen and Graham Wilcock. 2013. Open-domain information access with talking robots. In *14th Annual SIGdial Meeting on Discourse and Dialogue: Proceedings of the SIGDIAL 2013 Conference*, pages 360–362, Metz.

Kristiina Jokinen, Katri Hiovain, Niklas Laxström, Ilona Rauhala, and Graham Wilcock. 2016. DigiSami and digital natives: Interaction technology for the North Sami language. In *Proceedings of Seventh International Workshop on Spoken Dialogue Systems (IWSDS 2016)*, Saariselkä.

Niklas Laxström, Graham Wilcock, and Kristiina Jokinen. 2016. Internationalisation and localisation of spoken dialogue systems. In *Proceedings of Seventh International Workshop on Spoken Dialogue Systems (IWSDS 2016)*, Saariselkä.

Raveesh Meena, Kristiina Jokinen, and Graham Wilcock. 2012. Integration of gestures and speech in human-robot interaction. In *Proceedings of 3rd IEEE International Conference on Cognitive Infocommunications (CogInfoCom 2012)*, pages 673–678, Kosice.

Kenichi Okonogi, Graham Wilcock, and Seiichi Yamamoto. 2015. Nihongo WikiTalk no kaihatsu (Development of Japanese WikiTalk). In *Forum on Information Technology (FIT 2015)*, Matsuyama, Japan. (in Japanese).

Wikipedia. 2016. Robot Operating System — Wikipedia, The Free Encyclopedia. `https://en.wikipedia.org/wiki/Robot_Operating_System` [Online; accessed 24-August-2016].

Graham Wilcock and Kristiina Jokinen. 2015. Multilingual WikiTalk: Wikipedia-based talking robots that switch languages. In *Proceedings of the 16th Annual SIGdial Meeting on Discourse and Dialogue*, Prague.

Graham Wilcock, Niklas Laxström, Juho Leinonen, Peter Smit, Mikko Kurimo, and Kristiina Jokinen. 2016. Towards SamiTalk: a Sami-speaking Robot linked to Sami Wikipedia. In *Proceedings of Seventh International Workshop on Spoken Dialogue Systems (IWSDS 2016)*, Saariselkä.

Graham Wilcock. 2012. WikiTalk: A spoken Wikipedia-based open-domain knowledge access system. In *Proceedings of the COLING 2012 Workshop on Question Answering for Complex Domains*, pages 57–69, Mumbai.

Annotating Discourse Relations with The PDTB Annotator

Alan Lee[1], Rashmi Prasad[2], Bonnie Webber[3], Aravind Joshi[1]
[1]Department of Computer and Information Science, University of Pennsylvania
{aleewk, joshi}@seas.upenn.edu
[2]Department of Health Informatics and Administration, University of Wisconsin-Milwaukee
prasadr@uwm.edu
[3]School of Informatics, University of Edinburgh
Bonnie.Webber@ed.ac.uk

Abstract

The PDTB Annotator is a tool for annotating and adjudicating discourse relations based on the annotation framework of the Penn Discourse TreeBank (PDTB). This demo describes the benefits of using the PDTB Annotator, gives an overview of the PDTB Framework and discusses the tool's features, setup requirements and how it can also be used for adjudication.

1 Introduction

In recent years, discourse relations have become a topic of some interest and there has in effect been a rise in the number of corpora annotated for discourse relations. Following the release of the Penn Discourse TreeBank (PDTB) in 2008 (Prasad et al., 2008), a number of comparable corpora have since adapted the PDTB framework (Prasad et al., 2014), including the Hindi Discourse Relation Bank (Oza et al., 2009), the Leeds Arabic Discourse TreeBank (Al-Saif and Markert, 2010), the Biomedical Discourse Relation Bank (Prasad et al., 2011), the Chinese Discourse TreeBank (Zhou and Xue, 2012), the Turkish Discourse Bank (Zeyrek et al., 2013), the discourse layer of the Prague Dependency Treebank 3.0 (Bejček et al, 2013) and the TED-Multilingual Discourse Bank (TED-MDB) (Zeyrek et al., 2016).

Groups starting new discourse annotation projects have sought an openly available resource to support their work. To address this for annotation in the PDTB framework, we have packaged an updated version of our annotation tool - the PDTB Annotator - for use by the research community. Some of the potential benefits of using the PDTB Annotator include the following: i) the tool is Java-based and therefore works on a number of platforms; ii) it requires little external setup or preprocessing, minimally a set of (Unicode-encoded) text files; iii) with the use of Unicode text files, the tool works with a variety of writing systems and caters for a wide number of languages; iv) it lets a project define its own sense hierarchy; v) it doubles up as an adjudication tool - a pair of annotated file sets may be combined into an "adjudicator view" and the resulting adjudications saved into gold files; vi) each annotation is stored as a simple pipe-delimited text entry, allowing for easy retrieval or processing.

We briefly describe the PDTB annotation framework (Section 2), discuss existing annotation tools (Section 3), give a tour of the PDTB Annotator (Section 4), explain the kind of set-up and configuration for getting started (Section 5) and show how the tool can also be used for adjudication (Section 6).

2 The PDTB Annotation Framework

The PDTB follows a lexically-grounded approach for annotating discourse relations. Discourse relations can be realized explicitly in the text by *discourse connectives*. For example, the **Result** relation in (1) is annotated by marking the discourse connective *as a result* as the expression of the *Explicit* relation.

(1) *Despite the economic slowdown, there are few clear signs that growth is coming to a halt.* <u>As a result</u>, **Fed officials may be divided over whether to ease credit.** (0072)

This work has been supported by the National Science Foundation under grants RI 1422186 and RI 1421067.

Proceedings of COLING 2016, the 26th International Conference on Computational Linguistics: System Demonstrations, pages 121–125, Osaka, Japan, December 11-17 2016.

All relations are taken to have two arguments - Arg1 (shown in italics) and Arg2 (in bold). As per the revised argument-naming conventions in recent ongoing work on PDTB enrichment (Webber et al., 2016), the Arg2 in syntactically coordinated relations follows (i.e. is to the right of) Arg1, while the Arg2 in syntactically subordinated relations is (syntactically) subordinate to Arg1, regardless of textual order.

Discourse relations are not always realized as Explicit connectives. In such cases, a connective is left to be inferred by the annotator, who lexically encodes this inferred relation. This is shown in (2), where a **Reason** relation between the two adjacent sentences is annotated with *because* as the *Implicit* connective:

(2) *Also unlike Mr. Ruder, Mr. Breeden appears to be in a position to get somewhere with his agenda.* Implicit=because, **As a former White House [...], he is savvy in the ways of Washington.**. (0955)

Aside from Explicit vs Implicit relations, the PDTB framework allows for two other types of relations: *AltLex* for cases where the insertion of an Implicit connective to express an inferred relation leads to a redundancy due to the relation being alternatively lexicalized by some non-connective expression; *EntRel* for cases where only an entity-based coherence relation could be perceived between the sentences. A *NoRel* type is allowed for cases where no discourse relation or entity-based relation could be perceived between the sentences (Prasad et al., 2008).

Senses are annotated for Explicit, Implicit and AltLex relations. An annotator can also infer more than one sense between two arguments of a discourse relation. The tagset of senses is organized hierarchically into three levels. (See (Webber et al., 2016) for the latest PDTB sense hierarchy, which contains a number of refinements and improvements over the version used in PDTB 2.0.) Level 1, which contains four classes - **Temporal**, **Contingency**, **Comparison** and **Expansion**; a Level 2 subclass which further subcategorizes the Level 1 classes, and a Level 3 type, which conveys information about the *directionality* of Level 2 relations which are asymmetric. As an example, conditional relations are encoded as **Contingency** at Level 1, **Condition** at Level 2 and then either **Arg1-as-cond** (3) or **Arg2-as-cond** (4) at Level 3, depending on which argument of the relation serves as the antecedent of the conditional:

(3) *Call Jim Wright's office in downtown Fort Worth, Texas, these days* and **the receptionist still answers the phone "Speaker Wright's office.**

(4) *Insurance companies will offer a good rate* if **no one is sick**

The PDTB framework does not seek to establish links between discourse relations and makes no assumptions regarding higher-level discourse structures (e.g. as trees or graphs). Corpora annotated in the framework present a shallow representation of discourse structure and are well-suited as training material for the task of shallow discourse parsing (Xue et al., 2015).

3 Existing Annotation Tools

There does not exist at present a suitable tool for the annotation of discourse relations according to the PDTB framework. There are tools for annotating relations in the framework of Rhetorical Structure Theory (Mann and Thompson, 1988), like the ISI RST Annotation Tool (Marcu, n.d.), but these tools follow a different theoretical framework and a different set of assumptions - pre-segmentation of the text is required and all relations must be recursively structured into a single hierarchical tree. More recently, the Tree Editor (TrEd) for the Prague Dependency Treebank (PDT) (Bejček et al, 2013) was extended to allow for the annotation of discourse relations (Mírovský et. al., 2015) and was indeed used for developing the discourse layer of the PDT. However, while the discourse annotation in the PDT is inspired by the lexicalized approach of the PDTB, the discourse layer is overlaid on top of the existing tectogrammatical layer and does not stand off from the raw text.

There are more general-purpose text annotation tools which might conceivably be adapted for PDTB-style annotations, provided they allow for the free annotation of segments of text and then for customized linkings between these elements (e.g. MMAX2 (Müller and Strube, 2006), PALinkA (Orăsan, 2003)). However, general-purpose tools understandably require considerable customization and their output representations, typically in XML, often require more technical post-processing before in-depth analysis can proceed. In our experience, many annotation projects using the PDTB framework start off as pilots or prototypes with quick turnaround time requirements and cannot afford the disproportionate effort needed to customize complex multi-purpose tools.

4 The PDTB Annotator: A Brief Tour

The PDTB Annotator is a Java-based tool released as a runnable jar file and has been successfully used by Mac, Windows and Linux-based users running at least the 1.6 version of the Java Runtime Environment. The jar file is used in conjunction with a preconfigured file (called Options.cfg) which controls the sense tags as well as Implicit connectives available to the annotator (see Section 5).

The main window of the PDTB Annotator contains three sub-panels, as discussed below and shown in respective left-to-right order in Fig. 1.

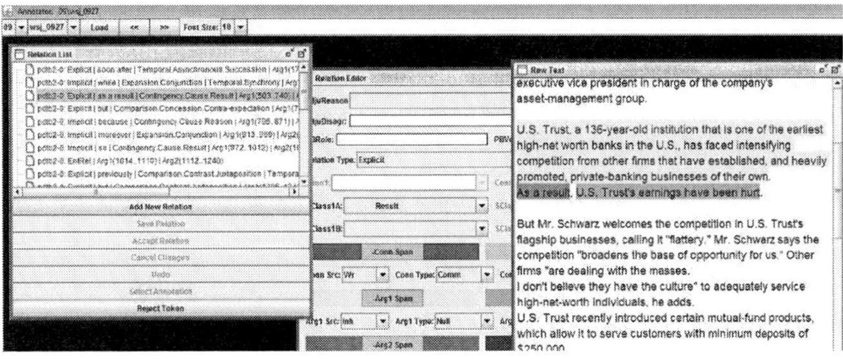

Figure 1: A view of the PDTB Annotator. Users may rearrange the subpanels as needed.

- The *Relation List panel* lists all annotation tokens for a particular text. Users also add new tokens, undo changes or reject a token here.
- The *Relation Editor panel* provides functionality for annotating the various features of a discourse relation - the relation type, the arguments of a relation (Arg1 and Arg2), the sense(s) of a relation, etc. Comments are also added on this panel.
- The *Raw Text panel* shows the actual text to be annotated. The annotator selects relevant portions of text using the mouse (discontinuous text spans are possible) and then switches to the Relation Editor to add the discourse relation features of the selected span.

Tokens are saved into a simple annotation file format, with one annotation file corresponding to each raw text file. Each token is represented by a pipe-delimited line of text and there are presently 34 fields in use. A description of each field can be found in The PDTB Group (2016). While most fields encode discourse relation features, a few additional ones are also used for adjudication and project management purposes (see Section 6). [1]

The original file format developed for PDTB 2.0 was designed for easy translation into Backus-Naur Form for use with the tools and APIs of the time. The difficulty of working with the older format led to the development of the simpler current format, where the pipe-delimited text entries can be easily processed by text-processing tools or imported into a spreadsheet.

5 Setup and Configuration

The PDTB Annotator makes use of three sets of files: i) text files; ii) annotation files; iii) comment files. Of these, only text files are obligatory. The resources needed for setting up an annotation project using the PDTB Annotator are minimal:

[1]Two fields - PB Role and PB Verb are specific to the PDTB. These were created to indicate links between certain PDTB tokens and semantic roles in the PropBank (Palmer, 2005). These fields can be left empty for other purposes.

- A set of text files. These should be raw text files and UTF-8 encoded.[2] A simple directory structure is assumed, consisting of a single base directory containing one or more sub-directories. The text files are distributed into these sub-directories. Naming conventions are up to the user.

- A base directory for annotation files. If an annotator is to annotate from scratch, this directory is left empty. An annotation file corresponding to each text file will be created dynamically as the annotation proceeds, mirroring the directory structure and file-naming convention of the text files.

The basic requirements aside, some common additional configuration or preprocessing steps include: i) defining a base directory for **comment files**, which lets the annotator comment on a token; ii) providing annotators with a set of **pre-annotated files**. For example, a set of explicit connectives might be pre-identified for annotation, automatically extracted from the raw texts and imported into the PDTB file format; iii) **Customizing the sense hierarchy**. This is done by simply modifying the text-based hierarchy provided in Options.cfg; iv) **Updating the list of implicit connectives** from the dropdown menu in the Relation Editor panel. This is also done by modifying Options.cfg, which contains by default a list of English connectives. A project might want to show connectives in a different language, for example.

6 Adjudication

The PDTB Annotator also doubles up as an adjudication tool. Using the tool this way, an adjudicator can evaluate corresponding tokens from two annotators.[3] For each pair of corresponding tokens, the adjudicator selects and potentially edits one of the tokens as the gold entry, then saves it into a gold file.

There is no additional setup needed to use the PDTB Annotator as an adjudication tool beyond specifying, upon launching the tool, the locations of the two sets of annotated files to be adjudicated. Figure 2 shows the "adjudicator view" of the Relation List panel introduced in Figure 1. Here, a list of gold tokens is shown and each node in the list can be expanded to show the pair of annotations being adjudicated, as shown for the third and fourth tokens. An unadjudicated gold token is displayed in red along with an agreement report - either "Annotators agree" (token #3), or "Disagreements" (tokens #2 and #4). Disagreements are reported for mismatches in sense, relation type or argument span. Adjudicated tokens are shown in black (token #1).

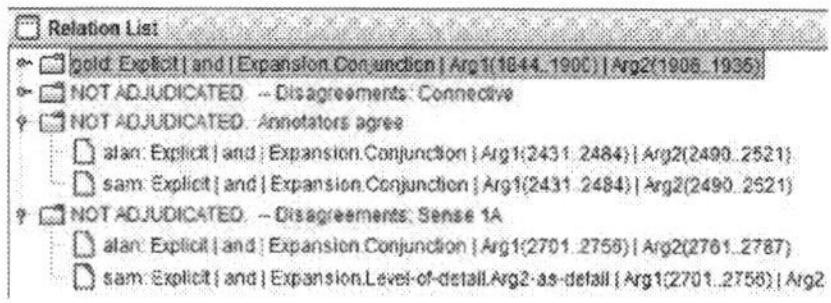

Figure 2: Adjudicator view of the Relation List panel

For each adjudicated token, the adjudicator can also specify the *reason* for the adjudication decision - e.g. due to annotator agreement, or the adjudicator agreed with one of the annotators, or corrections were made by the adjudicator, etc. For disagreeing tokens, the adjudicator can also specify the *type* of disagreement - e.g. a sense disagreement, a mismatch in argument spans, etc. There are fields reserved for these adjudication features in the annotation file format.

7 Conclusion

The latest version of the PDTB Annotator is designed to be convenient by serving the purposes of both annotation and adjudication. It can be run on many platforms and supports several writing systems and languages. By having control over the elements of some features, such as the sense hierarcy and implicit connectives, users can explore the suitability of other/additional senses or connectives for their corpus.

[2]By supporting UTF-8 encoded files, the PDTB Annotator works for a number of languages and writing systems. Romanized writing systems particularly benefit from the dynamic tokenization of the raw texts (by whitespace/punctuation), which makes it easier to select text spans using a mouse. Such tokenizations can be turned off for other writing systems.

[3]The current tool assumes at most two annotators, as agreement reports are based on a pair of annotators.

New features to record more fine-grained analyses during adjudication, such as the reason and type of disagreement, can be directly used to study task complexity in greater depth. The tool can be found at `http://www.seas.upenn.edu/~pdtb/annotator.html`. Any questions can be directed to the first author.

References

Al-Saif, A. and K. Markert. 2010. *The Leeds Arabic Discourse Treebank: Annotating discourse connectives for Arabic.* Proceedings of the 7th International Conference on Language Resources and Evaluation, Valletta.

Bejček, B., Hajičová, E., Hajič, J., Jínová, P., Kettnerová, V., Kolářová, V., Mikulová, M., Mírovský, J., Nedoluzhko, A., Panevová, J., Poláková, L., Ševčíková, M., Štěpánek, J. and Zikánová, S. 2013 *Prague Dependency Treebank 3.0.* Available at <http://ufal.mff.cuni.cz/pdt3.0/>

Mann, W. and S. Thompson 1988. *Rhetorical Structure Theory: A Theory of Text Organization.* Text 8(3):243281.

Marcu, D. n.d. Available at <http://www.isi.edu/licensedsw/RSTTool/index.html>

Mírovský, J., Jínová, P. and Poláková, L. *Discourse Relations in the Prague Dependency Treebank 3.0* Proceedings of COLING 2014, the 25th International Conference on Computational Linguistics: System Demonstrations, pp. 34-38

Müller, C. and M. Strube *Multi-Level Annotation of Linguistic Data with MMAX2.* In: Sabine Braun, Kurt Kohn, Joybrato Mukherjee (Eds.): Corpus Technology and Language Pedagogy. New Resources, New Tools, New Methods. Frankfurt: Peter Lang, pp. 197-214. (English Corpus Linguistics, Vol.3).

Orăsan, C. *PALinkA: A highly customisable tool for discourse annotation.* In Proceedings of the Fourth SIGdial Workshop of Discourse and Dialogue

Oza, U., R. Prasad, S. Kolachina, S. Meena, D. M. Sharma, and A. Joshi. 2009. *Experiments with annotating discourse relations in the Hindi Discourse Relation Bank.* Proceedings of the 7th International Conference on Natural Language Processing (ICON), Hyderabad.

Palmer M., P. Kingsbury P, D. Gildea 2005 *The Proposition Bank: An Annotated Corpus of Semantic Roles.* Computational Linguistics. 31 (1): 71106.

Prasad. R, N. Dinesh, A. Lee, E. Miltsakaki, L. Robaldo, A. Joshi, and B. Webber. 2008. *The Penn Discourse Treebank 2.0.* Proceedings of the 6th International Conference on Language Resources and Evaluation, Marrackech.

Prasad, R., S. McRoy, N. Frid, A. Joshi, and H. Yu. 2011. *The Biomedical Discourse Relation Bank.* The Biomedical Discourse Relation Bank. BMC Bioinformatics, 12(188):118.

The PDTB Group. 2016. *The PDTB Annotator.* <http://www.seas.upenn.edu/~pdtb/annotator.html>

Prasad, R., B. Webber and A. Joshi 2014. *Reflections on the Penn Discourse TreeBank, Comparable Corpora, and Complementary Annotation.* Computational Linguistics 49(4). pp. 921-950.

Webber, B., R. Prasad, A. Lee and A. Joshi 2016. *A Discourse-Annotated Corpus of Conjoined VPs.* Proceedings of the Tenth Linguistic Annotation Workshop (LAW). Berlin.

Xue, N., H. Ng, S. Pradhan, R. Prasad, C. Bryant and A. Rutherford 2015. *The CoNLL-2015 Shared Task on Shallow Discourse Parsing.* Proceedings of the Nineteenth Conference on Computational Natural Language Learning - Shared Task. Beijing.

Zeyrek, D., I. Demirşahin, A. Sevdik-Çallı and R. Çakıcı 2016. *Turkish Discourse Bank: Porting a discourse annotation style to a morphologically rich language.* Dialogue and Discourse, 4(2):174184.

Zeyrek, D., A. Mendes, S. Gibbon, Y. Grishina, M. Ogrodniczuk 2016. *TED-Multilingual Discourse Bank (TED-MDB): TED Talks annotated in the PDTB style..* (in preparation).

Zhou, Y. and N. Xue 2012. *PDTB-style discourse annotation of Chinese text.* Proceedings of the 50th Annual Meeting of the ACL, Jeju Island.

Opinion Retrieval Systems using Tweet-external Factors

Yoon-Sung Kim
Dept. of Computer Science
Korea University
Seoul, Korea
kys0205@korea.ac.kr

Young-In Song
Dept. of Computer Science
Korea University
Seoul, Korea
youngin.song@gmail.com

Hae-Chang Rim
Dept. of Computer Science
Korea University
Seoul, Korea
rim@korea.ac.kr

Abstract

Opinion mining is a natural language processing technique which extracts subjective information from natural language text. To estimate an opinion about a query in large data collection, an opinion retrieval system that retrieves subjective and relevant information about the query can be useful. We present an opinion retrieval system that retrieves subjective and query-relevant tweets from Twitter, which is a useful source of obtaining real-time opinions. Our system outperforms previous opinion retrieval systems, and it further provides subjective information about Twitter authors and hashtags to describe their subjective tendencies.

1 Introduction

Opinion mining is a natural language processing technique estimating an opinion from natural language text. This is useful for various users who report opinions in case of making reference to an opinion in various texts such as blogs, microblogs and forums. It can be used for identifying relevant opinions of customers about products or social issues. In addition, companies can utilize for analysis and establishing a marketing strategy using the analyzed results.

Analyzing sentiment for an entity from a large collection of data is costly. Therefore, an opinion retrieval system providing subjective and query-relevant documents can be useful. Especially, social network services such as Twitter are useful sources for estimating real-time public opinion. In case of social network services, there are limitations for retrieving subjective documents because of the limitations on the document length (Luo et al., 2012).

As a result of inherent document length limitations, several social search engine systems have been developed. The Sentiment140[1] system based on (Go et al., 2009) provides query-relevant and subjective documents in Twitter and the proportion of a collected and analysed sentiment. This system, however, does not perform sufficiently effective because it classifies documents using simple text features. Moreover, this system does not provide subjective information about Twitter authors and hashtags, although these features are useful for sentiment classification (Barbosa and Feng, 2010). Formerly, Twendz and Tweetfeel were the tools used for labeling Twitter polarity classification, however, these are no longer in service.[2]

We present a more powerful opinion retrieval system using tweet-external resources, which are used in state-of-the-art sentiment analysis approaches (Go et al., 2009; Luo et al., 2012; Luo et al., 2015). Our opinion retrieval system outperforms previous social network retrieval systems by adding features that are proposed in state-of-the-arts. In addition, our system provides information pursuant to subjectivity tendencies of Twitter authors and hashtags by showing sentiment statistics and tweet texts so that users can determine the opinion of the queries and subjective factors.

---

[1] http://www.sentiment140.com

[2] Twendz: http://twendz.waggeneredstrom.com, Tweetfeel: http://www.tweetfeel.com

Proceedings of COLING 2016, the 26th International Conference on Computational Linguistics: System Demonstrations, pages 126–130, Osaka, Japan, December 11-17 2016.

2 Opinion Retrieval System using Tweet-external Factors

Our opinion retrieval system retrieves subjective and query-relevant tweet documents. To provide the results, we use a learning-to-rank framework, utilizing several features that are helpful for opinion retrieval, as well as subjective information about each author and hashtag. Section 2.1 presents the opinion retrieval model, which forms the core of our system. Next, we describe how to use our opinion retrieval system in Section 2.2, and we show the architecture of our system in Section 2.3.

2.1 Opinion Retrieval Model using Learning-to-rank Framework

Our system performs opinion retrieval by re-ranking ad-hoc retrieval results. We re-rank our results using a learning-to-rank framework which is used in previous works (Luo et al., 2012). We use the features related to the document, author meta information, and Twitter-external information in our system.

Document features denote the characteristics that are observed in a tweet document. Several state-of-the-arts of polarity classification and opinion retrieval approaches use these features (Go et al., 2009; Barbosa and Feng, 2010; Luo et al., 2012; Luo et al., 2015). We use BM25 score, opinion word rate, and existence of link, hashtag, and mention.

Author-meta information is the information that we obtain from the author profile. It is useful for identifying subjectivity in Twitter (Luo et al., 2012). We use tweet number, follower number, friend number, and list number for author-meta features in our system.

Twitter-external information denotes the information that is related to Twitter-specific information such as the author of a tweet and hashtag in the tweet text. We aggregate the author-related tweet list written by the author wrote and we convert it into a document. In addition, we create a document based on the hashtag-related tweet list. which is the entire list of tweets using a particular hashtag (Kim et al., 2016). In this system, we use opinion word rate, retweet rate, pronoun rate, link rate, and average tweet length features in each aggregated document.

2.2 System Usage

In this section, we describe how to use our opinion retrieval system. Our system is composed of the components shown in Figure 1:

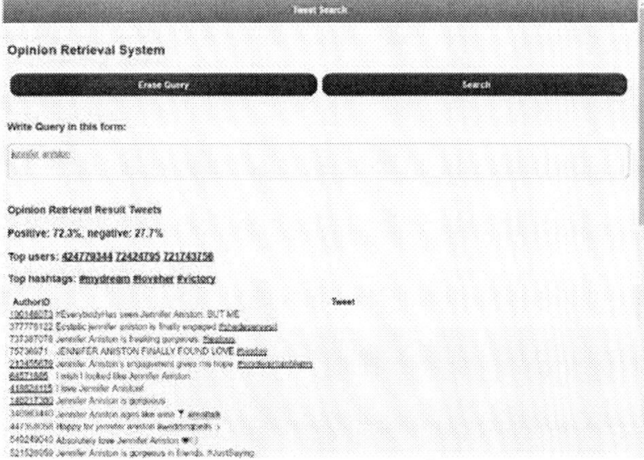

Figure 1. Screenshot of the main page of our proposed system

Figure 1 shows the screenshot of the main page of our site. On the main page, a user can write a query for retrieval. After writing such queries and deploying the search button, relevant and subjective results related to a query will be provided. As shown in Figure 1, the retrieved result consists of subjective information and the list of tweets. We provide polarity statistics, frequent authors and hashtags which have subjective information relevant to the authors' and hashtags' tendencies. Color marks in the tweet texts also give clues regarding the polarity (e.g., subjective lexicon).

The provided links for subjective author and subjective hashtags re-direct to a popup page. We provide the polarity information of the author and other subjective information and their tweet texts. Moreover, color marks of the texts are provided, which are same as the main tweet results.

2.3 System Architecture

In this section, we describe the architecture that comprises our system. Because of the absence of real-time Twitter API which provides hashtag text information, we use the English Twitter corpus using a Twitter public streaming API.

In our system, we first index the Twitter corpus for retrieval. We use Indri toolkit for indexing. Then, we extract features in the corpus for opinion retrieval, and create tweet lists for a tweet author, who wrote more than 100 tweets and hashtags which were used in more than 100 tweets. When a query is received, the retrieval system returns the top 500 tweets. We use BM25 algorithm for retrieving the queries. Then, we perform opinion retrieval by using the model described in Section 2.1. We use the ranking SVM algorithm from SVM Light toolkit. (Joachims, 1999). Finally, we provide the desired results and useful subjective information as described in Section 2.2. To provide sentiment statistics, we use a polarity classifier of (Barbosa and Feng, 2010). Finally, we utilize feature values for providing information of subjective authors and hashtags.

3 Experimental Result and Scenario

In this section, we describe the performance and effectiveness of the retrieval result of our system. In Section 3.1, we compare the performance to the previous opinion retrieval system, and in Section 3.2, we show an example of the retrieval result to explain the effectiveness of the retrieved results and the information of top users and hashtags.

3.1 Evaluation

To evaluate our system, we used the English Twitter corpus and the dataset in (Kim et al., 2016) The corpus was crawled during 1 month in 2012. The dataset was composed of tweets that are created by using Amazon Mechanical Turk. We utilized the corpus for composing the retrieval system, and then we evaluated the performance using the dataset. We used 10-fold cross validation for evaluation, and we used MAP metric. And, the Sentiment140 was used for our baseline system. We composed it using (Go et al., 2009). As shown in Table 1, our system significantly outperforms the baseline.

	Sentiment140	**Presented System**
MAP	0.2869	**0.3892**

Table 1. Performance of Sentiment140 and the presented system

3.2 Retrieval Scenario of our system

In this section, we show a scenario of retrieving a query to explain the effectiveness of our system and its usefulness in identifying the subjective tendency of the author and hashtag. Table 2 contains the top 10 retrieval results of our system when we search the query "Breaking Dawn", the name of a movie.

Rank	**Tweet Text**	**Author ID**
1	Going to watch breaking dawn #Lonely /:	Iam_princess123
2	#30GoodMovies is Twilight 6x New moon 6x Eclipse 6x Breaking Dawn part 1 6x Breaking Dawn part 2 6x #loveall	Vira_thecoldone
3	#5FavouriteFilms twilight, new moon, eclipse, breaking dawn part 1 and breaking dawn part 2	TeamKristen
4	cant wait for breaking dawn part 2 #ashamed (:	DutchZaynsters
5	#6favMovies twilight,new moon,eclipse,breaking dawn part 1,breaking dawn part 2 and welcome to the Riley's #Krisbian #Robstener #Robsesed!x	Nic_in_twiland
6	My moms face during Breaking Dawn #priceless lmao	KissaNicole
7	Twilight, New Moon, Eclipse, Breaking Dawn Part 1..& when it comes out, I'm sure Breaking Dawn Part 2 will be my fifth. ♥ #5FavouriteFilms.	fearlesskristen
8	#MoviesThatMadeMeCry breaking dawn LOL	AbbyFrasca
9	@TeamKristen: #5FavouriteFilms twilight, new moon, eclipse, breaking dawn part 1 and breaking dawn part 2 HahahaHahahaHahahaHahaha	jaythom93
10	#ReplaceMovieTitleWithSabaw : The Breaking #Sabaw (The Breaking Dawn)	_iM_sOnNy_

Table 2. Results of our system in case of retrieving "Breaking Dawn"

As shown in Table 2, we can figure out that the tweets containing opinion are in the top rank such as 1, 2, 3, 4, 5, 7, 8. The fact that the results with hashtags such as "#30GoodMovies", "#loveall", "#5FavouriteFilms" have higher ranks indicates the effectiveness of hashtag features because there are no clues about subjectivity except the hashtags.

In Table 3, we can see the lists of tweets for authors "TeamKristen" and "fearlesskristen" ranked 3 and 7 in Table 2, respectively. These tweets are about "Kristen Stewart", who is the actress of "Breaking Dawn", and the tweets are opinions about her and her movies. Table 4 shows the lists of tweets with hashtag "#30GoodMovies" and "#5FavouriteFilms" which rank 2 and 3 in Table 2, respectively. As shown in Table 4, there are subjective tweets about the movies for which these hashtags were used. Therefore, we can determine that the information provided by our subjective authors and relevant hashtags are useful for estimating subjectivity.

TeamKristen	**Fearlesskristen**
RT If you would go #LesbianForKristenStewart ;)	RT if your heart broke on 25th July 2012.
4 am and my love for Kristen is too big to let me sleep	"Ruperv." Lol omg, I love our fandom. :\')
I believe in Kristen. She's my role model for some reason.	#10PlacesIWantToGo: Kristen's house to tell her I love her. ♥ RT if you want to do that too.
IF YOU HATE KRISTEN STEWART UNFOLLOW ME, THANKS.	"You don't need to have the perfect face to be beautiful." - Kristen Jaymes Stewart. ♥
RT IF YOU STILL LOVE AND SUPPORT THE GIRL FROM MY ICON ♥	"Just follow your heart..you'll usually wind up where you want to be." - Kristen Stewart. ♥

Table 3. Examples of author-related tweets

#30GoodMovies	**#5FavouriteFilms**
I'm Legend #30GoodMovies	#5FavouriteFilms walk the line
Shaun the sheep #30GoodMovies	#5FavouriteFilms Batman: The Dark Knight
#30GoodMovies 6. Harry Potter and the half blood prince	#5FavouriteFilms the nutty professor, the original,,, jerry Lewis one
Harry Potter is one of #30GoodMovies	Oh no wait, I'm replacing Cool Runnings with Friends With Benefits #5FavouriteFilms
#30GoodMovies, anything and everything directed by Tim Burton.	#5FavouriteFilms inception - salt - 1984 - hunger games - beauty& the beast.

Table 4. Examples of hashtag-related tweets

4 Conclusion

We presented an opinion retrieval system for Twitter to find a subjective and query-relevant tweet related to a query. Our system outperformed previous opinion retrieval systems; it provides subjective information even about an individual user, which is not provided by other systems. In addition, our system can analyze the pros and cons of a product or service, which is certainly useful in the development of a marketing strategy. Unfortunately, we do not provide real-time tweet information due to the absence of a related Twitter API. If a Twitter is provided eventually, we will be able to provide real-time tweet service for real-time information of hashtag texts.

Acknowledgements

This research was supported by Next-Generation Information Computing Development Program through the National Research Foundation of Korea(NRF) funded by the Ministry of Science, ICT & Future Plannig (2012M3C4A7033344).

Reference

Barbosa L. and Feng J. 2010. *Robust Sentiment Detection on Twitter from Biased and Noisy Data*, Proceedings of the 23rd International Conference on Computational Linguistics, 36-44.

Go A., Bhayani R. and Huang L. 2009. *Twitter Sentiment Classification using Distant Supervision*, Technical Report, Stanford Digital Library

Joachim T. 1999. *Making large-Scale SVM Learning Practical.* Advances in Kernel Methods – Support Vector Learning, 169-184

Kim, Y., Song Y.-I., Rim H.-C. 2016. *Opinion Retrieval for Twitter Using Extrinsic Information*, Journal of Universal Computer Science, Volume 22, No 5, 608-629

Luo Z., Osborne M, and Wang T. 2012. *Opinion Retrieval in Twitter*, Proceedings of the Sixth International AAAI Conference on Weblogs and Social Media, 507-510

Luo Z., Yu Y., Osborne M. and Wang T. 2015. *Structuring Tweets for improving Twitter search*, Journal of the Association for Information Science and Technology, Volume 66, Issue 12, 2522-2539

TEXTPRO-AL: An Active Learning Platform for Flexible and Efficient Production of Training Data for NLP Tasks

Bernardo Magnini[1], Anne-Lyse Minard[1,2], Mohammed R. H. Qwaider[1], Manuela Speranza[1]
[1] Fondazione Bruno Kessler, Trento, Italy
[2] Dept. of Information Engineering, University of Brescia, Italy
{magnini,minard,qwaider,manspera}@fbk.eu

Abstract

This paper presents TEXTPRO-AL (Active Learning for Text Processing), a platform where human annotators can efficiently work to produce high quality training data for new domains and new languages exploiting Active Learning methodologies. TEXTPRO-AL is a web-based application integrating four components: a machine learning based NLP pipeline, an annotation editor for task definition and text annotations, an incremental re-training procedure based on active learning selection from a large pool of unannotated data, and a graphical visualization of the learning status of the system.

1 Background and Motivations

Text Mining technologies are becoming more and more requested, as they work "behind the shoulder" of widespread applications: search engines adopt semantic strategies to match user needs, virtual assistants provide help in task-driven conversations, trends on social media are discovered and analyzed in huge amounts of data. These applications take advantage of the recent progresses in Computational Linguistics, which, to a large extent, are based on a massive use of Machine Learning (ML) technology for Natural Language Processing (NLP) tasks.

A key aspect motivating our proposal is that ML systems need training data (i.e. annotated corpora), which in turn are based on high quality manual linguistic annotations. As a matter of fact, manual production of datasets for training is still a core step for developing concrete NLP applications and, as a consequence, there is a high demand for methodologies that make the process more flexible and efficient.

Specifically, we are interested in the following issues: (i) applications require high flexibility in the use of different labeling categories (e.g. general categories like `Person` as opposed to fine-grained categories like `Football-Player`); (ii) in addition, domain adaptation requires that a dataset developed for a general domain (e.g. calendar dates for news) is reused for a more specific domain (e.g. the legal domain) without loosing performance; (iii) there is an increasing demand for applications supporting different languages, some of which might not be well covered in terms of annotated data; (iv) finally, it is current practice in research (particularly in shared evaluation tasks) to develop training data independently of the performance they allow to obtain in a certain task, although this is not optimal for the production cycle of applications. In concrete cases, training data are updated and revised incrementally till performance for the task at hand is satisfactory.

2 Active Learning

The key choice in designing TEXTPRO-AL was to make use of Active Learning (AL) (Cohn et al., 1994; Settles, 2010) as the core technology for optimizing training production. The main principle underlying AL is that the selection of the textual portions to be manually annotated is much more effective when it is guided by strong criteria (typically, informativeness, representativeness, and diversity of selected instances) than when it is performed randomly, as in standard supervised learning.

Proceedings of COLING 2016, the 26th International Conference on Computational Linguistics: System Demonstrations, pages 131–135, Osaka, Japan, December 11-17 2016.

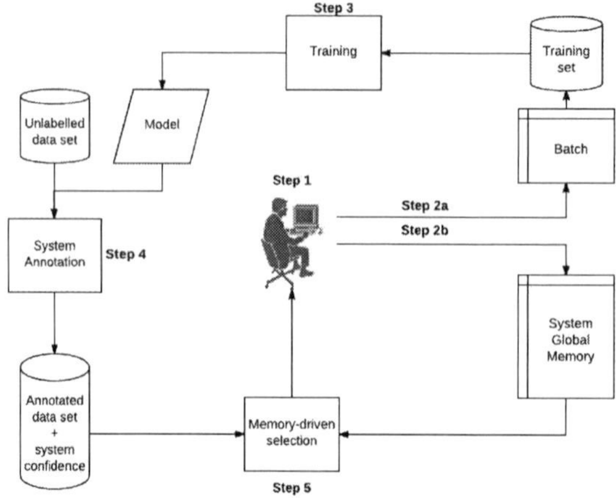

Figure 1: TEXTPRO-AL architecture.

These criteria are typically applied in an iterative way, following a re-training procedure, where instances are selected from a (usually large) pool of unlabeled texts. Although there are experimental evidences that AL allows for a significant reduction of the amount of training needed to achieve a certain performance (e.g. calculated in terms of F-measure), there is less experience and less consensus about the use of AL in practical contexts (Tomanek and Olsson, 2009).

In our implementation, the AL cycle (see Figure 1) starts with a human annotator providing supervision on a sample that has been tagged automatically by the system (step 1): the annotator is asked to either confirm the annotation (in case it is correct) or to revise it. The annotated instance is stored in a batch (step 2a), where it is accumulated with other instances for re-training and, as a result, a new model is produced (step 3). This model is used to automatically annotate a set of unlabeled documents and to assigns an estimated confidence score to each annotated instance (step 4).

In step 2b the manually supervised instance is stored in the Global Memory of the system (together with the revisions performed by the annotator). In step 5 a single instance is selected from the unlabeled dataset. The selected instance, as well as its relevant context, is removed from the unlabeled set and is presented to the human annotator to be revised.

Active Learning has been successfully experimented for a large variety of sequence labeling annotation tasks (an incomplete list includes (Shen et al., 2004) for Named Entity Recognition, (Ringger et al., 2007) for Part-of-Speech Tagging, and (Schohn and Cohn, 2000) for Text Classification), which guarantees the high portability of the approach we propose.

3 System Description

TEXTPRO-AL integrates four components in a single platform: (1) a ML-based *NLP pipeline*; (2) a web-based *annotation editor* for manually revising linguistic annotations; (3) an *AL package* which selects samples to be annotated from a large pool of non annotated documents and then re-trains the pipeline; (4) a *visualizer* of the internal learning status of the pipeline for the task at hand.

1. *NLP pipeline.* This is a set of tools for automatic text annotation based on ML classification. We assume that the pipeline is already available for a number of NLP tasks (e.g. part-of-speech tagging, named entity recognition), and that for each task the ML classifier already implements corresponding feature extractors (e.g. orthographic features for named entity recognition). We also assume that there are no hard coded linguistic categories for the NLP tasks (e.g. `Person` for NER), so that the pipeline builds a model for a labeling task by taking the categories directly from the training data. There are several linguistic pipelines of this type available, including CoreNLP[1] developed at

[1]`http://stanfordnlp.github.io/CoreNLP/`

Stanford University, the OpenNLP pipeline[2] and LingPipe[3]. For our demonstrator we use TextPro[4] (Pianta et al., 2008), a pipeline for English and Italian including several annotation layers, such as part-of-speech tagging, lemmatization, named entities recognition, dependency parsing and event extraction.

In order for a pipeline to be integrable with TEXTPRO-AL, it has to be able to produce an output in the IOB2 format[5] and to assign a confidence score to each labeled sequence.[6]

2. *Annotation editor.* This is a tool for manually inserting and revising linguistic annotations on a corpus. Required basic functions are the possibility to define a set of categories to be used for a certain annotation task and the capability to annotate a sequence of tokens with a certain category. Several open source annotation tools are available (e.g. Callisto,[7] WebAnno,[8] Brat,[9] and CAT[10]); among these, we selected MTEqual[11] (Girardi et al., 2014) (a tool developed for assessing the quality of machine translations) to integrate it in the current demonstrator, as it offers good editing features for online revisions. The use of MTEqual allows us to experiment the TEXTPRO-AL approach virtually on any sequence labeling annotation task.

3. *AL package.* This is a package for Active Learning which optimizes the selection of samples (from a large pool of unlabeled data) to be given for revision to the annotator. Only a small number of packages for AL are available (e.g. JCLAL[12]) and we preferred our own implementation, which is specifically targeted to NLP tasks.

4. *Learning visualizer.* This is a set of graphical tools allowing the annotator to monitor the learning status of the system. Specifically, we use learning curves produced with the Chart.js graphical package[13]. A learning curve shows the annotator the impact of the annotations on the performance of the system.

4 Novelty and Impact of the Platform

The TEXTPRO-AL platform aims at facilitating and making more efficient the development of training data for NLP tasks based on statistical machine learning. The goal is to give final users (e.g. companies) a platform which: (i) reduces the effort required to produce high quality training data; (ii) allows for easy and effective domain adaptation of existing classifiers; (iii) allows to monitor the performance of the classifier as the training data are incremented.

The technological novelty of the platform is the integration of three components, usually developed independently, in a single platform. To the best of our knowledge, this is the first system where a ML classifier, an annotation tool, and an active learning package are fully integrated. Particularly, while the role of AL has been scientifically investigated in controlled settings (e.g. (Shen et al., 2004) for named entity recognition, (Ringger et al., 2007) for part-of-speech tagging), the proposed platform allows for scientific experiments and uses in real settings, typically characterized by the presence of a huge (and uncontrolled) pool of unlabeled data.

Developing training data for new domains and new languages is of utmost importance for almost any text mining applications. As a consequence, reducing the time needed for data preparation may have

[2] http://opennlp.apache.org/index.html

[3] http://alias-i.com/lingpipe/index.html

[4] http://textpro.fbk.eu/

[5] The IOB2 tagging format is a common format for text chunking. B- is used to tag the beginning of a chunk, I- to tag tokens inside the chunk and O to indicate tokens not belonging to a chunk.

[6] Confidence scores can be obtained in terms of probabilities (e.g. with CRF algorithms), distance between a feature vector and the hyperplan (e.g. with SVM algorithms), etc.

[7] https://github.com/mitre/callisto

[8] https://webanno.github.io/webanno/

[9] http://brat.nlplab.org/index.html

[10] http://dh.fbk.eu/resources/cat-content-annotation-tool

[11] https://github.com/hltfbk/MT-EQuAl

[12] https://sourceforge.net/projects/jclal/

[13] http://www.chartjs.org

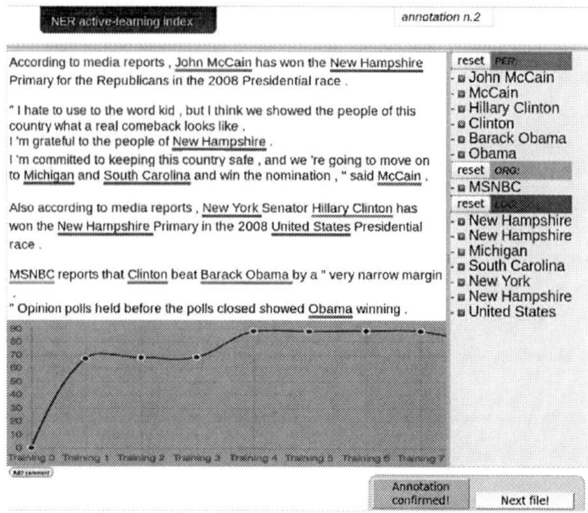

Figure 2: User interface of the TEXTPRO-AL platform.

a relevant impact on the overall production cycle of an application. In addition, the proposed platform enhances the user's experience by offering the human annotator the possibility of monitoring the impact of her/his work on the performance of the system.

5 The Platform at Work

The platform targets researchers and companies who need to develop training data for NLP applications, either from scratch or by extending existing datasets. The typical user of the system is a domain expert, whose goal is to produce a training set for a certain NLP task. In our experience, a user only needs a short training phase (in the order of one day) and some pilot annotations to learn how to use the system for most of the NLP tasks (e.g. part of speech tagging, named entities recognition, event detection). Particularly, the system targets NLP developers in a company, providing a stimulating environment where they can practice basic functionalities of ML applied to NLP.

The platform is delivered as a web application (see Figure 2) where multiple users are allowed to collaborate to the development of the same dataset. Through a graphical interface the user is guided to set up a project: this includes uploading unlabeled data, setting annotation categories, and setting re-training parameters (e.g. the frequency of the re-training). Then the user is presented with a document (e.g. a news story) selected from the unlabeled pool and is asked to revise the automatic annotation produced by the classifier with the model currently available. Once the user has confirmed the revisions, the system proposes a new document to be revised, on the basis of the AL selection procedures. At each moment the user can monitor the performance of the system on the task by consulting the learning curve and inspecting the content of the system memory (i.e. which errors are in the memory, how many times they have been considered, and whether the system considers them as solved or not).

We are not aware of any descriptions of similar platforms in the literature; while software packages for active learning do exist (for instance JCLAL) they are not integrated either with a graphical annotation tool or with an NLP pipeline. This is partly explained by the fact that in order to ensure replicability, research experiments on AL are typically performed on small annotated datasets and thus they do not need a real environment (with a real annotator). In concrete applications, on the other hand, more functionalities are needed as proposed in TEXTPRO-AL.

The TEXTPRO-AL platform is used in the context of four activities. The first is a collaboration with Euregio Srl[14] for developing a named entity recognition dataset for news in German from the South

[14]http://www.euregio.it

Tyrol area. In this case, the task and the categories used are standard, while the goal is to improve the performance on top of an existing dataset. The second experience is part of a research project on automatic analysis of live soccer commentaries in Italian (Minard et al., 2016b). In this case, the annotation categories (`player`, `goal`, etc.) were defined from scratch and the (non-expert) annotator was able to produce a dataset in seven working days. We also used the platform in a domain adaptation perspective for the annotation of named entities in tweets, where we annotated more than 2,000 tweets with the goal of adapting a system trained on news to social media texts (Minard et al., 2016a). Finally, we have been using TEXTPRO-AL for education purposes, to support an NLP introductory course.

6 Platform distribution

We currently offer the TEXTPRO-AL platform as an extension of the TextPro NLP pipeline (Pianta et al., 2008). TextPro is distributed under a dual licensing schema (i.e. free for research purposes, proprietary for commercial purposes). As we believe that domain adaptation is a major issue for extending the market of NLP applications, we are going to distribute the whole TEXTPRO-AL platform with the same dual schema adopted for TextPro.

Acknowledgments

This work has been partially supported by the EUCLIP (EUregio Cross LInguistic Project) project, under a collaboration between FBK and Euregio Srl.

References

David Cohn, Richard Ladner, and Alex Waibel. 1994. Improving generalization with active learning. In *Machine Learning*, pages 201–221.

Christian Girardi, Luisa Bentivogli, Mohammad Amin Farajian, and Marcello Federico. 2014. Mt-equal: a toolkit for human assessment of machine translation output. In *COLING 2014, 25th International Conference on Computational Linguistics, Proceedings of the Conference System Demonstrations, August 23-29, 2014, Dublin, Ireland*, pages 120–123.

Anne-Lyse Minard, Mohammed R.H. Qwaider, and Bernardo Magnini. 2016a. FBK-NLP at NEEL-IT: Active Learning for Domain Adaptation. In *Proceedings of the 5th Evaluation Campaign of Natural Language Processing and Speech Tools for Italian (EVALITA 2016)*.

Anne-Lyse Minard, Manuela Speranza, Bernardo Magnini, and Mohammed R.H. Qwaider. 2016b. Semantic interpretation of events in live soccer commentaries. In *Proceedings of the Third Italian Conference on Computational Linguistics CLiC-it 2016*.

Emanuele Pianta, Christian Girardi, and Roberto Zanoli. 2008. The TextPro Tool Suite. In *Proceedings of the 6th International Conference on Language Resources and Evaluation (LREC 2008)*, Marrakech, Morocco.

Eric Ringger, Peter McClanahan, Robbie Haertel, George Busby, Marc Carmen, James Carroll, Kevin Seppi, and Deryle Lonsdale. 2007. Active learning for part-of-speech tagging: Accelerating corpus annotation. In *Proceedings of the Linguistic Annotation Workshop*, LAW '07, pages 101–108, Stroudsburg, PA, USA. Association for Computational Linguistics.

Greg Schohn and David Cohn. 2000. Less is more: Active learning with support vector machines. In *Proceedings of the Seventeenth International Conference on Machine Learning*, ICML '00, pages 839–846, San Francisco, CA, USA. Morgan Kaufmann Publishers Inc.

Burr Settles. 2010. Active learning literature survey. Technical report.

Dan Shen, Jie Zhang, Jian Su, Guodong Zhou, and Chew-Lim Tan. 2004. Multi-criteria-based active learning for named entity recognition. In *Proceedings of the 42Nd Annual Meeting on Association for Computational Linguistics*, ACL '04, Stroudsburg, PA, USA. Association for Computational Linguistics.

Katrin Tomanek and Fredrik Olsson. 2009. A web survey on the use of active learning to support annotation of text data. In *Proceedings of the NAACL HLT 2009 Workshop on Active Learning for Natural Language Processing*, HLT '09, pages 45–48, Stroudsburg, PA, USA. Association for Computational Linguistics.

SideNoter: Scholarly Paper Browsing System based on PDF Restructuring and Text Annotation

Takeshi Abekawa and **Akiko Aizawa**
National Institute of Informatics
Tokyo, Japan
{abekawa,aizawa}@nii.ac.jp

Abstract

In this paper, we discuss our ongoing efforts to construct a scientific paper browsing system that helps users to read and understand advanced technical content distributed in PDF. Since PDF is a format specifically designed for printing, layout and logical structures of documents are indistinguishably embedded in the file. It requires much effort to extract natural language text from PDF files, and reversely, display semantic annotations produced by NLP tools on the original page layout. In our browsing system, we tackle these issues caused by the gap between printable document and plain text. Our system provides ways to extract natural language sentences from PDF files together with their logical structures, and also to map arbitrary textual spans to their corresponding regions on page images. We setup a demonstration system using papers published in ACL anthology and demonstrate the enhanced search and refined recommendation functions which we plan to make widely available to NLP researchers.

1 Introduction

In recent years, there has been significant progress in the digitization of scientific papers; it has become common to distribute papers in electronic format, from paper submissions to the hand of readers without passing through print media.

Major academic publishers have defined their own XML format and utilize a corresponding publishing process called single-source multi-use, in which conversion from an XML file to paper print or electronic formats such as PDF, HTML, and EPUB is realized. However, in many scholarly publishing arenas, no XML editing process is available yet – after publication, only the corresponding PDF files are stored by the publisher. PDF format was established with the objective of maintaining the same page layout on printed paper as on a computer screen. Consequently, PDF does not contain any information indicating the logical structure within the file format. This logical structure is very important for understanding the document, and humans do it effortlessly and intuitively. To replicate that, the difficult mechanical extraction process will necessarily involve heuristics.

We have developed a paper browsing system called SideNoter that runs in a web browser. Because most existing papers are distributed in PDF, the challenge lies in how to handle the file format of the fixed layout. In our system, the constraint of the fixed layout is utilized in a converse manner — the paper itself is displayed in the image and overlapping supplementary information obtained from the full-text is displayed on the page layout. We designed a workflow to structurally parse documents in PDF. Based on this, SideNoter provides several advanced search functions, including figures and tables search, related section search, and per-page information recommendation. We also implemented tools that associate the layout with logical and semantic structures of documents. This enables us to incorporate semantic annotations produced by NLP tools into the visualized document image shown in the browser. Currently, we are investigating the usability of the system under development using papers published in the ACL anthology. Figure 1 illustrates the overall flow of our proposed system.

Proceedings of COLING 2016, the 26th International Conference on Computational Linguistics: System Demonstrations, pages 136–140, Osaka, Japan, December 11-17 2016.

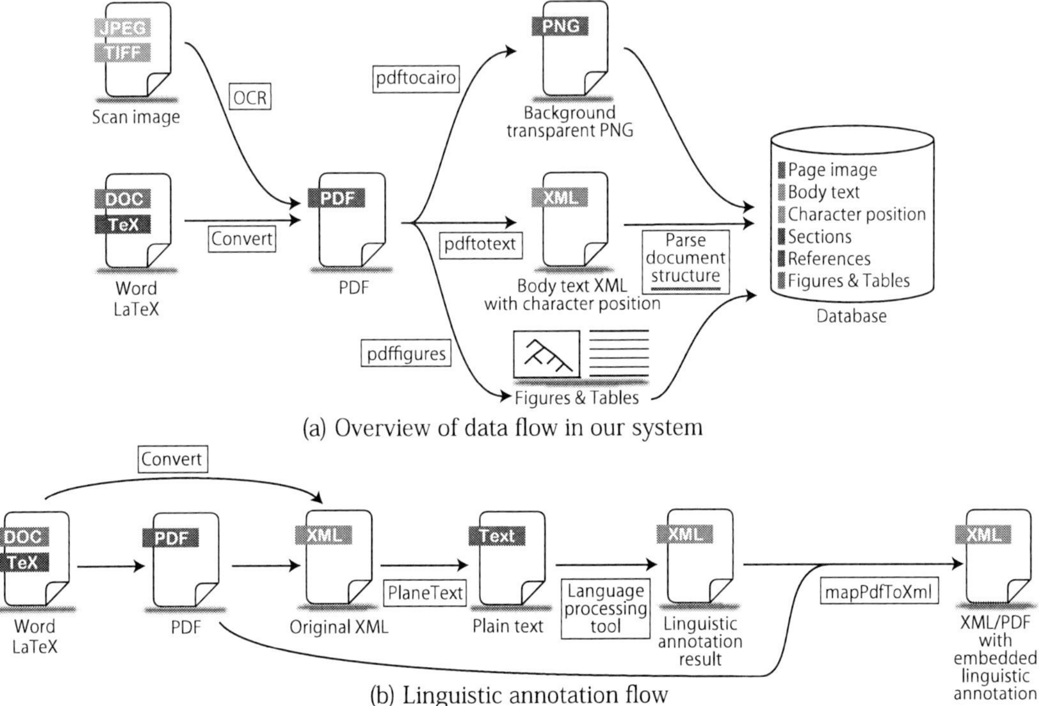

Figure 1: Overall workflow of the proposed system.

2 Related works

There are many systems for searching for papers. In the field of NLP, web services such as CiteSeerX[1] and ACL searchbench (Schäfer et al., 2011) are typical examples. To perform a flexible paper search in a specific field, it is necessary to extract the logical structure of the paper and its bibliographic information. Tools such as ParsCit (Councill et al., 2008), LA-PDFText (Ramakrishnan et al., 2012), PDFX (Constantin et al., 2013), and GROBID (Lopez, 2009) can be used to analyze the logical structure of papers. In addition, many frameworks that enable knowledge extraction from scholarly documents have been proposed, such as PDFMEF (Wu et al., 2015) and Dr. Inventor Project (Ronzano and Saggion, 2015). If the knowledge acquired from a paper could be displayed at the same time the paper is being read, readers' understanding of the paper would improve significantly. However, because a special viewer is often used to read PDF, it is difficult for other systems to add information to the same location as the PDF page.

3 Document Processing Work-flow

3.1 Document structure analysis flow

The system performs structural analysis of body text with the position coordinates obtained in the text extraction process, and obtains the logical structure of the paper. At this point, our system requires that the following three functions be realized: (a) font size and font name, (b) page coordinates of word units, and (c) in languages with a lack of space between words, such as CJK, the page coordinates of character units. We examined various open-source tools but could not find any that is sufficiently satisfactory. As a result, we decided to apply our own patch to *pdftotext* that is included in the Poppler library[2]. Because our objective is to adapt to other languages and other domains without having to prepare training data,

[1] http://citeseerx.ist.psu.edu/

[2] http://poppler.freedesktop.org/

we created our own rule-based structure analysis tool.

In this system, instead of displaying the PDF in a web browser, the image files converted from the PDF are displayed. To facilitate changes to the background color of the page, we utilize a transparent PNG background image format. In addition, our system uses the PDFFigures tool (Clark and Divvala, 2015) to extract figures and tables from papers. This tool can also recognize the corresponding caption text.

3.2 Linguistic annotation flow

We have developed a workflow to visualize and easily verify the annotation information generated by NLP tools on the page layout. First, the XML file of a paper is converted to plain text using our PlaneText framework[3] (Hara et al., 2014). PlaneText facilitates application of any NLP tools to target real-world documents containing structured text. Currently, a tool is also being developed to convert XML-tagged text into plain text sequences that can be directly inputted to NLP tools.

The annotation information is then applied to the resulting plain text using any of the NLP tools. In this case, the resulting generated file format is set to XML. Finally, the PDF layout information is embedded into the XML file using the mapPdfToXml[4] tool we are currently developing. This tool generates a new XML document by combining an original XML document and a PDF document that is converted from the original XML. The elements in the generated XML will have layout information that is extracted from the PDF: page number, position in the page, width, height, font name, font size, and color. Because SideNoter displays the page layout as an image, the annotation information generated by this workflow can be overlaid directly onto the paper's image.

4 Demonstration System: SideNoter for acl_anthology

4.1 XML-like advanced search functions

In this paper, search page used as the entrance to the system, a common search function is provided that facilitates full-text and metadata search such as paper title, author, conference name, and publication year. Search results display a facet list of the year of publication and the authors next to the paper list. The search results can also be narrowed to year of publication and author. In addition, the search can be limited to the text in the caption of figures and tables.

On clicking the paper title obtained in a search result, the outline of the paper is displayed onscreen. On the screen, thumbnails of each page, extracted figures and their captions, extracted section headings, and reference list are displayed. Relevant papers are listed by similarity with a vector space model weighted by TF-IDF on the right side of the screen. Clicking on sections in the section headings results in sections of other papers associated with the selected sections being listed.

4.2 Section-based retrieval

A click on the SideNoter icon in the search results or in outline view results in the screen transiting to paper browsing view. The system can display auxiliary information associated with the paper to facilitate reading comprehension as side-note columns on the left and right of the page. The system can also highlight specific terms or areas in the body text and draw an auxiliary line from a side-note column to the body text using an overlay over the image. The current system performs entity linking to Wikipedia articles, and displays explanatory text and images obtained from Wikipedia in a side-note column. It differs from other wikification systems in that it displays an image file that users simply look at to understand the meaning of a corresponding term. Thus, if a term is linked to the wrong entity, the user knows immediately that an error has occurred. Improving the accuracy of wikification is part of our future work.

In addition, the system utilizes a search API for terms and can dynamically display the search results. The current system searches for terms on video and slide-sharing sites, and displays the top results as side-notes.

[3] http://kmcs.nii.ac.jp/planetext/en/

[4] https://github.com/KMCS-NII/mapPdfToXml

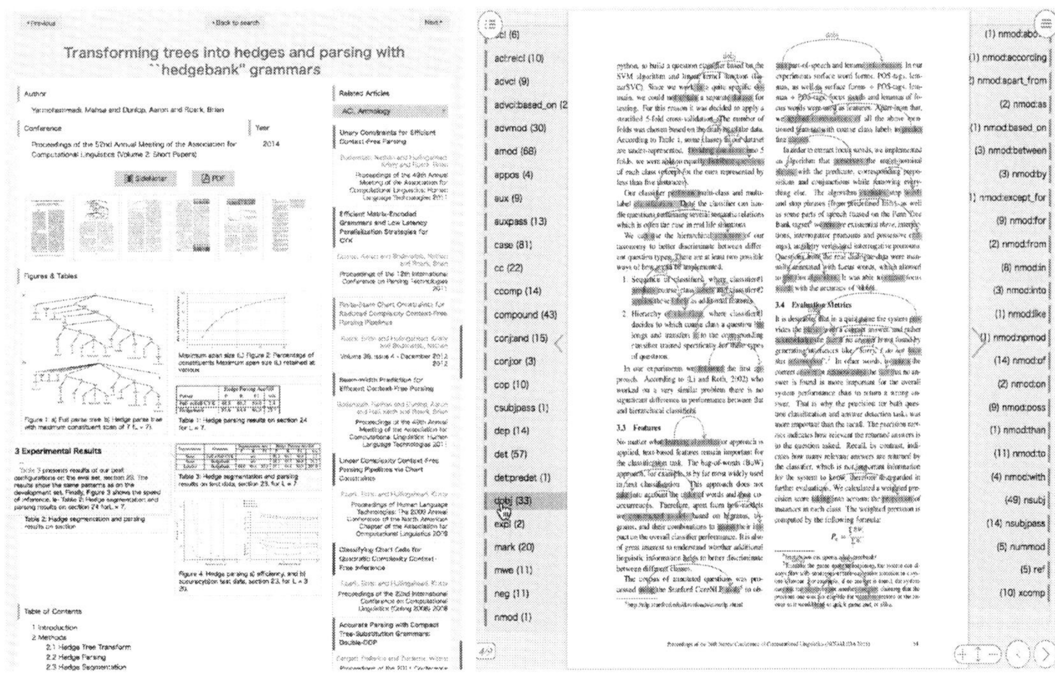

Figure 2: The screen shot of paper outline view (left) and dependency relation display (right).

4.3 Ability to seamlessly display linguistic annotation

As an example of this workflow, we annotated the dependency structure in the body text of a paper. In this workflow, the XML file annotated with dependency information was generated using the Stanford dependency parser (Chen and Manning, 2014) as the NLP tool. An example of the dependency relation displayed on SideNoter is shown in Figure 2. Conventionally, the dependency information has been discussed only in terms of one-sentence units. However, by viewing the overall relationship in the whole document, each of the dependencies occurring in the document and the density of the relationships can be understood.

5 Conclusion

In this paper, we presented a paper browsing system that displays a variety of information obtained from the body text of papers in side-note columns. In addition, we have developed a framework that displays annotation information obtained using an NLP tool on the paper layout. We believe that this platform will form a part of various useful NLP tools. This system will be published if a license can be obtained from ACL Anthology.

Acknowledgements

This work was supported by CREST, Japan Science and Technology Agency.

References

Danqi Chen and Christopher D Manning. 2014. A fast and accurate dependency parser using neural networks. In *the 2014 Conference on Empirical Methods in Natural Language Processing (EMNLP)*, pages 740–750.

Christopher Clark and Santosh Divvala. 2015. Looking beyond text: Extracting figures, tables, and captions from computer science papers. In *AAAI 2015, Workshop on Scholarly Big Data*.

Alexandru Constantin, Steve Pettifer, and Andrei Voronkov. 2013. Pdfx: Fully-automated pdf-to-xml conversion of scientific literature. In *the 2013 ACM symposium on Document engineering (DocEng2013)*, pages 177–180.

Isaac G. Councill, C. Lee Giles, and Min-Yen Kan. 2008. Parscit: An open-source crf reference string parsing package. In *the Language Resources and Evaluation Conference (LREC2008)*.

Tadayoshi Hara, Goran Topic, Yusuke Miyao, and Akiko Aizawa. 2014. Significance of bridging real-world documents and nlp technologies. In *Workshop on Open Infrastructures and Analysis Frameworks for HLT (OIAF4HLT)*, pages 44–52.

Patrice Lopez. 2009. Grobid: Combining automatic bibliographic data recognition and term extraction for scholarship publications. In *Proceedings of the 13th European Conference on Research and Advanced Technology for Digital Libraries*, ECDL'09, pages 473–474, Berlin, Heidelberg. Springer-Verlag.

Cartic Ramakrishnan, Abhishek Patnia, Eduard Hovy, and Gully APC Burns. 2012. Layout-aware text extraction from full-text pdf of scientific articles. *Source code for biology and medicine*, 7(1):1–10.

Francesco Ronzano and Horacio Saggion. 2015. Dr. inventor framework: Extracting structured information from scientific publications. In *Discovery Science*, volume 9356, pages 209–220. Springer International Publishing.

Ulrich Schäfer, Bernd Kiefer, Christian Spurk, Jörg Steffen, and Rui Wang. 2011. The acl anthology searchbench. In *the ACL-HLT 2011 System Demonstrations*, pages 7–13.

Jian Wu, Jason Killian, Huaiyu Yang, Kyle Williams, Sagnik Ray Choudhury, Suppawong Tuarob, Cornelia Caragea, and C. Lee Giles. 2015. Pdfmef: A multi-entity knowledge extraction framework for scholarly documents and semantic search. In *the 8th International Conference on Knowledge Capture (K-CAP2015)*.

Sensing Emotions in Text Messages: An Application and Deployment Study of EmotionPush

Shih-Ming Wang[1] **Chun-Hui Li**[1] **Yu-Chun Lo**[1]
Ting-Hao (Kenneth) Huang[2] **Lun-Wei Ku**[1]
[1] Academia Sinica, Taipei, Taiwan.
{ipod825, iamscli.tw}@gmail.com, howard.lo@nlplab.cc, lwku@iis.sinica.edu.tw
[2] Carnegie Mellon University, Pittsburgh, PA, USA. tinghaoh@cs.cmu.edu

Abstract

Instant messaging and push notifications play important roles in modern digital life. To enable robust sense-making and rich context awareness in computer mediated communications, we introduce *EmotionPush*, a system that automatically conveys the emotion of received text with a colored push notification on mobile devices. EmotionPush is powered by state-of-the-art emotion classifiers and is deployed for Facebook Messenger clients on Android. The study showed that the system is able to help users prioritize interactions.

1 Introduction

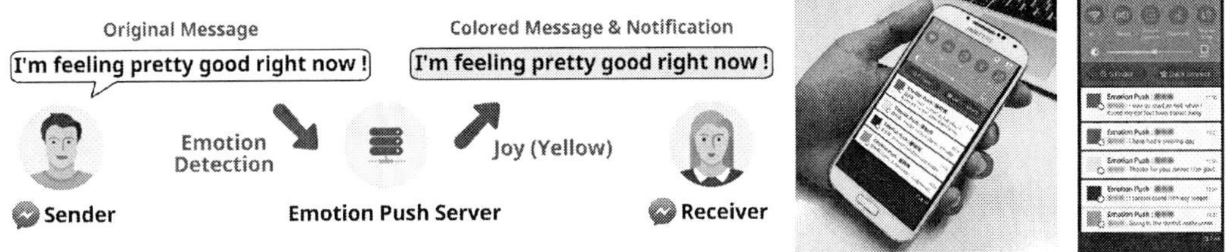

Figure 1: System overview and user scenario of EmotionPush. The server detects the emotion of the message and sends a colored notification to indicate the sender's emotion on the receiver's device.

Text-based communication plays a big part in computer mediated communications. With the advent of mobile devices, instant messaging and push notifications have become integral to modern digital life. However, text-based chatting is limited in both expressing emotions and building trust amongst users. Text-only chatting has been shown to result in worse communications and trust levels than face-to-face, video, and audio virtual communications (Bos et al., 2002). One study also demonstrated that knowing other people's emotions is crucial for collaboration, yet is surprisingly challenging for users via computer mediated communications (Eligio et al., 2012).

In response, previous works have attempted to automatically visualize emotions on text-based interfaces by visualizing the emotion dynamics in a document (Liu et al., 2003), providing haptic feedback via wearable equipment (Tsetserukou et al., 2009), or changing font sizes according to recognized emotions (Yeo, 2008). However, these explorations were primarily developed based on rule-based emotion detectors, which were shown to perform significantly worse than machine-learning algorithms (Wu et al., 2006). On the other hand, some researchers proposed to add new features, such as kinetic typography (Bodine and Pignol, 2003; Forlizzi et al., 2003; Lee et al., 2006; Lee et al., 2002), affective buttons (Broekens and Brinkman, 2009), and two-dimensional representations (Sánchez et al., 2005; Sánchez et al., 2006), on top of traditional chatting interfaces to allow users express emotions. Others studies have attempted to incorporate the user's body signals, such as fluctuating skin conductivity levels (DiMicco et al., 2002), thermal feedback (Wilson et al., 2016), or facial expression (El Kaliouby and

Proceedings of COLING 2016, the 26th International Conference on Computational Linguistics: System Demonstrations, pages 141–145, Osaka, Japan, December 11-17 2016.

Plutchik's Emotion Wheel

Emotion	Emotions in LJ40K	Color	Hex.	RGB
Anger	Aggravated, Annoyed, Frustrated, Pissed off	Red	#F70A0A	(247, 10, 10)
Joy	Happy, Amused, Cheerful, Chipper, Ecstatic, Excited, Good, Loved, Hopeful, Calm, Content, Crazy, Bouncy	Yellow	#FFFF00	(255, 255, 0)
Sadness	Sad, Bored, Crappy, Crushed, Depressed, Lonely, Contemplative, Confused	Navy Blue	#281A7A	(40,26,122)
Fear	Anxious	Green	#00FF00	(0, 255, 0)
Anticipation	Accomplished, Busy, Creative, Awake	Orange	#FF9A17	(255,154,23)
Tired	Cold, Exhausted, Drained, Tired, Sleepy, Hungry, Sick	Purple	#D32BFC	(211,43,252)
Neutral	Okay, Blah, Blank	(No Color)		

Figure 2: Visualizing emotion colors with Plutchik's Emotion Wheel. The 40 emotion categories of LJ40K are compacted into 7 main categories, each has a corresponding color on the emotion wheel.

Robinson, 2004), in instant messaging applications. However, after decades of research, these features are largely absent in modern instant messaging clients.

In this paper, we introduce ***EmotionPush***, a system that displays colored icons on push notifications (as shown in Figure 1) to signal emotions conveyed in received messages. EmotionPush is powered by machine learning technologies with state-of-the-art performances. Built on top of the long-lasting development of emotion detection, we applied the techniques to a real-world chatting environment to determine how well the system works for individual users. Our contribution is two-fold: 1) We created EmotionPush, the first system powered by modern machine-learning emotion classification technology to convey emotions for instant messages, and 2) we deployed the system on a widely-used instant messaging client on mobile devices, Facebook's Messenger, to examine the feasibility of the emotion feedback.

2 EmotionPush System

Similar to most mobile apps, EmotionPush adopted a client-server architecture (as shown in Figure 1.) When the user (receiver) receives a message via the instant messaging client, our system uses the text of the message to recognize its corresponding emotion, and then notifies the user (receiver) via push notification with a colored icon on his/her mobile device. We developed the EmotionPush *client* as an Android application[1], specifically for Facebook's Messenger (https://www.messenger.com/). The screen shot and user scenario of the app are shown in Figure 1. The EmotionPush *server* was implemented as a stand-alone web server powered by pre-trained emotion classification models.

Visualizing Emotions EmotionPush uses 7 colors to represent 7 emotions, as shown in Figure 2. This schema was designed as follows: First, we focused on emotions commonly connected with life events, unlike benchmarks such as (Nakov et al., 2016) which typically focus on general social media data. To simplify the mapping between emotions and text, we also decided to apply a *categorical representation* (e.g. *Anger*, *Joy*, etc.) (Klein et al., 2002) of emotions instead of a dimensional representation (valence, arousal) (Sánchez et al., 2006). Second, we utilized the emotion categories and data provided in *LiveJournal* (http://www.livejournal.com/). LiveJournal is a website where users post what they feel and tag each post with a corresponding emotion. The *LJ40k* corpus (Leshed and Kaye, 2006), a dataset that contains 1,000 blog posts for each of the 40 most common emotions on LiveJournal, was adopted to learn which emotions we should watch for in EmotionPush and to train the emotion classifiers. Finally, to reduce users' cognitive load, the original 40 emotions were compacted into 7 main emotions according to Plutchik's Emotion Wheel color theme (Plutchik, 1980), as shown in Figure 2.

Emotion Classification & Evaluation EmotionPush's 7 classifiers were trained on the LJ40k dataset with 7 compacted emotion labels. Each classifier is a binary classifier that indicates if the current message belongs to one of the 7 compacted emotions. The message was inputted into each classifier to obtain the probability of each compacted emotion label. Then the label of the highest probability was selected as the predicted emotion label of the current message.

To compare the performance of our approach with that of previous works on the LJ40k dataset (Yang and Liu, 2013), we replicated our classification method and features to predict the original *40* emotions

[1]EmotionPush is available at Google Play: https://play.google.com/store/apps/details?id=tw.edu.sinica.iis.emotionpush

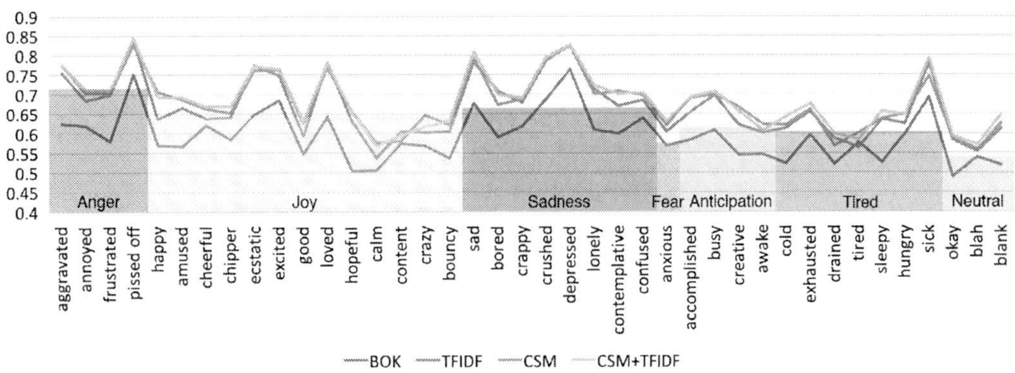

Figure 3: AUC scores of the binary classifiers corresponding to the 40 LiveJournal emotions and the 7 major emotions in EmotionPush.

in LJ40k. Forty binary-class classifiers (one emotion each) were developed by using LibSVM (Fan et al., 2008) with a radial basis function kernel. We chose to develop 40 classifiers instead of one 40-class classifier to a) better compare our results to Yang and Liu (2013), b) achieve better performance, and c) extend EmotionPush to a multi-labeling system in the future. To form a balanced training set for each emotion, we randomly selected 800 posts from LJ40K as positive examples and 800 posts of the other 39 emotions as negative examples. Aware of various features proposed for affect (Ku et al., 2009; Ku et al., 2011; Balahur et al., 2014; Poria et al., 2014; Tang et al., 2014; Xu et al., 2015), we used a 300-dimension word vectors trained on Google News (Mikolov et al., 2013) (https://code.google.com/archive/p/word2vec/) to represent each post. The model's parameters were tuned via a 10-fold cross-validation process.

The evaluations were performed on the held-out testing set that contains 8,000 posts (200 posts for each emotion). The AUC, the area under the receiver operating characteristic curve, was calculated. For the 40 emotions, our classifiers achieved an average AUC of 0.6788, which was comparable to the state-of-the-art performance, 0.6851, reported by (Yang and Liu, 2013). Figure 3 shows the performance of each emotion using different features. We observed that classifiers performed worse on *Blank*, *Okay*, *Drained*, and *Sleepy*. These low-performance emotions can be roughly classified into two categories: 1) *vague emotions*, such as *Blank* and *Okay*, are difficult to model, as people tend to interpret them differently, and 2) *similar emotions*, such as *Drained* and *Sleepy*, tend to overlap significantly, and thus hinder us from distinguishing them.

Furthermore, the colored bars in Figure 3 show the classification performances for the 7 compacted major emotions for EmotionPush. The classifiers of compacted emotions *Joy*, *Sadness* and *Anger* performed best among all 7 emotions, while *Neutral* and *Fear* performed worse, which might be because these two compacted emotions were made up of fewer LiveJournal emotions than others, as shown in Figure 2. This not only resulted in the lack of training data, but also brought in errors as these few emotions (including *Anxious*, *Okay*, *Blah*, and *Blank*) performed comparably less satisfactory (see Figure 3).

3 Deployment Study

In this study, we aimed to test whether EmotionPush can change the priority of interactions in instant messages on mobile devices. Therefore, we deployed EmotionPush to Google Play, and recruited 8 native English speakers who frequently used Facebook's Messenger app. The experiment lasted 12 days. We investigated the effect of EmotionPush by turning the color feedback off (for the first 5 days, noted as the *first week*) and on (for the latter 7 days, *second week*). We then analyzed changes in participants' priorities of reading and responding to messages.

During the entire study, we collected 6,288 messages in total, 3,844 read counts (first read of a message sequence) and 3,769 response counts (first response). The overall average score obtained from participants was above the average (2.375 over 4) for the question "EmotionPush can predict emotion colors correctly." Moreover, participants did not think wrongly predicted emotions would harm their chatting

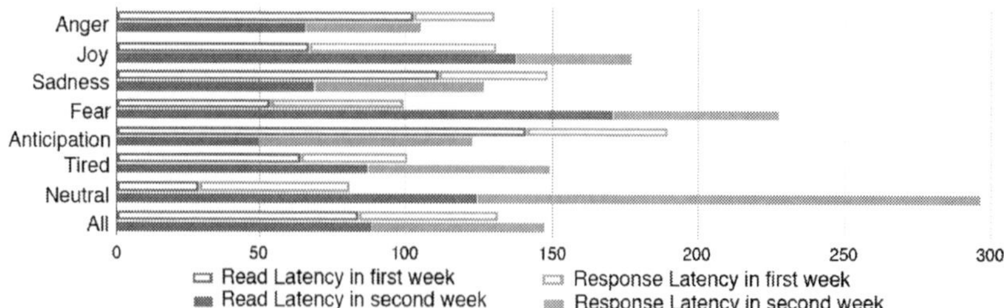

Figure 4: The results of two-week deployment study of EmotionPush. This chart shows the users' read and response latencies when color feedback is on (first week) and off (second week), respectively.

experience (average score 1.375 over 4).

From this study, we found that EmotionPush helps **prioritize interactions**. The average read latencies and response latencies for the first week and the second week are shown in Figure 4. We can observe that after the emotion colors were pushed, user's behavior changed accordingly. Especially for *Joy*, *Anger*, and *Sadness*, the priority of the instant message interactions changed in two interesting directions: 1) *Joy* (blue bar: with an increasing read latency from first week to second week) was read more slowly while *Sadness* and *Anger* (blue bar: with a decreasing read latency) was read more quickly, and 2) *Joy* was responded to more quickly (orange bar: with a decreasing response latency) while *Sadness* and *Anger* were responded to more slowly (orange bar: with an increasing response latency). The decreasing read latency of *Anger* ($p = 0.0019$) and the increasing response latency of *Sadness* ($p = 0.0486$) are significant. This might reveal that messages that are not urgent (*Joy*) can be put aside and read later, while participants are willing to read urgent messages (*Sadness* and *Anger*) earlier. On the other hand, users could casually respond to less urgent messages (i.e., with little thought), whereas urgent messages require more thought.

An interesting thing to mention is the changes of the response latency. Logically speaking, as participants read messages, they should realize the messages' emotions so that their response latency would not change after pushing emotion colors. However, we observed changes in Figure 4, and there is even a significant difference of the response latencies for *Sadness*. This suggests that the color feedback is not only notifying users, but also influencing their process of composing a response.

Overall, the feedback for using EmotionPush was positive. 78% of participants thought it is a good idea to add the feature of EmotionPush to Facebook's Messenger, and the other 22% wanted to add this feature eventually but just not immediately to wait for a better user interface and a better prediction performance for some emotion categories.

4 Conclusion and Future Work

We introduced EmotionPush, a system that automatically recognizes and pushes emotions of instant messages and visualizes them to the end-user, which enables the emotion sensing ability on messages and enriches the information in the communications. We believe this research can help us gain more insight into the effect of reinforcing the emotion sensing of robots. In the future, we plan to add this emotion sensing function in the message composing process and discuss the quality of conversations.

References

A. Balahur, R. Mihalcea, and A. Montoyo. 2014. Computational approaches to subjectivity and sentiment analysis: Present and envisaged methods and applications. *Computer Speech & Language*, 28(1):1–6.

K. Bodine and M. Pignol. 2003. Kinetic typography-based instant messaging. In *CHI'03 EA*. ACM.

N. Bos, J. Olson, D. Gergle, G. Olson, and Z. Wright. 2002. Effects of four computer-mediated communications channels on trust development. In *Proc. CHI'02*. ACM.

J. Broekens and W. Brinkman. 2009. Affectbutton: Towards a standard for dynamic affective user feedback. In *Proc. ACII'09*. IEEE, September.

J. M. DiMicco, V. Lakshmipathy, and A. T. Fiore. 2002. Conductive chat: Instant messaging with a skin conductivity channel. In *Proceedings of Conference on Computer Supported Cooperative Work*.

R. El Kaliouby and P. Robinson. 2004. Faim: integrating automated facial affect analysis in instant messaging. In *Proceedings of the 9th international conference on Intelligent user interfaces*, pages 244–246. ACM.

U. X. Eligio, S. E. Ainsworth, and C. K. Crook. 2012. Emotion understanding and performance during computer-supported collaboration. *Computers in Human Behavior*, 28(6).

R.-E. Fan, K.-W. Chang, C.-J. Hsieh, X.-R. Wang, and C.-J. Lin. 2008. Liblinear: A library for large linear classification. *The Journal of Machine Learning Research*, 9.

J. Forlizzi, J. Lee, and S. Hudson. 2003. The kinedit system: affective messages using dynamic texts. In *Proc. CHI'03*, pages 377–384. ACM.

J. Klein, Y. Moon, and R. W. Picard. 2002. This computer responds to user frustration:: Theory, design, and results. *Interacting with computers*, 14(2):119–140.

L.-W. Ku, T.-H. Huang, and H.-H. Chen. 2009. Using morphological and syntactic structures for chinese opinion analysis. In *Proc. EMNLP '09*, EMNLP '09, pages 1260–1269, Stroudsburg, PA, USA. ACL.

L.-W. Ku, T.-H. K. Huang, and H.-H. Chen. 2011. Predicting opinion dependency relations for opinion analysis. In *IJCNLP*, pages 345–353.

J. C. Lee, J. Forlizzi, and S. E. Hudson. 2002. The kinetic typography engine: an extensible system for animating expressive text. In *Proc. UIST'02*, pages 81–90. ACM.

J. Lee, S. Jun, J. Forlizzi, and S. E. Hudson. 2006. Using kinetic typography to convey emotion in text-based interpersonal communication. In *Proc. DIS '06*, DIS '06, pages 41–49, New York, NY, USA. ACM.

G. Leshed and J. Kaye. 2006. Understanding how bloggers feel: recognizing affect in blog posts. In *CHI'06 EA*.

H. Liu, T. Selker, and H. Lieberman. 2003. Visualizing the affective structure of a text document. In *CHI'03 EA*.

T. Mikolov, I. Sutskever, K. Chen, G. S. Corrado, and J. Dean. 2013. Distributed representations of words and phrases and their compositionality. In *Advances in neural information processing systems*, pages 3111–3119.

P. Nakov, A. Ritter, S. Rosenthal, F. Sebastiani, and V. Stoyanov. 2016. Semeval-2016 task 4: Sentiment analysis in twitter. In *Proceedings of the 10th international workshop on semantic evaluation (SemEval'16)*.

R. Plutchik. 1980. *Emotion: A psychoevolutionary synthesis*. Harpercollins College Division.

S. Poria, A. Gelbukh, E. Cambria, A. Hussain, and G.-B. Huang. 2014. Emosenticspace: A novel framework for affective common-sense reasoning. *Knowledge-Based Systems*, 69:108–123.

J. A. Sánchez, I. Kirschning, J. C. Palacio, and Y. Ostróvskaya. 2005. Towards mood-oriented interfaces for synchronous interaction. In *Proc. CLIHC '05*, CLIHC '05, New York, NY, USA. ACM.

J. A. Sánchez, N. P. Hernández, J. C. Penagos, and Y. Ostróvskaya. 2006. Conveying mood and emotion in instant messaging by using a two-dimensional model for affective states. In *Proceedings of VII Brazilian Symposium on Human Factors in Computing Systems*, IHC '06, pages 66–72, New York, NY, USA, November. ACM.

D. Tang, F. Wei, N. Yang, M. Zhou, T. Liu, and B. Qin. 2014. Learning sentiment-specific word embedding for twitter sentiment classification. In *ACL (1)*, pages 1555–1565.

D. Tsetserukou, A. Neviarouskaya, H. Prendinger, N. Kawakami, M. Ishizuka, and S. Tachi. 2009. ifeel_im! emotion enhancing garment for communication in affect sensitive instant messenger. In *Human Interface and the Management of Information. Designing Information Environments*. Springer.

G. Wilson, D. Dobrev, and S. A. Brewster. 2016. Hot under the collar: Mapping thermal feedback to dimensional models of emotion. In *Proc. CHI'16*, CHI'16, pages 4838–4849, New York, NY, USA. ACM.

C.-H. Wu, Z.-J. Chuang, and Y.-C. Lin. 2006. Emotion recognition from text using semantic labels and separable mixture models. *ACM transactions on Asian language information processing (TALIP)*, 5(2).

R. Xu, T. Chen, Y. Xia, Q. Lu, B. Liu, and X. Wang. 2015. Word embedding composition for data imbalances in sentiment and emotion classification. *Cognitive Computation*, 7(2):226–240.

Y.-H. Yang and J.-Y. Liu. 2013. Quantitative study of music listening behavior in a social and affective context. *IEEE Transactions on Multimedia*, 15(6).

Z. Yeo. 2008. Emotional instant messaging with kim. In *CHI'08 EA*, CHI EA '08, April.

Illinois Cross-Lingual Wikifier: Grounding Entities in Many Languages to the English Wikipedia

Chen-Tse Tsai and **Dan Roth**
University of Illinois at Urbana-Champaign
201 N. Goodwin, Urbana, Illinois, 61801
{ctsai12, danr}@illinois.edu

Abstract

We release a cross-lingual wikification system for all languages in Wikipedia. Given a piece of text in any supported language, the system identifies names of people, locations, organizations, and grounds these names to the corresponding English Wikipedia entries. The system is based on two components: a cross-lingual named entity recognition (NER) model and a cross-lingual mention grounding model. The cross-lingual NER model is a language-independent model which can extract named entity mentions in the text of any language in Wikipedia. The extracted mentions are then grounded to the English Wikipedia using the cross-lingual mention grounding model. The only resources required to train the proposed system are the multilingual Wikipedia dump and existing training data for English NER. The system is online at http://cogcomp.cs.illinois.edu/page/demo_view/xl_wikifier

1 Motivation

Wikipedia has become an indispensable resource in knowledge acquisition and text understanding for both human beings and computers. The task of wikification or Entity Linking aims at disambiguating mentions (sub-strings) in text to the corresponding titles (entries) in Wikipedia. For English text, this problem has been studied extensively. (Bunescu and Pasca, 2006; Cucerzan, 2007; Mihalcea and Csomai, 2007; Ratinov et al., 2011; Cheng and Roth, 2013) It also has been shown to be a valuable component of several natural language processing and information extraction tasks across different domains.

Recently, there has also been interest in the cross-lingual setting of Wikification: given a mention from a document written in a non-English language, the goal is to find the corresponding title in the English Wikipedia. This task is driven partly by the fact that a lot of information around the world may be written in a foreign language for which there are limited linguistic resources and, specifically, no English translation technology. Instead of translating the whole document to English, *grounding* the important entity mentions in the English Wikipedia may be a good solution that could better capture the key message of the text, especially if it can be reliably achieved with fewer resources than those needed to develop a translation system.

There are several language-specific Wikification systems but very few multilingual or cross-lingual systems. For instance, for English, there are Illinois Wikifier[1] and AIDA[2]. TagMe[3] supports Englsih, Italian, and German. RPI[4] developed systems for English, Spanish, and Chinese. However, even many widely spoken languages are not supported. Since these systems often use language-specific resources, it is hard to adapt these systems to a new language. The goal of the proposed system is to cover all 292 languages in Wikipedia and directly link mentions to the English Wikipedia titles using very little language-specific resource. That is, only using information in multilingual Wikipedia and some knowledge for tokenization, we are able to extract named entity mentions and ground them to the English Wikipedia for all languages in Wikipedia.

[1] http://cogcomp.cs.illinois.edu/page/demo_view/Wikifier
[2] http://github.com/yago-naga/aida
[3] http://tagme.d4science.org/tagme/
[4] http://blender04.cs.rpi.edu/~panx2/edl/

Proceedings of COLING 2016, the 26th International Conference on Computational Linguistics: System Demonstrations, pages 146–150, Osaka, Japan, December 11-17 2016.

Input Text:

Op 20 januari 2009 werd hij beëdigd als de 44e president van de Verenigde Staten. Hij is de eerste Amerikaan van Afrikaanse afkomst in deze functie. Tussen 3 januari 2005 en 16 november 2008 was Obama lid van de Senaat als vertegenwoordiger van Illinois en voordien was hij staatssenator in de wetgevende vergadering van zijn thuisstaat. Na het verslaan van de Republikeinse kandidaat John McCain tijdens de Amerikaanse presidentsverkiezingen 2008 werd hij op 20 januari 2009 tijdens de inauguratie op het Capitool

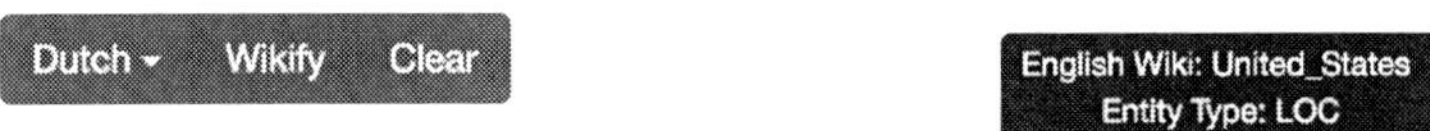

Op 20 januari 2009 werd hij beëdigd als de 44e president van de Verenigde Staten. Hij is de eerste Amerikaan van Afrikaanse afkomst in deze functie. Tussen 3 januari 2005 en 16 november 2008 was Obama lid van de Senaat als vertegenwoordiger van Illinois en voordien was hij staatssenator in de wetgevende vergadering van zijn thuisstaat. Na het verslaan van de Republikeinse kandidaat John McCain tijdens de Amerikaanse presidentsverkiezingen 2008 werd hij op 20 januari 2009 tijdens de inauguratie op het Capitool beëdigd als president.

Figure 1: Screen shot of Illinois Cross-Lingual Wikifier.

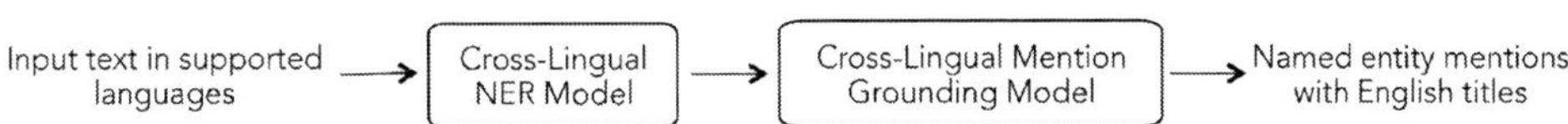

Figure 2: Pipeline of Illinois Cross-Lingual Wikifier.

2 System Description

Figure 1 shows the web interface of our system. The bottom part is its output. The extracted named entities (in blue) are hyperlinked to the corresponding English Wikipedia pages. If the cursor points to a mention (e.g., "Verenigde Staten"), the corresponding English title and the entity type will be shown.

Our system is based on two components that we proposed recently: a cross-lingual NER model (Tsai et al., 2016) and a cross-lingual mention grounding model (Tsai and Roth, 2016). Figure 2 shows an overview of the system. Given some text in a non-English language, the cross-lingual NER model extracts named entity mentions and the cross-lingual mention grounding model finds the corresponding English Wikipedia titles for each mention.

2.1 Cross-Lingual Named Entity Recognition

We use the direct transfer NER model proposed in Tsai et al. (2016). This model can be trained on one or several languages, depending on the availability of training data, and can be applied to other Wikipedia languages without changing anything in the model. The key idea is that the cross-lingual mention grounding model (Section 2.2) generates good language-independent NER features for each word in any Wikipedia language. More specifically, by grounding all n-grams in the input text to the English Wikipedia, we can describe each word using a set of FreeBase types and Wikipedia categories. Since these FreeBase types and Wikipedia categories are always in English, the features extracted based on these types can be used across different languages.

The features used in our model include the standard lexical features, gazetteer features, and the features based on the cross-lingual mention grounding model. Note that as concluded in Tsai et al. (2016), we only use all features when the target language uses Latin script. Otherwise, only the language-independent features (based on the cross-lingual mention grounding model) are active. The model is trained on the English training data from CoNLL 2003 shared task. Therefore it follows the named entity definitions of the shared task which use four entity types: PER, ORG, LOC, and MISC.

Note that we use white spaces and few common punctuations to tokenize the input text for most languages. For the languages which need special tokenization or word segmentation, we try to find publicly available tokenizers. Otherwise, we simply treat each character as a token.

Approach	Dutch	German	Spanish	Turkish	Tagalog	Yoruba	Bengali	Tamil
Our system	**61.56**	**48.12**	**60.55**	**47.12**	**65.44**	**36.65**	**43.27**	**29.64**
Täckström et al. (2012)	58.4	40.4	59.3	-	-	-	-	-
Zhang et al. (2016)	-	-	-	43.6	51.3	36.0	34.8	26.0

Table 1: Performance of the cross-lingual NER model. The numbers are F1 scores. We compare our system with two related work which also assume no training data for the target language.

	German	Spanish	French	Italian	Chinese	Hebrew	Thai	Arabic	Turkish	Tamil	Tagalog	Urdu
Prec@1	81.45	81.37	79.65	79.79	84.55	84.03	89.46	86.13	85.10	84.15	84.54	91.07

Table 2: Evaluation of the cross-lingual mention grounding model on the Wikipedia dataset.

2.2 Cross-Lingual Mention Grounding

We adapt the model proposed in Tsai and Roth (2016), which uses cross-lingual word and title embeddings to disambiguate the mentions extracted by the NER model to the English Wikipedia. The model consists of two steps:

Candidate Generation: The first step is to select a set of English title candidates for each foreign mention. The goal of this step is to produce a manageable number of candidates so that a more sophisticated algorithm can be applied to disambiguate them. This step is achieved by dictionaries built from the hyperlink structure and inter-language links in Wikipedia. That is, for each English title, we gather all possible strings in any language that can be used to refer to it.

Note that the limitation of this procedure is that it only retrieves titles that are in the intersection of the English Wikipedia and the target language Wikipedia. That is, the English titles that are linked to some titles in the target language Wikipedia. For example, since *Dan Roth* does not have a page in the Chinese Wikipedia, this process will not generate *Dan Roth*'s English Wikipedia page as a candidate when we see his name in Chinese. To overcome this limitation, we extend the candidate generation process with a transliteration model (Pasternack and Roth, 2009). The model is trained on the (target language name, English name) pairs obtained from the Wikipedia titles. If the original candidate generator fails to retrieve any candidate for a mention, we transliterate the mention into English and then query title candidates by this English transliteration.

Candidate Ranking: Given a mention and a set of English title candidates, we compute a score for each title which indicates how relevant the title is to the mention. We represent a pair of (mention, candidate) by a set of features which are various similarities between them. These features are computed based on cross-lingual word and title embeddings. We embed words and Wikipedia titles of English and the target language into the same semantic space. By representing the mention using several contextual clues, we can compute meaningful similarity between the mention and a English title using the cross-lingual embeddings. We train a linear ranking SVM model to combine these features for each language. The training examples are constructed from the hyperlinked phrases in Wikipedia articles.

2.3 Evaluation

Since our goal is to have broad coverage of languages, we try to evaluate our system on as many languages as possible. However, only a couple of languages have end-to-end wikification datasets that also follow the CoNLL named entity definitions. Therefore, we evaluate the two key components separately.

The cross-lingual NER model is evaluated on 8 lanugages and the results are shown in Table 1. For Dutch, German, and Spanish, we use the test data from CoNLL 2002/2003 shared tasks. The data for the other five low-resource languages are from the LORELEI and REFLEX packages[5]. Comparing

[5]LDC2015E13, LDC2015E90, LDC2015E83, and LDC2015E91

Approach	Spanish	Chinese
Top TAC'15 systems	80.4	83.1
Our System	80.93	83.63

Table 3: Performance of the cross-lingual mention grounding model on TAC 2015 Entity Linking diagnostic task (mentions are given as the input). The numbers are precision@1.

our system to two related work which also assume no training data for the target language, our system outperforms them on all 8 languages.

The cross-lingual mention grounding model is evaluated on the Wikipedia dataset of 12 languages created by Tsai et al. (2016). Results are listed in Table 2. In this dataset, since at least one third of the query mentions cannot be solved by the most common title, the baseline that predicts the most common title has precision@1 at most 66.67 for each language. We can see that our system is much better than this baseline. Table 3 compares our system with the top systems participated in TAC 2015 Entity Linking diagnostic tasks. Our system achieves slightly better scores than the best systems of Spanish and Chinese.

3 Related Work

Besides the language-specific systems that we discussed in Section 1, Babelfy[6] has the most similar goals to our system. Babelfy grounds words and phrases of 271 languages to BabelNet, a multilingual encyclopedic constructed from multiple resources, including Wikipedia, WordNet, VerbNet, and so on. For each mention, it also provides the corresponding English entry if there is any linked to the grounded target language entry. Therefore Babelfy can be viewed as a cross-lingual grounding system.

The main differences between our system and Babelfy are two folds. First, the target mentions are different. In our system, we focus on grounding named entities thus there is a multilingual named entity recognition module. Babelfy tries to disambiguate all linkable n-grams. For example, the string "president of United States" is linked to Wikipedia titles president_of_United_States, United_States, president, and United_(Phoenix_album), and the word "state" is linked to a sense in WordNet. From this example, we can see that grounding words inside a name entity may not be very useful. Second, Babelfy only grounds mentions to the entries in the target language, and shows the corresponding English entry if the English entry is linked to the target language entry. As discussed in Section 2.2, these inter-language links could be very sparse for many languages. Instead, our system uses a transliteration model to retrieve English candidates from the foreign mentions directly. Moreover, due to cross-lingual word and title embeddings, our ranking model can directly compute similarities between foreign mentions and English titles.

4 Conclusion and Future Work

We release Illinois Cross-Lingual Wikifier, a tool that extracts named entities for many languages, and also grounds the extracted entities to the English Wikipedia. The broad coverage of our system will help people and computers to understand text in many languages especially when machine translation technology is unavailable or unreliable.

There are various directions which one can pursue to improve our system. While the cross-lingual NER model covers many languages, its performance still can be improved significantly. One possible direction is to select a better or closer source language for each target language. Another is to incorporate target language specific knowledge into the model. For the cross-lingual mention grounding model, the candidate generation does not have good enough coverage for small languages. Currently we simply use an off-the-shelf transliteration model to retrieve possible English titles. While this works well for people's names, many organization and location names need to be translated instead of transliterated.

[6]http://babelfy.org/

Acknowledgments

This research is supported by NIH grant U54-GM114838, a grant from the Allen Institute for Artificial Intelligence (allenai.org), and Contract HR0011-15-2-0025 with the US Defense Advanced Research Projects Agency (DARPA). Approved for Public Release, Distribution Unlimited. The views expressed are those of the authors and do not reflect the official policy or position of the Department of Defense or the U.S. Government.

References

Razvan Bunescu and Marius Pasca. 2006. Using encyclopedic knowledge for named entity disambiguation. In *Proceedings of the European Chapter of the ACL (EACL)*.

Xiao Cheng and Dan Roth. 2013. Relational inference for wikification. In *Proc. of the Conference on Empirical Methods in Natural Language Processing (EMNLP)*.

Silviu Cucerzan. 2007. Large-scale named entity disambiguation based on Wikipedia data. In *Proceedings of EMNLP*, pages 708–716.

Rada Mihalcea and Andras Csomai. 2007. Wikify!: Linking documents to encyclopedic knowledge. In *Proceedings of ACM Conference on Information and Knowledge Management (CIKM)*, pages 233–242.

Jeff Pasternack and Dan Roth. 2009. Learning better transliterations. In *Proc. of the ACM Conference on Information and Knowledge Management (CIKM)*, 11.

Lev Ratinov, Dan Roth, Doug Downey, and Mike Anderson. 2011. Local and global algorithms for disambiguation to wikipedia. In *Proc. of the Annual Meeting of the Association for Computational Linguistics (ACL)*.

Oscar Täckström, Ryan T. McDonald, and Jakob Uszkoreit. 2012. Cross-lingual word clusters for direct transfer of linguistic structure. In *NAACL*.

Chen-Tse Tsai and Dan Roth. 2016. Concept grounding to multiple knowledge bases via indirect supervision. *Transactions of the Association for Computational Linguistics*, 2.

Chen-Tse Tsai, Stephen Mayhew, and Dan Roth. 2016. Cross-lingual named entity recognition via wikification. In *Proc. of the Conference on Computational Natural Language Learning (CoNLL)*.

Boliang Zhang, Xiaoman Pan, Tianlu Wang, Ashish Vaswani, Heng Ji, Kevin Knight, and Daniel Marcu. 2016. Name tagging for low-resource incident languages based on expectation-driven learning. In *NAACL*.

A Meaning-based English Math Word Problem Solver with Understanding, Reasoning and Explanation

Chao-Chun Liang, Shih-Hong Tsai, Ting-Yun Chang, Yi-Chung Lin and Keh-Yih Su
Institute of Information Science, Academia Sinica, Taiwan
{ccliang,doublebite,terachang621,lyc,kysu}@iis.sinica.edu.tw

Abstract

This paper presents a meaning-based statistical math word problem (MWP) solver with understanding, reasoning and explanation. It comprises a web user interface and pipelined modules for analysing the text, transforming both body and question parts into their logic forms, and then performing inference on them. The associated context of each quantity is represented with proposed *role-tags* (e.g., nsubj, verb, etc.), which provides the flexibility for annotating the extracted math quantity with its associated syntactic and semantic information (which specifies the physical meaning of that quantity). Those role-tags are then used to identify the desired operands and filter out irrelevant quantities (so that the answer can be obtained precisely). Since the physical meaning of each quantity is *explicitly* represented with those role-tags and used in the inference process, the proposed approach could explain how the answer is obtained in a human comprehensible way.

1 Introduction

The *math word problem* (MWP) is frequently chosen to study natural language understanding for the following reasons: (1) The answer to the MWP cannot be simply extracted by performing keyword/pattern matching. It clearly shows the merit of understanding and inference. (2) An MWP usually possesses less complicated syntax and requires less amount of domain knowledge, so the researcher can focus on the task of understanding and reasoning. (3) The body part of MWP (which mentions the given information for solving the problem) consists of only a few sentences. The understanding and reasoning procedure thus could be checked more efficiently. (4) The MWP solver has its own applications such as *Computer Math Tutor* and *Helper for Math in Daily Life*.

According to the approaches used to identify entities, quantities, and to decide operands and operations, previous MWP solvers can be classified as: (1) Rule-based approaches (Mukherjee and Garain, 2008; Hosseini et al., 2014), which make all related decisions based on a set of rules; (2) Purely statistics-based approaches (Kushman et al., 2014; Roy et al., 2015), in which all related decisions are done via a statistical classifier; and (3) Mixed approach (Roy and Roth, 2015), which identifies entities and quantities with rules, yet, decides operands and operations via statistical classifiers.

The main problem of the rule-based approaches is that a wide coverage rule-set is difficult and expensive to construct. Also, it is awkward in resolving ambiguity problem. In contrast, the main problems of the purely statistics-based approaches are that the performance deteriorates significantly when the MWP is complicated, and they are sensitive to the irrelevant information (Hosseini et al., 2014).

A meaning-based[1] statistical framework (Lin et al., 2015) is thus proposed to perform understanding and reasoning to avoid the problems mentioned above. The proposed *role-tags* (e.g., nsubj, verb, etc.) provides the flexibility for annotating extracted math quantities with their associated syntactic and se-

[1] According to the study reported by Pape (2004), the meaning-based approach for solving MWPs achieves the best performance among various behaviours adopted by middle school children.

Proceedings of COLING 2016, the 26th International Conference on Computational Linguistics: System Demonstrations, pages 151–155, Osaka, Japan, December 11-17 2016.

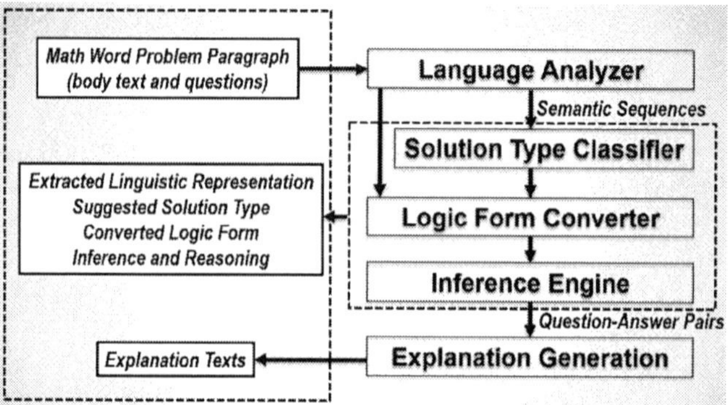

Figure 1: The block diagram of the MWP Solver

semantic (such as co-reference) information (in the context), which can be used to identify the desired operand, filter out irrelevant and perform inference to solve MWPs.

2 System Architecture

The block diagram of our English MWP solver is shown in Figure 1 (Lin et al., 2015). The sentences in a MWP are analyzed by the *Language Analyzer* (LA) module (i.e., Stanford CoreNLP suite (Manning et al., 2014)) to obtain corresponding linguistic representation (i.e., dependency trees and co-reference chains). Then, the *Solution Type Classifier* (STC), which is an SVM classifier adopting linear kernel functions, determines the solution type for each question in the MWP. According to the given solution type, the *Logic Form Converter* (LFC) transforms the linguistic representation into logic forms. Afterwards, based on the logic forms, the *Inference Engine* (IE) generates the answer for each question. Finally, the *Explanation Generator* (EG) module generates the explanation text to explain how the answer is obtained according to the given reasoning chain (Russell and Norvig, 2009).

2.1 Solution Type Identification

The solution type is the key math operation to solve a question in an MWP. In the classroom, children are usually taught with various MWPs of the same solution type, such as addition, multiplication, greatest common divisor, and so on. Teaching the MWPs of the same solution type at a time is helpful for learning because they share the similar patterns (in language usages or in logic representations/inferences). Once the solution type of an MWP is identified, solving the MWP becomes easier. Based on this strategy, the STC is adopted in our system to identify the solution type of MWPs.

The STC will select a math operation (that LFC should adopt to solve the problem) based on the global information across various input sentences. We classify the English MWPs into 6 main solution types: "*Addition*", "*Subtraction*", "*Multiplication*", "*Division*", "*Sum*" and "*TVQ*". The first five types are self-explained with their names. The last one "*TVQ*" means to get the initial/change/final value of a specific *Time-Variant-Quantity*. Currently, an SVM classifier with linear kernel functions (Chang and Lin, 2011) is used, and it adopts three different kinds of feature-sets: (1) Verb Category (Bakman, 2007; Hosseini et al., 2014) related features, (2) various *key-word indicators* (such as "*total*" and "*in all*" which frequently indicate an addition operation), and (3) indicators for various specified aggregative patterns (e.g. "*If the Body contains only two quantities, and their associated verbs are the same*" which frequently implies the "*Addition*" solution type).

2.2 Logical Form Transformation

A two-stage approach is adopted to transform the linguistic representation into logic forms for solving MWPs. In the first stage, the FOL predicates are generated by traversing the input linguistic representation. For example, "*Fred picked 36 roses.*" will be transformed into the following FOL predicates separated by the logic AND operator "&" and the first arguments, *v1*, *n1* and *n2*, are the identifiers.

verb(v1,pack)&nsubj(v1,n1)&dobj(v1,n2)&head(n2,rose)&nummod(n2,36)

In the second stage, crucial generic math facts associated with quantities and relations between quantities are generated. For example, the FOL function "*quan*(q_{id},*unit,object*)=*number*" is used to describe the facts about quantities. The first argument is a unique identifier to represent the quantity fact. The other arguments and the function value describe the meaning of this fact. For the above example, a quantity fact "*quan(q1,#,rose)=36*" is generated. Auxiliary domain-independent facts associated with domain-dependent facts like *quan(. . .)* are also created in this stage to help the IE find the solution. For example, the auxiliary fact "*verb(q1,pick)*" is created for *q1* to state "*the verb of q1 is pick*".

The FOL predicate "$qmap(map_{id}, q_{id1}, q_{id2})$", which denotes the mapping from q_{id1} to q_{id2}, is used to describe a relation between two quantity facts, where the first argument is a unique identifier to represent this relation. For example, *qmap(m1,q3,q4)* indicates that there is a relation between "100 candies" (*quan(q3,#,candidate)=100)* and "5 boxes" (*quan(q4,#,box)=5)* in the example of "*Pack 100 candies into 5 boxes*". The auxiliary fact "*verb(m1,pack)*" is created for *m1* to state "*the verb of m1 is pack*".

The questions in an MWP are transformed into FOL-like utility functions provided by the IE according to the suggested solution type. One utility function is issued for each question to find the answer. According to the solution type provided by the STC, the LFC will select an IE utility and instantiate its arguments. For example, if "*How many roses were picked in total?*" is labelled with "*Sum*" by the STC, the LFC will transform it to "*ASK Sum(quan(?q,rose),verb(?q,pick))*", which asks the IE to sum the values of all quantity facts of which verbs are "*pick*".

2.3 Logic Inference

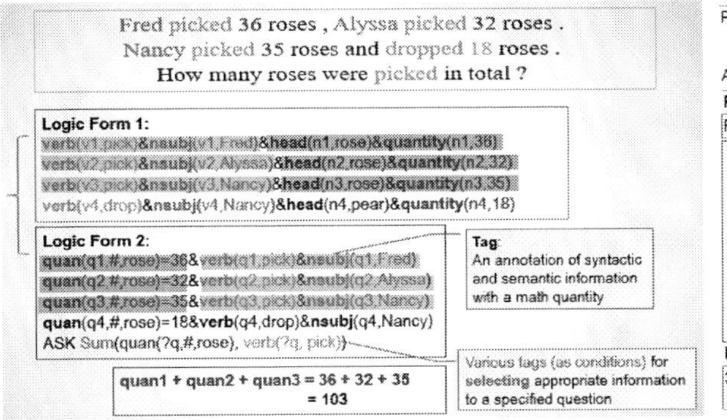

Figure 2: Logic form and logic inference of a *Sum* operation

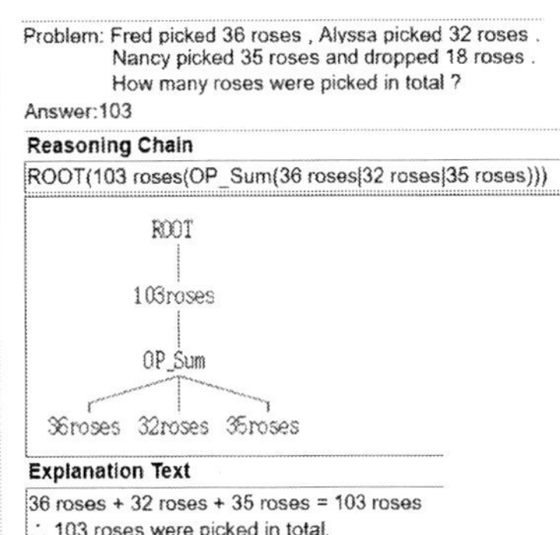

Figure3: The generated explanation tree and explanation text

The IE is used to find the solution of an MWP. Currently, IE provides 9 different utilities to perform simple arithmetical operations. It is responsible for providing utilities to select desired facts and then obtain the answer by taking math operations on those selected facts. For example, the Addition utility, "$Addition(value_1, value_2) = value$", returns the value of "$value_1 + value_2$", where $value_i$ could be a constant number, an FOL function value, or a value returned by a utility; and the Sum utility, "*Sum(function , condition)*", returns the sum of the values of FOL function instances which can be unified with the function arguments and satisfy the condition arguments. IE is also responsible for using inference rules to derive new facts from those facts which are directly derived from the description of the MWP. Consider the example shown in Figure 2, the IE will first select all qualified quantities which match "*quan(?q, #, rose)*" and with a "*pick*" verb-tag, and then performs a "*Sum*" operation on them. The irrelevant quantity "*quan(q4, #, rose)*" in that example is pruned out as its verb-tag is "*drop*", not "*pick*". The answer is then obtained by summing those quantities *q1*, *q2* and *q3*.

2.4 Explanation Generation

The EG is responsible for explaining the associated reasoning steps in fluent natural language based on the reasoning chain generated from IE. A math operation oriented approach (Huang et al., 2015) is adopted to explain how the answer is obtained. It first converts the given reasoning chain into its corresponding *Explanation Tree*, which represents the associated operations and operands for solving the MWP. After that, a specific template is used to generate the explanation text for each kind of operation. Consider the example shown in Figure 3, the explanation text "*36 roses + 32 roses + 35 roses = 103 roses. ∴103 roses were picked in total.*" will be generated to explain that the obtained answer is a summation of "*36 roses*", "*32 roses*" and "*35 roses*".

3 Experiments

	MA1	IXL	MA2	Total
3-fold Cross validation				
Our System	**94.8**	73.4	**88.4**	**85.3**
UIUC	-	-	-	78.0
ARIS	83.6	**75.0**	74.4	77.7
KAZB	89.6	51.1	51.2	64.0
Gold Solution Type				
Our System	99.3	97.8	95.0	97.5
STC accuracy	91.8	74.1	79.6	81.7

Table 1: Accuracy rates of different systems in AI2-395. "Total" denotes the micro-average performance. "Gold Solution Type" reports the accuracy from the gold solution type.

	IL-562
5-fold Cross validation	
Our System	**79.5**
UIUC	73.9
ARIS	-
KAZB	73.7

Table 2: Accuracy rates of different systems in IL-562 dataset.

We evaluate our system on two publicly available datasets, *AI2-395* and *IL-562*. **AI2-395** includes 395 *Addition* and *Subtraction* MWPs which are provided by Hosseini et al. (2014). It includes three sub-datasets (i.e., MA1, IXL and MA2) with different feature categories. **IL-562** is a collection of 562 arithmetic word problems released by Roy et al. (2015), and each of them can be solved with only one math operation among *Addition*, *Subtraction*, *Multiplication* or *Division*.

We compare our system with the rule-based approach ARIS (Hosseini et al., 2014), the purely statistical approach KAZB (Kushman et al., 2014), and the mixed approach UIUC system (Roy and Roth, 2015). We follow the same evaluation setting adopted in (Hosseini et al., 2014) and (Roy et. al, 2015). Table 1 and 2 show that our system significantly outperform theirs in overall performance.

4 Demonstration Outline

The MWP solver comprises a web user interface (Figure 4) and a processing server. The web interface is used to input the problem and display various outputs generated from the submitted MWP. The server will process the submitted problem to get the answer. After an MWP is submitted, various processing modules will be invoked in a pipelined manner (Figure 1) to solve the problem. Once the process is finished, the user can browse the outputs generated from each module: (1) Corresponding *dependency relations*, *co-reference chains* and *linguistic representations*, which are generated from *LA*. (2) Suggested *solution type*, which identifies the desired math operation. (3) Obtained *logical forms*, which are transformed from the linguistic representation and the specified solution type. (4) Generated *reasoning chain* and *explanation text* (Figure 3), which explains how the problem is solved. An online demo is available at: http://nlul.iis.sinica.edu.tw/EnglishMathSolver/mathDemo.py.

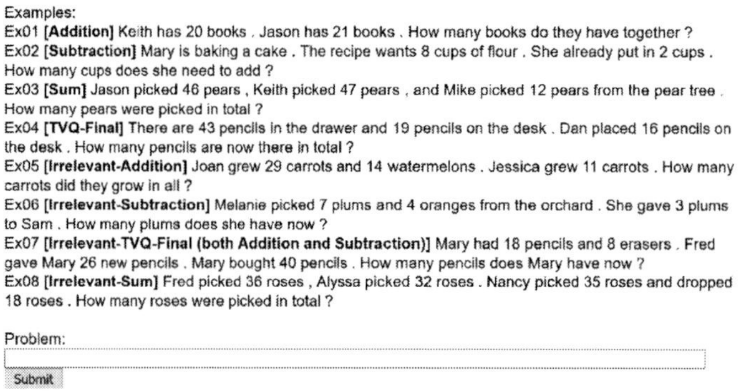

Examples:
Ex01 **[Addition]** Keith has 20 books . Jason has 21 books . How many books do they have together ?
Ex02 **[Subtraction]** Mary is baking a cake . The recipe wants 8 cups of flour . She already put in 2 cups . How many cups does she need to add ?
Ex03 **[Sum]** Jason picked 46 pears , Keith picked 47 pears , and Mike picked 12 pears from the pear tree . How many pears were picked in total ?
Ex04 **[TVQ-Final]** There are 43 pencils in the drawer and 19 pencils on the desk . Dan placed 16 pencils on the desk . How many pencils are now there in total ?
Ex05 **[Irrelevant-Addition]** Joan grew 29 carrots and 14 watermelons . Jessica grew 11 carrots . How many carrots did they grow in all ?
Ex06 **[Irrelevant-Subtraction]** Melanie picked 7 plums and 4 oranges from the orchard . She gave 3 plums to Sam . How many plums does she have now ?
Ex07 **[Irrelevant-TVQ-Final (both Addition and Subtraction)]** Mary had 18 pencils and 8 erasers . Fred gave Mary 26 new pencils . Mary bought 40 pencils . How many pencils does Mary have now ?
Ex08 **[Irrelevant-Sum]** Fred picked 36 roses , Alyssa picked 32 roses . Nancy picked 35 roses and dropped 18 roses . How many roses were picked in total ?

Problem:

Submit

Figure 4: A web interface of the MWP Solver

5 Conclusion

A meaning-based logic form represented with role-tags is first proposed to provide the flexibility for annotating the extracted math quantity with its associated syntactic and semantic information in the context. Those tags can be used to identify the desired operands and filter out irrelevant quantities. Since the physical meaning of each quantity is *explicitly* expressed and used during inference, the associated reasoning procedure is human comprehensible and could be easily explained to the user.

A statistical framework based on the above meaning-based logic form is then proposed in this paper to perform understanding and reasoning for solving the given MWP. The combination of the statistical framework and logic inference distinguishes the proposed approach from other approaches.

The main contributions of our work are: (1) Proposing a meaning-based logic representation so that the physical meaning of each quantity could be explicitly specified and used in getting the answer; (2) Proposing a statistical framework for performing reasoning from the given MWP text.

6 Future Works

Currently, the MWP solver assumes that the final answer can be directly obtained from those known quantity facts via only one arithmetic operation (i.e., merely handling one-step MWPs). It cannot solve the problem if multiple arithmetic operations are required. For example, "*Mary had 92 pieces of candy. She gave 4 pieces each to 9 friends. How many pieces of candy does Mary have left?*" is not handled now. A goal oriented approach for handling the above multi-step MWP is thus proposed and under test. Besides, the current system cannot handle some subtle referring relationships. For instance, the system does not know that "*customers*" refers to "*women*" and "*men*" in the following MWP "*A waiter had 6 tables he was waiting on, with 3 women and 5 men at each table. How many customers total did the waiter have?*". Advanced analysis is required to solve this kind of problems.

Reference

Yefim Bakman. 2007. Robust understanding of word problems with extraneous information. http://lanl.arxiv.org/abs/math.GM/0701393.

Chih-Chung Chang and Chih-Jen Lin. 2011. LIBSVM: a library for support vector machines. *ACM Transactions on Intelligent Systems and Technology*, 2(3):27:1–27:27. At http://www.csie.ntu.edu.tw/cjlin/libsvm.

Mohammad Javad Hosseini, Hannaneh Hajishirzi, Oren Etzioni, and Nate Kushman. 2014. Learning to solve arithmetic word problems with verb categorization. *EMNLP 2014, October 25-29, 2014, Doha, Qatar, A meeting of SIGDAT, a Special Interest Group of the ACL*, pages 523–533.

Chien-Tsung Huang, Yi-Chung Lin, and Keh-Yih Su. 2015. Explanation generation for a math word problem solver. *IJCLCLP*, 20(2):27–44.

Nate Kushman, Yoav Artzi, Luke Zettlemoyer, and Regina Barzilay. 2014. Learning to automatically solve algebra word problems. Baltimore, Maryland, June. *Association for Computational Linguistics*, page 271–281.

Yi-Chung Lin, Chao-Chun Liang, Kuang-Yi Hsu, Chien-Tsung Huang, Shen-Yun Miao, Wei-Yun Ma, Lun-Wei Ku, Churn-Jung Liau, and Keh-Yih Su. 2015. Designing a tag-based statistical math word problem solver with reasoning and explanation. *IJCLCLP*, 20(2):1–26.

Christopher D Manning, Mihai Surdeanu, John Bauer, Jenny Finkel, Steven J Bethard, and David McClosky. 2014. The Stanford CoreNLP natural language processing toolkit. In *ACL Demonstrations*.

Anirban Mukherjee and Utpal Garain. 2008. A review of methods for automatic understanding of natural language mathematical problems. *Artif Intell Rev*, 29(2):93–122.

Stephen J. Pape. 2004. Middle school children's problem-solving behavior: A cognitive analysis from a reading comprehension perspective. *Journal for Research in Mathematics Education*, 35(3):187–219.

Subhro Roy and Dan Roth. 2015. Solving general arithmetic word problems. *EMNLP*, pages 1743–1752.

Subhro Roy, Tim Vieira, and Dan Roth. 2015. Reasoning about quantities in natural language. *TACL*, 3:1–13.

Stuart Russell and Peter Norvig. 2009. *Artificial Intelligence*: A Modern Approach. Prentice Hall Press, Upper Saddle River, NJ, USA, 3rd edition.

Valencer: an API to Query Valence Patterns in FrameNet

Alexandre Kabbach and **Corentin Ribeyre**
University of Geneva
Department of Linguistics
5 Rue de Candolle, CH-1211 Genève 4
firstname.lastname@unige.ch

Abstract

This paper introduces Valencer: a RESTful API to search for annotated sentences matching a given combination of syntactic realizations of the arguments of a predicate – also called *valence pattern* – in the FrameNet database. The API takes as input an HTTP GET request specifying a valence pattern and outputs a list of exemplifying annotated sentences in JSON format. The API is designed to be modular and language-independent, and can therefore be easily integrated to other (NLP) server-side or client-side applications, as well as non-English FrameNet projects.

1 Introduction

The Berkeley FrameNet project (Baker et al., 1998) aims at creating a human and machine-readable lexical database of English, supported by corpus evidence annotated in terms of *frame semantics* (Fillmore, 1982). Its output takes the form of a database of corpus-extracted and annotated sentences specifying schematic representations of events, relations or entities called *frames*, frame-evoking words called *lexical units*, and semantic roles called *frame elements*. The latest data release contains about 1,200 frames, 10,000 frame elements, 13,000 lexical units and 200,000 manually annotated sentences (see Section 2 for examples of FrameNet annotated sentences).

Computational linguistics applications such as information extraction (Surdeanu et al., 2003), paraphrase recognition (Padó and Erk, 2005), question answering (Shen and Lapata, 2007) and parsing (Das et al., 2013) have made extensive use of FrameNet taxonomy and its documentation of the syntactic valence of the arguments of predicates. Information regarding predicate-argument structures – referred to as *valence patterns* in FrameNet (see Section 2) – could also benefit corpus linguists, alongside NLP applications, when searching for complex semantic and/or syntactic patterns not bounded by given lexical items, overcoming thereby the limitations of traditional concordancers (Manning, 2003).

However, given the current structure of FrameNet data (Baker et al., 2003), valence patterns cannot be searched directly and can only be accessed through the lexical units they refer to, although a given valence pattern may be realized in multiple lexical units across several distinct frames. Therefore, searching for all annotated sentences matching a given valence pattern, across lexical units and frames, requires some additional pre-processing of FrameNet data, beside the implementation of a specific search engine.

In this paper we address this issue and introduce Valencer: a RESTful API to search for annotated sentences matching a given valence pattern in the FrameNet database. The API takes as input an HTTP GET request specifying the queried valence pattern (see Section 3.3) and outputs a list of annotated sentences in JSON format (see Section 3.4). The Valencer API provides a lightweight server-side application compatible with modern W3C standards. It removes from potential users the burden of having to import and index FrameNet data, validate input queries and optimize the valence pattern search engine. Its JSON output, consistent with FrameNet data structure, makes the API easy to integrate into other (NLP) server-side or client-side applications. Finally, being language-independent, the API can be smoothly adapted to other FrameNet projects (e.g. Japanese (Ohara et al., 2004)), if they use the same XML data release format as the Berkeley FrameNet. Valencer is open-source, licensed under the MIT license and freely available at https://github.com/akb89/valencer.

Proceedings of COLING 2016, the 26th International Conference on Computational Linguistics: System Demonstrations, pages 156–160, Osaka, Japan, December 11-17 2016.

2 Valence Patterns in FrameNet

In FrameNet, syntactic realizations of frame elements are called *valences* and are represented as triplets FE.PT.GF of *frame element* (FE), *phrase type* (PT) and *grammatical function* (GF). *Valence patterns* refer to the range of combinatorial possibilities of valences for each lexical unit. Examples of valence patterns are given in (1) and (2) for the lexical unit *give*.v in the `Giving` frame. The two valence patterns differ in the morpho-syntactic realizations of their THEME and RECIPIENT frame elements.

(1) a. He gives local charities money

b. $[\text{He}]_{\text{Donor.NP.Ext}}$ **gives** $[\text{local charities}]_{\text{Recipient.NP.Obj}}$ $[\text{money}]_{\text{Theme.NP.Dep}}$

(2) a. He gives money to local charities

b. $[\text{He}]_{\text{Donor.NP.Ext}}$ **gives** $[\text{money}]_{\text{Theme.NP.Obj}}$ $[\text{to local charities}]_{\text{Recipient.PP[to].Dep}}$

In (1) and (2), 'NP' refers to a *noun phrase*, 'PP[to]' to a *prepositional phrase* headed by *to*, 'Ext' to an *external argument* (the subject), 'Obj' to an *object* and 'Dep' to a *dependent*.

3 API overview

3.1 Architecture

The `Valencer` API is a JavaScript Node.js-based RESTful web application relying on a MongoDB database. The workflow of the API follows: (1) receive an HTTP `GET` request specifying a valence pattern, (2) validate the query and its parameters, (3) retrieve and return the relevant data, and (4) output a collection of documents in JSON format. The output documents correspond to populated MongoDB entries. The technological choice of a document-based, JSON-oriented NoSQL database such as MongoDB is particularly relevant to our case as it allows us to keep consistency between the structure of the data output by the API and the structure of the data stored in the database. Additionally, the JSON format of the output makes the API particularly well-suited for integration with JavaScript web clients.

3.2 Underlying technologies

The choice of JavaScript, Node.js and MongoDB is primarily motivated by considerations of performance and maintainability. Performances of the V8 engine powering Node.js have turned JavaScript into a serious challenger of PHP for server-side technologies, especially when PHP is not used with a JIT compiler. Additionally, JavaScript asynchronous programming, especially when implemented with the async/await features of ECMAScript 2017, brings the benefits of concurrent programming without the traditional shortcomings of callbacks (see `http://callbackhell.com/`). It may even yield performance gains over traditional multi-threading approaches while avoiding complexity overhead. Finally, a multi-purpose technological environment, coded in a single programming language and able to handle both back-end and front-end computing as well as (XML) datasets imports greatly decreases refactoring and debugging complexity and improves long-term maintainability. Moreover, schemaless databases such as MongoDB provide a flexible architecture for handling sparse data, easy manipulation of complex tree-structures, and a seamless mapping to human-readable XML formats.

3.3 Input

The API takes as an entry point an HTTP `GET` request specifying a valence pattern 'vp'. For example, the query corresponding to the valence pattern in sentence (2b) is:

```
GET/annoSets?vp=Donor.NP.Ext Theme.NP.Obj Recipient.PP[to].Dep
```

The API is flexible and can process combinations of triplets FE.PT.GF in any order (e.g. PT.FE.GF, GF.PT.FE). It can also process partial triplets, with up to two non-specified elements (FE.PT, GF, PT.GF, etc.). This enables the API to process "semantic queries" – queries specifying only frame elements – such as `Donor Theme Recipient`, as well as "syntactic queries" – queries specifying only phrase types and/or grammatical functions – such as `NP.Ext NP.Obj PP[to].Dep`, and, of course, arbitrary combinations of both, such as `NP.Ext Theme Recipient.PP[to]`.

annotationSet document part 1/2


```
{"annotationSet": {
        "_id": 1632555,
        "sentence": {
                "_id": 1090710,
                "text": "He gives money to local
                        charities . ",
                ...
        },
        "lexUnit": {
                "_id": 4344,
                "name": "give.v",
        "frame": {
                "_id": 139,
                "name": "Giving",
                "lexUnits": [{
                        "_id": 4344,
                        "name": "give.v"}, {
                        "_id": 5344,
                        "name": "donate.v"}, {
                        ...
                }],
                "frameElements": [{
                        "_id": 1052,
                        "name": "Donor",
                        ...}, {
                ...
                }],
                ...
        },
        ...
```


annotationSet document part 2/2


```
        ...
        "pattern": {
                "_id": "57fc94026cc52246ae399541",
                "valenceUnits": [{
                        "_id": "57fc94026cc52246ae",
                        "FE": "Donor",
                        "PT": "NP",
                        "GF": "Ext"}, {
                        ...
                }]
        },
        "labels": [{
                "_id": "57fc94f96cc52246ae46e9ff",
                "name": "Donor",
                "type": "FE",
                "startPos": 0,
                "endPos": 1}, {
                "_id": "57fc94f96cc52246ae46ea05",
                "name": "NP",
                "type": "PT",
                "startPos": 0,
                "endPos": 1}, {
                "_id": "57fc94f96cc52246ae46ea02",
                "name": "Ext",
                "type": "GF",
                "startPos": 0,
                "endPos": 1}, {
                ...
        }]
}}
```


Figure 1: A sample output of the `Valencer` API: the annotationSet document corresponding to sentence (2a) "He gives money to local charities". For readability, the document is split into two parts.

3.4 Output

The `Valencer`API is primarily designed to output a collection of *annotationSet* documents (see Figure 1). In the original FrameNet XML data, annotationSet tags are found under two separate subgroups of the lexical unit entities: they connect the part which lists the syntactic realization of the arguments of the predicate (the valence patterns of the lexical unit) to the part which lists the annotated sentences exemplifying each valence pattern and their respective labels. In the `Valencer`, the annotationSet object merges all this information into one object: it centralizes information regarding a specific annotated sentence, its label, the lexical unit it refers to and the specific valence pattern it exemplifies. All original FrameNet ids are kept to potentially retrieve the original entities directly into the FrameNet database.

3.5 Authentication

The `Valencer` API follows a traditional HMAC-SHA1 key/secret authentication process to allow access to the API methods. The header of each HTTP request to the API must include a key, a Unix timestamp and a signature. The signature itself is the concatenation of the specified API route, the specified query and the Unix timestamp. It is hashed using a SHA1 algorithm and the secret corresponding to the key. At each HTTP request, the server recomputes the signature using the stored secret corresponding to the specified key and checks if it matches the signature passed to the header before accepting or rejecting the request. The timestamp is used to prevent man-in-the-middle attacks by setting a validation period for querys, disallowing thereby replay attacks using stolen keys, querys, and signatures.

4 Use Cases

By design the `Valencer` API is primarily intended to be integrated to other NLP systems or plugged to a web-based client, which is why all necessary information regarding an annotated sentence are gathered in a single annotationSet. However, to a human user, an annotationSet may include a lot of irrelevant information, such as object ids or references, which may render the analysis of the output of the API rather tedious. In order to better illustrate the functionalities of the `Valencer` API, we have implemented four additional routes in our middlewares, beside `GET/annoSets`, to extract and process only the necessary attributes of an annotationSet entity depending on specific use cases.

4.1 Get Lexical Units

`GET/lexUnits` returns a collection of lexical units, with their respective names and frame names, which contain at least one reference to the specified valence pattern given in input. It can be helpful, e.g., in searching for paraphrasing candidates, as FrameNet is characterized by relatively narrow-scope frames and frame elements. Indeed, by definition, lexical units sharing specific valence patterns should be relatively close semantically. For example, querying for the valence pattern `Donor.NP.Ext Theme.NP.Obj Recipient.PP[to].Dep` corresponding to sentence (2b) returns eleven lexical units, ten of which are in the `Giving` frame: *bequeath*.v, *contribute*.v, *donate*.v, *gift*.v, *give out*.v, *give*.v, *hand in*.v, *hand out*.v, *hand over*.v and *hand*.v. All verbs should therefore form valid sentences relatively close in meaning when replacing the verb *give* in sentence (2a): "He gives money to local charities". `GET/lexUnits` can also be used to analyze the "semantic scope" of a specific (syntactic) construction, by checking which lexical units match a given "syntactic" valence pattern, i.e., a valence pattern with unspecified frame elements. Querying, for instance, for the pattern `NP.Ext NP.Obj NP.Dep` corresponding to a prepositional indirect object construction returns a list of 346 unique lexical units (from a total of about 13,000) found in 206 frames (from a total of about 1,200).

4.2 Get Frames

`GET/frames` returns a collection of unique frame names corresponding to frames which contain lexical units which themselves contain at least one reference to the specified valence pattern given in input. Similarly to `GET/lexUnits`, `GET/frames` can be used to investigate the semantic scope of a given valence pattern (see Section 4.1). Additionally, `GET/frames` can be used to check which frames a frame element belongs to, an information that is not straightforwardly available in FrameNet (one has to search through all related frames to check whether or not it contains the frame element). Due to the diversity of semantic relations between frames in FrameNet – referred to as *frame relations* – frame elements can appear in more than one frame, and some (relatively abstract) frame elements can even appear in a significant number of frames. For instance, the DONOR and THEME frame elements of example (1) and (2) appear in 3 and 60 frames respectively.

4.3 Get Patterns

`GET/patterns` returns a collection of (valence) patterns – itself a collection of valenceUnit objects with FE, PT, GF attributes – matching the input. It is mostly useful for checking with which other valence units a given valence unit is realized. For example, querying for `Donor.NP.Ext` returns 81 unique patterns with 127 exemplifying sentences. There are currently 54,264 unique valence patterns in the FrameNet database.

4.4 Get Valence Units

`GET/valenceUnits` returns a collection of unique valenceUnit objects matching the input. It is particularly useful for checking all the syntactic realizations of a given frame element, or all the frame elements realized in a given syntactic valence. For example, querying for the frame element DONOR returns 12 unique valence units such as `Donor.PP[from].Dep` or `Donor.PP[of].Ext`. Querying for `PP[of].Ext` returns a list of 16 valence units including frame elements such as DONOR, TOPIC, MESSAGE or ENTITY. Querying then back for the output valence units with `GET/patterns`, `GET/frames` or `GET/lexUnits` provides more information about each pattern, frames and lexical units in which the valence units are realized.

5 Related Work

It is already possible to search for complex syntactic constructions within treebanks using tools such as TGrep2[1]. The main benefit of using FrameNet instead of treebanks lays in the theoretical background of *frame semantics* situated at the interface between syntax and semantics. It makes it possible to incorporate semantics and search for complex combinations of both syntactic *and* semantic constructions (see Section 3.3). FrameNet also brings a fine-grained classification of frames and frame elements, a strong advantage over PropBank (Palmer et al., 2005) for tasks such as paraphrase generation (see Section 4.1). Finally, FrameNet is free and machine readable, contrary to VDE (Herbst et al., 2004), theoretically noise-free as manually annotated, contrary to VALEX (Korhonen et al., 2006), and has a broader coverage than VerbNet (Schuler, 2005).

6 Conclusion

This paper introduced `Valencer`: a free, open-source and language-independent RESTful API to enable querying for valence patterns in the FrameNet database. The `Valencer` renders parts of FrameNet data more straightforwardly accessible and can also prove useful in non-FrameNet-specific tasks such as searching for complex semantic and syntactic constructions or generating high quality paraphrase.

References

Collin F. Baker, Charles J. Fillmore, and John B. Lowe. 1998. The Berkeley FrameNet Project. In *Proceedings of ACL-COLING*, pages 86–90, Montréal, Québec, Canada, August. Association for Computational Linguistics.

Collin F. Baker, Charles J. Fillmore, and Beau Cronin. 2003. The Structure of the FrameNet Database. *International Journal of Lexicography*, 16(3):281–296.

Dipanjan Das, Desai Chen, André F. T. Martins, Nathan Schneider, and Noah A. Smith. 2013. Frame-semantic parsing. *Computational Linguistics*, 40(1):9–56.

Charles J. Fillmore, 1982. *Frame semantics*, pages 111–137. Hanshin Publishing Co., Seoul, South Korea.

Thomas Herbst, David Heath, Ian F. Roe, and Dieter Götz. 2004. *A Valency Dictionary of English: A Corpus-Based Analysis of the Complementation Patterns of English Verbs, Nouns and Adjectives*, volume 40. Mouton de Gruyter.

Anna Korhonen, Yuval Krymolowski, and Ted Briscoe. 2006. A Large Subcategorization Lexicon for Natural Language Processing Applications. In *Proceedings of LREC*, volume 6.

Christopher D. Manning. 2003. Probabilistic Syntax. In Rens Bod, Jennifer Hay, and Stefanie Jannedy, editors, *Probabilistic Linguistics*, chapter 8. MIT Press.

Kyoko Hirose Ohara, Seiko Fujii, Toshio Ohori, Ryoko Suzuki, Hiroaki Saito, and Shun Ishizaki. 2004. The Japanese FrameNet Project: An Introduction. In *Proceedings of the Workshop on Building Lexical Resources from Semantically Annotated Corpora at LREC*, pages 9–11.

Sebastian Padó and Katrin Erk. 2005. To Cause Or Not To Cause: Cross-Lingual Semantic Matching for Paraphrase Modelling. In *Proceedings of the Cross-Language Knowledge Induction Workshop*.

Martha Palmer, Daniel Gildea, and Paul Kingsbury. 2005. The Proposition Bank: An Annotated Corpus of Semantic Roles. *Computational Linguistics*, 31(1):71–106.

Karin Kipper Schuler. 2005. *VerbNet: A broad-coverage, comprehensive verb lexicon*. Ph.D. thesis, University of Pennsylvania.

Dan Shen and Mirella Lapata. 2007. Using Semantic Roles to Improve Question Answering. In *Proceedings of EMNLP-CoNLL*, pages 12–21, Prague, Czech Republic, June. Association for Computational Linguistics.

Mihai Surdeanu, Sanda Harabagiu, John Williams, and Paul Aarseth. 2003. Using Predicate-Argument Structures for Information Extraction. In *Proceedings of ACL*, pages 8–15, Sapporo, Japan, July. Association for Computational Linguistics.

[1] `https://tedlab.mit.edu/~dr/Tgrep2/`

The Open Framework for Developing Knowledge Base And Question Answering System

Jiseong Kim, GyuHyeon Choi, Jung-Uk Kim, Eun-Kyung Kim, Key-Sun Choi
Machine Reading Laboratory
Semantic Web Research Center
Department of Computer Science
KAIST, Daejeon, Korea
{jiseong, wiany11, prismriver, kekeeo, kschoi}@kaist.ac.kr

Abstract

Developing a question answering (QA) system is a task of implementing and integrating modules of different technologies and evaluating an integrated whole system, which inevitably goes with a collaboration among experts of different domains. For supporting a easy collaboration, this demonstration presents the open framework that aims to support developing a QA system in collaborative and intuitive ways. The demonstration also shows the QA system developed by our novel framework.

1 Introduction

Recently, a system of a question answering capability, so-called question answering (QA) system, is on the rise by being applied on diverse domains, e.g., quiz show (IBM Watson), personal assistant (Apple Siri, Microsoft Cortana), home device (Amazon Echo), and so on.

Developing a QA system is a work of implementing and integrating modules of different technologies (e.g., natural language processing, disambiguation, graph manipulation), and then evaluating an integrated whole system. Each module is developed by different groups of specialists with such different technologies. All modules must be linked into one integrated system to reach a QA capability, which results in needs of a framework for collaboration.

It is not an easy work to collaborate among experts of different domains to build an integrated working system together. To ease the integration, for developers and researchers, a framework that supports logging I/O, exception handling, flexible system configuration, and so on is of need.

There has been many studies on a QA system over the past years. However, the integration environment for supporting collaborative developments is still lacking.

In this context, open knowledge base and question answering (OKBQA)[1] community has been developing a OKBQA framework for exchanging and harmonizing resources developed by different groups scattered over the world to promote an effective and efficient open collaboration for developing a QA system.

In this demonstration, we introduce the OKBQA framework with a state-of-the-arts-based novel QA pipeline, and the interfaces of the OKBQA framework that supports a development of a QA system in collaborative and intuitive ways.

In Section 2, we introduce the architecture and modules of the OKBQA framework in detail. In Section 4, we demonstrate interfaces of the OKBQA framework. Lastly, in Section 5, we conclude.

2 Architecture of The OKBQA Framework

The architecture of the OKBQA framework comprises a pipeline of OKBQA modules based on the state-of-the-art researches: template generation (Unger et al., 2012), graph search-based named entity disambiguation (Usbeck et al., 2014), SPARQL query generation (Jindong and Cohen, 2014), NLQ50 benchmark[2], and so on. Figure 1 shows the overall pipeline of the OKBQA framework that executes modules in a waterfall manner. The role of each module is detailed in the following section.

[1] http://www.okbqa.org
[2] http://2015.okbqa.org/nlq

Proceedings of COLING 2016, the 26th International Conference on Computational Linguistics: System Demonstrations, pages 161–165, Osaka, Japan, December 11-17 2016.

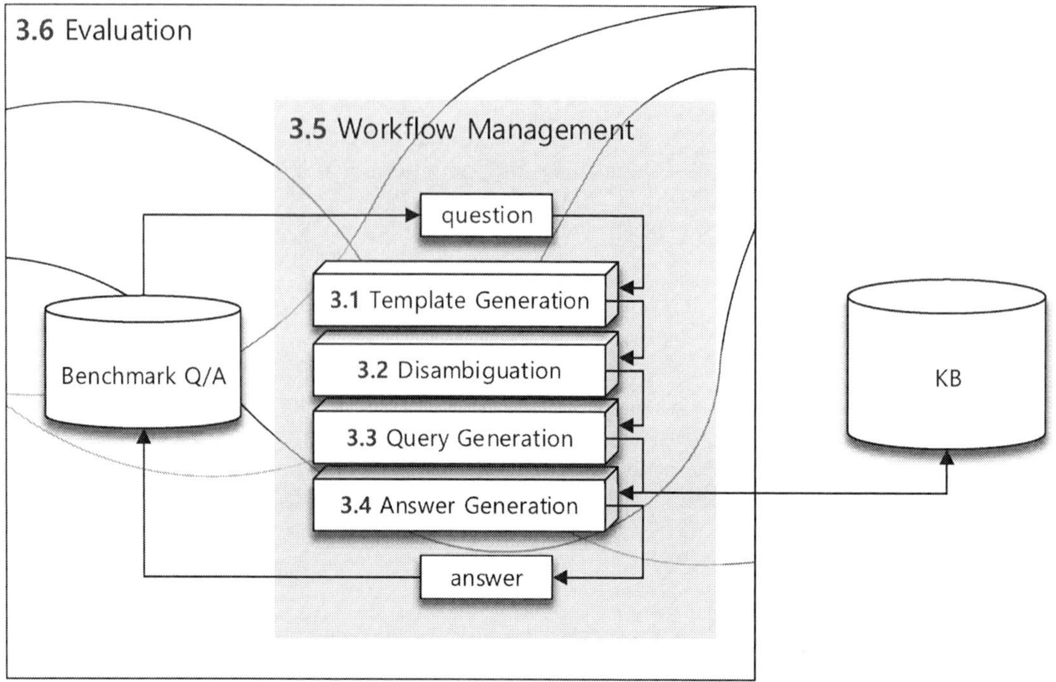

Figure 1: The architecture of the OKBQA framework: Each module is described in detail at each subsection of Section 3

3 OKBQA Modules

3.1 Template Generation

A template generation module (TGM) is for constructing a SPARQL query template from a question expressed in natural language. A *template* comprises *pseudo SPARQL query* and set of *slots*, which of a *pseudo SPARQL query* is a SPARQL query with unbounded variables for resources, classes, and properties specified in a KB, and a *slot* is description of variable. For example, the following shows an example of a template for a natural language question.

- Question: Which rivers flow through Seoul?
- Template:
  - Pseudo query: SELECT ?v4 WHERE { ?v4 ?v2 ?v6 ; ?v7 ?v3 . }
  - Slots (description of variables):
    1. v7 is bound to <http://lodqa.org/vocabulary/sort_of>.
    2. v6 is either a resource or a literal value.
    3. v6 is verbalized into "Seoul".
    4. v2 is a property.
    5. v2 is verbalized into "flow".
    6. v3 is a class.
    7. v3 is verbalized into "rivers".

A template is generated from a question by analyzing a semantic structure of a question from lexical entries and syntactic structure of a question (Unger et al., 2012).

3.2 Disambiguation

A disambiguation module (DM) is for identifying a URI (Uniform Resource Identifier) specified in a KB from verbalization of lexical entries on a question. For example, the following shows an example of disambiguated results.

- Question: Which rivers flow through Seoul?
- Disambiguated results:
  - The lexical entry "Seoul" means the entity <http://dbpedia.org/ontology/Seoul> defined in a KB.
  - The lexical entry "flow" means the entity <http://dbpedia.org/ontology/city> defined in a KB.
  - The lexical entry "rivers" means the entity <http://dbpedia.org/ontology/River> defined in a KB.

3.3 Query Generation

A query generation module (QGM) is for generating and ranking a candidate SPARQL query for a question using results of TGM and DM. For example, the following shows the most top-ranked candidate SPARQL query generated by QGM.

- Question: Which rivers flow through Seoul?
- SPARQL query:
- SELECT ?v4 WHERE {
  ?v4 <http://dbpedia.org/ontology/city> <http://dbpedia.org/resource/Seoul> .
  ?v4 ?v7 <http://dbpedia.org/ontology/River> .
  }

The above example query means retrive all entities can be bound to v4 that is a river and located in city "Seoul".

3.4 Answer Generation

After candidate SPARQL queries for an input question are generated, they are filtered and selected by scores to get the most right answers from a KB. An answer generation module (AGM) is for filtering and selecting final SPARQL queries from candidate SPARQL queries and retrieving answers for an input question from RDF (Resource Description Framework) KB.

3.5 Workflow Management

A control module (CM) supports a function of workflow management to link all of modules in collaborative and intuitive ways. CM constructs an integrated system of the QA capability. To ease collaboration, CM provides the functions of diverse pipeline configuration, inter-module linking, logging I/O flow and exceptional messages, and so on. Examples of the functions are shown in Section 4.

3.6 Evaluation

After a QA system is integrated, the pipeline of a QA system is evaluated to qualify the QA capability. An evaluation module (EM) is for evaluating an integrated whole QA system to measure an accuracy of a QA capability. To measure the accuracy, EM uses the NLQ50 benchmark dataset [3] to qualifying a QA system.

[3] http://2015.okbqa.org/nlq

4 Demonstration

The OKBQA framework supports Web-based interfaces for workflow management and evaluation. Developers can build and evaluate their own QA system with the interfaces in intuitive and collaborative ways. In the followings, we show the demonstration of the interfaces and QA results of a QA system developed by the OKBQA framework.

4.1 Web-based interface for workflow management

The Web-based CM interface[4] supports developers to build a custom QA pipeline with different configurations. The figure 2 shows a configuration page of the CM interface. Currently, the interface supports configuration of module address, execution sequence of modules, and the limit of the execution time of each module.

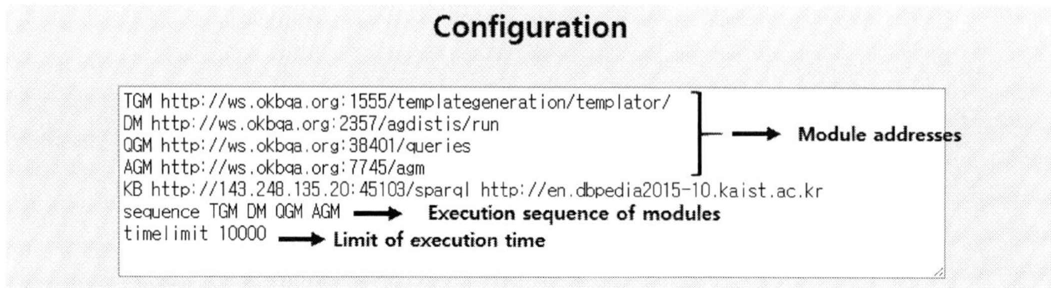

Figure 2: A configuration page of the interface of CM: The first field of each line is an configuration item to be configured and the remaining fields are configuration values for an item.

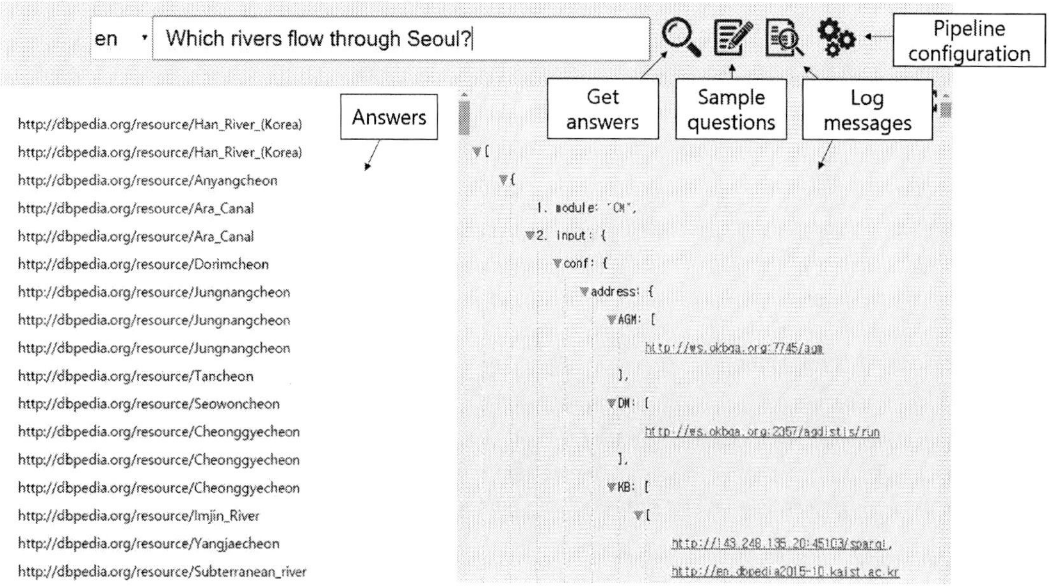

Figure 3: Results of a QA system developed by the OKBQA framework: Answers (left-side) of an input question with informative log messages (right-side) for collborative development

[4]http://ws.okbqa.org/web_interface

4.2 Web-based interface for evaluation

The Web-based EM interface supports measuring an accuracy of arbitrary QA pipelines. The interface uses CM to build a pipeline and evaluate with the NLQ50 benchmark dataset. The interface supports simple and intuitive design that can be checked on the Web page[5].

5 Conclusion

We showed the OKBQA framework with a state-of-the-arts-based novel QA pipeline and intuitive user interfaces for supporting a collaborative development and evaluation of a KB-based QA system. With our open framework, any developers can join the development of their own QA system with open collaboration. We argue that with our framework, a QA system can be built based on the sate-of-the-art researches and already implemented modules with the reduced efforts by decreased trial and error. Our already implemented modules are available on our repository[6], which can be a good starting point for beginners. We are persistently going to enhancing and qualifying supports of the framework with hoping to build a QA system of the qualified QA capability and the beyond.

Acknowledgements

This work was supported by Institute for Information & communications Technology Promotion(IITP) grant funded by the Korea government(MSIP) (No. R0101-16-0054, WiseKB: Big data based self-evolving knowledge base and reasoning platform). And also this work was supported by the Bio & Medical Technology Development Program of the NRF funded by the Korean government, MSIP(2015M3A9A7029735).

References

Unger, Christina and Bühmann, Lorenz and Lehmann, Jens and Ngonga Ngomo, Axel-Cyrille and Gerber, Daniel and Cimiano, Philipp. 2012. *Template-based question answering over RDF data. Proceedings of the 21st international conference on World Wide Web* (pp. 639–648). ACM.

Usbeck, Ricardo and Ngomo, Axel-Cyrille Ngonga and Röder, Michael and Gerber, Daniel and Coelho, Sandro Athaide and Auer, Sören and Both, Andreas. 2014. *AGDISTIS-graph-based disambiguation of named entities using linked data. International Semantic Web Conference* (pp.457-471). Springer.

Kim, J. D. and Cohen, K.. 2014. *Triple pattern variation operations for flexible graph search. Workshop on Natural Language Interfaces for Web of Data.*

[5]http://ws.okbqa.org/web_evaluation

[6]http://repository.okbqa.org

Linggle Knows: A Search Engine Tells How People Write

Jhih-Jie Chen[1], **Hao-Chun Peng**[2]
Mei-Cih Yeh[1], **Peng-Yu Chen**[1], **Jason S. Chang**[2]
[1]Department of Computer Science
[2]Institute of Information Systems and Applications
National Tsing Hua University
{jjc, henry.p, meicih, pengyu, jason}@nlplab.cc

Abstract

This paper presents *Linggle Knows*, an English grammar and linguistic search engine. *Linggle Knows* help people writing by displaying lexical and grammatical information extracted from a couple of large scale corpora, including Google Web 1T 5-gram, British National Corpus (BNC), New York Times Annotated Corpus (NYT), etc. It not only describes how a word is genuinely used, but also recommends various alternative collocations and word combinations. In addition, it gives real-world examples to better explain how a word is used in reality.

1 Introduction

It is estimated that roughly a billion people are learning and using English around the world (Graddol, 2003), most of which are second language (L2) learners. More specifically, further analysis reported that there are 375 million native speakers of English, and 750 million people use English as a second language (Crystal, 1997). Writing is probably the most difficult and profound among the four skills of language learning, even for a native speaker. For L2 Writer, much of the frustration in writing stems from the lack of vocabulary, misused preposition or verb, insufficient understanding of grammar, etc. Consequently, people have developed a variety of writing assisting tools to help writing.

Oxford Dictionaries contains extensive vocabularies along with explanations and examples. *NetSpeak* manipulates *Google Web 1T 5-gram* to provide a way of accessing n-gram information and is capable of filling the blank, reordering the text, choosing a better preposition, etc. Meanwhile, *Linggle* features better n-gram retrieval performance than *NetSpeak* and advances some ideas such as query with specific part of speech, and operator nesting (Boisson et al., 2013). *Grammarly* and *Ginger Software* check and correct grammatical errors, but only to the extent that is fairly narrow. *Write & Improve* gives corrective feedback sentence by sentence and assigns an overall grade for a submitted essay. On the other hand, *WriteAhead* proposed an interactive writing environment which suggests subsequent patterns or collocations while the user is writing away (Yen et al., 2015).

Each of the above tools indeed solves some writing problems in somewhat different ways. Yet there is no such an integrated system trying to solve all kinds of problems of writing considerately. As a result, we have to switch from one window to the other while trying to solve different kinds of writing problems. It is quite disturbing and sometimes upsetting, since it severely affect the efficiency and reduce the productivity of writing. Our objective is to develop a comprehensive tool which provides essential linguistic knowledge to help people obtain required information immediately and effortlessly.

We incorporate four mechanisms we considered the most important. N-gram search provides linguistic information in which you can fill the black or search for appropriate preposition. Pattern grammar enables giving instant writing suggestions while typing away. Rephrasing recommends correct or better use of words, while example sentence illustrate actual uses in real world.

In the following sections, we introduce the system design, interface, and underlying architecture. Next, we briefly describe each of the four subsystems. Finally, we exploit the great potential of the system and envision the future of writing.

Proceedings of COLING 2016, the 26th International Conference on Computational Linguistics: System Demonstrations, pages 166–169, Osaka, Japan, December 11-17 2016.

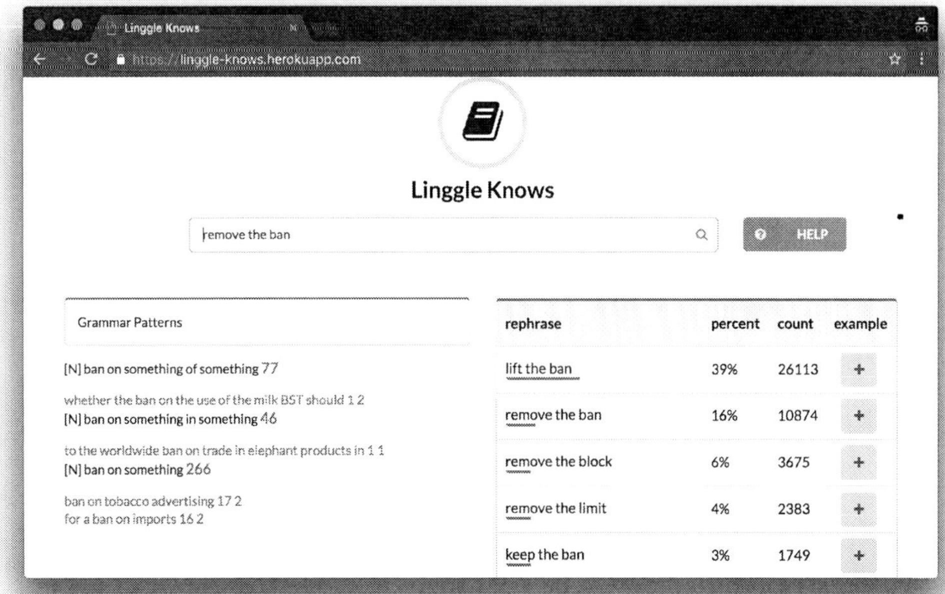

Figure 1: Example using *Linggle Knows* typing "remove the ban".

2 Linggle Knows

To establish user friendly, our design is to be simple and intuitive. Again, our objective is to develop a comprehensive tool helping people obtain information immediately and effortlessly. We build *Linggle Knows* as a web application, which can be accessed easily through browsers whenever using computer, laptop, or tablet. As shown in Figure 1, *Linggle Knows* is accessible at `https://linggle-knows.herokuapp.com`.

2.1 User Interface

Aiming at improving the productivity of writing, we design the interaction to be simple and intuitive. The interface purely consists of a search box and a result area. Instant feedback is received while entering words in the search box. The result is rendered in a clear and straightforward way so that users can find desired information right away. Moreover, n-gram search is very powerful but requires a certain understanding of linguistics, which is not innate in everyone. If one uses the query operator, n-gram information is displayed. Otherwise, our system shows writing suggestion based on grammar patterns and paraphrase recommendation. Interface characteristics described above reflects the design philosophy to be simple and intuitive.

2.2 System Architecture

To develop a robust and reliable system, we implement the four main components separately which can be accessed in a standard way. Each independent component can be accessed through RESTful API in JSON format, which is universal and can be easily utilized. The main system retrieves different information from the four independent subsystems through the universal interface mentioned above.

3 N-gram

We adopted the query functions described in (Boisson et al., 2013), whereas a different set of query operators is defined. The syntax of the patterns for n-grams is shown in Figure 2, and the explanation and examples are described in the following subsection.

Operators	Description	Example
*	match zero or more words	play * role
_	match any word	listen _ music
~	search for the similar words of TERM	~reliable person
?	search for TERM optionally	listen ?to music
/	either TERM1 or TERM2	receive/accept education
PoS.	search for word with specific part-of-speech tag. (v, n, adj, adv, prep, det, conj, pron)	v. det. report

Figure 2: Query operator instruction

3.1 Query Instruction

Wildcard enables the users to query zero, one or more arbitrary words up to five words in total. (i.e., "play * role" is intended to search for a maximum distance of three words.) Besides, the "?" operator before a word stands for a search of n-grams with or without the word. (i.e., one wanting to determine whether to use the word "to" between listen and music, then one can make the query "listen ?to music.") Yet another operation "/" is to search for information related to word choice. (i.e., "receive / accept * education" can be used to reveal that **receive education** is used much more often than **accept education**.) Finally, a set of PoS symbols is defined to support queries that need more precision than the symbol "_".

4 Pattern Grammar

Pattern grammar identifies the syntactic information of individual lexical terms (Hunston et al., 1996). As envisioned by(Hearst, 2015), writing software can be more effective if they can facilitate intensive interaction while writing in progress. (e.g., giving feedback for every word entered even with only partially written sentences or incomplete paragraphs). As described in (Yen et al., 2015), grammar patterns can be used to give instantaneous feedback while typing away, and such information can be extracted by generalizing the words nearby a term. In Figure 1, *Linggle Knows* provides writing suggestions by displaying extracted patterns along with examples.

5 Paraphrases and Corrections

Paraphrasing is the action of restating meaning using different words. It has been shown that for the English Language Leaners (ELLs) the inability in paraphrasing may hinder the writing skills and the ability of expression (Ismail and Maasum, 2009) . To help ELLs, a promising approach is automatic paraphrase generation (APG). In this section, we introduce a new strategy for extracting synonyms from large scale monolingual corpus, and then automatic paraphrase generation with corrections.

5.1 Synonyms Extraction

We separate this stage into two steps. First, we extract potential synonyms from a larges scale monolingual corpus (e.g., BNC), by exploiting different kinds of surface patterns (i.e., "ADJ and ADJ", "ADJ or ADJ", "NOUN but NOUN", etc.), to the extent of adjective, verb, adverb, and noun.

However, these extracted potential synonyms may contain some noise. In order to filter out non-synonyms, we apply rank ratio (RR) statistics (Deane, 2005) and adjust the overlap coefficients of our strategy. Finally, we tune both the RR and overlap coefficient thresholds to refine extracted synonyms.

5.2 Automatic Paraphrases Generation

We exploit Web-scale n-grams and word embedding to automatically generate paraphrases. First, we use large scale monolingual corpora to train a word2vec model (Mikolov et al., 2013a; Mikolov et al., 2013b). Second, we store each word with its corresponding vector, as well as its synonyms mentioned above into a database.

At run-time, words in the given query are substituted by their synonyms to derive candidate paraphrases. However, substituting blindly may lead to awkward phrases and sentences. To resolve this problem, we utilize Web-scale n-gram statistics via the linguistic search engine in section 3, to filter out improper candidate paraphrases. Next, we retrieve each word's vector from the database to construct the phrasal vector, then we compute the cosine similarity of the given query. Finally, we rerank the result based on cosine similarity and n-gram statistics.

6 Example Sentences

To help learners use the lexicon properly, examples are especially important. We collect a set of text data over 100 GB, and use *elastic search* (`github.com/elastic/elasticsearch`) to index sentences in several corpora, including NYT, VOA English, news crawl data from WMT16, etc.

6.1 Good Dictionary Example

Elasticsearch is not designed for indexing sentences and finding *good dictionary examples* (GDEX) as described in (Kilgarriff et al., 2008). Therefore, we apply the GDEX method to rank and select appropriate and representative sentences retrieved from Elasticsearch. The GDEX method considers sentence length, word frequency, the presence of pronouns, and most importantly collocations.

7 Conclusion and Future Work

Linggle Know shows the great potential of incorporating different approaches to help writing. Not only did they solve different kinds of writing problems, but also they complement and reinforce each other to be a complete and effective solution. Despite the extensive and multifaceted feedback and suggestion, writing is not all about syntactically or lexically well-written. It involves contents, structure, the certain understanding of the background, and many other factors to compose a rich, organized and sophisticated text. (e.g., conventional structure and idioms in academic writing). There is still a long way to go to accomplish the ultimate goal. We envision the future of writing to be a joyful experience with the help of instantaneous suggestion and constructive feedback.

References

Joanne Boisson, Ting-Hui Kao, Jian-Cheng Wu, Tzu-Hsi Yen, and Jason S Chang. 2013. Linggle: a web-scale linguistic search engine for words in context. In *ACL (Conference System Demonstrations)*.

David Crystal. 1997. English as a global language. *Cambridge University Press.*

Paul Deane. 2005. A nonparametric method for extraction of candidate phrasal terms. In *Proceedings of the 43rd Annual Meeting on Association for Computational Linguistics*, pages 605–613. Association for Computational Linguistics.

David Graddol. 2003. The decline of the native speaker. *Translation today: trends and perspectives. Clevedon: Multilingual Matters.*

Marti A Hearst. 2015. Can natural language processing become natural language coaching? In *Proceedings of the 53rd Annual Meeting of the Association for Computation Linguistics. ACL*, pages 1245–1252.

Susan Hunston, Gill Francis, and E Manning. 1996. Collins cobuild grammar patterns 1: verbs.

Syafini Ismail and N. R. Maasum. 2009. The effects of cooperative learning in enhancing writing performance. In *Proceedings of the language and culture:creating and fostering global communities.* SOLLS.INTEC 09 International Conference.

Adam Kilgarriff, Milos Husák, Katy McAdam, Michael Rundell, and Pavel Rychlý. 2008. Gdex: Automatically finding good dictionary examples in a corpus. In *Proceedings of the XIII EURALEX International Congress.*

Tomas Mikolov, Kai Chen, Greg Corrado, and Jeffrey Dean. 2013a. Efficient estimation of word representations in vector space. *arXiv preprint arXiv:1301.3781.*

Tomas Mikolov, Ilya Sutskever, Kai Chen, Greg S Corrado, and Jeff Dean. 2013b. Distributed representations of words and phrases and their compositionality. In *Advances in neural information processing systems.*

Tzu-Hsi Yen, Jian-Cheng Wu, Joanne Boisson, Jim Chang, and Jason Chang. 2015. Writeahead: Mining grammar patterns in corpora for assisted writing. *ACL-IJCNLP 2015.*

A Sentence Simplification System for Improving Relation Extraction

Christina Niklaus, Bernhard Bermeitinger, Siegfried Handschuh, André Freitas
Faculty of Computer Science and Mathematics
University of Passau
Innstr. 41, 94032 Passau, Germany
{christina.niklaus, bernhard.bermeitinger, siegfried.handschuh, andre.freitas }@uni-passau.de

Abstract

In this demo paper, we present a text simplification approach that is directed at improving the performance of state-of-the-art Open Relation Extraction (RE) systems. As syntactically complex sentences often pose a challenge for current Open RE approaches, we have developed a simplification framework that performs a pre-processing step by taking a single sentence as input and using a set of syntactic-based transformation rules to create a textual input that is easier to process for subsequently applied Open RE systems.

1 Introduction

Relation Extraction (RE) is the task of recognizing the assertion of relationships between two or more entities in NL text. Traditional RE systems have concentrated on identifying and extracting relations of interest by taking as input the target relations, along with hand-crafted extraction patterns or patterns learned from hand-labeled training examples. Consequently, shifting to a new domain requires to first specify the target relations and then to manually create new extraction rules or to annotate new training examples by hand (Banko and Etzioni, 2008). As this manual labor scales linearly with the number of target relations, this supervised approach does not scale to large, heterogeneous corpora which are likely to contain a variety of unanticipated relations (Schmidek and Barbosa, 2014). To tackle this issue, Banko and Etzioni (2008) introduced a new extraction paradigm named 'Open RE' that facilitates domain-independent discovery of relations extracted from text by not depending on any relation-specific human input.

Generally, state-of-the-art Open RE systems identify relationships between entities in a sentence by matching patterns over either its POS tags, e. g. (Banko et al., 2007; Fader et al., 2011; Merhav et al., 2012), or its dependency tree, e. g. (Nakashole et al., 2012; Mausam et al., 2012; Xu et al., 2013; Mesquita et al., 2013). However, particularly in long and syntactically complex sentences, relevant relations often span several clauses or are presented in a non-canonical form (Angeli et al., 2015), thus posing a challenge for current Open RE approaches which are prone to make incorrect extractions - while missing others - when operating on sentences with an intricate structure.

To achieve a higher accuracy on Open RE tasks, we have developed a framework for simplifying the linguistic structure of NL sentences. It identifies components of a sentence which usually provide supplementary information that may be easily extracted without losing essential information. By applying a set of hand-crafted grammar rules that have been defined in the course of a rule engineering process based on linguistic features, these constituents are then disembedded and transformed into self-contained simpler context sentences. In this way, sentences that present a complex syntax are converted into a set of more concise sentences that are easier to process for subsequently applied Open RE systems, while still expressing the original meaning.

Proceedings of COLING 2016, the 26th International Conference on Computational Linguistics: System Demonstrations, pages 170–174, Osaka, Japan, December 11-17 2016.

2 System Description

Referring to previous attempts at syntax-based sentence compression (Dunlavy et al., 2003; Zajic et al., 2007; Perera and Kosseim, 2013), the idea of our text simplification framework is to syntactically simplify a complex input sentence by splitting conjoined clauses into separate sentences and by eliminating specific syntactic sub-structures, namely those containing only minor information. However, unlike recent approaches in the field of extractive sentence compression, we do not delete these constituents, which would result in a loss of background information, but rather aim at preserving the full informational content of the original sentence. Thus, on the basis of syntax-driven heuristics, components which typically provide mere secondary information are identified and transformed into simpler stand-alone context sentences with the help of paraphrasing operations adopted from the text simplification area.

Definition of the Simplification Rules By analyzing the structure of hundreds of sample sentences from the English Wikipedia, we have determined constituents that commonly supply no more than contextual background information. These components comprise the following syntactic elements:

- **non-restrictive relative clauses** (e. g. *"The city's top tourist attraction was the Notre Dame Cathedral, which welcomed 14 million visitors in 2013."*)
- **non-restrictive** (e. g. *"He plays basketball, a sport he participated in as a member of his high school's varsity team."*) **and restrictive appositive phrases** (e. g. *"He met with former British Prime Minister Tony Blair."*)
- **participial phrases offset by commas** (e. g. *"The deal, titled Joint Comprehensive Plan of Action, saw the removal of sanctions."*)
- **adjective and adverb phrases delimited by punctuation** (e. g. *"Overall, the economy expanded at a rate of 2.9 percent in 2010."*)
- **particular prepositional phrases** (e. g. *"In 2012, Time magazine named Obama as its Person of the Year."*)
- **lead noun phrases** (e. g. *"Six weeks later, Alan Keyes accepted the Republican nomination."*)
- **intra-sentential attributions** (e. g. *"He said that both movements seek to bring justice and equal rights to historically persecuted peoples."*)
- **parentheticals** (e. g. *"He signed the reauthorization of the State Children's Health Insurance Program (SCHIP)."*)

Besides, both conjoined clauses presenting specific features and sentences incorporating particular punctuation are disconnected into separate ones.

After having thus identified syntactic phenomena that generally require simplification, we have determined the characteristics of those constituents, using a number of syntactic features (constituency-based parse trees as well as POS tags) that have occasionally been enhanced with the semantic feature of NE tag. For computing them, a number of software tools provided by the Stanford CoreNLP framework have been employed (Stanford Parser, Stanford POS Tagger and Stanford Named Entity Recognizer).[1] Based upon these properties, we have then specified a set of hand-crafted grammar rules for carrying out the syntactic simplification operations which are applied one after another on the given input sentence. In that way, linguistically peripheral material is disembedded, thus producing a more concise core sentence which is augmented by a number of related self-contained contextual sentences (see the example displayed in figure 1).

[1] http://nlp.stanford.edu/software/

Algorithm 1 Syntax-based sentence simplification

```
Input: sentence s
repeat
    r ← next rule ∈ R                                  # Null if no more rules
    if r is applicable to s then
        C, P ← apply r_extract to s                    # Identify the set of constituents C to extract from s, and their positions P in s
        for all constituents c ∈ C do
            context ← apply r_paraphrase to c          # Produce a context sentence
            contextSet ← add context                   # Add it to the core's set of associated context sentences
until R = ∅
core ← delete tokens in s at positions p ∈ P          # Reduce the input to its core
return core and contextSet                            # Output the core and its context sentences
```

Application of the Simplification Operations The simplification rules we have specified are applied one after another to the source sentence, following a three-stage approach (see algorithm 1). First, clauses or phrases that are to be separated out - including their respective antecedent, where required - have to be identified by pattern matching. In case of success, a context sentence is constructed by either linking the extractable component to its antecedent or by inserting a complementary constituent that is required in order to make it a full sentence. Finally, the main sentence has to be reduced by dropping the clause or phrase, respectively, that has been transformed into a stand-alone context sentence.

In this way, a complex source sentence is transformed into a simplified two-layered representation in the form of core facts and accompanying contexts, thus providing a kind of normalization of the input text. Accordingly, when carrying out the task of extracting semantic relations between entities on the reduced core sentences, the complexity of determining intricate predicate-argument structures with variable arity and nested structures from syntactically complex input sentences is removed. Beyond that, the phrases of the original sentence that convey no more than peripheral information are converted into independent sentences which, too, can be more easily extracted under a binary or ternary predicate-argument structure (see the example illustrated in figure 1).

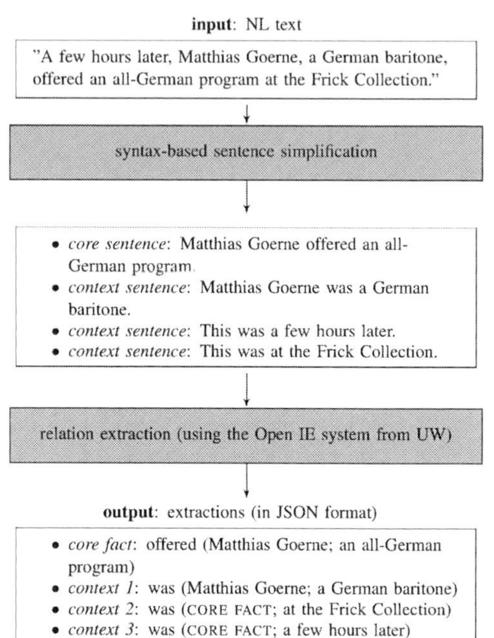

Figure 1: Simplification and extraction pipeline

3 Evaluation

The results of an experimental evaluation show that state-of-the-art Open RE approaches obtain a higher accuracy and lower information loss when operating on sentences that have been pre-processed by our simplification framework. In particular when dealing with sentences that contain nested structures, Open RE systems benefit from a prior simplification step (see figures 2 and 3 for an example). The full evaluation methodology and detailed results are reported in Niklaus et al. (2016).

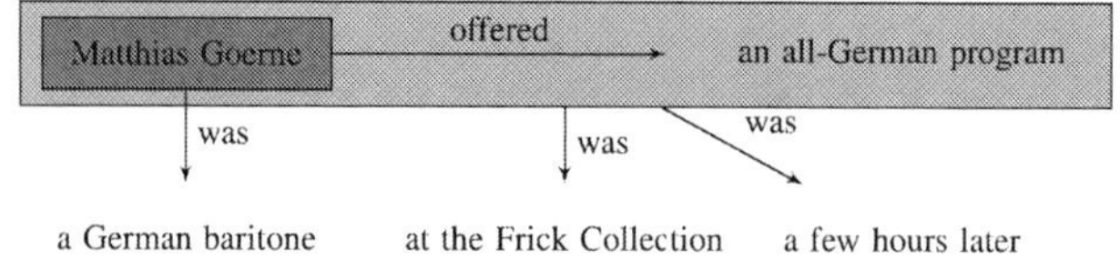

Figure 2: Extracted relations when operating on the simplified sentences

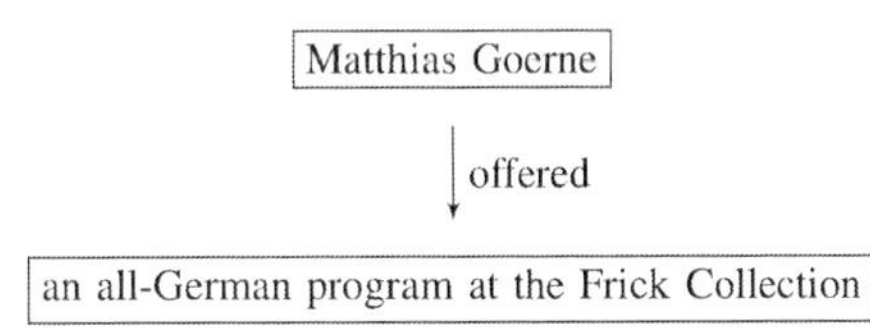

Figure 3: Result without a prior simplification step

4 Usage

The text simplification framework is publicly available[2] as both a library and a command line tool whose workflow is depicted in figure 1. It takes as input NL text in the form of either a single sentence or a file with line separated sentences. As described above, each input sentence is first transformed into a structurally simplified version consisting of 1 to n core sentences and 0 to m associated context sentences. In a second step, the relations contained in the input are extracted by applying the Open IE system[3] upon the simplified sentences. Finally, the results generated in this way are written to the console or a specified output file in JSON format. As an example, the outcome produced by our simplification system when applied to a full Wikipedia article is provided online.[4]

5 Conclusion

We have described a syntax-driven rule-based text simplification framework that simplifies the linguistic structure of input sentences with the objective of improving the coverage of state-of-the-art Open RE systems. As an experimental analysis has shown, the text simplification pre-processing improves the result of current Open RE approaches, leading to a *lower information loss* and a *higher accuracy* of the extracted relations.

References

Gabor Angeli, Melvin Johnson Premkumar, and Christopher D. Manning. 2015. Leveraging linguistic structure for open domain information extraction. In *Proceedings of the 53rd Annual Meeting of the Association for Computational Linguistics and the 7th International Joint Conference on Natural Language Processing*, pages 344–354. ACL.

Michele Banko and Oren Etzioni. 2008. The tradeoffs between open and traditional relation extraction. In *Proceedings of ACL-08: HLT*, pages 28–36. ACL.

Michele Banko, Michael J. Cafarella, Stephen Soderland, Matt Broadhead, and Oren Etzioni. 2007. Open information extraction from the web. In *Proceedings of the 20th International Joint Conference on Artificial Intelligence*, pages 2670–2676.

Daniel M. Dunlavy, John M. Conroy, Judith D. Schlesinger, Sarah A. Goodman, Mary Ellen Okurowski, Dianne P. O'Leary, and Hans van Halteren. 2003. Performance of a three-stage system for multi-document summarization.

Anthony Fader, Stephen Soderland, and Oren Etzioni. 2011. Identifying relations for open information extraction. In *Proceedings of the Conference on Empirical Methods in Natural Language Processing*, pages 1535–1545. ACL.

Mausam, Michael Schmitz, Robert Bart, Stephen Soderland, and Oren Etzioni. 2012. Open language learning for information extraction. In *Proceedings of the 2012 Joint Conference on Empirical Methods in Natural Language Processing and Computational Natural Language Learning*, pages 523–534. ACL.

Yuval Merhav, Filipe Mesquita, Denilson Barbosa, Wai Gen Yee, and Ophir Frieder. 2012. Extracting information networks from the blogosphere. *ACM Trans. Web*, 6(3):11:1–11:33.

[2] https://gitlab.com/nlp-passau/SimpleGraphene
[3] https://github.com/allenai/openie-standalone
[4] https://gitlab.com/nlp-passau/SimpleGraphene/tree/master/examples

Filipe Mesquita, Jordan Schmidek, and Denilson Barbosa. 2013. Effectiveness and efficiency of open relation extraction. In *Proceedings of the 2013 Conference on Empirical Methods in Natural Language Processing*, pages 447–457. ACL.

Ndapandula Nakashole, Gerhard Weikum, and Fabian Suchanek. 2012. Patty: A taxonomy of relational patterns with semantic types. In *Proceedings of the 2012 Joint Conference on Empirical Methods in Natural Language Processing and Computational Natural Language Learning*, pages 1135–1145. ACL.

Christina Niklaus, Siegfried Handschuh, and André Freitas. 2016. Improving relation extraction by syntax-based sentence simplification. `https://gitlab.com/nlp-passau/SimpleGraphene/blob/master/paper/improving-relation-extraction.pdf`.

Prasad Perera and Leila Kosseim. 2013. Evaluating syntactic sentence compression for text summarisation. In *Natural Language Processing and Information Systems - 18th International Conference on Applications of Natural Language to Information Systems*, pages 126–139.

Jordan Schmidek and Denilson Barbosa. 2014. Improving open relation extraction via sentence re-structuring. In *Proceedings of the Ninth International Conference on Language Resources and Evaluation*. ELRA.

Ying Xu, Mi-Young Kim, Kevin Quinn, Randy Goebel, and Denilson Barbosa. 2013. Open information extraction with tree kernels. In *Proceedings of the 2013 Conference of the North American Chapter of the Association for Computational Linguistics: Human Language Technologies*, pages 868–877. ACL.

David Zajic, Bonnie J. Dorr, Jimmy Lin, and Richard Schwartz. 2007. Multi-candidate reduction: Sentence compression as a tool for document summarization tasks. *Information Processing and Management*, 43(6):1549–1570.

Korean FrameNet Expansion Based on Projection of Japanese FrameNet

Jeong-uk Kim, Younggyun Hahm, and **Key-Sun Choi**
Machine Reading Lab, School of Computing
Korea Advanced Institute of Science and Technology (KAIST)
Daejeon, Republic of Korea
{prismriver, hahmyg, kschoi}@kaist.ac.kr

Abstract

FrameNet project has begun from Berkeley in 1997, and is now supported in several countries reflecting characteristics of each language. The work for generating Korean FrameNet was already done by converting annotated English sentences into Korean with trained translators. However, high cost of frame-preservation and error revision was a huge burden on further expansion of FrameNet. This study makes use of linguistic similarity between Japanese and Korean to increase Korean FrameNet corpus with low cost. We also suggest adapting PubAnnotation and Korean-friendly valence patterns to FrameNet for increased accessibility.

1 Introduction

Growing demand for natural language processing (NLP) inevitably requires large scale of proper training dataset. In this sense, Berkeley proposed FrameNet project of semantically analyzing sentences with several 'frames.'Based on Frame Semantics (Fillmore, 1982), event invoking words from sentences are selected to from a frame, with core roles of the event as frame elements. Such frame annotated dataset in FrameNet can be widely used as Semantic Role Labeling training set for Machine Translation, Information Extraction, Event Recognition and etc.

Since characteristics of target language must be considered to apply on the other NLP tasks, FrameNets have been developed in several languages. Most FrameNets like Japanese annotated sentences one by one (Ohara et al., 2003), but this procedure requires much time and effort of frame experts. On the other hand, utilizing existing corpus to easily generate FrameNet was also researched. For example, projection algorithm of English frame semantic data into Italian (Tonelli and Pianta, 2008) was suggested.

However, comparing to the abundant corpus in English FrameNet, FrameNets in other languages are containing relatively small dataset, or even missing. There was no Korean FrameNet until importing 4025 English FrameNet sentences into Korean using trained translators (Park et al., 2014). The translated sentences with frame information might be used for NLP in Korean with secured quality, but the quantity is rather too small for machine learning training data.

Focusing on the lack of frame annotated sentence, this study proposes much cost efficient method for expanding size of Korean FrameNet utilizing structural similarities between Japanese and Korean – use of postposition and interchangeable word order. After dividing original sentences into a set of word chunks, they were translated keeping the order of chunks putting the original frame information aside. This procedure did not require translators to learn frame semantics or to continue revisions of all frames. The projections of word chunks to frame elements were held on the translated sentences, with the extracted frame information. Furthermore, Korean FrameNet website introduces visualization of frame annotated sentences using PubAnnotation and valence patterns including postpositions.

Proceedings of COLING 2016, the 26th International Conference on Computational Linguistics: System Demonstrations, pages 175–179, Osaka, Japan, December 11-17 2016.

2 Expanding Korean FrameNet

For previous version of full-text annotations, Korean FrameNet contained 4025 sentences chosen from random categories of English FrameNet. They designed detailed guidelines to translate them into Korean (Park et al., 2014). The guidelines include keeping every frame elements, and preserving of frame element meanings even after the relocation. The translated sentences have high qualities with consecutive verifications with both expert translators and NLP majors, but the absolute size of the data is relatively small for NLP application.

Lexical units are the stemmed words that invoke frames in the full-text annotations. Part of speech tag for each lexical unit was chosen as the part of speech tag of the last morpheme of the stemmed words. In this way, 7130 lexical units were listed on the Korean FrameNet in the Korean alphabetic order.

Frame index contains brief definition of the frame, with its core or non-core frame elements for each lexical unit. Since the creation of Korean FrameNet used translation based approach, the frame index information is identical to that of English FrameNet. Therefore, Korean FrameNet makes use of 1019 frame index data from Berkeley as it is.

In order to expand the Korean FrameNet dataset, this study proposes machine aided projection approach from Japanese to Korean. The two languages both support flexible change of word order as role of each word is highly related to the attached preposition. With these advantages, new full-text annotated sentences can be achieved with low cost using the following approach.

2.1 Extract word chunks from Japanese FrameNet Corpus

Suppose a simple sentence "梅雨はすでに明け、九州地方は一気に夏模様である。" "The monsoon is already stopped, and summer seems to come in Kyusu area soon" from Japanese FrameNet. Its frame information is listed in Figure 1.

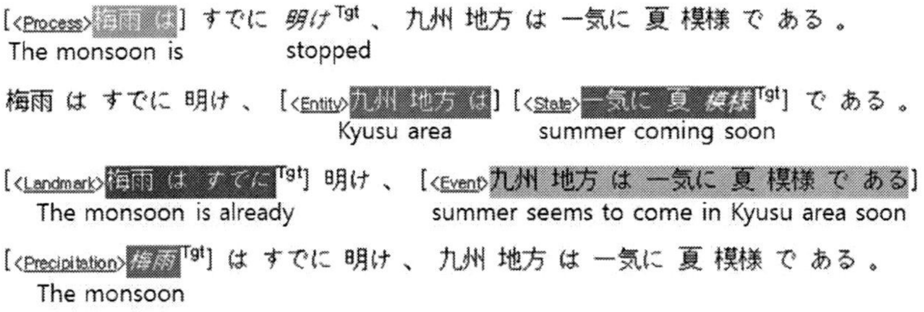

[<Process>梅雨 は] すでに 明け Tgt 、 九州 地方 は 一気に 夏 模様 で ある 。
The monsoon is stopped

梅雨 は すでに 明け 、 [<Entity>九州 地方 は] [<State>一気に 夏 模様 Tgt] で ある 。
Kyusu area summer coming soon

[<Landmark>梅雨 は すでに Tgt] 明け 、 [<Event>九州 地方 は 一気に 夏 模様 で ある] 。
The monsoon is already summer seems to come in Kyusu area soon

[<Precipitation>梅雨 Tgt] は すでに 明け 、 九州 地方 は 一気に 夏 模様 で ある 。
The monsoon

Figure 1: list of frames in an annotated sentence

Every start and end position of frame elements and lexical units become boundaries to split word chunks. Some positions can be used in different frames several times. Examples of sentences separated as word chunks shown in Figure 2. Frame information of the sentence is stored in a file for further use.

|梅雨 は| すでに| 明け| 、 九州 地方 は 一気に 夏 模様 で ある 。

梅雨 は すでに 明け 、| 九州 地方 は| 一気に 夏| 模様| で ある 。

|梅雨 は| すでに| 明け 、| 九州 地方 は 一気に 夏 模様 で ある| 。

|梅雨| は すでに 明け 、 九州 地方 は 一気に 夏 模様 で ある 。

Figure 2: list of word chunks separated with frame data

2.2 Translate extracted word chunks

Every boundary in section 2.1 are merged to a single sentence to be sent to expert translators unfamiliar with NLP, just liken in Figure 3. Positions of every frame element and lexical unit are kept as index of boundaries in its start and end position.

|梅雨| は| すでに| 明け| 、| 九州 地方 は| 一気に 夏| 模様| で ある| 。

Figure 3: sentence to be translated

Guidelines for translation include – meaning of the full sentence as well as each word in a boundary must be unchanged, boundary must not be removed, added, or relocated, and that the translated text in Korean must be natural. Result of the above example is shown in Figure 4.

The basic concept behind such division is that both Korean and Japanese are flexible for word ordering. Instead, role of each noun largely depends on the postposition of the word. For instance, 'は'(ha) in Japanese and '는'(neun) in Korean are both postpositions that represents the former noun chunk is a subject of the current sentence. In this way, no matter where the original sentence has subject, we can always make a correct Korean sentence with subject in the same relative position.

|장마| 는| 이미| 끝나| ,| 규슈 지방 은| 단숨에 여름| 이 올 듯한 모양| 이다| .

Figure 4: sentence translated with boundaries preserved

2.3 Retrieve annotated Korean sentences with frame information

The translated Korean sentence now requires to be reverted into frame annotated sentences. Stored frame information mapping word chunks indices to frame boundaries in the previous section is used to retrieve positions and frame index of frame elements and lexical units. An example of the result is shown in Figure 5. Frame annotated sentences in Korean are then added to the Korean FrameNet.

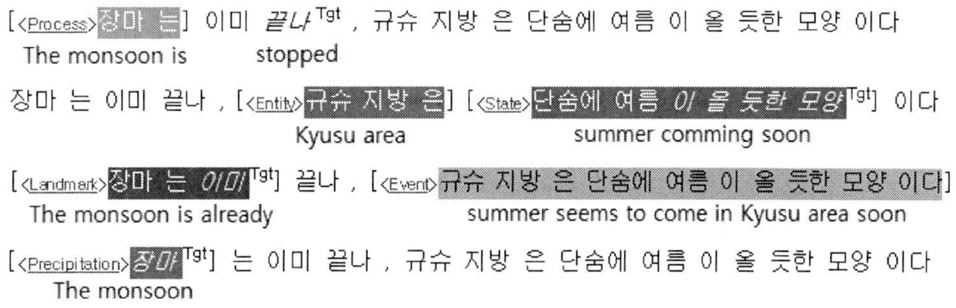

[<Process>장마 는] 이미 *끝나*^{Tgt} , 규슈 지방 은 단숨에 여름 이 올 듯한 모양 이다
The monsoon is stopped

장마 는 이미 끝나 , [<Entity>규슈 지방 은] [<State>단숨에 여름 *이 올 듯한 모양*^{Tgt}] 이다
Kyusu area summer comming soon

[<Landmark>장마 는 *이미*^{Tgt}] 끝나 , [<Event>규슈 지방 은 단숨에 여름 이 올 듯한 모양 이다]
The monsoon is already summer seems to come in Kyusu area soon

[<Precipitation>*장마*^{Tgt}] 는 이미 끝나 , 규슈 지방 은 단숨에 여름 이 올 듯한 모양 이다
The monsoon

Figure 5: frame annotated sentence in Korean

2.4 Quality Insurance

Double-checking policy of translators secures the quality of translation. In addition, we ask for any problems of unnatural sentences translated in the original order. However, there was no such case among total 1795 sentences supporting the correctness of our approach.

3 Demo Website

This version of Korean FrameNet also changes visualization of annotated sentences. Most FrameNet web service shows each frame element with unique color for frame index. However, for non-experts in this field, users must find the corresponding frame index from the color table. To get rid of this unnecessary work, we focused on the PubAnnotation.

PubAnnotation (Kim and Wang, 2012) introduced open source interface for annotation sharing. The system supports annotating part of the given sentence and linking two annotations as a relation. Frame information in Korean FrameNet website became more intuitive with the interface. Comparison of a same annotation with the two different approaches is shown in Figure 6 and 7. Lexical unit 'fell' is more noticeable using PubAnnotation by focusing on the origin of every relation. Roles of frame elements in the sentence are also easily seen with the annotation instead of mapping colors of frame elements to its roles in the frame.

[X] Aetna Life and Casualty Co. 's third - quarter net income FELL 22 % to $ 182.6 million , or $ 1.63 a share , reflecting the damages from Hurricane Hugo and lower results for some of the company 's major divisions .

Figure 6: frame information in English FrameNet

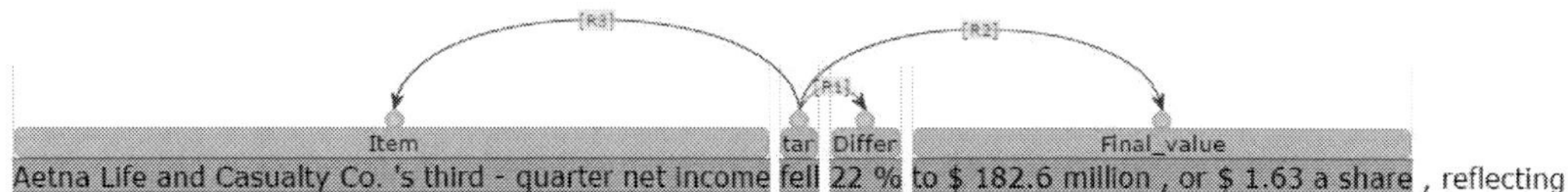

Figure 7: frame annotation using PubAnnotation

In addition, sentences with each lexical unit are categorized by their valence patterns. Originally, English FrameNet simply saves valences patterns as the order of frame elements. However, as mentioned above, postpositions play important roles in the meaning of a sentence. Valence patterns in Korean FrameNet are expressed with frame elements with part of speech tag of their prepositions like in Figure 8. For lexical unit '가' meaning 'go', the valence pattern shows a leading frame element 'theme' with a postposition for subject followed by 'time' without a postposition, 'goal' with a postposition for adverb, and the lexical unit. All FrameNet data is open to public in Korean FrameNet website[1].

[theme/JKS] + [time] + [goal/JKB] + 가

Figure 8: valence pattern with postposition

4 Conclusion

This study presents how to expand Korean FrameNet using Japanese FrameNet and to improve interface focused on Korean. Making use of linguistic characteristics dramatically reduces FrameNet transition costs with only few errors, and even more Japanese full-text annotations would be easily imported with reuse of parsing and error revision tools. Similar approaches can be applied to other language pair with the same characteristics. Combining FrameNet framework with PubAnnotation also lowers the accessibility of the public.

With richer annotation sets in Korean FrameNet and better visualization interface, Korean FrameNet has moved closer to the NLP researchers. Current Korean FrameNet might still be not enough for large scale NLP. However, Korean FrameNet would keep growing, and help researchers suffering from the lack of Korean dataset as a major resource of semantic role labeling.

[1] http://framenet.kaist.ac.kr

Acknowledgements

This work was supported by Institute for Information & communications Technology Promotion(IITP) grant funded by the Korea government(MSIP) (No. R0101-16-0054, WiseKB: Big data based self-evolving knowledge base and reasoning platform)

This work was supported by the Bio & Medical Technology Development Program of the NRF funded by the Korean government, MSIP(2015M3A9A7029735)

References

Collin F Baker, Charles J Fillmore, and John B Lowe. 1998. The berkeley framenet project. In *Proceedings of the 36th Annual Meeting of the Association for Computational Linguistics and 17th International Conference on Computational Linguistics-Volume 1*, pages 86–90. Association for Computational Linguistics.

Charles Fillmore. 1982. Frame semantics. *Linguistics in the morning calm*, pages 111–137.

Jin-Dong Kim and Yue Wang. 2012. Pubannotation: a persistent and sharable corpus and annotation repository. In *Proceedings of the 2012 Workshop on Biomedical Natural Language Processing*, pages 202–205. Association for Computational Linguistics.

Kyoko Hirose Ohara, Seiko Fujii, Hiroaki Saito, Shun Ishizaki, Toshio Ohori, and Ryoko Suzuki. 2003. The japanese framenet project: A preliminary report. In *Proceedings of pacific association for computational linguistics*, pages 249–254. Citeseer.

Jungyeul Park, Sejin Nam, Youngsik Kim, Younggyun Hahm, Dosam Hwang, and Key-Sun Choi. 2014. Frame-semantic web: a case study for korean. In *Proceedings of the 2014 International Conference on Posters & Demonstrations Track-Volume 1272*, pages 257–260. CEUR-WS. org.

Sara Tonelli and Emanuele Pianta. 2008. Frame information transfer from english to italian. In *LREC*.

A Framework for Mining Enterprise Risk and Risk Factors from Text Documents

Tirthankar Dasgupta
TCS Innovation Lab,
gupta.tirthankar@tcs.com

Lipika Dey
TCS Innovation Lab,
New Delhi
lipika.dey@tcs.com

Prasenjit Dey
IIT Kharagpur
prsnjt002@gmail.com

Rupsa Saha
TCS Innovation Lab,
Kolkata
rupsa.s@tcs.com

Abstract

Any real world events or trends that can affect the company's growth trajectory can be considered as *Risk*. There has been a growing need to automatically identify, extract and analyze risk related statements from news events. In this demonstration, we will present a risk analytics framework that processes enterprise project management reports in the form of textual data and news documents and classify them into valid and invalid risk categories. The framework also extracts information from the text pertaining to the different categories of risks like, their possible cause and impacts. Accordingly, we have used machine learning based techniques and studied different linguistic features like n-gram, POS, dependency, future timing, uncertainty factors in texts and their various combinations. A manual annotation study from management experts using risk descriptions collected for a specific organization was conducted to evaluate the framework. The evaluation showed promising results for automated risk analysis and identification.

1 Introduction

A real world event that has an associated probability of causing damage, injury, liability, loss or any other negative impact is termed as a risk(Lu et al., 2009; Slywotzky and Drzik, 2005; Beasley et al., 2005; Lu et al., 2009). Organizations are always on the look out for information related to such events caused by internal and external vulnerabilities such that the possible negative impacts may be avoided through preemptive action. Sources of risk can be many. The difficulty of risk identification arises from the diversity of the sources. Risks can arise from uncertainty in financial markets(Leidner and Schilder, 2010; Ykhlef and Algawiaz, 2014), industrial processes or due to project failures. Unexpected events like natural disasters, legal issues, deliberate attacks from adversaries or certain competitor moves can all lead to situations that can impact an organization and hence can be termed as risks.

Generally, a risk has the following characteristics: The risk type R_T or a name for the description of the risk that characterizes the nature of the adversarial potential, The *cause* R_C or the event that may cause the specified risk and the *impact* R_I that deals with the severity of the damage caused once it materialize.

Like all expert-driven activities that involve knowledge about handling uncertainties and predictive capabilities, risk analysis is a complex task that requires expertise that is acquired with experience. It is difficult to document. Besides, experts differ in their opinions. Sifting through a large number of such analyst reports and summarizing them is a tedious activity(Kogan et al., 2009). In this work, we present text mining techniques that can analyze large volumes of analyst reports to automatically extract risk statements, aggregate them and summarize them into risks of various categories.

As mentioned earlier, experts predict risks as probable future events that can impact business outcomes. The proposed methods employ machine learning based techniques to learn linguistic features

Proceedings of COLING 2016, the 26th International Conference on Computational Linguistics: System Demonstrations, pages 180–184, Osaka, Japan, December 11-17 2016.

and their dependencies from labeled samples of risk statements. The learned classifiers are applied to input text, wherein every sentence in the text is subjected to binary classification as "risk" or "not a risk".

The salient contributions of this demonstration are as follows:

1. A machine learning and computational linguistics based framework to analyze textual News events and classify them into true risk and false alarm categories,
2. Extract different categories of risk factors like *causes* and their possible *impacts*.

2 Proposed Risk Classification Framework

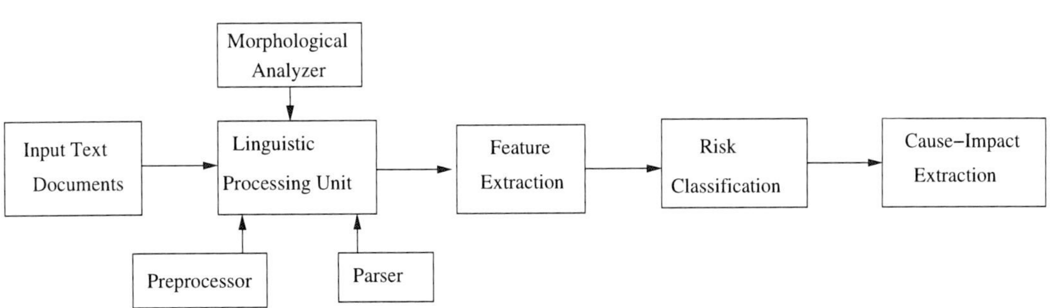

Figure 1: Architecture of the risk identification framework

The overall architecture of the risk classification and analysis framework is depicted in Figure 1. The proposed architecture has four primary modules: a) The *Linguistic pre-processing unit* b) *Feature extraction unit* c) *Risk classifier unit* and d) the *Risk analysis unit.* The input text is first passed to the preprocessing unit that removes html tags, and foreign language characters from the text. The preprocessed text is then passed to the Stanford parts-of-speech(POS) tagger and parser to label each word with their corresponding POS and to extract different dependency relations within the sentences. From the output of the POS tagger, root verbs are extracted and passed to an English morphological analyzer to identify the tense, aspect and modality of the root verb.

The syntactically analyzed text is then passed to the feature extraction unit. The features considered can be broadly classified into three types a) Future timing in texts, b) Uncertainty in texts and c) traditional linguistic features.

Future timing refers to the expressions that indicate (possible) upcoming events or states. For instance, the verb "expects" in the sentence *Testing of OCR division is expecting an overall fall in performance in the next few months*, indicate future timing.

Uncertainty mainly "concerned with the speaker's assumptions, or assessment of possibilities, and, in most cases, it indicates the speaker's confidence or lack of confidence in the truth of the proposition expected" (Coates, 1987). Various levels of uncertainty can be inferred from the expression. As a preliminary study, we have used only the presence of epistemic modal expressions like, modal auxiliaries, epistemic lexical verbs, adverb, adjectives and nouns to determine uncertainty in a text (Coates, 1987).

In *traditional linguistic* features we have considered *N-gram counts (N)*, *POS features(POS)*, *Dependency features (D)* that includes dependency length, and occurrence of adverbial clause modifier, auxiliary, negation modifier, marker, referent, open clausal complement, clausal complement, expletive, coordination, passive auxiliary, nominal subject, direct object, copula, and conjunct.

2.1 SVM based risk classification Model

Once the textual feedback is provided as an input to the system, it is first preprocessed and analyzed by the linguistic processing unit. The classifier learns each of the above linguistic features from a training sample of 5000 news articles collected from various online sources. We have primarily employed support vector machines (SVM) to develop a binary classifier that, given a news event would assign label "Risk" or "Not a risk" based on the textual properties. The SVM was implemented using the LIBSVM (Chang and Lin, 2011) software. Further, we have applied the SVM recursive feature elimination method (Duan et al., 2005) to significantly reduce the number of features from the training sample. We have tested four types of kernels namely linear, polynomial, radial basis and sigmoid on the data, but we have presented results against only linear and polynomial kernels as the other two functions were found to be significantly poor performers.

2.2 The risk analyzer

Once "risks" are identified, they are passed to the risk analysis module for the identification of risk causes and their possible impacts. For this, we have followed a similar technique as discussed in (Chang and Choi, 2004). The identified risk along with its associated metadata like cause, impact, and time of arrival are stored into the risk register to generate risk reports. Determination of cause-effect pair from the risk statement consists of two parts.(a) Sentence Segmentation,(b) Cause-Effect classifier

We define a probable candidate for cause or effect phrase as a verb-rooted syntactic tree, which connects one noun phrase to the other with causal relation. Here, we propose a novel and robust dependency tree based sentence segmentation algorithm which considers the syntactic variation in the sentences such as the passive and verbal chains to effectively extract the probable cause-effect phrases from a risk statement spread across a single long sentence or multiple sentences. The algorithm of the segmentation module is depicted as follows:

Algorithm 1 *

dependency tree based sentence segmentation algorithm

```
Input: Valid Risk statement: S;
Output: A set of causality candidates: C
POS tag S and get the dependency tree (or trees for multiple sentences) D of S
Q=set of nodes of D which are verbs(in any form or tense) and the root(s) node of D
C=""
Visited[q]=FALSE for all nodes q ;

for each node q ∈ Q do
    segment=TRAVERSE(q)
    C = C ∪ segment

end for

TRAVERSE (Node x)
S=x

for each child c of x do
    if (visited[c] = FALSEandc ∉ Q) then
        Visited[c]=TRUE
        S=S ∪ TRAVERSE (c)
    end if
end for
return S
```

end

The cause-effect classifier classifies the candidate $t_i \in T$ into cause (C_0) or effect (C_1) or none (C_2). In a long sentence or in a multiple sentence statement there may be some parts which expresses neither cause nor effect. To capture this, we have introduced the class C_2 which denotes neither cause nor effect. For example, in the sentence:

Requirements for a project may change over its lifetime. Change in requirements will lead to change in test cases and test data. This will affect the schedule planned for testing which in turn may lead to schedule-slippage of the entire project.

The cause/impact candidates we get are: t_1 : "Requirements for a project may change over its lifetime" , t_2 : "Change in requirements will lead", t_3 : "to change in test cases and test data" , t_4 : "This will affect the schedule" , t_5 : "planned for testing" , and t_6 : "which in turn may lead to schedule-slippage of the entire project". Here, the candidates t_1 and t_5 belongs to neither cause nor effect. Since, we are driven towards finding a solution using unsupervised learning method, it is difficult to learn the classifier parameter for C_2. Thus, we will compute the optimal class $C*$ of the candidate t_i as:

$$\begin{aligned} C* &= argmax_{C=C_0,C_1} P(C|t_i),\ if\ Dist(t_i) > \mu \\ &= C_2,\ otherwise \end{aligned} \tag{1}$$

Where,

$$Dist(t_i) = |\frac{log(P(C_0|t_i)) - log(P(C_1, t_i))}{log(P(C_0|t_i)) + log(P(C_1, t_i))}| \tag{2}$$

and,

$$P(C|t_i) = \frac{P(C) * P(t_i|C)}{P(t)} \approx P(T_i|C) \tag{3}$$

We have considered unigram, as the features of the candidate t_i. All these features are considered independent of each other. Therefore $P(t_i|C)$ can be written as $\prod_{k=1}^{k=|t_i|} P(W_{k,t_i}|c)$.

Where, $|t_i|$ denotes the total no of words in t_i after removal of stop words, and W_{k,t_i} denotes the kth word in t_i. All the above defined probabilities can be learn from the cause-effect annotated data-set. In this paper we have considered raw corpora instead of annotated corpora to automatically learn these probabilities. In the following subsection we will discuss the technique in details.

There are three training stages. In the first stage, initial probabilities of naive bayes classifier was learned from bootstrapping. From the raw corpora, we have extracted few cause-effect pair automatically using some predefined patterns. From these extracted cause-effect pairs, initial probabilities of the classifier are learned. For example, some of the sample pairs are as follows:

X may result Y , If X then Y , X will affect Y, Y because of X.

Here, X is the cause phrase and Y is the effect phrase. We compute the Unigram probability as,

$$P(w|c) = \frac{(No\ of\ occurrences\ of\ w\ in\ class\ c + 1)}{(N + |V|)} \tag{4}$$

where N= no of words in class c and V=vocabulary size of the corpus. The parameters are estimated with Laplace smoothing method for out of vocabulary words in the training data. The second stage is called the expectation step. The remaining training corpus where cause-effect pair are not been identified by bootstrapping is classified with the current classifier. The final training stage is called the maximization step. From the newly cause-effect classified data parameters are re-estimated. Parameters trained in EM are word probability $P(w_{k,t_i}|c)$. The parameters are estimated using Laplace smoothing method for words unseen in the training data. The expectation and maximization step are repeated while the classifier parameters improve.

3 Experimentation and Evaluation

We have collected a corpus of around 7000 risk descriptions of a specific organization over the period of seven months. Each of the chosen risk descriptions were manually annotated by a group of project management experts. The annotation process involves identifying risk statements, their potential causes and impacts. 60% of the data is used for training the model and the rest for testing. We have evaluated the performance of both the risk classification system and risk analysis system by comparing its output with that of the expert annotations. We quantify the performance score in terms of the precision(P), recall(Re), F-measure(F) and accuracy(A) values (See Table 1). We have tested four type of kernels namely linear, polynomial, radial basis and sigmoid on the data. However, we have presented results against only linear and polynomial kernels as the other two functions were found to be significantly poor performers. To evaluate the quality of the classifications for SVM, multiple correlations (R) have been used.

Table 1: Evaluating the risk classifier. ALL is the combination of U,POS, D and Un features.

	Linear					Polynomial				
Features	**P**	**Re**	**F**	**A**	**R**	**P**	**Re**	**F**	**A**	**R**
U	82	89	85	83	.51	74	71	72	68	.46
B	71	73	72	74	.43	67	77	71	69	.40
POS	57	66	61	55	.67	51	63	56	51	.23
D	67	78	72	68	.63	69	78	73	74	.27
Wn	65	41	50	43	.43	54	47	50	53	.21
S	79	81	80	81	.39	72	76	74	73	.56
Un	77	76	76	79	.67	70	79	74	70	.67
ALL	**86**	**90**	**88**	**87**	**.71**	80	88	84	85	.73

4 Conclusion

In this demonstration we have presented a framework that processes human-reported risk descriptions to classify them into true risk and false alarm categories. In order to achieve this, we have used the SVM based machine learning framework and studied different linguistic features to automatically identify and label text descriptions as valid and invalid risks. The present work also extracts information from the text to generate reports on different causes of risks and their possible impacts as stated by human experts in their assessments. We have evaluated the classification framework by comparing the output of the system with that of the expert annotated dataset. Our evaluation showed promising results for automated risk identification.

References

Mark S Beasley, Richard Clune, and Dana R Hermanson. 2005. Enterprise risk management: An empirical analysis of factors associated with the extent of implementation. *Journal of Accounting and Public Policy*, 24(6):521–531.

Du-Seong Chang and Key-Sun Choi. 2004. Causal relation extraction using cue phrase and lexical pair probabilities. In *International Conference on Natural Language Processing*, pages 61–70. Springer.

Chih-Chung Chang and Chih-Jen Lin. 2011. Libsvm: a library for support vector machines. *ACM Transactions on Intelligent Systems and Technology (TIST)*, 2(3):27.

Jennifer Coates. 1987. Epistemic modality and spoken discourse. *Transactions of the Philological society*, 85(1):110–131.

Kai-Bo Duan, Jagath C Rajapakse, Haiying Wang, and Francisco Azuaje. 2005. Multiple svm-rfe for gene selection in cancer classification with expression data. *IEEE transactions on nanobioscience*, 4(3):228–234.

Shimon Kogan, Dimitry Levin, Bryan R Routledge, Jacob S Sagi, and Noah A Smith. 2009. Predicting risk from financial reports with regression. In *Proceedings of Human Language Technologies: The 2009 Annual Conference of the North American Chapter of the Association for Computational Linguistics*, pages 272–280. Association for Computational Linguistics.

Jochen L Leidner and Frank Schilder. 2010. Hunting for the black swan: risk mining from text. In *Proceedings of the ACL 2010 System Demonstrations*, pages 54–59. Association for Computational Linguistics.

Hsin-Min Lu, Nina WanHsin Huang, Zhu Zhang, and Tsai-Jyh Chen. 2009. Identifying firm-specific risk statements in news articles. In *Intelligence and Security Informatics*, pages 42–53. Springer.

Adrian J Slywotzky and John Drzik. 2005. Countering the biggest risk of all. *Harvard Business Review*, 83(4):78–88.

Mourad Ykhlef and Danah Algawiaz. 2014. A new strategic risk reduction for risk management. *International Journal of Computational Intelligence Systems*, 7(6):1054–1063.

papago: A Machine Translation Service with Word Sense Disambiguation and Currency Conversion

Hyoung-Gyu Lee, Jun-Seok Kim, Joong-Hwi Shin, Jaesong Lee, Ying-Xiu Quan and Young-Seob Jeong
NAVER LABS, NAVER Corp., Seongnam-si, Gyeonggi-do, South Korea
{hg.lee, jun.seok, joonghwi.shin}@navercorp.com
{jaesong.lee, eungsoo.jun, pinode.waider}@navercorp.com

Abstract

In this paper, we introduce *papago* - a translator for mobile device which is equipped with new features that can provide convenience for users. The first feature is word sense disambiguation based on user feedback. By using the feature, users can select one among multiple meanings of a homograph and obtain the corrected translation with the user-selected sense. The second feature is the instant currency conversion of money expressions contained in a translation result with current exchange rate. Users can be quickly and precisely provided the amount of money converted as local currency when they travel abroad.

1 Introduction

papago[1] is a multi-language machine translator for mobile device that supports English, Japanese, Chinese and Korean. The mobile application is similar to Google Translate, Microsoft Translator and Baidu Translate.

With the spread of smartphones and increasing of overseas trips, the need of the translation service for mobile devices is increasing. As artificial intelligence technology develops, there are growing expectations of a translator among users.

Most translators take voice, text or images as an input, display the translated text and output the sound converted the text into speech. Therefore, the translation service requires use of high-level technologies including speech recognition, optical character recognition, machine translation and speech synthesis. *papago* can take voice, text or image as an input and provide both translation text and text-to-speech as outputs in common with other translators.

In addition, we introduce new features that can provide convenience for users as follows:

- **Word sense disambiguation (WSD) based on user feedback**: The translator suggests multiple meanings of a homograph in an input sentence. Users can select one meaning and obtain the re-translated sentence with the user-specified sense. Each sense is given as a simple picture within the translation result screen.

- **Instant currecy conversion**: If there is a money expression in an input sentence, our translator provides the instant currency conversion of money expressions with current exchange rate. Users can quickly and precisely be provided the amount of money converted as local currency during their traveling abroad.

In this paper, we focus on two features briefly described above. Section 2 explains the word sense disambiguation based on user feedback. Section 3 presents the instant currency conversion and the money information extraction. In section 4, we conclude the paper.

[1] https://play.google.com/store/apps/details?id=com.naver.labs.translator

Proceedings of COLING 2016, the 26th International Conference on Computational Linguistics: System Demonstrations, pages 185–188, Osaka, Japan, December 11-17 2016.

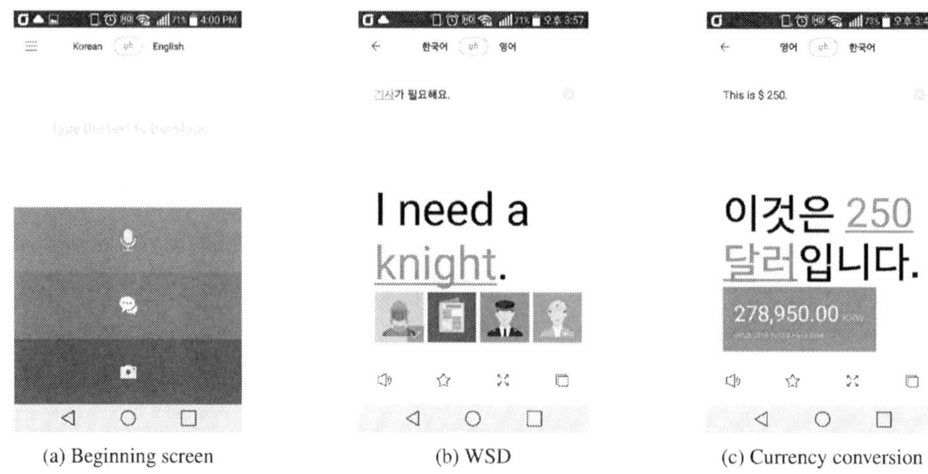

(a) Beginning screen (b) WSD (c) Currency conversion

Figure 1: Screenshots of *papago*

2 Word sense disambiguation based on user feedback

The first proposed feature, WSD[2] is needed by the following reasons:

- In mobile devices, translator users tend to input short and ambiguous sentences. If the input includes a homograph, it causes a lack of the word context and so its translation result can be different from user intention. For example, In Korean-to-English, the input '기사가 필요해요', whose meaning is 'I need 기사', has a homograph '기사' which has four senses, a knight, an article, a driver and an engineer. A translator cannot understand user intention, i.e. the precise meaning of '기사'.
- Users may want to correct only several words of an incorrect translation result.
- Users may want to verify if the translation of a homograph is correct or not.

To satisfy such demands, we propose the feature that helps users inspect which sense a homograph translation has, and change it to another translation. We also propose to use pictures when suggesting multiple meanings of a homograph to users. Picture is a great means to suggest word meanings to users, because users can easily understand word senses through pictures and they are applicable regardless of language. If user selects a picture, the application shows a new translation result. Figure 1b shows user interface for suggestions of WSD.

To implement this feature, we have to solve two technical problems:

1. Detecting a homograph and its translation from the input and output sentence pair.
2. Re-translating the input with user-selected sense, i.e. corresponding translation with the selected picture.

2.1 Detecting homograph and its translation

We detect both a homograph in an input (source sentence) and the translation of the homograph in the output (target sentence), based on dictionary-based matching after the translation decoding process. We determine whether each word contained in both source and target sentences is highlighted or not. We use the phrase alignment links acquired in the decoding process to recognize the connection between the homograph and its translation word to be highlighted. We can obtain the phrase alignment after decoding of each sentence, because our translator employs the (hierarchical) phrase-based(Koehn et al., 2003; Chiang, 2005) model as a core translation model.

[2]In natural language processing field, WSD generally refers to the task in which researchers determine a sense for each ambiguous word in a given sentence, fully automatically. We call the feature WSD, even if we manually disambiguate a word sense by users.

Korean	English	Chinese	Japanese	Picture
기사	article	记事	記事	기사_article.png
	knight	骑士	騎士	기사_knight.png
	driver	司机	運転手	기사_driver.png
	engineer	工程师	技師	기사_engineer.png

Table 1: Example of dictionary for WSD

We look a word up in the dictionary for WSD. It is a manually constructed list of pairs of a homograph and its translation for three language pairs: Korean-English, Korean-Chinese and Korean-Japanese. Therefore, we only support three directions for WSD. Table 1 shows a part of the dictionary for WSD.

Korean nouns were selected from the Standard Korean Language Dictionary of the National Institute of the Korean Language (NIKL)[3]. The dictionary was constructed through the following process:

1. Korean nouns with two or more senses are selected as entry candidates.
2. For each sense of each candidate, we find English, Chinese, and Japanese translations from a translation dictionary.
3. Save the word and its translations, if all translations of each sense are found, exclude it, otherwise.
4. Make a picture suitable for each sense and save it in the database.

We have finally acquired 931 Korean homographs and 2,050 translations of them for each target language: English, Chinese and Japanese[4]. We have constructed the entry with top-N frequent nouns of our corpus, so that it can cover as many homographs as possible.

2.2 Re-translating with user-selected sense

Our desired re-translation method is not a primitive word replacement but re-decoding a whole sentence. For example, if a user selects 'car' rather than 'tea' (picture) in the translation 'A cup of tea, please' of '차 좀 주세요', the translation should be corrected to 'Give me a car.' Thus, we propose a modified (hierarchical) phrase-based decoding method for re-translation.

If user selects a picture, i.e. a word sense, its corresponding translation, which can be a single or multi-word, is delivered to the translation decoder. For the reliable re-translation, we implemented online phrase filtering method for SMT decoder. SMT decoder recognizes the user request as (a list of) a source word index and its corresponding target word. When the decoder translates the source phrase containing the user-specified source index, it ignores every phrase pair whose target phrase does not contain the user-specified target word. Sometimes it is possible that there is no suitable phrase pair at all. In this case, we treat the specified source word as unknown word and replace it by the target word at post-processing. This guarantees the occurrence of the target word in translation result.

3 Instant currency conversion

International travelers commonly have needs of currency conversion. It may be useful for travelers to provide the currency-converted price in addition to translation result.

We propose the second feature that instantly converts the currency of the price contained in a money expression. If a translation result contains an expression of money, our translator highlights it and shows the price converted with the current exchange rate. The screenshot of this feature is shown in figure 1c. It is processed through the following process:

1. Translate the input sentence into target language.

[3] `http://stdweb2.korean.go.kr/main.jsp`

[4] Since the submission we have expanded the entry of our homograph list. We had acquired 455 homographs and 1,024 translations when we submitted this paper.

2. Detect and normalize money expressions from the translation result. (Described in section 3.1)

3. If one or more money expressions are detected, make an inquiry about current exchange rate[5].

4. Convert the amount of money obtained in 2. into the target currency.

Our policies for dectection and conversion of money expressions are as follows: We detect only currencies corresponding with source and target laguages of a translation result; e.g. US dollar and Korean won for English-to-Korean translation. And also, we convert the normailized value into the currency of opposite nation; e.g. Korean won to US dollar or US dollar to Korean won for English-to-Korean translation.

3.1 Detecting and normalizing money expression

We develop a module of money information extraction for the four languages: Korean, English, Chinese, and Japanese. It takes a raw sentence as an input, and generates a set of MONEY tags as an output. The MONEY tags convey some meta information about the money expressions. For the sentence "We borrowed 10 dollars from him", there will be one MONEY tag whose extent is '10 dollars'. The tag will also have a normalized amount of money (e.g., 10) and the corresponding currency (e.g., USD), where the format of currency follows ISO 4217[6]. The task of normalization of money expression is difficult due to the various ways of representing the same amount of money. For instance, the money expressions 'three dollars' and '3 bucks' mean the same amount of money. Moreover, some variations of money expressions are language-specific. The amount of money can be a real number in English, while it is not the case in some other languages (e.g., Korean). By taking these linguistic variations into account, the rules are carefully designed. To evaluate the rules, we construct the MONEY tagged corpus that consists of 300 - 500 sentences for each language. The evaluation results with the dataset show F1-scores higher than 94 in every language.

4 Conclusion

We introduced a machine translation service which is equipped with new features that can provide convenience for users. By using WSD based on user feedback, users can select one among word senses and obtain the corrected translation with the user-specified meaning. By using instant currency conversion, users can be quickly and precisely provided the amount of money converted as local currency when they travel abroad.

For the future work, we plan to also support English-to-X not only Korean-to-X for WSD. Moreover we try to design the database and the system architecture that can recognize multiple translations, i.e. synonyms for each sense in the dictionary for WSD.

Acknowledgements

We would like to thank Chang Song, NAVER LABS director for his advice and support.

References

David Chiang. 2005. A hierarchical phrase-based model for statistical machine translation. In *Proceedings of the 43rd Annual Meeting of the Association for Computational Linguistics (ACL).*

Philipp Koehn, Franz Josef Och, and Daniel Marcu. 2003. Statistical phrase-based translation. In *NAACL '03: Proceedings of the 2003 Conference of the North American Chapter of the Association for Computational Linguistics on Human Language Technology*, pages 48–54. Association for Computational Linguistics.

[5]We use the three exchange rates, Korean won per US dollar, Korean won per Chinese yuan and Korean won per Japanese yen. They are provided by KEB Hana Bank every hour. We can obtain the rates for all of 12 conversion directions between 4 languages from combinations of the three rates.

[6]`http://www.iso.org/iso/home/standards/currency_codes.htm`

TopoText: Interactive Digital Mapping of Literary Text

Randa El Khatib
Department of English
University of Victoria
British Columbia, Canada
khatib@uvic.ca

Julia El Zini
Department of Computer Science
American University of Beirut
Beirut, Lebanon
jwe0@4aub.edu.lb

David Wrisley
Department of English
American University of Beirut
Beirut, Lebanon
dw04@aub.edu.lb

Mohamad Jaber
Department of Computer Science
American University of Beirut
Beirut, Lebanon
mj54@aub.edu.lb

Shady Elbassuoni
Department of Computer Science
American University of Beirut
Beirut, Lebanon
se58@aub.edu.lb

Abstract

We demonstrate TopoText, an interactive tool for digital mapping of literary text. TopoText takes as input a literary piece of text such as a novel or a biography article and automatically extracts all place names in the text. The identified places are then geoparsed and displayed on an interactive map. TopoText calculates the number of times a place was mentioned in the text, which is then reflected on the map allowing the end-user to grasp the importance of the different places within the text. It also displays the most frequent words mentioned within a specified proximity of a place name in context or across the entire text. This can also be faceted according to part of speech tags. Finally, TopoText keeps the human in the loop by allowing the end-user to disambiguate places and to provide specific place annotations. All extracted information such as geolocations, place frequencies, as well as all user-provided annotations can be automatically exported as a CSV file that can be imported later by the same user or other users.

1 Overview

Spatial humanities researchers have long been utilizing digital mapping techniques in digital humanities. These visualizations are of interest because they uncover the internal spatial construction of works and often evoke arguments through patterns that may have otherwise eluded the reader through traditional close reading techniques. In this paper, we demonstrate TopoText, an interactive tool for digital mapping of literary texts in various languages such as English, German and Spanish. TopoText combines many NLP tools to provide the user with a comprehensive location-centered summary of a given text. First, it extracts all place names in the given text, which are then geoparsed and displayed on a map. In case of ambiguous place names, it provides a list of all the alternative locations that a place may be referring to (such as London England vs. London Ontario) with their geo-coordinates. The user can then pick the correct location the place is referring to, thereby introducing human intervention into automatic mapping in order to create the most accurate map possible. Moreover, TopoText calculates the number of times a place is mentioned in the text and plots it onto the map by having the points appear in different sizes. This results in a more meaningful map that is reflective of the content of the work rather than creating the illusion that all the places carry the same importance in the text.

TopoText goes beyond simply creating maps by instantly providing the user with word-place collocations that contextualize a place by offering the most recurring words related to it. These words can be faceted by part of speech tagging, which is useful because when tagging for nouns, for example, the resulting words would likely point to the general themes associated to this place. The word cloud can

Proceedings of COLING 2016, the 26th International Conference on Computational Linguistics: System Demonstrations, pages 189–193, Osaka, Japan, December 11-17 2016.

either show the word-place collocation in a specific passage (such as, the most frequent words around London in a user-highlighted text) or in the entire work (the most frequent words around London in Charles Dickenss Oliver Twist, or in his entire corpus). These word-place collocations can show how spatial representation of various places changes over time and across authors.

TopoText also allows the user to annotate places and the annotations are directly displayed on that place on the map. The annotations can range all the way from merely extracting specific passages to personal responses and analysis. This subjective element is crucial to humanities work and really opens up the system to many fields and drastically increases its scope. Finally, TopoText exports all the automatically geoparsed data, including place names, their geo-coordinates, and other attributes such as the frequencies and annotations, into a separate file that can be reused on other mapping platforms. This functionality counters commercial GIS tools and aligns with the open-source values that lie at the core of digital humanities practices. TopoText is fully implemented and is available as a free open-source tool under the GNU General Public License at `https://github.com/rkhatib/topotext/tree/v2`.

2 System Architecture

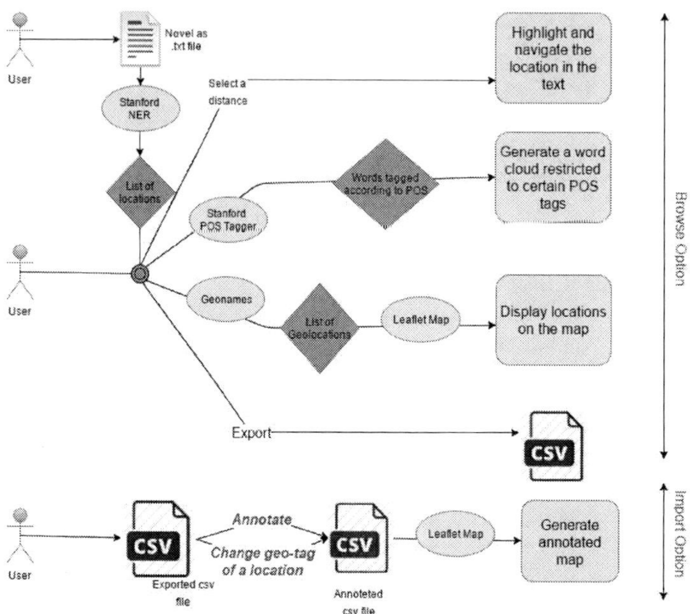

Figure 1: TopoText System Architecture

Figure 1 depicts the system architecture for TopoText. TopoText consists of two main components: a browse component and an import component. We will describe each separately next.

2.1 Browse Component

In the browse component, the user provides a piece of text, such as a novel or a biography article as a .txt file. The input text is then passed to the Stanford Named Entity Recognition (NER) Classifier (Finkel et al., 2005) which extracts all named entities in the text belonging to one of three classes: PERSON, ORGANIZATION and LOCATION. The list of places recognized (i.e. names tagged as LOCATION) are then extracted and provided back to the user, who has the following ways to explore these places:

- The user can select a place and track its occurrences in the text. TopoText highlights the user-selected place in the text and n words around it (distance in Figure 1). The user can also navigate to the next and previous occurrence of the place in the text. Figure 2 shows a snapshot of this feature.

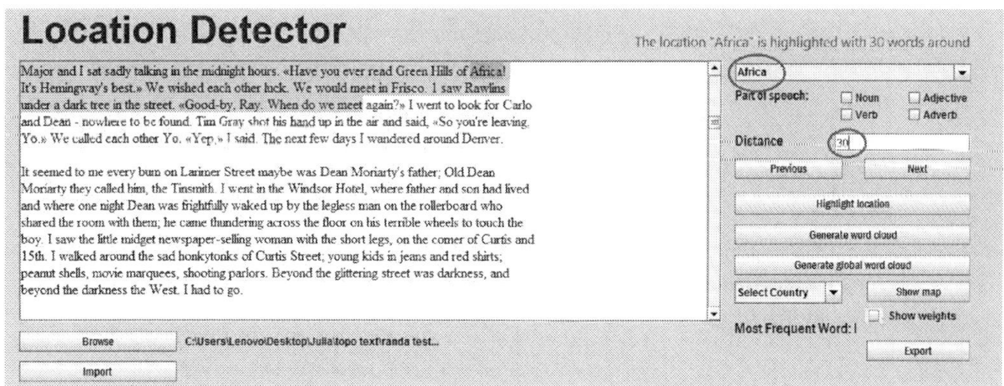

Figure 2: The selected place Africa is highlighted in the provided text along with a context of 30 words.

- The user can generate a map of all extracted places using Leaflet, which is an open-source JavaScript library for interactive maps (lea, 2016). To be able to do this, the extracted places by the NER tool are first geoparsed through the GeoNames web service (geo, 2016). GeoNames is the largest open gazetteer that is historical, multilingual, and provides alternative spellings for place names. This differentiates TopoText from many other mapping tools that rely on modern gazetteers such as Google Maps, thus excluding historical place names, alternative spellings (a common historical occurrence before the standardization of spelling and in works translated from other languages), and works written in other languages. In contrast, by relying on GeoNames, TopoText is able to extract these variations and provides the end-user with a list of all the alternative locations that a place may be referring to. The user can then specify which location a place refers to before it is rendered on the map. Additionally, the user can also view the weight of each place on the map, where the weight of a place is the frequency by which it appeared in the text. That is, the most frequent places mentioned in the text will have bigger markers on the map. An example map is shown in Figure 3.

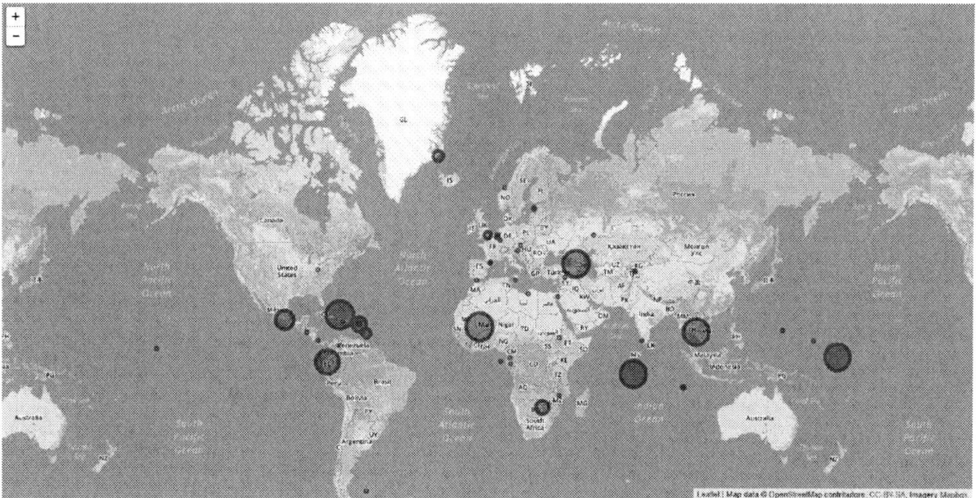

Figure 3: An example map generated by TopoText.

- The user can generate a Word Cloud for a given place. This word cloud can be a local word cloud from n words around the selected place or a global word cloud from all the words around the place in the text. In both cases, a web service provided by Wordle (wor, 2016) is used to generate the word cloud. Figure 4 shows a snapshot of an example word cloud. The user has also the option to select certain part of speech (POS) tags to include in the word cloud. The POS tags relevant in TopoText are: adjective, adverb, verb and noun. For instance, the user can exclude the adverbs from appearing in the word cloud, or select only the adjectives to have a better idea about the author's feelings about a certain place. To be able to do this, the text is POS tagged using the Stanford POS tagger (Toutanova and Manning, 2000).

- Finally, the user can also export all extracted information to a CSV file which contains every place extracted, their corresponding geo-coordinates, the country and an empty column where the user can provide annotations for places (see Import Component next). An example exported file is shown in Figure 5. This exported CSV file can be edited and reloaded by other users and can be re-used on other mapping platforms as well.

Figure 4: An example word cloud.

	A	B	C	D	E	F	G
1	Location N	Country	X	Y	weights	Annotation	
2	Franklin	United Sta	39.96118	-82.9988	5		
3	Franklin	New Zeala	-37.1667	175	5		
4	Franklin	Antarctica	-76.0833	168.3167	5		
5	Franklin	Australia	-33.6016	136.9415	5		
6	Franklin	Canada	45.04682	-73.9005	5		
7	England	United Kir	51.50853	-0.12574	27		
8	England	Jamaica	17.99358	-77.4661	27		
9	Neptune	Israel	29.54976	34.9563	1		
10	Neptune	Papua Ne	-4.49477	145.4554	1		
11	Neptune	Trinidad a	10.83333	-60.9	1		

Figure 5: An example exported CSV file.

2.2 Import Component

Using this component, the user can interact with a perviously exported CSV file. The user can, for instance, change the location a given place was mapped to by going through the list of alternative locations provided for that place, which are also included in the CSV file when it was exported. In addition, the user can provide any annotations for one or more places. Finally, the user can import this annotated CSV file, which will generate a map that displays all the places in the file along with their annotations.

3 Conclusion

We presented TopoText, an interactive digital mapping tool for literary texts in various language such as English, German and Spanish. TopoText utilizes various NLP tools and resources such as the Stanford NER, Leaflet, GeoNames and Wordle to provide users with a comprehensive location-centered summary of a given text. TopoText keeps the human in the loop by allowing the end-user to disambiguate places and to provide specific place annotations. TopoText is already available as an open source tool and has stirred wide interest in the digital humanities circuits.

In future work, we plan to extend TopoText to support other languages such as Arabic. This would involve finding or constructing appropriate gazetteers and NLP tools for such languages. We also plan to augment TopoText with an image retrieval component where place images are automatically retrieved from the Web and used to visually summarize the text. The images would be retrieved taken into consideration the context in which the place was mentioned, thus providing an accurate visual description of the place in context. Finally, we plan to develop a Web-based version of TopoText to increase its usability.

Acknowledgements

We would like to thank the American University of Beirut Research Board (URB) for their support in funding this project.

References

[Finkel et al.2005] Jenny Rose Finkel, Trond Grenager, and Christopher Manning. 2005. Incorporating non-local information into information extraction systems by gibbs sampling. In *Proceedings of the 43rd Annual Meeting on Association for Computational Linguistics*, ACL '05, pages 363–370, Stroudsburg, PA, USA. Association for Computational Linguistics.

[geo2016] 2016. The geonames geographical database. `http://www.geonames.org/`. Accessed: 2016-08-25.

[lea2016] 2016. Leaflet: an open-source javascript library for mobile-friendly interactive maps. `http://leafletjs.com/`. Accessed: 2016-08-25.

[Toutanova and Manning2000] Kristina Toutanova and Christopher D. Manning. 2000. Enriching the knowledge sources used in a maximum entropy part-of-speech tagger. In *Proceedings of the 2000 Joint SIGDAT Conference on Empirical Methods in Natural Language Processing and Very Large Corpora: Held in Conjunction with the 38th Annual Meeting of the Association for Computational Linguistics - Volume 13*, EMNLP '00, pages 63–70, Stroudsburg, PA, USA. Association for Computational Linguistics.

[wor2016] 2016. Wordle: Beautiful word clouds. `http://www.wordle.net/`. Accessed: 2016-08-25.

ACE: Automatic Colloquialism, Typographical and Orthographic Errors Detection for Chinese Language

Shichao Dong[1], Gabriel Pui Cheong Fung[2]
Binyang Li[4], Baolin Peng[1], Ming Liao[1], Jia Zhu[3] and Kam-fai Wong[1]

[1]Department of SEEM, The Chinese University of Hong Kong {scdong,blpeng,mliao,kfwong}@se.cuhk.edu.hk
[2]Director, Lab Viso Limited gabriel@labviso.com
[3]School of Computer Science, South China Normal University jzhu@m.scnu.edu.cn
[4]University of International RelationsUniversity of International Relations byli@uir.edu.cn

Abstract

We present a system called ACE for **A**utomatic **C**olloquialism and **E**rrors detection for written Chinese. ACE is based on the combination of N-gram model and rule-base model. Although it focuses on detecting colloquial Cantonese (a dialect of Chinese) at the current stage, it can be extended to detect other dialects. We chose Cantonese becauase it has many interesting properties, such as unique grammar system and huge colloquial terms, that turn the detection task extremely challenging. We conducted experiments using real data and synthetic data. The results indicated that ACE is highly reliable and effective.

1 Introduction

In general, there are two kinds of writing errors, typographical error (a.k.a. spelling errors) and orthographic error (a.k.a. cognitive error) (Damerau, 1964; Min et al., 2000). Typographical error means incorrectly substituting a right character with a wrong one, whereas orthographic error happens during the process of cognition. For colloquialism, there are two kinds as well: colloquial word and colloquial usage. For example, the word "返工" (means "back to work") is a colloquial Cantonese word. Its formal counterpart is "上班" (note: the characters of both words are completely different). On the other hand, the phrase "吃飯先" (go to dinner first), is a colloquial Cantonese usage and its formal counterpart is "先吃飯" (note: all characters in both words are the same but the position of the character "先" is different).

In this paper, we proposed a system called ACE (**A**utomatic **C**olloquialism and Spelling **E**rror Detector) to deal with all the errors stated previously. In ACE, there are three functions: (1) Identify the colloquial Cantonese words and usage; (2) Identify the potential spelling errors; (3) Provide correction suggestions.

To the best of our knowledge, there is no work related to automatically identify colloquial Cantonese. We do not aware any work on colloquialism in other language as well. For the work related to Chinese spelling error, (Lee et al., 2014) applied N-gram model and rule-based system to judge a sentence based on large number of data and experts knowledge. (Xie et al., 2015) builds a system using both N-gram model and Language model, and implements a dynamic programming to increase the efficiency. (Chang et al., 2015) implements a rule-base model and a linear regression model to tackle the task with the help of Chinese Orthographic Database. We observed that large training corpus is one of the key element for a reliable model (Tseng et al., 2015). Unfortunately, such setup is difficult to apply in our scenario because of the lack of Cantonese corpus.

2 System Description

ACE has two main modules: Cantonese detector and spelling error detector. Here is an outline of ACE: (Step 1) Identify over-segment parts in a sentence; (Step 2) Apply the Cantonese detector to check if there is any colloquial Cantonese (both usages and words); (Step 3) Apply the

Proceedings of COLING 2016, the 26th International Conference on Computational Linguistics: System Demonstrations, pages 194–197, Osaka, Japan, December 11-17 2016.

spelling error detector to check if there is any spelling error; (Step 4) Give correction suggestions for the errors detected in Step 2 and Step 3. In the followings we briefly describe the major elements within ACE.

2.1 Over-segment Parts

It is well proven that after sentence segmentation, the over-segment parts is an effective indicator to indicate potential spelling errors (Wu et al., 2010). Consider: "現在簡介有關香港電台數碼地面電視廣播法展概況", and its segmentation result: "現在/簡介/有關/香港電台 /數碼/地面/電視廣播/法/展/概況". The spelling error is "法" (the 4th last character). The correct character is"發". Note that the last four characters are segmented into three parts: "法/展/概況". If this sentence is written correctly as "... 發展概況", then the segmentation result will become ".../發展/概況". Hence two parts are resulted. By identifying the over-segment parts, we may have some cues if there is any potential spelling error. There are many different kinds of segmentation algorithms, such as HMM and Maximum Probability. In ACE, we use Maximum Probability as it performs that best empirically. Note that not all single-character word are regarded as over-segment part. Details will be discussed in Section 2.3.

2.2 Cantonese Detector

The Cantonese detector has two elements: (1) Build a large dictionary, and (2) Build a rule-base system. To build the large dictionary, apart from collecting the official Cantonese characters from the Hong Kong Information Office(http://www.gov.hk/tc/about/helpdesk) public education resources – "Hong Kong Extra Adding font collection", we further collect some "hot" and "trendy" Cantonese characters from online, such as Open-Rice(http://www.openrice.com/zh/hongkong). There are totally more than 11000 words in our Cantonese dictionary. To build the rule-base system, we apply some Cantonese linguistic rules and use pos-tagging to describe these rules. Accordingly, we build eight rules as a start for eight basic Cantonese sentence structure. A rule usually has two parts: a flag word and a part-of-speech-tagging pattern. For example: the phrase "吃飯先" has no Cantonese characters, and it can be tagged as "吃飯/v 先/d"(ACE follows the ICTCLAS(http://ictclas.nlpir.org) part-of-speech-tagging standards). The rule can be organized as "1-先 v/d", the "1" indicates the position of the flag character, in this case "先", and "v/d" is the part-of-speech-tagging pattern of a certain phrase.

2.3 Spelling Error Detector

To detect the spelling errors in a sentence and offer replacement suggestions, a typical way is to employ an recursion algorithm as follows: (1) Check if there is any single-character word. A single-character word will be regarded as an over-segment part; (2) Replace the characters in the over-segmented parts by their corresponding confusion sets one by one. The confusion set of a character is the set of characters that are similar to the character typographically or orthographically; (3) Reassemble a new sentence and justify if the character replacement is appropriate. Unfortunately, we encountered several problems with such approach. First, there are many single correct characters in a Chinese sentence. For example, "是" (mean"is"), "地" (similar to append " ing" in a word, mean something is continuing) and "的" (similar to append "'s" in a noun) are all single-character word and usually appear in a sentence. They will always be segmented as a single-character word. If we perform the recursion algorithm as stated above, the whole system will be slow down dramatically and become useless in practice because many correct single-character words are regarded as over-segment parts. Second, unnecessary replacements may happen, because some single-character words have high-frequent replacement candidates according to the training data. For example, word "白" has a replace candidate "的" from the confusion set, but "的" has much higher frequency comparing with "白" in the training data, then an unnecessary replacement from "白" to "的" may happen despite of the context.

	Precision	Recall	F1
High	0.4843	0.7764	0.5839
Medium	0.4239	0.7872	0.5368
Low	0.2647	0.7505	0.3770

Table 1: The performance for large corps

To deal with these problems, we assign a score to every sentence based on its segmented words after the sentence segmentation. The score is computed based on a language model: the more frequent a word appears in the training data (e.g., the word "是"), the higher score it is and the higher co-occurrence of words combinations get higher score. Setting thresholds has been proven a useful method (Ferraro et al., 2011). We regard a single-character word as an over-segment part if and only if its score is higher than a predefined threshold. The threshold is computed based on the minmax principle: the smallest score of the most frequent word in the training data. In addition, we set bias on the sentence scores, if the length of words list becomes shorter, which means the number of over-segmented parts in a sentence decrease, ACE will add a positive bias on the score to make it higher. In contrast, the score of the sentence will become lower with adding a negative bias if the list of words of the sentence become longer.

In addition, in ACE, unlike the existing approaches which usually try to do the character replacement immediately once they identified a potential spelling error, we regard the consecutive over-segment parts as one candidate set and perform the replacement for all characters within such set. This can effectively help us to identify some spelling errors where two characters in a word are both spelling wrong. For example, if "政策" is incorrectly written as "正束" (both characters are written incorrectly), then ACE is possible to detect the error, whereas the existing approaches may not necessary able to do so.

To justify whether a replacement is appropriate, we follow the existing approaches by: (1) Reassemble the sentence after character replacement, (2) Score the sentence, and (3) If the new score is higher than the previous score, we say that the replacement is justifiable.

3 Experiments

We conducted experiments on synthetic data and real data. For synthetic data, we collected 500 error-free compositions from school students. For each composition, we randomly pick N Chinese terms from a predefined dictionary and replace them with the corresponding colloquial Cantonese. Next, we randomly pick M characters from the composition and replace them with one of the characters from their corresponding confusion sets. We vary M and N to test the sensitiveness of ACE. We set $M+N$ equals to 4, 8, 10 to denote low, medium and high level of errors. For real error data, we collect 411 sentences from Hong Kong school students. Each of them may have more than one spelling errors or colloquial Cantonese usage.

3.1 Evaluation Results

We compute precision, recall and F-1 using true positive (the no. of spelling errors that are correctly detected), false positive (the no. of non-existent errors are identified) and false negative (the no. of spelling errors cannot be detected) . Table 1 shows the results using synthetic data. The result is satisfactory and comparable to the latest existing works.

Table 2 shows some sample results using the real data. For the sentence "從令天開始，我就成為一名小學生啦！", "今天" is written as "令天". The sentence "快到聖誕節了，我和媽媽一同去構買聖誕禮物。" shares similar error. The sentence "表姐專門來送結婚請貼給爸爸媽媽。", "請帖" is written as "請貼", the wrong character is **not** the first character of the word. This indicate the ACE could be able to select the best candidate using its recursion replacement algorithm. There are some sentences have colloquial Cantonese usages and spelling errors in the same sentence. For example, "今天返工，突然下起的大雨淋得他混身都濕透了。", "返工" is a

Sentence	Correction
從令天開始，我就成為一名小學生啦！	令 -> 今
我們不能隨便丟棄電弛，否則會污染環境。	弛 -> 池
快到聖誕節了，我和媽媽一同去構買聖誕禮物。	構 -> 購
今天返工，突然下起的大雨淋得他混身都濕透了。	返工 -> 下班, 混 -> 渾
我最愛吃媽媽包的交子啦！讓我吃飯先	交子 -> 餃子, 吃飯先 -> 先吃飯
表姐專門來送結婚請貼給爸爸媽媽。	請貼 -> 請帖
她是一位名付其實的好老師，學生們都很喜歡。	付 -> 符
常年累月的辛勞，使外公的腰越來越彎了。	常年累月 -> 長年累月
他誇耀自己的時候，總是眉飛色武，說個不停。	武 -> 舞

Table 2: Result Examples

colloquial word and "混身" is an error. ACE detects both errors successfully. ACE also detect the colloquial Cantonese *usage* (*not* Cantonese *word*). For example, "我最愛吃媽媽包的交子啦！讓我吃飯先", "交子" should be written as"餃子" and a colloquial usage "吃飯先". Finally, for a complex context such as "常年累月的辛勞，使外公的腰越來越彎了。", ACE could also detect the errors.

4 Conclusions

In this paper, we introduced ACE (**A**utomatic **C**olloquialism, Typographical and Orthographic **E**rror Detection) to detect the spelling errors and colloquial Cantonese from written Chinese, and to provide correction suggestions. The results indicated that ACE is effective and efficient.

Acknowledgment

This project is funded by the Hong Kong Applied Science and Technology Research Institute (ASTRI) (project code: 7050854), the fundamental research fund for the central universities (3262014T75, 3262015T70) and the National Natural Science Foundation of China (61502115, U1536207, 61370165, 61572043).

References

Tao-Hsing Chang, Cheng-Han Yang, and Hsueh-Chih Chen. 2015. Introduction to a proofreading tool for chinese spelling check task of sighan-8. In *ACL-IJCNLP 2015*, page 50.

Fred J Damerau. 1964. A technique for computer detection and correction of spelling errors. *Communications of the ACM*, 7(3):171–176.

Gabriela Ferraro, Rogelio Nazar, and Leo Wanner. 2011. Collocations: a challenge in computer assisted language learning. In *MTT*, pages 69–79.

Lung-Hao Lee, Liang-Chih Yu, Kuei-Ching Lee, Yuen-Hsien Tseng, Li-Ping Chang, and Hsin-Hsi Chen. 2014. A sentence judgment system for grammatical error detection. In *COLING*.

Kyongho Min, William H. Wilson, and Yoo-Jin Moon. 2000. Typographical and orthographical spelling error correction. In *LREC*.

Yuen-Hsien Tseng, Lung-Hao Lee, Li-Ping Chang, and Hsin-Hsi Chen. 2015. Introduction to sighan 2015 bake-off for chinese spelling check. In *ACL-IJCNLP 2015*, page 32.

Shih-Hung Wu, Yong-Zhi Chen, Ping che Yang, Tsun Ku, and Chao-Lin Liu. 2010. Reducing the false alarm rate of chinese character error detection and correction. In *CLP 2010*, pages 54–61.

Weijian Xie, Peijie Huang, Xinrui Zhang, Kaiduo Hong, Qiang Huang, Bingzhou Chen, and Lei Huang. 2015. Chinese spelling check system based on n-gram model. In *ACL-IJCNLP 2015*, page 128.

A Tool for Efficient Content Compilation

Boris Galitsky
Knowledge-Trail Inc
San Jose CA USA
bgalitsky@hotmail.com

Abstract

We build a tool to assist in content creation by mining the web for information relevant to a given topic. This tool imitates the process of essay writing by humans: searching for topics on the web, selecting content fragments from the found document, and then compiling these fragments to obtain a coherent text. The process of writing starts with automated building of a table of content by obtaining the list of key entities for the given topic extracted from web resources such as Wikipedia. Once a table of content is formed, each item forms a seed for web mining. The tool builds a full-featured structured Word document with table of content, section structure, images and captions and web references for all included text fragments.

Two linguistic technologies are employed: for relevance verification, we use similarity computed as a tree similarity between parse trees for a seed and candidate text fragment. For text coherence, we use a measure of agreement between a given and consecutive paragraph by tree kernel learning of their discourse trees.

The tool is available at http://animatronica.io/submit.html.

1 Introducing content compilation problem

In the modern society, writing and creating content is one of the most frequent human activity. An army of content creators, from students to professional writers produce various kinds of documents for various audiences. Not all of these documents are expected to be innovative, break-through or extremely important. The target of the tool being proposed is assistance with routine document creation process (Fig. 1) where most information is available on the web and needs to be collected, integrated and properly referenced.

A number of content generation software systems are available in specific business domains (Johnson 2016). Most of content generation software are template-based which limits their efficiency and volume of produced content (Hendrikx et al 2015). An interesting class of content generation system is based on verbalizing some numerical data. Also, content generation for computer game support turned out to be fruitful (Liapis et al 2013). Deep-learning – based generation of a sequence of words has a limited applicability for large scale content production industrial systems. The goal of this study is to build a content compilation assistance system that would meet the following criteria:

- Produces high volume cohesive text on a given topic in a domain-independent manner;
- Collects text fragments from the web and combines them to assist in research on a given topic, provide systematic references;
- Combines text, image and video resources in the resultant document;
- Suitable for producing a final report and manual editing by students, researchers in various fields in science, engineering, business and law.

On the bottom-left of Fig. 1 we show the main problem that needs to be solved to build a document from fragments collected from the web. For given two fragments, we need to determine if one can reasonably follow another in a cohesive manner. W build a discourse representation for each fragment an learn this representation to classify a pair of consecutive paragraphs as cohesive or not.

Proceedings of COLING 2016, the 26th International Conference on Computational Linguistics: System Demonstrations, pages 198–202, Osaka, Japan, December 11-17 2016.

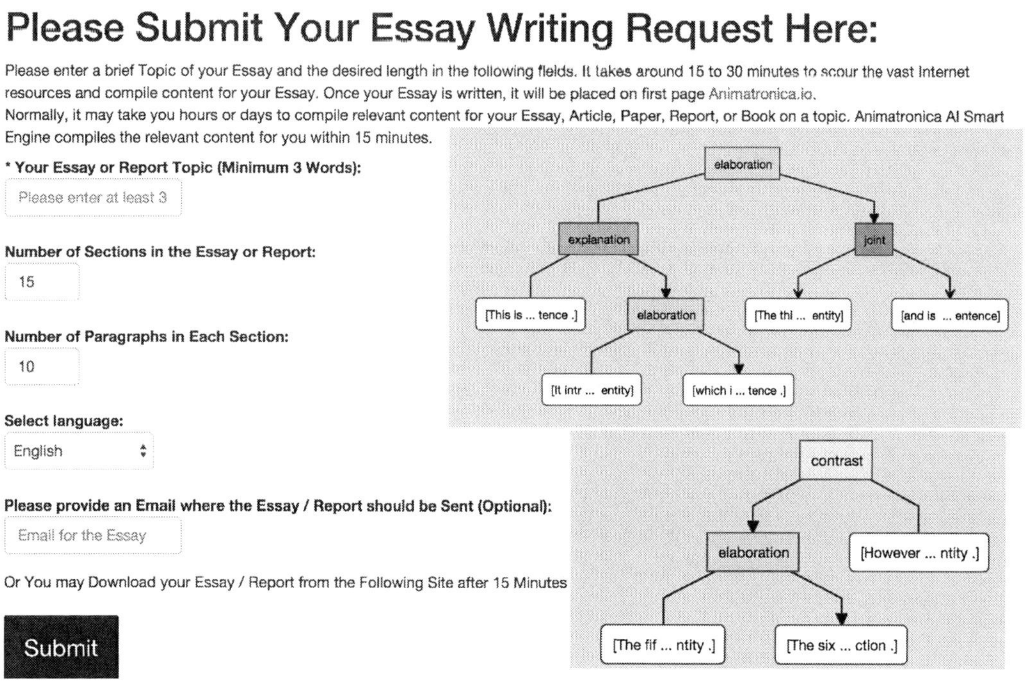

Please Submit Your Essay Writing Request Here:

Please enter a brief Topic of your Essay and the desired length in the following fields. It takes around 15 to 30 minutes to scour the vast Internet resources and compile content for your Essay. Once your Essay is written, it will be placed on first page Animatronica.io.
Normally, it may take you hours or days to compile relevant content for your Essay, Article, Paper, Report, or Book on a topic. Animatronica AI Smart Engine compiles the relevant content for you within 15 minutes.

* Your Essay or Report Topic (Minimum 3 Words):
Please enter at least 3

Number of Sections in the Essay or Report:
15

Number of Paragraphs in Each Section:
10

Select language:
English

Please provide an Email where the Essay / Report should be Sent (Optional):
Email for the Essay

Or You may Download your Essay / Report from the Following Site after 15 Minutes

Submit

elaboration
explanation
joint
[This is ... tence .]
elaboration
[The thi ... entity]
[and is ... entence]
[It intr ... entity]
[which i ... tence .]

contrast
elaboration
[However ... ntity .]
[The fif ... ntity .]
[The six ... ction .]

Figure 1: Content Compilation front end (on the left). The pair of discourse trees to find an appropriate sequence of mined text fragments (on the right-bottom)

2 Text Fragment Mining Algorithm

To write a document, we first create its table of contents (TOC). To do that, we mine the web for most important attributes associated with an entity we are writing about. For example, if we write a biography about a person, we find a biography page about a person of a similar kind (such as a writer or a scientist) and extract a TOC from it. Another option is two mine auto-complete values for this entity. For a scientist, it would be {*born, educated, researched, discovered, announced, became well known*}. Usually, Wikipedia is a good source of a structure of a TOC for a document on a given topic. TOC items will constitute a seed from which web search query will be formed.

The chart for text fragment mining algorithm is shown in Fig. 2. We start with the seed, one or multiple sentences each of which will form one or more paragraphs about the respective topics of the TOC. These seed sentences can be viewed as either headers or informational centroids of content to be compiled. We now iterate through each original sentence, build block of content for each and then merge all blocks, preceded by their seed sentences together, similar to (Sauper & Barzilay 2000).

To find relevant sentences on the web for a seed sentence, we form query as extracted significant noun phrases from this seed sentence: either longer one (three or more keywords, which means two or more modifiers for a noun, or an entity, such as a proper noun). If such queries do not deliver significant number of relevant sentences formed from search results, we use the whole sentence as a search engine query, filtering our content that is a duplicate to the seed.

The formed queries are run via search engine API or scraped, using Bing; search results are collected. We then loop through the parts of the snippets to see which sentences are relevant to the seed one and which are not. For all sentences obtained from snippets, we verify appropriateness to form content on one hand, and relevance to the seed sentence on the other hand. Appropriateness is determined based on grammar rules: to enter a paragraph cohesively, a sentence needs to include a verb phrase and be opinionated (Galitsky et al 2009). We filter out sentences that look like one or another form of advertisement, a call to buy a product, or encourages other user activity by means of an imperative verb.

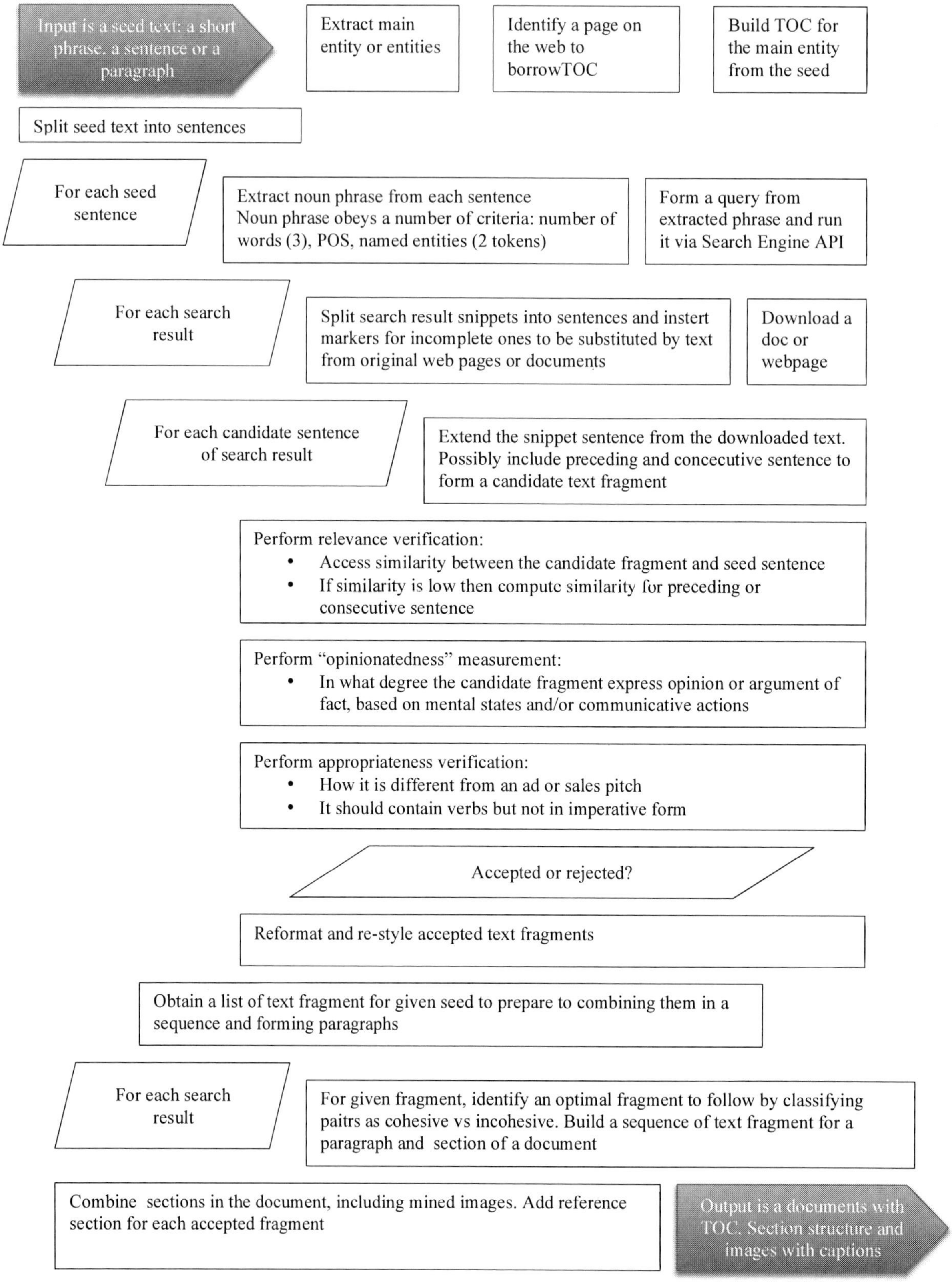

Input is a seed text: a short phrase, a sentence or a paragraph

Extract main entity or entities

Identify a page on the web to borrowTOC

Build TOC for the main entity from the seed

Split seed text into sentences

For each seed sentence

Extract noun phrase from each sentence
Noun phrase obeys a number of criteria: number of words (3), POS, named entities (2 tokens)

Form a query from extracted phrase and run it via Search Engine API

For each search result

Split search result snippets into sentences and instert markers for incomplete ones to be substituted by text from original web pages or documents

Download a doc or webpage

For each candidate sentence of search result

Extend the snippet sentence from the downloaded text. Possibly include preceding and concecutive sentence to form a candidate text fragment

Perform relevance verification:

- Access similarity between the candidate fragment and seed sentence
- If similarity is low then compute similarity for preceding or consecutive sentence

Perform "opinionatedness" measurement:

- In what degree the candidate fragment express opinion or argument of fact, based on mental states and/or communicative actions

Perform appropriateness verification:

- How it is different from an ad or sales pitch
- It should contain verbs but not in imperative form

Accepted or rejected?

Reformat and re-style accepted text fragments

Obtain a list of text fragment for given seed to prepare to combining them in a sequence and forming paragraphs

For each search result

For given fragment, identify an optimal fragment to follow by classifying paitrs as cohesive vs incohesive. Build a sequence of text fragment for a paragraph and section of a document

Combine sections in the document, including mined images. Add reference section for each accepted fragment

Output is a documents with TOC. Section structure and images with captions

Figure 2: Content compilation algorithm

Relevance is determined based on the operation of syntactic generalization (Galitsky et al 2012), where the bag-of-words approach is extended towards extracting commonalities between the syntactic parse trees of seed sentence and the text mined on the web. Syntactic generalization score is computed as a cardinality of maximal common sub-graph between the parse trees of the seed and candidate sentences or text fragments. Syntactic generalization allows a domain-independent semantic measure of topical similarity, delivering stronger relevance than the search engine itself or the keyword statistics.

In addition to syntactic generalization, the tool verifies common entities between seed and mined sentence, and applies general appropriateness metric. The overall score includes syntactic generalization score (the cardinality of maximal common system of syntactic sub-trees) and appropriateness score to filter out less suitable sentences. Finally, mined sentences are re-styled and re-formatted to better fit together. The following section explains how paragraphs are formed from text fragments.

3 Arranging Candidate Text Fragments

To form a coherent sections of a document, text fragments need to agree. For a given candidate fragment, we either find its optimal position in a section of a document for the receding and following fragment or paragraph of text, or reject it. To implement this functionality, we build a classifier for a pair of consecutive text fragments (paragraphs) and classify them as a valid (coherent, acceptable agreement) pair or an invalid one (Galitsky et al., 2015). We use a discourse trees representation (Joty et al 2013) where the parse tree information for each elementary discourse unit is retained. To form *<Fragment1, Fragment2>* pair one can combine the respective discourse trees into a single tree with the root RR (Fig.3). The discourse trees for these pairs are subject to tree kernel learning (Zhang & Lee 2003). We form a positive training set of classifier from the pairs of paragraph which actually follow each other and a negative training set - from the ones randomly selected from text (Yahoo! Answer corpus was used).

4 Conclusions

The discourse tree representation used in our content compilation system is a reduction of what is called parse thicket (Galitsky et al., 2015), a combination of parse trees for sentences with discourse-level relationships between words and parts of the sentence in one graph. The straight edges of this graph are syntactic relations, and curvy arcs – discourse relations, such as anaphora, same entity, sub-entity, rhetoric relation and communicative actions. This graph includes much richer information than just a combination of parse trees for individual sentences would. Parse thickets can be generalized at the level of words, relations, phrases and sentences (Fig. 3).

The tool has been advertised using Google AdWords and used by thousand of users searching for "free essay writing" to compile content for a variety of domains, including natural sciences and humanities.

The system is available for general audience at http://animatronica.io/submit.html. Examples of written documents on a wide variety of topics is available at http://mail3.fvds.ru/wrt_latest/.The source code can be obtained at https://github.com/bgalitsky/relevance-based-on-parse-trees under Apache Licence and is a sub-project of Apache OpenNLP https://opennlp.apache.org/.

Reference

Liapis, Antonios, Georgios N Yannakakis,and Julian Togelius. 2013. Sentient Sketchbook: Computer-aided game level authoring." InFDG, 213–220.

Johnson, MR, 2016. Procedural Generation of Linguistics, Dialects, Naming Conventions and Spoken Sentences. Proceedings of 1st International Joint Conference of DiGRA and FDG.

Galitsky, B., Ilvovsky, D., Kuznetsov, S. O. 2015. Text Classification into Abstract Classes Based on Discourse Structure. Proceedings of Recent Advances in Natural Language Processing, pages 200–207, Hissar, Bulgaria, Sep 7–9 2015.

Galitsky, B., MP González, CI Chesñevar.. A novel approach for classifying customer complaints through graphs similarities in argumentative dialogue. *Decision Support Systems*, Volume 46, Issue 3 717-729.

Galitsky, B., Gabor Dobrocsi, Josep Lluis de la Rosa, 2012. Inferring the semantic properties of sentences by mining syntactic parse trees. Data & Knowledge Engineering v81 pp 21-45.

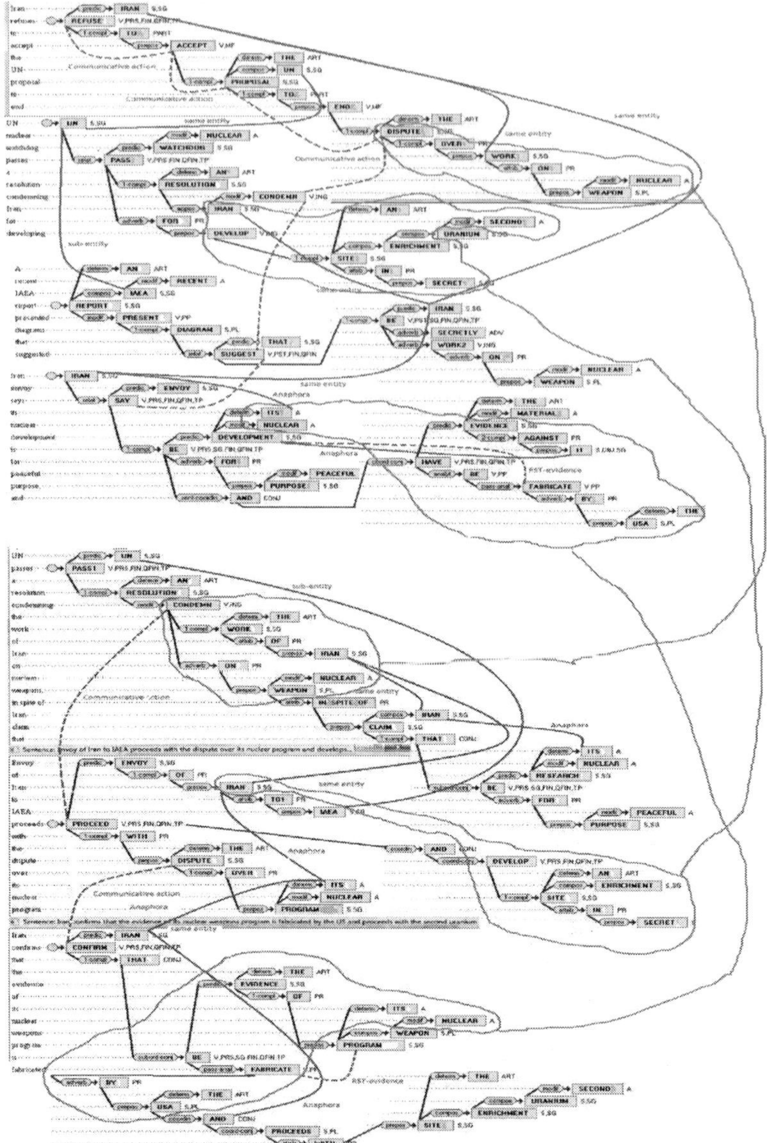

Figure 3: Parse thickets of two paragraphs assuring document cohesiveness

Hendrikx, Mark, Sebastiaan Meijer, Joeri Van Der Velden, and Alexandru Iosup. 2013. Procedural content generation for games: A survey. ACM Trans. Multimedia Comput. Commun. Appl. 9, 1, Article 1 22 pages.

Zhang, Dell and Wee Sun Lee. 2003. Question classification using support vector machines. In SIGIR '03: Proceedings of the 26th Annual International ACM SIGIR Conference on Research and Development in Information Retrieval, pages 26–32, New York, NY, USA, ACM.

Galitsky, B. 2013. Machine Learning of Syntactic Parse Trees for Search and Classification of Text. Engineering Application of Artificial Intelligence, dx.doi.org/10.1016/j.engappai.2012.09.017.

Joty, Shafiq R, Giuseppe Carenini, Raymond T Ng, and Yashar Mehdad. 2013. Combining intra-and multi- sentential rhetorical parsing for document-level dis- course analysis. In *ACL (1)*, pages 486–496.

Sauper, Cristina and Regina Barzilay. 2000. Automatically Generating Wikipedia Articles: A Structure-Aware Approach, Proceedings of ACL.

MAGES: A Multilingual Angle-integrated Grouping-based Entity Summarization System

Eun-kyung Kim and Key-Sun Choi
Semantic Web Research Center
Korea Advanced Institute of Science and Technology (KAIST)
Republic of Korea
{kekeeo,kschoi}@world.kaist.ac.kr

Abstract

This demo presents MAGES (multilingual angle-integrated grouping-based entity summarization), an entity summarization system for a large knowledge base such as DBpedia based on a entity-group-bound ranking in a single integrated entity space across multiple language-specific editions. MAGES offers a multilingual angle-integrated space model, which has the advantage of overcoming missing semantic tags (i.e., categories) caused by biases in different language communities, and can contribute to the creation of entity groups that are well-formed and more stable than the monolingual condition within it. MAGES can help people quickly identify the essential points of the entities when they search or browse a large volume of entity-centric data. Evaluation results on the same experimental data demonstrate that our system produces a better summary compared with other representative DBpedia entity summarization methods.

1 Introduction

The rapid increase in the number of triples in knowledge bases (KBs) has made it imperative to extract essential information from many relevant and similar facts that describe an entity comprising a set of entity–property–value triples (e.g., <Usain Bolt, nationality, Jamaican>, <Usain Bolt, birthPlace, Spanish Town>, <Usain Bolt, birthPlace, Jamaica>, <Usain Bolt, placeOfBirth, Jamaica>, <Usain Bolt, residence, Jamaica>, etc.). Therefore, entity summarization (Cheng et al., 2011), which creates a short summary from a set of triples from the description of an entity, has attracted much attention in recent years. This is a method designed to help people quickly identify the essential points of entities when searching or browsing a large volume of entity-centric data. Although several approaches have been proposed in (Cheng et al., 2011; Thalhammer and Rettinger, 2014; Gunaratna et al., 2015), their qualities are still far from ideal, and some approaches rely on external resources such as WordNet (Fellbaum, 1998).

This demo presents a multilingual angle-integrated grouping-based entity summarization system (MAGES), which is an entity summarization system for the DBpedia (Lehmann et al., 2014) based on the entity-group-bound ranking in an entity space. The intuition of this study is that property–value pairs—consecutively also called features—shared by an entity's group's members (neighborhoods) are considered more important for their identity than for the features they share with an entity that is not in their respective neighborhood. For example, there are two distinct groups: A = {"Usain Bolt", "Carl Lewis", "Michael Johnson"} and B = {"Babe Ruth", "Hyun-jin Ryu"}. Each group has distinguishing characteristics that can reveal underlying triples that generate entity summaries. Consider the difference between "Usain Bolt" in A and "Babe Ruth" in B for their typical player characteristics. "Usain Bolt" has essential properties such as "sport event" or "medal information," whereas "Babe Ruth" would have more emphasis on his "position" or "team."

There are many predefined semantic groups (i.e. types) of entities in DBpedia such as "Baseball Player," "Company," and "Film." However, although DBpedia has its own mechanisms for setting entity types, its coverage of the entity types is not sufficient. Moreover, the types of each entity, if they

Proceedings of COLING 2016, the 26th International Conference on Computational Linguistics: System Demonstrations, pages 203–207, Osaka, Japan, December 11-17 2016.

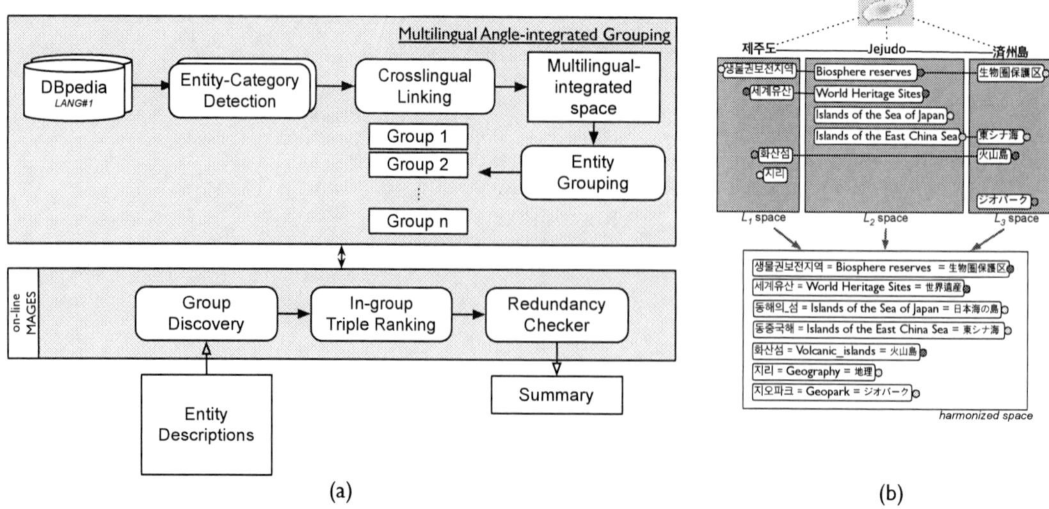

Figure 1: (a) The outline of the proposed multilingual angle-integrated grouping-based entity summarization system, (b) An example of multilingual topic integration: Collecting the scattered data (due to the different perspective) together to obtain the enriched knowledge of an entity in the DBpedia.

exist, are not stable enough to make a summary for the entity's description because of mismatches between defined type and actual entity descriptions. Therefore, new entity grouping is necessary, especially the grouping of entities in their multilingual angle integration to ensure that no relevant information is biased towards one specific language edition. DBpedia currently serves over 120 language editions extracted from language-specific Wikipedias that can contain different information from one language to another (Lehmann et al., 2014). In particular, language-specific editions can provide 1) more details about certain topics and 2) information missed in other DBpedia editions according to a specific cultural viewpoint. Unlike the prior studies of entity summarization, we particularly focus on methods for incorporating a variety of different lingual information scattered in Linked Open Data (Bizer et al., 2009) to enhance entities' topic detection. A multilingual angle-integrated space model can contribute to the creation of entity groups that are well-formed and more stable than the monolingual condition within it.

2 System Description

Figure 1 (a) shows the outline of the proposed system. It comprises the following steps: i) we mine all lingual category tags from multiple DBpedia language editions to create information about distinct entity groups, ii) Each feature is ranked based on the pertinent features of the in-group, and iii) We iteratively choose highly ordered and less similar facts by adopting a feature-ranking system.

2.1 Multilingual Angle-integrated Grouping

While observing the unstable manifestation of entity types in a KB's triples, category information will be used as a more stable source of clustering entities in a multilingual integrated space. We utilized the category tags to infer the topics of entities to build the entities' fine-grained semantic group. We integrated different languages' biased category tags into a single space that could help overcome missing categories and could help detect highly informative keywords for more stable entity grouping. For example, comparing the DBpedia Korean, English and Japanese editions of categories for "Jejudo" in Figure 1 (b), several categories are only in one monolingual edition: "Islands of the Sea of Japan" is only in the English edition and "지리[jili]" ("Geography") is only in the Korean edition.

Then, we induced a set of disjointed clusters in which each entity in DBpedia is categorized into a cluster (that represents an entity group) by executing a clustering process over the multilingual integrated entity space generated by weaving different category tags from several DBpedia language editions. The vector space of tokens from categories was used to identify the characteristics of an entity, such as "islands," "sea," and "japan," for a given entity "Jejudo" as in Figure 1 (b). We employed the k-means algorithm to accomplish this, because it is regarded as one of the simplest and most efficient unsupervised learning algorithms for clustering large data sets (J. A. Hartigan, 1979). The value of k for the k-means algorithm is determined by the number of types that exist in DBpedia.

2.2 In-Group Triple Ranking

In this step, all triples about each entity are ranked according to the in-group-relevance scoring formula. The working principle behind triple ranking is that we assign a higher score to triples that contain more relevant properties with high frequencies to reflect the importance of a property to a group, and more relevant values have higher correlations between two entities for a given triple. Hence, the score of a triple $t^e_{p,v}$ is defined as

$$\begin{aligned} score(t^e_{p,v}) &= p\_score(e,p) + v\_score(e,v) \\ &\quad + \lambda(p\_score(e,p) \times v\_score(e,v)), \end{aligned} \tag{1}$$

where $p\_score(e,p)$ is a weight assigned to the property p for the group of e, the $v\_score(e,v)$ is a correlation weight assigned to the value v for the entity e, and λ is a tuning parameter that determines the ratio of the synergy indicators. The p_score is derived by a property-weighting function that obtains the properties that interact most strongly in the in-group space for frequencies of labels of properties. This scheme is based on the label of an in-group property specifically influenced by the term frequency–inverse document frequency (TF-IDF) technique to obtain the top labels from each group. The v_score is derived by a correlation measure that is used in the case of two related entities; we assume that two entities are highly correlated when the fraction of triples that are in common with the total number of triples of both entities is higher.

2.3 Redundancy Checker

After the obtention of the triple ranking results, we focus on generating a summary of the triple collection by considering both relevance and anti-redundancy, until a given length of summary is reached. We attempt to iteratively measure the similarity of the next candidate triple to previously selected ones, and select a candidate if its similarity is below a threshold (user parameter) until the length limit of summary (σ) is reached. Given that a triple is much shorter than a sentence, most terms are specified within the KB. Therefore, a sequence matching procedure (Mount, 2004) provides the similarity measure among the words that appear in triples.

3 Experiments and Evaluation

We utilize the 10 largest languages in DBpedia—English, French, German, Italian, Spanish, Russian, Dutch, Polish, Portuguese, and Swedish—to project multilingual category information into a single space that provides integrated multi-angled semantics of each entity. All the category tags of the entities are tokenized and represented as vector stem words for entity grouping. Category tags marked in a different language are translated into English through the `owl:sameAs` link in the linked data. We assume that if two category tags are connected by means of this link, those categories can be considered to be the same.

As a current state-of-the-art method, FACeted Entity Summarization (FACES) (Gunaratna et al., 2015) aims to improve the coverage of its summarization using a conceptually different set of facts, called facets of an entity. The authors of FACES shared gold-standard entity summaries given by a group of human experts that consisted of 5 and 10 triples for each of the selected 50 entities in DBpedia. These are referred to as ideal summaries in our study.

Evaluations of the summarization systems use an ideal summary provided by multiple human annotators by counting the unit overlaps with the generated summary, which is regarded as the quality such as in Equation 2 (Cheng et al., 2011), where n is the number of human annotators required to produce the individual ideal summaries denoted by $Summ^I_i(e)$ for $i = 1, \ldots, n$, and the automatically generated summary is denoted by $Summ(e)$ for the entity e. The summary that achieves the highest quality score is considered to be the most similar to the ideal summary. Given $\sigma \in 5, 10$, an entity e and n ideal summaries received, their agreements (Cheng et al., 2011) averaged over all entities are 1.9596 and 4.6770 for $\sigma = 5$ and 10, respectively.

$$Quality(Summ(e)) = \frac{1}{n}\sum_{i=1}^{n}|Summ(e) \cap Summ_i^I(e)| \tag{2}$$

Table 1 shows the performance evaluation results of MAGES compared to FACES and other baselines. We considered several baselines to analyze the effectiveness of the entity group-based approaches. The simplest baseline was to build a group of entities utilizing the assigned entity types in KB (Typed). Another baseline that we considered was to build entity groups using monolingual categories (GES). It is clear from the Table 1 that our group-based summarization approach outperformed FACES in terms of the summarization quality. Moreover, a two-tailed paired t-test was performed to verify the statistical significance of the performance improvement. Significance was accepted at $p < 0.05$. For the top-5 and top-10 lists, the respective p values for MAGES against FACES were 0.02013 and 0.00152. Thus, our approach provides significantly better results than FACES. FACES provides a faceted summary of a given length by incorporating at least one feature from each facet. However, several important facts for a summary may be present in one facet; thus, a summary in each facet unit is not always ideal. Moreover, FACES expands each feature to obtain a set of words that rely on the external resource WordNet (e.g., hypernyms). However, WordNet does not always cover concepts in the KB, particularly relatively less popular concepts in English. For example, "Busan" is South Korea's second largest city after "Seoul," but the former is not indicated as such in WordNet. Thus "Busan" cannot be expanded as a "place" or "area" by the method used in FACES.

We also performed a random sampling analysis to verify the statistical significance of the integration of multiple lingual entity spaces, because an unbalanced number of tokens for clustering could affect the overall result. First, we selected 10,000 random tokens per system (GES and MAGES) to partition our original tokens into small- and same-sized token sets for the two approaches. Then, we executed clustering with these ingredients, and computed the Purity score (Amigó et al., 2009) for the clustering results of each system, in which the type information from DBpedia is gold standard. The average score of 100 random sampling experiments for MAGES (0.4777) was higher than that of experiments for GES (0.4607). A statistical evaluation using a two-sample paired t-test showed a p value equal to 2.28726×10^{-5}. MAGES exhibited a 0.03% improvement for the summary quality compared to the GES method for a top-five summary, as shown in Table 1. In other words, multilingual grouping comprises a signature to describe the main features of an entity in a group. In addition, it can help entities that are hidden in the long tail of a monolingual space.

Systems	$\sigma = 5$	$\sigma = 10$
FACES (state-of-the-art)	1.4611	4.3641
MAGES	**1.7082**	**4.5523**
GES	1.6727	4.4191
Typed	1.4651	4.1120

Table 1: Evaluation of the quality of summaries ($\lambda = 4.5$).

4 Conclusion

In this demo, we have presented MAGES, which is a system for configuring a summary within entity groups for entities of a data set in DBpedia. Our evaluation shows that the MAGES approach to summary generation outperforms another DBpedia entity summarization system when compared to the user-created benchmark. Moreover, MAGES can extract a particular group's stable signatures using multilingual angle integration, which can provide a useful strategy for identifying the nature of a described entity.

Acknowledgments

This work was supported by Institute for Information & communications Technology Promotion (IITP) grant funded by the Korea government (MSIP)(No. R0101-16-0054, WiseKB: Big data based self-evolving knowledge base and reasoning platform); the Bio & Medical Technology Development Program of the NRF funded by the Korean government, MSIP(2015M3A9A7029735).

References

Enrique Amigó, Julio Gonzalo, Javier Artiles, and Felisa Verdejo. 2009. A comparison of extrinsic clustering evaluation metrics based on formal constraints. *Information Retrieval*, 12(4):461–486.

Christian Bizer, Tom Heath, and Tim Berners-Lee. 2009. Linked Data - The story so far. *International Journal on Semantic Web and Information Systems*, 5(3):1–22.

Gong Cheng, Thanh Tran, and Yuzhong Qu. 2011. RELIN: Relatedness and informativeness-based centrality for entity summarization. In *Lecture Notes in Computer Science*, pages 114–129. Springer Berlin Heidelberg, Berlin, Heidelberg, October.

Christiane Fellbaum, editor. 1998. *WordNet - An Electronic Lexical Database*.

Kalpa Gunaratna, Krishnaprasad Thirunarayan, and Amit P. Sheth. 2015. Faces: Diversity-aware entity summarization using incremental hierarchical conceptual clustering. In Blai Bonet and Sven Koenig, editors, *AAAI*, pages 116–122. AAAI Press.

M. A. Wong J. A. Hartigan. 1979. Algorithm as 136: A k-means clustering algorithm. *Journal of the Royal Statistical Society. Series C (Applied Statistics)*, 28(1):100–108.

Jens Lehmann, Robert Isele, Max Jakob, Anja Jentzsch, Dimitris Kontokostas, Pablo N. Mendes, Sebastian Hellmann, Mohamed Morsey, Patrick van Kleef, Sören Auer, and Christian Bizer. 2014. DBpedia - a large-scale, multilingual knowledge base extracted from wikipedia. *Semantic Web Journal*.

David W. Mount, 2004. *Bioinformatics: Sequence and Genome Analysis*. Cold Spring Harbor Laboratory Press.

Andreas Thalhammer and Achim Rettinger. 2014. Browsing DBpedia entities with summaries. In *The Semantic Web: ESWC 2014 Satellite Events*, pages 511–515. Springer International Publishing, Cham, May.

Botta: An Arabic Dialect Chatbot

Dana Abu Ali and Nizar Habash
Computational Approaches to Modeling Language Lab
New York University Abu Dhabi, UAE
{daa389,nizar.habash}@nyu.edu

Abstract

This paper presents BOTTA, the first Arabic dialect chatbot. We explore the challenges of creating a conversational agent that aims to simulate friendly conversations using the Egyptian Arabic dialect. We present a number of solutions and describe the different components of the BOTTA chatbot. The BOTTA database files are publicly available for researchers working on Arabic chatbot technologies. The BOTTA chatbot is also publicly available for any users who want to chat with it online.

1 Introduction

Chatbots are conversational agents that are programmed to communicate with users through an intelligent conversation using a natural language. They range from simple systems that extract responses from databases when they match certain keywords to more sophisticated ones that use natural language processing (NLP) techniques. These conversational programs are commonly used for a variety of purposes from customer service and information acquisition to entertainment.

While chatbots remain English-dominated, the technology managed to spread successfully to other languages. The Arabic language is one of the under-represented languages in many NLP technologies, and chatbots are not an exception. The reason behind the slow progress in Arabic NLP is the complexity of the Arabic language, which comes with its set of challenges such as very rich morphology, high degree of ambiguity, common orthographic variations, and numerous dialects.

In this paper we present, BOTTA,[1] an Arabic dialect chatbot. BOTTA is a conversational companion that uses the commonly understood Egyptian Arabic (Cairene) dialect to simulate friendly conversation with users. To our knowledge, BOTTA is the first chatbot in an Arabic dialect. The BOTTA database files are publicly available for researchers working on Arabic chatbot technologies.[2] The BOTTA chatbot is also publicly available for any users who want to chat with it online.[3]

The rest of this paper is organized as follows. Next, we present related work in Section 2. We discuss the challenges for developing Arabic chatbots in Section 3. We then describe our approach and design decisions in some detail in Section 4 including presenting a conversation example and a preliminary user evaluation.

2 Related Work

As in many other NLP areas, there are two types of approaches to developing chatbots: using manually written rules (Wallace, 2003) or automatically learning conversational patterns from data (Shawar and Atwell, 2003; Sordoni et al., 2015; Li et al., 2016). Both approaches have some advantages and disadvantages. While manual rules allow more control over the language and persona of the chatbot, they are

[1]The name BOTTA (pronounced like but-ta) evokes the English word Bot as well as the Arabic friendly female nickname Batta (بطة), which can be translated as 'Ducky'.

[2]To obtain the BOTTA database files, go to http://camel.abudhabi.nyu.edu/resources/.

[3]To chat with BOTTA online, go to https://playground.pandorabots.com/en/clubhouse/ and search for 'Botta'. The current version (1.0) is under BotID dana33/botta.

Proceedings of COLING 2016, the 26th International Conference on Computational Linguistics: System Demonstrations, pages 208–212, Osaka, Japan, December 11-17 2016.

tedious to create and can be at times unnatural. Corpus-based techniques are challenged by the need to construct coherent personas using data created by different people. For BOTTA, we chose not to start with the corpus-based approach because we wanted to model certain aspects of the complexity of the Arabic language and address its challenges in a more controlled setting. We plan to make use of existing conversational corpora, such as Call Home Egyptian (Gadalla et al., 1997), in the future. But we are aware of many challenges: Call Home consists of recorded conversations between acquaintances, and BOTTA is supposed to talk to strangers; and not to mention that the speakers in Call Home vary in age and gender, while BOTTA is supposed to be a young woman. Another option is to get data from forums and Twitter, but the problem with that is that BOTTA will be borrowing different people's perspectives and personal opinions, which holds the risk of making her sound incoherent.

In the area of Arabic chatbots, little work has been done. Most notably, Shawar and Atwell (2004) developed a chatbot for question answering over Quranic text. Shawar (2011) described a question answering system focusing on the medical domain. Both of these efforts are in Standard Arabic (the first technically in Classical Arabic). AlHagbani and Khan (2016) discussed a number of challenges facing the development of an Arabic chatbot. They describe the challenges in detail but briefly describe the development of a simple chatbot.

In developing BOTTA, we make use of AIML (Artificial Intelligence Markup Language), a popular language used to represent dialogues as sets of patterns (inputs) and templates (outputs). ALICE, an award-winning free chatbot was created using AIML (Wallace, 2003). There are thousands of adaptations of ALICE made by botmasters who use her software as the base of their chatbots. One variation of ALICE is Rosie, a chatbot that was optimized for use on the Pandorabots online platform.[4] BOTTA aims to become the Rosie of Arabic dialects, providing future Arab botmasters with a base chatbot that contains basic greetings, general knowledge sets, and other useful features.

In the next section, we present a summary of the challenges we encountered developing BOTTA.

3 Arabic Natural Language Processing Challenges

The following are some of the main Arabic NLP challenges, with a focus on chatbots.

Dialectal Variation Arabic consists of a number of variants that are quite different from each other: Modern Standard Arabic (MSA), the official written and read language, and a number of dialects, the spoken forms of language (Habash, 2010). While MSA has official standard orthography and a relatively large number of resources, the various Arabic dialects have no standards and only a handful of resources. Dialects vary from MSA and each other in terms of phonology, morphology and lexicon. Dialects are not recognized as languages and not taught in schools in the Arab World. However, dialectal Arabic is commonly used in online chatting. This is why we find it more appropriate to focus on dialectal Arabic in the context of a chatbot. While BOTTA speaks in the Cairene Egyptian Arabic dialect, she recognizes common words and greetings in a number of other dialects.

Orthographic Ambiguity and Inconsistency Arabic orthography represents short vowels and consonantal doubling using optional diacritical marks, which most commonly are not included in the text. This results in a high rate of ambiguity. Furthermore, Arabic writers make very common mistakes in spelling a number of problematic letters such as Alif-Hamza forms and Ta-Marbuta (Zaghouani et al., 2014). The issue of orthography is exacerbated for Arabic dialects where no standard orthographies exist (Habash et al., 2012; Eskander et al., 2013).

Morphological Richness Arabic words are inflected for a large number of features such as gender, number, person, voices, aspect, etc., as well as accepting a number of attached clitics. In the context of a chatbot system this proves very challenging. Verbs, adjectives, and pronouns are all gender specific, which requires the chatbot to have two different systems of responses – one for male users and another for female users.

[4]http://www.pandorabots.com/.

Idiomatic Dialogue Expressions As with any other language, Arabic has its own set of unique idiomatic dialogue expressions. One common class of such expressions is the modified echo greeting responses, e.g., while the English greeting 'Good Morning' gets an echo response of 'Good Morning', the equivalent Arabic greeting صباح الخير *SbAH Alxyr*[5] 'lit. Morning of Goodness' gets a modified echo response of صباح النور *SbAH Alnwr* 'lit. Morning of Light'.

Because of all these challenges, an Arabic-speaking chatbot requires its unique databases, as opposed to a machine translation wrapper around an existing English-speaking chatbot.

Next, we discuss BOTTA's design and components.

4 Botta

BOTTA's persona is that of a friendly female chatbot, who aims to simulate conversation and connect with as many Arab users as she can. She is the first chatbot that converses in an Arabic dialect, which supports her purpose of entertaining users who are accustomed to chatting in the dialect. We created BOTTA using AIML and launched it on the Pandorabots platform. BOTTA's knowledge base is made up of AIML files that store the categories containing its responses to the user inputs, set files of themed words and phrases, and map files that pair up related words and phrases.

4.1 AIML Files

The main file here is the greetings file, which divides the basic greetings in a number of Arabic dialects into categories. The templates, or responses, in these categories also contain questions that allow BOTTA to learn basic information about the user, such as age, gender, and nationality. BOTTA retrieves that information when needed, such as when formulating gender-inflected responses. Another AIML file stores BOTTA's bio, explaining her background to users and asking them questions about themselves in return to maintain conversations. Other AIML files are linked to map and set files, which will be discussed next. The categories in the AIML files have certain patterns that would initiate the extraction of information from the other files.

4.2 Set Files

Sets in AIML are simple lists that are used to store words and phrases that fall under one theme. BOTTA has been equipped with certain lists that provide her with some general knowledge, which she can use to continue the conversation and entertain users. Some of these sets have been directly translated from Rosie's sets, such as the countries' set. Other sets have been modified according to what is used in Arabic dialects. For example, months in Arabic have different names depending on the regional dialect; therefore, BOTTA has separate sets of months based on each dialect it recognizes. BOTTA also has unique sets, storing dialectal bad language that offend her, words that indicate the dialect of the users, and other regional knowledge.

4.3 Map Files

Maps in AIML are lists of key-value pairs that are used to relate words to certain words and phrases. Keys in maps should be stored in sets for the mapping to work. Sets and maps have to be called within the AIML files; otherwise, they remain idle in the chatbot memory. BOTTA has a `nation2capital` map, a translated version from the same Rosie file. BOTTA also has the `word2proverb map`, which allows her to generate a funny Arabic dialect proverb when she matches on a word but does not understand the phrase. One of the most important maps BOTTA has is the `name2gender` map, which is used to determine the user's gender, and thus the gender-inflected responses. AIML files are used to activate sets and maps. One example of this is the `guessingthegender.aiml` file, which would be used when a user provides BOTTA with a name. BOTTA searches for the name in the `names.set`; if the name is found, she searches for the corresponding gender in the `name2gender.map` file. After confirming

[5] Arabic transliteration is presented in the Habash-Soudi-Buckwalter scheme (Habash et al., 2007) .

Figure 1: A sample conversation between a user (U) and BOTTA (B).

the guessed gender with the user, BOTTA sets the gender variable and starts using the correct gender-inflected responses during the conversation. If the name is not found in the `names.set` file, BOTTA asks for that information from the user instead – see the example conversation in Figure 1, where BOTTA does not recognize the user's name.

4.4 Orthography Handling

In BOTTA, we use orthographic normalization to overcome the inconsistent spelling variations of certain characters. Some of the changes we made were borrowed from the Conventional Orthography of Dialectal Arabic (Habash et al., 2012), which is an internally consistent and coherent convention for writing dialectal Arabic. While BOTTA does not use normalized text in its responses, changing user inputs to that form enhances the matching liklihood. Rosie uses this technique for reductions and contractions. BOTTA performs the following orthographic transformations:

- The word-final Alif-Maqsura letter ى *ý* is often used in Egypt to write word-final Ya ي *y*, and vice versa (Eskander et al., 2013). In BOTTA, we change every Alif-Maqsura to Ya.
- We change every Ta-Marbuta ة *ħ* to Ha ه *h*, since these two letters are often confused in word-final positions.
- The misspelling of the Alif-Hamza forms (أ Â, إ Ǎ and ا A) is the most common spelling mistake in Arabic, with a 38.5% frequency rate (Eskander et al., 2013). We normalize all Alif-Hamza forms (أ Â, إ Ǎ) to bare Alif (ا A).

By performing the above-mentioned transformations, BOTTA's pattern matching will be able to overcome 85.1% of the spelling mistakes found in spontaneous Arabic typing (Eskander et al., 2013).

4.5 Preliminary User Evaluation

We asked three native Arabic speakers to chat with BOTTA and evaluate the naturalness of the conversation. Two of them are native Egyptian Arabic speakers, and one is a Levantine Arabic speaker. They all agreed that they found her entertaining and wanted the conversation to last longer. They commented that her Egyptian Arabic sounds authentic. Not being informed of BOTTA's purpose beforehand, they all guessed that she was created to carry out a conversation and not perform tasks. They pointed out that she gets repetitive sometimes, and makes out-of-context statements. Their suggestions include having her talk about herself more, asking the user more questions, and leading the conversation by introducing new topics.

5 Conclusions and Future Work

We have presented BOTTA, the first Arabic dialect chatbot and described the challenges and some solutions to building chatbots in Arabic. The BOTTA files are publicly available for researchers working on Arabic chatbot technologies. In the future, we plan to enhance BOTTA's pattern matching using corpus-based machine learning techniques. Further development will also include exploiting existing tools for Egyptian Arabic processing (Pasha et al., 2014) to perform morphological analysis on the input and to experiment with lemma-based pattern matching.

References

Eman Saad AlHagbani and Muhammad Badruddin Khan. 2016. Challenges facing the development of the Arabic chatbot. In *First International Workshop on Pattern Recognition*, pages 100110Y–100110Y. International Society for Optics and Photonics.

Ramy Eskander, Nizar Habash, Owen Rambow, and Nadi Tomeh. 2013. Processing Spontaneous Orthography. In *Proceedings of the 2013 Conference of the North American Chapter of the Association for Computational Linguistics: Human Language Technologies (NAACL-HLT)*, Atlanta, GA.

Hassan Gadalla, Hanaa Kilany, Howaida Arram, Ashraf Yacoub, Alaa El-Habashi, Amr Shalaby, Krisjanis Karins, Everett Rowson, Robert MacIntyre, Paul Kingsbury, David Graff, and Cynthia McLemore. 1997. CALLHOME Egyptian Arabic Transcripts. In *Linguistic Data Consortium, Philadelphia.*

Nizar Habash, Abdelhadi Soudi, and Tim Buckwalter. 2007. On Arabic Transliteration. In A. van den Bosch and A. Soudi, editors, *Arabic Computational Morphology: Knowledge-based and Empirical Methods*. Springer.

Nizar Habash, Mona Diab, and Owen Rabmow. 2012. Conventional Orthography for Dialectal Arabic. In *Proceedings of LREC*, Istanbul, Turkey.

Nizar Habash. 2010. *Introduction to Arabic Natural Language Processing*. Morgan & Claypool Publishers.

Jiwei Li, Michel Galley, Chris Brockett, Jianfeng Gao, and Bill Dolan. 2016. A persona-based neural conversation model. *arXiv preprint arXiv:1603.06155.*

Arfath Pasha, Mohamed Al-Badrashiny, Ahmed El Kholy, Ramy Eskander, Mona Diab, Nizar Habash, Manoj Pooleery, Owen Rambow, and Ryan Roth. 2014. MADAMIRA: A Fast, Comprehensive Tool for Morphological Analysis and Disambiguation of Arabic. In *In Proceedings of LREC*, Reykjavik, Iceland.

Bayan Abu Shawar and Eric Atwell. 2003. Using dialogue corpora to train a chatbot. In *Proceedings of the Corpus Linguistics 2003 conference*, pages 681–690.

Abu Shawar and ES Atwell. 2004. An Arabic chatbot giving answers from the Qur'an. In *Proceedings of TALN04: XI Conference sur le Traitement Automatique des Langues Naturelles*, volume 2, pages 197–202. ATALA.

Bayan Abu Shawar. 2011. A chatbot as a natural web interface to Arabic web qa. *iJET*, 6(1):37–43.

Alessandro Sordoni, Michel Galley, Michael Auli, Chris Brockett, Yangfeng Ji, Margaret Mitchell, Jian-Yun Nie, Jianfeng Gao, and Bill Dolan. 2015. A neural network approach to context-sensitive generation of conversational responses. *arXiv preprint arXiv:1506.06714.*

Richard Wallace. 2003. The elements of AIML style. *Alice AI Foundation.*

Wajdi Zaghouani, Behrang Mohit, Nizar Habash, Ossama Obeid, Nadi Tomeh, Alla Rozovskaya, Noura Farra, Sarah Alkuhlani, and Kemal Oflazer. 2014. Large scale Arabic error annotation: Guidelines and framework. In *LREC*, pages 2362–2369.

What's up on Twitter? Catch up with TWIST!

Marina Litvak and **Natalia Vanetik** and **Efi Levi** and **Michael Roistacher**
Department of Software Engineering
Sami Shamoon College of Engineering
Beer Sheva, Israel
{marinal,natalyav}@sce.ac.il
{efilvefi,mikiroistacher}@gmail.com

Abstract

Event detection and analysis with respect to public opinion and sentiment in social media is a broad and well-addressed research topic. However, the characteristics and sheer volume of noisy Twitter messages make this a difficult task. This demonstration paper describes a TWItter event Summarizer and Trend detector (TWIST) system for event detection, visualization, textual description, and geo-sentiment analysis of real-life events reported in Twitter.

1 Introduction

Twitter grows rapidly. Efficient, accurate, and scalable real-time analysis of Twitter content is in demand and requires integration of sophisticated approaches for natural language processing, signal processing, and more. Instead of considering single tweets, Twitter events[1] are detected and analysed in many existing approaches (Becker et al., 2011; Long et al., 2011; Weng and Lee, 2011; Cordeiro, 2012; Osborne et al., 2014; Preotiuc-Pietro et al., 2012). Our method is directed toward *unspecified event detection*, where an event has not been previously identified. Because no prior information is available, the classic approach to detection of such events exploits temporal bursts of Twitter stream features such as *hashtags* and specific words. TWIST defines an event as a collection of hashtags and extends the Event Detection with Clustering of Wavelet-based Signals (EDCoW) algorithm of Weng and Lee (2011) by performing an additional text analysis of tweets. This extension enables TWIST to distinguish between events that occur at the same time and share similar wavelet signals, but have a different content. After events are detected, each event can be summarized using both internal content from Twitter, and external sources. Finally, all detected events are analysed by their sentiment distribution over a world map, and visualized in the resolution of countries. This feature enables the TWIST user to see whether and how the geolocation of Twitter users affects their opinions, and how the sentiments and opinions regarding the same political or other event can be different over different countries. TWIST utilizes unsupervised learning for most of its stages, except sentiment analysis. TWIST does not rely on external ontologies. It incoporates external sources, automatically retrieved, for summarizing events. Also, TWIST detects geolocation of event-related tweets (and not geolocation of events) and visualizes their sentiments on a map. TWIST architecture is flexible, its implementaion uses the JavaScript Object Notation (JSON) format for the processed data that enables other domains to be easily integrated. All this makes TWIST convenient for a potentially wide range of users, from private individuals and businesses, to data scientists and other professionals dealing with different kinds of data analysis.

2 System description

Our system is written in C#, as a standalone application, and it uses a MySQL database. The system (see Figure 1) is composed of several modules that are described below.

2.1 The Twitter stream

The dataset object of analysis is retrieved using the Twitter streaming API that, using the default access level, returns a random sample of all public tweets. This access level provides a small proportion of

[1]A Twitter event is a collection of tweets and re-tweets that discuss the same subject in a relatively short (minutes, hours or days) time period.

Proceedings of COLING 2016, the 26th International Conference on Computational Linguistics: System Demonstrations, pages 213–217, Osaka, Japan, December 11-17 2016.

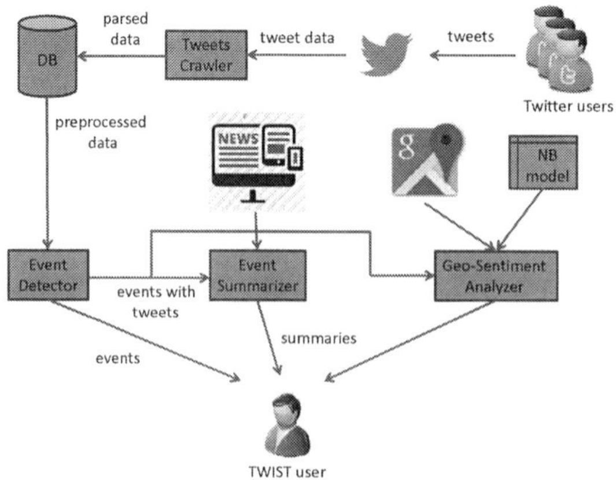

Figure 1: Data flow of TWIST.

all public tweets (1%). The data are returned in JSON, as a set of documents, one per tweet. Given the average number of 140 million tweets sent per day in Twitter, the size of the data retrieved by the streaming API in a 24 hour time span is roughly 1,400,000 tweets. The 140 character limit of tweets gives an expected data stream of 196 MBytes per day or 2269 bytes per second. The Tweets Crawler uses Tweetinvi[2] to retrieve tweets data and store it in a database. We are mainly interested in hashtags, as an explicit annotation of a tweet's main theme.

2.2 Event detector

This component detects events by operating hashtag wavelets, following three stages of the EDCoW algorithm enumerated below, and integrated with text analysis. The system enables a user to follow after the evolution of the event detection process by visualizing the results of each simple stage. The configuration file enables a user to set multiple parameters of the event detector, such as time period to work on, sampling time interval, and the hashtag minimal count threshold.

Wavelet analysis

A wavelet is a wave-like oscillation with an amplitude that begins at zero, increases, and then decreases back to zero. The EDCoW algorithm detects events by grouping a set of hashtags with similar burst patterns. This algorithm has three components: (1) signal construction, (2) filtering and cross-correlation computation, and (3) graph partitioning.

The **first** stage of the EDCoW algorithm constructs a signal for each individual hashtag that appears in tweets, using its *tf-idf* values. The **second** part of signal processing builds the smooth signal with the help of a sliding window that covers a number of initial sample points. We use the Savitzky-Golay filter (Press and Teukolsky, 1990). After autocorrelation is computed, irrelevant signals (with low values) are discarded, thereby efficiently eliminating noise from the meaningful data. The values of cross-correlation (similarity) for the remaining signals are stored in a matrix. Correlation values that are too low are set to zero[3]. The **third** stage of the algorithm views event detection as a graph-partitioning problem for a weighted graph whose adjacency matrix is the wavelet cross-correlation matrix. TWIST uses the Girvin-Newman algorithm (2006). After modularity-based graph partitioning (third stage), the clusters of hashtag wavelets representing events are displayed to the user. TWIST extends the EDCoW algorithm by analysing the textual content of tweets. The latter requires text pre-processing that is performed on all collected tweets before they are stored in a database and then analysed.

Text preprocessing

We perform the following preprocessing steps for each collected tweet: (1) tokenization, (2) part-of-speech tagging and filtering, (3) stop-words removal, and (4) stemming for remaining words (Porter, 1980). The result of preprocesing is a collection of normalized terms and hashtags, linked to their tweets. The frequency-based statistics (term frequency–inverse document frequency) are then calculated

[2]A Twitter C# library `https://tweetinvi.codeplex.com/`

[3]TWIST uses *median value* as a boundary in both cases

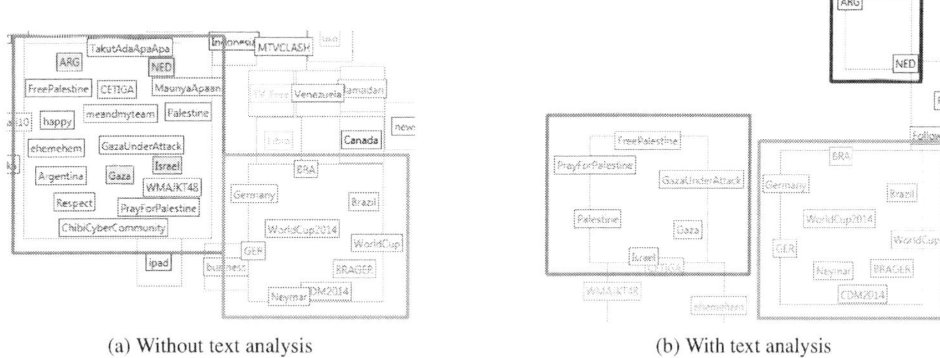

(a) Without text analysis (b) With text analysis

Figure 2: Events detected by TWIST

and also stored in our database.

Text similarity analysis for better event detection

Our system extends the third stage of the EDCoW algorithm by integrating a text similarity knowledge between tweets into a graph representation. The motivation behind this idea was dictated by a possible situation where two or more unrelated events evolve at the same time, following the same burst pattern. In such a case, a wavelet analysis will not distinguish between these events, and only analysing the *content* of tweets may point to the differences between them.

In TWIST, the weights on graph edges are calculated as a weighted linear combination of cross-correlation values computed during the second stage, together with *textual similarity* scores for every pair of signals. Every signal is represented by the texts of all tweets belonging to it. TWIST enables the end user to choose between two classic metrics for textual similarity–Jaccard and cosine similarity. Given a cross-correlation score cc_{ij} and a similarity score sim_{ij} between signals i and j, the weight on edge between signal nodes is computed as $w_{ij} = \alpha \times cc_{ij} + (1 - \alpha) \times sim_{ij}$, where $0 \leq \alpha \leq 1$ is a system parameter. Figure 2 shows different clusters, representing events, that were detected without taking tweet text into account (by using hashtag wavelets only), and with analysis of tweets.

2.3 Event summarizer

This module enables a user to obtain a summary of an event of interest. A user can choose to see either an *internal profile* for the selected event, which includes the most salient hashtags, keywords, and tweets, or an *external profile* that contains sentences from the most salient external links mentioned in tweets. The module enables a user to configure multiple internal parameters that affect the summary quality. The summarization approach in both cases follows a strictly extractive principle, as being most appropriate for the Twitter domain, both in terms of accuracy and efficiency. We used two state-of-the-art algorithms in the summarization process – TextRank (Mihalcea and Tarau, 2004) and Lingo (Osiski et al., 2004) – for text ranking and clustering, respectively. The following subsections describe adaptation of those algorithms in our system.

2.3.1 Internal profile

The internal profile is built from the most salient hashtags, keywords, and tweets. The tweets with the highest PageRank score are retrieved from a weighted tweets graph, with nodes standing for tweets, according to the TextRank method. A tweets graph is built on the tweets that are filtered by length and keywords coverage in order to reduce graphs size and TextRank processing time. Hashtags are considered as extremely important keywords and give a higher impact to a coverage score. A similarity between tweets for weighting the graphs edges can be calculated by either Jaccard similarity between sets of tweets terms or cosine similarity between their tf-idf vectors. The keywords and hashtags are ranked by their *tf-idf* score and the top-ranked ones are extracted.

2.3.2 External profile

The external profile of the detected event is compiled by extracted parts from the relevant external sources. This profile is created in TWIST by (1) retrieving the relevant sources; (2) preprocessing and ranking relevant sources; and (3) summarizing the top-ranked sources.

The relevant sources for each detected event are retrieved by collecting, analyzing, and filtering links appearing in tweets. The sources that do not contain enough meaningful text are filtered. Then, the document graph, with nodes standing for sources and edges for lexical similarity between them, is built, and the eigenvalue centrality is computed. For final ranking of external sources, their eigenvalue centrality, the keyword coverage, and link frequency counts are used.

The summarization is performed by (1) selecting theme sentences, and then (2) ranking and selecting theme sentences into a summary. We consider theme to be a group of lexically similar sentences, and retrieve all event-related themes by a clustering of sentences collected from relevant sources. We use the Lingo clustering algorithm that, in addition to clusters, also provides a label and a score for each cluster. Then, given clusters, we select theme sentences closest to cluster centroids as representatives of their clusters. A summary that describes the detected event must cover as many its important themes as possible. Given theme sentences, we rank them using the TextRank approach–an undirected graph of sentences with the lexical similarity relationships is built from event theme sentences, and the PageRank algorithm is applied to find sentence scores–and compile a summary from the top-ranked sentences.

2.4 Geo-sentiment analyser

The geo-sentiment analyser is the only module of TWIST that needs annotated data for supervised learning. It uses the NaiveBayes algorithm, as one of the most simple and reliable classification methods for textual data. The textual data is preprocessed and represented in a bag-of-words format, per tweet. Each bag is labeled by a particular detected event (event detector output) and country (we filter out tweets that lack geolocation data). Then a trained model[4] of NaiveBayes is used for a sentiment classification of tweets, and the resulting statistics are displayed on the world map. A user can choose to see majority sentiment, with corresponding color, and full distribution statistics for the event of interest. We use the Google GeoChart API for a map visualization.

3 Pilot study and experiments

We performed a pilot study over a two day period, during which $7,549,339$ tweets, published between 08/07/14 24:00 and 10/07/14 24:00, and covering 95889 hashtags, were collected. The data collection fell during the period of the Football World Cup 2014 and the Israeli Protective Edge Operation in Gaza (Wikipedia, 2014). There is a need to stress that we collected tweets only until midnight, so it is likely that we collected only partial events (for instance, the football game between Argentina and Holland took place in the late hours of the evening, and, therefore, only some of the tweets about the game were collected).

Using pure wavelet similarity according to the EDCoW algorithm resulted in inaccurate event detection, when different unrelated events mistakenly fell into the same category. As an example, signals related to the football game between Holland and Argentina fell in the same cluster with signals hashtagged by Gaza. The system detected one event perfectly–the World Cup 2014. The clique contains BRA, GER, WorldCup2014, Brazil, and similar hashtags. However, the Protective Edge Operation event was not detected. After the text analysis component was activated, Gaza and World Cup 2014 were detected as separate unrelated events. The Protective Edge Operation event is detected properly. The event contains hashtags such as PrayForPalestine, GazaUnderAttack, and FreePalestine. The demo video of TWIST demonstrates its usage in the demo mode, on the data described above, with results for all stages, including: event detection, summarization of main events, and their geo-sentiment analysis. The video can be found here: `https://youtu.be/JH4-YU8mL9A`. One can also run TWIST in a regular mode, where a new data will be collected and analysed in a real time.

The accuracy of NaiveBayes classifier for the sentiment classification was evaluated on the Sentiment140 dataset and resulted in 76%, using 10-fold cross validation. The experimental results for the TextRank summarizer can be found in its original paper (Mihalcea and Tarau, 2004). The improvement in event detection, using text analysis, was determined by human evaluation during our pilot study. It takes approximately one minute for TWIST to analyse over 7 million tweets.

[4]trained on the Sentiment140 dataset (`http://www.sentiment140.com`)

4 Conclusions and future work

In this work we present a system we call TWIST, which aims at detecting and describing events in Twitter during a pre-defined period of time. TWIST extends the EDCoW algorithm by Weng and Lee (2011) by text analysis of tweets. As a pilot study showed, the proposed extensions improve the quality of event detection. Also, TWIST applies summarization techniques for describing the detected events and performs their geo-sentiment analysis.

In future, we intend to experiment with more sophisticated summarization techniques and methods for linking news to Twitter events (see (Guo et al., 2013)). Also, we plan to evaluate TWIST performance using human evaluations.

Acknowledgments

We want to thank Daniel Miles, Dror Binder, and Shahar Sabag for their contribution to TWIST implementation and support.

References

Hila Becker, Mor Naaman, and Luis Gravano. 2011. Beyond trending topics: Real-world event identification on twitter. *ICWSM*, 11:438–441.

Mário Cordeiro. 2012. Twitter event detection: Combining wavelet analysis and topic inference summarization. In *Doctoral Symposium on Informatics Engineering, DSIE*.

Weiwei Guo, Hao Li, Heng Ji, and Mona Diab. 2013. Linking tweets to news: A framework to enrich short text data in social media. In *Proceedings of the 51st Annual Meeting of the Association for Computational Linguistics*, pages 239–249.

Rui Long, Haofen Wang, Yuqiang Chen, Ou Jin, and Yong Yu. 2011. Towards effective event detection, tracking and summarization on microblog data. In *Web-Age Information Management*, pages 652–663. Springer.

Rada Mihalcea and Paul Tarau. 2004. Textrank: Bringing order into texts. In *Proceedings of the Conference on Empirical Methods in Natural Language Processing (EMNLP)*.

Mark EJ Newman. 2006. Modularity and community structure in networks. *Proceedings of the National Academy of Sciences*, 103(23):8577–8582.

M. Osborne, S. Moran, R. Mccreadie, A. Von Lunen, M. Sykora, E. Cano, N. Ireson, C. Macdonald, I. Ounis, Y. He, T. Jackson, F. Ciravegna, , and A. OBrien. 2014. Real-time detection, tracking, and monitoring of automatically discovered events in social media. In *52nd Annual Meeting of the Association for Computational Linguistics: System Demonstrations*, pages 37–42.

Stanisaw Osiski, Jerzy Stefanowski, and Dawid Weiss. 2004. Lingo: Search results clustering algorithm based on singular value decomposition. In *Advances in Soft Computing, Intelligent Information Processing and Web Mining, Proceedings of the International IIS: IIPWM04 Conference*, pages 359–368.

M.F. Porter. 1980. An algorithm for suffix stripping. *Program*, 14(3):130137.

Daniel Preotiuc-Pietro, Sina Samangooei, Trevor Cohn, Nicholas Gibbins, and Mahesan Niranjan. 2012. Trendminer: An architecture for real time analysis of social media text. In *Workshop on Real-Time Analysis and Mining of Social Streams (RAMSS), International AAAI Conference on Weblogs and Social Media (ICWSM)*.

William H Press and Saul A Teukolsky. 1990. Savitzky-golay smoothing filters. *Computers in Physics*, 4(6):669–672.

Jianshu Weng and Bu-Sung Lee. 2011. Event detection in twitter. *ICWSM*, 11:401–408.

Wikipedia. 2014. Protective edge operation. `http://en.wikipedia.org/wiki/2014_IsraelGaza_conflict`.

Praat on the Web: An Upgrade of Praat for Semi-Automatic Speech Annotation

Mónica Domínguez, Iván Latorre,
Mireia Farrús, Joan Codina-Filbà
Universitat Pompeu Fabra,
C. Roc Boronat, 138
08018 Barcelona, Spain
monica.dominguez|ivan.latorre|
mireia.farrus|joan.codina@upf.edu

Leo Wanner
ICREA and Universitat Pompeu Fabra,
Barcelona, Spain
leo.wanner@upf.edu

Abstract

This paper presents an implementation of the widely used speech analysis tool Praat as a web application with an extended functionality for feature annotation. In particular, Praat on the Web addresses some of the central limitations of the original Praat tool and provides (i) enhanced visualization of annotations in a dedicated window for feature annotation at interval and point segments, (ii) a dynamic scripting composition exemplified with a modular prosody tagger, and (iii) portability and an operational web interface. Speech annotation tools with such a functionality are key for exploring large corpora and designing modular pipelines.

1 Motivation and Background

Automatic annotation of speech often involves dealing with linguistic and acoustic information that needs to be conveniently organized at different levels of segmentation (i.e., phonemes, syllables, words, phrases, sentences, etc.). Even though laboratory experiments on speech are controlled to a certain extent (e.g., minimal word pairs, short sentences, read speech) and are usually annotated manually, the increasing trend to analyze spontaneous speech, especially in human-machine interaction, requires tools to facilitate semi-automatic annotation tasks with a compact visualization for manual revision, presentation of results and versatile scripting capabilities.

The Praat software (Boersma, 2001) is one of the most widely used open-source tools for audio signal processing and annotation in the speech community. Praat has a dedicated text format called *TextGrid*, where stackable lines, called *tiers*, are mapped to the whole time-stamp of the associated sound file (cf. Figure 1). Accordingly, tiers account for the temporal nature of speech and take one compulsory parameter: the time-stamp of the *segments*, which are the smallest unit in a TextGrid. A time-stamp can be of two kinds: an interval (specifying the beginning and end time of each segment) or a point in time. This sequence of time-stamps is encoded in tiers as consecutive segments. Once (interval or point) segments are marked, they can take an optional string parameter, called *label*.

While suitable for a coarse-grained glance at the acoustic profile of speech, Praat shows two major limitations when it comes to more detailed annotation that also involves linguistic information. Firstly, Praat's segment annotations are opaque blocks of strings, and there is no function for a linguistic analysis of the labels. For instance, if an interval segment for the word *places* (as in the example shown in Figure 1) includes morphological information within the same label (e.g., "places: noun = plural"), there is no function in Praat that would allow the division of the string *places: noun = plural* into tokens of any kind, for example, *places — noun — plural*. Secondly, Praat is not modular, i.e., all automatic routines a user is interested in (e.g., detection of silent and voiced parts, annotation of intensity peaks and valleys, computing relative values, etc.) must be programmed together in a single script. No user need-driven composition of stand-alone off-the-shelf scripts for dedicated subroutines is possible, which implies that for any new constellation of the subroutines a new script must be programmed.

Proceedings of COLING 2016, the 26th International Conference on Computational Linguistics: System Demonstrations, pages 218–222, Osaka, Japan, December 11-17 2016.

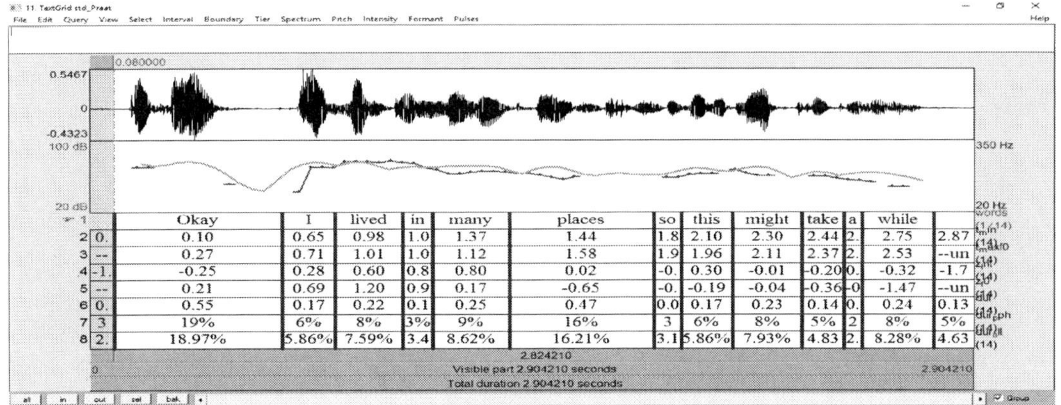

Figure 1: Standard Praat visualization:Annotation using tiers.

In order to remedy these limitations, advanced users have found workarounds. Thus, the first limitation is remedied by either extracting information to an external file, as ProsodyPro (Xu, 2013) does, or by annotating in parallel tiers with cloned time segments and different labels, as shown in Figure 1. To circumvent the second limitation, experienced users tend to program in external platforms and call Praat for performing specific speech processing routines. For example, Praaline (Christodoulides, 2014) extracts acoustic information from Praat for analysis in the R statistic package (R Core Team, 2013) and visualization in the Sonic visualizer (Cannam et al., 2010). However, these workarounds make the use of Praat cumbersome.

The Praat on the Web tool presented in this paper aims to address the aforementioned Praat limitations. More precisely, it upgrades Praat along the lines observed in state-of-the-art natural language processing (NLP) annotation interfaces as encountered for SEMAFOR[1] (Tsatsaronis et al., 2012), Brat[2] (Stenetorp et al., 2012), or GATE[3] (Cunningham et al., 2011). Such an upgrade is instrumental for prosody studies, among other, which are described as a combination of features (not only acoustic, but also linguistic) and therefore benefit greatly from a versatile semi-automatic approach to annotation and a compact visualization of those features.

Praat on the Web involves three main technical aspects: (i) a multidimensional feature vector within segment labels (see Figure 2 for illustration), (ii) a web-based implementation, and (iii) an operational interface for modular script composition exemplified as a prosody tagger. Given that many Praat scripts are freely available and shared in the speech community for different specialized tasks, one of the advantages of modular scripting within the same platform is keeping a library of scripts for easy replacement of independent subtasks within a larger pipeline. The dynamic composition approach presented in this paper, thus, promotes tests on how different configurations affect the final output of the architecture, and positively impacts reproducibility of experiments in a user-friendly web environment.

Praat on the Web is available for extended feature annotation, but compatible with the original Praat format, as a web application[4] and as a local version;[5] source code and all scripts mentioned in this paper as well as a tutorial are available in a Github account.[6] and distributed under a GNU General Public Licence.[7]

[1]http://www.cs.cmu.edu/ ark/SEMAFOR/
[2]http://brat.nlplab.org/
[3]https://gate.ac.uk/
[4]http://kristina.taln.upf.edu/praatweb/
[5]implemented for Praat v.6.0.11
[6]https://github.com/monikaUPF
[7]http://www.gnu.org/licenses/

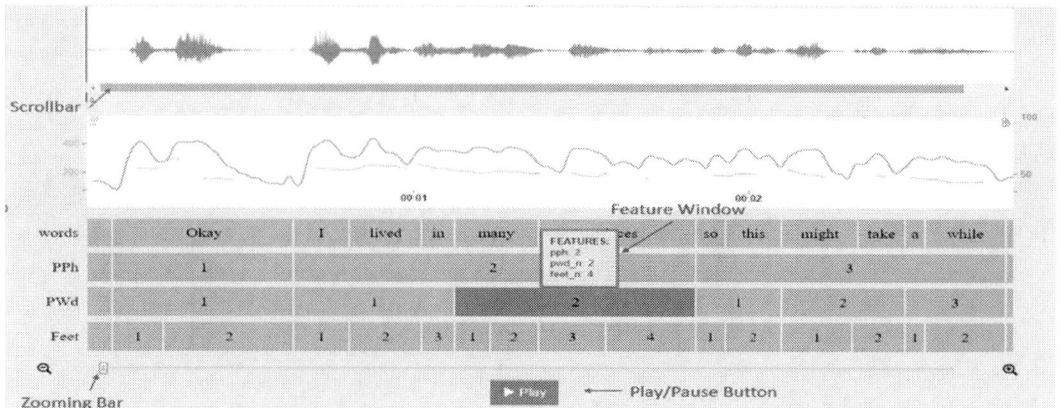

Figure 2: Praat on the Web's visual enhancement of the standard Praat.

2 Annotating in parallel tiers versus using features

Annotations in tiers are convenient for studying nested elements in the speech signal. For example, Selkirk (1984) proposes a hierarchical structure of intonation where smaller units (e.g., prosodic feet) are embedded in larger ones (e.g., prosodic words and prosodic phrases), as Figure 2 shows. However, if each layer needs to be annotated in stacked tiers with cloned times as previously shown in Figure 1, a long collection of repeated tiers for each new layer information blurs visual presentation and makes manual revision tasks harder.

Praat on the Web's main menu on our webpage includes a first demo (accessible by clicking on the button "Enter Demo 1"), where the user can upload their own audio and TextGrid files for visualization and playback. Sample files with feature annotations, which can serve as inspiration or examples, are also provided in the demo. Waveform, fundamental frequency (F0) and intensity curves are displayed on the screen together with the annotated tiers. There are some practical differences with respect to the standard Praat, which are summarized in Table 1. Whereas standard Praat uses keyboard commands to perform actions during annotation such as zooming and playback, Praat on the Web has dedicated buttons for these actions, as illustrated in Figure 2.

Action	Standard Praat	Praat on Web
Zooming	keyboard shortcuts (ctrl+i/o/n)	sliding bar signaled with amplifying glass symbol
Audio playback	shift button or segment + time bar click	play/pause button or segment + waveform click
Scroll left/right	scrollbar below TextGrid	scrollbar below waveform

Table 1: Comparison: actions in standard Prat and Praat on Web.

Further demonstration of visualization capabilities using automatic scripts for merging tiers and splitting features (Demos 3 and 4 respectively) are also available in the online demo webpage. Users can upload their own cloned TextGrids entering Demo 3 and click on the 'run' button to automatically annotate selected cloned tiers as features. In Demo 4, this action is reversed, i.e., feature vectors are converted to cloned tiers. All TextGrids generated in Praat on the Web are displayed in the browser and can also be downloaded for local use clicking on the "Download" button.

3 Dynamic Scripting Composition

Entering Demo 2 through the main menu of Praat on the Web, an example of dynamic scripting composition can be run on available samples or uploaded files. The configuration of the automatic prosody tagger[8] appears in the right part of the screen (see Figures 3 and 4). The pipeline varies depending on

[8]Further information on the prosody tagger' methodology, technical specifications and evaluation is provided in Domínguez et al. (2016).

the selected configuration.

The prosody tagger is made up of a total of eight modules, three of which (from Module 1 to 3) are common for the two possible configurations:

1. Word segments (see Figure 3): when clicking on this button, six modules will appear in the "Selected modules" box. Modules 5 and 6 predict boundaries and prominence respectively on both acoustic information annotated in Modules 1 to 3 and word segments exported by Module 4. A TextGrid with the word alignment needs to be provided to run this configuration.

2. Raw speech (see Figure 4): when clicking on this button, five modules will appear in the "Selected modules" box. Prediction is performed on acoustic information and thus, Module 4 is not in the pipeline and alternative Modules 5 and 6 are chosen for this pipeline.

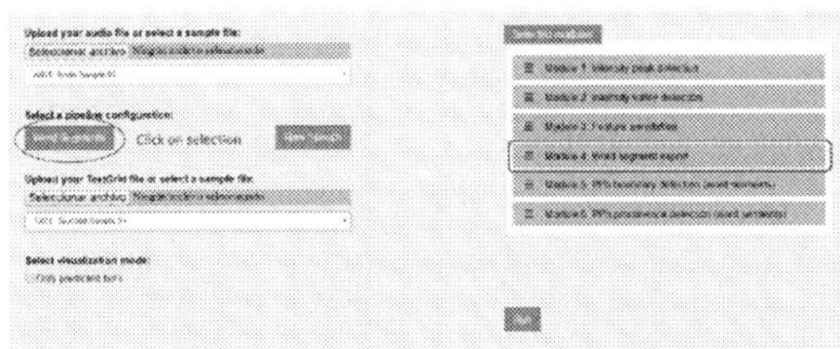

Figure 3: Configuration with word segments.

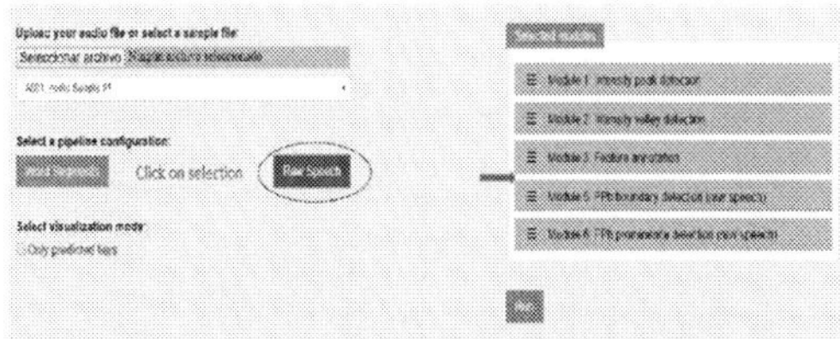

Figure 4: Configuration for raw speech.

The users can select in the web interface the output of the prosody tagger by ticking the option "only predicted tiers" displayed at the bottom left side of the screen. If that option is not ticked, all tiers generated by each module are shown. The output of the tagger (including annotated features of each segment) is displayed on screen in the browser; it can also be downloaded in TextGrid format for local use.

A further add-on of Praat on the Web is that includes a centralized repository of scripts and data. The action of selecting modules for the sample prosody tagger has been scripted in this demonstration to be automatically done, and the web interface allows moving around modules to prove that modules are also manually interchangeable.

4 Conclusions

We have presented the tool Praat on the Web, which aims to take speech annotations to meet the increasingly demanding requirements in the field of speech technologies. In such a scenario, user-friendly semi-automatic annotation tools within one versatile common platform are key to make steady progress in the study of complex events, like prosody, over large amounts of data. Praat on the Web shows several advantages over standard Praat in that it offers: (i) intuitive visualization of segment annotations using features displayed in a dedicated window; (ii) easy modularity of computational tasks within the same Praat platform; (iii) ready-to-use web environment with no pre-installation requirements for presentation of results. The two first characteristics are achieved including functionality for feature annotation. Consequently, the smallest unit in a Praat TextGrid is no longer an opaque string label, but a well-structured linguistic unit containing a *head*, a *feature name* and a *feature value*.

At the time of publication, Praat on the Web runs with sample or uploaded files for visualization, playback and automatic prediction of PPh boundaries and prominence. In the future, user account management will be introduced for researchers to upload their scripts and create their own pipeline configurations. The web interface is well-suited for annotation and demos (like this one) and teaching purposes; we also plan to extend it with online edition of manual annotations.

Praat on the Web is a first step in the transformation of speech annotation tools to meet the standards already set in other branches of computational linguistics. A move in this direction is especially needed for integrative research and reproducibility that require user-friendly tools for designing automatic processes with enhanced visualization capabilities.

Acknowledgements

This work is part of the KRISTINA project, which has received funding from the *European Unions Horizon 2020 Research and Innovation Programme* under the Grant Agreement number H2020-RIA-645012. It has been also partly supported by the Spanish Ministry of Economy and Competitiveness under the Maria de Maeztu Units of Excellence Programme (MDM-2015-0502). The third author is partially funded by the Spanish Ministry of Economy and Competitivity through the *Juan de la Cierva* program.

References

P. Boersma. 2001. Praat, a system for doing phonetics by computer. *Glot International*, 5(9/10):341–345.

C. Cannam, C. Landone, and M. Sandler. 2010. Sonic visualiser: An open source application for viewing, analysing, and annotating music audio files. In *Proceedings of the ACM Multimedia 2010 International Conference*, pages 1467–1468, Firenze, Italy, October.

G. Christodoulides. 2014. Praaline: Integrating tools for speech corpus research. In *Proceedings of the 9th International Conference on Language Resources and Evaluation*, Reykjavik, Iceland.

H. Cunningham, D. Maynard, K. Bontcheva, V. Tablan, N. Aswani, I. Roberts, G. Gorrell, A. Funk, A. Roberts, D. Damljanovic, T. Heitz, M. A. Greenwood, H. Saggion, v Petrak, Y. Li, and W. Peters. 2011. *Text Processing with GATE (Version 6).*

M. Domínguez, M. Farrús, and L. Wanner. 2016. An automatic prosody tagger for spontaneous speech. In *Proceedings of COLING*, Osaka, Japan.

R Core Team, 2013. *R: A Language and Environment for Statistical Computing.* R Foundation for Statistical Computing, Vienna, Austria.

E. O. Selkirk. 1984. *Phonology and Syntax: The relation between sound and structure.* The MIT Press, Cambridge, Massachussetts.

P. Stenetorp, S. Pyysalo, G. Topić, T. Ohta, S. Ananiadou, and J. Tsujii. 2012. Brat: A web-based Tool for NLP-assisted Text Annotation. In *Proceedings of the Demonstrations at the 13th Conference of the European Chapter of the Association for Computational Linguistics*, EACL '12, pages 102–107, Stroudsburg, PA, USA. Association for Computational Linguistics.

G. Tsatsaronis, I. Varlamis, and K. Nørvåg. 2012. Semafor: Semantic document indexing using semantic forests. In *Proceedings of the 21st ACM International Conference on Information and Knowledge Management*, CIKM '12, pages 1692–1696, New York, NY, USA. ACM.

Y. Xu. 2013. Prosodypro a tool for large-scale systematic prosody analysis. In *Proceedings of Tools and Resources for the Analysis of Speech Prosody (TRASP)*, pages 7–10, Aix-en-Provence, France.

YAMAMA: Yet Another Multi-Dialect Arabic Morphological Analyzer

Salam Khalifa, Nasser Zalmout and Nizar Habash
Computational Approaches to Modeling Language Lab
New York University Abu Dhabi, UAE
{salamkhalifa,nasser.zalmout,nizar.habash}@nyu.edu

Abstract

In this paper, we present YAMAMA, a multi-dialect Arabic morphological analyzer and disambiguator. Our system is almost five times faster than the state-of-the-art MADAMIRA system with a slightly lower quality. In addition to speed, YAMAMA outputs a rich representation which allows for a wider spectrum of use. In this regard, YAMAMA transcends other systems, such as FARASA, which is faster but provides specific outputs catering to specific applications.

1 Introduction

The Arabic language poses many challenges for Natural Language Processing (NLP). First, Arabic is morphologically rich, having a large number of inflections per lemma. Secondly, Arabic is orthographically ambiguous, having about 12 full morphological analyses per word on average. Finally, Arabic has a number of linguistic varieties among which Modern Standard Arabic (MSA) is the official primary written standard with numerous resources, while the other varieties are the unofficial primarily spoken Dialects of Arabic (DA). For more on Arabic NLP, see (Habash, 2010). Table 1 presents an example that showcases the aspect of morphological ambiguity which is shared across all varieties of Arabic.[1]

هل سينجح بين أفليك في دور باتمان ؟ hl synjH byn Âflyk fy dwr bAtmAn Will Ben Affleck be a good Batman?		
POS	**Diac**	**Gloss**
PV+PVSUFF_SUBJ:3MS	bay∼ana	He demonstrated
PV+PVSUFF_SUBJ:3FP	bay∼an∼a	They demonstrated
NOUN_PROP	biyn	Ben
ADJ	bay∼in	Clear
PREP	bayn	Between, among
NOUN_PROP	bi+yan	with a Yen
15 more analysis ...		

Figure 1: Possible analyses produced by the morphological analyzer of the word بين *byn*. The correct analysis is highlighted in gray.

Previous efforts on morphological analysis and disambiguation have led to the creation of a number of state-of-the-art tools with high accuracy, such as MADAMIRA (Pasha et al., 2014). MADAMIRA produces a rich output (diacritization, tokenization, part-of-speech (POS), lemmatization, gloss, and all inflected features), but it is slow. Other systems such as FARASA (Darwish and Mubarak, 2016) are very fast but focus on specific types of output with high quality performance (tokenization). Clearly, there is always a tradeoff between speed, quality and richness. Our system, YAMAMA (Yet Another Multi-Dialect Arabic Morphological Analyzer; Arabic يمامة 'Barbary Dove'), is an alternative to MADAMIRA and FARASA: it offers a faster performance than MADAMIRA but with all of MADAMIRA's rich output at a reasonable tradeoff of quality that varies depending on the specific feature.[2]

2 Related Work

There has been a considerable amount of work on MSA and DA morphological analysis, disambiguation, POS tagging, tokenization, lemmatization and diacritization. One of the most notable efforts is MADAMIRA (Pasha et al., 2014). MADAMIRA produces a rich feature set for each word, containing

[1] Arabic transliteration is presented in the Habash-Soudi-Buckwalter scheme (Habash et al., 2007).
[2] To obtain YAMAMA (Version 1.0), go to http://camel.abudhabi.nyu.edu/resources/.

Proceedings of COLING 2016, the 26th International Conference on Computational Linguistics: System Demonstrations, pages 223–227, Osaka, Japan, December 11-17 2016.

more than 14 morphological and lexical features. It also provides different tokenization schemes. Additionally, MADAMIRA has two modes for MSA and Egyptian Arabic (EGY). The speed of MADAMIRA however is relatively slow (420 words/sec in stand-alone mode, and 1,013 words/sec in server mode) especially for NLP tasks where speed may be critical. Recently, Darwish and Mubarak (2016) and Abdelali et al. (2016) presented a new Arabic segmenter, FARASA. They reported much faster running times than MADAMIRA with similar accuracy on toekniztion. FARASA produces word segmentations only as opposed to MADAMIRA's richer output; and it currently does not handle any Arabic dialect. Our system, YAMAMA, uses some components from MADAMIRA, in particular the morphological analyzers (out-of-context readings) but has its own disambiguation models. This allows YAMAMA to maintain the richness of MADAMIRA, but increase the speed. The disambiguation modeling components are inspired by FARASA's design. In this paper, we compare to both systems in terms of quality and speed.

3 YAMAMA

Motivation We were motivated by the FARASA approach (Darwish and Mubarak, 2016; Abdelali et al., 2016). FARASA achieves very high tokenization accuracy at a very high speed by not using any context. It relies on simple probabilistic models of stems, prefixes, suffixes and their combinations. While this approach will be limiting for complex tasks such as POS tagging, it is sufficient for tokenization, particularly when it comes to specific applications such as machine translation (MT) and information retrieval (IR) (Abdelali et al., 2016). Our goal for YAMAMA is to create a system that combines the rich output of MADAMIRA with fast and simple out-of-context analysis selection comparable to FARASA's approach. For in-vocabulary words, YAMAMA uses a pre-computed maximum likelihood model to assign an analysis to every word. For out-of-vocabulary words, YAMAMA ranks all of the analyses for such words using two unigram language models of the lemma and the Buckwalter POS tag. In both cases, YAMAMA reduces the text to types and makes decisions in type space, thus benefiting from the low type to token ratio.[3]

Datasets For the training and development of our system, we used the same settings as those used for MADAMIRA. For MSA, we used the Penn Arabic Treebank (PATB parts 1,2 and 3) (Maamouri et al., 2004), and for EGY, the ARZ Treebank (Maamouri et al., 2014) . We followed the data splits recommend by Diab et al. (2013) for both treebanks.

Maximum Likelihood Model We created the maximum likelihood model based on the ATB *Train* dataset by selecting the most frequent analysis for each word token in the dataset. The selected analyses are then stored in a dictionary that is loaded once the system starts running. The analyses include all the morphological and lexical features as in MADAMIRA.

Analysis and Disambiguation For the OOV words, we run a morphological analyzer (same analyzer used in MADAMIRA). For MSA we used the SAMA database (Graff et al., 2009), and for EGY we used the CALIMA ARZ database (Habash et al., 2012). The analyses of each word are ranked using the multiplication of their lemma probability and their semi-lexicalized Buckwalter tag probability. Both probabilities are estimated using the training data. The highest ranking analysis is selected; and the word and analysis are added to the loaded analysis dictionary.

Tokenization YAMAMA currently produces a detailed segmentation consisting of the undiacritized morphemes from the Buckwalter tag analysis (BWTagTok). For the analysis dictionary the BWTagTok segmentation is generated for each word ahead of time. Whereas for OOV words, the segmentation is generated after disambiguation.

Output Generation Although all analyses are determined in type space, the output has to be generated in token space. YAMAMA's output is in the same format as MADAMIRA's.

[3]In a text of 80 words, the type to token ratio is 89%, whereas in a text of 8M words, the type to token ratio is only 3.7%.

4 Evaluation

We present next two sets of experiments. The first set targets accuracy and speed and the second set targets machine translation quality. In both sets, we try to compare YAMAMA[4] to MADAMIRA[5] and FARASA[6] both, when possible.

4.1 Accuracy and Speed Evaluation

Experimental Setup While MADAMIRA and YAMAMA share similar output, they are different from FARASA. To allow us to compare them, we conducted three experiments. First, we compared MADAMIRA and YAMAMA in terms of accuracy of their rich output. Second, we compared all systems in terms of accuracy of the specific tokenization output of FARASA. Finally, we compared all three systems in terms of speed on a very large corpus. We also report speeds in the first two experiments, although the test sets are relatively small. For the accuracy evaluation we used the Test sets recommended by Diab et al. (2013) of the Penn Arabic Treebank (PATB parts 1,2 and 3) (Maamouri et al., 2004) (for MSA) and the ARZ Treebank (Maamouri et al., 2014) (for EGY).

	MDMR		YMM	
	MSA	EGY	MSA	EGY
BWTagTok	98.5	93.8	98.4	94.0
LEX	96.8	87.5	96.1	87.8
POS	96.8	92.5	96.1	91.9
DIAC	88.0	83.6	81.0	85.3
ALL	86.0	78.4	78.8	79.3
Time (s)	57.7	51.2	15.4	31.1

Table 1: Evaluation results for MADAMIRA (**MDMR**) and YAMAMA (**YMM**) on the two tests **MSA** (ATB) and **EGY** (ARZ-ALL) using a number of morphological features: Buckwalter POS Tag tokenization (BWTagTok), Lemma (LEX), Part-of-Speech (POS), Diacritization (DIAC) and all features together (ALL). We also report running time.

Results First, in Table 1, we compare YAMAMA to MADAMIRA in terms of accuracy over the (a) Buckwalter POS tag segmentation, which is an undiacritized segmentation based on the morphemes in the Buckwalter analysis, (b) Lemma, (c) POS, (d) Diacritization, and (e) ALL features. We also report the time the systems took to complete the task. To give an example of the various features evaluated, the word المجموعة *Almjmwςħ* 'collection/group' may have a correct analysis with the BWTagTok `Al+mjmwE+p`, the lemma `majomuwEap`, the POS `noun`, and the diacritization `AlmajomuwEapi`. The ALL condition would include all of these in addition to `prc3:0 prc2:0 prc1:0 prc0:Al_det per:na asp:na vox:na mod:na gen:f num:s stt:d cas:g enc0:0`. For MSA, YAMAMA performs very closely to MADAMIRA except for DIAC, which explains the drop in ALL. However, in EGY, YAMAMA beats MADAMIRA in almost all aspects, except for POS. YAMAMA is four times faster than MADAMIRA in the MSA setting, and two times faster in EGY; due to the large size of the CALIMA ARZ database which is three times larger than SAMA, hence more loading time. Also, the speed of YAMAMA is sensitive to the ratio of OOV types, where it uses the morphological analyzer.

Second, in Table 2 we compare to MADAMIRA and YAMAMA to FARASA in terms of FARASA's tokenization scheme (FarasaTok), which is similar but not exactly the same as the BWTagTok. We automatically converted the MADAMIRA and YAMAMA outputs as well as the MSA and EGY test sets to FarasaTok to be able to compare in the same tokenization space. We also report on an Alif, Ya and Ta-Marbuta normalized version of FarasaTok (FarasaTokNorm) for all test conditions. In addition to the test sets reported on earlier, we add the MSA WikiNews test set that was reported on by Darwish and Mubarak (2016). Across all conditions, YAMAMA and MADAMIRA behave very similarly. In MSA WikiNews, all three systems behave similarly. However, as would be expected, YAMAMA and MADAMIRA beat FARASA on the EGY set by a large margin. YAMAMA and MADAMIRA also have higher performance than FARASA on the MSA set. In terms of speed, YAMAMA outperforms in all modes except for EGY. The speeds of YAMAMA are competitive with FARASA except for EGY for the reasons mentioned earlier.

[4] YAMAMA:Version: 1.0.

[5] MADAMIRA: Released on May 16, 2016, version 2.1.

[6] FARASA: Downloaded on May 27, 2016.

	MSA			EGY			MSA-Wiki		
	MDMR	**YMM**	**FRS**	**MDMR**	**YMM**	**FRS**	**MDMR**	**YMM**	**FRS**
FarasaTok	98.7	98.7	89.6	94.3	94.4	73.3	98.5	98.0	98.7
FarasaTok Norm	99.2	99.2	98.4	96.5	96.6	86.6	98.9	98.8	98.7
Time (s)	58.1	15.7	17.7	51.4	31.2	16.8	43.8	9.9	14.8

Table 2: Evaluation results for MADAMIRA (**MDMR**), YAMAMA (**YMM**) and FARASA (**FRS**) on the three tests **MSA** (ATB), **EGY** (ARZ-ALL) and **MSA-Wiki** (WikiNews) using FARASA tokenization scheme in basic (**FarasaTok**) and normalized forms (**FarasaTok Norm**). We also report running time.

Finally, we ran all systems through a large dataset of 7.5 million words from Gigaword (Parker et al., 2009). The reported running times for MADAMIRA (standalone mode), YAMAMA and FARASA are 2,305s, 398s and 99s, respectively. YAMAMA is five times faster than MADAMIRA and FARASA is four times faster than YAMAMA.

4.2 Machine Translation Evaluation

Experimental Setup We used the Moses toolkit (Koehn et al., 2007) with default parameters to develop the Statistical Machine Translation (SMT) systems. For alignment, we used GIZA++ (Och and Ney, 2003). And for language modeling, we used KenLM (Heafield et al., 2013) to build a 5-gram language model. We evaluate using BLEU (Papineni et al., 2002) and METEOR (Banerjee and Lavie, 2005). We apply statistical significance tests using the paired bootstrapped resampling method (Koehn, 2004). We used the Arabic-English parallel component of the UN Corpus (Eisele and Chen, 2010), with about 9 million lines for the English language model (~286 million words), 200 thousand parallel lines for training (~5 million words), 2000 lines for tuning, and 3000 lines for testing. The English content was tokenized using the default English tokenizer at Moses, and the Arabic texts were tokenized through YAMAMA, MADAMIRA and FARASA into the same Arabic Treebank tokenization scheme. For YAMAMA, we used the TOKAN tool (Habash et al., 2009) to do the tokenization. The Arabic dataset we used had English text segments covering UN resolutions numbers and named entities; so we applied Moses' English whitespace tokenization scripts on the Arabic files in advance of the Arabic tokenization for the three systems to be of a better match to the English reference.

	With OOV		Without OOV	
	BLEU	**METEOR**	**BLEU**	**METEOR**
YAMAMA	39.49	0.3618	38.00	0.3448
MADAMIRA	39.52	0.3627	37.65	0.3435
FARASA	37.73	0.3301	37.76	0.3436

Table 3: Machine translation results

Results and Analysis The results of the SMT experiments are presented in Table 3, with YAMAMA and MADAMIRA showing a statistically significant performance improvement relative to FARASA. For a better understanding of the results, we analyzed the output files and observed that FARASA transliterates English words with Arabic letters and deletes the vowels, most likely the result of an internal minor transliteration error. This behavior is problematic for SMT, as Moses would pass such English Out-of-Vocabulary (OOV) words in Arabic letters. To facilitate a better comparison ignoring the effect of different OOV handling, we performed additional SMT experiments that drop the OOV words from all three systems' output. Results are also in Table 3, with YAMAMA outperforming the other two systems slightly but with statistical significance. MADAMIRA and FARASA performed closely, with a statistically insignificant difference. As a general observation, we conclude that the variations among the different systems don't have a profound impact on the SMT quality.[7]

5 Conclusions and Future Work

We presented YAMAMA, a multi-dialect Arabic morphological analyzer and disambiguator. YAMAMA is almost five times faster than MADAMIRA, with slightly lower quality. YAMAMA outputs a rich representation which allows for a wider spectrum of use, transcending other systems, such as FARASA,

[7]We would like to thank the Farasa team, specifically, Kareem Darwish, Hamdy Mubarak, and Ahmed Abdelali for helpful conversations. We have provided them with feedback and they have since released an updated version of Farasa.

which is faster but provides specific outputs catering to specific applications. There is yet much room for enhancing the speed and the quality of YAMAMA, which we plan to investigate.

References

Ahmed Abdelali, Kareem Darwish, Nadir Durrani, and Hamdy Mubarak. 2016. Farasa: A fast and furious segmenter for Arabic. In *Proceedings of the 2016 Conference of the North American Chapter of the Association for Computational Linguistics: Demonstrations*, pages 11–16, San Diego, California.

Satanjeev Banerjee and Alon Lavie. 2005. METEOR: An Automatic Metric for MT Evaluation with Improved Correlation with Human Judgments. In *Proceedings of the ACL 2005 Workshop on Intrinsic and Extrinsic Evaulation Measures for MT and/or Summarization.*

Kareem Darwish and Hamdy Mubarak. 2016. Farasa: A new fast and accurate Arabic word segmenter. In *Proceedings of the Tenth International Conference on Language Resources and Evaluation (LREC 2016).*

Mona Diab, Nizar Habash, Owen Rambow, and Ryan Roth. 2013. LDC Arabic treebanks and associated corpora: Data divisions manual. *arXiv preprint arXiv:1309.5652.*

Andreas Eisele and Yu Chen. 2010. Multiun: A multilingual corpus from united nation documents. In *Proceedings of the Language Resources and Evaluation Conference (LREC)*, pages 2868–2872.

David Graff, Mohamed Maamouri, Basma Bouziri, Sondos Krouna, Seth Kulick, and Tim Buckwalter. 2009. Standard Arabic Morphological Analyzer (SAMA) Version 3.1. Linguistic Data Consortium LDC2009E73.

Nizar Habash, Abdelhadi Soudi, and Tim Buckwalter. 2007. On Arabic Transliteration. In A. van den Bosch and A. Soudi, editors, *Arabic Computational Morphology: Knowledge-based and Empirical Methods*. Springer.

Nizar Habash, Owen Rambow, and Ryan Roth. 2009. MADA+TOKAN: A toolkit for Arabic tokenization, diacritization, morphological disambiguation, POS tagging, stemming and lemmatization. In Khalid Choukri and Bente Maegaard, editors, *Proceedings of the Second International Conference on Arabic Language Resources and Tools*. The MEDAR Consortium, April.

Nizar Habash, Ramy Eskander, and Abdelati Hawwari. 2012. A Morphological Analyzer for Egyptian Arabic. In *Proceedings of the Twelfth Meeting of the Special Interest Group on Computational Morphology and Phonology*, pages 1–9, Montréal, Canada.

Nizar Y Habash. 2010. *Introduction to Arabic natural language processing*, volume 3. Morgan & Claypool Publishers.

Kenneth Heafield, Ivan Pouzyrevsky, Jonathan H. Clark, and Philipp Koehn. 2013. Scalable modified Kneser-Ney language model estimation. In *Proceedings of the 51st Annual Meeting of the Association for Computational Linguistics*, pages 690–696, Sofia, Bulgaria, August.

Philipp Koehn, Hieu Hoang, Alexandra Birch, Christopher Callison-Burch, Marcello Federico, Nicola Bertoldi, Brooke Cowan, Wade Shen, Christine Moran, Richard Zens, Christopher Dyer, Ondrej Bojar, Alexandra Constantin, and Evan Herbst. 2007. Moses: open source toolkit for statistical machine translation. In *Proceedings of the 45th Annual Meeting of the Association for Computational Linguistics Companion Volume Proceedings of the Demo and Poster Sessions*, pages 177–180, Prague, Czech Republic.

Philipp Koehn. 2004. Statistical significance tests for machine translation evaluation. In *Proceedings of EMNLP 2004*, pages 388–395, Barcelona, Spain, July. Association for Computational Linguistics.

Mohamed Maamouri, Ann Bies, Tim Buckwalter, and Wigdan Mekki. 2004. The Penn Arabic Treebank: Building a Large-Scale Annotated Arabic Corpus. In *NEMLAR Conference on Arabic Language Resources and Tools*, pages 102–109, Cairo, Egypt.

Mohamed Maamouri, Ann Bies, Seth Kulick, Michael Ciul, Nizar Habash, and Ramy Eskander. 2014. Developing an Egyptian Arabic Treebank: Impact of Dialectal Morphology on Annotation and Tool Development. In *Proceedings of the Ninth International Conference on Language Resources and Evaluation (LREC-2014)*. European Language Resources Association (ELRA).

Franz Josef Och and Hermann Ney. 2003. A Systematic Comparison of Various Statistical Alignment Models. *Computational Linguistics*, 29(1):19–52.

Kishore Papineni, Salim Roukos, Todd Ward, and Wei-Jing Zhu. 2002. BLEU: a Method for Automatic Evaluation of Machine Translation. In *Proceedings of the 40th Annual Meeting of the Association for Computational Linguistics*, pages 311–318, Philadelphia, PA.

Robert Parker, David Graff, Ke Chen, Junbo Kong, and Kazuaki Maeda. 2009. Arabic Gigaword Fourth Edition. LDC catalog number No. LDC2009T30, ISBN 1-58563-532-4.

Arfath Pasha, Mohamed Al-Badrashiny, Ahmed El Kholy, Ramy Eskander, Mona Diab, Nizar Habash, Manoj Pooleery, Owen Rambow, and Ryan Roth. 2014. MADAMIRA: A Fast, Comprehensive Tool for Morphological Analysis and Disambiguation of Arabic. In *In Proceedings of LREC*, Reykjavik, Iceland.

CamelParser: A System for Arabic Syntactic Analysis and Morphological Disambiguation

Anas Shahrour, Salam Khalifa, Dima Taji, Nizar Habash
Computational Approaches to Modeling Language (CAMeL) Lab
New York University Abu Dhabi, UAE
{anas.shahrour,salamkhalifa,dima.taji,nizar.habash}@nyu.edu

Abstract

In this paper, we present CamelParser, a state-of-the-art system for Arabic syntactic dependency analysis aligned with contextually disambiguated morphological features. CamelParser uses a state-of-the-art morphological disambiguator and improves its results using syntactically driven features. The system offers a number of output formats that include basic dependency with morphological features, two tree visualization modes, and traditional Arabic grammatical analysis.

1 Introduction

Automatic processing of Arabic is challenging for several reasons (Habash, 2010). Arabic is morphologically rich and highly ambiguous. The morphological analyzer we use represents Arabic words with 15 features, such as gender, number, person, state, case, etc. (Pasha et al., 2014). And due to Arabic's optional diacritization orthography, words have an average of 12 analyses per word (Pasha et al., 2014). Furthermore, Arabic morphology and syntax have complex agreement rules. For example, a noun may get its case by being the subject of a verb and its state by being the head of an Idafa (possessive) construction; while adjectives modifying this noun agree with it in its case, their state is determined by the state of the last element in the Idafa construction chain the noun heads.

In this paper, we present CamelParser, a system for Arabic syntactic dependency analysis aligned with contextually disambiguated morphological features. CamelParser uses a state-of-the-art morphological disambiguator, MADAMIRA (Pasha et al., 2014), and improves its results using syntactically driven features. The system offers a number of output formats that include basic Columbia Arabic Treebank dependency (Habash and Roth, 2009) with morphological features, two tree visualization modes, and traditional Arabic grammatical analysis. CamelParser is publicly available for research purposes.[1]

2 Related Work

In related work on modeling Arabic syntax and morphology, Habash et al. (2007a) demonstrated that given good syntactic representations, case prediction can be done with a high degree of accuracy. Alkuhlani et al. (2013) later extended this work to cover all morphological features. Marton et al. (2013) explored the contribution of different POS tag sets and several lexical and inflectional morphology features to dependency parsing of Arabic. Building on all of these previous efforts, Shahrour et al. (2015) presented an approach for improving the quality of several morphological features using syntax. They demonstrated that predicted syntax can significantly improve the full morphological analysis choice, particularly for case and state. Our system, CamelParser, further builds on their approach and improves on it by optimizing the syntactic parsing and by offering output in several formats including aligned syntax and morphology, traditional Arabic grammatical analysis (إعراب *ÂiςrAb*),[2] tree visualization, and tree annotation output compatible with the dependency annotation tool TrEd (Pajas, 2008).

[1] CamelParser can be downloaded from `http://camel.abudhabi.nyu.edu/resources/`.
[2] Arabic transliteration is presented in the Habash-Soudi-Buckwalter scheme (Habash et al., 2007b).

Proceedings of COLING 2016, the 26th International Conference on Computational Linguistics: System Demonstrations, pages 228–232, Osaka, Japan, December 11-17 2016.

3 System Description

3.1 Overview

CamelParser is based on the system proposed by Shahrour et al. (2015) and uses the same data splits (*Train*, *Dev* and *Test*) described by Diab et al. (2013) for the Penn Arabic Treebank (PATB, parts 1, 2 and 3) (Maamouri et al., 2004), and the same morphological feature representations derived from the PATB analyses following the approach used in the MADAMIRA Arabic morphological analysis and disambiguation system (Pasha et al., 2014). We trained an Arabic dependency parser using MaltParser (Nivre et al., 2007) on the Columbia Arabic Treebank (CATiB) version of the PATB (Habash and Roth, 2009). We used an enriched data format that includes all our morphological features and three POS tag sets with different degrees of granularity: CATiBex (Marton et al., 2013), Kulick (Kulick et al., 2006), and Buckwalter (Buckwalter, 2002).

CamelParser improves on the morphological disambiguation done in MADAMIRA using the syntactic analysis information to predict the case and state features with an unlexicalized machine learning model. The predicted case and state are used to select a new morphological analysis. The final output consists of the syntax in CATiB style aligned with the MADAMIRA morphology features for each token (see the list of features exemplified in Table 1). The output formats are discussed in section 3.4.

3.2 Syntactic Parser Optimization

For parser optimization, we divided the *Dev* set into two parts with nearly equal number of tokens: *DevTune* (35,759 words) and *DevTest* (35,750 words). During the optimization, the parser was trained on *Train* (with gold morphological features) and evaluated against *DevTune* (with predicted morphological features). *DevTest* is reserved for future development.

The optimization was performed in two stages. The first stage is using MaltOptimizer (Ballesteros and Nivre, 2012), a tool for optimizing MaltParser for a specific dataset. MaltOptimizer does not allow the user to use separate train and test sets, a feature that we need to train the parser on gold features and evaluate against predicted features. For this reason, we used a modified version of MaltOptimizer that allows the user to provide separate train and test sets.[3]

While MaltOptimizer optimizes for the parsing algorithm, the learning algorithm, and the feature model, it doesn't optimize for the set of morphological features used. That is, it cannot produce an optimal subset of morphological features, it can either conclude that it helps to include all features or that it helps to exclude them all. This is why a second stage of optimization is performed to optimize for the morphological feature set. The lemma is the exception as it is represented in a separate column in the CoNLL-X format, and so MaltOptimizer can optimize for it separately. In the second stage of optimization, we use MaltParser in the optimal settings from the first stage. The optimization is done in a greedy way starting with an empty morphological feature set or with the lemma if it was selected in the first stage. At each round of optimization, we decide which of the remaining morphological features score is the highest when added to the current feature set, and if the added feature gives an improvement to the labeled attachment score, a new feature set is determined and the optimization continues. Otherwise, the new feature is dropped and the optimization round is concluded.

3.3 Arabic Grammatical Analysis

To facilitate the use of this system in the context of Arabic grammar education, the CamelParser output is mapped to the traditional way of expressing Arabic grammatical analyses (إعراب *ǍiςrAb*). The system traverses the syntactic tree and uses a collection of grammatical analysis and morphology rules to translate the syntactic and morphological information to the traditional grammatical analysis representation. The output is provided in plain text or tabular HTML format. Figure 1.(iii) shows an example grammatical analysis output. The grammatical analysis output for the noun أرباح *ÂrbAH* 'profits', which is the subject in the example translates to the following: *the subject with a nominative case indicated by the 'Damma' ending, and it is the head of an Idafa construct.*

[3]We are thankful to Miguel Ballesteros and Joakim Nivre for providing us with the modified version of MaltOptimizer.

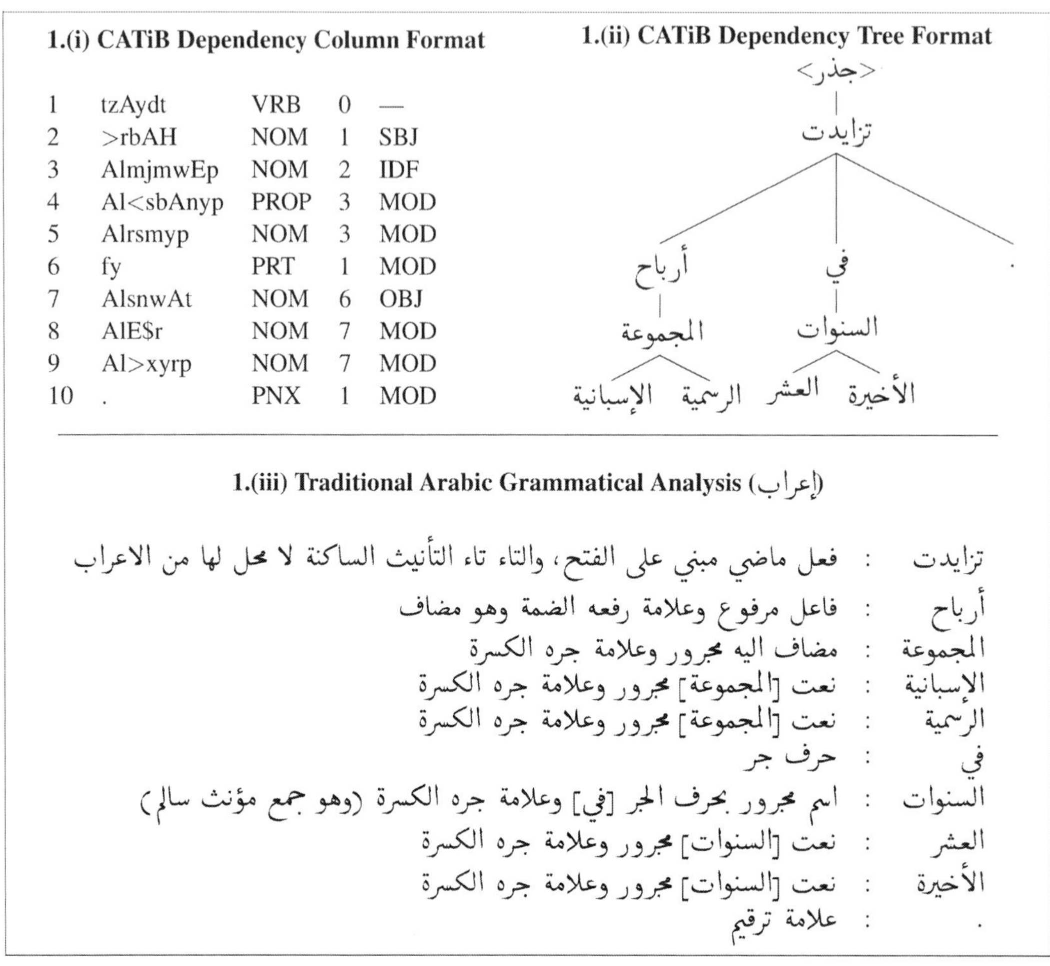

Figure 1: CamelParser Output Formats. Morphological features are not shown due to space limitations. The example sentence is .تزايدت أرباح المجموعة الإسبانية الرسمية في السنوات العشر الأخيرة *tzAydt ÂrbAH AlmjmwEħ AlĂsbAnyħ Alrsmyħ fy AlsnwAt Alςšr AlÂxyrħ* (Lit. *increased profits the-group the-Spanish the-official in the-years the-ten the-last.*) 'The profits of the official Spanish group increased in the last ten years.' The output in **1.(i)** is in the Buckwalter Transliteration scheme (Habash et al., 2007b).

3.4 Output Formats

The CamelParser produces the following output formats:

- Syntactic analysis in the CATiB dependency representation (Habash and Roth, 2009) aligned with the morphology of each token in the feature-value pair format used in MADAMIRA (Pasha et al., 2014). Table 1 shows the features and their values for one example word. For more details on Arabic morphological features, see (Habash, 2010).
- Traditional Arabic grammatical analysis format.
- Tree visualization in PDF format.
- Tree file in `.fs` format for annotation in the TrEd tree editor (Pajas, 2008).

Additionally, as a side product, CamelParser generates an improved morphological disambiguation file in `.mada` format (MADAMIRA tool output), and a corresponding `ATB4MT` tokenization file (Arabic Treebank tokenization scheme). Figure 1 shows the same analysis in the first three output formats discussed above.

	Feature	Value	Description of Feature and Value
1	tok	AlmjmwEp	Arabic Treebank token form (Buckwalter Transliteration)
2	toknorm	AlmjmwEp	Alif/Ya normalized token (Buckwalter Transliteration)
3	toklex	majomuwEap	Lemma of token (Buckwalter Transliteration)
4	tok_utf8	المجموعة	Arabic Treebank token (UTF8)
5	toknorm_utf8	المجموعة	Alif/Ya normalized token form (UTF8)
6	toklex_utf8	مَجْمُوعَة	Lemma of token (UTF8)
7	catib4	NOM	A coarser version of CATiB POS (PROP is mapped to NOM, and VRB-PASS is mapped to VRB)
8	catibex	Al-NOM-p	CATiBEX POS tag (Marton et al., 2013)
9	pos	noun	MADAMIRA's POS tag (Pasha et al., 2014)
10	gloss	collection;group;bloc	English Gloss
11	prc3	0	Proclitic 3 (question proclitic), with value *0*
12	prc2	0	Proclitic 2 (conjunction proclitic), with value *0*
13	prc1	0	Proclitic 1 (preposition proclitic), with value *0*
14	prc0	Al_det	Proclitic 0 (article proclitic), with value *Al_det* for the determiner ال *Al* 'the'
15	per	na	Person, with value *N/A*
16	asp	na	Aspect, with value *N/A*
17	vox	na	Voice, with value *N/A*
18	mod	na	Mood, with value *N/A*
19	gen	f	Gender, with value *f* for *feminine*
20	num	s	Number, with value *s* for *single*
21	stt	d	State, with value *d* for *definite*
22	cas	g	Case, with value *g* for *genitive*
23	enc0	0	Enclitic 0 (pronominals), with value *0*
24	rat	y	Rationality (currently under development; defaulting to *y*)
25	catib6	NOM	CATiB POS tag (Habash and Roth, 2009)
26	penpos	DT+NN	Penn POS tag (Habash, 2010)
27	bw	DET+NOUN+NSUFF_FEM_SG +CASE_DEF_GEN	Buckwalter POS tag (Buckwalter, 2002)

Table 1: The features generated by CamelParser for the word المجموعة *Almjmwςħ 'the group'* from the example shown in Figure 1, and their values and descriptions. The system's transliterated Arabic values are in the Buckwalter scheme (Habash et al., 2007b). The exact output line from CamelParser is:

```
3 AlmjmwEp NOM 2 IDF tok:AlmjmwEp toknorm:AlmjmwEp toklex:majomuwEap tok_utf8:المجموعة
toknorm_utf8:المجموعة toklex_utf8:مَجْمُوعَة catib4:NOM catibex:Al-NOM-p pos:noun
gloss:collection;group;bloc prc3:0 prc2:0 prc1:0 prc0:Al_det per:na asp:na
vox:na mod:na gen:f num:s stt:d cas:g enc0:0 rat:y catib6:NOM pennpos:DT+NN
bw:DET+NOUN+NSUFF_FEM_SG+CASE_DEF_GEN.
```

4 Evaluation

Parsing Accuracy We compare the performance of CamelParser to the parser described in Shahrour et al. (2015), henceforth, Baseline Parser. The two systems use the same training data (*Train*) and report on the same testing data (*Test*) in predicted morphology setting. CamelParser, however, uses more features and has been optimized as discussed above. In terms of labeled attachment, unlabeled attachment, and label accuracy, CamelParser achieves 83.8%, 86.4%, and 93.2%, respectively. These are significant improvements over the Baseline Parser's respective scores of 81.6%, 84.6%, and 92.0%. Previously reported state-of-the-art results by Marton et al. (2013) are 81.7%, 84.6%, and 92.8% (again, for labeled attachment, unlabeled attachment, and label accuracy, respectively). We present their numbers here although it is hard to conduct a fair comparison because of differences in training and testing data sets.

Morphological Disambiguation Accuracy We compare the performance of the morphological disambiguation produced by CamelParser to that of the MADAMIRA system which CamelParser uses. All the results are reported on the same data set (*Test*). There are many metrics that can be used, but we focus here on two harsh metrics: full word diacritization accuracy and all morphological feature selection. The MADAMIRA system produces 88.1% and 86.1% for these two metrics respectively. CamelParser's use of syntax to improve morphological analysis raises the scores to 90.8% and 88.7%.

5 Conclusion

We presented CamelParser, a system for improved syntactic analysis and morphological disambiguation of Arabic. The system uses an optimized syntactic parser and produces morphologically-enriched syntactic dependencies, along with tree visualizations, TrEd file outputs for annotation, and traditional grammatical analyses.

References

Sarah Alkuhlani, Nizar Habash, and Ryan Roth. 2013. Automatic morphological enrichment of a morphologically underspecified treebank. In *HLT-NAACL*, pages 460–470.

Miguel Ballesteros and Joakim Nivre. 2012. Maltoptimizer: an optimization tool for maltparser. In *Proceedings of the Demonstrations at the 13th Conference of the European Chapter of the Association for Computational Linguistics*, pages 58–62. Association for Computational Linguistics.

Tim Buckwalter. 2002. Buckwalter Arabic Morphological Analyzer Version 1.0. Linguistic Data Consortium, University of Pennsylvania, 2002. LDC Catalog No.: LDC2002L49.

Mona Diab, Nizar Habash, Owen Rambow, and Ryan Roth. 2013. LDC Arabic treebanks and associated corpora: Data divisions manual. *arXiv preprint arXiv:1309.5652*.

Nizar Habash and Ryan M Roth. 2009. CATiB: The Columbia Arabic Treebank. In *Proceedings of the ACL-IJCNLP 2009 Conference Short Papers*, pages 221–224. Association for Computational Linguistics.

Nizar Habash, Ryan Gabbard, Owen Rambow, Seth Kulick, and Mitchell P Marcus. 2007a. Determining case in Arabic: Learning complex linguistic behavior requires complex linguistic features. In *EMNLP-CoNLL*, pages 1084–1092.

Nizar Habash, Abdelhadi Soudi, and Tim Buckwalter. 2007b. On Arabic Transliteration. In A. van den Bosch and A. Soudi, editors, *Arabic Computational Morphology: Knowledge-based and Empirical Methods*. Springer.

Nizar Habash. 2010. *Introduction to Arabic Natural Language Processing*. Morgan & Claypool Publishers.

Seth Kulick, Ryan Gabbard, and Mitch Marcus. 2006. Parsing the Arabic Treebank: Analysis and Improvements. In *Proceedings of the Treebanks and Linguistic Theories Conference*, pages 31–42, Prague, Czech Republic.

Mohamed Maamouri, Ann Bies, Tim Buckwalter, and Wigdan Mekki. 2004. The Penn Arabic Treebank: Building a Large-Scale Annotated Arabic Corpus. In *NEMLAR Conference on Arabic Language Resources and Tools*, pages 102–109, Cairo, Egypt.

Yuval Marton, Nizar Habash, and Owen Rambow. 2013. Dependency parsing of modern standard Arabic with lexical and inflectional features. *Computational Linguistics*, 39(1):161–194.

Joakim Nivre, Johan Hall, Jens Nilsson, Atanas Chanev, Gülsen Eryigit, Sandra Kübler, Svetoslav Marinov, and Erwin Marsi. 2007. MaltParser: a language-independent system for data-driven dependency parsing. *Natural Language Engineering*, 13(02):95–135.

Petr Pajas. 2008. Tred: Tree editor. http://ufal.mff.cuni.cz/ pajas/tred.

Arfath Pasha, Mohamed Al-Badrashiny, Ahmed El Kholy, Ramy Eskander, Mona Diab, Nizar Habash, Manoj Pooleery, Owen Rambow, and Ryan Roth. 2014. MADAMIRA: A Fast, Comprehensive Tool for Morphological Analysis and Disambiguation of Arabic. In *In Proceedings of LREC*, Reykjavik, Iceland.

Anas Shahrour, Salam Khalifa, and Nizar Habash. 2015. Improving Arabic diacritization through syntactic analysis. In *Proceedings of the 2015 Conference on Empirical Methods in Natural Language Processing, EMNLP 2015, Lisbon, Portugal, September 17-21, 2015*, pages 1309–1315.

Demonstrating Ambient Search: Implicit Document Retrieval for Speech Streams

Benjamin Milde[1,2], **Jonas Wacker**[1], **Stefan Radomski**[2], **Max Mühlhäuser**[2], and **Chris Biemann**[1]

[1] Language Technology Group / [2] Telecooperation Group
Computer Science Department
Technische Universität Darmstadt, Germany

Abstract

In this demonstration paper we describe Ambient Search, a system that displays and retrieves documents in real time based on speech input. The system operates continuously in ambient mode, i.e. it generates speech transcriptions and identifies main keywords and keyphrases, while also querying its index to display relevant documents without explicit query. Without user intervention, the results are dynamically updated; users can choose to interact with the system at any time, employing a conversation protocol that is enriched with the ambient information gathered continuously. Our evaluation shows that Ambient Search outperforms another implicit speech-based information retrieval system. Ambient search is available as open source software.

1 Introduction

In the recent past, personal assistants like Siri or Google Now emerged, providing a natural voice-based interface for querying and finding information. These developments have been made possible by recent advances in Automated Speech Recognition (ASR) and Natural Language Understanding (NLU). Typically, these systems are actively triggered by users and are constrained to an ever–growing, yet finite set of hard-wired commands and question types. However, people may want to look up helpful information or check facts during a conversation or while listening to a lecture. In these situations, the interaction with a personal assistant or searching the web for the information hampers the flow of the discussion, respectively leads to distraction. In this work, we demonstrate Ambient Search. The system displays relevant information on-the-fly, solely based on speech input streams. In contrast to the above-mentioned personal assistants, our system does not require explicit interaction, as it unobtrusively listens to speech streams in the background, updating relevant results as time progresses. As a proof of concept, we make use of TED talks to demonstrate our system.

2 Related Work

The Remembrance Agent (Rhodes and Starner, 1996) is an early prototype of a continuously running automated information retrieval system, implemented as a plugin for the text editor Emacs. Given a collection of user-accumulated email and personal files, it attempts to find those documents that are most relevant to the user's current context. Rhodes and Maes (2000) also defined the term *just-in-time information retrieval agents* as "a class of software agents that proactively present information based on a person's context in an easily accessible and non-intrusive manner". Dumais et al. (2004) introduced an implicit query (IQ) system, which serves as a background system when writing emails. It also uses Term Frequency – Inverse Document Frequency (TF-IDF) scores for keyword extraction, like the Remembrance Agent. The most similar system to *Ambient Search* was presented by Habibi and Popescu-Belis (2015), extending earlier work on an Automatic Content Linking Device (Popescu-Belis et al., 2000).

3 System Description

Our system is based on the following processing steps. They are carried out in real-time:

Proceedings of COLING 2016, the 26th International Conference on Computational Linguistics: System Demonstrations, pages 233–237, Osaka, Japan, December 11-17 2016.

Speech decoding. We stream the speech signal into an ASR system, emitting partial sentence hypotheses and predicting sentence boundaries. We use Kaldi (Povey et al., 2011), an open-source speech recognition framework and acoustic models based on the TED-LIUM corpus (Rousseau et al., 2014) and the TEDLIUM 4-gram language model (LM) from Cantab Research (Williams et al., 2015). We make use of kaldi-gstreamer-server[1], which wraps a Kaldi model into a streaming server that can be accessed with websockets. This provides a bi-directional communication channel, where audio is streamed to the server application and partial and full sentence hypothesis and boundaries are simultaneously returned.

Keyword and keyphrase extraction. Once a full sentence has been hypothesized, new keywords and keyphrases are extracted in the current sentence, if available. A keyphrase, as opposed to a single keyword, can consist of serveral words that refer to one concept. We first precompute a DRUID (Riedl and Biemann, 2015) dictionary on a recent Wikipedia dump with scores for noun phrases. DRUID is a state-of-the-art unsupervised measure for multiword expressions (MWEs) using distributional semantics and precomputed dictionaries for English can be downloaded from the JoBimText project website[2]. All keyphrases with a DRUID score over a certain threshold (e.g. 0.7, see also Section 4) and all remaining words that are adjectives and nouns, as determined by an off-the-shelf part of speech (POS)-tagger[3], are used as candidate terms.

Candidate term ranking. We score candidate terms according to a Word2Vec (Mikolov et al., 2013) and TF-IDF ranking measure. We first precompute IDF and lookup tables for all unique words in the Simple English Wikipedia and for all multiword terms in our DRUID dictionary. Word2Vec (CBOW) is our source of semantic similarity. We train it on stemmed text and treat multiwords as opaque units. We then compute the average Word2Vec vector over all candidate terms. Finally, we score each candidate term according to the cosine distance of each term word vector to the average word vector of the last 10 sentences and multiply this with the TF-IDF score of the given term.

Index queries. We use Elastic Search[4] and stream2es[5] to build an index of the Simple English Wikipedia[6]. We build an OR query of all top query terms (e.g. up to the top 10 query words), assigning the computed scores to the individual terms in the query. Eventually, the returned documents are also aggregated, i.e. older documents found with previous sentences decay their score over time (multiplied with $d = 0.9$) and newer documents are sorted into a list of n best documents. This list is thus sorted by topical relevance of the documents and by time, with newer documents having precedence. Finally, the n best relevant documents are presented to the user and updated as soon as changes become available.

Implementation Details. We encapsulate the processing steps into the following Python programs: (1) A Kaldi client program, that either uses the system's microphone or an audio file, streaming it in real time to obtain partial and full transcription hypothesis. (2) A relevant event generator program, that searches for new keywords and keyphrases and queries the elastic search index to obtain relevant documents. (3) The Ambient Search server, which sends out appropriate events to the browser view, to display the current top n relevant documents and to move older documents into a timeline. We connect the individual modules with message passing through a common channel on a redis-server[7]. Through it, modules can send and receive events and act accordingly, e.g. to the availability of a new utterance hypothesis from the recognition module. Word2Vec and TF-IDF vectors are computed with the Gensim (Řehůřek and Sojka, 2010) package. The Ambient Search web page is implemented in HTML5/JS and connects to a server instance running on the Python micro-framework Flask[8], making use of Server Sent Events (SSE) to push new information from the server to the web browser. This enables a reversed information channel, where the server pushes descriptions of new relevant documents to the browser client as it becomes available.

3.1 Visual Presentation

Figure 1 gives a visual impression of our system, after it had been listening for a few minutes to Alice Bows Larkin's TED talk on climate change[9]. On the bottom of the page, we show excerpts of up to four

[1] https://github.com/alumae/kaldi-gstreamer-server [2] jobimtext.org/components/druid/
[3] http://spacy.io [4] https://elastic.co/ [5] https://github.com/elastic/stream2es
[6] https://simple.wikipedia.org [7] http://redis.io/ [8] http://flask.pocoo.org/
[9] http://ted.com/speakers/alice_bows_larkin

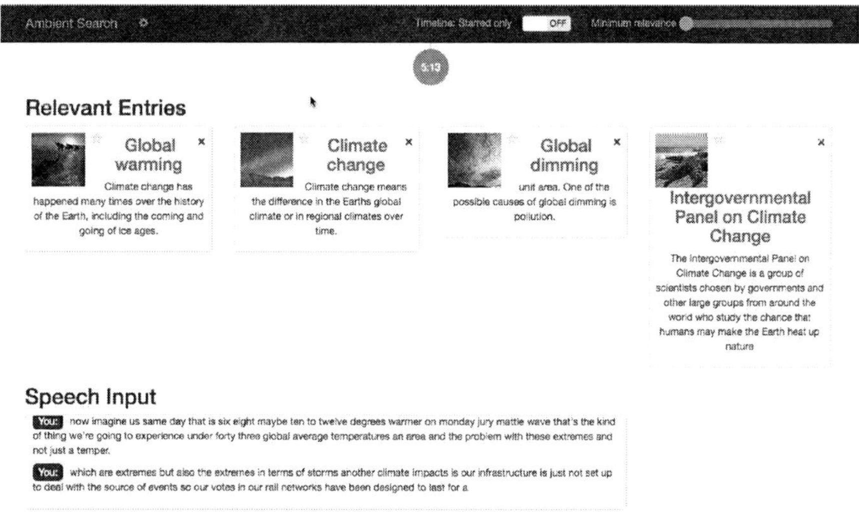

Figure 1: Screenshot of the system after listening to five minutes of the TED talk "We're too late to prevent climate change - here is how we adapt" by Alice Bows Larkin [9]

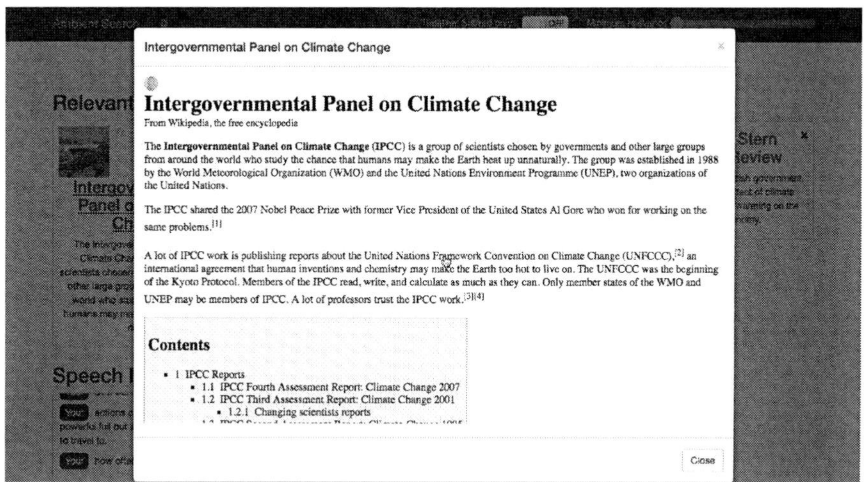

Figure 2: Screenshot of the modal dialog that opens after clicking on a relevant item, that can be used to read one of the proposed Wikipedia articles.

relevant Wikipedia documents to the user. Clicking on such a document opens up a modal view to read the Wikipedia article, as depicted in Figure 2. When newer and more relevant articles are retrieved, older articles move into a timeline, which is constructed above the currently retrieved articles. While the user is at the bottom of the page, the page keeps automatically scrolling to the end, like a terminal.

In the timeline (see also Figure 3), users can go back to previously displayed relevant entries and can adjust the minimal relevance of the shown elements, to filter entries by the systems confidence. Elements can also be bookmarked, to quickly retrieve them later. This can be used to quickly mark interesting articles to be read later, e.g. while Ambient Search is being used listening to a talk and the user only briefly interacts with it while listening. The displayed entries can also be removed from the web page at any time by clicking on the X in the boxes.

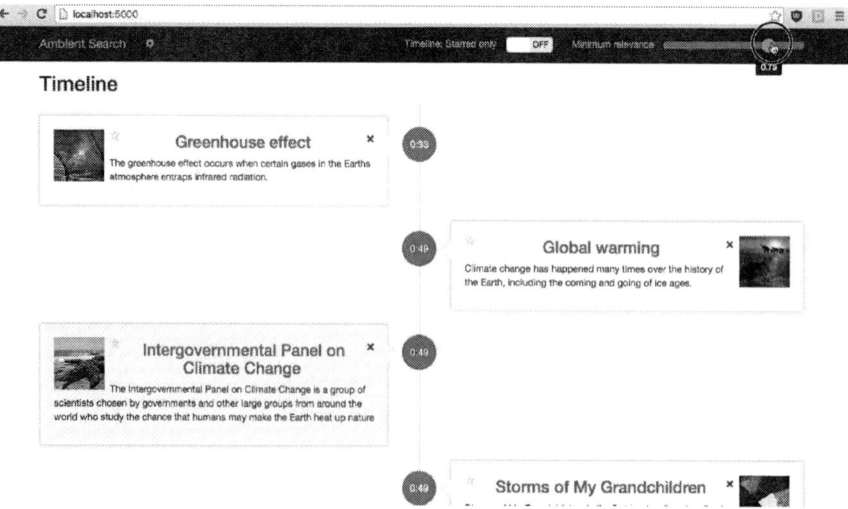

Figure 3: Screenshot of the timeline that constructs above the relevant entries, showing previously displayed relevant entries. Users can also adjust the minimal relevance bar at the top right of the screen, to filter entries by the systems confidence.

4 Evaluation

We directly measure how relevant the retrieved documents are: We focus on an evaluation of the top-ranked documents returned by the IR system for a particular TED talk fragment transcription, since only top documents are suggested to the user. The Normalized Discounted Cumulative Gain (NDCG) measure (Järvelin and Kekäläinen, 2002) is a popular choice to evaluate search engines and also takes into account the ranking of the proposed documents. We evaluate on the top-5 returned documents of the complete system, with two annotators and a standard relevance scale from 0-3. For computing NDCG, we pool all judgments across systems, obtaining an average of 27.7 relevance judgments per fragment, following standard practices for IR evaluations (Clarke et al., 2012).

Method	NDCG (std. dev.)
(1) TF-IDF baseline no MWEs	0.426 (27.8%)
(2) Habibi and PB original implementation	0.427 (28.0%)
(3) Habibi and PB our prep.	0.465 (24.1%)
(4) Habibi and PB our prep., **gold trans.**	0.476 (21.7%)

Method	NDCG (std. dev.)
(5) Our proposed method with MWEs (c=0.7)	0.471 (26.1%)
(6) Our proposed method without MWEs	**0.481 (26.8%)**
(7) Our proposed method without MWEs, **gold trans.**	0.578 (25.2%)
(8) Our proposed method with MWEs (c=0.7), **gold trans.**	0.602 (22.1%)

Table 1: NDCG comparison of TF-IDF baseline keyword and keyphrase extraction methods, the proposed LDA based keyword extraction method by Habibi and Popescu-Belis (2015) and our proposed method based on DRUID, Word2vec and TF-IDF.

In Table 1, we show a comparison of different methods for automatic keyword extraction on TED talk transcriptions (as produced by kaldi-gstreamer-server). All methods use the same resources, i.e. they are all pretrained on the same Simple English Wikipedia dump from May 2016. We allow each system to produce an equal number of 10 terms per query. We did see good results using the method proposed by Habibi and Popescu-Belis (2015), beating our TF-IDF baseline (1). However, we noticed that the publicly available Matlab implementation of this method[10] did only remove stopwords as part of its preprocessing (2). When we use our preprocessing as input (3), we can improve both keyword and NDCG evaluation scores significantly. The best NDCG score using speech transcripts was obtained with our proposed

[10] https://github.com/idiap/DocRec

method *without* using multiwords (6). We experimented with different values of c: 0.3, 0.5 and 0.7, which all lowered NDCG scores. However, making our pipeline multiword-aware raised our NDCG score on manual (gold) transcriptions, cf. experiments (7 vs. 8). We have done further experiments and an in-depth error analysis in Milde et al. (2016), including further experiments on manual transcriptions.

5 Conclusion

We demonstrated *Ambient Search*, a system that can show and retrieve relevant documents for speech streams. As a proof-of-concept we indexed Wikipedia pages, as this provides an universal coverage of different topics and a large document collection for testing purposes. Our approach compares favorably over previous methods of topic discovery and keyword extraction in speech transcriptions. Our proposed term extraction and ranking method using Word2Vec (CBOW) embeddings and TF-IDF is simple to implement. It can also be adapted quickly to other languages without the need for any labeled training data. The only barrier of entry can be the availability of a speech recognition system in the target language.

As the proposed use of multiword terms seems to be somewhat dependent on the quality of the transcription, we consider including likelihood information of the speech recognition system in the future. Ambient search is published on Github [11] as an open source software licensed under the Apache 2.0 license. A demonstration video is also available, along all pretrained models, evaluation files and scripts that are necessary to repeat and reproduce the results presented in this paper.

Acknowledgments. This work was partly supported by the Bundesministerium für Bildung und Forschung (BMBF), Germany, within the Dialog+ project within the program KMU-innovativ. We also want to thank Alexander Hendrich for contributing to improve the HTML5/JS display client and Michelle Sandbrink for helping out with the relevance judgements of the retrieved documents.

References

C. Clarke, N. Craswell, and E. Voorhees. 2012. Overview of the TREC 2012 Web Track. In *Proc. TREC*, Gaithersburg, MD, USA.

S. Dumais, E. Cutrell, R. Sarin, and E. Horvitz. 2004. Implicit Queries (IQ) for Contextualized Search. In *Proc. SIGIR*, page 594, Sheffield, UK.

M. Habibi and A. Popescu-Belis. 2015. Keyword Extraction and Clustering for Document Recommendation in Conversations. *IEEE/ACM Transactions on Audio, Speech, and Language Processing*, 23(4):746–759.

K. Järvelin and J. Kekäläinen. 2002. Cumulated Gain-based Evaluation of IR Techniques. *ACM Trans. Inf. Syst.*, 20(4):422–446.

T. Mikolov, I. Sutskever, K. Chen, G. Corrado, and J. Dean. 2013. Distributed Representations of Words and Phrases and their Compositionality. In *Proc. NIPS*, pages 3111–3119, Lake Tahoe, NV, USA.

B. Milde, J. Wacker, S. Radomski, M. Mühlhäuser, and C. Biemann. 2016. Ambient Search: A Document Retrieval System for Speech Streams. In *Proc. COLING*, Osaka, Japan.

A. Popescu-Belis, J. Kilgour, P. Poller, A. Nanchen, E. Boertjes, and J. De Wit. 2000. Automatic Content Linking: Speech-based Just-in-time Retrieval for Multimedia Archives. In *Proc. SIGIR*, page 703, Athens, Greece.

D. Povey, A. Ghoshal, G. Boulianne, L. Burget, O. Glembek, N. Goel, M. Hannemann, P. Motlicek, Y. Qian, P. Schwarz, J. Silovsky, G. Stemmer, and K. Vesely. 2011. The KALDI Speech Recognition Toolkit. In *Proc. IEEE ASRU*, Waikoloa, HI, USA.

R. Řehůřek and P. Sojka. 2010. Software Framework for Topic Modelling with Large Corpora. In *Proc. LREC*, pages 45–50, Valletta, Malta.

B. Rhodes and P. Maes. 2000. Just-in-time Information Retrieval Agents. *IBM Systems Journal*, 39(3):686.

B. Rhodes and T. Starner. 1996. Remembrance Agent: A Continuously Running Automated Information Retrieval System. In *Proc. Practical Application Of Intelligent Agents and Multi Agent Technology*, pages 487–495.

M. Riedl and C. Biemann. 2015. A Single Word is not Enough: Ranking Multiword Expressions Using Distributional Semantics. In *Proc. EMNLP*, pages 2430–2440, Lisbon, Portugal.

A. Rousseau, P. Deléglise, and Y. Estève. 2014. Enhancing the TED-LIUM Corpus with Selected Data for Language Modeling and More TED Talks. In *Proc. LREC*, pages 3935–3939, Reykjavik, Iceland.

W. Williams, N. Prasad, D. Mrva, T. Ash, and T. Robinson. 2015. Scaling Recurrent Neural Network Language Models. In *Proc. ICASSP*, pages 5391–5395, Brisbane, Australia.

[11] `https://github.com/bmilde/ambientsearch`

ConFarm: Extracting Surface Representations of Verb and Noun Constructions from Dependency Annotated Corpora of Russian

Nikita Mediankin
Institute of Formal and Applied Linguistics
Charles University in Prague, Czech Republic
Faculty of Mathematics and Physics
12800, Praha 2, Sekaninova 14
`nikita.medyankin@gmail.com`

Abstract

ConFarm is a web service dedicated to extraction of surface representations of verb and noun constructions from dependency annotated corpora of Russian texts. Currently, the extraction of constructions with a specific lemma from SynTagRus and Russian National Corpus is available. The system provides flexible interface that allows users to fine-tune the output. Extracted constructions are grouped by their contents to allow for compact representation, and the groups are visualised as a graph in order to help navigating the extraction results. ConFarm differs from similar existing tools for Russian language in that it offers full constructions, as opposed to extracting separate dependents of search word or working with collocations, and allows users to discover unexpected constructions as opposed to searching for examples of a user-defined construction.

1 Introduction

Certain modern schools of linguistic thought focus on constructions as the means of investigating word meaning. This paradigm, along with rapidly developing capabilities for data-driven research, have recently spawned numerous studies of Russian constructions. For these, specialized resources and tools are required, such as manually annotated frame banks and lexicons, tools for automated or semi-automated expansion of said frame banks, as well as tools for extraction of constructions from large corpora.

The main goal of the presented system is to provide linguists with the means for automatic extraction of verb and noun constructions from dependency annotated treebank of Russian texts. The scope of the system does not include semantic frame labeling, and is restricted to the extraction of surface representation. One of the supposed applications of the system is to help in ongoing development of Russian FrameBank (Lyashevskaya, 2010) by both adding examples to existing constructions and discovering new ones.

2 Difference from Existing Systems

ConFarm differs from similar existing tools that can be used for Russian language, such as SketchEngine (`https://www.sketchengine.co.uk/`), RNC Sketches (`http://ling.go.mail.ru/synt/`), and search in syntactically annotated part of Russian National Corpus (`http://ruscorpora.ru/search-syntax.html`), in the following aspects:

1. For each sentence with search word, ConFarm provides a combination of all extracted dependents. Therefore, it offers full constructions, as opposed to extracting dependents of search word separately or working with collocations.

2. The existing tools mostly allow users to search for examples of a user-defined construction, while ConFarm can be used to discover unexpected constructions by leaving the extraction option about the desirable syntactic relations unspecified in the interface.

Proceedings of COLING 2016, the 26th International Conference on Computational Linguistics: System Demonstrations, pages 238–242, Osaka, Japan, December 11-17 2016.

3 Corpora

ConFarm allows to extract constructions from two corpora, SynTagRus in its 2015 state (`http://ruscorpora.ru/instruction-syntax.html`), and recent dump of Russian National Corpus (`http://www.ruscorpora.ru`). SynTagRus is a manually annotated dependency treebank of Russian texts. It was automatically converted both for the use by ConFarm and to provide training for MaltParser model used in RU Syntax NLP pipeline (`http://web-corpora.net/wsgi3/ru-syntax/`). Texts from Russian National Corpus were automatically annotated using RU Syntax pipeline. The details on SynTagRus conversion, and RU Syntax pipeline can be found in (Medyankin, Droganova, 2016).

4 Interface

ConFarm extraction page is used both for specifying extraction options and for presenting the results. It allows user to enter lemma, choose part of speech (currently verb or noun), impose a number of restrictions, and choose a number of options for post processing of extracted constructions. Screenshot of the interface is shown in Figure 1. It should be noted that if nothing is specified in 'only with' options, that means no restriction is imposed, e.g., if 'only with syntactic relations' field is left blank, constructions with any syntactic relations will be extracted, thus allowing to discover unexpected constructions.

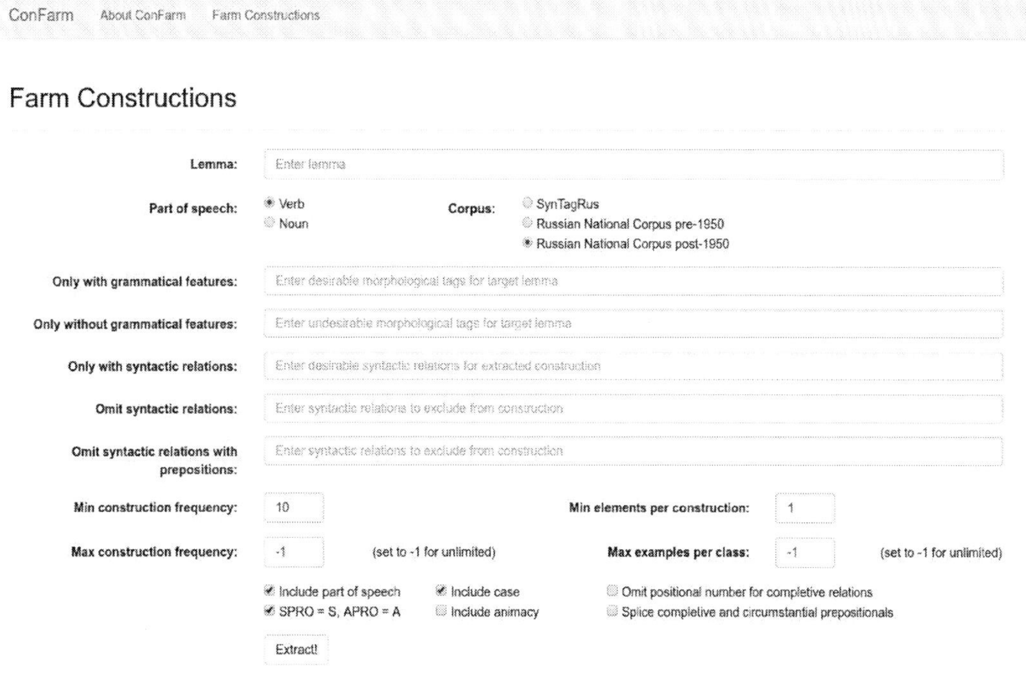

Figure 1: Extraction interface.

The results are presented as both graph and list of extracted constructions grouped by construction contents. Each entry in the list is expandable to show all extracted examples. Each example is shown as a full sentence with extracted construction marked in color. A click on a word opens a popup with information about its lemma, tags, head, and dependency relation label. Figure 2 shows a partial list of constructions extracted for verb *грузить* 'load' from pre-1950 subcorpus of Russian National Corpus.

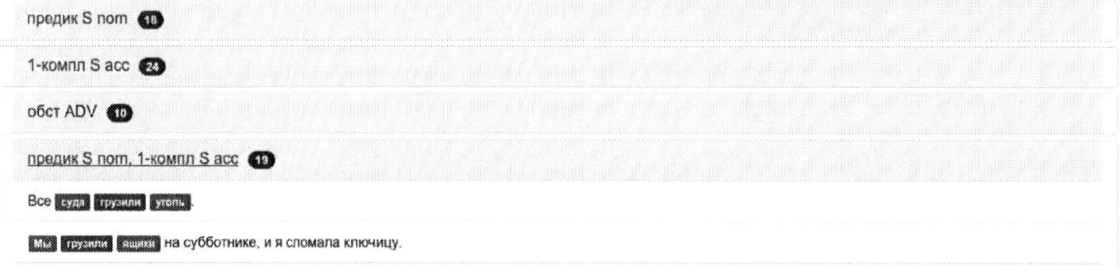

Figure 2: Partial example of extracted constructions list.

5 Extraction and Classification

Extraction process is rule-based and is performed by a Python3 module specifically written for this purpose.

Immediate and prepositional dependent of search word is always extracted, unless user specifically states in extraction options to exclude dependents with this dependency label. This allows users to fine-tune the balance between recall and precision.

Extraction of other parts of construction is based on a set of rules designed to prevent overextraction and includes additional extraction of dependents of search word's head if it is a verb or a short adjective, and extraction of potential object at the start of coordinated or subordinated chain.

Extracted constructions are grouped by the set of dependency labels present among the parts of the construction. These groups are then viewed as a partially ordered set by inclusion and their relationship is visualized by a Hasse diagram to help navigating the extraction results. The example of the diagram for the constructions with verb *грузить* 'load' extracted from post-1950 subcorpus of Russian National Corpus is shown in Figure 3 (only constructions with frequency more than 10 in the corpus were considered).

Figure 3: An example of classification diagram.

6 Evaluation and Discussion

For the purposes of evaluation, the following test has been conducted. 200 examples of different verb constructions with their verb in any form but participle, each with an illustrative chunk of text from Russian National Corpus, were chosen at random from Russian FrameBank (`http://framebank.ru/`). Only arguments were considered part of construction, no adjuncts were included. Each illustrative chunk was then ran through the same stages as though it was annotated for ConFarm and a construction was extracted from it, i.e., annotated with RU Syntax and passed to the Python3 function used to extracts constructions from a sentence. The following settings were chosen as a tradeoff between precision and recall: exclude circumstantial dependents without preposition, exclude parenthetic, delimitative, and expository dependents. This was done in order to reduce adjuncts in the results. Since no exactly similar systems are available for Russian language to compare the results to, a simple baseline was developed: extract all nouns, infinitive verbs, and prepositions directly preceding them within ±5 context window or sentence boundaries, whatever is met first.

FrameBank	Baseline	ConFarm
subject	Noun nom Verb inf	Noun nom, predicative Verb inf, predicative
object	Noun acc Verb inf	Noun acc, completive Verb inf, completive
periphery	Noun other case Prep + Noun other case	Noun other case, completive Prep + Noun other case, completive

Table 1: FrameBank to Baseline to ConFarm match for labeled scores.

The results were then manually compared with FrameBank annotations. First, unlabeled scores were calculated: (1) if given token is present both in FrameBank annotation and extracted construction, it is considered true positive, disregarding its dependency label and FrameBank labeling; (2) if it is present in FrameBank annotation, but not in extracted construction, it is considered false negative; (3) if it is not present in FrameBank annotation, but is present in extracted construction, it is considered false positive; (4) if it is not present in FrameBank annotation, nor in extracted construction, it is considered true negative. Unlabeled precision, recall and accuracy were then calculated following standard definitions. Second, labeled scores were calculated: same as above but given token was only considered a hit if (a) its case (for nouns) or infinitiveness (for verbs) matched FrameBank, and (b) its dependency label corresponded to its FrameBank rank as shown in Table 1. For baseline, only (a) was considered when calculating labeled scores. The scores are shown in Table 2.

	Unlabeled			Labeled		
	precision	recall	accuracy	precision	recall	accuracy
Baseline	51%	77%	85%	44%	67%	82%
ConFarm	75%	79%	93%	64%	68%	89%

Table 2: Test results.

With both labeled and unlabeled scores, ConFarm showed much higher precision and slightly higher recall, compared to the baseline. Detailed examination of the results showed that better precision was due to ConFarm filtering out irrelevant nouns and infinitives, and the recall was higher because of detected distant parts of construction that did not get to the context window, but not by the large margin because a number of relevant completive dependents were erroneously marked as circumstantial and therefore filtered out.

7 Availability

ConFarm web-service is available for unconditional use at `http://www.confarm.online`.

8 Conclusion

This article presented a web-service ConFarm that provides extraction and initial classification of surface representations of verb and noun constructions from two dependency annotated Russian corpora: SynTagRus and Russian National Corpus, the latter of which was automatically dependency annotated specifically for the purpose of using it in ConFarm. The web-interface allows users to fine-tune the output by specifying a number of various extraction options. The system was evaluated on 200 different verb constructions from Russian FrameBank and results compared to a simple baseline set up without using dependency annotation. For both labeled and unlabeled scores, ConFarm showed much higher precision and slightly higher recall than the baseline. Further improvements can be made to the system by both obtaining better automated annotation for Russian National Corpus and by refining the rules for extracting parts of the construction that are not immediate or prepositional dependents of the search word.

Acknowledgements

This work was partially funded by the Ministry of Education, Youth and Sports of the Czech Republic under the project SVV project 260 333. It used language resources stored and distributed by the LINDAT/CLARIN project of the Ministry of Education, Youth and Sports of the Czech Republic (project LM2015071).

References

Olga Lyashevskaya. 2010. *Bank of Russian constructions and valencies.* LREC 2010. Malta, Valletta, May 19-21, 2010.

Nikita Medyankin, Kira Droganova. 2016. *Building NLP Pipeline for Russian with a Handful of Linguistic Knowledge.* Online proceedings of the Workshop "Computational linguistics and language science" (CLLS) Moscow 2016, CEUR Workshop Proceedings (in print, manuscript is available at http://web-corpora.net/wsgi3/ru-syntax/static/downloads/Medyankin_Droganova_CLLS_2016.pdf).

ENIAM: Categorial Syntactic-Semantic Parser for Polish

Wojciech Jaworski **Jakub Kozakoszczak**
Institute of Computer Science, Polish Academy of Sciences
University of Warsaw
wjaworski@mimuw.edu.pl jkozakoszczak@gmail.com

Abstract

This paper presents ENIAM, the first syntactic and semantic parser that generates *semantic representations* for sentences in Polish. The parser processes non-annotated data and performs tokenization, lemmatization, dependency recognition, word sense annotation, thematic role annotation, partial disambiguation and computes the semantic representation.

1 Introduction

ENIAM is a syntactic and semantic parser that generates *semantic representations* for sentences in Polish. It is publicly available under the address `http://eniam.nlp.ipipan.waw.pl` and licensed under GPL 3. The parser processes non-annotated data and performs all the necessary steps: tokenization, lemmatization, dependency recognition, word sense annotation, thematic role annotation, partial disambiguation and computes the semantic representation. It is the first semantic parser for Polish.

The system was developed within the CLARIN-PL project (`http://clarin-pl.eu`) which aims at creating a research infrastructure intended for the humanities and social sciences dealing with large collections of Polish texts. The range of applications of the system is wide and includes all the language processing tasks that involve the semantic level, in particular Information Retrieval, Question Answering, Recognizing Textual Entailment. An example of a QA task is the processing of biograms for knowledge extraction and for answering questions of the type "Who publishes in a journal edited by themselves?".

2 System Description

The text processing steps are executed in a fuzzy pipeline. The system doesn't disambiguate the output of every step immediately but makes a compact representation of the ambiguous outcome and passes it to next stages. Structure sharing assures that the growth of the representation is polynomial with respect to the length of the sentence, although the number of interpretations growths exponentially. The disambiguation is perform near the and of the pipeline, when all syntactic and semantic constraints are applied to data.

The reason for the fuzzy pipeline approach is that disambiguation is never 100% accurate and a single error during disambiguation after one stage of processing often makes it impossible to perform the next stage of processing. The other reason is that we consider ambiguity as a property of natural language that should be modeled under equal terms with other linguistic phenomena.

During the preprocessing (all stages before finding the dependency structure) the text is represented as a graph whose edges correspond to running words (tokens). For each interpretation of a token another alternative edge is being added, e.g.:

Proceedings of COLING 2016, the 26th International Conference on Computational Linguistics: System Demonstrations, pages 243–247, Osaka, Japan, December 11-17 2016.

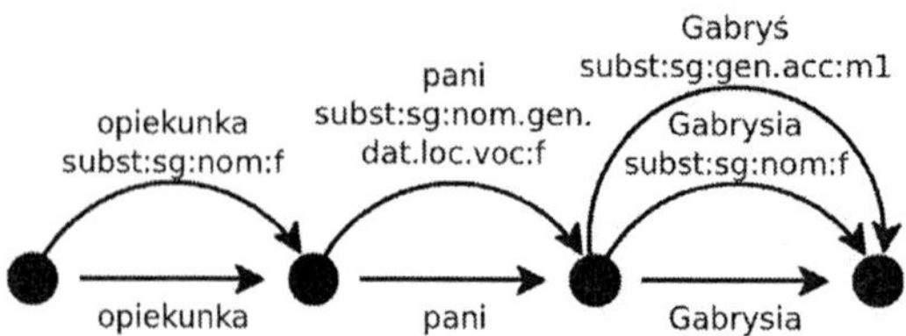

Preprocessing includes character-level analysis (tokenization, haplology of punctuation), word-level analysis (lematization, morphosyntactic tagging, word sense annotation, subcategorization, semantic valence annotation) and phrase-level analysis (abbreviation extension, MWE recognition, Named Entity Recognition).

Lemmatization is based on the dictionaries SGJP (Zygmunt et al., 2015) and Polimorf (Wolinski et al., 2012). All possible lemmata and morphosyntactic tags are deduced from the endings. Then, if there is at least one known lemma among deduced lemmata, the unknown lemmata are being discarded. If none of the lemmata is known, all of them are returned.

Named entity annotation is also done with the help of SGJP and Polimorf which associate proper names with a general type of their referent, e.g. toponym, surname and such. Capitalized nouns that are not classified as proper names in the dictionaries are treated as proper names of unknown type.

Word senses taken from Słowosieć (the Polish WordNet) (Maziarz et al., 2014) are ascribed to lexemes. Each sense is represented in the WordNet style as a lemma with a number . The senses of proper names are their types.

The valency of the lexemes in the sentence is determined with the valency dictionary Walenty (Przepiórkowski et al., 2014). Walenty covers most verbs and many nouns, adjectives and adverbs. Each entry comprises syntactic schemata that include detailed syntactic description of the obligatory dependents, and semantic frames that give their semantic characteristic, namely thematic roles and selectional preferences expressed as synsets from Słowosieć. The schemata and the frames are mapped many-to-many.

Preliminary disambiguation tries to crudely match selectional preferences of all the possible heads with hypernyms of all the possible dependents. If a selectional preference is not a hypernym of any lexeme in the sentence, it is discarded, and if a hypernym is not a preference of any of the lexemes, it is discarded as well. The slots in the syntactic schemata in Walenty correspond to traditional argument positions (such as subject or object). The system adds slots for remaining dependents if needed (e.g. locative modifiers)

Syntactic Analysis Preprocessing is followed by the construction of the syntactic tree done in Type Logical Categorial Grammar (TLCG) (Morrill, 2010). To parse a sentence is to give a proof in a non-commutative intuitionistic linear logic, therefore fragments of the proof system can be implemented to obtain quick parsers with guaranteed correctness. The lexicon is generated dynamically for each query from SGJP and Walenty entries.

The categorial grammar doesn't play further role in building the semantic representation. The full lexicalization of categorial grammars facilitates integration with the resources: morphological and valence dictionaries. The choice of TLCG instead of the standard CCG (Bos et al., 2004) is motivated by the wider choice of connectives that express important information, like ambiguity or polymorphism.

Parser The parser is based on the CKY algorithm and is a direct implementation of a fragment of the proof system for linear logic. It has the expressiveness of context-free grammar. Since the categorial framework allows for inflectional ambiguity representation, the size of the generated lexicon is exponentially smaller than a context-free grammar that models the same language. The dependency structure between tokens is generated in a lazy way. The ambiguity is expressed in the form of a compressed tree. Fragments of the parse tree are compressed immediately after obtaining.

Semantic valence In order to better handle the ambiguities caused by the variety of senses and thematic roles that are assigned to lexemes, no semantic information is introduced to the categorial grammar and thus no semantic representation is immediately obtained together with the dependency structure. The alternating meanings and valency frames are added in the maximally local way. Thus this approach leads towards Universal Dependencies (De Marneffe and Manning, 2008), where non-semantic prepositions, numerals, auxiliary verbs etc. becomes dependents of their traditional arguments.

Disambiguation Disambiguation is done in stages. First, we check the satisfiability of selectional restrictions, then we select the most likely lemmas on the basis of a list of NKJP1M (Adam Przepiórkowski and Lewandowska-Tomaszczyk, 2012) lemma frequency list, and at the end, we choose word senses. Other types of ambiguity, such as eg. PP attachment ambiguity remains currently ambiguous. For the purpose of the presentation in the demo, 10 unambiguous dependency structures are drawn.

Semantics Semantic representation is built upon dependency trees augmented with concepts from Słowosieć (which is an ontology for our meaning representation) and relations between concepts that extend the set of thematic roles defined in Walenty.

The semantic analysis is shallow in that it describes the world in accordance to its view imprinted in the language:

- The intensions of lexemes are concepts.
- The concepts provide truth conditions for the referents of the words.
- Relations between the referents are provided by valency dictionary or given in the syntactic relations.

Its main merit is that it requires little resources for a complete semantic representation.

However, the presented shallow semantic analysis is a starting point for further development, mainly through enrichment with domain-specific theories.

Metalanguage We assume an extended version of FOL with one meta-predicate DSCR that binds a formula with its identifier. The logical formulae are presented on the form of semantic graphs.

(1) *Słoń* *trąbi.*
Elephant trumpets.
'An elephant trumpets.'

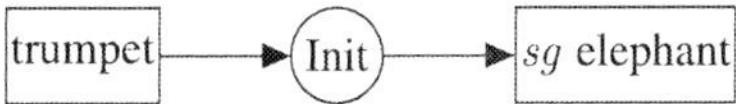

The boxes represent entities mentioned in the text. One is the *elephant* and another is the action of *trumpeting*. [1] The symbol sg is a quantifier that define the count of the entities exactly one.

The circles represent relations between the entities. The Init relation says that the *elephant* is the initiator of *trumpeting*. The ingoing arrow leads from the first argument and the outgoing one leads to the second.

The graph is equivalent to the logical formula

$$\exists(s, \text{TYPE}(s, \text{elephant}) \wedge |s| = 1, \exists(t, \text{TYPE}(t, \text{trumpet}) \wedge \text{INITIATOR}(t, s))) \quad (2)$$

where each entity is identified by a variable. The predicate $\text{TYPE}(x, \mathrm{t})$ assigns a type t to a variable x, i.e. it states that set of objects denoted by x belongs to the ontological category t.

Variables are always assigned to sets of entities. Singular number is denoted by the statement that a set is a singleton, and plural number by the statement that it has quantity greater than 1.

Proper names are represented using predicate $\text{HASNAME}(x, '\mathrm{name}')$ which connects a string 'name' with a set of objects denoted by x. In semantic graphs quotation marks indicate the property of being a proper name. Those names don't define an ontological type of the referent but identify it by assigning a label.

[1]For the convenience of non Polish speaking readers all presented logical formulae are translated into English and are therefore not identical to the parser output. In particular the parser presents concept names in Polish.

We consequently reify all concepts. Every lexeme (or MWE) which is not a quantifier, conjunct or non-semantic item is translated into a TYPE or HASNAME predicate. The reasons for this are: the possibility of modifiers for virtually every part of speech in Polish, uniformization of all parts of speech for the clarity of the Semantic Metalanguage and for further processing.

Apart from the above two predicates we have a fixed number of binary predicates that denote relations between concepts such as Init (Initiator), Thme (Theme), etc.

We also extend FOL with special quantifiers existing in the language, e.g. *co dziesiąty* ('every tenth') or *prawie każdy* ('almost every').

(3) *Słoń codziennie trąbi.*
Elephant everyday trumpets.
'An elephant trumpets everyday.'

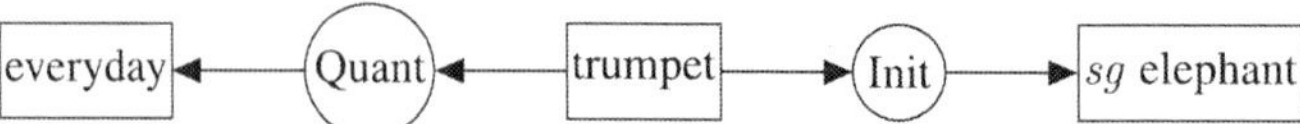

$$\exists(s, \text{TYPE}(s, \text{elephant}) \wedge |s| = 1, \text{EVERYDAY}(t, \text{TYPE}(t, \text{trumpet}) \wedge \text{INITIATOR}(t, s))) \quad (4)$$

Quantifiers are ordered according to words in the sentence. This solution to the problem of quantifier scope ambiguity is motivated by the fact that Polish is nearly free word order language.

Properties Properties are typically expressed by adjectives and adverbs.

(5) *Intensywnie różowy słoń trąbi.*
Deeply pink elephant trumpets.
'An elephant in deep pink trumpets.'

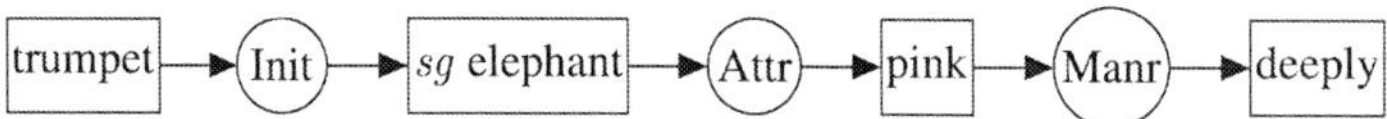

The name of the property is bound with the name of the entity that has the property with the predicate Attribute for adjectives and Manner for adverbs. Individuals have properties and properties also have properties.

Time and space descriptions Time and space is usually given in adverbs and prepositional phrases. Prepositions of location and direction give the relations between locations and temporal prepositions give the relations between points and or intervals in time taken separately or in sets. Those relations undergo reification because they can be modified, e.g. *dość głęboko w szafie* 'quite deep in the closet'. The predicate Location indicates the location of a situation / an event. The predicates Location Source, Location Goal, Path indicate the presence of movement, its location and direction. The predicates Time and Duration give information about the temporal location of an entity (typically an event) and about its duration. The Ref predicate binds a proposition with its dependent.

(6) *Z Poznania jedzie pociąg przez Warszawę.*
From Posen-GEN goes train-NOM through Warsaw-ACC.
'A train goes from Posen through Warsaw.'

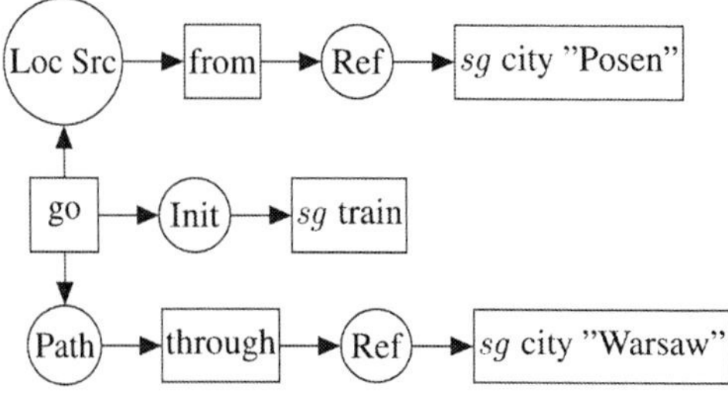

Inner models A proposition in a subordinate clause doesn't need to be implied by the whole sentence. We place it in a separate box in order to indicate that its truth value ought to be determined against the subjective point of view:

(7) *Jan wierzy, że słoń trąbi.*
Jan believes, that elephant trumpets.
'Jan believes that an elephant trumpets.'

A meta-predicate DSCR is added to the logical notation is a tool for representing relations between embedded models in the subject language .

$$\exists(w, \text{TYPE}(w, \text{believe}) \wedge \exists(j, \text{TYPE}(j, \text{person}) \wedge \text{HASNAME}(j, \text{'Jan'}) \wedge |j| = 1, \text{INITIATOR}(w, j)) \wedge \exists(x, \text{TYPE}(x, \text{that}) \wedge \text{DSCR}(x, \exists(s, \text{TYPE}(s, \text{elephant}) \wedge |s| = 1, \exists(t, \text{TYPE}(t, \text{trumpet}) \wedge \text{INITIATOR}(t, s)))), \text{CONDITION}(w, x)))$$

3 Conclusions

Presented system is novel not only as a tool for semantic processing of Polish. ENIAM introduces the fuzzy pipeline approach to language processing and implements a subset of LCG form large scale language processing. It also takes advantage of huge semantic resources (such as Słowosieć and Walenty) which were created as a part of CLARIN-PL project. The fact that ENIAM does not require any prior annotation of processed sentences make it universal and ready to use tool.

Acknowledgements

Work financed as part of the investment in the CLARIN-PL research infrastructure funded by the Polish Ministry of Science and Higher Education.

References

Rafał L. Górski Adam Przepiórkowski, Mirosław Bańko and Barbara Lewandowska-Tomaszczyk. 2012. National corpus of polish. *Wydawnictwo Naukowe PWN, Warsaw*, pages 51–58.

Johan Bos, Stephen Clark, Mark Steedman, James R Curran, and Julia Hockenmaier. 2004. Wide-coverage semantic representations from a ccg parser. In *Proceedings of the 20th international conference on Computational Linguistics*, page 1240. Association for Computational Linguistics.

Marie-Catherine De Marneffe and Christopher D Manning. 2008. Stanford typed dependencies manual. Technical report, Technical report, Stanford University.

Marek Maziarz, Maciej Piasecki, Ewa Rudnicka, and Stan Szpakowicz. 2014. plwordnet as the cornerstone of a toolkit of lexico-semantic resources. In *Proceedings of the Seventh Global Wordnet Conference*, pages 304–312.

Glyn Morrill. 2010. *Categorial grammar: Logical syntax, semantics, and processing*. Oxford University Press.

Adam Przepiórkowski, Elżbieta Hajnicz, Agnieszka Patejuk, and Marcin Woliński. 2014. Extended phraseological information in a valence dictionary for NLP applications. In *Proceedings of the Workshop on Lexical and Grammatical Resources for Language Processing (LG-LP 2014)*, pages 83–91, Dublin, Ireland. Association for Computational Linguistics and Dublin City University.

Marcin Wolinski, Marcin Milkowski, Maciej Ogrodniczuk, and Adam Przepiórkowski. 2012. Polimorf: a (not so) new open morphological dictionary for polish. In *LREC*, pages 860–864.

Saloni Zygmunt, Woliński Marcin, Wołosz Robert, Gruszczyński Włodzimierz, and Skowrońska Danuta. 2015. Grammatical dictionary of polish.

Towards Non-projective High-Order Dependency Parser

Wenjing Fang and **Kenny Q. Zhu** and **Yizhong Wang** and **Jia Tan**
Shanghai Jiao Tong University
{littlebeanfang,kzhu}@sjtu.edu.cn and {eastonwyz,tjtanjia.tan}@gmail.com

Abstract

This paper demonstrates a novel high-order dependency parsing framework that targets non-projective languages. It imitates how a human parses sentences in an intuitive way. At every step of the parse, it determines which word is the easiest to process among all the remaining words, identifies its head word and then folds it under the head word. This greedy framework achieves competitive accuracy on WSJ evaluation set and shows additional advantage on the non-projective corpus. Further, this work is flexible enough to be augmented with other parsing techniques. [1]

1 Introduction

Dependency parse trees, as the most commonly used syntax representation, is a preliminary part in many Natural Language Processing(NLP) tasks. Existing data-driven dependency parsers are divided into two classes, graph-based and transition-based. As typical graph-based parsers, MSTParser and its variants (McDonald et al., 2005) presently enjoy high accuracy at some cost of parsing time. However, such exact inference approach limits the range of features that can be extracted (McDonald and Nivre, 2007). MaltParser (Nivre, 2003), which is the most representative of transition-based parsers, carries out a sequence of greedy actions determined by a classifier trained from parsing sequences. Transition-based parsing is done incrementally by processing smaller word spans into subtrees first before combining smaller subtrees into bigger ones. Consequently, MaltParser has not met much success with non-projective parsing.[2]

Studies in psycholinguistics revealed how humans comprehend a sentence. Humans tend to perform a rapid and shallow recognition of major phrases, which guide the understanding process from the easiest relations to the more difficult ones (Townsend and Bever, 2001). By folding modifiers under their head words, we can gradually grasp the sentence structure and incorporate the already built structures for later parse. There is an earlier attempt inspired by the same intuition (Goldberg and Elhadad, 2010), whose framework is an adaptation of transition-based parser. However, it inherits the same problem as MaltParser in which candidate heads are all locally determined and can only deal with projective parsing.

This paper builds a parsing framework that follows the above intuition. It has two key components. The *sequence predictor* generates a permutation of words in the input sentence, which indicates the processing order, from the easy to the hard. The *head mapper* takes each word from the sequence and maps the head for each word in that order. Our current implementation generates transition-based processing sequence to guide a greedy high order graph-based decoder. It outperforms the easy-first parser in that it achieves similar accuracies with projective parsing (Kong and Smith, 2014), but can also deal with non-projective cases. In this paper, we use the idea of *parsing sequence* to bridge the gap between transition-based and graph-based methods under one framework.

[1]Kenny Q. Zhu is the corresponding author and is partially supported by NSFC Grant No. 61373031.

[2]The later proposal of SWAP action ameliorates some of this problem. But training a classifier for this action is hard due to limited resources of training data.

Proceedings of COLING 2016, the 26th International Conference on Computational Linguistics: System Demonstrations, pages 248–252, Osaka, Japan, December 11-17 2016.

2 Framework

The general architecture of the parser is shown in Figure 1 and is divided into training phase and parsing phase.

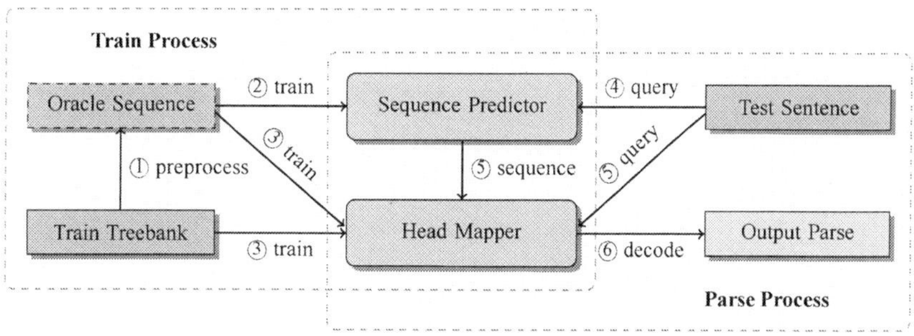

Figure 1: Sequence Based Parser Framework

Training: The preprocessing step generates oracle sequences from the gold standard parse trees. Only the word forms and the POS tags in these parse trees are used. Here, we assume that a child node is easier to process than its parent node and it is supposed to be attached before its parent. [3] We then train respectively a graph-based head mapper (a.k.a. decoder) from the gold sequences and the gold parses, and a sequence predictor from the gold sequences.

Parsing: Given an input sentence, the sequence predictor outputs a feasible decoding sequence, which is a permutation of the words in the input. For each word in this sequence, the head mapper returns its best head word according to a scoring function while employing a cycle detection mechanism. The process continues until all words in the sentence have found their heads. The procedure guarantees to produce a tree structure eventually.

In the current implementation, we generate the decoding sequence by *stackproj* algorithm (Nivre, 2009) in MaltParser and scorer-based greedy head mapper.

3 System Architecture

In the following, we present the preliminary investigation on the two key components of the our parser: head mapper and sequence predictor .

3.1 Head Mapper

Figure 2 shows the decoding process of the head mapper for a non-projective example sentence (McDonald et al., 2005): "*John saw a dog yesterday which was a Yorkshire Terrier*". A head mapper takes the lexical information of a sentence and a permutated sequence of words in that sentence as inputs. Suppose the sequence is:

$John_1 \rightarrow a_3 \rightarrow dog_4 \rightarrow yesterday_5 \rightarrow Yorkshire_9 \rightarrow a_8 \rightarrow was_7 \rightarrow which_6 \rightarrow Terrier_{10} \rightarrow saw_2$.

The subscript stands for the position of the word in original sentence. At step one, we look for the head of *John*. At this point, all other words are potential candidate heads. In order to measure the probabilities of these candidate arcs, we introduce a scorer, which is the key idea of graph-based parsers. By comparing the scores printed on every black arc in Figure 2, the red arc was eventually selected, i.e. saw is made the head of $John$. The process continues for the word *a*, etc.

In practice, we ensure that there are no cycles of nodes generated during parsing, so that the final output is a dependency tree structure starting from the ROOT node[4]. We also build a parse agenda to

[3] By this rule, multiple gold sequences can be generated from one dependency tree. In this paper, when a parent node has multiple children, we generate the sequence by a left-to-right order.

[4] A manually introduced node in dependency parsing task, it is the root of a dependency tree.

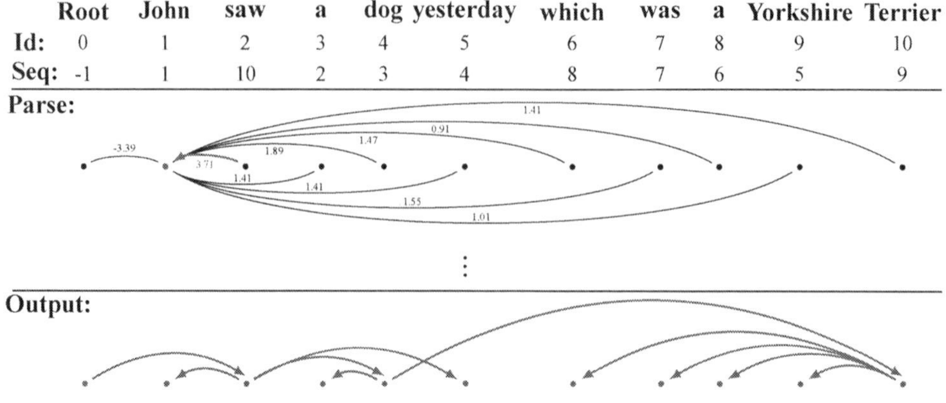

Figure 2: Example Parse of head mapper

record the existing arcs, which provides the high order information for our scorer. For example, after adding arc:$saw \rightarrow John$, all the attachment on these two nodes will take this arc into consideration.

We introduce a linear arc scorer to measure the score of a directed arc. The sum of all arc scores gives the final score of the whole parse tree. We currently use the typical high-dimensional binary features, including second order features (McDonald and Pereira, 2006). Because of the deterministic decoding in our framework, we can make use of existing arcs to guide later head mapping. This kind of decoder gives us the flexibility of applying any high order features explored by previous works (Carreras, 2007; Koo and Collins, 2010; Ma and Zhao, 2012).

The arc scorer is trained by the iterative online training framework MIRA (Margin Infused Relaxed Algorithm) (Crammer and Singer, 2003). In each iteration, we update the feature weights based on one sentence. The decoder gives a greedy parse according to current feature weights. By scoring the gold dependency tree and the current parse, along with the number of incorrect arcs in the current parse, MIRA keeps updating the weights until it eventually converges to an optimal scorer. The learning algorithm typically terminates after a few iterations.

3.2 Sequence Predictor

The intuition of sequence predictor is to rank words according to the ease of head word attaching. Words that are easy to handle can be processed earlier without high order features. To decide whether process a word immediately, we imitate the action classifier in MaltParser.

In fact, we can understand the action classifier in a different way that it can reflect the relative priority between the top two words on processing stack. We translate the actiones as:

- LA - process the word on the top of stack;
- RA - process the second word in stack;
- SH - postpone the process of both the two words on top of stack.

In this way, a word sequence can be inferred rather straightforwardly from the action sequence.

4 Demo

We build this sequence-based non-projective dependency parser and the part of the work is licensed under the GNU General Public License.

We evaluate our demo systsem on the WSJ test set under english[5] and five non-projective treebanks in different languages.[6] [7]

[5]the training set is sections 2-21 of WSJ corpus and test set is sections 00-01

[6]http://ilk.uvt.nl/conll/post_task_data.html

[7]http://www.nltk.org/nltk_data/

Table 1 shows the results of our system(nonproj), MaltParser and MSTParser. Generally, we outperform MaltParser in non-projective treebanks, which indicates that our framework tolerates free word order better. Our accuracy is not as good as MSTParser, because of the greedy decoding strategy. Nevertheless, this strategy gives rise to improvement in parsing time and flexibility in defining high order features than MSTParser.

Table 1: End-to-end accuracies on 8 languages

Language	nonproj	MSTParser	MaltParser
basque	77.45%	81.81%	74.88%
dutch	81.43%	85.66%	77.28%
danish	86.84%	89.39%	85.65%
portuguese	86.93%	88.63%	85.97%
slovene	78.26%	80.16%	76.09%
WSJ	89.50%	90.64%	90.23%

Further, we compare the accuracies of the non-projective arcs in the test data in Table 2. The system produces reasonable accuracies and outperforms MaltParser and MSTParser on parsing non-projective arcs.

Table 2: Accuracy of non-projective arcs in 5 languages

	basque			dutch			danish			portuguese			slovene		
parser	correct	total	accuracy	correct	total	accuracy	correct	total	accuracy	correct	total	accuracy	correct	total	accuracy
nonproj	225	569	0.395431	339	529	0.640832	79	121	0.652893	104	191	0.544503	101	263	0.3840304
MaltParser	200	569	0.351494	300	529	0.567108	58	121	0.479339	103	191	0.539267	98	263	0.3726236
MSTParesr	204	569	0.358524	204	529	0.385633	63	121	0.520661	90	191	0.471204	109	263	0.4144487

Given a CoNLL formatted training data and test data, our demo can parse out the dependency tree. Figure 1 is the snapshot of the demo showing the parsing result on the multilingual corpus.

Nonproj Dependency Parser

Enter a sentence to be parsed: Language: Dutch

Iedereen loopt een zeker risico, dat_wil_zeggen een kans op gezondheidsschade.

Random Parse

Parse Result

su (loopt-2, Iedereen-1)
ROOT (Root-0, loopt-2)
det (risico-5, een-3)
mod (risico-5, zeker-4)
obj1 (loopt-2, risico-5)
punc (risico-5, ,-6)
mod (risico-5, dat_wil_zeggen-7)
det (kans-9,een-8)
body (dat_wil_zeggen-7, kans-9)
mod (kans-9, op-10)
obj1 (op-10, gezondheidsschade-11)
punc (gezondheidsschade-11, .-12)

Figure 3: Example Parse of head mapper

5 Conclusion

We develop a novel sequence-based dependency parsing framework. It shows promising results despite of an unoptimized implementation. The key idea is that a good parsing sequence can be predetermined and can contribute to good parsing accuracy and substantial speedup. Although only a few simple approaches are attempted to train the sequence predictor, the framework allows the integration of better and more advanced models, which may lead to results closer to an upper bound 93.59% [8] for the WSJ test set.

Even though the current classifier based sequence predictor produces better results among our preliminary attempts, the parsing accuracy is limited by the rather localized or even incorrect sequence order produced. More importantly, we discovered that the parsing accuracy is very sensitive to the quality of parsing sequence. Future work can be focused on developing better sequence predictors that outperform this classifier based method.

Graph-based methods spend most of the time extracting features. Some work attempted to save time by displaying arc filter (Bergsma and Cherry, 2010; Rush and Petrov, 2012). We can incorporate some of these techniques to speed up the parsing. Furthermore, Beam search works well in a left-to-right head attaching. We can also adapt beam search to our framework so as to relax its strictly greedy nature.

References

[Bergsma and Cherry2010] Shane Bergsma and Colin Cherry. 2010. Fast and accurate arc filtering for dependency parsing. In *Proceedings of the 23rd International Conference on Computational Linguistics (Coling 2010)*, pages 53–61.

[Carreras2007] Xavier Carreras. 2007. Experiments with a higher-order projective dependency parser. In *EMNLP-CoNLL*, pages 957–961.

[Crammer and Singer2003] Koby Crammer and Yoram Singer. 2003. Ultraconservative online algorithms for multiclass problems. *The Journal of Machine Learning Research*, 3:951–991.

[Goldberg and Elhadad2010] Yoav Goldberg and Michael Elhadad. 2010. An efficient algorithm for easy-first non-directional dependency parsing. In *NAACL HLT*, pages 742–750.

[Kong and Smith2014] Lingpeng Kong and Noah A Smith. 2014. An empirical comparison of parsing methods for stanford dependencies. *arXiv preprint arXiv:1404.4314*.

[Koo and Collins2010] Terry Koo and Michael Collins. 2010. Efficient third-order dependency parsers. In *ACL*, pages 1–11.

[Ma and Zhao2012] Xuezhe Ma and Hai Zhao. 2012. Fourth-order dependency parsing. In *COLING (Posters)*, pages 785–796. Citeseer.

[McDonald and Nivre2007] Ryan T McDonald and Joakim Nivre. 2007. Characterizing the errors of data-driven dependency parsing models. In *EMNLP-CoNLL*, pages 122–131.

[McDonald and Pereira2006] Ryan T McDonald and Fernando CN Pereira. 2006. Online learning of approximate dependency parsing algorithms. In *EACL*.

[McDonald et al.2005] Ryan McDonald, Fernando Pereira, Kiril Ribarov, and Jan Hajič. 2005. Non-projective dependency parsing using spanning tree algorithms. In *HLT/EMNLP*, pages 523–530.

[Nivre2003] Joakim Nivre. 2003. An efficient algorithm for projective dependency parsing. In *IWPT*.

[Nivre2009] Joakim Nivre. 2009. Non-projective dependency parsing in expected linear time. In *ACL-IJCNLP: Volume 1-Volume 1*, pages 351–359.

[Rush and Petrov2012] Alexander M Rush and Slav Petrov. 2012. Vine pruning for efficient multi-pass dependency parsing. In *NAACL HLT*, pages 498–507.

[Townsend and Bever2001] David J Townsend and Thomas G Bever. 2001. *Sentence comprehension: The integration of habits and rules*, volume 1950. MIT Press.

[8]Take the sequence inferred the oracle actions from MaltParser as both training sequence and parsing sequence and define only first and second order features in MSTParser for head mapper to get this raw bound

Using Synthetically Collected Scripts for Story Generation

Takashi Ogata
Iwate Prefectural University
/ 152-52, Sugo, Takizawashi,
Iwate, 020-0693 Japan
t-ogata@iwate-pu.ac.jp

Tatsuya Arai
Iwate Prefectural University
/ 152-52, Sugo, Takizawashi,
Iwate, 020-0693 Japan
g0311011@s.iwate-pu.ac.jp

Jumpei Ono
Iwate Prefectural University
/ 152-52, Sugo, Takizawashi,
Iwate, 020-0693 Japan
g236m001@s.iwate-pu.ac.jp

Abstract

A script is a type of knowledge representation in artificial intelligence (AI). This paper presents two methods for synthetically using collected scripts for story generation. The first method recursively generates long sequences of events and the second creates script networks. Although related studies generally use one or more scripts for story generation, this research synthetically uses many scripts to flexibly generate a diverse narrative.

1 Introduction

A script, originally related to a type of schema in Gestalt psychology (Bartlett 1923), is a knowledge-representation method in cognitive science and artificial intelligence (AI) (Schank and Abelson 1977). The authors use a script as one of the methods or techniques to generate stories in an Integrated Narrative Generation System (INGS), an automated NGS architecture that is already operating through incremental development (Ogata 2016). Ogata, Arai, and Ono (2016) comprehensively introduced how to use a script in INGS. The script is organically positioned as one of the story-generation techniques, especially for detailed episodic sequences of events or a character's sequential actions.

This paper presents two methods for synthetically using collected scripts for story generation in INGS. The first method recursively generates long sequences of events and the second creates script networks. Related studies deal with one or more scripts for story generation. In contrast, this research synthetically uses many scripts to flexibly generate a diverse narrative. Although this paper does not discuss the semantic aspects of a script, we will add semantic mechanisms to the proposed formal methods in the future.

Kybartas and Bidarra (2016) classified 67 types of narrative-generation systems based on the degree of automatic generation in a story and components in the story. The degree is divided into five steps (the degree for story are "Manual", "Structure", "Template", "Constrained", "Automated", and the degree for components are "Manual", "Modification", "Simulation", "Constrained", "Automated"). INGS is positioned as "constrained" (level 4 of the five steps) in both points of view. In the evaluation, a story and components are fully generated.

2 Scripts and INGS

Narratology (Prince 1982) divides a narrative into structural elements (story and discourse). A story refers to temporally ordered events. Though temporal order is a category of semantic techniques that organically combines events, the semantic mechanism includes other techniques types. A discourse means ordered events in which a story is narrated and also includes surface text; it is constructed using many techniques, e.g., causal relation and macro narrative structures. INGS is designed based on this idea (Figure 1). A narrative-generation process is conducted through the following mechanisms: story generation, discourse, and surface representation. INGS has knowledge mechanisms, including conceptual dictionaries (Ogata 2015) and language-notation dictionaries. Moreover, INGS has narrative-content knowledge bases to store basic fragmental, patternal, and structural knowledge. A detailed description of the current version can be found in (Ogata 2016).

This paper focuses on story generation. A story can be constructed at various levels of detail. "Taro eats sushi at a restaurant" can certainly be an event in a story. More detailed sequences of events for "eating at a restaurant" can also be elements in a story. Each of the scripts extends an event into a sequence of events to solidify or detail the process.

Proceedings of COLING 2016, the 26th International Conference on Computational Linguistics: System Demonstrations, pages 253–257, Osaka, Japan, December 11-17 2016.

In related studies, a story grammar (Rumelhart 1975) hierarchically details a story from the macro structure to the micro one. A goal-plan (Newell and Simon 1972; Schank and Abelson 1977) details an event or a sequence of events using a planning action toward a character's goal. Scripts, story grammars, and goal-plans are major structural techniques that solidify part of a story or the story itself. In INGS, the techniques for each generation and their order are not predetermined. Different techniques are flexibly, collectively, and co-operatively used. Additionally, though the *StoryNet* scripts by Singh, Barry, and Liu (2004) have a branch structure, INGS scripts have a simple pattern with no branches. Moreover, though Fujiki, Nanba, and Okumura (2002) acquire two terms per script, INGS has an unlimited number of terms in scripts.

A story in INGS is described using a hierarchical tree structure that uses relations to combine the sub-structures. At the lowest level, events and states are organized temporally. A script is also one of the relations. Techniques for story generation are called story techniques. They are basically defined by a story's relations, and each relation uses the corresponding information in the story-content knowledge base. A script technique is also a story technique. Figure 2 shows the script technique mechanism. Each script is stored in the script-content knowledge base. Ogata, Arai, and Ono (2016) provide a detailed explanation.

INGS inputs a parameter that defines the story structure. All story techniques are selected based on this parameter. A story technique inputs a node from the story-tree structure and outputs a sub-tree that is structured by relations corresponding to the technique. In particular, a script technique outputs a sub-tree structure constructed of three or more events. A story tree is expanded by substituting the nodes in the sub-tree. In Figure 2, the "E2" node is substituted by the output sub-tree.

3 Collecting Scripts and their Synthetic Use in INGS

Various script-collection or acquisition methods are available. Manual acquisition directly writes scripts using rules and limitations, imagination and experience, or narrative analyses. Automatic acquisition has also been explored (Fujiki, Nanba, and Okumura 2002). Automatic organization in this paper means that new script knowledge is generated based on previously acquired scripts.

3.1 Collecting Scripts

Scripts were collected using the following process:

1) Two-hundred seventy-six university students freely wrote 873 natural language scripts based on simple examples, without special semantic constraints. We collected 860 scripts by checking each event's flow.

2) We transformed the natural-language scripts into the corresponding INGS case structures using a semi-automatic script-description tool (Arai, Ono, and Ogata 2016). Specifically, a user decides the meaning of each verb concept in a script from candidates in the verb-conceptual dictionary. The tool checks the consistency using the case structures and stores the completed script in the script-content knowledge base.

3) We set each script's name to correspond to a verb-concept name included in the verb-conceptual dictionary.

The original 860 script names overlapped extensively. Only 332 script names remained when the overlapping ones were removed. The verb-conceptual dictionary includes 11,951 verb concepts. About 2.78% of the verb concepts have been scripted. In the future, we intend to convert all the verb concepts to scripts.

3.2 Recursively Combining the Collected Scripts

A script is expanded by a recursive combination process from the first element (Figure 3). If the verb concept in a script event equals the name of another script, the original script is expanded by the latter script. We cannot repeat a previously used script. Table 1 shows the result of an experiment.

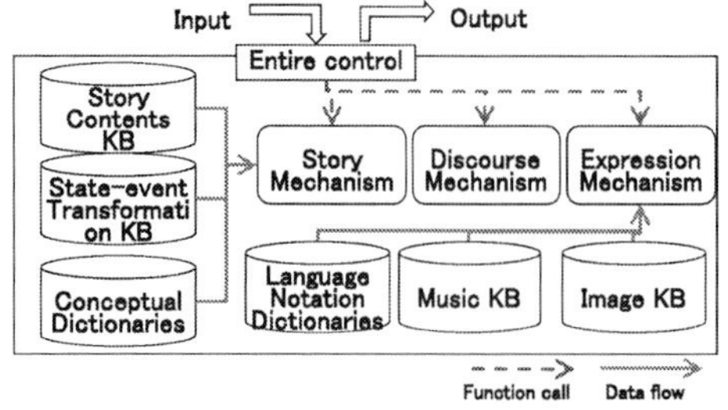

Figure 1. Overview of INGS Architecture

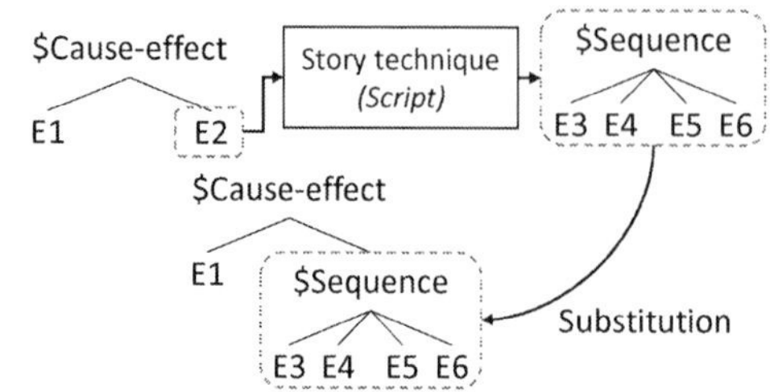

Figure 2. IO Structure of Script Technique

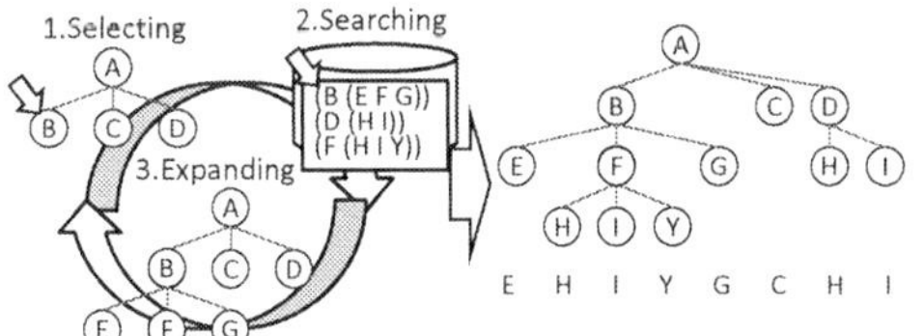

Figure 3. Recursive Script Combination

Table 1. Experimental Results of Script Combination

Timing	Script length		
	Min	Max	Average
Before	2	15	6.85
After	2	190	43.96

3.3 Generating Script Networks using the Collected Scripts

We generated script networks using the collected scripts. Basically, the next script for each script is based on a verb concept. In particular, this method pairs all scripts in a temporal order. If overlapping pairs for a script overlap, only one pair is used. Figure 4 shows the four-step process with a concrete example. *Cytoscape* is an open-source software product for visualizing network graphs by the U.S. National Institute of General Medical Sciences.

Figure 5 (left) shows the entire generated script networks that including five networks. Figure 5 (right) zooms in on a part of the main network that includes 1127 verb concepts. The "average path length" in Table 2 means the average distance between any two nodes. The dispersion in the values' variance is relatively small. Table 3 shows the characteristics of elements in the networks. The "starting node" and "terminal node" respectively mean the arrows from a node and to a node. If the "harmonic mean" value is higher, the verb concept appears more frequently in the starting point, middle points, and terminal point in a script.

3.4 Using Generated Scripts for Story Generation in INGS

We present an overview of using synthesized scripts for story generation. There are two methods—1) recursive generation and 2) script networks—and two techniques—a) detailing and b) inclusion—for a total of four script techniques (1-a, 1-b, 2-a, and 2-b). The former technique (a) expands or substitutes an event in a story by a sequence of detailed events, and the latter (b) expands or substitutes an event in a story by a sequence in which the event is included (Figure 6).

In addition, we insert adequate values into each event case in all scripts using a semi-automatic script-description tool and give a name to each script. The case values are associated with the conceptual dictionaries in INGS. As many scripts are very long, part of a script can be cut to make it shorter. For example, the average number of events in 50 "have-a-meal1" scripts is 32.

1-a: A target event in a story is expanded by detailing it with a script sharing the name of the verb concept in the event.

1-b: A target event in a story is expanded using a script in which the verb concept of the target event is included. Figure 7 shows an example of a script structure generated by this method.

2-a: A target event in a story is expanded by substituting part of it with a script in the network that

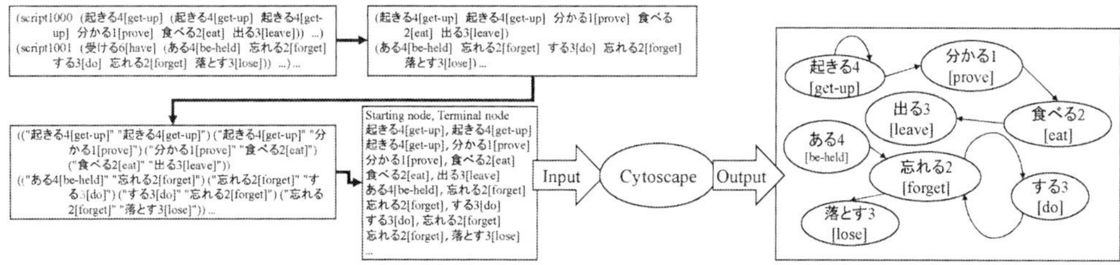

Figure 4. Script-Network Generation Process

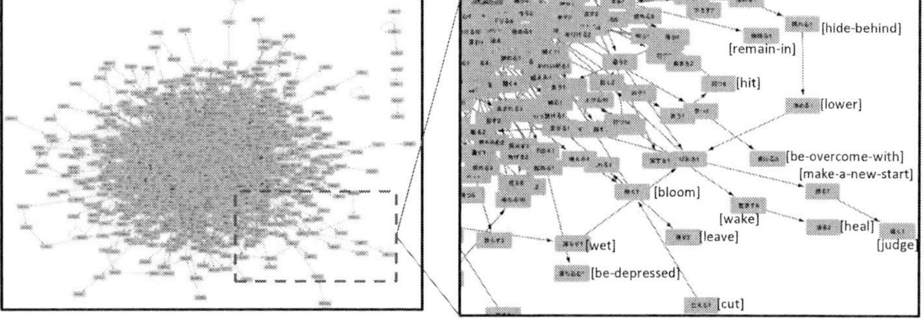

Figure 5. Five Script Networks and the Focused Part

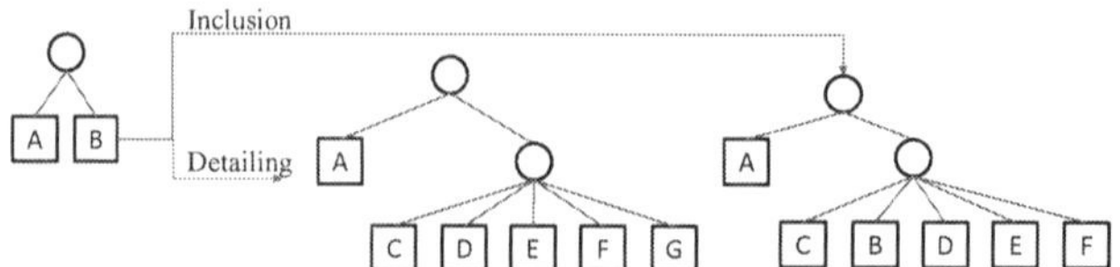

Figure 6. Using the Combined Script

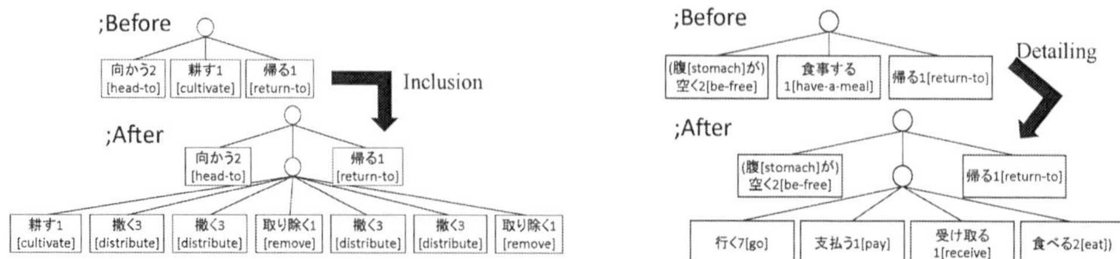

Figure 7. Generated Structure (1-b)

Figure 8. Generated Structure (2-a)

shares the name of the verb concept in the event. Figure 8 shows an example of the structure generated using this method and Figure 9 shows the script.

2-b: A target event in a story is expanded by using a script in which the verb concept in the target event is included.

Before

```
($継起[sequence]
 (event 空く 2[be-free] (type action) (ID 1) (time (time1 time2)) (agent age%青年[young-
        man]#1) (location loc%家[house]#1) (object obj%腹[stomach]#1))
 (event 食事する 1[have-a-meal] (type action) (ID 2) (time (time2 time3)) (agent age%青年
        [young-man]#1) (location loc%家[house]#1))
 (event 帰る 1[return-to] (type action) (ID 6) (time (time6time7)) (agent age%青年[young-
        man]#1) (from loc%料理屋[restaurant]#1) (to loc%家[house]#1)))
```

After

```
($継起[sequence]
 (event 空く2[be-free] (type action) (ID 1) (time (time1 time2)) (agent age%青年[young-man]#1) (loca-
        tion loc%家[house]#1) (object obj%腹[stomach]#1))
  ($継起[sequence]
   (event 行く7[go] (type action) (ID 2) (time (time2 time3)) (agent age%青年[young-man]#1) (location
        loc%家[house]#1) (object obj 買い物[shopping]#1))
   (event 支払う1[pay] (type action) (ID 3) (time (time3 time4)) (agent age%青年[young-man]#1) (coun-
        ter-agent age%店員[clerk]#1) (location loc%料理屋[restaurant]#1))
   (event 受け取る 1[receive] (type action) (ID 4) (time (time4 time5))(agent age%青年[young-man]#1)
        (location loc%料理屋[restaurant]#1) (object obj%ハンバーグ[hamburg]#1) (from age%店員
        [clerk]#1))
   (event 食べる2[eat] (type action) (ID 5) (time (time5 time6)) (agent age%青年[young-man]#1) (loca-
        tion loc%料理屋[restaurant]#1) (object obj%ハンバーグ[hamburg]#1)))
 (event 帰る1[return-to] (type action) (ID 6) (time (time6time7)) (agent age%青年[young-man]#1) (from
        loc%料理屋[restaurant]#1) (to loc%家[house]#1)))
```

Figure 9. Generation Example (2-a)

Table 2. Script Network Characteristics (1)

	Number of verb concepts	Average path length	Variance		Number of verb concepts	Average path length	Variance
Network1	1127	4.30	0.33	Network4	2	1.00	0.00
Network2	3	1.33	0.02	Network5	1	0.00	0.00
Network3	2	1.00	0.00				

Table 3. Script Networks Characteristics (2)

Verb concept	Starting node	Terminal node	Harmonic mean	Verb concept	Starting node	Terminal node	Harmonic mean
食べる 2[eat]	148	182	163.25	死ぬ 1[die]	0	5	0.00
出る 3[leave]	116	152	131.58	寛ぐ 1[relax]	0	3	0.00
行く 7[go]	144	91	111.52	盛る 3[incorporate]	0	3	0.00
乗る 1[ride]	112	104	107.85	悲しむ 1[feel-sad]	0	2	0.00
洗う 2[wash]	79	77	77.99	出す 12[give]	0	2	0.00
見る 2[visit]	64	67	65.47	起きる 2[break-out]	4	0	0.00
買う 2[incur]	70	57	62.83	減る 2[run-short]	3	0	0.00
帰る 2[come-home-from]	44	97	60.54	思う 5[think]	3	0	0.00
行く 3[go-from]	70	44	54.04	張る 3[fill]	2	0	0.00
選ぶ 1[choose]	50	47	48.45	惚れる 1[fall-in-love]	2	0	0.00

4 Conclusions

INGS included two methods for using synthetically collected scripts for story generation. The first recursively generated a long sequence of events and the second created script networks. This paper implemented both methods and showed their effectiveness in the INGS architecture through actual generated examples. Future issues include semantic consideration, automated script acquisition, etc.

Reference

Arai T., Ono J. and Ogata T. 2016. Semi-automatic generation of events sequence knowledge for narrative generation: The use in an integrated narrative generation system, *Proc. 30th Annual Conf. of the Japanese Society for Artificial Intelligence*, 3P1-1in2.

Bartlett F. C. 1923. *Psychology and Primitive Culture*, Cambridge University Press, England.

Fujiki T., Nanba H. and Okumura M. 2002. Automatic acquisition of a script knowledge from a text collection, *Proc. of the Forum on Information Technology*, 2002 (2): 123–124.

Kybartas B. and Bidarra R. 2016. A survey on story generation techniques for authoring computational narratives, *IEEE Transactions on Computational Intelligence and AI in Games*, 99.

Newell A. and Simon H. A. 1972. *Human Problem Solving*. Prentice Hall, UK.

Ogata T. 2015. Building Conceptual Dictionaries for an Integrated Narrative Generation System, *Journal of Robotics, Networking and Artificial Life*, 1 (4): 270–284.

Ogata T. 2016. Computational and cognitive approaches to narratology from the viewpoint of narrative generation, Ogata T. and Akimoto T. (Eds.). *Computational and Cognitive Approaches to Narratology*, USA: IGI Global Publishing, 1–73.

Prince G. 1982. *Narratology*, Walter de Gruhter & Co., Berlin.

Rumelhart D. E. 1975. Notes on a schema for stories, Bobrow D. G. and Collins A. M. (Eds.), *Representation and Understanding: Studies in Cognitive Science*, Academic Press, The Netherlands.

Schank R. C. and Abelson R. P. 1977. *Scripts, Plans, Goals, and Understanding*, Lawrence Erlbaum, NJ.

Singh P., Barry B. and Liu H. 2004. Teaching machines about everyday life, *BT Technology Journal*, 22 (4): 227–240.

CaseSummarizer: A System for Automated Summarization of Legal Texts

Seth Polsley **Pooja Jhunjhunwala*** **Ruihong Huang**
Department of Computer Science and Engineering, Texas A&M University
spolsley, pj861992, huangrh@cse.tamu.edu

Abstract

Attorneys, judges, and others in the justice system are constantly surrounded by large amounts of legal text, which can be difficult to manage across many cases. We present CaseSummarizer, a tool for automated text summarization of legal documents which uses standard summary methods based on word frequency augmented with additional domain-specific knowledge. Summaries are then provided through an informative interface with abbreviations, significance heat maps, and other flexible controls. It is evaluated using ROUGE and human scoring against several other summarization systems, including summary text and feedback provided by domain experts.

1 Introduction

Legal systems across the world generate massive amounts of unstructured text everyday; judges, lawyers, and case workers process and review millions of cases each year in the United States alone. These case files may be very long, often including hundreds of pages of dense legal text. Some form of automating or simplifying the review process could help legal workers manage this workload better. In this work, we consider automated text summarization as one means to this end.

Summarization is a challenging sub-task of the broader text-to-text generation field of natural language processing (NLP). Summaries are usually generated by extracting 'important' portions of the text. Extraction-based methods are often used because abstraction-based summarization is an open problem in NLP. Abstraction-based summarization is intended to generate summaries based on abstract representations of the text, inspired by how humans generate summaries based on their own understanding of text; there is a great deal of ongoing research devoted to developing these methods (Moratanch and Chitrakala, 2016).

In extraction-based methods, the most relevant sentences or phrases of a document may be found through a metric like TF*IDF (Nenkova and McKeown, 2012), and while this is a useful approach to general text summarization, it can miss a lot of critical information in certain domains. For instance, legal documents have a large amount of technical content. Domain-specific summarizing systems have been developed for many different fields as one means of addressing this limitation of general summarizers; they use knowledge of the content specifically in that domain to boost performance. CaseSummarizer is a summary engine specific to the legal domain that builds on existing methods paired with domain-specific constructs to present an interface with scalable summary text, lists of entities and abbreviations from the document, and a significance heat map of the entire text.

2 Background

Several systems have been built for the explicit purpose of summarizing legal documents. One of the earliest works in this area is the "Fast Legal EXpert CONsultant" (FLEXICON) system developed by Gelbart and Smith (Gelbart and Smith, 1991a). FLEXICON is keyword-based, referencing against a large database of terms to find important regions of text (Gelbart and Smith, 1991b). Moens et al. later introduced SALOMON which uses cosine similarity to group regions of the text that are similar (Moens et al., 1999). The goal of this approach is to extract relevant portions of different topics in the text, similar to some other abstraction-oriented methods (Barzilay and Elhadad, 1999; Erkan and Radev, 2004). LetSum, developed by Farzindar and Lapalme, more closely resembles a keyword-based system, employing a set of "cue phrases" to identify portions of the text associated with specific themes like 'Introduction', 'Context', and 'Conclusion' (Farzindar and Lapalme, 2004). While LetSum performed relatively well against the human-provided summaries, the shortened text was found to be too long. Other extraction-based

*Software Engineer, Google Inc.

Proceedings of COLING 2016, the 26th International Conference on Computational Linguistics: System Demonstrations, pages 258–262, Osaka, Japan, December 11-17 2016.

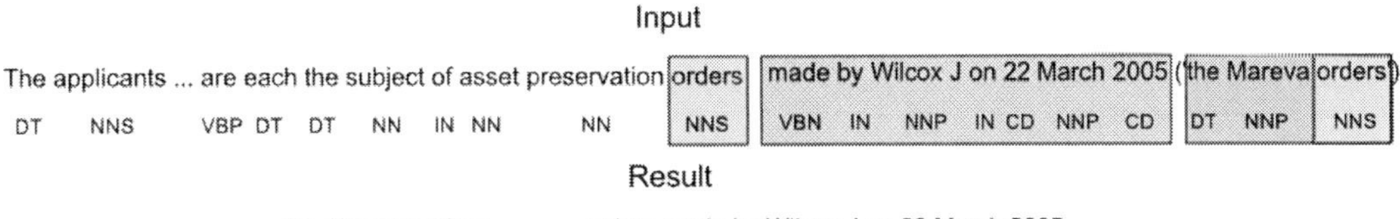

Figure 1: An example of an abbreviation being extracted with its source text. The algorithm attempts to match the POS of the head word of a parenthetical phrase with the first matching POS before the abbreviation.

methods have been developed to overcome a reliance on language-dependent keywords using graph-based ranking (Mihalcea, 2005; Wong et al., 2008).

A large body of recent work has been presented by Galgani and Hoffmann through LEXA, a system which uses citation analysis to generate summaries (Galgani et al., 2012a; Galgani and Hoffmann, 2010). LEXA includes an interface for continued system learning using Ripple-down Rules (RDR), which allows domain experts to evaluate sentence selections live and agree or disagree with the selections. When the experts agree on a relevant sentence, a new extraction pattern is added (Galgani et al., 2015). Galgani et al. continued their work in this domain with the development of a multi-technique approach to summarization, including 'catchphrase' analysis (Galgani et al., 2012b). CaseSummarizer is a multi-technique approach with a goal of providing a comprehensive interface that pairs scalable controls with supplemental details like abbreviations and significance heat maps.

3 Implementation

CaseSummarizer's internal pipeline consists of three distinct steps: preprocessing, scoring of sentence relevance, and domain processing; summaries are then presented externally through the user interface.

3.1 Internal Pipeline

CaseSummarizer is built in Python and uses the feature-rich Natural Language ToolKit (NLTK) module for preprocessing by splitting documents into sentences which are stemmed, lemmatized, case-normalized, and cleared of stop words (Bird et al., 2009). Sentences are scored using a TF*IDF matrix built from thousands of legal case reports, which counts term frequency using $TF * IDF_t = TF_t * 1/\log \frac{N}{DF_t}$ where N refers to the number of documents, TF_t is the total count of term t, and DF_t is the number of documents in which t appears. These scores are summed over each sentence and normalized by the sentence length. This normalization step ensures the system does not bias long sentences.

In order to include additional domain information, CaseSummarizer first extracts a list of all entities from the text. Parties can be extracted from case titles because of the document structure. Similarly, abbreviations of entity names are identified by CaseSummarizer to aid the reader's understanding of summaries. This is done by determining the Part-Of-Speech (POS) of the head words of parenthetical phrases and reading right-to-left until the earliest non-consecutive occurrence of that POS is found in the text. See Figure 1 as an example.

CaseSummarizer does not use specific cue words or catchphrases, but adjusts sentence scores using occurrences of known entities, dates, and proximity to section headings. The adjustment function is $w_{new} = w_{old} + \sigma(0.2d + 0.3e + 1.5s)$, where σ is the standard deviation among sentence scores, d refers to the number of dates present, e is the number of entity mentions, and s is a boolean indicating the start of a section. The weights primarily were selected through trial-and-error to reflect the relative importance of each term, e.g. dates are less useful than entities, and feedback from experts indicated that section headings should carry heavier weight.

3.2 User Interface

User interaction is performed through a web interface which provides all extracted information and some adjustable controls. After selecting the case to summarize, the fields are populated with the parties and date, followed by the list of all recognized entities. A listing of abbreviations matches all phrases to their original full form in the text; this information can help the reader quickly discern which entities are being referenced when an abbreviation appears. These fields are shown in Figure 2.

The sentence scores are manifest in two forms: the summaries themselves and significance heat maps. The summaries are fully scalable using a slider, allowing the user to show only the most important sentences at any compression level. The significance heat map presents the full document text but assigns a color to each sentence based on the pertinence score it received during the weighting stage. By using the summary text and the heat map together, CaseSummarizer provides a helpful reference to users for identifying important regions in the text. See Figure 3 for an example.

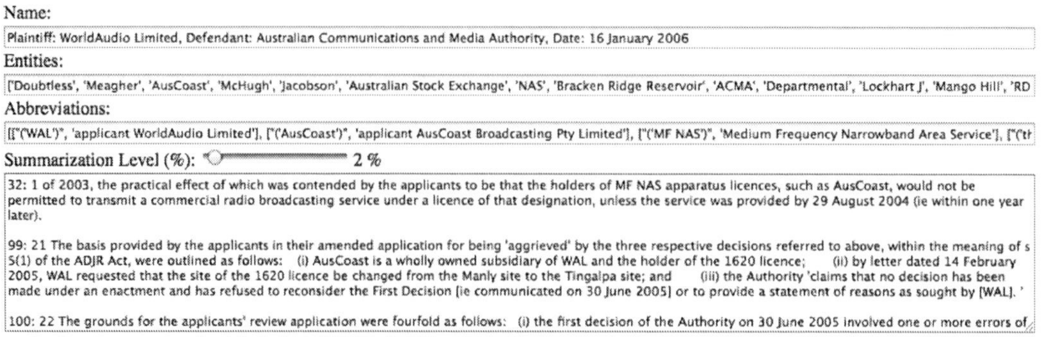

Name:

Plaintiff: WorldAudio Limited, Defendant: Australian Communications and Media Authority, Date: 16 January 2006

Entities:

['Doubtless', 'Meagher', 'AusCoast', 'McHugh', 'Jacobson', 'Australian Stock Exchange', 'NAS', 'Bracken Ridge Reservoir', 'ACMA', 'Departmental', 'Lockhart J', 'Mango Hill', 'RD

Abbreviations:

[["('WAL')", 'applicant WorldAudio Limited'], ["('AusCoast')", 'applicant AusCoast Broadcasting Pty Limited'], ["('MF NAS')", 'Medium Frequency Narrowband Area Service'], ["('th

Summarization Level (%): 2 %

32: 1 of 2003, the practical effect of which was contended by the applicants to be that the holders of MF NAS apparatus licences, such as AusCoast, would not be permitted to transmit a commercial radio broadcasting service under a licence of that designation, unless the service was provided by 29 August 2004 (ie within one year later).

99: 21 The basis provided by the applicants in their amended application for being 'aggrieved' by the three respective decisions referred to above, within the meaning of s 5(1) of the ADJR Act, were outlined as follows: (i) AusCoast is a wholly owned subsidiary of WAL and the holder of the 1620 licence; (ii) by letter dated 14 February 2005, WAL requested that the site of the 1620 licence be changed from the Manly site to the Tingalpa site; and (iii) the Authority 'claims that no decision has been made under an enactment and has refused to reconsider the First Decision [ie communicated on 30 June 2005] or to provide a statement of reasons as sought by [WAL]. '

100: 22 The grounds for the applicants' review application were fourfold as follows: (i) the first decision of the Authority on 30 June 2005 involved one or more errors of

Figure 2: The extracted fields for a sample case, showing the names of parties, entities, a listing of abbreviations and their full forms, and the scalable summary text.

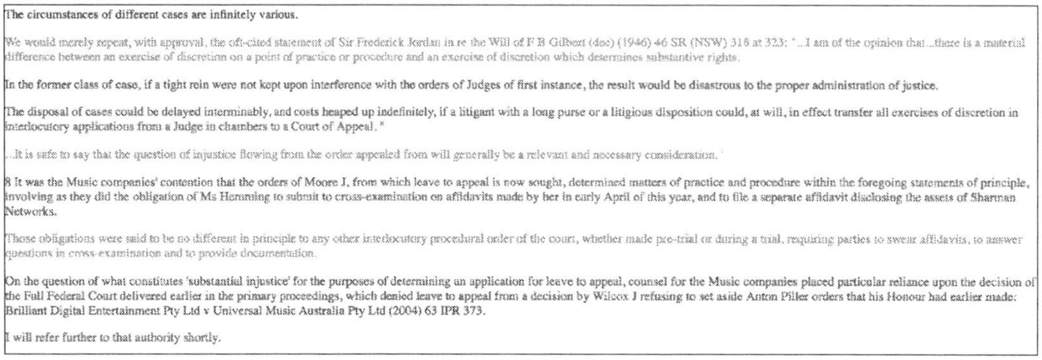

The circumstances of different cases are infinitely various.

We would merely repeat, with approval, the oft-cited statement of Sir Frederick Jordan in re the Will of F B Gilbert (dec) (1946) 46 SR (NSW) 318 at 323: "...I am of the opinion that...there is a material difference between an exercise of discretion on a point of practice or procedure and an exercise of discretion which determines substantive rights.

In the former class of case, if a tight rein were not kept upon interference with the orders of Judges of first instance, the result would be disastrous to the proper administration of justice.

The disposal of cases could be delayed interminably, and costs heaped up indefinitely, if a litigant with a long purse or a litigious disposition could, at will, in effect transfer all exercises of discretion in interlocutory applications from a Judge in chambers to a Court of Appeal."

...it is safe to say that the question of injustice flowing from the order appealed from will generally be a relevant and necessary consideration.'

8 It was the Music companies' contention that the orders of Moore J, from which leave to appeal is now sought, determined matters of practice and procedure within the foregoing statements of principle, involving as they did the obligation of Ms Hemming to submit to cross-examination on affidavits made by her in early April of this year, and to file a separate affidavit disclosing the assets of Sharman Networks.

Those obligations were said to be no different in principle to any other interlocutory procedural order of the court, whether made pre-trial or during a trial, requiring parties to swear affidavits, to answer questions in cross-examination and to provide documentation.

On the question of what constitutes 'substantial injustice' for the purposes of determining an application for leave to appeal, counsel for the Music companies placed particular reliance upon the decision of the Full Federal Court delivered earlier in the primary proceedings, which denied leave to appeal from a decision by Wilcox J refusing to set aside Anton Piller orders that his Honour had earlier made: Brilliant Digital Entertainment Pty Ltd v Universal Music Australia Pty Ltd (2004) 63 IPR 373.

I will refer further to that authority shortly.

Figure 3: A snippet of the case's full text in the significance heat map. Each sentence is color-coded based on the its score, ranging from low (blue) to high (red).

4 Evaluation

Because summaries are very subjective, evaluation can be difficult; Lin et al. introduced a set of metrics called the ROUGE package in (Lin, 2004) that provide a pairwise comparison method for evaluating candidate summaries against human-provided ones. The ROUGE metric has multiple variants and may be applied at the word, phrase, or sentence level. In this case, we used ROUGE-N, which measures the overlap of n-grams between summaries, with N = 1, 2, 3, and 4. We also computed the ROUGE-L score, a metric similar to an F-measure based on sentence-level similarity of two summaries. In addition to ROUGE scores, we asked domain experts to rate several summaries using a set of six evaluation questions based on the original set of questions presented by Liu and Liu for ranking summaries in (Liu and Liu, 2008). We also consulted the experts for feedback on the system.

CaseSummarizer uses the same data set as LEXA, which was created and released by Galgani et al. It contains 3890 legal cases from the Federal Court of Australia (FCA) from the years 2006-2009. Evaluation was performed on a set of 5 randomly-selected documents. Six automated tools were chosen for comparison. Four were online programs, AutoSummarizer, TextSummarizer, SplitBrain, and SMMRY[1]. The other two were Apple Inc.'s Summarizer program and Galgani et al.'s summaries included with the data set. We also asked domain experts to provide summaries for randomly selected cases. For consistency in the ROUGE metrics, we selected a compression rate of 3% in the automated systems. The domain experts were asked to generate sentence-level summaries by extracting approximately 3% of the sentences from the document.

Table 1 shows the ROUGE scores of each system against the expert summaries. We can see that CaseSummarizer performs very favorably against the other systems when evaluated against expert summaries. The domain expert ratings are shown in Figure 4 alongside each evaluation question. While the automated summaries are still lacking across the board when compared to the expert-generated ones, CaseSummarizer is most effective in capturing a coherent flow of events and obtaining a good coverage of important points in a case. It also received the best average rating among all the automatic systems.

[1] autosummarizer.com, textsummarization.net/text-summarizer, splitbrain.org/services/ots, and smmry.com/, respectively

Table 1: ROUGE scores indicating the similarity between automatically-generated summaries and the expert-generated summaries.

	CaseSum	AutoSum	TextSum	SplitBrain	SMMRY	Apple Sum	Galgani et al.
Rouge-1	0.194	0.207	0.183	0.241	0.248	0.175	0.132
Rouge-2	0.114	0.089	0.072	0.146	0.137	0.097	0.049
Rouge-3	0.091	0.059	0.049	0.123	0.104	0.075	0.026
Rouge-4	0.085	0.048	0.043	0.117	0.090	0.068	0.019
Rouge-L	0.061	0.017	0.015	0.056	0.062	0.033	0.017

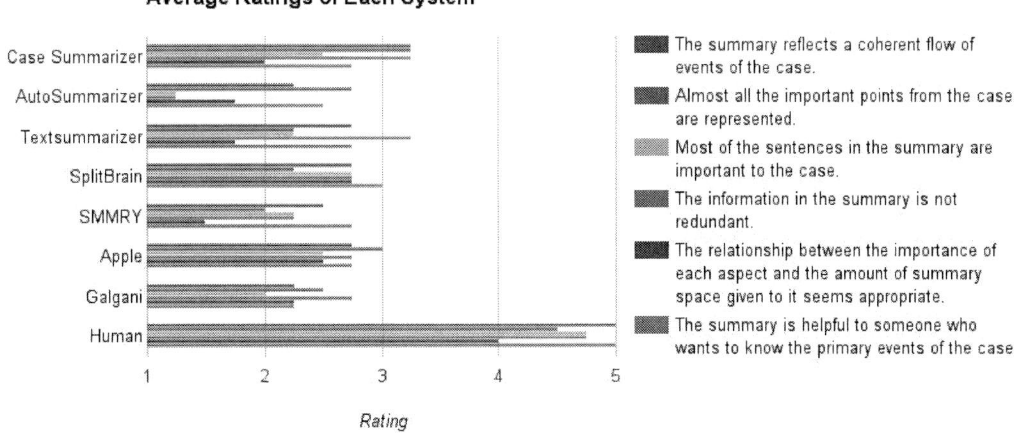

Figure 4: Domain expert ratings of each summary, including the expert-generated ones. The evaluation questions are shown on the right-hand side with the average scores for each method shown on the left-hand side.

5 Future Work

One of the most interesting findings from the summary scoring study is that the expert-generated summaries received very high ratings from other experts, as shown in Figure 4. These summaries were also generated entirely from sentence extraction, like the automated systems. This indicates both the value of sentence-level summarization on legal documents and provides some validation that sentence extraction methods can indeed generate helpful summaries. However, the disparaty between expert summary scores and the automated systems highlights the need for future improvements in summarization methods. To further explore these ideas, we consulted with domain experts regarding the CaseSummarizer system. The following points outline some of their primary suggestions.

- Extracted sentences need to be more representative of the different sections of a case file, e.g. premise, arguments, findings, judgements, etc.
- A considerable amount of repetition of ideas was observed in the summaries generated by the system, which should be discouraged.
- Most domain-experts believed that a better summary would be generated by selecting sentences that are closer to the end of the document as these sentences often tend to summarize the points discussed in the whole document.
- Experts also pointed out the need for different kinds of summaries in the legal field. For instance, in one use case, a lawyer may wish to have highlights of key factual points to refresh his or her memory of the details of a case, but another attorney may wish to see only the findings to determine the relevance to some current proceedings.

6 Conclusion

We found that CaseSummarizer performs favorably against non-domain specific summarizers. The summaries generated are able to provide a reasonable idea about the context of a case, even though some important points are missed. While not able to perform as well as human experts, it fared the best among several other systems when evaluated by humans, and the domain experts suggested several improvements we hope to explore in the future work. Foremost, we seek to dissuade repetition by penalizing similar sentences. We also plan to add incentives to favor sentences near the end of documents as they may include vital information, and finally, we wish to explore extracting better representations of different sections using cue words. CaseSummarizer shows a promising start in combining summarization techniques into a multi-faceted interface with domain-inspired information.

Acknowledgments

The authors would like to thank each of the domain experts who provided high-quality summaries and ratings on the systems, as well as all those who gave feedback on CaseSummarizer's various iterations.

References

Regina Barzilay and Michael Elhadad. 1999. Using lexical chains for text summarization. *Advances in automatic text summarization*, pages 111–121.

Steven Bird, Ewan Klein, and Edward Loper. 2009. *Natural Language Processing with Python*. O'Reilly Media.

Günes Erkan and Dragomir R Radev. 2004. Lexrank: Graph-based lexical centrality as salience in text summarization. *Journal of Artificial Intelligence Research*, 22:457–479.

Atefeh Farzindar and Guy Lapalme. 2004. Letsum, an automatic legal text summarizing system. *Legal knowledge and information systems, JURIX*, pages 11–18.

Filippo Galgani and Achim Hoffmann. 2010. Lexa: Towards automatic legal citation classification. In *AI 2010: Advances in Artificial Intelligence*, pages 445–454. Springer.

Filippo Galgani, Paul Compton, and Achim Hoffmann. 2012a. Citation based summarisation of legal texts. In *PRICAI 2012: Trends in Artificial Intelligence*, pages 40–52. Springer.

Filippo Galgani, Paul Compton, and Achim Hoffmann. 2012b. Combining different summarization techniques for legal text. In *Proceedings of the Workshop on Innovative Hybrid Approaches to the Processing of Textual Data*, pages 115–123. Association for Computational Linguistics.

Filippo Galgani, Paul Compton, and Achim Hoffmann. 2015. Lexa: Building knowledge bases for automatic legal citation classification. *Expert Systems with Applications*, 42(17):6391–6407.

Daphne Gelbart and JC Smith. 1991a. Flexicon, a new legal information retrieval system. *Can. L. Libr.*, 16:9.

Dephne Gelbart and JC Smith. 1991b. Beyond boolean search: Flexicon, a legal tex-based intelligent system. In *Proceedings of the 3rd international conference on Artificial intelligence and law*, pages 225–234. ACM.

Chin-Yew Lin. 2004. Rouge: A package for automatic evaluation of summaries. In *Text summarization branches out: Proceedings of the ACL-04 workshop*, volume 8.

Feifan Liu and Yang Liu. 2008. Correlation between rouge and human evaluation of extractive meeting summaries. In *Proceedings of the 46th Annual Meeting of the Association for Computational Linguistics on Human Language Technologies: Short Papers*, pages 201–204. Association for Computational Linguistics.

Rada Mihalcea. 2005. Language independent extractive summarization. In *Proceedings of the ACL 2005 on Interactive poster and demonstration sessions*, pages 49–52. Association for Computational Linguistics.

Marie-Francine Moens, Caroline Uyttendaele, and Jos Dumortier. 1999. Abstracting of legal cases: the potential of clustering based on the selection of representative objects. *Journal of the Association for Information Science and Technology*, 50(2):151.

N Moratanch and S Chitrakala. 2016. A survey on abstractive text summarization. In *Circuit, Power and Computing Technologies (ICCPCT), 2016 International Conference on*, pages 1–7. IEEE.

Ani Nenkova and Kathleen McKeown. 2012. A survey of text summarization techniques. In *Mining Text Data*, pages 43–76. Springer.

Kam-Fai Wong, Mingli Wu, and Wenjie Li. 2008. Extractive summarization using supervised and semi-supervised learning. In *Proceedings of the 22nd International Conference on Computational Linguistics-Volume 1*, pages 985–992. Association for Computational Linguistics.

WISDOM X, DISAANA and D-SUMM: Large-scale NLP Systems for Analyzing Textual Big Data

Junta Mizuno Masahiro Tanaka Kiyonori Ohtake Jong-Hoon Oh
Julien Kloetzer Chikara Hashimoto Kentaro Torisawa
Data-driven Intelligent System Research Center (DIRECT), NICT / Kyoto, Japan
{junta-m, mtnk, kiyonori.ohtake, rovellia, julien, ch, torisawa}@nict.go.jp

Abstract

We demonstrate our large-scale NLP systems: WISDOM X, DISAANA, and D-SUMM. WISDOM X provides numerous possible answers including unpredictable ones to widely diverse natural language questions to provide deep insights about a broad range of issues. DISAANA and D-SUMM enable us to assess the damage caused by large-scale disasters in real time using Twitter as an information source.

1 Introduction

This paper describes three large-scale NLP systems we have developed at NICT: WISDOM X, DISAANA, and D-SUMM. The first system, WISDOM X[1], is an open-domain question-answering (QA) system for Japanese using 4-billion web pages as an information source. It was designed to enable users to obtain a wide and deep perspective on a broad range of issues. The range of questions that humans can pose is unlimited and web texts are a valuable information source for compiling a comprehensive list of answers. Such answers are expected to include *unknown unknowns* in the infamous words of Donald Rumsfeld, which are things that "we don't know we don't know" (Torisawa et al., 2010). For instance, even though global warming is a severe and widely discussed problem that might result in devastating *unknown unknowns* for many people in the future, no exhaustive list of answers has been compiled to the question: "What happens if global warming worsens?" Although many documents available on the web actually describe the possible consequences of global warming, only a few can be discovered using commercial search engines because they merely provide a huge number of documents that users have to read. By contrast, WISDOM X, for instance, provides hundreds of answers to the question, and furthermore suggests new questions related to the first question to have deeper knowledge related to the issue.

Our other two systems, DISAANA[2] and D-SUMM[3], were developed to help disaster victims and rescue workers in the aftermath of large-scale disasters. One lesson from the 2011 Great East Japan Earthquake was that a large-scale disaster can destroy a wide range of infrastructure, disrupt lives, and cause many unpredictable situations. Immediately after the disaster, much useful information was transmitted into cyberspace, especially for such social media as Twitter. Nevertheless, because most people were overwhelmed by the huge amount of information, they were unable to make proper decisions and much confusion ensued. DISAANA provides a list of answers to questions such as "What is in short supply in City X?" and displays locations related to each answer on a map (e.g., locations where food is in short supply) in real time using Twitter as an information source. D-SUMM summarizes the disaster reports from a specified area in a compact format and enables rescue workers to quickly grasp the disaster situations from a *macro* perspective. In the 2016 Kumamoto Earthquake (M7.0), DISAANA was actually used by the Japanese government[4] and provided a wide range of useful information, including such unpredictable one as the shortage of *Halal foods*[5].

[1]publicly available at http://wisdom-nict.jp (in Japanese)

[2]publicly available at http://disaana.jp (in Japanese)

[3]publicly available at http://disaana.jp/d-summ (in Japanese)

[4]"Analyzing tweets to comprehend necessities," Yomiuri Shimbun Evening edition, p.1, 2016, May 11.

[5]The Muslim population in Japan is quite small.

Proceedings of COLING 2016, the 26th International Conference on Computational Linguistics: System Demonstrations, pages 263–267, Osaka, Japan, December 11-17 2016.

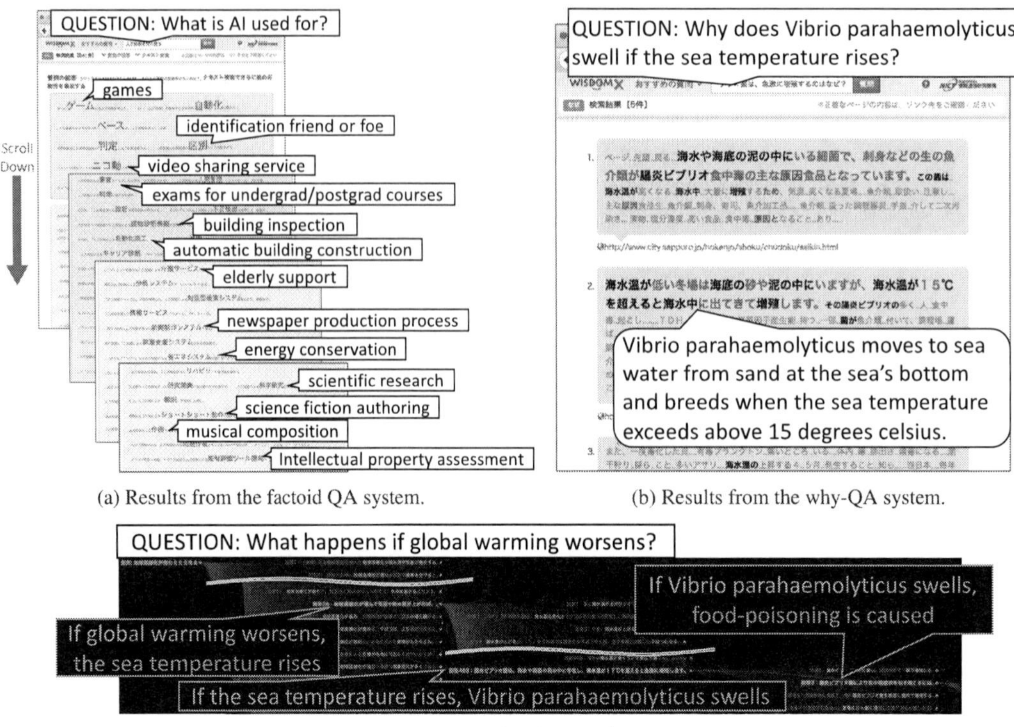

(a) Results from the factoid QA system.

(b) Results from the why-QA system.

(c) Results from the what-happens-if QA system.

Figure 1: Example screenshots of WISDOM X.

In the following, we provide an overview of WISDOM X, DISAANA, and D-SUMM.

2 WISDOM X: Information Analysis System

WISDOM X, which discovers answers to given questions from about 4-billion web pages by several kinds of deep semantic processing, consists of four QA systems, each of which deals with different types of questions: factoid (e.g., What prevents global warming?), why-type (Oh et al., 2012; Oh et al., 2013; Oh et al., 2016) (e.g., Why did the global warming worsen?), what-happens-if-type (Hashimoto et al., 2012; Hashimoto et al., 2014) (e.g., What happens if global warming worsens?), and definition type (e.g., What is global warming?). It also has a functionality that suggests questions to users. These QA systems use a large-scale knowledge base for entailment recognition(Saeger et al., 2009; Hashimoto et al., 2009; Saeger et al., 2011; Hashimoto et al., 2011; Kloetzer et al., 2013; Sano et al., 2014; Kloetzer et al., 2015) and semantic noun clusters (Kazama and Torisawa, 2008). We also developed a middleware RaSC (Tanaka et al., 2016) to efficiently run various NLP tools on hundreds of computation nodes.

We designed WISDOM X to provide a wide range of pin-point answers, e.g., a noun phrase for factoid questions and a sentence for what-happens-if-type questions. This feature constitutes a major difference from commercial search engines, which merely give web pages for a given query and rely on human effort to ascertain pin-point answers. In addition, WISDOM X can provide numerous answers to a given question. For instance, the current version of WISDOM X provides around 800 answers to the question, "What is AI used for?" (Figure 1a). Since all the answers are presented as noun phrases, it is relatively easy to find useful or interesting answers from them. It would be extremely difficult to find 800 answers for the same question by reading the documents provided by search engines. This feature of WISDOM X is expected to be useful for the discovery of relatively unknown ideas in AI applications, for instance, and for the creation of novel and innovative ideas using such unknown but already written ideas as hints. WISDOM X also enables us to search for relatively unknown future risks, such as the undesirable side effects of the Tokyo Olympic games in 2020.

Moreover, WISDOM X enables us to create valuable hypotheses, which are not described in our information source, i.e., 4 billion web pages. Figure 1c portrays the process of hypothesis creation. Initially, a user poses a question, "What happens if global warming worsens?" and one answer is that "the sea temperature will rise." If the user clicks on that answer, the system suggests another question, "What happens if the sea temperature rises?" and the answer includes "Vibrio parahaemolyticus swells." By repeating this process, the user can create the following hypothesis: "if global warming worsens, the sea temperature rises and an increase of food poisoning will be caused by Vibrio parahaemolyticus." This is actually a chain of causalities. Although we were unable to find any web pages that describe the entire hypothesis in our web archive, Baker-Austin et al. (2013) partly confirmed it.

In the above hypothesis creation process, the question suggestion played an important role. WISDOM X suggests other types of questions as well, including "Why does Vibrio parahaemolyticus swell if the sea temperature rises?" (Figure 1b) and "What is Vibrio parahaemolyticus?" The first question can be regarded as a question asking for textual support for the causality between the rise of the sea temperature and Vibrio parahaemolyticus. Such questions can be used to identify highly reliable answers among those provided by WISDOM X. In addition, when a user gives a keyword instead of a question as a query, WISDOM X lists answerable questions related to it. For example, when a user inputs "smartphone," WISDOM X suggests roughly five hundred questions, such as "What can smartphones resolve?"

WISDOM X sorts the answers according to their confidence scores, whose computation varies depending on the question type. For instance, the scores of answers to the why-type questions are provided by a supervised classifiers (Oh et al., 2013). In addition, semantically similar answers to factoid questions are grouped together as far as possible to help users to find answers that are valuable to them. The semantic similarities are computed using unsupervised word clustering (Kazama and Torisawa, 2008).

3 DISAANA and D-SUMM: Disaster Information Analyzer and Summarizer

DISAANA analyzes tweets in real time, discovers disaster-related information, and presents it in organized formats. It has two modes: QA and problem-listing. In the QA mode, for example, a user can enumerate goods in short supply in Kumamoto merely by asking, "What is in short supply in Kumamoto?" (Figure 2a). The answers are classified by such semantic categories as *medical supplies* for readability. A user can also enumerate them on a map (Figure 2c). In the problem-listing mode, a user can obtain a list of problems, such as "people were buried alive," which are occurring in a specified area (prefecture, city or town) without questions by using Varga et al. (2013)'s method (Figure 2b).

We constructed a million-scale location DB, which includes *part-of* relations between locations (e.g., Mashiki town is *part-of* Kumamoto prefecture) and each latitude and longitude of locations, to identify locations in tweets and display them related to the answers on a map. We did not use geotags attached to tweets because only a small fraction of them are actually geotagged due to privacy issues and the reported locations are often different from the locations from which users post tweets. When an area is specified in queries, the answers and problems related to the subparts are also presented to users. This is yet another function that has not been provided by commercial search engines.

One problem with DISAANA is that it often provides too many answers, which are difficult to grasp instantly. To address this problem, we developed D-SUMM (Figure 3), which summarizes the list of problems in a specified area provided by DISAANA. Similar problem reports such as "buildings collapsed" and "houses were demolished" were merged into a single problem report. In addition, the reports were classified according to their subparts of a specified area.

Another important issue is false rumors. In past disaster situations, numerous false rumors were spread widely on Twitter (e.g., "Drinking iodine protects against radiation" during the 2011 Great East Japan Earthquake). DISAANA and D-SUMM give an alert to users by retrieving not only answers but also information that contradicts the answers by using a modality analyzer (Mizuno et al., 2015) and contradictory patterns (Kloetzer et al., 2013). For example, when "acid rain" is one of the answers to the question, "What happened in a petrochemical complex?" and there is a tweet that contradicts the answer such as "Acid rain in the petrochemical complex is a false rumor," DISAANA presents it alongside the original tweet: the source of the answer. By examining such contradictory information, users can notice

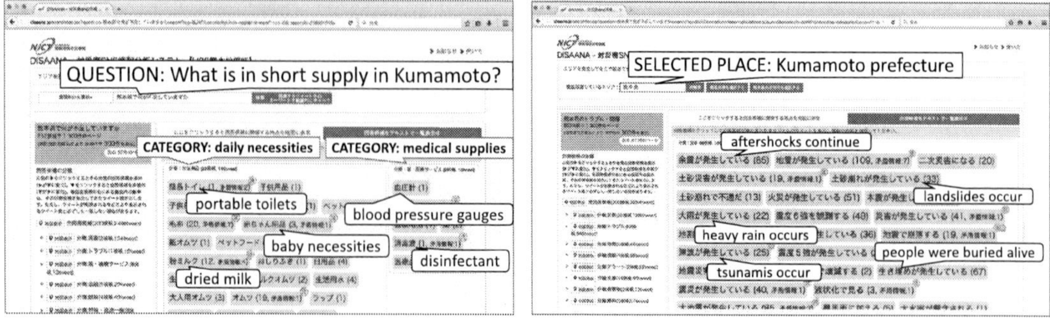

(a) Results from the QA mode.

(b) Results from the problem-listing mode.

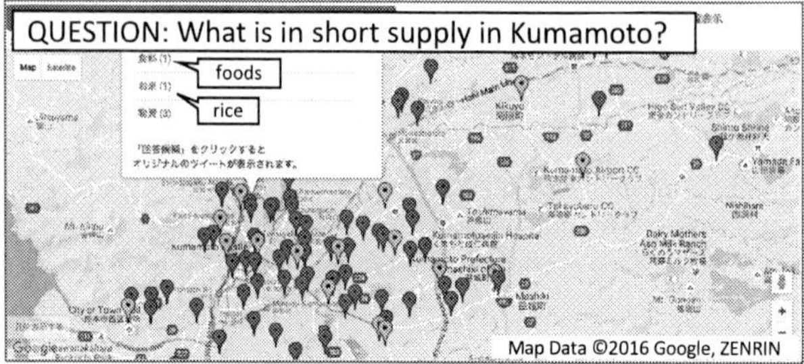

(c) Results from the QA mode located on a map.

Figure 2: Example screenshots of DISAANA.

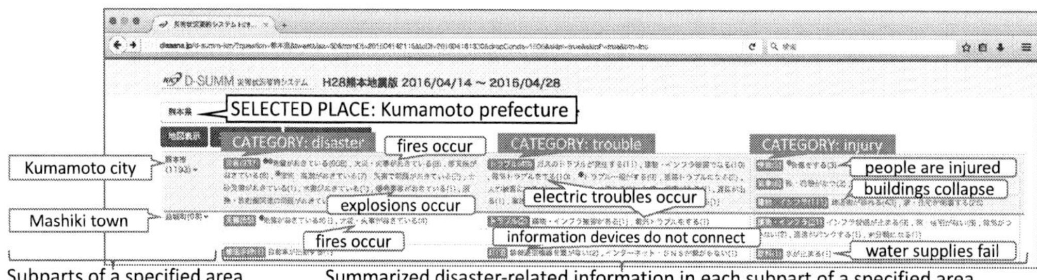

Figure 3: Example screenshot of D-SUMM.

the possibility of false rumors.

4 Conclusion

In this paper, we introduced three systems: WISDOM X, DISAANA and D-SUMM. We are going to add more intelligent functionality to the systems, such as more advanced reasoning mechanisms (Hashimoto et al., 2015) and such highly accurate linguistic analysis tools as anaphora resolution (Iida et al., 2016).

Acknowledgments

This work was partially supported by the Council for Science, Technology and Innovation (CSTI) through the Cross-ministerial Strategic Innovation Promotion Program (SIP), titled "Enhancement of societal resiliency against natural disasters" (Funding agency: JST).

References

Craig Baker-Austin, Joaquin A. Trinanes, Nick G. H. Taylor, Rachel Hartnell, Anja Siitonen, and Jaime Martinez-Urtaza. 2013. Emerging Vibrio risk at high latitudes in response to ocean warming. *Nature Climate Change*, pages 3:73–77.

Chikara Hashimoto, Kentaro Torisawa, Kow Kuroda, Stijn De Saeger, Masaki Murata, and Jun'ichi Kazama. 2009. Large-scale verb entailment acquisition from the web. In *Proceedings of EMNLP 2009*, pages 1172–1181.

Chikara Hashimoto, Kentaro Torisawa, Stijn De Sager, Jun'ichi Kazama, and Sadao Kurohashi. 2011. Extracting paraphrases from definition sentences on the web. In *Proceedings of ACL-HLT 2011*, pages 1087–1097.

Chikara Hashimoto, Kentaro Torisawa, Stijn De Saeger, Jong-Hoon Oh, and Jun'ichi Kazama. 2012. Excitatory or inhibitory: A new semantic orientation extracts contradiction and causality from the web. In *Proceedings of EMNLP-CoNLL 2012*, pages 619–630.

Chikara Hashimoto, Kentaro Torisawa, Julien Kloetzer, Motoki Sano, István Varga, Jong-Hoon Oh, and Yutaka Kidawara. 2014. Toward future scenario generation: Extracting event causality exploiting semantic relation, context, and association features. In *Proceedings of ACL 2014*, pages 987–997.

Chikara Hashimoto, Kentaro Torisawa, Julien Kloetzer, and Jong-Hoon Oh. 2015. Generating event causality hypotheses through semantic relations. In *Proceedings of AAAI-15*, pages 2396–2403.

Ryu Iida, Kentaro Torisawa, Jong-Hoon Oh, Canasai Kruengkrai, and Julien Kloetzer. 2016. Intra-sentential subject zero anaphora resolution using multi-column convolutional neural network. In *Proceedings of EMNLP 2016 (to appear)*.

Jun'ichi Kazama and Kentaro Torisawa. 2008. Inducing gazetteers for named entity recognition by large-scale clustering of dependency relations. In *Proceedings of ACL08: HLT*, pages 407–415.

Julien Kloetzer, Stijn De Saeger, Kentaro Torisawa, Chikara Hashimoto, Jong-Hoon Oh, and Kiyonori Ohtake. 2013. Two-stage method for large-scale acquisition of contradiction pattern pairs using entailment. In *Proceedings of EMNLP 2013*, pages 693–703.

Julien Kloetzer, Kentaro Torisawa, Chikara Hashimoto, and Jong-Hoon Oh. 2015. Large-scale acquisition of entailment pattern pairs by exploiting transitivity. In *Proceedings of EMNLP 2015*, pages 1649–1655.

Junta Mizuno, Canasai Kruengkrai, Kiyonori Ohtake, Chikara Hashimoto, Kentaro Torisawa, and Julien Kloetzer. 2015. Recognizing complex negation on Twitter. In *Proceedings of PACLIC 2015*, pages 544–552.

Jong-Hoon Oh, Kentaro Torisawa, Chikara Hashimoto, Takuya Kawada, Stijn De Saeger, Jun'ichi Kazama, and Yiou Wang. 2012. Why question answering using sentiment analysis and word classes. In *Proceedings of EMNLP-CoNLL 2012*, pages 368–378.

Jong-Hoon Oh, Kentaro Torisawa, Chikara Hashimoto, Motoki Sano, Stijn De Saeger, and Kiyonori Ohtake. 2013. Why-question answering using intra- and inter-sentential causal relations. In *Proceedings of ACL 2013*, pages 1733–1743.

Jong-Hoon Oh, Kentaro Torisawa, Chikara Hashimoto, Ryu Iida, Masahiro Tanaka, and Julien Kloetzer. 2016. A semi-supervised learning approach to why-question answering. In *Proceedings of AAAI-16*, pages 3022–3029.

Stijn De Saeger, Kentaro Torisawa, Jun'ichi Kazama, Kow Kuroda, and Masaki Murata. 2009. Large scale relation acquisition using class dependent patterns. In *Proceedings of ICDM'09*, pages 764–769.

Stijn De Saeger, Kentaro Torisawa, Masaaki Tsuchida, Jun'ichi Kazama, Chikara Hashimoto, Ichiro Yamada, Jong-Hoon Oh, István Varga, and Yulan Yan. 2011. Relation acquisition using word classes and partial patterns. In *Proceedings of EMNLP 2011*, pages 825–835.

Motoki Sano, Kentaro Torisawa, Julien Kloetzer, Chikara Hashimoto, István Varga, and Jong-Hoon Oh. 2014. Million-scale derivation of semantic relations from a manually constructed predicate taxonomy. In *Proceedings of COLING 2014*, pages 1423–1434.

Masahiro Tanaka, Kenjiro Taura, and Kentaro Torisawa. 2016. Low latency and resource-aware program composition for large-scale data analysis. In *Proceedings of CCGrid 2016*, pages 325–330.

Kentaro Torisawa, Stijn de Saeger, Jun'ichi Kazama, Asuka Sumida, Daisuke Noguchi, Yasunari Kakizawa, Masaki Murata, Kow Kuroda, and Ichiro Yamada. 2010. Organizing the web's information explosion to discover unknown unknowns. *New Generation Computing*, 28(3):217–236.

István Varga, Motoki Sano, Kentaro Torisawa, Chikara Hashimoto, Kiyonori Ohtake, Takao Kawai, Jong-Hoon Oh, and Stijn De Saeger. 2013. Aid is out there: Looking for help from tweets during a large scale disaster. In *Proceedings of ACL 2013*, pages 1619–1629.

Multilingual Information Extraction with POLYGLOTIE

Alan Akbik, Laura Chiticariu, Marina Danilevsky, Yonas Kbrom, Yunyao Li, Huaiyu Zhu
IBM Research - Almaden
{akbika,chiti,mdanile,yktbrom,yunyaoli,huaiyu}@us.ibm.com

Abstract

We present POLYGLOTIE, a web-based tool for developing extractors that perform Information Extraction (IE) over multilingual data. Our tool has two core features: First, it allows users to develop extractors against a *unified abstraction* that is shared across a large set of natural languages. This means that an extractor needs only be created once for one language, but will then run on multilingual data without any additional effort or language-specific knowledge on part of the user. Second, it embeds this abstraction as a set of views within a declarative IE system, allowing users to quickly create extractors using a mature IE query language. We present POLYGLOTIE as a hands-on demo in which users can experiment with creating extractors, execute them on multilingual text and inspect extraction results. Using the UI, we discuss the challenges and potential of using unified, crosslingual semantic abstractions as basis for downstream applications. We demonstrate multilingual IE for 9 languages from 4 different language groups: English, German, French, Spanish, Japanese, Chinese, Arabic, Russian and Hindi.

1 Introduction

Information Extraction (IE) is the task of automatically extracting structured information from text (Sarawagi, 2008). Current IE approaches mostly focus on monolingual data and use language-specific feature sets to create extractors (Mintz et al., 2009; Surdeanu and Ji, 2014; Rocktäschel et al., 2015). A downside of such approaches is that extractors need to be separately created for each new language of interest, potentially blowing up costs.

With this demo, we present POLYGLOTIE, a web-based tool that allows users to create extractors over a *unified, crosslingual abstraction* of shallow semantics. The core advantage of our approach is that extractors need only be created once for one language against this abstraction, but can then automatically extract information from multilingual text.

We base our approach on previous work in multilingual semantic parsing (Akbik et al., 2015; Akbik and Li, 2016a; Akbik and Li, 2016b). In this research, we created a semantic role labeler (SRL) capable of predicting shallow semantic frame and role labels from the English Proposition Bank (Palmer et al., 2005) for 9 languages from 4 different language groups. We propose to utilize these semantic labels as the shared feature set against which users develop extractors. This, we argue, has two advantages: First, semantic role labels have human readable, shallow semantic descriptions (such as *buyer*, *thing bought*, and *price paid*) allowing users even without a background in linguistics to develop extractors. Second, since the same English labels are detected across all languages, users need not be language experts in a target language to create extractors. For instance, an English speaker might use this abstraction to create extractors for Chinese or Japanese.

The purpose of the demo is twofold: a) We demonstrate how extractors can be formulated against a shared abstraction based on frame semantics, and illustrate how they extract information from multilingual text. b) We illustrate the challenges and potential of using a frame-semantic abstraction for crosslingual applications.

Proceedings of COLING 2016, the 26th International Conference on Computational Linguistics: System Demonstrations, pages 268–272, Osaka, Japan, December 11-17 2016.

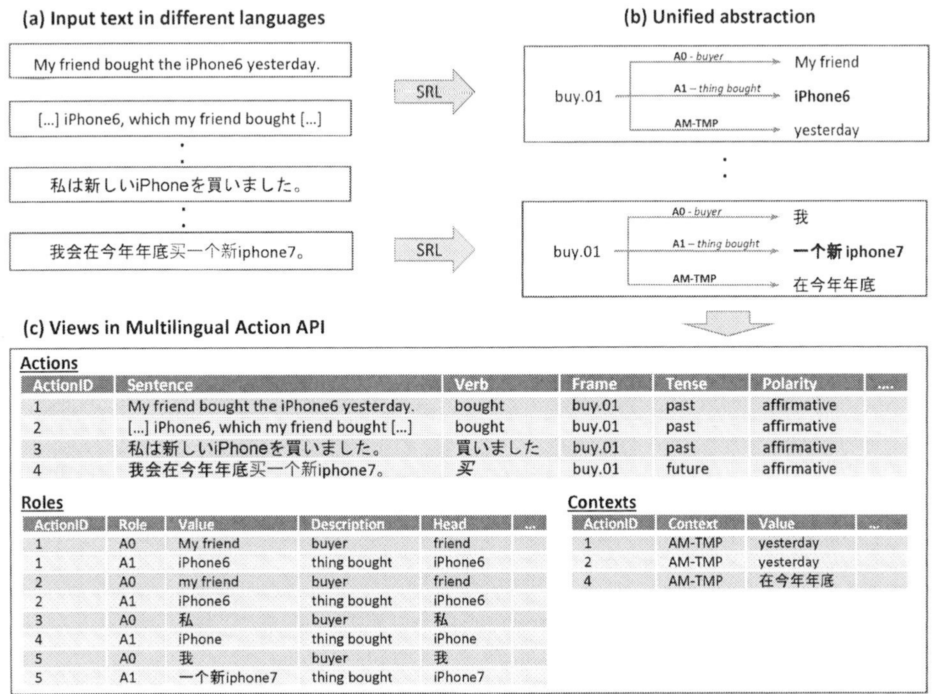

Figure 1: A multilingual text collection consisting of English, Japanese and Chinese sentences **(a)** parsed into the unified shallow semantic abstraction given by PropBank labels **(b)**. The abstraction is exposed through three views in POLYGLOTIE **(c)**.

2 A Unified Crosslingual Abstraction

Frame semantics as language-independent abstraction. We utilize POLYGLOT (Akbik and Li, 2016a), a semantic role labeler that predicts English Proposition Bank frame and role labels for sentences in one of 9 different languages. The SRL is trained with target language data that was automatically labeled with English PropBank labels using an annotation projection approach (Akbik et al., 2015; Akbik and Li, 2016b).

Refer to Figure 1 for an illustration of this process. Input text in three different languages **(a)** is parsed into a frame-semantic representation with English labels. The representation is illustrated in Figure 1 **(b)** for two of the four input sentences, an English and a Chinese sentence. In all sentences, the BUY.01 frame is recognized, together with the roles *buyer* and *thing bought* and a temporal context. Crucially, after parsing into the unified abstraction, no language specific shallow semantic features remain.

Exposing Views. We execute POLYGLOT over the multilingual corpus and expose the frame-semantic representation of all sentences through a simple, programmable API in three views. See Figure 1 **(c)** for an illustration of these views. Each view carries a number of attributes: An ACTIONS view that exposes information on frame-evoking verbs, including the frame (BUY.01), the tense (past, present, future) and the polarity (affirmative or negative). A ROLES view that exposes the primary arguments of verbs (PropBank roles A0 through A4), including information on syntactic argument structure. And a CONTEXTS view that exposes information about adjuncts of verbs such as temporal, location and manner contexts, corresponding to optional roles in PropBank.

3 Declarative Information Extraction Against the Unified Abstraction

We create extractors in a declarative fashion against these views. In declarative IE, extractors are fundamentally SQL-like queries against views that create other views that are either output as extraction results or embedded in other extractors (Chiticariu et al., 2010). This approach has the advantages of providing

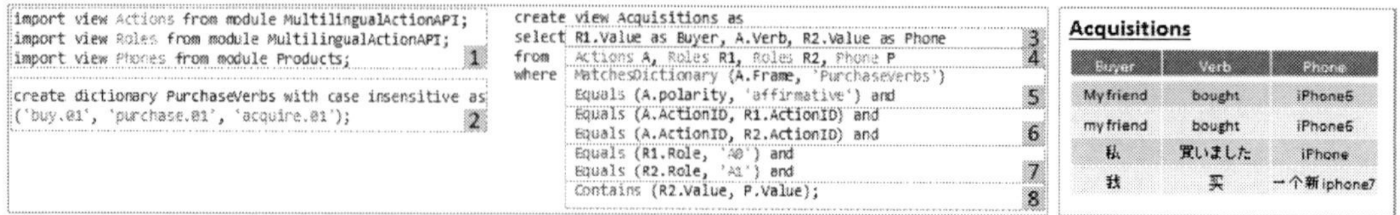

Figure 2: Multilingual extractor for smartphone acquisitions. AQL rule and extraction results.

a standard IE language and data model, and allowing for the creation of succinct and embeddable views, further simplifying the process of developing multilingual extractors.

For an example of a declarative extractor, refer to Figure 2. This extractor searches for instances of a relation between buyers and the smartphone they purchase. To illustrate how the extractor works, we give details on each block of lines, referred to by the numbered blocks (**1**)-(**8**) in the figure. We first import a series of *views* (previously defined extractors or NLP components) through the import statements in block (**1**): Those views are the ACTIONS and ROLES views as defined in section 2, as well as the PHONES view, a previously created NER for smartphones. We then define a *dictionary* of acquisition-evoking frames (**2**), such as BUY.01 and PURCHASE.01. We then define the extractor as a view called ACQUISITION (**4**), which we create using the previously imported views (ACTIONS, ROLES and PHONES), with several constraints: ACTIONS need to be part of the previously defined dictionary (since we are only interested in *buying* actions) and the *polarity* should be positive (to discard negated actions such as *will not buy*) (**5**). ACTIONS is joined with two copies of ROLES to retrieve two roles for each frame (**6**), which we require to be 'A0' and 'A1' respectively (**7**). A final constraint is that the latter role should contain a mention of a smartphone, which we add by matching it to the PHONES view (**8**). Finally, we define the extractor output as the buyer, verb and phone retrieved from the relevant attributes in the input views (**3**). For example output of this extractor, refer to the "Acquisitions" table in Figure 2 (right hand side).

Background on the query language. The example was created using only two statements that make use of multiple built-in constructs of the Annotation Query Language (AQL): dictionary matching (CREATE DICTIONARY and MATCHESDICTIONARY constructs), span operations (the EQUALS and CONTAINS built-in predicates), and relational operations such as selection, projection and join (the SELECT, FROM and WHERE clauses). AQL is part of the SystemT (Chiticariu et al., 2010) framework for expressing NLP algorithms with both rules and machine learning constructs. For further reading, please refer to the ACL Reference[1].

4 Multilingual IE Web Interface and Demo Scenarios

We present our web tool as a hands-on demo where users can create extractors and execute them on multilingual text. Refer to Figure 3 for an illustration of the web UI. In the top row, users can enter multilingual text (**1**) and create or modify an AQL rule that defines an output view (**2**). Upon hitting the extract button, the rule is executed over the input and the results are visualized in two ways (**3**): In the annotated text view, the extractions are annotated as labels in the input text. In the extractions view, the results are given in table format that shows the view as produced by the extractor.

We will use two demonstration scenarios. The first scenario involves the retail domain to identify purchase behavior similar to the smartphone acquision extractor discussed in Figure 1. The second scenario involves event extraction focused on the sports domain.

5 Discussion and Outlook

With this demonstration, users explore declarative IE rules over a unified, frame-semantic abstraction to create multilingual extractors. A point of discussion and current research is the coverage of semantic constructs required for IE applications. For instance, in its current form, the API is verb-centric, but

[1]The AQL Reference is available at: `http://ibm.co/2bNuweC`

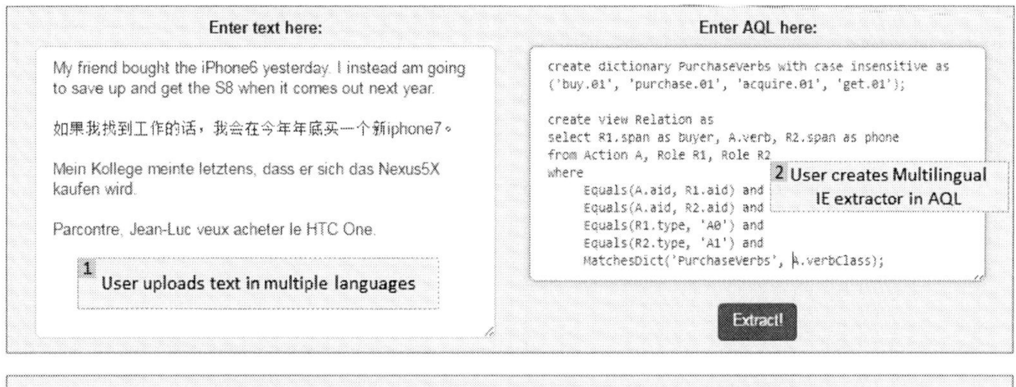

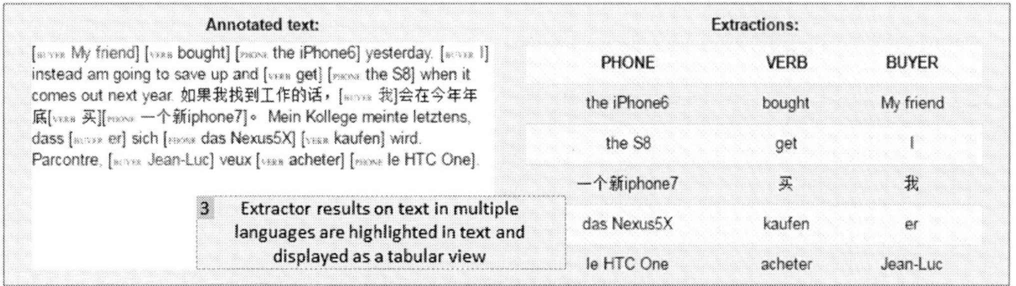

Figure 3: Screenshot of the POLYGLOTIE web interface.

current work on frame-semantic abstractions (Banarescu et al., 2012; Bonial et al., 2014) focuses on other types of frame-evoking elements such as complex predicates. Furthermore, while our abstraction currently captures the semantic roles of constituents, lexical values often diverge between languages (the city of Milan for instance is called Milano in Italian and Mailand in German). Accordingly, we will focus on broadening our multilingual parsing to entity-level concepts, similar to entity-level annotations in abstract meaning representations (Banarescu et al., 2012).

References

A. Akbik and Y. Li. 2016a. Polyglot: Multilingual semantic role labeling with unified labels. In *ACL*.

Alan Akbik and Yunyao Li. 2016b. Towards semi-automatic generation of proposition banks for low-resource languages. In *EMNLP*.

Alan Akbik, Laura Chiticariu, Marina Danilevsky, Yunyao Li, Shivakumar Vaithyanathan, and Huaiyu Zhu. 2015. Generating high quality proposition banks for multilingual semantic role labeling. In *ACL*, pages 397–407.

L. Banarescu, C. Bonial, S. Cai, M. Georgescu, K. Griffitt, U. Hermjakob, K. Knight, P. Koehn, M. Palmer, and N. Schneider. 2012. Abstract meaning representation (amr) 1.0 specification. In *EMNLP*.

Claire Bonial, Julia Bonn, Kathryn Conger, Jena D Hwang, and Martha Palmer. 2014. Propbank: Semantics of new predicate types. In *LREC*, pages 3013–3019.

Laura Chiticariu, Rajasekar Krishnamurthy, Yunyao Li, Sriram Raghavan, Frederick Reiss, and Shivakumar Vaithyanathan. 2010. SystemT: An algebraic approach to declarative information extraction. In *ACL*, pages 128–137.

M. Mintz, S. Bills, R. Snow, and D. Jurafsky. 2009. Distant supervision for relation extraction without labeled data. In *ACL/AFNLP*, pages 1003–1011.

Martha Palmer, Daniel Gildea, and Paul Kingsbury. 2005. The proposition bank: An annotated corpus of semantic roles. *Computational linguistics*, 31(1):71–106.

Tim Rocktäschel, Sameer Singh, and Sebastian Riedel. 2015. Injecting logical background knowledge into embeddings for relation extraction. In *HTC-NAACL*.

Sunita Sarawagi. 2008. Information extraction. *Foundations and trends in databases*, 1(3):261–377.

M. Surdeanu and H. Ji. 2014. Overview of english slot filling track at TAC KB population evaluation. In *TAC*.

WordForce: Visualizing Controversial Words in Debates

Wei-Fan Chen Fang-Yu Lin Lun-Wei Ku
Institute of Information Science,
Academia Sinica, Taipei, Taiwan.
viericwf@iis.sinica.edu.tw, nis50122806@gmail.com, lwku@iis.sinica.edu.tw

Abstract

This paper presents WordForce, a system powered by the state of the art neural network model to visualize the learned user-dependent word embeddings from each post according to the post content and its engaged users. It generates the scatter plots to show the force of a word, i.e., whether the semantics of word embeddings from posts of different stances are clearly separated from the aspect of this controversial word. In addition, WordForce provides the dispersion and the distance of word embeddings from posts of different stance groups, and proposes the most controversial words accordingly to show clues to what people argue about in a debate.

1 Introduction

Word embeddings have been widely used in deep neural networks and have achieved promising results. Compared to the traditional n-gram feature, which represents each document as a high dimensional sparse vector, the word embedding is representing with the low dimensional and dense vector. Hence using embeddings has its merits on decreasing training time and reducing complexity, and many papers have introduced different compositions of word embeddings in their work for comparison (Chen et al., 2015; Lai et al., 2015). However, one drawback of using word embeddings is that human cannot interpret its meaning as when using n-gram feature. In previous work, one solution is to visualize the word embeddings by reducing them into two-dimensional vectors on a x-y plot to view the semantic distribution of words. For example, in Iyyer et al.'s work we see people's names would cluster together when they have the same jobs or positions, e.g., presidents of United States, prime ministers or emperors (Iyyer et al., 2014); ScholarOctopus[1] and tsnejs[2] visualize research articles embeddings and word embeddings, respectively; Mikolov also shows the semantics can be calculated using this kind of two dimensional plot (Mikolov and Dean, 2013); the semantic word cloud based on word embedding visualizes the word usage in product reviews (Xu et al., 2016). All these show the distance between word embeddings reveals semantic relations.

In a time that social media becomes part of our life, we attempt to observe the user-dependent word embeddings in a debate to analyze user-dependent semantics. In the past, incorporating meta data to train neural network models for sentiment analysis on product reviews and social media texts has been shown to be effective. For example, our UTCNN integrates users, topics and comments information in Facebook posts (Chen and Ku, 2016); Dong et al. consider topics and add an adaptive layer in their recursive neural network for target-dependent Twitter sentiment (Dong et al., 2014); Tang et al.'s UPNN incorporates users and products (Tang et al., 2015). In this paper, to see how this kind of word embeddings can be further utilized, we consider users who posted or liked the post in the process of training word embeddings in addition to a pure text-based neural network models (Kim, 2014). Such learned word embeddings for the same word would differ among posts when the engaged users are different.

[1] http://cs.stanford.edu/people/karpathy/scholaroctopus/

[2] http://cs.stanford.edu/people/karpathy/tsnejs/wordvecs.html

Proceedings of COLING 2016, the 26th International Conference on Computational Linguistics: System Demonstrations, pages 273–277, Osaka, Japan, December 11-17 2016.

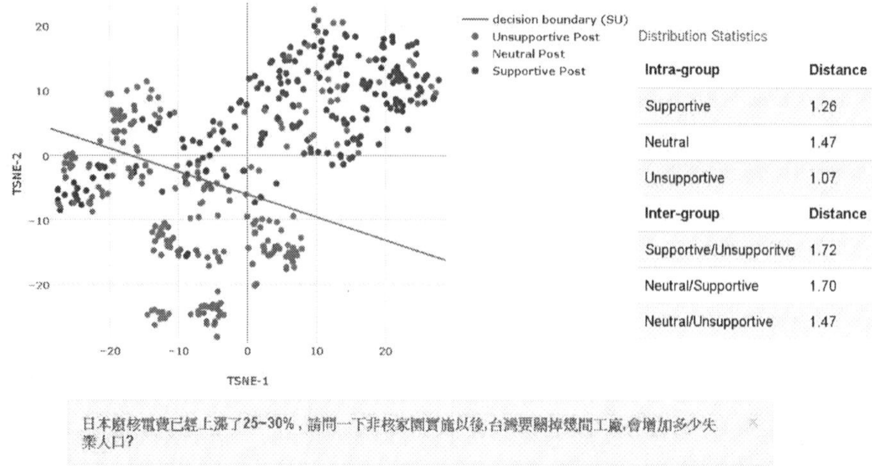

Figure 1: The WordForce interface showing the results of the controversial word 上漲(rise). The selected post comments that after the implement of non-nuclear policy, the electricity rate in Japan has risen 25-30%; if we follow, how many factories will be closed and how many unemployed people will we have?

Therefore, we may investigate their semantic difference and how they can contribute to the analysis of the stance classification problem in debates.

For this purpose, we present the web-based system, WordForce[3], where users can query an arbitrary corpus word to get its visualization and statistic information. Figure 1 shows the query result of searching the word 上漲(rise) in the nuclear power plant construction debate. The left-hand side shows the two-dimensional visualization including its word embedding in each post and a decision boundary between the supportive and unsupportive stance (if applicable). Supportive/unsupportive posts were those in support of or against anti-reconstruction; neutral posts were those evincing a neutral standpoint on the topic, or were irrelevant. The stance of the post where the word embedding is from is indicated by different dot colors: blue for supportive, gray for neutral, and red for unsupportive. The plot here suggests that the word *rise*, referring to the rise of electric charge in the nuclear power debate, has different semantics between the supportive and unsupportive posts as we expect. The right-hand side shows distribution statistics. Further clicking on any dot will show the original post content below the plot, e.g., after clicking a red dot, the unsupportive post arguing that the abandon of nuclear power will rise the electricity rate shows below.

2 Learning User-Dependent Word Embeddings

To learn the user-dependent word embeddings for stance classification and visualization, we train the 50-dimensional word embeddings via GloVe (Pennington et al., 2014). These embeddings are then transformed via a user-dependent matrix embedding U_k as in equation 1.

$$x'_w = U_k \cdot x_w \tag{1}$$

where x_w and x'_w are the word embeddings of word w trained by GloVe and the transformed word embeddings, respectively. The user-dependent matrix embedding models the user's preference for reading certain semantics where the "user" denotes a pseudo user on behalf of all likers and authors in a given post. Then the transformed word embeddings x'_w are used as the input of a convolutional neural network and fed into a fully connected network to yield the final post stance. The detail descriptions of the proposed neural network model is included in the paper of UTCNN (Chen and Ku, 2016).

We collect data from anti-nuclear-power Chinese Facebook fan groups in one year period of time, including posts and their author and liker IDs. There are a total of 2,496 authors, 505,137 likers and

[3]WordForce is available at `http://doraemon.iis.sinica.edu.tw/wordforce`

	Supportive	Neutral	Unsupportive	all
Annotation	7,504	24,816	275	32,595
Stance Classification	.698	.957	.571	.755

Table 1: Annotation results and f-scores of stance classification of Facebook dataset.

32,595 posts. We annotate the stance of all posts as *supportive*, *neutral*, or *unsupportive*. The annotation results are shown in the first row of Table 1. On average, 161.1 users are engaged to one post. The maximum is 23,297 and the minimum is one (the author). Experimental results show that the proposed model achieves good results on the Chinese Facebook fans group material as shown in the second row of Table 1 (Chen and Ku, 2016). For comparison, this model is also tested on the English open benchmark CreateDebate for stance classification and it outperforms the state of the art by achieving the accuracy 0.842 against 0.735 (Sridhar et al., 2015; Chen and Ku, 2016).

3 WordForce

On top of the word embeddings obtained from the state of the art neural network model for stance classification, WordForce visualize these embeddings for debatable issues to provide useful information for research surveys or industrial applications. WordForce can illustrate each corpus word by displaying a two-dimensional word embedding distribution plot as well as the inter- and intra-group distances (dispersion and distance, respectively), where a "group" is a set of word embeddings from posts of the same stance label. Furthermore, with these statistics, WordForce can propose different types of controversial words ,i.e., aspects or events that people of different stance are arguing about.

From Controversial Word Visualization to Suggestion After training, we gather all the word embeddings from the user-dependent transformation. For each corpus word, we collect their transformed word embeddings x'_w and project them into a two-dimensional space via t-SNE (Maaten and Hinton, 2008). The two dimensions of the t-SNE plot implicitly present latent sentiment or semantic so that similar words would have similar vector representations as in many related work (Iyyer et al., 2014; Melamud et al., 2015).

Now with the positions of embeddings of one word, WordForce can further calculate their intra- and inter-group distance. The intra-group distance (dispersion) of group g is defined as the average Euclidean distance to the group mean shown in equation 2.

$$Dispersion\,(g) = \frac{1}{N_g} \sum_n \|v_{n,g} - \mu_g\| \tag{2}$$

where N_g is the size (number of dots) of this group, $v_{n,g}$ is the n-th vector, and μ_g is the mean of the group g, respectively. The inter-group distance (distance) is the average link between two groups as in equation 3.

$$Distance\,(g_i, g_j) = \frac{1}{N_{g_i} \cdot N_{g_j}} \sum_{v_n \in g_i, v_m \in g_j} \|v_n - v_m\| \tag{3}$$

where N_{g_i} and N_{g_j} are the sizes of group i and j, respectively; v_n and v_m are the n-th vector of group i and the m-th vector of group j, respectively. A low dispersion value indicates posts and their engaged users of the same stance group agree in its semantic, while a high distance value indicates posts and their engaged users vary a lot among groups and can be separated. With the dispersion and distance value of each word calculated from its embeddings, WordForce is then able to propose controversial words by ordering their dispersion value ascendingly and the distance value discendingly.

Table 2 shows some words with a high inter-group distance, a low intra-group dispersion or a high TFIDF value, which confirms that WordForce can propose different controversial words in addition to the conventional topical words. WordForce also lists these words for users to see their word embedding distribution plots and statistics.

Controversial Word Type	Example (Translation)
Top high TFIDF	龍門(lonmen), 絶食(hunger strike), 夏天(summer)
Top high distance	日光(solar),廢氣(air pollution), 煙囪(chimney)
Top low dispersion	核融合(nuclear fusion),國庫(exchequer), 偵檢器(radiation-detector)

Table 2: Example controversial words proposed by WordForce.

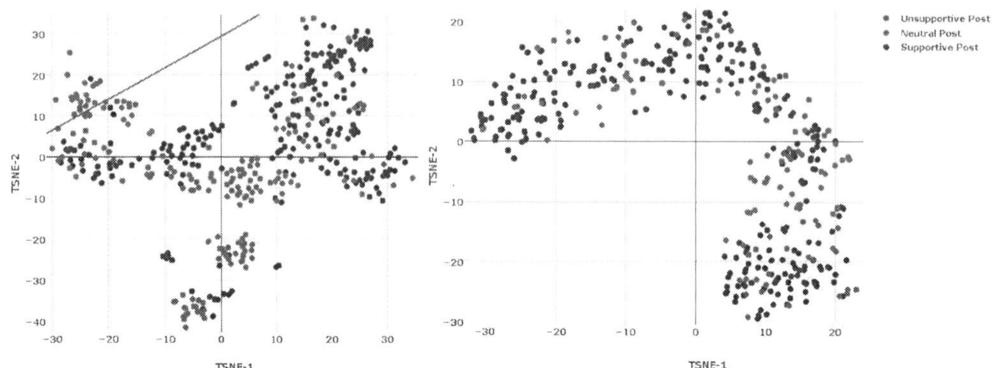

Figure 2: Word embedding distribution plots for 絶食(hunger strike) and 廢氣(air pollution).

Discussion We select some cases to illustrate WordForce. Figure 1 shows the plot and statistics of the word 上漲(rise). The dispersion of the neutral group is much larger than that of both the supportive group and the unsupportive groups, and the large inter-group distance tells that supportive to unsupportive posts are more different than neural to supportive or neutral to unsupportive posts. The trend these numbers tell can be easily captured by reading the plot. From the plot we also find that the unsupportive posts are clustered into several sub-groups. These sub-groups represent different related arguments. For example, the sub-group on the far right collects news articles discussing the disadvantages of abandoning nuclear, while the one in the middle includes some personal criticisms. All these observations confirm that WordForce can facilitate deeper analysis.

In Figure 2 we show another two word embedding examples: 絶食(hunger strike) at the right-hand side and 廢氣(air pollution) at the left-hand side. The word 絶食(hunger strike) seems to be unrelated to the nuclear issue but the word embeddings tell differently and are clearly separated: going deeper we find a former politician has organized a hunger strike against the nuclear power. Hence some related posts support the hunger strike to opt for the anti-nuclear, and the others say the hunger strike is a publicity stunt so that to be against the anti-nuclear.

Unlike hunger strike, air pollution is related as the thermal generation supplies most electricity in Taiwan but produces much air pollution. However, the word embeddings from posts of different stances are mixed up. Going deeper we find that both supportive and unsupportive posts express the same opinion towards it: air pollution is a disaster. In supportive posts, users dislike air pollution and suggest to use clean energy such as the solar or hydroelectric power. On the other hand in unsupportive posts, users dislike air pollution either but suggest to use nuclear power as it produce almost no air pollution.

4 Conclusion

We present WordForce, a user-dependent word embedding visualization and analysis system for debate issues, to demonstrate how to analyze transformed word embeddings from the stance aspect. WordForce can provide two-dimensional scatter plots as well as the dispersion and the distance values to demonstrate the word force for debatable topics. In the future, we plan to apply it on the research problems related to more debate issues.

Acknowledgements

Research of this paper was partially supported by Ministry of Science and Technology, Taiwan, under the contract MOST 104-2221-E-001-024-MY2.

References

Wei-Fan Chen and Lun-Wei Ku. 2016. UTCNN: a deep learning model of stance classification on social media text. In *COLING (to appear)*. auspices of the International Committee on Computational Linguistics.

Wei-Fan Chen, Yann-Hui Lee, and Lun-Wei Ku. 2015. Topic-based stance mining for social media texts. In *International Conference on HCI in Business*, pages 22–33. Association for Computing Machinery.

Li Dong, Furu Wei, Ming Zhou, and Ke Xu. 2014. Adaptive multi-compositionality for recursive neural models with applications to sentiment analysis. In *Proceedings of the Conference of the Association for the Advancement of Artificial Intelligence*. AAAI.

Mohit Iyyer, Jordan L Boyd-Graber, Leonardo Max Batista Claudino, Richard Socher, and Hal Daumé III. 2014. A neural network for factoid question answering over paragraphs. In *Proceedings of the 2014 Conference on Empirical Methods in Natural Language Processing*, pages 633–644. Association for Computational Linguistics.

Yoon Kim. 2014. Convolutional neural networks for sentence classification. In *Proceedings of the Conference on Empirical Methods in Natural Language Processing*, pages 1746–1751. Association for Computational Linguistics.

Siwei Lai, Liheng Xu, Kang Liu, and Jun Zhao. 2015. Recurrent convolutional neural networks for text classification. In *Proceedings of the Conference of the Association for the Advancement of Artificial Intelligence*, pages 2267–2273. AAAI.

Laurens van der Maaten and Geoffrey Hinton. 2008. Visualizing data using t-sne. *Journal of Machine Learning Research*, 9(Nov):2579–2605.

Oren Melamud, Omer Levy, Ido Dagan, and Israel Ramat-Gan. 2015. A simple word embedding model for lexical substitution. In *Proceedings of the 1st Workshop on Vector Space Modeling for Natural Language Processing*, pages 1–7.

T Mikolov and J Dean. 2013. Distributed representations of words and phrases and their compositionality. *Advances in neural information processing systems*.

Jeffrey Pennington, Richard Socher, and Christopher D. Manning. 2014. Glove: Global vectors for word representation. In *Proceedings of the Conference on Empirical Methods in Natural Language Processing*, pages 1532–1543. Association for Computational Linguistics.

Dhanya Sridhar, James Foulds, Bert Huang, Lise Getoor, and Marilyn Walker. 2015. Joint models of disagreement and stance in online debate. In *Proceedings of the 53rd Annual Meeting of the Association for Computational Linguistics*, pages 116–125. Association for Computational Linguistics.

Duyu Tang, Bing Qin, and Ting Liu. 2015. Learning semantic representations of users and products for document level sentiment classification. In *Proceedings of the 53rd Annual Meeting of the Association for Computational Linguistics and the 7th International Joint Conference on Natural Language Processing*, pages 1014–1023. Association for Computational Linguistics.

Jin Xu, Yubo Tao, and Hai Lin. 2016. Semantic word cloud generation based on word embeddings. In *2016 IEEE Pacific Visualization Symposium (PacificVis)*, pages 239–243. IEEE.

Zara: A Virtual Interactive Dialogue System Incorporating Emotion, Sentiment and Personality Recognition

Pascale Fung, Anik Dey, Farhad Bin Siddique, Ruixi Lin, Yang Yang, Dario Bertero, Wan Yan, Ricky Chan Ho Yin, Chien-Sheng Wu
Human Language Technology Center
Department of Electronic and Computer Engineering
Hong Kong University of Science and Technology, Hong Kong
pascale@ece.ust.hk,
[adey, fsiddique, rlinab, yyangag, dbertero, ywanad]@connect.ust.hk,
eehychan@ust.hk, b01901045@ntu.edu.tw

Abstract

Zara, or 'Zara the Supergirl' is a virtual robot, that can exhibit empathy while interacting with an user, with the aid of its built in facial and emotion recognition, sentiment analysis, and speech module. At the end of the 5-10 minute conversation, Zara can give a personality analysis of the user based on all the user utterances. We have also implemented a real-time emotion recognition, using a CNN model that detects emotion from raw audio without feature extraction, and have achieved an average of 65.7% accuracy on six different emotion classes, which is an impressive 4.5% improvement from the conventional feature based SVM classification. Also, we have described a CNN based sentiment analysis module trained using out-of-domain data, that recognizes sentiment from the speech recognition transcript, which has a 74.8 F-measure when tested on human-machine dialogues.

1 Introduction

As the availability of interactive dialogue systems is on a rise, people are getting more accustomed to talking to machines. Modern systems are equipped with better statistical and machine learning modules in order to help them get better over time. People have started expecting the machines to understand different aspects of dialogues, like intent, humor, sarcasm, etc. We want the system to connect with us more, by recognising our emotions. This requires machines to have an empathy module in them, that will enable them to give more emotional responses during the interaction with users (Fung, 2015).

We have developed a prototype system that is a web program that can be rendered on a browser, and is a virtual robot with a cartoon character to represent itself (Fung et al., 2015). It can converse with a user by asking a few questions related to the user's personal experiences, and can give a personality analysis based on the responses after a 5-10 minute conversation. At each round of interaction, the response to the user utterance is chosen based on the emotion and sentiment recognition results, some examples are shown below:

Zara: *How was your last vacation?*

User: *I went on a vacation last month and it was pretty bad, I lost all my luggage.*

Response: *That doesn't sound so good. Hope your next vacation will be a good one.*

User: *My last vacation was amazing, I loved it!*

Response: *That sounds great. I would like to travel with you.*

Conventional methods of emotion recognition require feature engineering (Schuller et al., 2009; Schuller et al., 2010), which is too slow for a task like this, and so cannot be used in interactive dialogue systems. Therefore, we use a Convolutional Neural Network (CNN) model that bypasses the feature extraction and extracts emotion from raw-audio in real-time.

Proceedings of COLING 2016, the 26th International Conference on Computational Linguistics: System Demonstrations, pages 278–281, Osaka, Japan, December 11-17 2016.

2 System Description

2.1 Design

The main task of our system right now is the assessment of MBTI personality at the end of the conversation with the user (Polzehl et al., 2010). We have designed 6 unique classes of questions asking the user about their childhood memories, last vacation, work challenges, creativity in telling a story, companionship, and also their opinion on human-robot interactions. Each class is termed as a 'state' and each state consists of an opening question and other follow up questions, depending on the user response. Zara can be used using an URL link rendered on a browser, with the use of a microphone and a camera.

The conversation flow is controlled via the dialogue management system that keeps track of the various states. It also decides between two different types of conversation, one is where Zara asks the question, or machine-initiative, and the other is user-initiative questions or challenges to Zara.

2.2 Facial and Speech Recognition

At the initial stage, when the system is started, a snapshot of the user's face is taken, and the facial recognition algorithm tries to identify the user's gender and ethnicity, along with a confidence score.

For speech recognition, we collected acoustic data from different public domain and LDC corpora, which makes a total of 1385 hours of speech. The acoustic models are trained by the Kaldi speech recognition toolkit (Povey et al., 2011), using the raw audio together with encode-decode parallel audio to train Deep Neural Network - Hidden Markov Models (DNN-HMMs). We apply sequence discriminative training using state Minimum Bayes Risk (sMBR) criterion, and layer wise training of restricted Boltzmann machines (RBMs), along with frame cross-entropy training via mini-batch stochastic gradient descent (SGD). We use text data, that includes Cantab filtering sentences on Google 1 billion word LM benchmark (Chelba et al., 2013), acoustic training transcriptions, and other web crawled news, and music and weather domain queries, making a total of around 90M sentences. Our decoder supports streaming of raw audio or CELP encoded data via TCP/IP or HTTP protocol, and performs decoding in real time. The ASR system achieves 7.6% word error rate on our clean speech test data[1].

2.3 Real-Time Emotion Recognition from Raw Audio

Most of the benchmark systems on classification of Emotional speech (Mairesse et al., 2007) or music genres or moods (Schermerhorn and Scheutz, 2011), involves feature extraction and classifier learning, which is both time-consuming and requires a lot of hand tuning. Therefore, we have developed a Convolutional Neural Network model that can recognise emotions directly from time-domain audio signal, bypassing the feature engineering. This is suitable for use in applications like interactive dialogue systems, which have real-time requirements.

We built a dataset from the TED-LIUM corpus release 2 (Rousseau et al., 2014), that includes 207 hours of speech extracted from 1495 TED talks. After initially annotating the data using a commercially available API, we hand-corrected the annotations. Six categories of emotions are used: criticism, anxiety, anger, loneliness, happiness, and sadness, and the audio data is divided into 13 second segments for annotations.

Using 8kHz as the sampling rate, and a single filter in the CNN, we set the convolutional window size to be 200, which is 25 ms, and an overlapping step size of 50, equivalent to 6 ms. The convolutional layer uses the differences between neighbouring and overlapping frames, and also performs its own feature extraction from the raw audio. Max pooling is done later that gives an output of a segment-based vector, which is then fed to a fully connected layer that acts like a Deep Neural Network (DNN), thereby mapping the output to a probabilistic distribution over the emotion categories via a final softmax layer.

For baseline, we use Support Vector Machine (SVM) classifier with a linear kernel using the INTERSPEECH 2009 emotion feature set (Schuller et al., 2009). The results are shown in Table 1. By using a single filter CNN architecture, we achieve real-time decoding, around 1.62 ms on average for each segment of longer than 13s, and also we achieve a notable 4.5% improvement on average when compared to the baseline SVM method.

[1] `https://catalog.ldc.upenn.edu/LDC94S13A`

Emotion class	SVM (%)	CNN (%)
Criticism/Cynicism	55.0	61.2
Defensiveness/Anxiety	56.3	62.0
Hostility/Anger	72.8	72.9
Loneliness/Unfulfillment	61.1	66.6
Love/Happiness	50.9	60.1
Sadness/Sorrow	71.1	71.4
Average	61.2	**65.7**

Table 1: Accuracies obtained in the Convolutional Neural Network model for emotion classification from raw audio samples.

2.4 Sentiment Recognition from Text

Previous research by Kim (2014) has shown that Convolutional Neural Networks (CNNs) can perform impressively in the sentiment classification task. We use word embedding vectors (Word2Vec) trained on the Google News corpus (Mikolov et al., 2013) of size 300, to train a CNN with one layer of convolution and max pooling (Collobert et al., 2011). Using convolutional sliding window of sizes 3, 4 and 5 to represent different features, we apply a max-pooling operation on the output vectors from the convolutional layer. Two different CNN channels are used, one that keeps the word vectors static throughout, and the other fine tunes the vectors via back-propagation (Kim, 2014). The two sentence encoding vectors from the two channels are fed to the final softmax layer, that gives as output the probability distribution over the binary sentiment classification of the transcribed speech text. To improve the performance accuracy, we have used a larger Twitter sentiment 140[2] dataset, and have compared to the original Movie Review dataset used in Kim (2014). Results are shown in Table 2.

Model	Accuracy	Precision	Recall	F-score
Movie Review	67.8%	91.2%	63.5%	74.8
Twitter	72.17%	78.64%	86.69%	82.47

Table 2: Sentiment analysis results tested on human-machine conversations when trained from Twitter and Movie Review datasets

2.5 Personality Analysis

Our task is to identify the user personality from sixteen different MBTI personality types[3], and we designed six different domain specific personal questions for the classification. A group of training users were asked to fill up the original MBTI personality test questionnaire, that contains about 70 questions, and this was used as the gold standard label for training. The user responses to Zara's questions were used to calculate scores in four personality dimensions (Introversion - Extroversion, Intuitive - Sensing, Thinking - Feeling, Judging - Perceiving). Based on previous research done by Mairesse et al. (2007), we use the scores from the emotion and sentiment recognition as speech and linguistic cues to calculate the personality dimension scores.

3 Handling Challenges

Sometimes users can respond in a way that does not answer the question directly, and therefore impose a challenge on Zara. From a preliminary study on the recorded responses, it was found that 12.5% of users asked irrelevant questions to Zara, 24.62% challenged Zara in some other way, and 37.5% tried to avoid the topic. According to Wheeless and Grotz (1977), such cases are also common in human-human conversations.

[2] www.sentiment140.com

[3] https://www.personalitypage.com/html/high-level.html

Most common challenges were avoidance of topic, followed by usage of abusive language. Although Zara is made empathetic in nature, it is also given some witty traits, for example, if multiple swearing or use of inappropriate language is detected, then Zara stops conversing with the user unless they apologise. A general question to Zara (like "What is the capital of China?") will be answered from a general knowledge database using a search engine API.

4 Conclusion

We have described our prototype system, Zara the Supergirl, that uses real-time emotion and sentiment recognition to converse with a user by attempting to give emotionally intelligent responses. Such systems will help future robots to have a better and more advanced empathy module in them, thereby enabling them to build an emotional connection with humans. Also, we have shown that current research on deep learning can help come up with better and faster models to recognise different aspects of human behaviour like personality, in real-time conversations. This advancement can help us build robots that will help humans in the future, and instead of bringing mischief, they can be our companions and caregivers.

References

Ciprian Chelba, Tomas Mikolov, Mike Schuster, Qi Ge, Thorsten Brants, Phillipp Koehn, and Tony Robinson. 2013. One billion word benchmark for measuring progress in statistical language modeling. *arXiv preprint arXiv:1312.3005*.

Ronan Collobert, Jason Weston, Léon Bottou, Michael Karlen, Koray Kavukcuoglu, and Pavel Kuksa. 2011. Natural language processing (almost) from scratch. *The Journal of Machine Learning Research*, 12:2493–2537.

Pascale Fung, Anik Dey, Farhad Bin Siddique, Ruixi Lin, Yang Yang, Wan Yan, and Ricky Chan Ho Yin. 2015. Zara the supergirl: An empathetic personality recognition system.

Pascale Fung. 2015. Robots with heart. *Scientific American*, pages 60–63.

Yoon Kim. 2014. Convolutional neural networks for sentence classification. *arXiv preprint arXiv:1408.5882*.

Francois Mairesse, Marilyn A. Walker, Matthias R. Mehl, and Roger K. Moore. 2007. Using linguistic cues for the automatic recognition of personality in conversation and text. *Journal of Artificial Intelligence Research*, pages 457–500.

Tomas Mikolov, Ilya Sutskever, Kai Chen, Greg S Corrado, and Jeff Dean. 2013. Distributed representations of words and phrases and their compositionality. In *Advances in neural information processing systems*, pages 3111–3119.

Tim Polzehl, Sebastian Möller, and Florian Metze. 2010. Automatically assessing personality from speech. In *Semantic Computing (ICSC), 2010 IEEE Fourth International Conference on*, pages 134–140. IEEE.

Daniel Povey, Arnab Ghoshal, Gilles Boulianne, Lukas Burget, Ondrej Glembek, Nagendra Goel, Mirko Hannemann, Petr Motlicek, Yanmin Qian, Petr Schwarz, et al. 2011. The kaldi speech recognition toolkit. In *IEEE 2011 workshop on automatic speech recognition and understanding*, number EPFL-CONF-192584. IEEE Signal Processing Society.

Anthony Rousseau, Paul Deléglise, and Yannick Estève. 2014. Enhancing the ted-lium corpus with selected data for language modeling and more ted talks. In *LREC*, pages 3935–3939.

Paul Schermerhorn and Matthias Scheutz. 2011. Disentangling the effects of robot affect, embodiment, and autonomy on human team members in a mixed-initiative task. In *Proceedings from the International Conference on Advances in Computer-Human Interactions*, pages 236–241.

Björn Schuller, Stefan Steidl, and Anton Batliner. 2009. The interspeech 2009 emotion challenge. In *INTERSPEECH*, volume 2009, pages 312–315. Citeseer.

Björn Schuller, Stefan Steidl, Anton Batliner, Felix Burkhardt, Laurence Devillers, Christian A Müller, and Shrikanth S Narayanan. 2010. The interspeech 2010 paralinguistic challenge. In *INTERSPEECH*, volume 2010, pages 2795–2798.

L. R. Wheeless and J. Grotz. 1977. The measurement of trust and its relationship to self-disclosure. *Human Communication Research*, 3(3):250–257.

NL2KB: Resolving Vocabulary Gap between Natural Language and Knowledge Base in Knowledge Base Construction and Retrieval

Sheng-Lun Wei, Yen-Pin Chiu, Hen-Hsen Huang, and Hsin-Hsi Chen
Department of Computer Science and Information Engineering
National Taiwan University, Taipei, Taiwan
{weisl, ypchiu, hhhuang}@nlg.csie.ntu.edu.tw; hhchen@ntu.edu.tw

Abstract

Words to express relations in natural language (NL) statements may be different from those to represent properties in knowledge bases (KB). The vocabulary gap becomes barriers for knowledge base construction and retrieval. With the demo system called **NL2KB** in this paper, users can browse which properties in KB side may be mapped to for a given relational pattern in NL side. Besides, they can retrieve the sets of relational patterns in NL side for a given property in KB side. We describe how the mapping is established in detail. Although the mined patterns are used for Chinese knowledge base applications, the methodology can be extended to other languages.

1 Introduction

Knowledge bases (KBs) such as YAGO (Suchanek et al., 2007) and DBpedia (Lehmann et al., 2014) are useful resources in various applications such as question answering (Yih et al., 2015). KBs contain rich information of entities and their properties. A fact in a KB is usually represented as the form (*entity*1, *property*, *entity*2). Most KBs rely on manpower for editing and maintenance, so it is challenging to keep them up-to-date. Frank et al. (2012) point out the latency issue in knowledge base update. How to construct and update the knowledge base automatically is indispensable.

Mining facts from natural language (NL) statements and introducing them to knowledge base becomes a trend. In the sentence "蜜雪兒歐巴馬嫁給巴拉克奧巴馬" (Michelle Obama is married to Barack Obama), there are the two entities, i.e., 蜜雪兒歐巴馬 (Michelle Obama) and 巴拉克奧巴馬 (Barack Obama), and a relation 嫁給 (is married to) between them. In DBpedia, the relation 嫁給 (is married to) is represented as the property <spouse>. In other words, 嫁給 (is married to) in NL side is an NL relational pattern of the property <spouse> in KB side.

The vocabulary gap not only affects knowledge base construction, but also knowledge retrieval applications such as question answering. English relational patterns like PATTY (Nakashole et al., 2012) show efficacy on related applications (Dutta et al., 2015). In this work, we present a system for Chinese relation extraction and release a collection of human-verified Chinese relational patterns as a resource. We also demonstrate the applications of relational patterns on the demo website.

This paper is organized as follows. Section 2 surveys the related work. Section 3 describes the methodology. Section 4 shows and discusses the results. Section 5 demonstrates the **NL2KB** system.

2 Related Work

Information extraction (IE) models like ReVerb (Fader et al., 2011) automatically extract information from unstructured or semi-structured documents. Given an English sentence, ReVerb identifies two arguments and their relation in the form of (*argument*1, *relation*, *argument*2). PATTY (Nakashole et al., 2012) is a taxonomy system of relational patterns in English. From Wikipedia and the New York Times, 127,811 relational patterns are mined to describe 225 DBpedia properties, and 43,124 relational patterns are mined to describe 25 YAGO's properties. However, the coverage is still an issue.

Most open IE systems are developed for English, and few are for other languages. ZORE (Qiu et al., 2014) is a model that extracts relations from Chinese articles and presents them in the format of ReVerb style. However, this system does not deal with vocabulary mapping between NL and KB sides.

Proceedings of COLING 2016, the 26th International Conference on Computational Linguistics: System Demonstrations, pages 282–286, Osaka, Japan, December 11-17 2016.

3 Method

In this paper, we extract relational patterns from the Chinese Wikipedia corpus and map them to the properties defined in DBpedia. In other words, the mapping between NL and KB is established. The DBpedia dataset used in our system was released on 8th May, 2014, and the dump of Chinese Wikipedia was released on 25th March, 2015. Figure 1 shows an overview of Chinese pattern extraction.

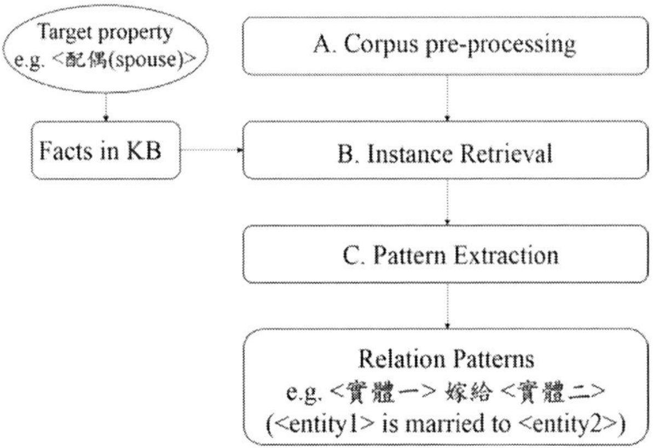

Figure 1: System overview.

3.1 Corpus Pre-processing

We discard all non-text information from the Chinese Wikipedia corpus such as html tags, xml tags, and cited tags, and perform sentence segmentation. Three punctuations, i.e., period, question mark, and exclamation mark, are regarded as sentence delimiters. After segmentations, we index each sentence into a search engine based on Solr[1] in order to do instance retrieval in the following step.

3.2 Alias Expansion

People may refer to an entity in different ways. For example, 貝拉克奧巴馬 (Barack Obama) is also called 巴拉克歐巴馬 (Barack Obama) and 巴拉克海珊歐巴馬二世 (Barack Hussein Obama II). We construct an alias dictionary for entities by collecting redirect pages from Wikipedia. The alias dictionary consisting of 1,317,829 entities is consulted for entity expansion to retrieve more instances from the corpus.

3.3 Instance Retrieval

If a sentence contains two entities and these two entities are connected with a property, we regard this sentence is an instance of the property. For each fact in DBpedia, we search the instances that describe the same fact in Chinese Wikipedia and extract relational patterns from these instances. All the sentences that contain the entity pair in the fact are retrieved. Figure 2 considers the target property "spouse" as an example to describe the process of instance retrieval.

3.4 Pattern Extraction

The instances retrieved by the method specified in Section 3.3 have some similar manifestations that are valuable to extract relational patterns from them. Figure 3 shows the process of pattern extraction in detail. First, Stanford toolkit[2] is performed to generate the dependency parse tree of each instance. Then, we find the shortest path between the two entities in the dependency tree, and regard the words in the shortest path as a relational pattern. Figure 4 shows the shortest path from 李雪主 (Ri Sol-ju) to 金正恩 (Kim Jong-un) is 李雪主 (Ri Sol-ju) => 嫁给 (is married to) =>金正恩 (Kim Jong-un). Thus, we regard (<*entity*1>, 嫁給 (is married to), <*entity*2>) as a relational pattern of the property <spouse>.

[1] http://lucene.apache.org/solr/
[2] http://stanfordnlp.github.io/CoreNLP/

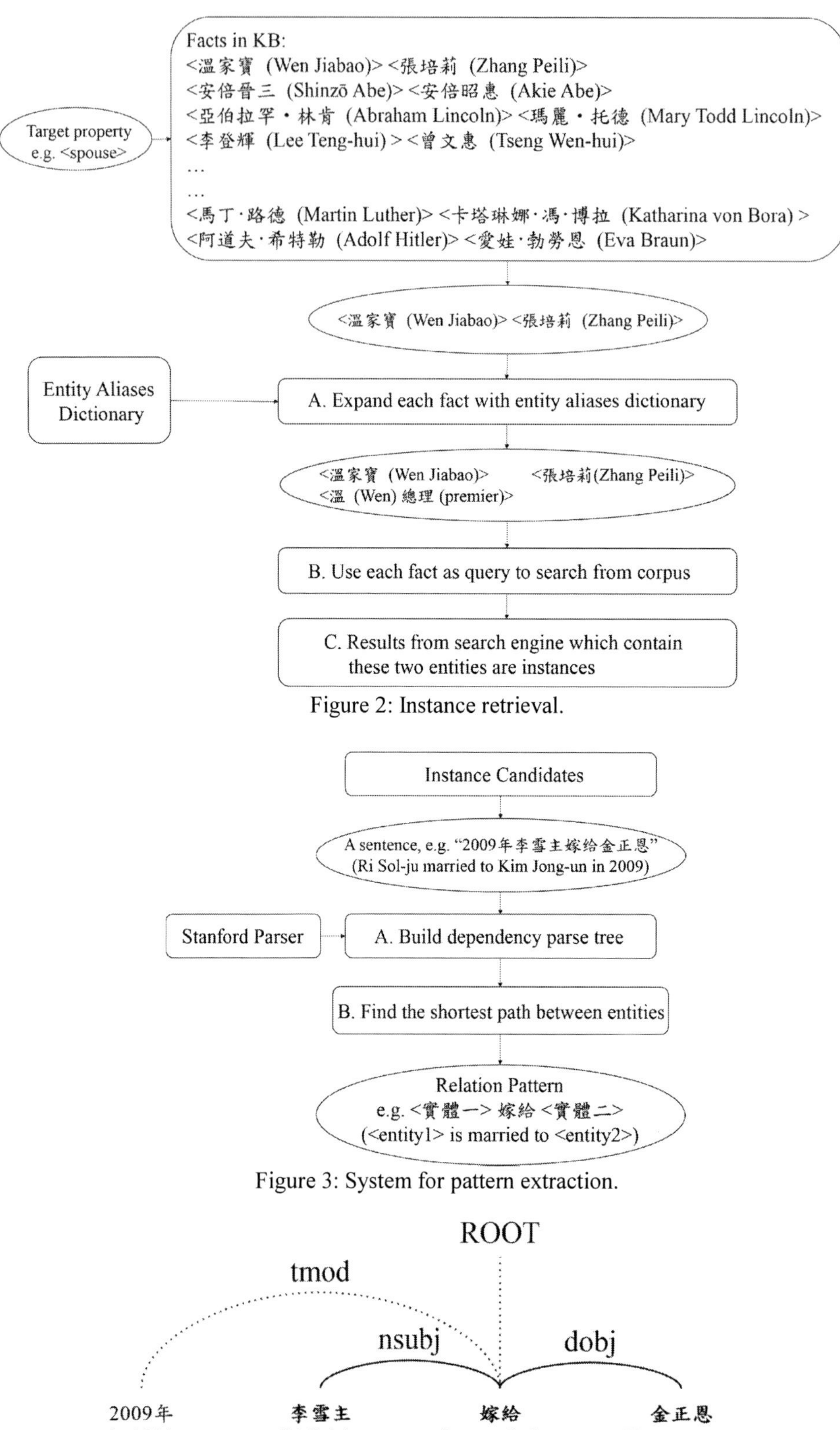

Figure 2: Instance retrieval.

Figure 3: System for pattern extraction.

Figure 4: Dependency parse tree for a Chinese example.

4 Experiments and Analysis

There are 2,614 properties that contain at least 10 facts found in DBpedia. We exclude the properties <subdivisionType>, <subdivisionName>, and the properties related to <time zone>. A total of 2,608 properties remain as our target. We extract relational patterns for all of them. A minimum support threshold is set to 5 for each pattern, and the top 15 patterns for each property are selected. Finally, a total of 7,139 relational patterns covering 1,087 properties are collected.

To evaluate the performance of our method, each relational pattern is verified by three annotators, and the majority is taken as ground-truth. The Fleiss' kappa among the annotators is 0.52 (moderate agreement). P@5, P@10, and P@15 are 0.6, 0.597, and 0.587, respectively. The relational patterns can be downloaded from the website– http://nlg.csie.ntu.edu.tw/nlpresource/nl2kb/.

We also evaluate our relational patterns based on their part of speech (POS) tags. We focus on nouns and verbs. The results are shown in Table 1. "Verb" means the relational pattern consists of a single verb such as (<*entity*1>, 加盟 (join), <*entity*2>). "Noun" means the relational pattern consists of a single noun such as (<*entity*1>, 妻子 (wife), <*entity*2>). "Partial Verb" means the relational pattern consists of multiple words and contains a verb like (<*entity*1>, 運動員 (athlete) 效力 (play for), <*entity*2>). "Partial Noun" means the relational pattern consists of multiple words and contains a noun such as (<*entity*1>, 電視劇 (TV show) 主演 (starring), <*entity*2>). Obviously, the relational patterns containing verbs are more accurate than the noun-based patterns.

For each property, we search all instances of its facts. The more facts for a property, the more instances we retrieve. We divide our relational patterns into three groups, i.e., "Frequent", "Medium", and "Infrequent", by the number of facts. "Frequent" covers properties containing at least 1,000 facts such as <starring>, <author>, and <spouse>. "Medium" covers properties contain at least 100 facts and less than 999 facts such as <education>, <currency>, and <mother>. "Infrequent" covers properties containing at least 10 facts and less than 99 facts. Table 2 shows the results. For each group, the top 5 patterns always outperform the top 10 and top 15 ones. The group "Frequent" has the best performances, while "Infrequent" has the lowest ones. In other words, the more the facts, the more the reliable patterns.

POS Tags	# Patterns	P@15
Verb	1,311	**0.709**
Partial Verb	1,305	**0.641**
Noun	3,897	0.547
Partial Noun	1,718	0.575
All	7,139	0.587

Table 1: Performances in different POS tags.

	Frequent	Medium	Infrequent	All
# Patterns	2,333	3,481	1,325	7,139
P@5	**0.671**	0.602	0.534	0.600
P@10	**0.652**	0.596	0.523	0.597
P@15	**0.636**	0.581	0.515	0.587

Table 2: Performances in numbers of facts.

5 A Demo System

We demonstrate an application of our relational patterns on our website: http://nlg.csie.ntu.edu.tw/nlpresource/nl2kb/. Given a sentence in Chinese, our system will extract all the possible properties to which the relation in the sentence is mapped. As shown in Figure 5, the input sentence is first word segmented and POS tagged by the Stanford toolkit. Then pattern matching is applied to identify relations in the sentence, and the possible KB properties of each relation are recommended. We measure the score of each property by multiplying its support value and its confidence value. Finally, we show the results ranked by the scores.

Three functions shown as follows are demonstrated:

(1) Select a property and find all its relational patterns along with their support and confidence.
(2) Select a relational pattern and find all its properties along with their support and confidence.

(3) Enter a sentence and find which properties it contains. That is a fundamental task for knowledge base construction and retrieval.

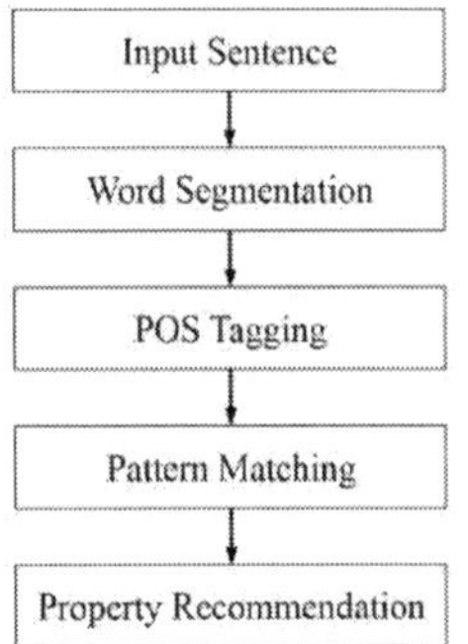

1989 年 (in 1989) 江澤民 (Jiang Zemin) 當選/VV (was elected) 中共(CPC) 總書記 (general secretary)

1989 年/NT 江澤民/NR 當選/VV 中共/NR 總書記/NN

Property	Relational pattern	Support	Confidence
incumbent	<Entity1> 當選 <Enity2>	65	0.289
office	<Entity1> 當選 <Enity2>	47	0.209
party	<Entity1> 總書記 <Enity2>	39	0.250
leader1Name	<Entity1> 總書記 <Enity2>	36	0.231

Figure 5: The workflow for our demo system.

6 Conclusion

In this study, we create a Chinese relational pattern resource based on properties in the DBpedia knowledge base. We propose a system that extracts relational patterns by using the syntactic information. A total of 7,139 relational patterns that cover 1,087 properties are extracted and verified. We release the human-verified Chinese relational patterns as a resource (http://nlg.csie.ntu.edu.tw/nlpresource/nl2kb/), which can be utilized in various tasks such as knowledge base acceleration and question-answering. Although our system is designed for mining Chinese relational patterns, the methodology can be extended to other languages.

7 Acknowledgements

This research was partially supported by Ministry of Science and Technology, Taiwan, under grants MOST-102-2221-E-002-103-MY3 and MOST-105-2221-E-002-154-MY3, and National Taiwan University under grant NTU-ERP-104R890858.

References

Arnab Dutta, Christian Meilicke, and Heiner Stuckenschmidt. 2015. Enriching Structured Knowledge with Open Information. In *Proceeding of the 24th International Conference on World Wide Web (WWW)*, pages 267-277.

Anthony Fader, Stephen Soderland, and Oren Etzioni. 2011. Identifying relations for open information extraction. In *Proceedings of the 2011 Conference on Empirical Methods in Natural Language Processing (EMNLP)*, pages 1535–1545.

John R. Frank, Max Kleiman-Weiner, Daniel A. Roberts, Feng Niu, Ce Zhang, Christopher Ré, and Ian Soboroff. 2012. Building an Entity-Centric Stream Filtering Test Collection for TREC 2012. In *Proceedings of the Twenty-First Text REtrieval Conference*.

Jens Lehmann, Robert Isele, Max Jakob, Anja Jentzsch, Dimitris Kontokostas, Pablo N. Mendes, Sebastian Hellmann, Mohamed Morsey, Patrick van Kleef, Soren Auer, and Christian Bizer. 2012. DBpedia – A Large-scale, Multilingual Knowledge Base Extracted from Wikipedia. *Semantic Web Journal* 1:1–29.

Ndapandula Nakashole, Gerhard Weikum, and Fabian Suchanek. 2012. PATTY: A Taxonomy of Relational Patterns with Semantic Types. In *Proceedings of the 2012 Joint Conference on Empirical Methods in Natural Language Processing and Computational Natural Language Learning*, pages 1135–1145.

Likun Qiu and Yue Zhang. 2014. ZORE: A Syntax-based System for Chinese Open Relation Extraction. In *Proceedings of the 2014 Conference on Empirical Methods in Natural Language Processing (EMNLP)*, pages 1870–1880.

Fabian M. Suchanek, Gjergji Kasneci, and Gerhard Weikum. 2007. Yago: A Core of Semantic Knowledge. In *Proceedings of the 16th International Conference on World Wide Web (WWW)*, pages 697–706.

Wen-tau Yih, Ming-Wei Chang, Xiaodong He, and Jianfeng Gao. 2015. Semantic Parsing via Staged Query Graph Generation: Question Answering with Knowledge Base. *Proceedings of the 53rd Annual Meeting of the Association for Computational Linguistics and the 7th International Joint Conference on Natural Language Processing*, pages 1321–1331.

PKUSUMSUM : A Java Platform for Multilingual Document Summarization

Jianmin Zhang, Tianming Wang and Xiaojun Wan
Institute of Computer Science and Technology, Peking University
The MOE Key Laboratory of Computational Linguistic (Peking University)
Beijing 100871, China
{zhangjianmin2015, wangtm, wanxiaojun}@pku.edu.cn

Abstract

PKUSUMSUM is a Java platform for multilingual document summarization, and it supports multiple languages, integrates 10 automatic summarization methods, and tackles three typical summarization tasks. The summarization platform has been released and users can easily use and update it. In this paper, we make a brief description of the characteristics, the summarization methods, and the evaluation results of the platform, and also compare PKUSUMSUM with other summarization toolkits.

1 Introduction

Automatic document summarization has drawn much attention in the fields of natural language processing, information retrieval and text mining for a long time. It is very useful to help users quickly get main information from a long document or a large number of documents, and thus save users' reading time. In the past years, document summarization has become an active research area and various document summarization methods have been proposed. A well-designed and well-developed document summarization platform will greatly help both researchers and developers in this area, and more in-depth researches and real applications can be easily conducted and realized based on this platform. However, there are several major shortcomings in existing document summarization toolkits, e.g., low coverage of summarization methods, no support of multiple tasks and multiple languages, poor scalability, etc. Therefore, we aim at developing a more competitive document summarization platform in order to satisfy various kinds of research and development needs in this area.

Our summarization toolkit is called PKUSUMSUM (PKU's SUMmary of SUMmarization methods), which is a Java platform for multilingual document summarization. It is developed in Java and supports single-document, multi-document and topic-focused multi-document summarizations in multiple languages. More importantly, it covers a number of various summarization methods.

Main features of PKUSUMSUM include:

- It integrates stable and various summarization methods, and the performance is good enough.
- It supports three typical summarization tasks, including simple-document, multi-document and topic-focused multi-document summarizations.
- It supports Western languages (e.g. English) and Chinese language.
- It integrates English tokenizer, stemmer and Chinese word segmentation tools.
- The Java platform can be easily distributed on different OS platforms, like Windows, Linux and MacOS.
- It is open source and developed with modularization, so that users can add new methods and modules into the toolkit conveniently.

The above features makes PKUSUMSUM have significant advantages over existing automatic summarization tools which only partially fulfill the requirements illustrated above.

Proceedings of COLING 2016, the 26th International Conference on Computational Linguistics: System Demonstrations, pages 287–291, Osaka, Japan, December 11-17 2016.

2 Summarization Methods for Different Summarization Tasks

PKUSUMSUM is a powerful Java platform for multilingual document summarization. It integrates 10 popular summarization methods, supports for multiple languages, and can tackle three typical document summarization tasks. The performance values of the methods implemented in PKUSUMSUM are competitive. To be specific, PKUSUMSUM integrates the following 10 unsupervised summarization methods (including baselines):

Lead: This baseline method takes the first sentences one by one in the single document or the first document in the collection, where documents in the collection are assumed to be ordered by name.

Coverage: This baseline method takes the first sentence one by one from the first document to the last document in the collection.

Centroid: In centroid-based summarization (Radev et al., 2004a), a pseudo-sentence of the document called centroid is constructed. The centroid consists of words with TFIDF scores above a predefined threshold. The score of each sentence is defined by summing the scores based on different features including cosine similarity of the sentence with the centroid, position weight and cosine similarity with the first sentence. We also added an additional feature of cosine similarity between the sentence and the topic for the topic-based multi-document summarization task.

TextRank: TextRank (Mihalcea et al., 2004) builds a graph and adds each sentence as vertices, the overlap of two sentences as relations that connect sentences. Then the graph-based ranking algorithm is applied until convergence. Sentences are sorted based on their final score and a greedy algorithm is employed to impose diversity penalty on each sentence and select summary sentences.

LexPageRank: LexPageRank (Erkan et al., 2004) computes sentence importance based on the concept of eigenvector centrality in a graph representation of sentences. In this model, a connectivity matrix based on intra-sentence cosine similarity is used as the adjacency matrix of the graph representation of sentences.

ClusterCMRW: Given a document set covering a few topic themes, usually the sentences in an important theme cluster are deemed more salient than the sentences in a trivial theme cluster. The Cluster-based Conditional Markov Random Walk Model (ClusterCMRW) (Wan and Yang, 2008) makes use of the link relationships between sentences in the document set and fully leverages the cluster-level information.

ManifoldRank: The manifold-ranking method is a typical method for topic-focused multi-document summarization (Wan et al., 2007). The ranking score is obtained for each sentence in the manifold-ranking process to denote the biased information richness of the sentence. Then a greedy algorithm is employed to impose diversity penalty on each sentence.

ILP: Integer linear programming (ILP) approaches (Gillick et al., 2009) cast document summarization as a combinatorial optimization problem. An ILP model selects sentences by maximizing the sum of frequency-induced weights of bigram concepts contained in the summary. Here we use the open source tool lp_solve[1] for Java to solve the ILP problem.

Submodular: Using submodular function is a very competitive approach in multi-document summarization. It performs summarization by maximizing submodular functions under a budget constraint. The submodularity hidden in the coverage, diversity and non-redundancy can be reflected in a class of submodular functions. We use two submodular functions for document summarization tasks (Lin and Bilmes, 2010; Li at el, 2012). In particular, **Submodular1** implements the algorithm proposed in (Li at el, 2012) and uses formula (7) in the paper. **Submodular2** makes some modifications on the functions in (Lin and Bilmes, 2010).

As mentioned earlier, PKUSUMSUM can tackle three typical summarization tasks, and Table 1 shows which tasks can be solved by each method. "Yes" means that the method can solve the certain task. Note that Centroid, ILP and Submodular1&2 were originally proposed for multi-document summarization, and we directly apply them for single-document summarization in this study.

For evaluating the performance of PKUSUMSUM, we use the DUC benchmark datasets. We use the DUC 2002 (Task 1) dataset for evaluating single-document summarization, the DUC 2004 (Task 2) dataset for evaluating multi-document summarization and the DUC 2006 dataset for evaluating topic-focused multi-document summarization. The ROUGE metrics (Lin and Hovy, 2003) are used to auto-

[1] http://lpsolve.sourceforge.net/5.5/

matically evaluate the quality of produced summaries given the gold-standard reference summaries. We use the ROUGE-1.5.5 toolkit to perform the evaluation, and report the F-scores of the following metrics in the experimental results: ROUGE-1, ROUGE-2, and ROUGE-SU4. The scores of different methods in PKUSUMSUM for different tasks are shown in Tables 2-4, respectively. We can see that Lead is hard to defeat for single-document summarization, and most methods proposed for multi-document summarization (e.g. ILP, Submodular1&2) do not perform well for single document summarization. For multi-document summarization, Submodular1&2 outperforms all other methods, and for topic-focused multi-document summarization, ManifoldRank outperforms the two baselines and the centroid method.

Method	Single-document	Multi-document	Topic-focused Multi-document
Lead	Yes	Yes	Yes
Coverage	-	Yes	Yes
Centroid	Yes	Yes	Yes
TextRank	Yes	Yes	-
LexPageRank	Yes	Yes	-
ClusterCMRW	-	Yes	-
ManifoldRank	-	-	Yes
ILP	Yes	Yes	-
Submodular1	Yes	Yes	-
Submodular2	Yes	Yes	-

Table 1. The correspondence between summarization tasks and methods

Method	ROUGE-1	ROUGE-2	ROUGE-SU4
Lead	0.4770	0.2242	0.2407
Centroid	0.4755	0.2230	0.2389
TextRank	0.4562	0.1930	0.2155
LexPageRank	0.4502	0.1851	0.2093
ILP	0.4756	0.2214	0.2386
Submodular1	0.4592	0.1893	0.2122
Submodular2	0.4604	0.1924	0.2148

Table 2. F-scores for single-document summarization on DUC 2002 (Task 1)

Method	ROUGE-1	ROUGE-2	ROUGE-SU4
Lead	0.3182	0.0645	0.1023
Coverage	0.3392	0.0757	0.1152
Centroid	0.3668	0.0876	0.1268
TextRank	0.3725	0.0863	0.1272
LexPageRank	0.3607	0.0755	0.1202
ILP	0.3601	0.0743	0.1185
Submodular1	0.3841	0.0949	0.1348
Submodular2	0.3839	0.0958	0.1355
ClusterCMRW	0.3760	0.0908	0.1308

Table 3. F-scores for multi-document summarization on DUC 2004 (Task 2)

Method	ROUGE-1	ROUGE-2	ROUGE-SU4
Lead	0.3458	0.0589	0.1132
Coverage	0.3502	0.0643	0.1218
ManifoldRank	0.4028	0.0812	0.1387
Centroid	0.3578	0.0580	0.1134

Table 4. F-scores for topic-based multi-document summarization on DUC 2006

3 Availability, License, Usage and Scalability

The PKUSUMSUM toolkit has been released and the open-source software can be freely downloaded[2] and used under the GNU GPL license.

PKUSUMSUM is developed with Java. The Java platform can be easily distributed on different operating systems, like Windows, Linux and MacOS, so users who are used to different operating systems can use PKUSUMSUM with no barrier.

Both the source code and the Java executable package of PKUSUMSUM are provided. If users are not familiar with the Java source code or do not want to re-compile the code, they can use command line to run the Java package. The parameters in different summarization methods can be conveniently set by users and they all have default values.

We integrate some pre-processing or post-processing modules into the platform, like English tokenizer[3], stemmer[4] and Chinese word segmenter[5]. Other western languages are also supported. Users can easily obtain summaries for documents without extra processing.

PKUSUMSUM is developed with modularity and it is easy to add new modules to the platform. For example, we create an independent class for each data processing unit or summarization method, so users can add new classes for other methods without altering the structure of the platform.

4 Comparison with Other Toolkits

We compared PKUSUMSUM with the following existing automatic summarization toolkits:

MUSEEC (MUltilingual SEntence Extraction and Compression) (Litvak et al., 2016): This summarization tool implements only three extractive summarization techniques as MUSE based on a genetic algorithm (GA), POLY based on linear programming (LP), and an extension of POLY named WECOM. Although it can support multiple western languages, the three homogeneous methods it implements are not adequate and it is not easy to modify.

MEAD[6] (Radev et al., 2004b): The methods it implements are very limited and simple. It can tackle single and multi-document summarization tasks, but does not support topic-focused multi-document summarization task.

SUMMA (Horacio Saggion, 2008): It depends on the GATE platform (Cunningham et al., 2002), and only supports one method.

In addition, there are some simple tools coding by Python, such as **sumpy**, which can support four simple methods, and **summa**, which can only support TextRank. The existing systems have several of the following problems: 1) low coverage of summarization methods; 2) no support of different tasks; 3) no support of multiple languages; 4) poor scalability; 5) lack of platform independence.

5 Conclusion

We introduced the PKUSUMSUM platform for document summarization, which has been released. It has powerful ability and it supports multi-language, integrates 10 automatic summarization methods and can tackle three popular summarization tasks. In our future work, we will add more supervised summarzation methods into the platform.

Acknowledgements

This work was supported by National Natural Science Foundation of China (61331011), National Hi-Tech Research and Development Program (863 Program) of China (2015AA015403) and IBM Global Faculty Award Program. Xiaojun Wan is the corresponding author of this paper.

Reference

[2] http://www.icst.pku.edu.cn/lcwm/wanxj/files/PKUSUMSUM.zip

[3] Stanford Tokenizer, http://nlp.stanford.edu/software/tokenizer.html

[4] The Porter Stemming Algorithm, http://tartarus.org/~martin/PorterStemmer/

[5] Ansj toolkit, https://github.com/NLPchina/ansj_seg

[6] http://www.summarization.com/mead/

Hamish Cunningham, Diana Maynard, Kalina Bontchva and Valentin Tablan. 2002. A framework and graphical development environment for robust NLP tools and applications. *ACL*.

Günes Erkan, and Dragomir R. Radev. 2004. LexPageRank: Prestige in Multi-Document Text Summarization. *EMNLP*.

Dan Gillick, and Benoit Favre. 2009. A scalable global model for summarization. *Proceedings of the Workshop on Integer Linear Programming for Natural Language Processing*.

Jingxuan Li, Lei Li, and Tao Li. 2012. Multi-document summarization via submodularity. *Applied Intelligence* 37.3: 420-430.

Chin-Yew Lin and Eduard Hovy. 2003. Automatic evaluation of summaries using n-gram co-occurrence statistics. *NAACL*.

Hui Lin and Jeff Bilmes. 2010. Multi-document summarization via budgeted maximization of submodular functions. *HLT-NAACL*.

Marina Litvak, Natalia Vanetik, Mark Last, and Elena Churkin. 2016. MUSEEC: A Multilingual Text Summarization Tool. *ACL*.

Rada Mihalcea, and Paul Tarau. 2004. TextRank: Bringing order into texts. *EMNLP*.

Dragomir R. Radev, Hongyan Jing, Małgorzata Stys, Daniel Tam. 2004a. Centroid-based summarization of multiple documents. *Information Processing & Management* 40.6: 919-938.

Dragomir R. Radev, Timothy Allison, Sasha Blair-Goldensohn, et al. 2004b. MEAD-A Platform for Multidocument Multilingual Text Summarization. *LREC*.

Horacio Saggion. 2008. A robust and adaptable summarization tool. Traitement Automatique des Langues 49.2.

Xiaojun Wan, Jianwu Yang, and Jianguo Xiao. 2007. Manifold-Ranking Based Topic-Focused Multi-Document Summarization. *IJCAI*.

Xiaojun Wan and Jianwu Yang. 2008. Multi-document summarization using cluster-based link analysis. *SIGIR*.

Kotonush: Understanding Concepts Based on Values behind Social Media

Tatsuya Iwanari
University of Tokyo

Kohei Ohara
University of Tokyo

Naoki Yoshinaga
IIS, University of Tokyo

Nobuhiro Kaji
Yahoo Japan Corporation

Masashi Toyoda
IIS, University of Tokyo

Masaru Kitsuregawa
IIS, University of Tokyo
NII, Japan

Abstract

Kotonush, a system that clarifies people's values on various concepts on the basis of what they write about on social media, is presented. The values are represented by ordering sets of concepts (*e.g.*, *London*, *Berlin*, and *Rome*) in accordance with a common attribute intensity expressed by an adjective (*e.g.*, *entertaining*). We exploit social media text written by different demographics and at different times in order to induce specific orderings for comparison. The system combines a text-to-ordering module with an interactive querying interface enabled by massive hyponymy relations and provides mechanisms to compare the induced orderings from various viewpoints. We empirically evaluate Kotonush and present some case studies, featuring real-world concept orderings with different domains on Twitter, to demonstrate the usefulness of our system.

1 Introduction

When we want to investigate unfamiliar entities or concepts (*e.g.*, iPhone SE) as consumers, or inversely, intend to supply new concepts as vendors, we typically endeavor to understand the value of a given concept by comparing or ordering it with familiar concepts (*e.g.*, Xperia X or Galaxy S7) from various perspectives (*e.g.*, *user-friendliness*). At present, people often spend a substantial amount of time wading through massive social media text to get an overview of others' perceptions, or spend a lot of money to call for votes from experts in order to come up with a convincing ordering.

In this study, we present **Kotonush**, a system that induces people's values on given concepts from social media text as concept orderings on the basis of common attribute intensity expressed by an adjective. Our system enables users to interactively ask queries (concepts and an adjective) and compare the induced orderings for deeper understanding of the concepts. Assuming that a user has at least one target concept (or entity) in mind, our querying interface helps the user to interactively list similar entities using massive hyponymy relations (Sumida et al., 2008). Receiving a query, a text-to-ordering module (Iwanari et al., 2016) collects posts from social media text written by specific (gender, region) users and at a certain time of interest (say, *domain*) to induce concept orderings specific to the chosen domain. Our ordering visualizer then provides intelligent interfaces to compare orderings from various perspectives to gain a deeper insight into the domain-specific values of concepts.

Our system is beneficial not only in practical terms for understanding entities from others' values (orderings with related entities) to make correct decisions (*e.g.*, ordering smartphones in terms of *user-friendliness*) but also in sociological terms for inversely understanding common views shared by a certain demographic and/or from a certain period of time. We conclude this work with a handful of interesting case studies comparing concept orderings in different domains taken from our 4-year Twitter archive.

2 Related Work

There have been no attempts other than our own previous work (Iwanari et al., 2016) on ordering concepts on the basis of the intensity of their attributes. Although aspect-based sentiment analysis mines reviews

Proceedings of COLING 2016, the 26th International Conference on Computational Linguistics: System Demonstrations, pages 292–296, Osaka, Japan, December 11-17 2016.

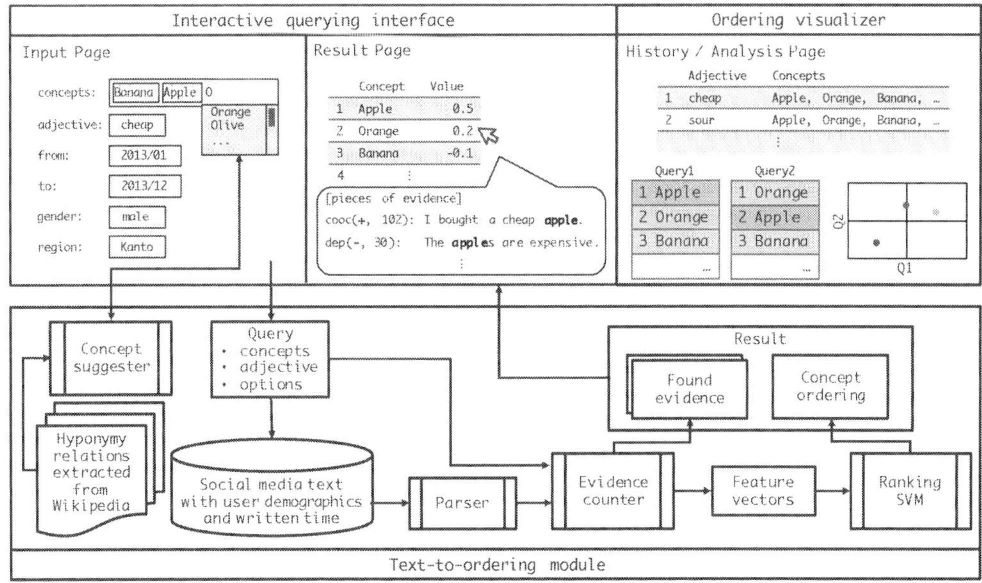

Figure 1: Overview of Kotonush, the system we developed to acquire values from social media text.

or other texts for opinions on entities (Pang and Lee, 2008), such analysis focuses on the polarity of specific aspects (i.e., whether the '*atmosphere*' of a restaurant is good or not), while our system supports not only the polarity but also the intensity of attributes (a restaurant is *cozy* or *lively*).

Iwanari et al. (2016) initiated the task of ordering concepts and proposed methods that order concepts by gathering various pieces of evidence from social media text and integrating them with a supervised learning. They confirmed that it is possible to obtain common views from the text people write. However, there are a couple of issues when it comes to using their method for our purpose of understanding the target concepts. First, it is not easy to conceive other concepts to compare with the target concept. Second, monolithic orderings induced from entire social media texts do not provide a deeper insight into the target concepts. To address these issues, we have built a system that suggests to users other concepts in the same category as the target concepts along with tools to understand the values in different domains.

3 System Architecture

Our system consists of three parts: (1) an interactive querying interface, (2) a text-to-ordering module, and (3) an ordering visualizer (Figure 1). Our querying interface enables users to interactively input a set of concepts and an adjective as a query (Figure 2a) and then sends them to the text-to-ordering module. The querying interface accepts several options that specify domains, such as the gender and region of social media users as well as the time periods of interest. After receiving a query, the text-to-ordering module collects posts from social media text in the domain and returns a convincing ordering along with the pieces of evidence used (to justify the ordering). The system keeps track of the results of asked queries so that users can compare the (cached) results with other queries on our system's History / Analysis page (Figure 2b and 2c). This enables us to compare concepts from various viewpoints (adjectives) or to observe differences of ordering in each domain to see which factors affect orderings.

Note here that the domain analyses provide deeper and closer insight into not only target concepts but also target domains (*e.g.*, *women in Japan like Disney movies better than action movies*, as we will reveal in the following case studies). In the following, we describe the workflow of our system in more detail.

Preprocessing We assume a search engine to retrieve posts that include concepts and adjectives and have built a simple inverted index-based search engine for that purpose. This search engine can easily be replaced with other search engines such as the Twitter API (to obtain up-to-date orderings), since all the text analyses to collect evidence on concept ordering are done online.

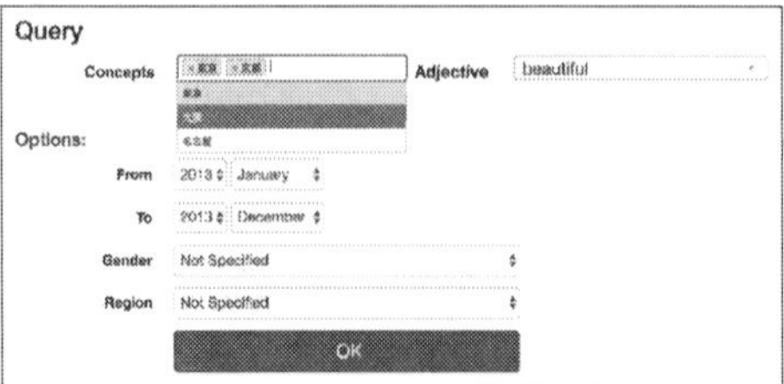

(a) Interactive querying interface accepts a set of concepts, an adjective, and options. The system suggests concepts in the same category.

Cached Queries

select queries to compare

Id	Adjective	Concepts	From	To	Gender	Region	Actions
1	entertaining	京都,大阪,東京,福岡	2013/01	2013/12	Male	Not Specified	
2	entertaining	京都,大阪,東京,福岡	2013/01	2013/12	Not Specified	Kanto	
3	entertaining	京都,大阪,東京,福岡	2013/01	2013/12	Not Specified	Kansai	
5	entertaining	京都,大阪,東京,福岡	2013/01	2013/12	Not Specified	Kyushu	

(b) History page keeps cached query results.

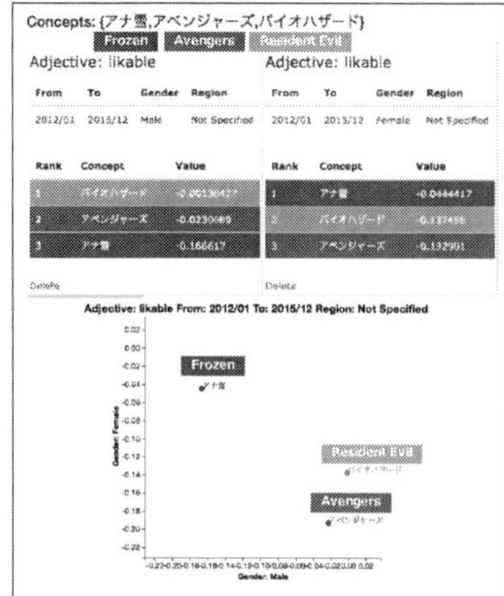

(c) Users can compare orderings with different settings. This example compares movies (Frozen, Avengers, and Resident Evil) in terms of 'likable' with two genders.

Figure 2: Snapshots of our system for ordering objects on the basis of common attribute intensity.

As with the indexing, we briefly identify the gender and location (prefecture) of social media users from their posts and profiles for domain analyses and then associate text with those attributes. Since this process is outside the focus of this study, here we just use existing methods based on bag-of-words.

Interactive querying Users input a query by adding concepts one by one and selecting an adjective from a (short) list that meets the users' practical demands. The list prompts users to compare concepts in different ways that might not come to mind on their own. Users can also specify domains (Figure 2a).

Although users can input any concepts they want, they may not conceive of concepts they might wish to compare. For example, when you browse rental movies at a shop, you may not be able to remember appropriate movies for comparison. The same applies here. To help such users, Kotonush suggests concepts related to given concepts. We exploit hyponymy relations extracted from Wikipedia (Sumida et al., 2008) to suggest concepts that share the same hypernym with the given concepts.

Concept ordering After receiving a query, the text-to-ordering module retrieves posts including one or more of the given concepts and the adjective from social media text in the specified domain. The posts are then online parsed with J.DepP, a state-of-the-art dependency parser for Japanese (Yoshinaga and Kitsuregawa, 2014), to process massive text online ($>10,000$ sentences/s).

The parsed text is given to our implementation of Iwanari et al. (2016) to induce a concept ordering. The method uses four types of evidence to capture the common view on concepts from social media text: (1) co-occurrences of a concept and an adjective (*e.g.*, How large that whale is!), (2) dependencies from a concept to an adjective (*e.g.*, A whale is so big.), (3) similes (*e.g.*, He is brave as a lion.), and (4) comparative expressions (*e.g.*, Whales are larger than cats.). The first three implicitly suggest attribute intensity and can be understood as capturing the absolute intensity of the attribute that the concept has. The fourth directly captures the relative attribute intensity, which directly indicates the order of a subset of a concept set. The method encodes these four types of evidence as real-valued features by using point-wise mutual information (PMI) of the pairs of a concept and adjective for each piece of evidence and then performs an ordering based on ranking SVM. Finally, the text-to-ordering module returns the joint results of the outputs of found pieces of evidence so that users can know what social media users say about each item along with the ordering obtained by ranking SVM with scores computed for each item.

Ordering visualizer By keeping the results of past queries in our system, users can review and compare them on the History / Analyze page. This page provides complete sets of cached results as a table and tools to analyze queries with different settings such as bump charts (top of Figure 2c). With bump

Table 1: Correlations between Twitter user orderings and gold-standard orderings.

	Male	Female	All
Avg. ρ	0.681	0.674	0.661

Table 2: Spearman's ρ against gold-standard orderings.

	BASELINE		DOMAIN-UNAWARE		DOMAIN-AWARE	
	MALE	FEMALE	MALE	FEMALE	MALE	FEMALE
Avg. ρ	0.262	0.339	0.308	0.322	0.309	0.337

charts, users can, for example, determine the best season for each flower by varying periods.

In addition to bump charts, we implemented an interface of scatter plots on the page (bottom of Figure 2c). Although users can compare two or more queries at once with bump charts, scatter plots provide a more intuitive way of comparing two queries when a user wants to know the relative strength of the attribute intensity of each concept (*e.g, lemons are much more sour than apples and dorians, i.e., lemon* $\gg$ *apple* $>$ *dorian*), compare orderings with different attributes (*e.g., 'cheap' and 'delicious' for restaurants*), or compare ordering in a different domain (*e.g., male vs. female*).

4 Evaluation

We conducted experiments to evaluate Kotonush with our archive of 25 billion Twitter posts in terms of correlation between system-generated and gold-standard orderings. We used LIBLINEAR (`https://www.csie.ntu.edu.tw/~cjlin/liblinear/`) as an implementation of ranking SVM.

4.1 Settings

We prepared 28 queries with the same process in Iwanari et al. (2016), which used a word clustering-based method. They cover a wide variety of queries: from concepts (*e.g.*, '*car*') to instances (*e.g.*, '*Kinkaku-ji*', a shrine) and from objective adjectives (*e.g.*, '*fast*') to subjective ones (*e.g.*, '*likable*').

To prepare gold-standard orderings for training and testing Kotonush, we used a crowdsourcing service (`https://crowdworks.jp/`) to ask 53 Twitter users (workers) to answer (rank) each query. The users had various demographics: gender (24 males and 29 females), age (from 20s to 60s), location (29 out of 47 prefectures in Japan) and occupation (students, homemakers, office workers, etc.). We generated gold-standard orderings for each gender by choosing an ordering, in all permutations of concepts, that maximized the average of Spearman's rank correlation coefficient ρ against the orderings of the workers by gender, in addition to gold-standard orderings for all workers.

Table 1 shows the average correlations between the human and gold-standard orderings for three domains: all users, male users, and female users. The human-generated orderings have strong correlations and show higher correlations when we restrict workers in specific domains. By looking into these domain-specific orderings in detail, we can understand their values on concept orderings, *e.g.*, males' preferences regarding alcohol are quite different compared with those of females. The evaluation datasets will be available on `http://www.tkl.iis.u-tokyo.ac.jp/~nari/coling-16/`.

We have explored two different ways to train ranking SVM. Domain-unaware training uses the gold-standard orderings computed from the orderings given by all the workers, while domain-aware training uses the gold-standard orderings for individual domains (male and female). In domain-aware training, the number of training examples is multiplied by the number of domains (here, two) and the quality of the gold-standard orderings (correlations against human orderings) is higher than domain-unaware training, although it could suffer from a data sparseness problem. In testing, we input statistics collected from Twitter posts (Jan. 2012 - Dec. 2015) in each domain to obtain domain-specific orderings.

4.2 Results

Table 2 shows the experimental results obtained by leave-one-out cross-validation with the aforementioned datasets. We evaluated the system-generated orderings for each domain by computing Spearman's ρ against the gold-standard ordering in the domain. Here, BASELINE refers to the baseline

Table 3: Case studies in different settings.

(a) Flower (Beautiful): Three seasons

	Mar. - May	*Jun. - Aug.*	*Sep. - Nov.*
1	Cherry	Sunflower	Mum
2	Sunflower	Cherry	Sunflower
3	Mum	Mum	Cherry

(b) Disease (Fearful): Years

	2013	2014
1	Influenza	Dengue
2	Malaria	Influenza
3	Dengue	Malaria

(c) Fruit (Delicious): Regions

	Tohoku	*Shikoku*
1	Apple	Tangerine
2	Tangerine	Apple
3	Strawberry	Strawberry

method adopted in (Iwanari et al., 2016), which scores each concept on the basis of noun-adjective co-occurrences, i.e., the first evidence our system uses. The baseline method outperformed the proposed method in female domain because similes were hardly observed in posts written by female. The domain-aware training obtained better Spearman's ρ than the domain-unaware training.

5 Case Studies

This section presents four case studies that demonstrate the effectiveness of our system. We used the ranking SVM obtained by domain-unaware training along with statistics collected from Twitter posts. Even though we implemented the system to process all of the tasks in a single thread, it processes posts fast enough (about 10,000 posts in less than 5 sec), and they can be improved easily because all the tasks are perfectly parallel. We have hereafter translated the Japanese system outputs into English.

The first case study captures common views on movies in terms of gender (Figure 2c). In Japan, men tend to like action movies better than Disney movies and women vice versa. The next case compares three seasonal flowers – (Japanese) cherry, sunflower, and Chrysanthemum (mum) – in terms of beauty in different seasons (Table 3a). The results clearly show the blooming season (best time) of each flower. The third shows the time-series fearfulness of three diseases: Influenza, Malaria, and Dengue fever. The rise of Dengue fever from 2013 to 2014 reflects its spreading over Japan in 2014. Table 3c shows the region-parameterized results of '*Fruit (Delicious)*', which is reasonable for Japanese because the Tohoku (north) and Shikoku (south) areas are famous for the production of apples and tangerines, respectively.

6 Conclusion

We presented **Kotonush**, a system that acquires and compares orderings of concepts on the basis of intensity of their common attributes. Our system enables us to easily obtain concept orderings specific to a certain demographic and period from social media text. We empirically confirmed that our system outperformed the baseline based on noun-adjective co-occurrences, and we provided some case studies that compare concept orderings induced from a different domain in our 4-year Twitter archive.

We are now working to support languages other than Japanese, since a cross-lingual comparison between orderings obtained from text in different languages will reveal the differences of perception of different language speakers. We will release the codes of Kotonush for the academic and industrial communities under BSD License at `http://www.tkl.iis.u-tokyo.ac.jp/~nari/coling-16/`.

Acknowledgments

This work was partially supported by JSPS KAKENHI Grant Number 16K16109 and 16H02905.

References

T. Iwanari, N. Yoshinaga, N. Kaji, T. Nishina, M. Toyoda, and M. Kitsuregawa. 2016. Ordering concepts based on common attribute intensity. In *IJCAI-16*.

B. Pang and L. Lee. 2008. *Opinion Mining and Sentiment Analysis*. Now Publishers Inc.

A Sumida, N Yoshinaga, and K Torisawa. 2008. Boosting precision and recall of hyponymy relation acquisition from hierarchical layouts in wikipedia. In *LREC-08*.

N. Yoshinaga and M. Kitsuregawa. 2014. A self-adaptive classifier for efficient text-stream processing. In *COLING-14*.

Exploring a Continuous and Flexible Representation of the Lexicon

Pierre Marchal
ERTIM, INaLCO
2 rue de Lille
F-75007 PARIS
pierre.marchal@inalco.fr

Thierry Poibeau
LaTTiCe, CNRS – ENS – Université Paris III
PSL – USPC
1 rue Maurice Arnoux
F-92120 MONTROUGE
thierry.poibeau@ens.fr

Abstract

We aim at showing that lexical descriptions based on multifactorial and continuous models can be used by linguists and lexicographers (and not only by machines) so long as they are provided with a way to efficiently navigate data collections. We propose to demonstrate such a system.

1 Background and Motivations

"You shall know a word by the company it keeps!" (Firth, 1957). This all too well-known citation motivates any lexicographic work today: it is widely accepted that word description cannot be achieved without the analysis of a large number of contexts extracted from real corpora. However, this is not enough.

The recent success of deep learning approaches has shown that discrete representations of the lexicon are no longer appropriate. Continuous models offer a better representation of word meaning, because they encode intuitively valid and cognitively plausible principles: semantic similarity is relative, context-sensitive and depends on multiple-cue integration.

At this point, one may say that it doesn't matter if these models are too abstract and too complex for humans as they are used by machines. We think this argument is wrong. If continuous models offer a better representation of the lexicon, we must conceive new lexical databases that are usable by humans and have the same basis as these continuous models. There are arguments to support this view.

For example, it has been demonstrated that semantic categories have fuzzy boundaries and thus the number of word meanings per lexical item is to a large extent arbitrary (Tuggy, 1993). Although this still fuels lots of discussions among linguists and lexicographers, we think that a description can be more or less fine-grained while maintaining accuracy and validity. Moreover, it has been demonstrated that lexical entries in traditional dictionaries overlap and different word meanings can be associated with a sole example (Erk and McCarthy, 2009), showing that meaning cannot be sliced into separate and exclusive word senses.

The same problem also arises when it comes to differentiating between arguments and adjuncts. As said by Manning (2003): "There are some very clear arguments (normally, subjects and objects), and some very clear adjuncts (of time and 'outer' location), but also a lot of stuff in the middle". A proper representation thus need to be based on some kind of continuity and should take into consideration not only the subject and the object, but also the prepositional phrases as well as the wider context.

Some applications already address some of the needs of lexicographers in the era of big data, *i.e.* big corpora in this context. The most well-known application is the SketchEngine (Kilgarriff et al., 2014). This tool has already provided invaluable services to lexicographers and linguists. It gives access to a synthetic view of the different usages of words in context. For example, the SketchEngine can give a direct view of all the subjects or complements of a verb, ranked by frequency or sorted according to various parameters. By exploding the representation, this tool provides an interesting view of the lexicon. However, in our opinion, it falls short when it comes to showing the continuous nature of meaning.

Proceedings of COLING 2016, the 26th International Conference on Computational Linguistics: System Demonstrations, pages 297–301, Osaka, Japan, December 11-17 2016.

Here we propose a system that combines the advantages of existing tools (a wide coverage database offering a synthetic view of a large vocabulary) with those of a dynamic representation. We focus on verbs since these lexical items offer the most complex syntactic and semantic behaviors. More specifically, we examine Japanese verbs, as Japanese is a language that presents a complex system of case markers that are generally semantically ambiguous.

2 Outline of our approach

When building a verb lexicon, numerous challenges arise such as the notion of lexical item – that is, how many entries and subentries are necessary to describe the different meanings of a given verb? – and the distinction between arguments and adjuncts – that is, what complements are necessary to describe a particular meaning of a given verb? Following up on studies in natural language processing and linguistics, we embrace the hypothesis of a continuum between ambiguity and vagueness (Tuggy, 1993), and the hypothesis that there is no clear distinction between arguments and adjuncts (Manning, 2003). Although this approach has been applied and evaluated for Japanese, the theoretical framework to compute the argumenthood of a complement, or build the hierarchical structure of the lexical entries, is partially independent.

We assume a list of verbal structures that have been automatically extracted from a large representative corpus. A verbal structure is an occurrence of a verb and its complements (expressed as syntactic dependencies); a complement is an ordered pair of a lexical head and a case marker.

Computing the argumenthood of complements Following up on previous studies on the distinction between arguments and adjuncts (Manning, 2003; Merlo and Esteve Ferrer, 2006; Fabre and Bourigault, 2008; Abend and Rappoport, 2010), we propose a new measure of the degree of argumenthood of complements, derived from the famous TF-IDF weighting scheme used in information retrieval:

$$\text{argumenthood}(v, c) = (1 + \log \text{count}(v, c)) \log \frac{|V|}{|\{v' \in V : \exists(v', c)\}|} \tag{1}$$

where c is a complement (*i.e.* an ordered pair of a lexical head and a case particle); v is a verb; $\text{count}(v, c)$ is the number of cooccurrences of the complement c with the verb v; $|V|$ is the total number of unique verbs; $|\{v' \in V : \exists(v', c)\}|$ is the number of unique verbs cooccurring with this complement. That is, we are dealing with complements instead of terms, and with verbs instead of documents. This measurement captures two important rules of thumb for distinguishing between arguments and adjuncts. The first part of the formula $(1 + \log \text{count}(v, c))$ takes the idea that complements appearing frequently with a given verb tend to be arguments; the second part of the formula $\log \frac{|V|}{|\{v' \in V : \exists(v', c)\}|}$, that complements which appear with a large variety of verbs tend to be adjuncts.

The proposed measure assigns a value between 0 and 1 to a complement – 0 corresponds to a prototypical adjunct; 1 corresponds to a prototypical argument – and thus model a continuum between arguments and adjuncts.

Enriching verb description using shallow clustering A verbal structure corresponds to a specific sense of a given verb; that is, the sense of the verb is given by the complements selected by the verb. Yet a single verbal structure contains a very limited number of complements. So as to obtain a more complete description of the verb sense, we propose to merge verbal structures corresponding to the same meaning of a given verb into a minimal predicate-frame using reliable lexical clues. We call this technique *shallow clustering*. Our method relies on the principles that *i)* two verbal structures describing the same verb and having at least one common complement might correspond to the same verb sense, and that *ii)* some complements are more informative than others for a given sense.

As for the second principle, the measure of argumenthood, introduced in the previous section, serves as a tool for identifying the complements which contribute the most to the verb meaning. Our method merges verbal structures in an iterative process – beginning with the most informative complements (*i.e.* complements yielding the highest argumenthood value) – as shown in Algorithm 1.

```
Data: A set W of verbal structures (v, D), where v is a verb and D is a list of complements
Result: A set W' of minimal predicate-frames (v, D') such that |W'| ⩽ |W|
W' ← ∅;
foreach verb v in {v : ∃(v, D) ∈ W} do
    /* Let C' be the list of complements cooccurring with v sorted
       by argumenthood values in non-increasing order                    */
    C ← {c : ∃(v, D) ∈ W ∧ c ∈ D};
    C' ← (c : c ∈ C ∧ argumenthood(v, C'[i]) ⩾ argumenthood(v, C'[i + 1]));
    for i ← 0 to length(C') − 1 do
        /* Let D' be a subset of {D : ∃(v, D) ∈ W}                          */
        D' ← ∅;
        foreach list of complements D in {D : ∃(v, D) ∈ W} do
            if C'[i] ∈ D then
                add D to D';
                remove (v, D) from W;
            end
        end
        foreach list of complements D in {D : ∃(v, D) ∈ W} do
            if ∃X ∈ D' such that D ⊂ X then
                add D to D';
                remove (v, D) from W;
            end
        end
        if |D'| ⩾ 2 then add the minimal predicate-frame (v, D') to W';
    end
end
```

Algorithm 1: Shallow clustering of verbal structures.

Modeling word senses through hierarchical clustering We propose to cluster the minimal predicate-frames built during the *shallow clustering* procedure into a dendrogram structure. A dendrogram allows the definition of an arbitrary number of classes (using a threshold) and thus fits nicely with our goal of modeling a continuum between ambiguity and vagueness. A dendrogram is usually built using a hierarchical clustering algorithm, with a distance matrix as its input. So as to measure the distance between minimal predicate-frames, we propose to represent minimal predicate-frames as vectors which would then serve as arguments of a similarity function.

Following previous studies on semantic composition, we suppose that "the meaning of a whole is a function of the meaning of the parts and of the way they are syntactically combined" (Partee, 1995) as well as all the information involved in the composition process (Mitchell, 2011). The following equation summarizes the proposed model of semantic composition:

$$p = f(\mathbf{u}, \mathbf{v}, R, K) \tag{2}$$

where $\mathbf{u}$ and $\mathbf{v}$ are two lexical components; R is the syntactic information associated with $\mathbf{u}$ and $\mathbf{v}$; K is the information involved in the composition process.

Following the principles of distributional semantics (Harris, 1954; Firth, 1957), lexical heads can be represented in a vector space model (Salton et al., 1975). Case markers (or prepositions) can be used as syntactic information. Finally, we propose to use our argumenthood measure to initialize the K parameter as it reflects how important a complement is for a given verb.

The proposed model of semantic composition is applied recursively to all the complements of a given minimal predicate-frame so as to produce a single vector. Hierarchical clustering is then applied to vector

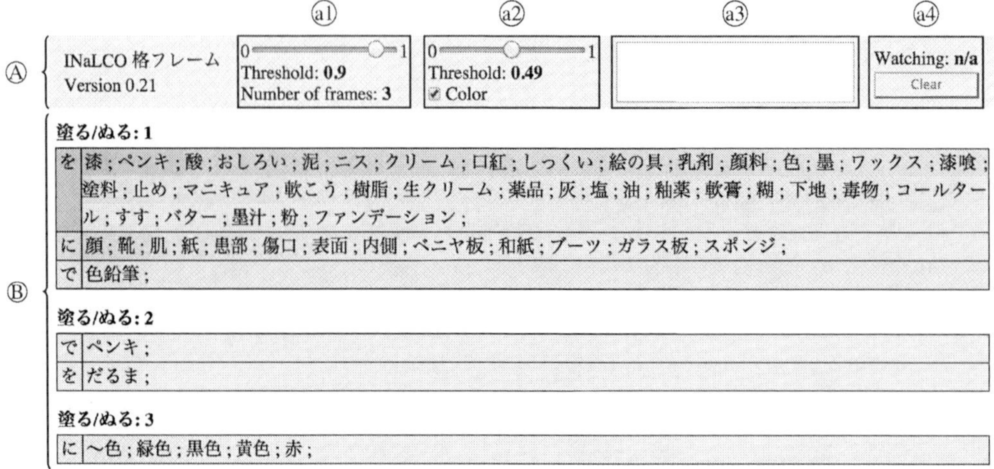

Figure 1: Screen capture of our visualization tool – Ⓐ control panel: ⓐ1 slider for partitioning subentries; ⓐ2 slider for selecting complements; ⓐ3 notification zone; ⓐ4 subentry identifier. – Ⓑ subentry panel. Here, we present the entry for the verb 塗る *nuru* "to smear". The threshold values reveal the locative alternation XにYを塗る *X ni Y wo nuru* "smear Y on X" ↔ XをYで塗る *X wo Y de nuru* "smear X with Y".

representation of the minimal predicate-frames so as to build a dendrogram for each verb in our data. The dendrogram serves as a model of the continuum between ambiguity and vagueness.

3 Overview of the visualization tool

In order to make the resource usable by humans, it is necessary to provide the end user with a graphical interface to navigate and explore the data in more detail. Our goal is to build a resource that reflects the subtleties of continuous models but avoids the complexity of a multifactorial analysis and offers a simple interface that allows a lexicographer or a linguist to navigate the data collection easily.

After many attempts, we managed to create a simple interface where the multifactorial analysis is abstracted as a double continuum: a continuum between ambiguity and vagueness, and a second continuum between arguments and adjuncts. Figure 1 shows a screen capture of our visualization tool[1].

Slider ⓐ1 represents the continuum between ambiguity and vagueness. It sets a threshold on the dendrogram of the subentries; subentries whose distance is less than the threshold are merged so as to make a single subentry. When the threshold is set to 0, each minimal predicate-frame corresponds to a distinct subentry; when set to 1 all minimal predicate-frames are merged into a single subentry. Slider ⓐ2 represents the continuum between arguments and adjuncts. It sets a threshold so as to only select complements that exhibit a certain argumenthood value. When the threshold is set to 0, all complements are displayed; when set to 1, only the complement with the highest degree of argumenthood is visible. Also, a color is assigned to each lexical head so as to indicate its degree of argumenthood: a light color indicates a value close to 0 (an adjunct); a dark color indicates a value close to 1 (an argument).

The user can move the two sliders back and forth to dynamically increase or decrease the number of subentries and complements. As the number of subentries can be substantial, we implemented various functionalities to track changes in the subentry panel. The notification panel ⓐ3 displays information about subentries that have merged or split, appeared or disappeared. We also implemented a mechanism to automatically focus and lock the subentry panel on a particular subentry (in which case the subentry number is given in ⓐ4).

[1]Our results are available online: `http://marchal.er-tim.fr/ikf`. Data is distributed under a Creative Commons licence (CC-BY-SA 4.0).

4 Discussion

First experiments with lexicographers have shown that exploration of the lexicon in the manner described above makes it possible to find new verb usages. The interface we have created is intuitive enough to allow the user to gradually unveil the meanings of verbs, starting with discriminative syntactic patterns (*e.g.* transitive versus intransitive) or broad semantic classes of complements (*e.g.* literal versus figurative), to finally uncover – as constraints on the partitioning of subentries and on the selection of complements are released – more fine-grained and domain-dependant meanings of the verbs. This exploration method also allows the user to observe linguistic phenomena at the syntax/semantics interface – such as diathesis alternations, as shown in Figure 1 with the locative alternation of the verb 塗る *nuru* "to smear" –, and verify prior assumptions that have been formulated in a different framework, particularly the status of certain complements (*i.e.* arguments versus adjuncts), or account for the productivity of some fixed expressions.

5 Conclusion

In this paper we have shown that is is possible to build lexical resources, based on continuous models, that can be useful not only to machines but also to humans. A more formal evaluation of both the interface and the lexical resource is currently underway, involving both linguists and lexicographers. This evaluation has already proved that our resource and its interface is useful, efficient and sufficiently powerful for professional end users.

Acknowledgements

Pierre Marchal's research has been partially funded by a "contrat doctoral" from the French Ministry of Higher Education and Research (Doctoral School 265). The authors wish to thank Ms. Jennifer Lewis-Wong (ERTIM, INaLCO) who assisted in the proof-reading of this paper.

References

Omri Abend and Ari Rappoport. 2010. Fully unsupervised core-adjunct argument classification. In *Proceedings of the 48th Annual Meeting of the Association for Computational Linguistics*, pages 226–236.

Katrin Erk and Diana McCarthy. 2009. Graded word sense assignment. In *Proceedings of the 2009 Conference on Empirical Methods in Natural Language Processing*, pages 440–449.

Cécile Fabre and Didier Bourigault. 2008. Exploiter des corpus annotés syntaxiquement pour observer le continuum entre arguments et circonstants. *Journal of French Language Studies*, 18(1):87–102.

John R. Firth, 1957. *A Synopsis of Linguistic Theory 1930–1955*, pages 1–32. Basil Blackwell, Oxford.

Zellig S. Harris. 1954. Distributional structure. *Word*, 10:146–162.

Adam Kilgarriff, Vít Baisa, Jan Bušta, Miloš Jakubíček, Vojtěch Kovář, Jan Michelfeit, Pavel Rychlý, and Vít Suchomel. 2014. The sketch engine: ten years on. *Lexicography*, 1(1):7–36.

Christopher D. Manning. 2003. Probabilistic syntax. In S. Jannedy R. Bod, J. Hay, editor, *Probabilistic Linguistics*, pages 289–341. MIT Press, Cambridge, MA.

Paola Merlo and Eva Esteve Ferrer. 2006. The notion of argument in prepositional phrase attachment. *Computational Linguistics*, 32(3):341–377.

Jeffrey Mitchell. 2011. *Composition in Distributional Models of Semantics*. Ph.D. thesis, University of Edinburgh.

Barbara H. Partee, 1995. *Lexical Semantics and Compositionality*, pages 311–360. The MIT Press, Cambridge, MA.

G. Salton, A. Wong, and C. S. Yang. 1975. A vector space model for automatic indexing. *Communications of the ACM*, 18(11):613–620.

David Tuggy. 1993. Ambiguity, polysemy, and vagueness. *Cognitive Linguistics*, 4(3):273–290.

Automatically Suggesting Example Sentences of Near-Synonyms for Language Learners

Chieh-Yang Huang Nicole Peinelt Lun-Wei Ku
Institute of Information Science,
Academia Sinica, Taipei, Taiwan.
appleternity@iis.sinica.edu.tw, nis50122806@gmail.com, lwku@iis.sinica.edu.tw

Abstract

In this paper, we propose `GiveMeExample` that ranks example sentences according to their capacity of demonstrating the differences among English and Chinese near-synonyms for language learners. The difficulty of the example sentences is automatically detected. Furthermore, the usage models of the near-synonyms are built by the GMM and Bi-LSTM models to suggest the best elaborative sentences. Experiments show the good performance both in the fill-in-the-blank test and on the manually labeled gold data, that is, the built models can select the appropriate words for the given context and vice versa.

1 Introduction

Integrating new words into active vocabulary requires language learners to make connections between the new lexical items and their previous knowledge. The acquisition of (near-)synonyms is especially challenging as learners need to know in which respects the words are similar and in which ways they differ from each other in order to make correct lexical choices while composing sentences. While absolute synonymy, i.e., interchangeability of words in any context, is generally a rare linguistic phenomenon, near-synonyms, which are similar words that differ in mostly only one aspect, are relatively common and often confuse learners with small nuances between them (DiMarco et al., 1993).

In order to assist language learners with the acquisition of near-synonyms, we previously developed `GiveMeExample` (Chieh-Yang and Lun-Wei, 2016) , a system that allows users to search for a pair of similar words and obtain a number of ranked example sentences which best highlight the difference between the words. Based on these examples, learners can derive the different usage patterns. In this paper, we introduce the enhanced edition, including the basic functions with the added language support for Chinese, an automatic difficulty scorer, an improved word usage model and a visualization feature for all the ranked example sentences. The online `GiveMeExample` system is available at `http://givemeexample.com/GiveMeExample/`.

2 Example Sentence Suggestion

`GiveMeExample` recommends useful and clear example sentences in two stages: first filtering out complicated sentences by the **automatic difficulty scorer** and then ranking the remained sentences by their **clarification ability**, which indicates the capability of a sentence to clear up confusion of words. We start from introducing the materials for the system design.

Experimental Material and Automatic Difficulty Scorer For the English version, the sentence pool is assembled using example sentences from Vocabulary.com[1]. On the other hand, the Chinese pool is composed of sentences collected from two balanced corpora, the Lancaster Corpus of Mandarin Chinese (McEnery and Xiao, 2003) and the UCLA Written Chinese Corpus (Tao and Xiao, 2007). All of the

[1]Text from Vocabulary.com (`https://www.vocabulary.com`), Copyright ©1998–2016 Thinkmap, Inc. All rights reserved.

Proceedings of COLING 2016, the 26th International Conference on Computational Linguistics: System Demonstrations, pages 302–306, Osaka, Japan, December 11-17 2016.

sentences here are utilized to train the word usage model, but in order to provide useful example sentences for learners, we further filter out complicated sentences and build with remaining sentences the simple sentence pool, from which the final example sentences are chosen.

To filter out complicated sentences, we build the automatic difficulty scorer based on the work of Pilán et al. (2014) but with several modifications. First, in order to assign to each sentence a score (as opposed to a class) we use a linear regression model instead of SVM. Second, the Swedish-specific features introduced by Pilán et al. (2014) are omitted. The training data for English sentence difficulty scorer is manually labeled by a native speaker who grades sentences from two aspects, the difficulty of wording and the complexity of sentence structure, ranging from 1 to 4. The sentence difficulty score ranging from 2 to 8 is then obtained by summing up these two scores. However, for the Chinese sentence difficulty scorer, the training data is collected from mock tests for Hanyu Shuiping Kaoshi (HSK), a Chinese Proficiency Test, and the difficulty degree of a extracted sentence corresponds to the proficiency degree of the content that this sentence comes from.

Measuring Clarification Ability of Sentences When searching for useful example sentences for the target word w_i in a word confusion set W, there are two related factors: (1) **Fitness**: the probability $P(s|w_i)$, whether w_i is appropriate for the example sentence s given a slot to put w_i. $P(s|w_i)$ is calculated by the word usage model. (2) **Relative Closeness**: the summation of the differences of between probabilities $P(s|w_i)$ and $P(s|w_j)$, i.e., $\sum_{w_j \in W - w_i} P(s|w_i) - P(s|w_j)$. A high relative closeness score denotes a better fit of s to w_i and a worse fit to $W - w_i$. We then calculate the clarification score with the multiplication of the fitness score and the relative closeness score:

$$score(s|w_i) = P(s|w_i) * (\sum_{w_j \in W - w_i} P(s|w_i) - P(s|w_j)) \quad (1)$$

where $score(s|w_i)$ denotes the clarification score of the example sentence s for w_i. We generate recommendations by ranking sentences in the simple sentence pool by their clarification scores. Then we repeat this procedure for all words in word confusion set W to find their elaborative example sentences. Next, we describe the calculation of the probability $P(s|w_i)$.

Word Usage Model To estimate $P(s|w)$ for an observed sentence s, we build a word usage model for the word w. The word usage model is built as an one-class classifier to recognize target samples from an unknown sample space and to process dynamically requested word confusion sets without retraining the models. We introduce two word usage models, the Gaussian Mixture Model (GMM) (Xu and Jordan, 1996) with contextual feature and the Bi-directional Long Short Term Memory neural network (Bi-LSTM) (Graves et al., 2013; Schuster and Paliwal, 1997; Hochreiter and Schmidhuber, 1997).

To build the GMM model, for each sentence $s = w_1 \cdots w_{t-k} \cdots w_t \cdots w_{t+k} \cdots w_n$, where w_t is the target word and k is the window size, we take the k words preceding and following the target word and represent them as well as their adjacent combinations in sequence using the summation of their word embeddings (Pennington et al., 2014). For example, the feature extracted by the windows size $k = 2$ is $\{e_{w_{i-2}} e_{w_{i-1}} e_{w_{i-2,i-1}} e_{w_{i+1}} e_{w_{i+2}} e_{w_{i+1,i+2}}\}$, where e_w denotes the summation of word embeddings of word sequence w. Next, GMM applies Expectation–Maximization algorithm to estimate its parameters and approximate to the data distribution. Empirically, we find that the GMM model with $k = 2$ and $number$ (of mixture) $= 50$ achieves the best performance. To train the GMM model for the target word w_t, a total of 5,000 corresponding sentences are used as the training samples.

To build the Bi-LSTM model, following the same idea of using contextual features, we take words adjacent to the target word into account. However, rather than using the information limited in a small window, Bi-LSTM exploits all the preceding and the following words of the target word in the sentence by a forward LSTM and a backward LSTM respectively. Then the output vectors of these two LSTM are concatenated together to form the sentence embedding, which is also a kind of contextual feature of the given sentence. At last, we add two fully connected layers as the binary classifier to predict whether w_t is appropriate for s. To train a Bi-LSTM model for w_t, we use 5,000 sentences containing w_t as the positive samples. For the negative samples, we randomly choose another 50,000 sentences (10 times of the positive samples) which do not contain w_t. In the end, a total of 55,000 sentences are used to train the Bi-LSTM model for each w_t.

3 System

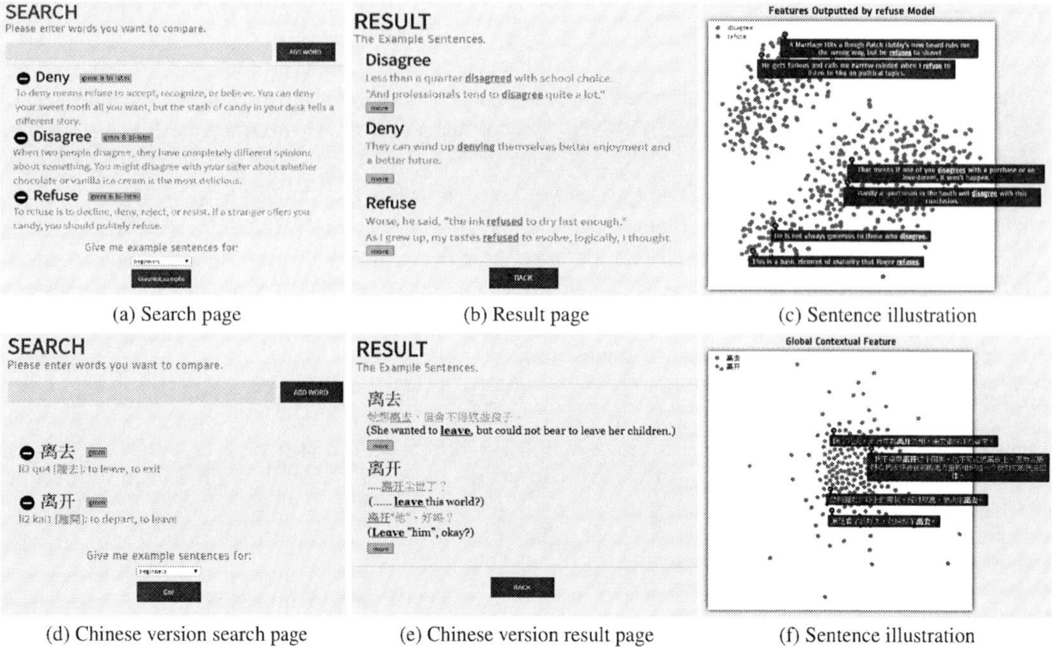

(a) Search page (b) Result page (c) Sentence illustration

(d) Chinese version search page (e) Chinese version result page (f) Sentence illustration

Figure 1: The user interface of `GiveMeExample`

Near-Synonym Set Search Interface Fig. 1a and Fig. 1d show the search interface. On the search page, learners can type in the words they want to compare easily and dynamically. In addition, `GiveMeExample` also offers a brief explanation of each word. The "gmm &bi-lstm" flag on the right side of the searched word indicates that `GiveMeExample` can provide example sentences suggested by both two models. Furthermore, learners can adjust the difficulty level with a drop-down list to find example sentences according to their language proficiency.

Fig. 1b and Fig. 1e show the result interface where the system-suggested example sentences are listed. `GiveMeExample` provides a "more" button to retrieve additional elaborative sentences. This function facilitates learners to reach more example sentences to generalize the usage and make inference about their difference. In Fig. 1b, learners can conclude that only "refuse" is followed by "to Verb" but the other two words are not. However, example sentences of "disagree" and "deny" do not demonstrate explicit usage. As a result, more example sentences are needed for learners to infer the correct usage of these two words. A similar situation occurs in Fig. 1e. Learners can conclude that only "离开" can be followed by an object, but "离去" cannot. However, for "离去", learners may need more example sentences.

Example Sentence Illustration In the example sentence illustration page, each sentence is turned into a two dimensional point by applying t-Distributed Stochastic Neighbor Embedding (t-SNE) (Maaten and Hinton, 2008) on its contextual feature vector (either from the GMM or Bi-LSTM model). When Bi-LSTM model is used, we will generate one figure for each word because each Bi-LSTM word usage model has it own feature extractor. One confusing word will have different feature vector in different word models. Therefore, for a confusion word set, we will have several figures for one confusing word from several word models. Fig. 1c illustrates the figure on the near-synonym set {refuse, disagree} generated by the Bi-LSTM word usage model of "refuse". `GiveMeExample` displays the sentence represented by each point when the user hovers the mouse over it. With this function, learners can easily search for either different or similar usage patterns of a set of confusing words. For instance, in Fig. 1c, the top two blue points of "refuse" both show the usage "someone refuses to do something" of this word and thus are grouped together, while the red-blue mixed small group at the lower left corner of the figure showing similar usage "someone refuses/disagrees" of the two confusing words "refuse" and "disagree".

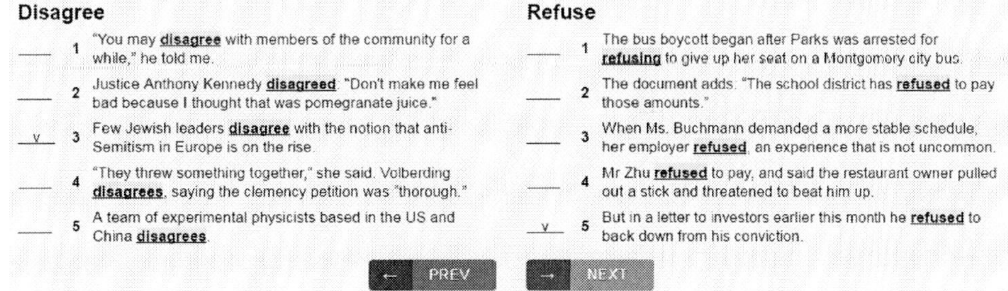

Figure 2: An example question for learners. Learners need to select the best sentence pair, one from the left column and one from the right, to best illustrate the difference between {refuse, disagree}.

In this figure learners can easily find that the example sentences are roughly grouped into three clusters, suggesting in general there are three major usages of these two words.

Differing Aspect	Near-synonym Pair	Score	Differing Aspect	Near-synonym Pair	Score
abstract vs. concrete	blunder - error	7/10	low vs. high degree	mist - fog	2/10
	维护 - 保护	6/10		经常-往往	3/10
formal vs. informal	child - kid	6/10	pejorative vs. favorable	skinny - slim	3/10
	购买 - 买	9/10		产生-造成	8/10

Table 1: How useful the recommended example sentences can help discriminate near-synonyms.

Evaluation We first evaluate Fitness by the FITB test, which assesses whether the proposed fitness score can identify the appropriate context for a given word. A FITB question contains a sentence with a blank field to be filled in by several near-synonym candidate answers. We adopt Edmonds benchmark for evaluation. Edmonds (1997) suggests the FITB test on 1987 Wall Street Journal (WSJ) and defines 7 near-synonym sets, and after that it becomes a benchmark. Among the one-class models ever reported in the literature, the 5-gram language model is the best (acc 69.90%) (Islam and Inkpen, 2010). However, results show our proposed GMM and Bi-LSTM both outperform it by achieving the accuracy 70.26% and 73.05%, respectively.

Then we evaluate Clarification by the Learner Glod standard (LG) experiment. We define 10 near-synonym sets, where each set contains 2 near-synonym verbs, for evaluation. For each near-synonym set we build 20 questions. Fig. 2 shows an example question for the word confusion set {refuse, disagree}. Each question contains 5 randomly chosen example sentences for each confusing word. The sentences are listed in parallel, 5-to-5, in each question and 6 learners are requested to choose the best sentence pair, one sentence for each word. The pair selected by learners are treated as the gold answer and thus each question has at most six gold pairs from learners. Then the `GiveMeExample` system answers each question by regarding it as question of 25 sentence-pair choices. The sytem will rank all these 25 choices and among them the rank of best gold pair are used to calculate the mean reciprocal rank (MRR). The MRR of GMM and Bi-LSTM are 0.502, 0.500 respectively, and both outperform the random-ordered baseline (0.423) and first-seen baseline(0.429).

Discussion In order to investigate how helpful the proposed system is, we conduct a case study for a number of Chinese and English near-synonym pairs that differ in certain linguistic aspects (abstract vs. concrete, formal vs. informal, low vs. high degree and pejorative vs. favorable) as proposed by DiMarco et al. (1993). The ten highest ranked sentences from the system are manually scored for their suitability to discriminate each two confusing words, conferring one point on a good example sentence and zero points if the sentence did not highlight a difference between the two near-synonyms. The main criterion we employ for this decision is whether the synonyms are mutually exchangeable without altering the meaning and normality of the original statement (Cruse, 1986). According to our results, the system makes good suggestions for the abstract vs. concrete and formal vs. informal word pairs (Table 1) with 60 to 90 percent of helpful example sentences. Especially the formal and informal difference is the most recognizable from the example sentences, e.g. "Would you let your kids smoke pot?" vs. "The New York City Children's Chorus will perform during the worship service." Results for the pejorative vs. favorable word pairs are mixed, while the suggested sentences for the near-synonyms with varying degrees are found to be less distinctive by their associated context. The difference in performance seems largely related to the extend to which the words differ from each other, making "mist - fog" more difficult to distinguish than "error - blunder".

The analysis of the recommended sentences also shows that the system picks up two additional aspects in which near-synonyms may differ. First, many suggested sentences contain collocational patterns which are helpful to distinguish similar words, such as fixed expressions e.g. "error bars" but not "blunder bars" and common arguments e.g. "维护平衡" vs. "保护鸟种". Second, the system can demonstrate monofunctional vs. polyfunctional properties of near-synonyms, e.g. "error" can only serve as noun, but "blunder" can function as a noun ("What a jolly blunder Police Headquarters would make!") as well as a verb ("Ye blundering idiot!").

4 Conclusion

We have proposed the `GiveMeExample` system to help language learners understand English and Chinese near-synonyms by utilizing learners' ability to learn implicitly from the comparison of good example sentences. We have shown that `GiveMeExample` has the design to support the online comparison of arbitrary words and can perform satisfactory. In the future, we plan to support the analysis of phrases and further investigate the effect from the learning side.

Acknowledgements

Research of this paper was partially supported by Ministry of Science and Technology, Taiwan, under the contract MOST 104-2221-E-001-024-MY2.

References

Huang Chieh-Yang and Ku Lun-Wei. 2016. Givemeexample: Learning confusing words by example sentences.

D Alan Cruse. 1986. *Lexical semantics*. Cambridge University Press.

Chrysanne DiMarco, Graeme Hirst, and Manfred Stede. 1993. The semantic and stylistic differentiation of synonyms and near-synonyms. In *AAAI Spring Symposium on Building Lexicons for Machine Translation*, pages 114–121.

Philip Edmonds. 1997. Choosing the word most typical in context using a lexical co-occurrence network. In *Proceedings of EACL 1997*, pages 507–509. Association for Computational Linguistics.

Alex Graves, Abdel-rahman Mohamed, and Geoffrey Hinton. 2013. Speech recognition with deep recurrent neural networks. In *2013 IEEE ICASSP*, pages 6645–6649. IEEE.

Sepp Hochreiter and Jürgen Schmidhuber. 1997. Long short-term memory. *Neural computation*, 9(8):1735–1780.

Aminul Islam and Diana Inkpen. 2010. Near-synonym choice using a 5-gram language model. *Research in Computing Sciences*, 46:41–52.

Laurens van der Maaten and Geoffrey Hinton. 2008. Visualizing data using t-sne. *Journal of Machine Learning Research*, 9(Nov):2579–2605.

Tony McEnery and Richard Xiao. 2003. The lancaster corpus of mandarin chinese.

Jeffrey Pennington, Richard Socher, and Christopher D Manning. 2014. Glove: Global vectors for word representation. In *EMNLP*, volume 14, pages 1532–1543.

Ildikó Pilán, Elena Volodina, and Richard Johansson. 2014. Rule-based and machine learning approaches for second language sentence-level readability. In *BEA Workshop 2014*, pages 174–184.

Mike Schuster and Kuldip K Paliwal. 1997. Bidirectional recurrent neural networks. *IEEE Transactions on Signal Processing*, 45(11):2673–2681.

Hongyin Tao and Richard Xiao. 2007. The ucla chinese corpus (2nd edition).

Lei Xu and Michael I Jordan. 1996. On convergence properties of the em algorithm for gaussian mixtures. *Neural computation*, 8(1):129–151.

Kyoto-NMT: a Neural Machine Translation implementation in Chainer

Fabien Cromières
Japan Science and Technology Agency [†*]
Kawaguchi-shi, Saitama 332-0012
fabien@pa.jst.jp

Abstract

We present Kyoto-NMT, an open-source implementation of the Neural Machine Translation paradigm. This implementation is done in Python and Chainer, an easy-to-use Deep Learning Framework.

1 Introduction

1.1 Neural Machine Translation

Neural Machine Translation (NMT) is a new approach to Machine Translation (MT) that, although recently proposed, has quickly achieved state-of-the-art results (Bojar et al., 2016). It is now growingly popular and might become the main focus of MT research in the next few years. Kyoto-NMT implements the Sequence-to-Sequence model with Attention mechanism first proposed in (Bahdanau et al., 2015) as well as some more recent improvements. It is intended to evolve incrementally to include new improvements as they are found.

1.2 The RNN-Search model

We describe here briefly the (Bahdanau et al., 2015) model that forms the basis of Kyoto-NMT, but for details one should check the original paper. As shown in figure 1, an input sentence is first converted into a sequence of vector through an embedding layer; these vectors are then fed to two LSTM layers (one going forward, the other going backward) to give a new sequence of vectors that encode the input sentence. On the decoding part of the model, a target-side sentence is generated with what is conceptually a Recurrent Neural Network Language Model: an LSTM is sequentially fed the embedding of the previously generated word, and its output is sent through a deep softmax layer to produce the probability of the next word. This decoding LSTM is also fed a context vector, which is a weighted sum of the vectors encoding the input sentence, provided by the attention mechanism.

2 Kyoto-NMT workflow

There are essentially three steps in the use of Kyoto-NMT: data preparation (`make_data.py`), training (`train.py`), evaluation (`eval.py`).

2.1 Data Preparation

The required training data is a sentence-aligned parallel corpus that is expected to be in two utf-8 text files: one for source language sentences and the other target language sentences. One sentence per line, words separated by whitespaces[1]. Additionally, some validation data should be provided in a similar form (a source and a target file). This validation data will be used for early-stopping, as well as to

[†]Work done during a project taking place in Kyoto University.

[1]One is here free to choose any concept of "word". For Japanese, they could correspond to individual characters, or units obtained from automatic segmentation.

Proceedings of COLING 2016, the 26th International Conference on Computational Linguistics: System Demonstrations, pages 307–311, Osaka, Japan, December 11-17 2016.

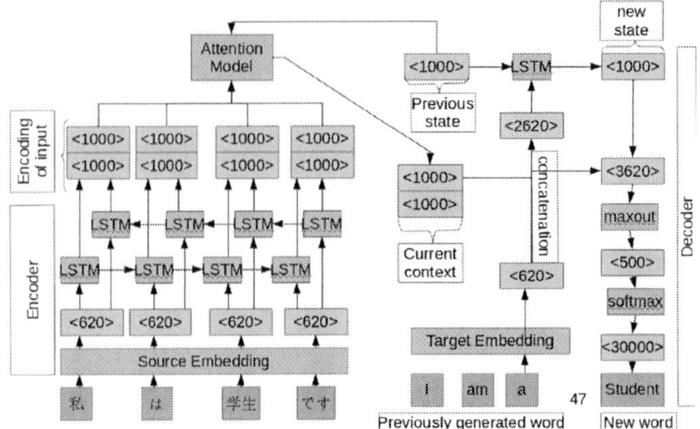

Figure 1: The structure of a NMT system with Attention, as described in (Bahdanau et al., 2015) (but with LSTMs instead of GRUs). The notation "<1000>" means a vector of size 1000. The vector sizes shown here are the ones suggested in the original paper.

visualize the progress of the training. One should also specify the maximum size of vocabulary for source and target sentences.

```
./make_data.py train.src train.tgt data_prefix
    --dev_src valid.src --dev_tgt valid.tgt
    --src_voc_size 100000 --tgt_voc_size 30000
```

As a result of this call, two dictionaries indexing the n and m most common source and target words are created (with a special index for out-of-vocabulary words). The training and validation data are then converted to integer sequences according to these dictionaries and saved in a gzipped JSON file[2] prefixed with `data_prefix`.

2.2 Training

Training is done by invoking the `train.py` script, passing as argument the data prefix used in the data preparation part.

```
./train.py data_prefix train_prefix
```

This simple call will train a network with size and features similar to those used in the original (Bahdanau et al., 2015) paper (except that LSTMs are used in place of GRUs). However, there are many options to specify different aspects of the network: embedding layer size, hidden states size, number of lstm stacks, etc. The training settings can also be specified at this point: weight decay, learning rate, training algorithm, dropout values, minibatch size, etc.

`train.py` will create several files prefixed by `train_prefix`. A JSON file `train_prefix.config` is created, containing all the parameters given to `train.py` (used for restarting an interrupted training session, or using a model for evaluation). A file `train_prefix.result.sqlite` is also created, containing a SQLite database that will keep track of the training progress. Furthermore, model files containing optimized network parameters will be saved regularly. Every n minibatches (by default n = 200), an evaluation is performed on the validation set. Both perplexity and BLEU scores are computed. The BLEU score is computed by translating the validation set with a greedy search[3]. The models that have given the best

[2] As a design principle, all files generated are in JSON format, except for the trained parameters which are saved in `numpy`'s npz format

[3] Greedy search translation will take a few seconds for a validation set of 1000 sentences. On the other hand, beam search can take several dozens of minutes depending on the parameters, and thus cannot be used for frequent evaluation

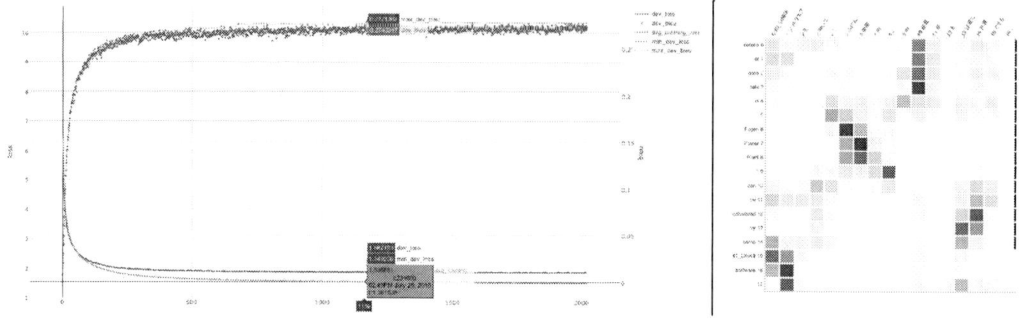

Figure 2: **Left:** Visualisation of the training evolution with plotly. blue dots represent validation BLEU, blue line represents validation loss and green line represents training loss over last 200 minibatches. **Right:** Visualization of the attention in a translation.

BLEU and best perplexity so far are saved in files `train_prefix.model.best.npz` and `train_prefix.model.best_loss.npz` respectively. This allows to have early stopping based on two different criterions: validation BLEU and validation perplexity.

The SQLite database keep track of many information items during the training: validation BLEU and perplexity, training perplexity, time to process each minibatch, etc. An additional script can use this database to generate a plotly[4] graph showing the evolution of BLEU, perplexity and training loss, as shown in figure 2. This graph can be generated while training is still in progress and is very useful for monitoring ongoing experiments.

2.3 Evaluation

Evaluation is done by running the script `eval.py`. It allows, among other things, to translate sentences by doing a beam search with a trained model. The following command will translate `input.txt` into `translations.txt` using the parameters that gave the best validation BLEU during training:

```
./eval.py train_prefix.config train_prefix.model.best.npz input.txt
     translations.txt--mode beam_search --beam_width 30
```

We usually find that it is better to use the parameters that gave the best validation BLEU rather than the ones that gave the best validation loss. Although it can be even better to do an ensemble translation with the two. The `eval.py` script has many options for tuning the beam search, ensembling several trained models, displaying the attention for each translation (as in figure 2), etc.

When an Out-of-Vocabulary index is generated by the decoder, it is tagged with the source position on which attention is the most focused. This allows the replacement of the OOV item with the translation of the corresponding source word using an external dictionary. This type of approach was first proposed by (Luong et al., 2015). They were actually using a specific annotation to retrieve the source position instead of relying on the attention, but we found that their annotation is not very suitable for language pairs with very different word orders such as Japanese and English.

3 Implementation and Performances

3.1 Chainer

Chainer[5] is a Deep Learning framework based on Python. Its approach is somehow opposite to Theano[6] and Tensorflow[7], who use Python instructions to define a computation graph that will then be compiled

[4]https://github.com/plotly

[5]http://chainer.org/

[6]http://deeplearning.net/software/theano/

[7]https://www.tensorflow.org/

and executed. On the other hand, in Chainer, the definition of the computation and its execution happens concurrently. The "precompiled computation graph" paradigm has advantages in term of performances, but make it more difficult to follow the control flow of a program. In particular, in Theano, applying a recurrent network to a variable-length input can require the use of complex ad-hoc instructions like Theano's *scan*. On the other hand, in Chainer, it can be done with a simple Python for-loop:

```
for x in input:
   cell, state = lstm(cell, state, x)
```

We thus believe that our implementation is easier to understand and modify than those based on Theano or Tensorflow.

3.2 Other NMT implementations

The authors of (Bahdanau et al., 2015) have made their implementation available, based on the Theano Deep Learning framework. Since then, we are aware of several re-implementation/improvements that have been made available[8]: The Deep Learning for MT Tutorial's code, Tensorflow's NMT implementation, the Lamtram toolkit (Neubig, 2015), chainn, chainer_nmt and the implementation of the authors of (Luong and Manning, 2016). We are however not familiar with all of these implementations, and a systematic comparison of features and performances between all of them would go well beyond the scope of this paper.

3.3 Performances

This implementation was used as a basis for a participation to the MT shared tasks of the Workshop on Asian Translation[9] (WAT). This let us confirm we could obtain state-of-the-art results. For example, on the ASPEC Japanese-to-English task, a simple, carefully trained, single-layer LSTM could already obtain a BLEU score of 22.86, while the official Moses Baseline score for WAT2015 was only 20.36 (Nakazawa et al., 2015). Using ensembling and training more complex models, we could obtain a score of 26.22, higher than the best score reported for WAT2015 (which was 25.41). We could obtain similarly good results for the three other language directions (involving Japanese-English and Japanese-Chinese). A fuller description of these experiments can be found in (Cromières et al., 2016).

In terms of computation time, the training speed is about one minibatch per seconds on a Geforce Titan X (Maxwell) for a network with one LSTM layer. The Theano-Groundhog implementation with similar network size (yet with GRUs instead of LSTMs) can on the other hand process roughly two minibatches per seconds. The relative performance gap can be reduced as network size increase, but is still important, even considering LSTMs can be slower than GRUs for the same output size. Theano's use of precompiled computation graphs will necessarily have a performance advantage over a library like Chainer (at the price of the intuitivity of the control flow), but we have identified some bottleneck and are hopeful that training time can be brought to within 20% difference with that of Theano or Tensorflow implementations.

4 Conclusion and Future Work

We have developped an implementation of Neural-MT that obtained competitive results in the translation shared-tasks to which we participated. The focus of this implementation is to make it straightforward, with just one or two command line instructions, to use the most relevant best practices and advances for MT (early-stopping, unknown word replacement, ensembling, etc.). We are releasing[10] the code under a GPL License[11] in the hope it will be useful for comparison of implementations and results, and as a potential basis for extensions. Future work will include speed and memory optimizations and addition of more state-of-the-art features as research on NMT progresses.

[8]respectively: github.com/lisa-groundhog/GroundHog, github.com/nyu-dl/dl4mt-tutorial, www.tensorflow.org/, github.com/neubig/lamtram, github.com/philip30/chainn, github.com/odashi/chainer_nmt, github.com/lmthang/nmt.hybrid

[9]http://lotus.kuee.kyoto-u.ac.jp/WAT/

[10]https://github.com/fabiencro/knmt

[11]We are considering releasing it under a more permitive license (MIT or LGPL)

Acknowledgements

Work supported by the Japan Science and Technology Agency.

References

Dzmitry Bahdanau, Kyunghyun Cho, and Yoshua Bengio. 2015. Neural machine translation by jointly learning to align and translate. In *ICLR 2015*.

Ondrej Bojar, Rajen Chatterjee, Christian Federmann, Yvette Graham, Barry Haddow, Matthias Huck, Antonio Jimeno Yepes, Philipp Koehn, Varvara Logacheva, Christof Monz, et al. 2016. Findings of the 2016 conference on machine translation (wmt16). In *Proceedings of WMT 2016*.

Fabien Cromières, Chenhui Chu, Toshiaki Nakazawa, and Sadao Kurohashi. 2016. Kyoto university participation to wat 2016. In *Third Workshop on Asian Translation (WAT2016)*.

Minh-Thang Luong and Christopher D. Manning. 2016. Achieving open vocabulary neural machine translation with hybrid word-character models. In *Association for Computational Linguistics (ACL)*, Berlin, Germany, August.

Minh-Thang Luong, Ilya Sutskever, Quoc V Le, Oriol Vinyals, and Wojciech Zaremba. 2015. Addressing the rare word problem in neural machine translation. In *Proceedings of ACL 2015*.

Toshiaki Nakazawa, Hideya Mino, Isao Goto, Graham Neubig, Sadao Kurohashi, and Eiichiro Sumita. 2015. Overview of the 2nd Workshop on Asian Translation. In *Proceedings of the 2nd Workshop on Asian Translation (WAT2015)*, pages 1–28, Kyoto, Japan, October.

Graham Neubig. 2015. lamtram: A toolkit for language and translation modeling using neural networks. http://www.github.com/neubig/lamtram.